Fodor's 1992 Affordable Germany

Portions of this book appear in *Fodor's Germany '92*.

Fodor's Travel Publications, Inc.
New York London Toronto

ISBN 0-679-02141-8

First Edition

Fodor's Affordable Germany

Editors: Craig Seligman, Paula Consolo
Area Editors: Graham Lees, Robert Tilley
Contributors: Charles Barr, Hampton Binden, Robert Blake, Sheila Brownlee, Hannah Clements, Michael Cresswell, Birgit Gericke, Andrew Heritage, Liz Hulme, Helmut Koenig, Tony Peisley, Anita Peltonen, Isabelle Pöhlman, Linda K. Schmidt, Susan Williams
Art Director: Fabrizio La Rocca
Cartographers: David Lindroth, R. R. Donnelly and Sons Co.
Cover Photograph: Weinberg-Clark/Image Bank

Design: Vignelli Associates

Special Sales

Fodor's Travel Publications are available at special discounts for bulk purchases (100 copies or more) for sales promotions or premiums. Special editions, including personalized covers, excerpts of existing guides, and corporate imprints, can be created in large quantities for special needs. For more information write to Special Marketing, Fodor's Travel Publications, 201 East 50th St., New York, NY 10022; or call 800/800-3246. Inquiries from Canada should be sent to Random House of Canada, Ltd., Marketing Dept., 1265 Aerowood Dr., Mississauga, Ontario L4W 1B9. Inquiries from the United Kingdom should be sent to Fodor's Travel Publications, 20 Vauxhall Bridge Rd., London, England SW1V 2SA.

MANUFACTURED IN THE UNITED STATES OF AMERICA
10 9 8 7 6 5 4 3 2 1

Contents

Maps

Foreword

The Affordables are aimed at people like you and me—people with discriminating tastes and limited budgets.

This is a new series that combines essential budget travel information with all the great editorial features of a Fodor's gold guide: quality writing, authoritative hotel and restaurant reviews, detailed exploring tours, and wonderful maps.

The idea behind these guides is that you, the budget traveler, have the same curiosity, good taste, and high expectations as those who travel first class, and you need information with the same depth and detail as readers of Fodor's gold guides. But as a budget traveler you also need to know about low-cost activities, meals, and lodging, and especially how to get around by train or bus.

Some of you, of course, will spend a bit more on a hotel with full service and amenities but will eat simply; others will be willing to go the hostel route in order to splurge on meals; yet others will save by sticking to public transportation and picnic lunches in order to do some serious shopping. We've tried to include enough options so that each of you can spend your money in the way you most enjoy spending it.

The Affordables, therefore, tell you about activities you can enjoy for free—or close to it. They also place a special emphasis on bargain shopping—what to buy and where to find it.

These are not guides for the hotdog-on-the-run-it's-okay-to-sleep-on-a-park-bench crowd, but for those of you who insist on at least two good, healthy meals a day and a safe, comfortable place to put your head at night. The hotels we recommend offer good value, and there are no dives, thank you—only clean, friendly places with an acceptable level of comfort, convenience, and charm. There's also a wide range of inexpensive and moderately priced dining options, mostly small, family-run restaurants offering healthy, home-cooked, regional cuisine.

Equally important, the Affordables organize all travel according to convenient train and bus routes, and include point-to-point directions that get you to each town and attraction. No matter how you're traveling—by car, train, or bus—your Fodor's Affordable will tell you exactly how to get there. We even locate train routes on maps—a feature every cost-conscious traveler will appreciate, but which (if we may wave our own flag) you won't find in any other budget guide.

Fodor's has made every effort to provide you with accurate, up-to-date information, but time always brings change, and consequently the publisher cannot accept responsibility for errors that may occur. Hours and admission fees in particular may change, so, when it matters to you, we encourage you to call ahead.

We also encourage you to write and share your travel experiences with us—pleasant and unpleasant. When a hotel or restaurant fails to live up to its billing, please let us know, and we'll investigate the complaint and revise our entries when the facts warrant it. Send your letters to The Editor, Fodor's Affordables, 201 East 50th Street, New York, NY 10022.

Have a great trip!

Michael Spring
Editorial Director

Fodor's Choice

No two people will agree on what makes a perfect vacation, but it's fun and helpful to know what others think. We hope you'll have a chance to experience some of Fodor's Choices during your visit to Germany. For detailed information about each entry, refer to the appropriate chapter of the book.

Castles

Burg Eltz, Mosel

Heidelberg Schloss

Kaiserburg, Nürnberg

Neuschwanstein Castle, Füssen

The Residenz, Würzburg

Schwerin Palace, Schwerin

Wartburg Castle, Eisenach

Museums

Ägyptisches Museum, Berlin

Alte Pinakothek, Munich

Deutsches Museum, Munich

Deutsches Schiffahrtsmuseum, Bremerhaven

Domschatzkammer, Aachen

Gemäldegalerie, Berlin

Gemäldegalerie Alte Meister, Dresden

Kunsthalle, Hamburg

Museum der Bildenden Kunste, Leipzig

Römisch-Germanisches Museum, Köln

Churches

Dom St. Bartholomäus, Frankfurt

Frauenkirche, Munich

Kölner Dom, Köln

Münster, Freiburg

Trier Dom, Trier

Vierzehnheiligen, Franconia

Wieskirche, Upper Bavaria

Zinsterzienser-Klosterkirche, Bad Doberan

Places Where Time Stands Still

Bad Wimpfen

Hameln

Passau

Rothenburg-ob-der-Tauber

Rügen and Usedom islands

Bargain Dining

Adriatic Grill, Berlin

Alte Schwede, Wismar

Historische Wurstküche, Regensburg

Ratsweinkeller, Hamburg

Straubinger Hof, Munich

Weinhaus Uhle, Schwerin

Zur Herrenmühle, Heidelberg

Zur Schranke, Nürnberg

Bargain Lodging

Dreiflüssehof, Passau

Gasthof Spezial, Bamberg

Haus der Jugend, Deutschherrnufer, Frankfurt

Jugendtouristhotel aboard the ship *Frieden*, Rostock

Pension Arco, Berlin

Pension Beck, Munich

Tannenberg, Bad Tölz

Memorable Sights

Brandenburger Tor and Wall remains, Berlin

Dreiflusseck (confluence of the Inn, Ilz, and Danube rivers), Passau

Oktoberfest, Munich

Reeperbahn, Hamburg

The Rhine in Flames fireworks

Semper Opera House, Dresden

Wilhelmshöhe park, Kassel

Unforgettable Excursions

A boat ride on Bavaria's Königsee

A boat ride on the Danube River from Regensburg to Weltenburg

A cable-car ride to the summit of the Zugspitze, Germany's highest mountain, outside Garmisch

A combination (train and boat) family ticket from Munich to the Starnbergersee and Ammersee lakes

A one-day tour of the Romantic Road, from Würzburg to Füssen

A steam-train ride on the *Molli* from Bad Doberan to the Baltic Sea

Germany
0
100 miles
0
150 km
N
North Sea
Baltic Sea
DENMARK
POLAND
HOLLAND
GERMANY
Rügen
Fehmarn
Elbe
Elbe
Ems
Oder
Oder
Neisse
FORMER BORDER BETWEEN EAST AND WEST GERMANY
Flensburg
Husum
Kiel
Neustadt
Rostock
Barth
Stralsund
Greifswald
Anklam
Cuxhaven
Caroliensiel
Norden
Wilhelmshaven
Emden
Bremerhaven
Hamburg
Lübeck
Wismar
Schwerin
Güstrow
Teterow
Neubrandenburg
Waren
Neustrelitz
Neustadt-Glewe
Ludwigslust
Pritzwalk
Perleberg
Wittenberge
Neuruppin
Oranienburg
Oldenburg
Bremen
Meppen
Salzwedel
Stendal
Berlin
Potsdam
Brandenburg
Wolfsburg
Hannover
Braunschweig
Osnabrück
Rheine
Minden
Frankfurt
Magdeburg
Bielefeld
Hildesheim
Münster
Halberstadt
Bernburg
Dessau
Wittenberg
Lübben
Cottbus
Bitterfeld
Essen
Duisberg
Dortmund
Hagen
Göttingen
Nordhausen
Halle
Leipzig
Mühlhausen
Görlitz

Köln
Aachen
Bonn
Rhine
Siegen
Marburg
Giessen
BELGIUM
Koblenz
Erfurt
Weimar
Eisenach
Bad Hersfeld
Alsfeld
Fulda
Suhl
Meiningen
Saalfeld
Gera
Zwickau
Chemnitz
Plauen
Hof
Münchberg
Coburg
Wiesbaden
Mainz
Frankfurt-am-Main
Bingen
Bad
Kreuznach
Mosel
Trier
LUX.
Darmstadt
Main
Würzburg
Bamberg
Bayreuth
CZECHOSLOVAKIA
Mannheim
Ludwigshafen
Heidelberg
Rothenburg-
o-d-Tauber
Fürth
Nürnberg
Speyer
Saarbrücken
Heilbronn
Karlsruhe
Regensburg
Straubing
Deggendorf
Stuttgart
Baden-Baden
Passau
Danube
Tübingen
Isar
Offenburg
Ulm
Neu-Ulm
Augsburg
Munich
Rhein
FRANCE
Biberach
Inn
Memmingen
Freiburg
Tuttlingen
Ravensburg
Wangen
Bad Reichenhall
Berchtesgaden
Rheinfelden
Konstanz
Friedrichshafen
Garmisch-
Partenkirchen
AUSTRIA
SWITZERLAND

German Rail Lines

CZECHOSLOVAKIA
AUSTRIA
SWITZERLAND
FRANCE
BELGIUM
LUX.
Danube
Rhine
Rhein
Main
Mosel
Isar
Inn
Köln
Aachen
Bonn
Siegen
Marburg
Giessen
Koblenz
Wiesbaden
Mainz
Frankfurt-am-Main
Bingen
Bad Kreuznach
Trier
Darmstadt
Mannheim
Ludwigshafen
Heidelberg
Speyer
Saarbrücken
Karlsruhe
Heilbronn
Stuttgart
Baden-Baden
Tübingen
Offenburg
Freiburg
Rheinfelden
Konstanz
Tuttlingen
Biberach
Ulm
Neu-Ulm
Memmingen
Ravensburg
Wangen
Friedrichshafen
Erfurt
Weimar
Eisenach
Bad Hersfeld
Alsfeld
Fulda
Suhl
Meiningen
Saalfeld
Coburg
Gera
Zwickau
Chemnitz
Plauen
Hof
Münchberg
Bayreuth
Bamberg
Würzburg
Rothenburg-o-d-Tauber
Fürth
Nürnberg
Regensburg
Straubing
Deggendorf
Passau
Augsburg
Munich
Bad Reichenhall
Berchtesgaden
Garmisch-Partenkirchen

Introduction

by Graham Lees

British-born Graham Lees has lived in Germany for the past decade and reports on German and central European political and social issues for a variety of foreign publications.

Germany is an expensive country. Its cost of living matches its standard of living—high. While some basic foodstuffs and utilities cost no more than in other parts of the West, such services as hotels, restaurants, and public transportation can be extremely pricey. The good news for the foreign traveler is that, at press time at least, the reunification of East and West Germany had weakened the value of the Deutschemark (DM) against other major currencies. In late 1991 the dollar was worth around DM 1.64, compared with DM 1.51 at the end of 1990. Fluctuations between the pound and the mark haven't been so extreme, because those two currencies are now bound within the European Economic Community's financial structures; at press time the pound was worth DM 2.90. How long the mark will stay weak is anybody's guess, given the volatility of the international money markets, but clearly the cost of unification will continue to drain the German national coffers for some time to come.

The reunification—which took place on October 3, 1990, after a political division of more than 40 years—didn't prompt universal cheers. A united Germany would pose a threat to the military stability of Europe, warned the critics. German economic power could steamroll across the Continent, moaned the sceptics. Germans are pushy, domineering, and workaholic, jeered Teutonophobes worldwide. But the "new" Germans have been confounding them all. The nation steadfastly stuck to constitutional strictures limiting the use of its armed forces to the NATO arena and refused to deploy them in the Persian Gulf conflict. The federal government, which once showered money on the Soviet Union and elsewhere, vastly underestimated the cost of rebuilding the east and was forced to raise domestic taxes to help stem the downward spiral in eastern employment and the huge migration west. And a comprehensive social survey revealed that the average German had some unexpected aspirations for the year 2000.

Conducted by a German research institute for a national daily newspaper and published in January 1991, the survey found that a majority of Germans would like to be less competitive and to work fewer hours per week. It revealed, among other things, that 75% of Germans reject the idea of German participation in any international conflicts—only 6% want their reunited country to play a greater political or military role abroad. Far from being isolationist and xenophobic, a massive 83% want their borders thrown open completely, and 71% are ready for Germany to be absorbed in a United States of Europe. More than three-quarters of the population believes that protecting the environment should become the highest priority of government and industry, and more than 50%—this in a country with more cars per capita than anywhere outside the United States—want less road traffic by the year 2000. Reflecting this sentiment, the federal government has warned car manufacturers that it might impose a beer bottle–style deposit surcharge on new cars, to be passed from owner to owner and eventually, when the vehicle is scrapped, refunded to the final owner by the manufacturer—the idea being to make the industry more responsible for the millions of tons of nonrecyclable scrap it creates every year. This almost obsessional urge to clean up the environment is an extension of the house-proud tidiness you can see reflected in the nation's clean streets and subways and its spic-and-span countryside.

But while the physical divisions of the Berlin Wall and the Iron Curtain are gone, Germany remains two separate countries in many ways—not least in the glaring difference in standards of living. The infrastructure of eastern Germany is woefully dilapidated; driving east, you can still tell when you've crossed the old Iron Curtain border—the roads get bumpier. Economists and sociologists predict that it could take a generation to fuse the two halves. Today, Germans in the west refer disparagingly to their kinfolk in the east as "Ossies" (easterners), implying that 40 years of Communism have made them different. Perhaps—but there were always differences. To outsiders, Germans are Germans whether they live in Berchtesgaden or Berlin. But Prussians are as different from Bavarians, or Saxons from Rhinelanders, as Alaskans are from Texans.

The lingering differences provide a fascinating and disturbing background for today's traveler. But although many historic buildings—indeed, whole towns—in eastern Germany are crumbling after a half-century of Stalinist mismanagement, the picture isn't all grim: The Communists, even when they were cash-strapped, took pride in their country's architectural and cultural heritage. Weimar, home at one time or another to Goethe, Schiller, Herder, Liszt, Bach, and other cultural giants, is still a showplace. The medieval heart of Erfurt emerged from World War II with barely a scratch and sparkles today. The Baltic coast island of Rügen floats in a picturesque time warp, suspended in the 1920s.

The former East Germany—from the forests of Thuringia and Saxony, south of Leipzig and Dresden, to the Baltic coast—is cheaper, on the whole, than what was West Germany. Lodging in the east (except in the big city hotels) is easier on the pocket; meals are far less expensive (as long as you steer clear of fancy hotel restaurants); and public transportation is cheaper and more plentiful than in the car-clogged west. The down side is that hotels and restaurants in the east are both shabbier and sparser than in the holiday playgrounds of the west.

Costs vary tremendously across the reunited country. The big cities—Berlin, Munich, Hamburg, Frankfurt—are the most expensive; attractive but less populated areas, such as Franconia in northern Bavaria and even the German Alpine region, can be surprisingly economical. For example: a half-liter (¾ pint) of beer in the center of Munich might cost DM 4.20; in Bamberg, 150 miles to the north, the same half-liter (albeit from a different brewery!) will cost half that. In the picturesque medieval towns of Fulda, Alsfeld, Passau, Regensburg, and Coburg, you can buy a three-course lunch for less than the price of an entrée in Frankfurt. As a general rule, it's cheaper to order a cup of coffee at a *Stehcafe* (stand-up café) than to sit down and be served; some city cafés offer both options, and the price can vary from DM 1.70 to DM 2.80. In some sit-down cafés you can order coffee only by the pot (usually just over two cups), which can cost up to DM 4.50. A small glass of mineral water in a café or restaurant can cost up to DM 3—but you can buy a liter bottle in a supermarket for just over DM 1. The same goes for other drinks; a half-liter bottle of beer can cost as little as 85 pfennigs in a Munich supermarket.

In the big cities—especially in popular tourist destinations such as Munich—it's increasingly difficult to find a double room for a night for less than DM 75. But shop around the same town and you can still find a solid two-course lunch for under DM 20—which, in rural Franconia, will buy you three courses and a beer. Eating and sleeping costs aside, though, it's the big cities that offer the most free or almost-free attractions. For a few marks you can spend whole days exploring superb museums and art galleries. Most of the cities' architectural delights cost nothing to feast your eyes on. Only at the theater or concert hall do prices become prohibitive for the budget traveler.

Whatever the uncertainties brought by reunification, one hallmark of the German character remains constant: a nationwide love affair with beer. The merging of the two Germanys has actually led, for the first time in several years, to an increase in brewing, generated mainly by eastern Germans' demand for the superior western brews they had been so long denied. The result: In 1991 the Germans regained their world title for per capita consumption of beer, downing an average of 144 liters (254 pints) each—just ahead of the Czechoslovakians and Belgians and way ahead of the British (197 pints) and Americans (165 pints).

The Bavarians—who consumed a staggering 200 liters (352 pints) each—took the gold medal.

Money-saving Tips

- **Choose when to travel.** European tourism peaks over the summer, and prices are accordingly high. If you're at all flexible, plan to travel during the low season—between November and March—or else the shoulder season—April, May, and mid-September through October. Since many people begin their vacations on Friday or Saturday, airfares are usually more expensive on weekends, so try to travel midweek. Also, since city hotels are often filled with business travelers during the week, you may save money by arranging to stop in big cities over the weekend when the rates may be less expensive. (*See* When to Go in Chapter 1.)

- **Consult discount travel clubs and agencies.** Before going away, you may want to look into organizations that specialize in discounted hotel and airfares. Some travel clubs are especially good at arranging cut-rate deals with suppliers. Other clubs and agencies offer smaller discounts through partial rebates of commissions. Several such organizations are **Discount Travel International** (114 Forrest Ave., Narberth, PA 19072, tel. 215/668–7184); **Moment's Notice** (425 Madison Ave., New York, NY 10017, tel. 212/486–0503); **Travelers Advantage** (CUC Travel Service, 49 Music Square West, Nashville, TN 37203, tel. 800/548–1116); and **Worldwide Discount Travel Club** (1674 Meridian Ave., Miami Beach, FL 33139, tel. 305/534–2082).

- **Stay in cheaper regions.** You can save money by spending more time off-the-beaten track, in regions that tend to accommodate fewer tourists. This means less time in Berlin and Munich, but vacations in the countryside can be equally rewarding.

- **Avoid the single supplement fee.** Solo travelers looking to reduce their expenses can contact one of several organizations that help to match up travel companions. All of these groups charge a fee—usually between $20 and $40. Some publish a newsletter and let readers get in touch with one another, others match companions according to their interests. Organizations include: **Odyssey Network** (118 Cedar St., Wellesley, MA 02181, tel. 617/237-2400) and **Partners in Travel** (Box 491145, Los Angeles, CA 90049).

- **Think about buying the *Half Price Europe* book.** This book includes discount coupons for hotels, restaurants, rental cars, shops, tours, and special events. However, it's fairly expensive—$65 at the time of writing, plus postage and handling—and some travel experts feel that the hotel coupons are the only worthwhile deals in the book. Even so, if you have your heart set on a specific hotel at a particular time, you may be disappointed; many hotels offer a limited number of rooms at discount prices. Send $65 to **Entertain-**

ment Publications (2125 Butterfield Rd., Troy, MI 48084, tel. 800/477–3234), or order by phone; MasterCard and Visa accepted.

- **Make a budget.** Allow yourself a certain amount of spending money each day and try not to exceed that limit. There's no reason to set the same limit every day; you may want to live the spartan life for a while, then indulge yourself later. But make a habit of adhering to your daily allowances, so the cost of your trip can be kept below a predetermined sum.

- **Categorize expenses.** Travel expenses generally fall into these categories: accommodation, food, transportation, and cultural or recreational activities. Use these headings as guidelines for setting your priorities when you're deciding where you want to cut back. Eating sandwiches and staying at a youth hostel, for example, may save enough for a concert or a night at the theater.

- **Ask about discounts.** Not all discounts are advertised, so make an effort to ask about discounts before paying. Watch for weekend rates, student and age-related reductions, and promotional deals.

- **Be creative about accommodations.** A cheap hotel is *not* your only option for inexpensive lodging. You can have a more authentic German experience at a *Pension*. Other possibilities include youth hostels (not just for youths), country inns, and rooms in private homes. (*See* Lodging in Chapter 1.)

- **Go camping.** If you enjoy the outdoors, try spending some or all of your nights at the very affordable campsites located throughout Germany. Equipment is likely to be less expensive at home, so buy what you need before you go.

- **Save money on food.** *Gaststätten* and *Gasthöfe* offer hearty German food and drink at affordable prices. You're likely to find less expensive restaurants in the countryside, or on the outskirts of town, away from the heavily populated areas. You can also buy your food at a store, or find an attractive park or roadside spot and have a picnic lunch or an early dinner. In big cities especially, this is the best way to lower dining expenses without resorting to fast food. (*See* Dining in Chapter 1.)

- **Save on money exchange.** Inquire with someone at your hotel or at a tourist office about banks that specialize in changing money. Whatever you do, don't cash your traveler's checks at shops, hotels, or tourist attractions. (*See* Changing Money in Chapter 1.)

- **Don't make phone calls from your hotel.** If you make a call from your hotel room, you'll have to pay a surcharge. When calling home, prepare yourself with lots of change or phonecards, then find a pay phone and dial your call directly. This may be an inconvenience, but it's cheaper than an operator-assisted call.

- **Shop wisely.** Some of the best bargains can be found at factory shops. The cities, with their high prices and attractive items, are often frustrating for budget travelers, but ask at your hotel or at the tourist office about the street markets around town.

- **Use the VAT refund.** You can claim a refund on Germany's 14% Value Added Tax (*Mehrwertsteuer*) when you shop. Ask for a customs form along with your bill, as some stores offer the service only upon request, if they offer it at all. The form must be stamped by German customs when you leave the country, and then sent, together with the bill, back to the shop, which will mail you the refund minus handling costs. A few stores issue forms that allow you to collect your refund as you exit the country.

- **Consider your rail-travel needs.** Individual tickets aren't always more expensive than the pass you may be considering. If you don't plan to cover a lot of ground, it can be cheaper to pay for your trips individually. (*See* Rail Passes *and* Student and Youth Travel in Chapter 1.)

- **Travel at night.** Keep in mind that overnight rail travel saves money on accommodations. But take the necessary precautions against thieves, such as sleeping on top of your wallet or valuables, if you decide to spend the night on a train.

- **Consider a public-transportation pass.** In some cities you can buy passes for unlimited travel, good for a certain number of days on city buses and trains; in others, you can save money by purchasing several tickets at a time. If you plan to rely at all on public transportation inside a city, passes or multiple purchases will save you money.

- **Compare car-rental companies.** The multinational American companies don't always offer the best deals. You may do better with North American tour operators that arrange for cars from European rental companies. These tour operators include **Auto Europe, Connex, Europe by Car, Foremost Euro-Car,** and **Kemwell.** (*See* Car Rentals in Chapter 1.) Weekly touring packages offer unlimited mileage and a much better rate than the day-to-day deals. To qualify for most of these touring rates, you need to keep the car for at least five days, so plan your itinerary accordingly.

- **Find out about the arts for free.** Before spending your money on high-priced culture and entertainment, find out what's being offered for free. Most museums, churches, and commercial art galleries don't charge admission fees. You can look through local newspapers and magazines for free events, such as outdoor concerts and festivals.

1 Essential Information

Before You Go

Government Tourist Offices

Contact the German National Tourist Office at 747 Third Avenue, New York, NY 10017, tel. 212/308–3300; or 444 South Flower Street, Suite 2230, Los Angeles, CA 90071, tel. 213/688–7332.

In Canada Box 417, 2 Fundy, Place Bonaventure, Montreal H5A 1B8, tel. 514/878–9885.

In the United Kingdom Nightingale House, 65 Curzon Street, London W1Y 7PE, tel. 071/495–0081.

Tour Groups

Package tours are typically the most economical way to visit Germany. Thanks to the volume of passengers tour operators handle, they can negotiate significantly lower prices with airlines, hotels, and other travel suppliers than you can get on your own. There are, of course, potential drawbacks—you might find yourself dining with 20 people you don't particularly care for or being forced to march to the beat of someone else's drum. The key to a successful vacation is finding the tour that best suits your personal style, so ask a lot of questions. How many people are in the group? How much free time is there? Is there a special-interest tour I might find appealing?

The tours listed below should give you some idea of the wealth of programs available. Some are good introductory tours, some are more in-depth, others leave you to organize much of your own itinerary. For additional resources, contact your travel agent or the German National Tourist Office.

When considering a tour, be sure to find out (1) exactly what expenses are included, particularly tips, taxes, side trips, meals, and entertainment; (2) the ratings of all hotels on the itinerary and the facilities they offer; (3) the additional cost of single, rather than double, accommodations if you are traveling alone; and (4) the number of travelers in your group. Note whether the tour operator reserves the right to change hotels, routes, or even prices after you've booked, and check out the operator's policy regarding cancellations, complaints, and trip-interruption insurance. Many tour operators request that packages be booked through a travel agent; there is generally no additional charge for doing so.

General-interest Tours For a basic but good overview of the country, consider the 12-day "Best of Germany" from **Caravan Tours** (401 N. Michigan Ave., Chicago, IL 60601, tel. 312/321–9800 or 800/621–8338). Caravan's "Gothic Splendor" is a little less hectic, featuring a four-day Rhine cruise. **Globus-Gateway** (150 S. Los Robles Ave., Suite 860, Pasadena, CA 91101, tel. 818/449–0919 or 800/556–5454) runs a good, comprehensive tour, "Romantic Germany," as well as a new United Germany trip. **Olson-Travelworld** (100 N. Sepulveda Blvd., Suite 1010, El Segundo, CA 90245, tel. 213/615–0711 or 800/421–2255) offers "Fairy-tale Germany" (11 days) and "Storybook Germany" (17 days), both strong on Old World charm. "From Berlin to Leningrad" follows an intriguing itinerary that includes Berlin and heads east through

Poland to Moscow. **American Express Vacations** (Box 5014, Atlanta, GA 30302, tel. 800/241–1700 or 800/282–0800 in Georgia) is a veritable supermarket of tours. You name it, they've either got it packaged or can customize a package for you. **Maupintour** (Box 807, Lawrence, KS 66044, tel. 913/843–1211 or 800/255–4266) has a comprehensive 17-day tour of eastern and western Germany, as well as a leisurely 12-day tour that includes a Mosel River cruise. **Delta Air Lines** (tel. 800/338–2010) has a 13-day motorcoach tour that includes stops in Berlin, Heidelberg, Dresden, Köln, Hamburg, and Munich.

Special-interest Tours

Art/Architecture **Esplanade Tours** (581 Boylston St., Boston, MA 02116, tel. 617/266–7465) offers several in-depth art and architecture tours led by noted lecturers.

Barge Cruising Drift in leisure and luxury down the Rhine, Lahn, and Mosel rivers (crossing into France) with **Floating Through Europe** (271 Madison Ave., New York, NY 10016, tel. 212/685–5600).

Health/Fitness **DER Tours** (11933 Wilshire Blvd., Los Angeles, CA 90025, tel. 213/479–4140 or 800/937–1234) offers spa packages at five classic spas in the Black Forest and Bavaria.

Music **Dailey-Thorp Travel** (315 W. 57th St., New York, NY 10019, tel. 212/307–1555) offers deluxe opera and music tours, including "Musical Heartland of Europe." The tour features operas in Berlin, Dresden, and Prague (Czechoslovakia). Itineraries vary according to available performances.

Wine/Cuisine **Travel Concepts** (373 Commonwealth Ave., Suite 601, Boston, MA 02115–1815, tel. 617/266–8450) offers the "German Wine Academy." Usually based at Kloster Eberbach, a 12th-century monastery, the program includes tastings and visits to vineyards and wine cellars in seven of Germany's 11 wine-producing regions. **DER Tours** (*see above*) offers a tour called "Romantic Rhine and Wine."

Package Deals for Independent Travelers

DER Tours (*see* Tour Groups, *above*) specializes in independent packages. Travelers can choose from a variety of air, transportation, and overnight options. The company also offers bed-and-breakfast packages.

Delta Air Lines (*see* General-interest Tours, *above*) offers fly/drive and fly/rail packages, as well as five-night "city sprees," in Munich and Hamburg. All include round-trip airfare.

Europabus. The German railways section of this European-wide network offers several attractive German tours, including Romantic Germany and Eastern Germany (both seven days). Contact GermanRail in the United States or Deutsche Touring, Frankfurt (*see* Rail Passes, *below*).

Lufthansa German Airlines (750 Lexington Ave., New York, NY 10022, tel. 718/895–1277) offers air/hotel packages throughout the country, as does **TWA Getaway Vacations** (tel. 800/GET-AWAY).

Pan Am Holidays (tel. 800/843–8687) offers special rates at select hotels in Berlin, Frankfurt, Hamburg, and Munich when you fly round-trip on Pan Am and stay at the hotel a minimum of three nights.

When to Go

The tourist season in Germany runs from May to late-October, when the weather is at its best. Lodging prices are highest nationwide during July and August, and in winter holiday areas from Christmas to mid-January. The winter sports season in the Bavarian Alps runs from Christmas to mid-March. However, most resorts offer out-of-season (*Zwischensaison*) and "edge-of-season" (*Nebensaison*) rates, and tourist offices can provide lists of hotels that offer special low-price inclusive weekly packages (*Pauschalangebote*). Similarly, many winter ski resorts offer low rates for the periods between mid-January (after local school holidays) and Easter. The other advantage of out-of-season travel is that crowds are very much less in evidence. The disadvantages of visiting out of season, especially in winter, are that the weather is cold and, apart from ski resorts, some tourist attractions, especially in rural areas, are closed or have shorter hours.

Climate Germany's climate is temperate, although cold snaps can plunge the thermometer well below freezing, particularly in the Alps, the Harz region of Lower Saxony, and the higher regions of north Franconia. Summers are usually sunny and warm, though be prepared for a few cloudy and wet days. The south is normally always a few degrees warmer than the north. As you get nearer the Alps, however, the summers get shorter, often not beginning until the end of May. Fall is sometimes spectacular in the south: warm and soothing. The only real exception to the above is the strikingly variable weather in South Bavaria caused by the *Föhn,* an Alpine wind that gives rise to clear but very warm conditions. The Föhn can occur in all seasons. Sudden atmospheric pressure changes associated with the Föhn give some people headaches.

The following are the average daily maximum and minimum temperatures for Munich.

Jan.	35F	1C	**May**	64F	18C	**Sept.**	67F	20C
	23	-5		45	7		48	9
Feb.	38F	3C	**June**	70F	21C	**Oct.**	56F	14C
	23	-5		51	11		40	4
Mar.	48F	9C	**July**	74F	23C	**Nov.**	44F	7C
	30	-1		55	13		33	0
Apr.	56F	14C	**Aug.**	73F	23C	**Dec.**	36F	2C
	38	3		54	12		26	-4

WeatherTrak provides information on more than 750 cities around the world at 900/370–8728 (cost: 95¢ per minute). The number plays a taped message that tells you to dial a three-digit access code for the destination in which you're interested. The code is either the area code (in the United States) or the first three letters of the foreign city. For a list of all access codes, send a self-addressed stamped envelope to Cities, 9B Terrace Way, Greensboro, NC 27403. For more information, call 800/247–3282.

Festivals and Seasonal Events

Contact the **German National Tourist Office** for exact dates and additional information.

January	**Fasching season:** Carnival events, including proclamations of carnival princes, street fairs, parades, masked balls, and more, take place in Munich, Köln, Bonn, Düsseldorf, Offenburg, and around the Black Forest. Festivities reach their peak just prior to Ash Wednesday.
February	**Internationale Filmfestspiele** in Berlin is Germany's premier film festival. **Frankfurt International Fair** is a major consumer goods trade fair.
March	**Munich Fashion Week** is a popular trade fair of the latest fashions.
April	**German International Tennis Championships** are held in Hamburg.
May	**Mozart's Heritage in Dresden** celebrates the composer with opera, symphony, and chamber music concerts.
Early June–August	**Frankfurt Summertime Festival** features outdoor activities throughout the city.
July	**Richard Wagner Festival** is a major musical event in Bayreuth.
August	**Castle Festival** features open-air theater presentations at the castle in Heidelberg.
September	**Wine festivals** are held throughout the Rhineland. **Oktoberfest** in Munich attracts millions of visitors from throughout Germany, Europe, and abroad.
October	**Frankfurt Book Fair** is a famous annual literary event.
November	**St. Martin's Festival,** with children's lantern processions, is celebrated throughout the Rhineland and Bavaria.
December	**Christmas markets** are held in Augsburg, Munich, Heidelberg, Hamburg, Nürnberg, Lübeck, Freiburg, Berlin, Essen, and numerous smaller towns.

What to Pack

Pack light—luggage restrictions on international flights are tight. Airlines generally allow two pieces of check-in luggage and one carry-on piece per passenger. No piece of check-in luggage can exceed 62 inches (length + width + height) or weigh more than 70 pounds. The carry-on luggage cannot exceed 45 inches (length + width + height) and must fit under the seat or in the overhead luggage compartment. Passengers in first and business classes are also allowed to carry on one garment bag. It is always best, however, to check with your airline ahead of time to find out about its luggage restrictions.

What you pack depends more on the time of year than on any particular dress code. Winters can be bitterly cold; summers are warm but with days that suddenly turn cool and rainy. In the summer, take a warm jacket or heavy sweater for the Bavarian Alps, where the nights can be chilly even during the height of summer.

For the cities, pack as you would for an American city: dressy outfits for formal restaurants and nightclubs, casual clothes elsewhere. Jeans are as popular in Germany as anywhere else, and are perfectly acceptable for sightseeing and informal dining. In the evening, men will probably feel more comfortable wearing a jacket and tie in more expensive restaurants. Many German women are extremely fashion-conscious and wear stylish outfits to restaurants and the theater, especially in the larger cities.

If you plan to swim in a pool, take a bathing cap. They're obligatory in Germany, for both men and women. For stays in budget hotels, take your own soap. Many do not provide soap or provide only one small bar. You will need an electrical adapter for your hair dryer or other small appliances. The current is 220 volts, 50 cycles.

Taking Money Abroad

Traveler's checks and major U.S. credit cards, particularly Visa, are accepted in large cities and resorts. In smaller towns and rural areas, you'll need cash. Many small restaurants and shops in the cities also tend to operate on a cash basis. You won't get as good an exchange rate at home as abroad, but it's wise to exchange a small amount of money into German Deutschemarks before you go to avoid lines at airport currency-exchange booths. Most U.S. banks will exchange your money for Deutschemarks. If your local bank can't provide this service, you can exchange money through **Thomas Cook Currency Service.** To find the office nearest you, contact them at 29 Broadway, New York, NY 10006, tel. 212/635–0515.

For safety and convenience, it's always best to take traveler's checks. The most recognized traveler's checks are **American Express, Barclay's, Thomas Cook,** and those issued through such major commercial banks as **Citibank** and **Bank of America.** Some banks will issue the checks free to established customers, but most charge a 1% commission fee. Buy part of the traveler's checks in small denominations to cash toward the end of your trip. This will save you from having to cash a large check and ending up with more foreign money than you need. You can also buy traveler's checks in Deutschemarks—a good idea if the dollar is falling and you want to lock into the current rate. Remember to take the addresses of offices where you can get refunds for lost or stolen traveler's checks. *The American Express Traveler's Companion,* a directory of offices to contact worldwide in case of loss or theft of American Express Traveler's checks, is available at most American Express travel offices. In Germany, to report lost American Express traveler's checks, call the Brighton, England, office at 0273/21242.

The best places to change money are banks and bank-operated currency-exchange booths in airports and railway stations. You will generally be charged a DM 1–DM 2 commission for the transaction. Changing money in hotels is not a good idea—the commission can be exorbitant.

Getting Money from Home

There are at least three ways to get money from home: (1) Have it sent through a large commercial bank with a branch in the town where you're staying. The only drawback is that you must have an account with the bank; if not, you'll have to go through your own bank and the process will be slower and more expensive. (2) Have it sent through American Express. If you are a cardholder, you can cash a personal check or a counter check at an American Express office for up to $1,000; $200 will be in cash and $800 in traveler's checks. Goldcard holders can receive up to $5,000: $500 in cash and $4,500 in traveler's checks. There is a 1% commission on the traveler's checks. American Express also offers a service called **American Express MoneyGram,** which allows you to receive an unlimited amount of money. It works this way: You call home and ask someone to go to an American Express office or an American Express MoneyGram agent located in a retail outlet, and fill out an American Express MoneyGram. It can be paid for with cash or any major credit card. The person making the payment is given a reference number and telephones you with that number. The American Express MoneyGram agent calls an 800 number and authorizes the transfer of funds to an American Express office or participating agency in the town where you're staying. In most cases, the money is available immediately on a 24-hour basis. You pick it up by showing identification and giving the reference number. Fees vary according to the amount of money sent. For $1,000, the fee is $70; for $500, the fee is $45. For the American Express MoneyGram location nearest your home and to find out where the service is available overseas, call tel. 800/543–4080. You do not have to be a cardholder to use this service. (3) Have it sent through **Western Union,** U.S. telephone number 800/325–6000. If you have a MasterCard or Visa, you can have money sent for any amount up to your credit limit. If not, have someone take cash or a certified cashier's check to a Western Union office. The money will be delivered within two business days to a post office in the city where you're staying. Fees vary with the amount of money sent. For $1,000 the fee is $59 if paying with cash, $64 if you use a credit card; for $500, the fee is $49 with cash, $54 with a credit card.

German Currency

The unit of currency in Germany is the Deutschemark (DM), divided into 100 pfennings (pf). Bills are DM 1,000, 500, 200, 100, 50, 20, and 10. Coins are DM 5, 2, and 1, and 50, 10, 5, 2, and 1 pf. At press time the exchange rate was about DM 1.64 to the U.S. dollar, DM 1.44 to the Canadian dollar, and DM 2.90 to the pound sterling.

The Deutschemark became the official currency of united Germany in July 1990. However, great discrepancies still exist in the standard—and cost—of living between western and eastern Germany.

What It Will Cost

Germany's standard of living is one of the highest in Europe—and so is its cost of living. But within the overall statistics, prices can vary tremendously, especially between west and east. Except for room rates at international-class hotels and restaurants, prices in East Germany used to run about half of those in West Germany, but with a common currency and free-market economy, everything is in a tremendous state of flux. You will find that coffee, beer, snacks, and local public transportation will be noticeably cheaper in eastern Germany than in western. (Be prepared for prices quoted in this guide to have changed drastically by the time you travel.)

Buses are cheaper than trains, but the railroad network is more extensive and more convenient. Rail costs can be kept down if you take advantage of one of the special discount offers available to foreign visitors (*see* Rail Passes *and* Student and Youth Travel, *below*).

The following sample prices are meant only as a general guide; you can expect substantial variations.

Small-town bed-and-breakfast for two, without private bath (Gasthof Spezial, Bamberg): DM 65.

City budget hotel for two, without private bath (Hotel Dittberner, Berlin): DM 92.

City budget dinner for two, without drinks (Straubinger Hof, Munich): DM 33.50.

Cheapest Frankfurt concert ticket: DM 25.

Coca-Cola, budget restaurant: DM 2.50.

Cup of coffee, budget restaurant: DM 2.50.

Street-stand snack (two sausages and a roll): DM 2.70.

Glass of wine, budget restaurant (¼-liter): DM 4.50.

City taxi ride (3 miles, plus tip): DM 7.

Subway ticket (one way): DM 2.40.

Movie ticket: DM 9.50.

Daily newspaper (U.S. or U.K.): DM 2.60.

½-liter glass of beer, city: DM 3.80.

½-liter glass of beer, country: DM 2.70.

Round-trip rail ticket (Munich–Garmisch, special day-trip price): DM 24.50.

Taxes

Mehrwertsteuer (Value Added Tax) goes into most service bills, including car hire, lodging, and dining. You may be unaware of the extra charge since it's built into the end price. At press time (fall 1991) the rate was 14%, but it may soon rise to 16% as part of European Economic Community standardization. Nowadays airport tax is generally a hidden extra included in the price of your ticket. Some holiday centers, such as Garmisch in the Bavarian Alps, charge a local accommodation tax—usually only a few marks per person.

Passports and Visas

Americans All U.S. citizens require a passport to enter Germany. Applications for a new passport must be made in person; renewals can be obtained in person or by mail (*see below*). First-time applicants should apply to one of the 13 U.S. Passport Agency offices well in advance of their departure date. In addition, local county courthouses, many state and probate courts, and some post offices accept passport applications. Necessary documents include: (1) a completed passport application (Form DSP-11); (2) proof of citizenship (birth certificate with raised seal or naturalization papers); (3) proof of identity (unexpired driver's license, employee ID card, or any other document with your photograph and signature); (4) two recent, identical 2-inch-square photographs (black-and-white or color); (5) $42 application fee for a 10-year passport (those under 18 pay $27 for a five-year passport). If you pay in cash, you must have the exact amount, as no change is given. Passports are mailed to you within about 10 working days.

To renew your passport by mail, you'll need a completed Form DSP-82, two recent, identical passport photographs, a passport issued less than 12 years ago, and a check or money order for $35.

A tourist/business visa is not required for U.S. citizens staying up to three months in Germany, but longer stays generally require a visa. Check with the Embassy of the Federal Republic of Germany, 4645 Reservoir Rd. NW, Washington, DC 20007, tel. 202/298–4000.

Canadians All Canadian citizens require a passport to enter Germany. Send your completed application (available at any post office or passport office) to the **Bureau of Passports,** Suite 215, West Tower, Guy Favreau Complex, 200 René Lévesque Blvd. West, Montreal, Quebec H2Z1X4. Include $25, two photographs, a guarantor, and proof of Canadian citizenship. Applications can also be made in person at the regional passport offices in Edmonton, Halifax, Montreal, Toronto, Vancouver, or Winnipeg. Passports are valid for five years and are nonrenewable.

Visas are not required for Canadian citizens to enter Germany for stays of up to three months.

Britons All British citizens require a passport to enter Germany. Application forms are available from travel agencies and main post offices, or from the **Passport Office** (Clive House, 70 Petty France, London SW1H 9HD, tel. 071/279–3434). Send the completed form to a regional passport office or apply in person at a main post office. The application must be countersigned by your bank manager, or by a solicitor, barrister, doctor, clergyman, or justice of the peace who knows you personally. In addition, you'll need two photographs and a £15 fee. The occasional tourist might opt for a British Visitors' passport. It is valid for one year, costs £7.50 and is nonrenewable. You'll need two passport photographs and identification. Apply at your local post office.

Visas are not required for British citizens to enter Germany.

Customs and Duties

On Arrival There are three levels of duty-free allowance for visitors to Germany.

Entering Germany from a non-European country, the allowances are (1) 400 cigarettes or 100 cigars or 500 grams of tobacco, (2) 1 liter of spirits more than 22% proof or 2 liters of spirits less than 22% proof, (3) 2 liters of wine, (4) 50 grams of perfume and ¼ liter of toilet water, and (5) other goods to the value of DM 115.

Entering Germany from a country belonging to the EC, the allowances are (1) 200 cigarettes (300 if not bought in a duty-free shop) or 75 cigars or 400 grams of tobacco, (2) 1 liter of spirits more than 22% proof (1.5 liters if not bought in a duty-free shop), or 3 liters of spirits less than 22% proof, (3) 5 liters of wine, (4) 75 grams of perfume and ⅓ liter of toilet water, and (5) other goods to the value of DM 780.

Entering Germany from a European country not belonging to the EC (Austria or Switzerland, for example), the allowances are (1) 200 cigarettes or 50 cigars or 250 grams of tobacco, (2) 1 liter of spirits more than 22% proof or 2 liters of spirits less than 22% proof, (3) 2 liters of wine, (4) 50 grams of perfume and ¼ liter of toilet water, and (5) other goods to the value of DM 115.

Tobacco and alcohol allowances are for visitors aged 17 and over. Other items intended for personal use can be imported and exported freely. There are no restrictions on the import and export of German currency.

On Departure

U.S. Customs

If you are bringing any foreign-made equipment from home, such as cameras, it's wise to carry the original receipt with you or register it with U.S. customs before you leave (Form 4457). Otherwise you may end up paying duty on your return. U.S. residents may bring home duty-free up to $400 worth of foreign goods, as long as they have been out of the country for at least 48 hours and haven't made an international trip in 30 days. Each member of the family is entitled to the same exemption, regardless of age, and exemptions can be pooled. For the next $1,000 worth of goods, a flat 10% rate is assessed; above $1,400, duties vary with the merchandise. Included for travelers 21 or older are 1 liter of alcohol, 100 cigars (non-Cuban), and 200 cigarettes. Only one bottle of perfume trademarked in the United States may be imported. However, there is no duty on antiques or art over 100 years old. Anything exceeding these limits will be taxed at the port of entry, and may be taxed additionally in the traveler's home state. Gifts valued at under $50 may be mailed to friends or relatives at home duty-free, but not more than one package per day to any one addressee may be sent, and packages may not include perfumes costing more than $5, tobacco, or liquor.

Canadian Customs

Canadian residents have an exemption ranging from $20 to $300, depending on the length of stay out of the country. For the $300 exemption, you must have been out of the country for one week. For any given year, you are allowed one $300 exemption. You may also bring in duty-free up to 50 cigars, 200 cigarettes, 2.2 pounds of tobacco, and 40 ounces of liquor, provided these are declared in writing to customs on arrival and accompany the traveler in hand or in checked-through baggage. Personal gifts should be mailed as "Unsolicited Gift—Value under $40." Request the Canadian customs brochure "I Declare" for further details.

British Customs

Returning to the United Kingdom, a traveler aged 17 or over can take home (1) 200 cigarettes or 100 cigarillos or 50 cigars or 250 grams of tobacco; (2) two liters of still table wine and, in addition, (a) one liter of alcoholic drink over 22% volume (most spirits) or (b) two liters of alcoholic drink under 22% by volume (fortified or sparkling wines) or (c) two more liters of table wine; (3) 60 milliliters of perfume and 250 milliliters of toilet water; (4) other goods to a value or £32, but not more than 50 liters of beer or 25 lighters.

In the first category, you may import duty-free (1) 200 cigarettes or 100 cigarillos or 50 cigars or 250 grams of tobacco (*Note:* If you live outside Europe, these allowances are doubled), (2) 1 liter of alcoholic drinks over 22% volume or 2 liters of alcoholic drinks not over 22% volume or fortified or sparkling wine, (3) 2 liters of still table wine, (4) 60 milliliters of perfume, (5) 250 milliliters of toilet water, and (6) other goods to the value of £32.

In the second category, you may import duty-free (1) 300 cigarettes or 150 cigarillos or 75 cigars or 400 grams of tobacco, (2) 1.5 liters of alcoholic drinks over 22% volume or 3 liters of alcoholic drinks not over 22% volume or fortified or sparkling wine, (3) 5 liters of still table wine, (4) 90 milliliters of perfume, 375 milliliters of toilet water, and (6) other goods to the value of £250. (*Note:* Though it is not classified as an alcoholic drink by EC countries for customs' purposes and is thus considered part of the "other goods" allowance, you may not import more than 50 liters of beer.)

In addition, no animals or pets of any kind may be brought into the United Kingdom. The penalties for doing so are severe and are strictly enforced.

Language

The Germans are great linguists, and you'll find that English is spoken in virtually all hotels, restaurants, airports, and stations, museums, and other places of interest. However, English is not always widely spoken in rural areas; this is especially true of the eastern part of Germany.

Unless you speak fluent German, you may find some of the regional dialects hard to follow, particularly in Bavaria. While most Germans can speak "high," or standard, German, some older country people will only be able to speak in their dialect.

Staying Healthy

Sanitation and health standards in Germany are as high as those anywhere in the world, and there are no serious health risks associated with travel there. If you have a health problem that might require purchasing prescription drugs while in Germany, have your doctor write a prescription using the drug's generic name. Brand names vary widely from one country to another.

The **International Association for Medical Assistance to Travelers** (IAMAT) is a worldwide association that offers a list of approved physicians and clinics whose training meets British and American standards. For a list of German physicians and clinics that are part of this network, contact IAMAT (417 Center St., Lewiston, NY 14092, tel. 716/754–4883; in **Canada,** 40 Regal Rd., Guelph, Ontario N1K 1B5; in **Europe,** 57 Voirets, 1212 Grand-Lancy, Geneva, Switzerland). Membership is free.

Inoculations are not required for entry to Germany.

Insurance

Travelers may seek insurance coverage in three areas: health and accident, loss of luggage, and trip cancellation. Your first step is to review your existing health and homeowner policies; some health-insurance plans cover health expenses incurred while traveling, some major-medical plans cover emergency transportation, and some homeowner policies cover the theft of luggage.

Health and Accident Several companies offer coverage designed to supplement existing health insurance for travelers:

Carefree Travel Insurance (Box 310, 120 Mineola Blvd., Mineola, NY 11501, tel. 516/294–0220 or 800/323–3149) provides coverage for emergency medical evacuation and accidental death and dismemberment. It also offers 24-hour medical phone advice.

International SOS Assistance (Box 11568, Philadelphia, PA 19116, tel. 215/244–1500 or 800/523–8930), a medical assistance company, provides emergency evacuation services, worldwide medical referrals, and optional medical insurance.

Travel Guard International, underwritten by Transamerica Occidental Life Companies (1145 Clark St., Stevens Point, WI 54481, tel. 715/345–0505 or 800/782–5151), offers reimbursement for medical expenses with no deductibles or daily limits, as well as emergency-evacuation services.

Wallach and Company, Inc. (243 Church St., NW, Suite 100D, Vienna, VA 22180, tel. 703/281–9500 or 800/237–6615), offers comprehensive medical coverage, including emergency evacuation services worldwide.

Lost Luggage Luggage loss is usually covered as part of a comprehensive travel-insurance package that includes personal accident, trip cancellation, and sometimes default and bankruptcy insurance. Several companies offer comprehensive policies: **Access America, Inc.,** a subsidiary of Blue Cross-Blue Shield (Box 11188, Richmond, VA 23230, tel. 800/334–7525 or 800/284–8300); **Near Services,** (450 Prairie Ave., Suite 101, Calumet City, IL 60409, tel. 708/868–6700 or 800/654–6700); and **Travel Guard International** (*see* Health and Accident Insurance, *above*).

Trip Cancellation Flight insurance is often included in the price of a ticket when paid for with American Express, Visa, and other major credit and charge cards. It is usually included in combination travel-insurance packages available from most tour operators, travel agents, and insurance agents.

Rail Passes

The **EurailPass,** valid for unlimited first-class train travel through 17 countries, including Germany, is an excellent value if you plan to travel around the Continent. The ticket is available for periods of 15 days ($390), 21 days ($498), one month ($616), two months ($840), and three months ($1,042). Three people traveling together can purchase the 15-day pass for $298 each. During the off-season (Oct.–Mar.) two people can enjoy the cut-price deal. For those under 26, there is the **Eurail Youthpass,** for one or two months' unlimited second-class train travel at $425 and $560.

For travelers who like to spread out their train journeys, there is the **Eurail Flexipass.** With the 15-day pass ($230), travelers get five days of unlimited first-class train travel spread out over a 15-day period; a 21-day pass gives you nine days of travel ($398), and a one-month pass gives you 14 days ($498).

The EurailPass is available only if you live outside Europe or North Africa. The pass must be bought from an authorized agent before you leave for Europe. Apply through your travel agent, or contact **GermanRail** (747 3rd Ave., New York, NY 10017, tel. 212/308–3102).

The new GermanRail (DB) Flexipass, now valid for the entire German rail network, is available to non-Europeans and must be purchased outside of Europe. The "flexible" nature of the pass allows you to spread your days of train travel over a month-long period. A second-class pass costs $130 for five days, $200 for 10 days, and $250 for 15 days. A Youthpass (second-class only) for people aged 12–26 ranges from $90 to $150 (*see* Student and Youth Travel, *below*). GermanRail passes can be used on buses operated by the DB, as well as on tour routes along the Romantic and Castle roads served by Deutsche Touring (*see* Getting Around by Bus in Staying in Germany, *below*). Cruises on the Rhine, Main, and Mosel rivers operated by the Köln-Düsseldorfer (KD) Line are also included with the pass.

Student and Youth Travel

The **International Student Identity Card** (ISIC) entitles students to youth rail passes, special fares on local transportation, Intra-European student charter flights, and discounts at museums, theaters, sports events, and many other attractions. If purchased in the United States, the $14 cost of the ISIC also includes $3,000 in emergency medical insurance, $100 a day for up to 60 days of hospital coverage, and a collect phone number to call in case of emergencies. Apply to the **Council on International Student Exchange** (CIEE, 205 E. 42nd St., New York, NY 10017, tel. 212/661–1414). In Canada, the ISIC is available for CN$12 from **Travel Cuts** (187 College St., Toronto, Ont. M5T 1P7, tel. 416/979–2406).

The **Youth International Educational Exchange Card** (YIEE), issued by the **Federation of International Youth Travel Organizations** (FIYTO, 81 Islands Brugge, DK-2300 Copenhagen S, Denmark), provides similar services to nonstudents under the age of 26. In the United States, the card is available from CIEE (*see above*). In Canada, the YIEE is available from the **Canadian Hostelling Association** (CHA, 1600 James Naismith Drive, Suite 608, Gloucester, Ont. K1B 5N4, tel. 613/748–5638).

An **International Youth Hostel Federation** (IYHF) membership card is the key to inexpensive dormitory-style accommodations at more than 5,000 youth hostels in 68 countries around the world. Hostels provide separate sleeping quarters for men and women at rates ranging from $7 to $20 a night per person and are situated in a variety of facilities, including converted farmhouses, villas, and restored castles, as well as specially constructed modern buildings. IYHF membership is available in the United States through American Youth Hostels (AYH, Box 37613, Washington, DC 20013, tel. 202/783–6161) and in Canada through the **Canadian Hostelling Association** (*see above*). The cost for a first-year membership is $25 for adults 18–54. Renewal thereafter is $15 a year. For youths (17 and under), the rate is $10 a year, and for senior citizens (55 and older) the rate is $15 a year. Family membership is available for $35 a year.

Council Travel, a CIEE subsidiary, is the foremost U.S. student travel agency, specializing in low-cost charters and serving as the exclusive U.S. agent for many student airfare bargains and student tours. CIEE's 80-page *Student Travel*

Catalog and "Council Charter" brochure are available free from any Council Travel office in the United States (enclose $1 postage if ordering by mail). Contact the CIEE headquarters (205 E. 42nd St., New York, NY 10017) for the branch office nearest you.

The **Educational Travel Center** (438 N. Frances St., Madison, WI 53703, tel. 608/256–5551) is another student travel specialist worth contacting for information on student tours, bargain fares, and bookings.

Students who would like to work abroad should contact CIEE's **Work Abroad Department** (205 E. 42nd St., New York, NY 10017, tel. 212/661–1414, ext. 1130). The council arranges various types of paid and voluntary work experiences overseas for up to six months. CIEE also sponsors study programs in Europe, Latin America, and Asia, and publishes many books of interest to the student traveler. These include *Work, Study, Travel Abroad: The Whole World Handbook* ($10.95 plus $1 book-rate postage or $2.50 first-class postage); and *Volunteer! The Comprehensive Guide to Voluntary Service in the U.S. and Abroad* ($6.95 plus $1 book-rate postage or $2.50 first-class postage).

The Information Center at the **Institute of International Education** (IIE) has reference books, foreign university catalogs, study-abroad brochures, and other materials, which may be consulted by students and nonstudents alike, free of charge. The Information Center (809 UN Plaza, New York, NY 10017, tel. 212/984–5413) is open Monday–Friday 10–4. It is not open on holidays.

IIE administers a variety of grant and study programs offered by U.S. and foreign organizations, and publishes a well-known annual series of study-abroad guides, including *Academic Year Abroad, Vacation Study Abroad,* and *Study in the United Kingdom and Ireland.* The institute also publishes *Teaching Abroad,* a book of employment and study opportunities overseas for U.S. teachers. For a current list of IIE publications with prices and ordering information, write to Publications Service, Institute of International Education, 809 UN Plaza, New York, NY 10017. Books must be purchased by mail or in person; telephone orders are not accepted.

General information on IIE programs and services is available from its regional offices in Atlanta, Chicago, Denver, Houston, San Francisco, and Washington, DC.

A **German Rail Youthpass** (second-class only), for people aged 12–26, costs between $90 and $150. The pass can be purchased anywhere outside Germany, but these favorable prices are available only in the United States. Travelers under 26 who have not invested in any of the other rail passes should inquire about discount travel fares under a Billet International Jeune (BIJ) scheme. The special one-trip tariff is offered by Euro-Train International, with offices in London, Dublin, Paris, Madrid, Lisbon, Rome, Zurich, Athens, Brussels, Budapest, Hanover, Leiden, Vienna, and Tangier. You can purchase a Eurotrain ticket at one of these offices or at travel-agent networks, mainline rail stations, and specialist youth-travel operators.

Students with valid ID can obtain 50% reductions on entry charges to virtually all galleries and museums. Students also qualify for 10% discounts on Europabus fares and most trains other than ICE trains.

Traveling with Children

Publications ***Family Travel Times*** is a newsletter published 10 times a year by **TWYCH** (Travel with Your Children, 80 Eighth Ave., New York, NY 10011, tel. 212/206–0688). Subscription costs $35 and includes access to back issues and twice-weekly opportunities to call in for specific advice.

Young People's Guide to Munich is a free pamphlet available from the German National Tourist Office (747 Third Ave., New York, NY 10017, tel. 212/308–3300).

Hotels A likely choice for families is any one of the Schloss (castle) hotels in Germany; many have parklike grounds. U.S. representatives are **Europa Hotels and Tours** (tel. 800/523–9570) and **DER Tours Inc.** (tel. 800/937–1234).

Home Exchange Exchanging homes is a surprisingly low-cost way to enjoy a vacation abroad, especially a long one. The largest home-exchange service, **International Home Exchange Service** (Box 190070, San Francisco, CA 94119, tel. 415/435–3497) publishes three directories a year. Membership, which costs $45, entitles you to one listing and all three directories. **Loan-a-Home** (2 Park La., 6E, Mount Vernon, NY 10552, tel. 914/664–7640) is popular with academics on sabbatical and businesspeople on temporary assignment. There's no annual membership fee or charge for listing your home, however one directory and a supplement costs $35. Loan-a-Home publishes two directories (in December and June) and two supplements (in March and September) each year. The set of four books costs $45 per year.

Getting There On international flights, children under two years not occupying a seat pay 10% of adult fare. Various discounts apply to children from ages two to 12. Reserve a seat behind the bulkhead of the plane, which offers more legroom and can usually accommodate a bassinet (which some airlines will supply). At the same time, inquire about special children's meals or snacks, offered by most airlines. (See "TWYCH's Airline Guide," in the February 1990 and 1992 issues of *Family Travel Times*, for a rundown on children's services offered by 46 airlines.)

Regulations about infant travel on airplanes are in the process of changing. Until they do, however, if you want to be sure your infant is secure, you should buy a separate ticket and bring your own infant car seat (but check with the airline in advance—some don't allow them). Some airlines allow babies to travel in their own car seats at no charge if there's a spare seat available; otherwise, safety seats will be stored and the child will have to be held by a parent. For the booklet *Child/Infant Safety Seats Acceptable for Use in Aircraft*, write to the **Federal Aviation Administration** (800 Independence Ave., SW, Washington, DC 20591, tel. 202/267–3479). If you opt to hold your baby on your lap, do so with the infant outside the seat belt so he or she won't be crushed in case of a sudden stop.

Baby-sitting Services First check with the hotel desk for recommended child-care arrangements. Also, most local tourist offices in Germany maintain updated lists of baby-sitters. The baby-sitters have all been screened. Expect to pay approximately DM 25 per hour. In Munich, for a tourist-office-approved service offering sitters who speak English, call 089/229–291 or 089/394–507. Also, contact the **Munich American High School** (Cincinnatistr. 61A, Munich, tel. 089/622–98354). The **American Women's Club of Frankfurt** (Abrams Bldg., Frankfurt, West Germany, APO, NY 09757) runs a child-care center at the military base near the Abrams Building (tel. 069/55–3129).

Hints for Disabled Travelers

The **Information Center for Individuals with Disabilities** (Fort Point Pl., 1st floor, 27–43 Wormwood St., Boston, MA 02210, tel. 617/727–5540; TDD 617/727–5236) offers useful problem-solving assistance, including lists of travel agents that specialize in tours for the disabled.

Moss Rehabilitation Hospital Travel Information Service (1200 West Tabor Rd., Philadelphia, PA 19141–3009, tel. 215/456–9600; TDD 215/456–9603) provides (for a small fee) information on tourist sights, transportation, and accommodations in destinations around the world.

Mobility International USA (Box 3551, Eugene, OR 97403, tel. 503/343–1284), an internationally affiliated organization, coordinates exchange programs for disabled people around the world and offers information on accommodations and organized study programs. The annual fee is $20.

The **Society for the Advancement of Travel for the Handicapped** (26 Court St., Penthouse, Brooklyn, NY 11242, tel. 718/858–5483) offers access information. Annual membership costs $45, or $25 for senior travelers and students. Send a stamped, self-addressed envelope.

Travel Industry and Disabled Exchange (TIDE, 5435 Donna Ave., Tarzana, CA 91356, tel. 818/368–5648) provides (for a $15 per-person annual membership fee) a quarterly newsletter and a directory of travel agencies and tours to Europe, Canada, New Zealand, and Australia, all specializing in travel for the disabled.

The Itinerary (Box 2012, Bayonne, NJ 07002, tel. 201/858–3400) is a bimonthly travel magazine for the disabled. Subscriptions cost $10 for one year, $20 for two. ***Access to the World: A Travel Guide for the Handicapped,*** by Louise Weiss, offers tips on travel and accessibility around the world. It is available from Henry Holt & Co. for $12.95 (tel. 800/247–3912; the order number is 0805001417).

Hints for Older Travelers

The **American Association of Retired Persons** (AARP, 1909 K St. NW, Washington, DC 20049, tel. 202/662–4850) has two programs for independent travelers: (1) the "Purchase Privilege Program," which offers discounts on hotels, airfare, car rentals, and sightseeing; and (2) the "AARP Motoring Plan," provided by Amoco, which offers emergency aid and trip-routing information for an annual fee of $33.95 per couple. The AARP also arranges group tours, including apartment living in Europe, through **American Express Vacations** (Box 5014, Atlanta, GA 30302, tel. 800/241–1700 or 800/637–6200 in GA).

AARP members must be 50 or older. Annual dues are $5 per person or per couple.

When using an AARP or other identification card, ask for a reduced hotel rate at the time you make your reservation, not when you check out. At participating restaurants, show your card to the maitre d' before you're seated, since discounts may be limited to certain set menus, days, or hours. When renting a car, be sure to ask about special promotional rates which may offer greater savings than the available discount.

Elderhostel (75 Federal St., 3rd floor, Boston, MA 02110–1941, tel. 617/426–7788) is an innovative educational program for people 60 and older. Participants live in dorms on some 1,200 campuses around the world. Mornings are devoted to lectures and seminars; afternoons, to sightseeing and field trips. The all-inclusive fee for two- to three-week trips, including room, board, tuition, and round-trip transportation, ranges from $1,800 to $4,500.

National Council of Senior Citizens (925 15th St. NW, Washington, DC 20005, tel. 202/347–8800) is a nonprofit advocacy group with some 5,000 local clubs across the country. Annual membership is $12 per person or per couple. Members receive a monthly newspaper with travel information and an ID card for reduced-rate hotels and car rentals.

Mature Outlook (6001 N. Clark St., Chicago, IL 60660, tel. 800/336–6330), a subsidiary of Sears Roebuck & Co., is a travel club for people over 50, with hotel and motel discounts and a bimonthly newsletter. Annual membership is $9.95 per couple. Instant membership is available at participating Holiday Inns.

Holders of British Rail Senior Citizens' Rail Cards can buy an "add-on" **European Senior Citizens' Rail Card** that permits half-price train travel in most European countries, including Germany. Senior citizens from other countries who intend to stay in Germany for some time should consider buying the DB **Senioren-Pass.** This is available in two forms: the Senioren Pass "A" (which costs DM 75) allows half-price travel Mon.–Thurs. and Sat., while Senioren B (DM 110) permits half-price travel any day of the week. Both are valid for a year and can be bought before going to Germany.

Senior citizens with proof of age generally qualify for 50% reductions on entrance fees at most German galleries and museums.

Arriving and Departing

From North America by Plane

Since the air routes between North America and Germany are heavily traveled, the passenger has a choice of many airlines and fares. But fares change with stunning rapidity, so consult your travel agent on what bargains are currently available.

Be certain to distinguish among (1) nonstop flights—no changes, no stops; (2) direct flights—no changes but one or more stops; and (3) connecting flights—two or more planes, two or more stops.

Discount Flights The major airlines offer a range of tickets that can increase the price of any given seat by more than 300%, depending on the day of purchase. As a rule, the further in advance you buy the ticket, the less expensive it is and the greater the penalty (up to 100%) for canceling. Check with airlines for details.

The best buy is not necessarily an APEX (advance purchase) ticket on one of the major airlines. APEX tickets carry certain restrictions: They must be bought in advance (usually 21 days); they restrict your travel, usually with a minimum stay of seven days and a maximum of 90; and they also penalize you for changes—voluntary or not—in your travel plans. But if you can work around these drawbacks, they are among the best-value fares available.

Charter flights offer the lowest fares but often depart only on certain days, and seldom on time. Though you may be able to arrive at one city and return from another, you may lose all or most of your money if you cancel your ticket. Don't sign up for a charter flight unless you've checked with a travel agency about the reputation of the packager. It's particularly important to know the packager's policy concerning refunds should a flight be canceled. One of the most popular charter operators to Europe is **Council Charter** (205 E. 42nd St., New York, NY 10017, tel. 800/223-7402 or 212/661-0311), a division of CIEE (Council on International Education Exchange). Other companies advertise in the Sunday travel section of newspapers.

Somewhat more expensive—but up to 50% below the cost of APEX fares—are tickets purchased through companies known as consolidators, which buy blocks of tickets on scheduled airlines and sell them at wholesale prices. Here again, you may lose all or most of your money if you change plans, but at least you will be on a regularly scheduled flight with less risk of cancellation than on a charter. Once you've made your reservation, call the airline to make sure you're confirmed. Among the best known consolidators are **UniTravel** (Box 12485, St. Louis, MO 63132, tel. 800/325-2222 or 314/569-2501) and **Access International** (101 W. 31st St., Suite 1104, New York, NY 10001, tel. 212/465-0707 or 800/825-3633). Others advertise in the Sunday travel section of newspapers as well.

A third option is to join a travel club that offers special discounts to its members. Three such organizations are **Moment's Notice** (425 Madison Ave., New York, NY 10017, tel. 212/486-0503); **Discount Travel International** (114 Forrest Ave., Narberth, PA 19072, tel. 215/668-7184); and **Worldwide Discount Travel Club** (1674 Meridian Ave., Suite 300, Miami Beach, FL 33139, tel. 305/534-2082). These cut-rate tickets should be compared with APEX tickets on the major airlines.

Airlines The U.S. airlines that serve Germany are **Northwest Airlines** (tel. 800/447-4747), which flies to Frankfurt; **Delta** (tel. 800/241-4141), which flies to Frankfurt, Stuttgart, and Munich; **TWA** (tel. 800/892-4141), which flies to Frankfurt, Stuttgart, Munich, and Berlin; **Pan Am** (tel. 800/221-1111), which flies to Frankfurt, Stuttgart, Munich, Berlin, Hamburg, Nürnberg, Düsseldorf, and Hannover; and **American Airlines** (tel. 800/433-7300), which flies to Frankfurt, Berlin, Hamburg, Munich, and Nürnberg. **Lufthansa** (tel. 800/645-3880), the German national airline, flies direct to Düsseldorf, Frankfurt, Köln/Bonn, Hamburg, Munich, and Stuttgart. Another German carrier, **LTU International Airways** (tel. 800/888–0200), flies from New York, Miami, San Francisco, and Los Angeles to Frankfurt, Munich, and Düsseldorf.

Flying Time The flying time to Frankfurt from New York is 7.5 hours; from Chicago, 10 hours; from Los Angeles, 12 hours.

Enjoying the Flight If you're lucky enough to be able to sleep on a plane, it makes sense to fly at night. Many experienced travelers, however, prefer to take a morning flight to Europe and arrive in the evening, just in time for a good night's sleep. Since the air on a plane is dry, it helps to drink a lot of nonalcoholic liquids; drinking alcohol contributes to jet lag. Feet swell at high altitudes, so it's a good idea to remove your shoes while in flight. Sleepers usually prefer window seats to curl up against; those who like to move about the cabin should ask for aisle seats. Bulkhead seats (located in the front row of each cabin) have more legroom, but seat trays are attached to the arms of your seat rather than to the back of the seat in front of you. Bulkhead seats are generally reserved for the disabled, the elderly, and parents traveling with infants.

Smoking Regulations You can request a nonsmoking seat during check-in or when you book your ticket. If a U.S. airline tells you there are no seats available in the nonsmoking section, insist on one: Department of Transportation regulations require U.S. carriers to find seats for all nonsmokers on the day of the flight, provided they meet check-in time restrictions.

From the United Kingdom by Plane

The main charter-plane company, Air Europe, went bust in 1991, and so far no new airline has stepped in to fill the gap. **Dan Air** continues to offer the cheapest and most regular charter flights, from Gatwick. The airline flies five times a week to Berlin and Munich, and twice weekly to Hamburg, Frankfurt, Düsseldorf, and Stuttgart.

British Airways and **Lufthansa** are the other main airlines flying from London to Germany. Between them, they serve nine German destinations—10, including Münster, to which Lufthansa's subsidiary airline, **DLT**, flies. Both airlines set aside a percentage of seats on all routes for APEX discount flights. In some cases, these must be booked two weeks ahead of travel.

The main gateways to Germany by air are Düsseldorf, Köln, Frankfurt, Munich, and Berlin. British Airways and Lufthansa each have up to two flights a day into Köln, with a flying time of 1¼ hours and a minimum round-trip fare of £90. British Airways has up to seven flights and Lufthansa six flights into Frankfurt from London, with a flying time of 1 hour and 25 minutes and a minimum fare of £95. Each airline has three flights into Munich, with a 1 hour and 40 minute flying time and a minimum fare of £125. British Airways has up to three nonstop and three one-stop flights into Berlin, with a nonstop flying time of 1 hour and 40 minutes and a minimum fare of £135. Lufthansa inaugurated flights into Berlin in late 1990.

The airlines also fly to Bremen, Hannover, and Stuttgart, and Lufthansa also has one flight a day into Nürnberg.

Commuter-style airline **Connectair** flies twice a day from Gatwick to Düsseldorf with an £80 cheapest round-trip fare. **Air UK** flies weekdays from London's third airport, Stansted, to Frankfurt (1 hour and 55 minutes flying time) and DLT's other Gatwick service also goes to Frankfurt.

Another airline that flies into Berlin is **Pan Am,** which can also fly you into Frankfurt, Hamburg, and Munich as a continuation of its transatlantic flights into London.

Increasing competition has brought fares down to lower levels than still exist on other European routes from the United Kingdom, and further improvement is expected now that British Midland, the U.K. independent airline, flies from Heathrow to Düsseldorf and Frankfurt.

For reservations: **British Airways** (tel. 081/897–4000); **Air UK** (tel. 0345/666777); **Lufthansa** (tel. 071/408–0442); **Pan Am** (tel. 071/409–0688); **Connectair** (tel. 0293/862971); **Dan Air/GTF** (tel. 071/229–2474).

From the United Kingdom by Train

British Rail operates up to 10 services a day to Germany under its Rail Europe banner. Eight of the departures are from Victoria (via the Dover-Ostend ferry or jetfoil) with the other two from Liverpool Street (via Harwich–Hook of Holland).

The services, involving train changes (usually at Köln), include Köln, Koblenz, Frankfurt, Osnabruck, Hannover, Hamburg, Stuttgart, and Munich, with the journey time to Köln usually 9 hours via jetfoil, 12 hours via the Dover–Ostend ferry, and 13 hours via the Harwich–Hook route. To Munich, the times vary from 14 to 23 hours depending on the time of departure and route. The fastest train leaves Victoria at about 8 AM. Rail fares can be more expensive than plane fares.

Berlin is reached via Hannover in about 20 hours, with up to four departures a day—two from Victoria, two from Liverpool Street.

The cheapest round-trip fares to Köln and Munich are £72 and £145, with the ordinary fares set at £85 and £188. These apply to the Victoria departures; Liverpool Street services are more expensive.

A one-way fare to Berlin is £80; the round-trip fare is £160. Book through British Rail travel centers (tel. 071/834–2345).

From the United Kingdom by Bus

Traveling to Germany by bus is generally cheaper than by rail, though if your visit is part of a wider European tour the Eurailpass is a better deal. The fastest service is by **Europabus,** which has up to three departures a day from London's Victoria coach station. The buses cross the Channel on Sealink's Dover-Zeebrugge ferry service and then drive via the Netherlands and Belgium to Köln (14½ hours), Frankfurt (17½ hours), Mannheim (18¾ hours), Stuttgart/Nürnberg (20½ hours), and Munich (22¾ hours). One-way and round-trip fares are: Köln (£36/£59), Frankfurt (£38/£65), Mannheim (£41/£70), Stuttgart/Nürnberg (£48/£76), and Munich (£52/£86). For a full schedule of international services connecting with German destinations contact Deutsche Touring (Am Römerhof 17, 6000 Frankfurt am Main 90, tel. 069/79030).

Bookings can also be made through **Transline** (tel. 0708/864911), which runs a service to 35 smaller towns in West Germany. There are up to four departures a week, also from Victoria, and the buses cross either via P&O European Ferries' Dover-Ostend or Sally Line's Ramsgate-Dunkerque services. Destinations include Hannover, Dortmund, Essen, and Düsseldorf as well as the smaller towns. Fares range from £32 to £36 one way and £59 to £66 round-trip.

From the United Kingdom by Car

The choice of Channel crossing from the United Kingdom when driving to Germany, and not using the direct Harwich-Hamburg link, will depend on the final destination. If north Germany is the destination, then ports in the Netherlands are the most convenient. For central and south Germany, the Belgian entry ports are best.

A sample of the mileages confirms this. For Berlin and Hannover, the Hook of Holland is considerably closer at 476 and 282 miles than Ostend at 520 and 387 miles respectively; for Munich, Ostend is 23 miles closer at 530. For Köln and Frankfurt, the two ports are almost equidistant. Both are considerably closer than the French ports.

For the Hook of Holland, ferries depart from Harwich—the east coast port reached from London via the A-12 (about 2½ hours' drive). **Sealink** operates one ferry daily and one overnight; both sail year-round. It is an eight-hour crossing, and passengers' fares start at £27 (£9 supplement for first-class travel), car rates range from £32 to £63, and a two-berth cabin costs from £6 to £14.

Like Sealink, **Olau Line** operates newer, high-quality ships on its Netherlands route. There is one daily and one overnight departure from the north Kent port of Sheerness (two hours from London via A2/M2) to Vlissingen. The fare is £22; car rates start at £25.

P&O European Ferries operates services from Dover to both Zeebrugge (up to six a day) and Ostend, 19 miles southwest down the coast. Crossing time to Ostend is four hours, half an hour longer to Zeebrugge. Passengers' fares to both Belgian ports are £13, with car rates from £24 to £78.

All four ports mentioned are between one and two hours' drive of the German border. From the Hook, take the A-12 to Arnhem and then the A-1 toward Dortmund, Essen, and so on. From Vlissingen, take the A-58 and then the A-67 to Düsseldorf.

Both Zeebrugge and Ostend are a short drive from the E-5, from which you can turn off onto the E-3 at Ghent for Düsseldorf and Essen, or stay on and join the A-61 for Bonn and, farther south, Koblenz, Wiesbaden, Frankfurt, and Mannheim.

P&O also operates a ferry service into Zeebrugge from Felixstowe (another English east coast port just north of Harwich); while **North Sea Ferries** operates from much farther north at Hull to Zeebrugge and Rotterdam Europoort, two miles south of the Hook.

There is a **Motorail** service from Paris to Munich. A distance of 575 miles, the journey takes 10 hours and there is one departure a day.

For ferry reservations: **Sealink,** tel. 01/834–8122; **P&O,** tel. 01/734–4431; **Olau,** tel. 0795/666666; **North Sea Ferries,** tel. 0482/795141; **French Motorail,** tel. 071/409–3518 (information only).

It is recommended that motorists acquire a green card from their insurance companies. This gives comprehensive insurance coverage for driving in Germany. The most comprehensive breakdown insurance and vehicle and personal security coverage is sold by the **Automobile Association** (AA) in its Five Star scheme.

Staying in Germany

Getting Around

The best public transportation in Germany is the extensive and highly efficient rail network, which reaches into most of the corners of the country and even high into the Alps. Standard fares can be expensive, but there are many Rover, discount, and group deals (a group can be as few as four people traveling together), which can slash prices by up to 40% (*see below*).

Buses serve as backup, usually in rural areas remote from railheads. There is no long-distance network on a par with Greyhound in the United States. Most of the long distance buses are operated by Europabus (*see below*).

Germany also has an excellent air network, operated almost exclusively by Lufthansa; but unless you need to get somewhere urgently, fares are generally prohibitive. A Munich–Berlin round-trip, for example, runs DM 640.

By Train If you are planning much train travel, take advantage of the heavily discounted **Rover** tickets, which you must buy before you arrive in the country (*see below*). The **Deutsches Bundesbahn (DB),** or German Federal Railways, runs trains in what used to be West Germany; trains in the east are still operated by the **Reichsbahn.** The two systems are expected to merge in the near future; in the meantime they are increasingly integrating their networks, and there are now many more trains linking the eastern cities of Leipzig, Dresden, Halle, Magdeburg, Potsdam, Rostock, and Schwerin—as well as Berlin—with destinations in the western half. DB offers a range of discounted fares and inclusive tickets, from family Rovers to Senior Citizen Cards. But the most flexible and economical deal for the foreign visitor is probably the new German Rail Pass (*see* Rail Passes in Before You Go, *above*).

All major cities in western Germany are linked by fast **InterCity** services, which run hourly and offer first- and second-class cars. Even faster **InterCity Express (ICE)** trains, capable of speeds up to 265 kilometers per hour (165 miles per hour), came into service in late 1991. Travel times are being cut by 30% on these wider, more comfortable trains, reducing the journey from Hamburg to Munich from eight hours to under six. If you buy a train ticket locally, you will automatically be given second class unless you request first class. First-class fares generally cost 50% more for slightly bigger seats with more leg room.

There is a surcharge of up to DM 24 (depending on distance) for traveling on ICE trains, which may be worthwhile if you're trying to save time or if you place a high value on comfort. A surcharge of DM 6 (DM 10 first class) is added, regardless of distance, on all InterCity journeys, but seat reservations—on both ICE and InterCity trains—are free if you make them in advance. These trains will not carry bikes.

If you are going a long distance—say, Hamburg to Munich—you can cut hotel costs by traveling overnight and booking a couchette bed. The lowest-price deal is in a six-berth coed compartment: DM 28, including a sleeping bag–style sheet. All long-distance routes have restaurant cars, and overnight InterCity trains have sleeper cars. There are also slower long-distance (Inter-Regio) trains operating between western cities, and E-trains make the run over shorter distances.

Trains in eastern Germany remain slower because of the poor condition of the tracks and of many bridges. The Reichsbahn, like the DB, usually offers first- and second-class cars, and dining cars or buffet facilities on longer routes. Since fewer people in the east have automobiles, trains there are more heavily used. We strongly advise you to make seat reservations for long journeys.

Special train maps on platform notice boards give details of the layout of each IC train arriving on that line, showing where first- and second-class cars and the restaurant car are situated, as well as where they will stop along the length of the platform. If you have a reservation, it will give the number of the car with your seats; locate this car on the map so that you can stand on the platform exactly where your car will stop when the train pulls in. It is possible to check your baggage for Frankfurt Airport from any of 52 Intercity stations throughout Germany. Except on weekends, there is guaranteed overnight delivery.

Note that in high season you will frequently encounter lines at ticket offices for seat reservations. Unless you are prepared to board the train without a reserved seat, taking the chance of a seat being available, the only way to avoid these lines is to make an advance reservation by phone. Call the ticket office (*Fahrkarten Schalter*) of the rail station from which you plan to depart. Here again, you will probably have to make several attempts before you get through to the reservations section (*Reservierungen-Platzkarten*), but you will then be able to collect your seat ticket from a special counter without having to wait in line.

Tourist Rail Cards

DB Regional Rail Rovers (**Tourenkarten**) cover some 73 areas, including all the main tourist regions. They are excellent value for the money. Valid for any 10 days within a 21-day vacation period, they cost around DM 50 for one person, DM 68 for two people traveling together, and DM 83 for a family (one or two parents, plus any number of unmarried children under 18 and grandparents). Unless you are going to Germany on a vacation run by the railways themselves, the Tourenkarte has to be bought when you arrive in Germany. However, there is one catch: To be eligible you must travel at least 250 kilometers (155 miles) on a German train to reach your vacation area and the same distance when you leave. So check distances carefully on your map—it may be worth making a slight detour to qualify.

For further information, contact **GermanRail** (747 Third Ave., New York, NY 10017, tel. 212/308–3106).

By Bus Bus fares within Germany are on the high side. The trip from Frankfurt to Munich costs DM 86 (round-trip DM 155); from Heidelberg to Munich, DM 56 (round-trip DM 101). A large proportion of services are operated by the railways (**Bahnbus**) and are closely integrated with train services, while on less busy rail lines, services are run by buses in off-peak periods—normally mid-day and weekends. Rail tickets are valid on these services. The railways, in the guise of **Deutsche Touring,** also operate the German sections of the Europabus network. Contact them at Am Römerhof 17,6000-Frankfurt/Main 90, for details about a range of 2–7-day package tours.

Bus travel, unlike train travel, offers only one class of service. Europabus offers discounts on 10-day round-trip tickets. All Deutsches Bundesbahn train passes (Eurail included) are valid on Europabus services within Germany. Students and people under 26 get 10% reductions on Europabus fares, but the bus network is far smaller than the rail network.

One of the best services is provided by the Romantic Road bus between Würzburg (with connections to and from Frankfurt and Wiesbaden) and Füssen (with connections to and from Munich, Augsburg, and Garmisch-Partenkirchen). This is an all-reserved-seats bus with a stewardess, offering one- or two-day tours in each direction in summer, leaving in the morning and arriving in the evening. Details and reservations are available from Deutsche Touring (*see above*) or big-city tourist offices.

All towns of any size operate their own local buses. For the most part, those link up with local trams (streetcars), electric railways services (S-bahn), and subways (U-bahn). Fares vary according to distance, but a ticket usually allows you to transfer freely between the various forms of transportation. Some cities issue 24-hour tickets at special rates.

By Car Roads in the western part of the country are generally excellent, but many surfaces in eastern Germany, where an urgent improvement program is under way, are in poor condition. Gasoline (petrol) costs are between DM 1.17 and DM 1.32 per liter. As part of antipollution efforts, many German cars now run on lead-free fuel (which is cheaper than leaded because the government has kept taxes on it down). Some older cars may not run especially well on it, but it makes no difference at all to the performance of newer models. German filling stations are highly competitive and bargains are often available if you shop around, but *not* at autobahn filling stations. Self-service, or *SB-Tanken*, stations are cheapest. Pumps marked *Bleifrei* contain unleaded gas.

As elsewhere in Western Europe, in Germany you drive on the right, and road signs give distances in kilometers. Political reunification did not bring a consensus to the rules of the road, however. In the western part of Germany, unlimited speeds on the autobahns continue, while in former East Germany—the five new states of Thüringia, Saxony, Saxony-Anhalt, Brandenburg, and Mecklenburg—a top limit of 100 kph (60 mph) remains in force (80 kph on other country roads). Speed limits on non-autobahn country roads in western areas vary from 80 to 100 kph. Germany charges motorists no toll on its autobahns.

Note that seat belts must be worn at all times by front- *and* back-seat passengers.

An absolute ban on alcohol is strictly enforced for drivers in the east, but drivers in the west can still legally sit behind the wheel after drinking two small beers or wine. These inconsistencies are expected to be resolved soon.

Entry formalities for motorists are few: All you need is proof of insurance, an international car-registration document, and an international driver's license. If you or your car are from an EC country, or from Austria, Norway, Switzerland, Sweden, or Portugal, all you need is your domestic license and proof of insurance. *All* foreign cars must have a country sticker.

Car Rentals Rental rates vary widely, depending on size and model, number of days you use the car, insurance coverage, and whether special drop-off fees are imposed. In most cases, rates quoted include unlimited free mileage and standard liability protection. Not included are collision damage waiver (CDW), which eliminates your deductible payment should you have an accident; personal accident insurance; gasoline; and European value added taxes (VAT), which at press time was 14% throughout Germany. A national car-rental firm will charge about DM 60 per day, DM 415 per week, including insurance and unlimited mileage, for a small two-door, four-seat model such as a Volkswagen Polo. (If you want to avoid a collision deductible of DM 4,000, insurance will run you an extra DM 20–DM 38 per day.) You'll be expected to return the car with a full tank of gas; otherwise you'll be charged for the gas, at the rental firm's high rate. Gasoline costs vary considerably, especially in cities and even between service stations belonging to big chains such as Esso and BP, so shop around if you have the time (and always avoid buying gas on the autobahns).

If you're flying into a major German city you can save money by arranging to pick up and return your car at the airport. You'll have to weigh the added expense of renting a car from a major company with an airport office against the savings on a car from a budget company with offices in town. You could waste precious hours trying to locate the budget company in return for only a small financial savings. If you're arriving and departing from different airports, look for a one-way car rental with no return fees. If you're traveling to more than one country, make sure your rental contract permits you to take the car across borders and that the insurance policy covers you in every country you visit. Be prepared to pay more for a car with an automatic transmission. Since these cars aren't as readily available as those with manual transmission, you should reserve them in advance.

Driver's licenses issued in the United States, Canada, and Britain are valid in Germany. You might also take out an international driving permit before you leave, to smooth out difficulties if you have an accident or as an additional identification. Permits are available for a small fee through local offices of the American Automobile Association (AAA) and the Canadian Automobile Association (CAA), or from their main offices (**AAA,** 8111 Gatehouse Rd., Falls Church, VA 22047–0001, tel. 703/AAA–6000; **CAA,** 2 Carlton St., Toronto, Ontario M5B 1K4, tel. 416/964–3170).

It's best to arrange a car rental before you leave. You won't save money by waiting until you arrive in Germany, and you may find that the type of car you want is not available at the last minute. Rental companies usually charge according to the exchange rate of the dollar at the time the car is returned or when the credit-card payment is processed. Three companies guaranteeing advertised rates if you pay in advance are **Budget Rent-a-Car** (3350 Boyington St., Carrollton, TX 75006, tel. 800/527–0700), **Connex Travel International** (983 Main St., Peekskill, NY 10566, tel. 800/333–3949), and **Cortell International** (770 Lexington Ave., New York, NY 10021, tel. 800/223–6626 or 800/442–4481 in NY).

Other budget rental companies serving Germany include **Europe by Car** (1 Rockefeller Plaza, New York, NY 10020, tel. 800/223–1516 or 800/252–9401 in CA), **Auto Europe** (Box 1097 Sharps Wharf, Camden, ME 04843, tel. 800/223–5555, or 800/342–5202 in ME, or 800/237–2465 in Canada), **Foremost Euro-Car** (5430 Van Nuys Blvd., Van Nuys, CA 91404, tel. 800/423–3111), and **Kemwel** (106 Calvert St., Harrison, NY 10528, tel. 800/678–0678).

Other companies include **Avis** (tel. 800/331–1212); **Hertz** (tel. 800/223–6472 or 800/522–5568 in NY); and **National** or **Europcar** (tel. 800/CAR–RENT).

GermanRail offers Rail and Drive packages, which combine a train Flexipass (*see* Rail Passes, *above*) with three days of unlimited-mileage car rental. Packages start at $185 (for a five-day Flexipass and three-day car rental over a month-long period).

By Plane Services are operated by **Lufthansa** and by Germany's leading charter company, **LTU.** Details of all internal services are available from travel agents; otherwise, contact Lufthansa at Frankfurt airport (tel. 069/690–71222; 069/690–30509).

Lufthansa also runs an excellent train, the "Lufthansa Express," linking Düsseldorf, Köln, Bonn, and Frankfurt airports and acting as a supplement to existing air services. Only passengers holding air tickets may use the train, but there is no extra charge for it. Service is first class. Luggage is automatically transferred to your plane on arrival at the airport. German Railways operates a similar service called "Rail and Fly," and trains on the Köln-Munich line stop at Frankfurt airport instead of at Wiesbaden for connections with flights to and from Frankfurt.

By Boat River and lake trips are among the greatest delights of a vacation in Germany, especially along the Rhine, Germany's longest river. The Rhine may be viewed at a variety of paces: by fast hydrofoil, by express boat, by sedate motorship, or by romantic paddle steamer. For those in a hurry, there is a daily hydrofoil service from Düsseldorf right through to Mainz. It is advisable to book in advance for this. German cruise ships also operate on the Upper Rhine as far as Basel, Switzerland; on the Main between Frankfurt and Mainz; on the Danube to Linz and on to Vienna; on the Europe Canal joining the Main and the Danube; on the Elbe and Weser and their estuaries; on the Inn and Ilz; and on the Ammersee, Chiemsee, Königsee, and Bodensee.

EurailPasses are valid on all services of the KD German Rhine Line and on the Mosel between Trier and Koblenz. (If you use the fast hydrofoil, a supplementary fee has to be paid.) DB Tourist Card holders are given a 50% reduction on KD ships. Regular rail tickets are also accepted, meaning that you can go one way by ship and return by train. All you have to do is pay a small surcharge to KD Rhine Line and get the ticket endorsed at one of the landing stage offices. But note that you have to buy the rail ticket first and *then* get it changed.

One of the best and most attractive ways of seeing the glories of the Rhine and the Moselle is on one of the traditional KD old-time paddle steamers or on one of their large modern motor vessels. During the summer there are good services between Bonn and Koblenz and between Koblenz and Bingen; both trips take around five hours.

KD German Rhine Line now operates two luxury cruises on the Elbe River from May through October: a five-day trip from Bad Schandau to Magdeburg, and a seven-day journey from Bad Schandau to Hamburg. Ports of call include Dresden, Meissen, and Wittenberg. The cruises, aboard modern power vessels, are in great demand, so reservations are necessary several months in advance.

KD has several budget deals, too; for example, on Sunday or holidays, children between 4 and 14 accompanied by adults pay only DM 5. Likewise, senior citizens pay only half price on Monday. If it's your birthday, you travel free. For details of all KD services, contact the company in the United States at 170 Hamilton Avenue, White Plains, NY 10601–1788, tel. 914/948–3600, and at 323 Geary Street, San Francisco, CA 94102–1860, tel. 415/392–8817; in Germany contact Köln-Düsseldorfer Deutsche Rheinschiffahrt AG, Frankenwerft 15, 5000–Köln 1, tel. 0221/20880.

By Bike Information on all aspects of cycling in Germany is available from the **Bund Deutscher Radfahrer,** the Association of German Cyclists (Otto-Fleck-Schneise 4,6000 Frankfurt 71). There are no formalities governing the importation of bikes into Germany, and no duty is required. Bikes can also be carried on most trains—though *not* on ICE or InterCity trains (*see above*)—if you buy a *Fahrradkarte,* or bicycle ticket. These cost DM 6.50 per journey and can be bought at any train station. Those under 26 with a "Tramper Ticket"—a monthly Rover that costs DM 234—can take bikes free of charge. Full details are given in the German railway's brochure *Fahrrad am Bahnhof.*

Bicycles are available for rental at more than 270 train stations throughout the country, most of them in south Germany. The cost is DM 10–DM 12 per day, DM 6–DM 8 if you have a valid rail ticket. They can be returned to most other stations; there's a drop-off fee of DM 4.60 per bike.

The most popular areas for bicycle touring are Franconia, The Rhineland, and the Black Forest. For the best advice on low-traffic routes, and for specially marked bike-route maps, write the **Allgemeiner Duetscher Fahrrad Club** (Am Dobben 91, 2800 Bremen 1), or call the club at tel. 0421/74052.

Telephones

Local Calls Local public phones charge a minimum 30 pfennigs per call (for five minutes). Public phones take 10-pfennig, DM 1, and DM 5 coins. If you plan to make an out-of-town call, take along a good supply of DM 1 coins. Most phone booths have instructions in English as well as German; if yours doesn't, simply lift the receiver, put the money in, and dial.

Card phones are rapidly replacing coin-operated ones, accounting for as many as half the pay phones in some city-center areas. You can buy cards from post offices for DM 12 or DM 50 (depending on the amount of phone time you need); they'll save you up to 20%.

International Calls These can be made from public phones bearing the sign "Inlands and Auslandsgespräche." They take 10 pfennigs, DM 1, and DM 5 coins; a four-minute call to the United States costs DM 15. To avoid weighing yourself down with coins, however, make international calls from post offices; even those in small country towns will have a special booth for international calls. You pay the clerk at the end of your call. Never make international calls from your hotel room; rates will be at least double the regular charge.

Operators and Information The western German telephone system is fully automatic, and it's unlikely that you'll have to employ the services of an operator (except to reach certain rural eastern German areas). If you do, dial 01188, or 00118 for international calls. If the operator doesn't speak English (also unlikely), you'll be passed to one who does.

Mail

Postal Rates Airmail letters to the United States and Canada cost DM 1.40; postcards cost 90 pfennigs. All letters to the United Kingdom cost DM 1; postcards cost 60 pfennigs.

Receiving Mail You can arrange to have mail sent to you in care of any German post office; have the envelope marked "Postlagernd." This service is free. Alternatively, have mail sent to any American Express office in Germany. There's no charge to cardholders, holders of American Express traveler's checks, or anyone who has booked a vacation with American Express. Otherwise, you pay DM 2 per collection (not per item).

Tipping

The service charges on lodging bills suffice for most tips, though you should tip bellhops and porters; DM 2 per bag or service is ample. Whether you tip the desk clerk depends on whether he or she has given you any special service.

Service charges are included in all restaurant bills (listed as *Bedienung*), as is tax (listed as *MWST*). Nonetheless, it is customary to round out the bill to the nearest mark or to leave about 5% (give it to the waiter or waitress as you pay the bill; don't leave it on the table).

In taxis, round out the fare to the nearest full mark as a tip. Only give more if you have particularly cumbersome or heavy luggage (though you will be charged 50 pfennigs for each piece of luggage anyway).

Opening and Closing Times

Banks Times vary from state to state and city to city, but banks are generally open weekdays from 8:30 or 9 to 3 or 4 (5 or 6 on

Thursday). Branches at airports and main train stations open as early as 6:30 AM and close as late as 10:30 PM.

Museums Most museums are open from Tuesday through Sunday 9–6. Some close for an hour or more at lunch, and some are open on Monday.

Shops Times vary slightly, but generally shops are open 9 or 9:15–6:30 Monday through Friday and until 2 PM on Saturday, except for the first Saturday in the month, when the bigger stores stay open until 6 in winter and 4 in summer. Many shops also now remain open on Thursday evenings until 8:30.

National Holidays January 1; April 17 (Good Friday); April 19 (Easter); April 20 (Easter Monday); May 1 (May Day); May 28 (Ascension Day); June 8 (Pentecost Monday); October 3 (Day of German Unity); November 18 (Day of Repentance and Prayer); December 25, 26 (Christmas).

Lodging

The cost of accommodation in Germany varies tremendously between city and countryside. A simple double room in a budget hotel in, say, Frankfurt or Munich can cost DM 150, while bed-and-breakfast in a private guest house in the rural Rhineland or on the Baltic coast might be under DM 40 for two.

But the cities are not without their bargains. The best bets are places that prefix their names with the term *Pension*; there you can find city lodgings at under DM 100 for a double—sometimes even with a private bath.

In the country there are also numerous *Gasthöfe* or *Gasthäuser*, which are country inns that serve food and also have rooms; *Fremdenheime* (guest houses); and, at the lowest end of the scale, *Zimmer*, meaning simply "rooms," normally in private houses (look for the sign reading *Zimmer frei* or *zu vermieten* on a green background, meaning "to rent"; a red sign reading *besetzt* means that there are no vacancies).

Lists of German hotels are available from the German National Tourist Office and all regional and local tourist offices. (Most hotels have restaurants, but those listed as *Garni* will provide breakfast only.) Tourist offices will also make bookings for you at a nominal fee, but they may have difficulty doing so after 4 PM in high season and on weekends, so don't wait until too late in the day to begin looking for your accommodations. (If you do get stuck, ask someone who looks local—a postman, policeman, or waitress, for example—for a Zimmer zu vermieten or Gasthof; in rural areas especially you'll find that people are genuinely helpful). A hotel reservation service is also operated by **ADZ** (Corneliusstr. 34, W–6000 Frankfurt/Main, tel. 069/740767). It is able to make reservations in many hotels throughout the country for a small fee.

Many major American hotel chains—Hilton, Sheraton, Holiday Inn, Arabella, Canadian Pacific, Ramada, Preferred—have hotels in the larger German cities.

Rentals Bungalows or apartments (*Ferienwohungen* or *Ferienapartments*), usually accommodating two to eight people, can be rented throughout Germany. Rates are low, with reductions for longer stays. There is usually an extra charge for gas and electricity, and sometimes water. There is also normally a charge for linen, though you may also bring your own.

Details of rentals in all regions of the country are available from the regional and local tourist offices. In addition, the German Automobile Association issues listings of family holiday apartments; write **ADAC Reisen** (Am Westpark 8, 8000 Munich 70).

Farm Vacations *Urlaub auf dem Bauernhof,* or vacations down on the farm, have increased dramatically in popularity throughout Germany over the past five years, and almost every regional tourist office now produces a brochure listing farms in its area that offer bed and breakfast, apartments, and entire farmhouses to rent. In addition, the German Agricultural Association (DLG) produces an illustrated brochure listing over 1,500 farms, all inspected and graded, from the Alps to the North Sea, that offer accommodations. It costs DM 7.50 (send an international reply coupon if writing from the United States) and is available from **DLG Reisedienst, Agratour** (Zimmerweg 16, D–6000 Frankfurt/Main 1).

Camping Campsites—some 2,000 in all—are scattered the length and breadth of Germany. The **DCC,** or German Camping Club (Mandlstr. 28, D–8000 Munich 40) produces an annual listing of 1,600 sites; it also details sites where trailers and mobile homes can be rented. Similarly, the German Automobile Association (*see* Rentals, *above,* for address) publishes a listing of all campsites located at autobahn exits. In addition, the German National Tourist Office publishes a comprehensive and graded listing of campsites.

Sites are generally open from May through September, though about 400 are open year-round for the very rugged. Most sites get crowded during high season, however. Prices range from around DM 10 to DM 15 for a car, trailer, and two adults; less for tents. If you want to camp elsewhere, you must get permission from the landowner beforehand; ask the police if you can't track him or her down. Drivers of mobile homes may park for one night only on roadsides and in autobahn parking-lot areas, but may not set up camping equipment there.

Youth Hostels Germany's youth hostels—*Jugendherbergen*—are probably the most efficient, up-to-date, and proportionally numerous of any country's in the world. There are more than 700 in all, many located in castles that add a touch of romance to otherwise utilitarian accommodations. Since unification, many eastern German youth hostels have closed down. An effort is being made, however, to keep as many open as possible, and renovations are currently underway to bring eastern hostels up to the standards of their western counterparts.

Apart from Bavaria, where there is an age limit of 27, there are no restrictions on age, though those under 20 take preference when space is limited. You'll need an International Youth Hostel card, valid for one year, for reduced rates, usually about DM 12 to DM 18 for youth under 27 and DM 13.50 to DM 22 for adults (breakfast included), which must be paid in cash. Cards are available from the **American Youth Hostels Association** (Box 37613, Washington, DC 20013) and the **Canadian Hostelling Association** (333 River Rd., Ottawa, Ontario K1L 8H9). For listings of German youth hostels, contact the **Deutsches Jugendherbergswerk Hauptverband** (Bismarckstr. 8, D–4930

Detmold, tel. 05231/74010) or the German National Tourist Office.

Ratings This guide uses two categories of accommodation rates: one for cities, the other for smaller towns, villages, and the countryside. Rates given are for a double room, but not necessarily one with a private bath or shower.

Category	Cities and Expensive Regions	Less Expensive Regions
Moderate	under DM 180 ($110)	under DM 150 ($90)
Inexpensive	under DM 130 ($80)	under DM 110 ($65)
Budget	under DM 90 ($55)	under DM 70 ($45)

Dining

Almost every city street has its *Gaststätte*, a sort of combination diner and pub, and every village its *Gasthof*, or inn. The emphasis in both is on the characteristic German preference for *gutbürgerliche Küche*, or good home cooking, with simple food, wholesome rather than sophisticated, at reasonable prices. These are also places where people meet in the evening for a chat, a beer, and a game of cards, so you needn't feel compelled to leave as soon as you have eaten. They normally serve hot meals from 11:30 AM to 9 or 10 PM; some places stop serving hot meals between 2 and 6 PM, although you can still order cold dishes. Lunch rather than dinner is the main meal in Germany, a fact reflected in the *Tageskarte*, or suggested menu, every lunchtime. And at a cost of DM 12 to DM 15, in either a Gaststätte or Gasthof, for soup, a main course, and simple dessert (though this is not always offered), it's excellent value. Coffee is generally available, and it's perfectly acceptable to go into a Gaststätte or country pub and order just a pot of coffee outside busy lunch periods. Some, though not all, expensive restaurants also offer a table d'hôte (suggested or special) daily menu. Prices will be much higher than in a Gaststätte or Gasthof, but considerably cheaper than à la carte.

Regional specialties are given in the Dining sections of individual chapters. For names of German foods and dishes, *see* the Menu Guide at the end of this book.

Budget Eating Tips
Ethnic Restaurants Germany has a vast selection of moderately priced Italian, Greek, Chinese, and—largely as a result of the number of Yugoslav workers in Germany—Balkan restaurants. All are good value, though you may find the food in Balkan restaurants spicy. Italian restaurants are about the most popular of all specialty restaurants in Germany—the pizza-to-go is as much a part of the average German's diet as *Bratwurst* or a hamburger. You'll find that Chinese restaurants in particular offer special tourist and lunch menus.

Stand-up Snack Bars Often located in pedestrian zones, *Imbiss* stands can be found in almost every busy shopping street, in parking lots, train stations, and near markets. They serve *Wurst* (sausage), grilled, roasted, or boiled, of every shape and size, and rolls filled with cheese, cold meat, or fish. Prices range from DM 3 to DM 6 per portion.

Department Stores For lunch, restaurants in local department stores (*Kaufhäuser*) are especially recommended for wholesome, appetizing, and inexpensive food. **Kaufhof, Karstadt, Horton,** and **Hertie** are names to note, as well as the enormous **KaDeWe** in Berlin.

Butcher Shops Known as *Metzgerei,* these often have a corner that serves warm snacks. The **Vinzenz-Murr** chain in Munich and throughout Bavaria have particularly good-value food. Try *warmer Leberkäs mit Kartoffelsalat,* a typical Bavarian specialty, which is a sort of baked meat loaf with sweet mustard and potato salad. In north Germany, try *Bouletten,* small hamburgers, or *Currywurst,* sausages in a piquant curry sauce.

Fast Food A number of fast-food chains exist all over the country. The best are **Wienerwald, McDonald's,** and **Burger King.** There are also **Nordsee** fish bars, serving hot and cold fish dishes.

Picnics Buy some wine or beer and some cold cuts and rolls (*Brötchen*) from a department store, supermarket, or delicatessen and turn lunchtimes into picnics. You'll not only save money, but you'll also be able to enjoy Germany's beautiful scenery. Or leave out the beer and take your picnic to a beer garden, sit down at one of the long wood tables, and order a *Mass* (liter) of beer.

Ratings We have compiled two rating systems: one for dining in cities, the other for smaller towns, villages, and the countryside. Prices are per person for two courses, without drinks.

Category	Cities and Expensive Regions	Less Expensive Regions
Moderate	under DM 40 ($24)	under DM 30 ($18)
Inexpensive	under DM 30 ($18)	under DM 20 ($12)
Budget	under DM 20 ($12)	under DM 15 ($9)

Credit Cards

The following credit card abbreviations are used: AE, American Express; DC, Diners Club; MC, Mastercard; V, Visa.

Popular Itineraries

The Castles of Ludwig II

Munich tour operators offer day trips to the four famous castles of Bavaria's flamboyant King Ludwig II, but for those who want to get to know them without distracting interruptions, there's no alternative but to strike out on your own. The castles are set in magnificent countryside that invites the visitor to linger and complete a stay with a walk or a hike undisturbed by the demands of a tour operator's timetable.

Length of Trip 4 to 5 days

Getting Around **By car:** From Munich, this is a 340-kilometer (210-mile) round-trip drive.

By public transportation: Three of the four castles are close together near the town of Füssen, at the western end of the Bavarian Alps. Regular train service connects Munich with this pretty town, which is within walking or bicycling distance of Neuschwanstein and Hohenschwangau. Travelers based in Garmisch-Partenkirchen can take a bus from the train station there to Schwangau (adjoining Hohenschwangau) and Füssen. The same bus stops in the monastery village of Ettal for connections with another bus to Linderhof castle.

The Main Route **Two nights: Füssen.** Neuschwanstein and Hohenschwangau (Ludwig's childhood home) can both be reached by bus from Füssen. Alternatively, hire bikes from the local station. Allow at least a full day to see both castles.

One night: Ettal. Buses run from the picturesque mountain village of Ettal to Linderhof (which some class as the finest product of Ludwig's imagination). Oberammergau is a 10-minute bus ride away.

Two nights: Chiemsee. The unfinished Herrenchiemsee palace stands on Herren Island in the Chiemsee. Passenger boats offer regular service to the island (and to the smaller, equally charming Fraueninsel) from the lakeside resorts of Prien and Gstadt. It's easier to reach Chiemsee on public transportation by returning to Munich, picking up an express train to Salzburg, getting off at Prien, and connecting there with the ferry to Herren Island. The trip can be done in one day. By car, take the scenic route along mountain byways from Füssen.

Information *See* Chapters 3 and 4.

Through Central Germany to the North Sea

The Germans have always waxed romantic about their rivers, and not just about the Rhine and the Danube. At the idyllic point where the rivers Werra and Fulda join to become the Weser there's a granite stone with an inscription in verse that, loosely translated, reads:

Where Werra and Fulda gently kiss
and thereby lose their right to be,
The stately Weser is born by this
Embrace and flows on to the far-off sea.

The Weser is truly stately, one of Germany's most beautiful rivers, bordered by sleepy towns with medieval streets of half-timbered houses running down to the water's edge, and spilling into the North Sea. The Grimm brothers lived and worked and soaked up the inspiration for their immortal stories in the central part of this route. Our itinerary diverges from theirs, however, beginning on the banks of another great German river, the Main, at Aschaffenburg with its magnificent Renaissance palace, the former seat of the electors of Mainz. Behind Aschaffenburg rise the wild, wooded heights of the Spessart plateau, much of which is a protected national park. You'll leave the Spessart at the picturesque little town of Steinau an der Strasse, where the Grimm brothers spent their childhood. From there, you continue on to Münden, where the Fulda "embraces" the Werra and travels onward as the Weser to the North Sea.

Length of Trip 6 to 8 days

Getting Around **By car:** From Frankfurt, take Autobahn A-3 (direction Würzburg and Munich) to Aschaffenburg, then follow the well-marked "Rhön- und Spessfahrt" route through the Spessart and Rhön to Fulda. From Fulda, follow the Fulda River valley road to Bad Hersfeld, Rotenburg an der Fulda, and Kassel. From Kassel, follow the Wesertal road to Bremen and the sea.

By public transportation: All the main points on the route—Aschaffenburg, Fulda, Kassel, and Bremen—can be reached by regular InterCity trains from Frankfurt.

The Main Route

One night: Aschaffenburg. Spare a morning or an afternoon to tour the mighty Elector's Palace, the Renaissance-style Johannisburg.

Two nights: Take your time traveling through the **Spessart,** pulling in to spend the night at bed-and-breakfast farmhouses along the way.

One night: Fulda, with an evening stroll through its Baroque quarters.

One night: Kassel. You'll need an entire day to appreciate fully the beauty of the Wilhelmshöhe park and palace.

Two nights: Weser valley. From Kassel, if you're driving, follow the Weser River valley northward through the Pied Piper's town of Hameln and on to Bremen. By public transport, you can take a train to Hameln and pick up a fast InterCity to the coast; or you can take the local train from Kassel to Münden and do the Weser valley in style, chugging up to Hameln aboard a leisurely riverboat.

One night: Bremen—and at least one day to sit back and take stock of the trip. Take a morning or afternoon excursion to the fishing-boat harbor of Bremerhaven.

Information *See* Chapters 11 and 12.

Rivers of Wine

The Rhine and Mosel need no introduction, but who knows the attractions of their tributaries—the rivers Saar and Nahe? A tour of the four "rivers of wine" will take you from the crowds and crush of the Rhine of picture-postcard fame to the less dramatic but much more peaceful valley of the Saar. The high road across the Hunsrück range of hills, which is bordered by all four rivers, leads you back at your own pace to the point where the well-trodden tourist trail picks up again on the Nahe River. In little more than a week, you'll have skirted (and perhaps visited) Germany's most famous vineyards—and you should have tasted some of the country's finest wines.

Length of Trip 10 to 12 days

Getting Around

By car: It's a 454-kilometer (280-mile) round-trip drive from Wiesbaden.

By public transportation: The rail journey along the Rhine between Bingen and Koblenz is Germany's most spectacular train ride. Riverboats also make the journey, and you can stop off at any point on the way. From Koblenz, the rail line hugs the contours of the Mosel River to Trier; alternatively, you can again choose to travel the river by boat. A combination of train and bus will complete the itinerary along the Saar and across the Hunsrück to the Nahe River. Bus tours are offered by travel agencies in Wiesbaden, Bingen, Koblenz, and Trier.

The Main Route **Two nights:** The **Rheingau** region, between Eltville and Rüdesheim. Visit the vineyards of the Rheingau (they produce Germany's finest wine), and Bingen, at the mouth of the Nahe River.

Four nights: Along the **Rhine** between Rüdesheim and Koblenz. See the vineyards of Bacharach, Boppard, Brey, Kaub, Lorch, Oberwesel, Spay, and St. Goar, and the castles (or what remains of them) of Ehrenfels, Katz, Reichenstein, Rheinstein, Schönburg, and Sooneck.

Four nights: Along the **Mosel** between Koblenz and Trier. Take excursions to the Deutsche Eck (where the Mosel and Rhine meet) and to the vineyards of Alken, Bernkastel-Kues, Bremm (Europe's steepest vineyard), Ediger, Kobern-Gondorf, Kröv, Nehren, Neumagen (Germany's oldest wine town, praised by the 4th-century Roman poet Ausonius in his work *Mosella*), Piesport, Traben-Trarbach, Winningen (its August wine festival is one of Germany's oldest), Zell, and to the castles of Cochem, Ehrenburg, Eltz (a medieval picture-book castle so treasured by the Germans that they've engraved its image on their DM 500 bank notes), and Thurant.

Two nights: Trier. Explore Trier and follow the Saar River to Saarburg, Mettlach, and as far as the great, "Saar Bend," a spectacular point where the river nearly doubles back on itself.

Two nights: Idar-Oberstein. Venture into the Hunsrück hills and along the Nahe River to Bad Kreuznach. Take a day tour of the "Precious Stones Route," a well-marked 30-mile itinerary, starting and ending in Idar Oberstein, where precious stones are still mined and polished.

Information *See* Chapter 10.

White Sands of the Baltic Coast

Between the former East-West border town of Lübeck and the Polish frontier, Germany's other coastline is now wide open to the foreign visitor. As East Germany's window on the sea, the area was largely isolated until the end of 1989; and so miles of sandy coastline, peppered with chalk cliffs and charming coves, escaped the attention of developers. But there is more to this region than sea breezes and sand—a wealth of architectural delights awaits inspection. The tour takes in several of the old ports of the former Hanseatic League, the powerful merchants' organization that dominated trade on the Baltic in the Middle Ages and whose wealth financed the fine buildings still standing today.

Length of Trip 7 to 10 days

Getting Around **By car:** The route runs 478 kilometers (298 miles) from Lübeck to Ahlbeck, on the island of Usedom along the Polish border.

By public transportation: A solid rail network links the places mentioned below. You can start in Lübeck and make your way east; or you could base yourself in Rostock, which has excellent train connections, and embark on a series of excursions. You can make two side trips by 19th-century steam train: one from Bad Doberan to the coast, and the other on the island of Rügen.

The Main Route **One night: Lübeck.** A walk through the old town gates of the famous Holstentor, pictured on every DM 50 bank note, is highly recommended, and so is a stroll around the colonnaded market square, one of the prettiest in Europe.

One night: Schwerin. The capital of the region is well worth the 64-kilometer (40-mile) detour, if only to marvel at the opulence of the lake-island palace of the Mecklenburg princes. A boat trip on the 18-kilometer (11-mile) Schwerinsee lake is a relaxing diversion. Be sure to explore Wismar and inspect the ornate 1602 pump house on the town square, on your way to or from Schwerin.

Two nights: Bad Doberan-Rostock. Make Rostock your base for several excursions to the coast, and allow time to explore this shipbuilding port's old town. Don't miss a ride on *Molli*, a 106-year-old steam train that chugs through the streets of Bad Doberan to the seaside resort of Kühlungsborn.

One night: Stralsund. This bustling, centuries-old port, whose center retains a medieval air, is the gateway to the island of Rügen. Accommodations are scarce, but the local tourist office has listings for bed-and-breakfast lodgings.

Two nights: Rügen. You could easily spend two or more days on this enchanting island, relaxing on one of the many sandy beaches or discovering your own private cove.

One night: Usedom. From Rügen, you can complete the tour in a day, ending up on this island. Try to reserve a room at one of the seaside lodgings in Ahlbeck or Heringsdorf; or hunt out a bed-and-breakfast through the local tourist office.

Information *See* Chapters 12 and 15.

Germany at a Glance: A Chronology

c 5000 BC Primitive tribes settle in the Rhine and Danube valleys.

c 2000–800 BC Distinctive German Bronze Age culture emerges, with settlements ranging from coastal farms to lakeside villages.

c 450–50 BC Salzkammergut people, whose prosperity is based on abundant salt deposits (in the area of upper Austria), trade with Greeks and Etruscans; they spread as far as Belgium and have first contact with the Romans.

9 BC–AD 9 Roman attempts to conquer the "Germans"—the tribes of the Cibri, the Franks, the Goths, and the Vandals—are only partly successful; the Rhine becomes the northeastern border of the Roman Empire (and remains so for 300 years).

---

212 Roman citizenship is granted to all free inhabitants of the Empire.

c 400 Pressed forward by Huns from Asia, German tribes such as the Franks, the Vandals, and the Lombards migrate to Gaul (France), Spain, Italy, and North Africa, scattering the Empire's populace and eventually leading to the disintegration of central Roman authority.

486 The Frankish kingdom is founded by Clovis; his court is in Paris.

497 The Franks convert to Christianity.

---

776 Charlemagne becomes king of the Franks.

800 Charlemagne is declared Holy Roman Emperor; he makes Aachen capital of his realm, which stretches from the Bay of Biscay to the Adriatic and from the Mediterranean to the Baltic. Under his enlightened patronage, there is an upsurge in art and architecture—the Carolingian renaissance.

843 The Treaty of Verdun divides Charlemagne's empire among his three sons: West Francia becomes France; Lotharingia becomes Lorraine (territory to be disputed by France and Germany into the 20th century); and East Francia takes on, roughly, the shape of modern Germany.

911 Five powerful German dukes (of Bavaria, Lorraine, Franconia, Saxony, and Swabia) establish the first German monarchy by electing King Conrad I.

962 Otto I is crowned Holy Roman Emperor by the Pope; he establishes Austria—the East Mark. The Ottonian renaissance is marked especially by the development of Romanesque architecture.

1024–1125 The Salian Dynasty is characterized by a struggle between emperors and Church that leaves the empire weak and disorganized; the great Romanesque cathedrals of Speyer, Trier, Mainz, and Worms are built.

1138–1254 Frederick Barbarossa leads the Hohenstaufen Dynasty; there is temporary recentralization of power, underpinned by strong trade and Church relations.

1158 Munich, capital of Bavaria, is founded by Duke Henry the Lion; Henry is deposed by Emperor Barbarossa, and Munich is presented to the House of Wittelsbach, which rules it until 1918.

1241 The Hanseatic League is founded to protect trade; Bremen, Hamburg, Köln, and Lübeck are early members. Agencies soon extend to London, Antwerp, Venice, and the Baltic and North seas; a complex banking and finance system results.

mid-1200s The Gothic style, exemplified by the grand Köln Cathedral, flourishes.

1456 Johannes Gutenberg (1397–1468) prints first book in Europe.

1471 The painter Albrecht Dürer (dies 1528) is born into—the Renaissance. The Dutch-born philosopher Erasmus (1466–1536), and the painters Hans Holbein the Younger (1497–1543), Lucas Cranach the Elder (1472–1553), and Albrecht Altdorfer (1480–1538) help disseminate the new view of the world. Increasing wealth among the merchant classes leads to strong patronage for the revived arts.

1517 The Protestant Reformation begins in Germany when Martin Luther (1483–1546) nails his "Ninety-Five Theses" to a church door in Wittenberg, contending that the Roman Church has forfeited divine authority through the corrupt sale of indulgences. Though Luther is outlawed, his revolutionary doctrine splits the church; much of north Germany embraces Protestantism.

1524–25 The (Catholic) Hapsburgs rise to power; their empire spreads throughout Europe (and as far as North Africa, the Americas, and the Philippines). In 1530, Charles V (a Hapsburg) is crowned Holy Roman Emperor; he brutally crushes the Peasants' War, one in a series of populist uprisings in Europe.

1545 The Council of Trent marks the beginning of the Counter-Reformation. Through diplomacy and coercion, most Austrians, Bavarians, and Bohemians are won back to Catholicism, but the majority of Germany remains Lutheran; persecution of religious minorities grows.

1618–48 Germany is the main theater for combat in the Thirty Years' War. The powerful Catholic Hapsburgs are defeated by Protestant forces, swelled by disgruntled Hapsburg subjects and the armies of King Gustav Adolphus of Sweden. The bloody conflict ends with the Peace of Westphalia (1648); Hapsburg and papal authority are severely diminished.

1689 Louis XIV of France invades the Rhineland Palatinate and sacks Heidelberg. Elsewhere at the end of the 17th century, Germany consolidates its role as a center of scientific thought.

1708 Johann Sebastian Bach (1685–1750) becomes court organist at Weimar and launches his career; he and Georg Friederic Händel (1685–1759) fortify the great tradition of German music. Baroque and, later, Rococo art and architecture flourish.

1740–86 Reign of Frederick the Great of Prussia; his rule sees both the expansion of Prussia (it becomes the dominant military force in Germany) and the growth of Englightenment thought.

c 1790 The great age of European orchestral music is raised to new heights in the work of Joseph Haydn (1732–1809), Wolfgang Amadeus Mozart (1756–1791), and Ludwig van Beethoven (1770–1827).

---

early 1800s Johann Wolfgang von Goethe (1749–1832) helps initiate Romanticism. Other German Romantics include the writers Friedrich Schiller (1759–1805) and Heinrich von Kleist (1777–1811); the composers Robert Schumann (1810–1856), Hungarian-born Franz Liszt (1811–1886), Richard Wagner (1813–1883), and Johannes Brahms (1833–1897); and the painter Casper David Friedrich (1774–1840). In architecture, the severe lines of neoclassicism become popular.

1806 Napoléon's armies invade Prussia; it briefly becomes part of the French Empire.

1807 The Prussian prime minister Baron vom und zum Stein frees the serfs, creating a new spirit of patriotism; the Prussian army is rebuilt.

1813 The Prussians defeat Napoléon at Leipzig.

1815 Britain and Prussia defeat Napoléon at Waterloo. At the Congress of Vienna, the German Confederation is created as a loose union of 39 independent states, reduced from more than

300 principalities. The *Bundestag* (national assembly) is established at Frankfurt. Already powerful Prussia increases, gaining the Rhineland, Westphalia, and most of Saxony.

1848 The "Year of the Revolutions" is marked by uprisings across the fragmented German Confederation; Prussia uses the opportunity for further expansion. A national parliament is elected, taking the power of the Bundestag to prepare a constitution for a united Germany.

1862 Otto von Bismarck (1815–1898) becomes Prime Minister of Prussia; he is determined to wrest German-populated provinces from Austro-Hungarian (Hapsburg) control.

1866 Austria-Hungary is defeated by the Prussians at Sadowa; Bismarck sets up the Northern German Confederation in 1867. A key figure in Bismarck's plans is Ludwig II of Bavaria (the Dream King). Ludwig—a political simpleton—lacks successors, making it easy for Prussia to grab his lands.

1867 Karl Marx (1818–1883) publishes *Das Kapital.*

1870–71 The Franco-Prussian War: Prussia lays siege to Paris. Victorious Prussia seizes Alsace-Lorraine but eventually withdraws from all other occupied French territories.

1871 The four south German states agree to join the Northern Confederation; Wilhelm I is proclaimed first Kaiser of the united Empire.

1882 Triple Alliance is forged between Germany, Austria-Hungary, and Italy. Germany's industrial revolution blossoms, enabling it to catch up with the other great powers of Europe. Germany establishes colonies in Africa and the Pacific.

c 1885 Daimler and Benz pioneer the automobile.

1890 Kaiser Wilhelm II (rules 1888–1918) dismisses Bismarck and begins a new, more aggressive course of foreign policy; he oversees the expansion of the Navy.

1890s A new school of writers, including Rainer Maria Rilke (1875–1926), emerges. Rilke's *Sonnets to Orpheus* gives German poetry new lyricism.

1905 Albert Einstein (1879–1955) announces his theory of relativity.

1906 Painter Ernst Ludwig Kirchner (1880–1938) helps organize *Die Brücke*, a group of artists that along with *Der Blaue Reiter* forge the avant-garde art movement Expressionism.

1907 Great Britain, Russia, and France form the Triple Entente, which, set against the Triple Alliance, divides Europe into two armed camps.

1914–18 Austrian Archduke Franz-Ferdinand is assassinated in Serbia. The attempted German invasion of France sparks off World War I; Italy and Russia join the Allies, and four years of pitched battle ensue. By 1918, the Central Powers are encircled and must capitulate.

1918 Germany is compelled by the Versailles Treaty to give up its overseas colonies and much European territory (including Alsace-Lorraine to France) and to pay huge reparations to the Allies; the tough terms leave the new democracy (the Weimar Republic) shaky.

1919 The Bauhaus school of art and design, the brainchild of Walter Gropius (1883–1969), is born. Thomas Mann (1875–1955) and Hermann Hesse (1877–1962) forge a new style of visionary intellectual writing—until quashed by Nazism.

1923 Germany suffers runaway inflation. Adolf Hitler's "Beer Hall Putsch," a rightist revolt, fails; leftist revolts are frequent.

1925 Hitler publishes *Mein Kampf* ("My Struggle").

1932 The Nazi Party gains the majority in the Bundestag.

1933 Hitler becomes chancellor; the Nazi "revolution" begins.

1934 President Paul von Hindenburg dies; Hitler declares himself *Führer* (leader) of the Third Reich (empire). Nazification of all German social institutions begins, spreading a policy that is virulently racist and anti-Communist. Germany recovers industrial might and rearms.

1936 Germany signs anti-Communist agreements with Italy and Japan, forming the Axis; Hitler reoccupies the Rhineland.

1938 The *Anschluss* (annexation): Hitler occupies Austria; Germany occupies the Sudetenland in Czechoslovakia.

1939–40 In August, Hitler signs a pact with the Soviet Union; in September he invades Poland; war is declared by the Allies. Over the next three years, there are Nazi invasions of Denmark, Norway, the Low Countries, France, Yugoslavia, and Greece. Alliances form between Germany and the Baltic states.

1941–45 Hitler launches his anti-Communist crusade against the Soviet Union, reaching Leningrad in the north and Stalingrad and the Caucasus in the south. In 1944, the Allies land in France; their combined might brings the Axis to its knees. In addition to the millions killed in the fighting, over 6 million have died in Hitler's concentration camps. Germany is again in ruins. Hitler kills himself. Berlin (and what becomes East Germany) is occupied by the Soviet Union.

1945 At the Yalta Conference, France, the United States, Britain, and the Soviet Union divide Germany into four zones; each country occupies a sector of Berlin. The Potsdam Agreement expresses the determination to rebuild Germany as a democracy.

1948 The Soviet Union tears up the Potsdam Agreement and attempts, by blockade, to exclude the three other Allies from their agreed zones in Berlin. Stalin is frustrated by a massive airlift of supplies to West Berlin.

1949 The three Western zones are combined to form the Federal Republic of Germany (DDR); the new West German parliament elects Konrad Adenauer as chancellor (a post held until his retirement in 1963). Soviet-held East Germany becomes the Communist German Democratic Republic.

1950s West Germany, aided by the financial impetus provided by the Marshall Plan, rebuilds its devastated cities and economy—the *Wirtschaftswunder* (economic miracle) gathers pace.

1957 The Treaty of Rome heralds the formation of the European Economic Community (EEC); Germany is a founding member.

1961 Communists build the Berlin Wall to stem the outward tide of refugees. The writers Heinrich Böll and Günter Grass emerge.

1969–1974 The vigorous chancellorship of Willy Brandt pursues Ostpolitik, improving relations with Eastern Europe, the Soviet Union, and recognizing East Germany's sovereignty.

mid-1980s The powerful German Green Party emerges as the leading environmentalist voice in Europe.

1989 Discontent in East Germany leads to a flood of refugees westward and to mass demonstrations; Communist power collapses across Eastern Europe; the Berlin Wall falls.

1990 Political instability ushers in the year. In March the first free elections in East Germany bring a center-right government to power. The Communists, faced with corruption scandals, suffer a big defeat, but are represented in the new, democratic parliament. The World War II victors hold talks with the two German governments and the Soviet Union gives its support for reunification. Economic union takes place on July 1, with full political unity on October 3. Five new states are created out of the former German Democratic Republic. In December, in the first democratic national German elections for 58 years, Chancellor Helmut Kohl's three-party coalition is reelected. Support for the Green Party wanes, and the Communists—renamed the Democratic Socialists—win 17 seats in the new parliament.

1991 Nine months of emotional debate about the future capital of the reunited country finally ends on June 20, when parliamentary representatives vote in favor of quitting Bonn—seat of the West German government since 1949—and moving to Berlin, which was the capital until the end of World War II.

2 Munich

With Tours of Downtown and Schloss Nymphenburg

Given the choice, the city most Germans would live in is Munich. One of its major attractions is its location, only 70 kilometers (44 miles) from the year-round playground of the Alps (in summer, hiking and swimming in the mountain lakes; in winter, skiing). But it's more than just the southern location that makes Munich, the third largest of Germany's cities, so attractive. Munich is an uncommon mixture of culture and kitsch, of beautiful Baroque architecture and bawdy beer halls. The more sober-minded Germans in the north sometimes shake their heads in dismay: How can a city that claims to be Germany's cultural capital, with its internationally acclaimed opera, cinema industry, and art galleries, stage such a gross, beer-swigging event as the annual Oktoberfest? But that paradox may be what sets the capital of Bavaria and its 1.3 million inhabitants apart.

Munich is proud of its beery tradition. Where else would an opera house have a special beer brewed for it? How many other cities have universities that can boast a department devoted to beer research? If Munich is eccentric by "normal" German standards, then its chief flag bearer must be Ludwig II, one of the last of the Wittelsbachs, the royal dynasty that for almost 750 years ruled over Munich and southern Germany, until the monarchy was abolished in 1918. For while Bismarck was striving from his Berlin power base to create a modern unified Germany, "Mad" Ludwig—also nicknamed the "Dream King"—was almost bankrupting the state's treasury by building a succession of fairy-tale castles and remote summer retreats in the mountains and countryside.

Munich is undoubtedly Germany's prettiest big city. In addition to its architecture, there are spacious and gracious parks with lakes and beer gardens—most notably the Englischer Garten, which is like a long green lung extending from near the city center to the northern outskirts alongside the River Isar. But Munich isn't just beauty and beer. Much of its wealth comes from the high-tech industries that have sprung up in the proximity of two of Germany's most famous business names: Siemens and BMW. Munich is probably also Germany's most expensive city; it boasts some of the most upscale restaurants and shops in Europe. If you have the money, you can easily spend it on a $250 hotel room or a $150 dinner. A new pair of shoes could cost you $300, a sports jacket $1,000.

But such extravagance notwithstanding, it's possible to spend a few highly enjoyable days in Munich without busting your budget.

Essential Information

Important Addresses and Numbers

Tourist Information The **Fremdenverkehrsamt** (central tourist office) is located in the heart of the city (Sendlingerstr. 1, tel. 089/23911), just around the corner from Marienplatz. This office can help with room reservations; if you arrive after hours, call for a recorded message detailing hotel vacancies. (Open Mon.–Thurs. 8:30–3, Fri. 8:30–2.) Longer hours are kept by the city tourist office at the **Hauptbahnhof** train station (at the entrance on Bayerstr., tel. 089/239–1256; open 8 AM–11 PM. There are also tourist offices at the **Rathaus** (city hall), on Marienplatz (open weekdays 9–5), and at Munich's new airport.

For information on the Bavarian mountain region south of Munich, contact the **Fremdenverkehrsverband München-Oberbayern** (Upper Bavarian Regional Tourist Office) on Sonnenstrasse 10 (tel. 089/597–347).

An official monthly listing of upcoming events, the *Monatsprogramm,* is available at most hotels and newsstands and all tourist offices for DM 1.80. Information in English about museums and galleries can be obtained round-the-clock by dialing 089/239–162, and about castles and city sights by dialing 089/239–172.

Where to Change Money The most economical place to change money is at the main train station (Hauptbahnhof). An exchange office in the righthand corner of the front main entrance, open daily 7 AM–11 PM, charges only DM 1 per transaction. Money-exchange offices are also located in both the arrivals and departures halls at the airport.

Consulates **U.S. Consulate General,** Königstrasse 5, tel. 089/23011. **British Consulate General,** Amalienstrasse 62, tel. 089/394–015. **Canadian Consulate,** Tal 29, tel. 089/222–661.

Emergencies **Police:** tel. 089/110. **Fire department:** tel. 089/112. **Ambulance:** tel. 089/19222. **Medical emergencies:** tel. 089/558–661. **Pharmacy emergency service:** tel. 089/594–475. The **Internationale Inter-Apotheke** (corner of Luisenstr. and Elisenstr., tel. 089/595–444) stocks American and British products (open Mon.–Fri. 8

AM–6 PM, Sat. 8 AM–1 PM), or go to the Internationale Apotheke, Neuhauserstrasse 8, tel. 089/260–3021.

English-language Bookstores The **Anglia English Bookshop** (Schellingstr. 3, tel. 089/283–642) has the largest selection of English-language books in Munich. Other selections can be found at the **Internationale Presse** store at the main train station, or at **Hugendubel** bookshop, 2nd floor, at Marienplatz.

Travel Agencies **American Express,** Promenadenplatz 6, tel. 089/21990. **ABR,** the official Bavarian travel agency, has outlets all over Munich; call 089/12040 for information.

Lost and Found **Fundstelle der Stadtverwaltung** (city lost-property office), Ruppertstrasse 19, tel. 089/2331. **Fundstelle der Bundesbahn,** (railway lost-property office), Hauptbahnhof, Bahnhofplatz 2, tel. 089/128–6664.

Car Rental **Avis:** Airport Riem, tel. 089/9211–8350; Nymphenburgerstrasse 61, tel. 089/1260–0020; Balanstrasse 74, tel. 089/497–301.
Europcar: Airport Schwanthalerstrasse 10A, tel. 089/5947–2325.
Hertz: Airport Riem, tel. 089/908–744; Nymphenburgerstrasse 81, tel. 089/129–5001.
Sixt-Budget: Seitzstrasse 9, tel. 089/223–333.

All car-rental firms operating at Riem will be at the new airport. Reservations will automatically be transferred from the old to the new airport when Riem shuts down, as will (initially) all telephone calls to the old Riem locations.

Arriving and Departing by Plane

At press time, Munich's big new **Franz Josef Strauss Airport,** 28 kilometers (17 miles) northeast of the city, was on schedule for its May 1992 opening, but full service and connection details were not available. The new airport, one of the most advanced in Europe, has been under construction for 10 years and will be capable of handling up to 14 million passengers a year. It replaces the much smaller **Riem Airport,** which had become too small for the volume of traffic but may still be functioning when you visit.

Between the Airport and Downtown A new fast train line (the S-8) will link Franz Josef Strauss with Munich's main train station (Hauptbahnhof) every 20 minutes; the journey will take 38 minutes. Riem is nearer to the city and linked by bus and train. A service bus (DM 5.50 one-way) runs every 20 minutes between the domestic and international terminals and the main train station and takes about 25 minutes, depending on traffic. The train connection is slower and not direct, but marginally cheaper if you plunge straightaway into the city's strip-ticket system (cancel 2 strips; *see* Getting Around, *below*). Take bus No. 37 from the Arrivals terminal to the Riem S-bahn train station for links to Marienplatz and Hauptbahnhof.

Arriving and Departing by Train and Bus

By Train All regional and InterCity trains arrive and depart from Munich's main train station, the Hauptbahnhof, at Bahnhofplatz, a five-minute walk from the pedestrianized old town center. For telephone advice on routes and timetables, call 089/

592–991; or visit the newly refurbished information office, located in the center of the concourse, where you can pick up simple, single-sheet timetables for individual destinations throughout Germany and the rest of Europe. You can also get details about current special offers at the information office.

By Bus Munich, like many other German towns and cities, has no bus terminal. However, most national and international buses serving the city stop in Arnulfstrasse, the wide street abutting the northern side of the train station. For detailed information on buses arriving and departing Munich, call the local office of Deutsche Touring, Arnulfstr. 3, 8000 Munich 2, tel. 089/591-824.

Getting Around

On Foot Downtown Munich is only a mile square and is easily explored on foot. Almost all of the major sights in the city center are on the interlinking web of pedestrian streets that runs from Karlsplatz by the main train station to Marienplatz and the Viktualienmarkt and extends north around the Frauenkirche and up to Odeonsplatz. The central tourist office issues a free map with suggested walking tours. For sights and attractions away from the city center, make use of the excellent public transportation system.

By Public Transportation Munich has an efficient and well-integrated public transportation system consisting of the **U-bahn** (subway), the **S-bahn** (suburban railway), the **Strassenbahn** (streetcars), and **buses.** All U-bahn and S-bahn lines connect with the central trio of underground stations in the heart of the city: Marienplatz, Karlsplatz, and Hauptbahnhof. Services start around 5 AM and run until about midnight, although some central subway lines stay open until about 1:30 AM. For a clear explanation in English of how the system works, pick up a copy of *Rendezvous mit München*, available free from any tourist office.

Fares are uniform for the entire system. As long as you are traveling in the same direction, you can transfer from one mode of transportation to another on the same ticket. You can also interrupt your journey as often as you like, and time-punched tickets are valid for up to two hours. The system used to calculate the fares, however, is complex. In essence, it's based upon the number of zones you cross. A basic **Einzelfahrkarte** (one-way ticket) costs DM 2.50 (DM 1.10 for children under 15) for a ride in the inner zone; if you plan to take a number of trips around the city, you'll save money by buying a **Mehrfahrtenkarte,** or multiple "strip" ticket. The zonal system was recently changed, and red strip tickets are now valid for children under 15 only. Blue strips cover adults. DM 9.50 buys a 10-strip ticket. Most inner-area journeys cost 2 strips, which must be canceled at one of the many time-punching machines at stations or on buses and trams. For a short stay, the best deal is the **Tageskarte** ticket, which provides unlimited travel on all public transportation from 9 AM till 4 AM. Costs are DM 8 (DM 2.50 for children under 15) for an inner-zone ticket and DM 16 (DM 4.50 for children under 15) for the entire network.

All tickets can be purchased from the blue dispensers at U- and S-bahn stations and at bus and streetcar stops. Bus and streetcar drivers, all tourist offices, and Mehrfahrtenkarten booths (which display a white *K* on a green background) also sell tick-

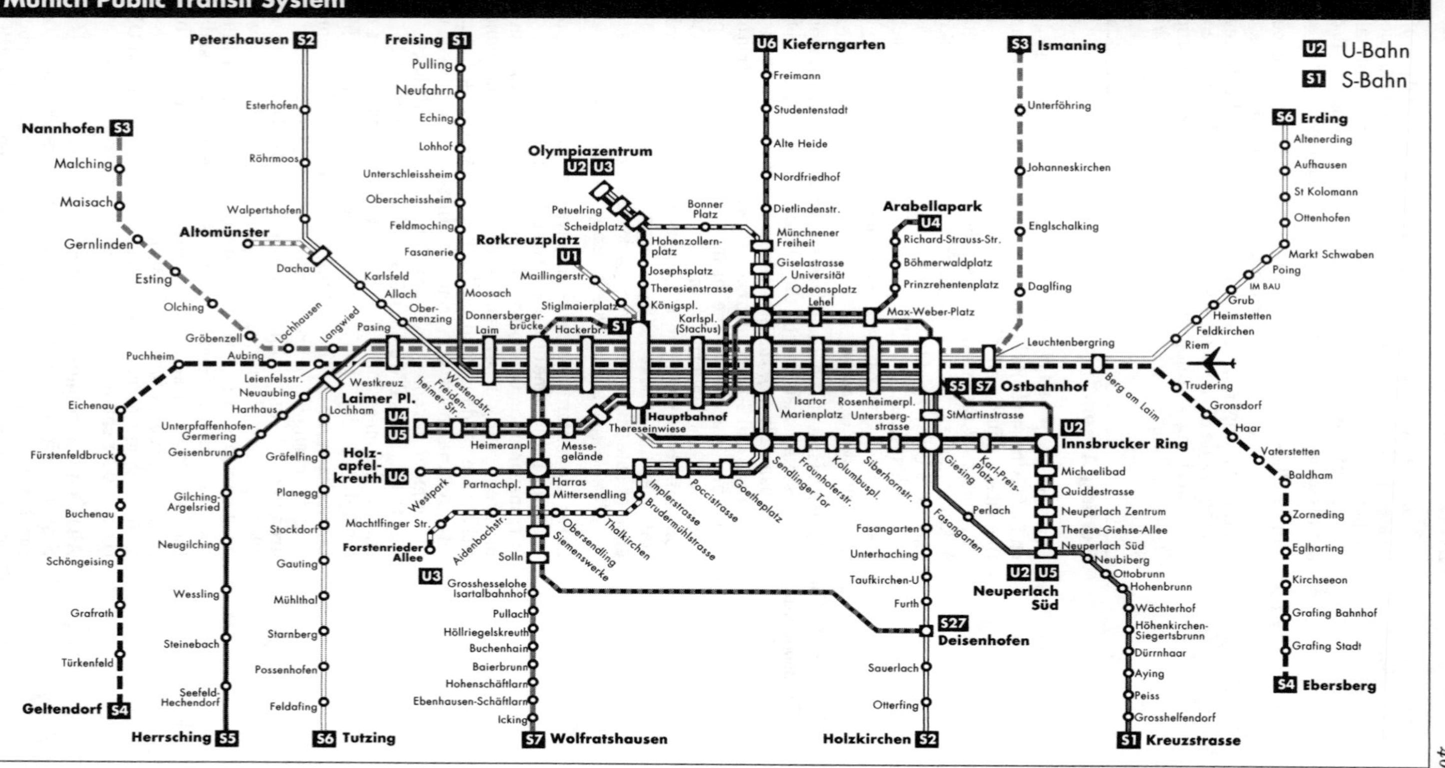
Munich Public Transit System
U2 U-Bahn
S1 S-Bahn
Petershausen S2
Esterhofen
Röhrmoos
Walpertshofen
Dachau
Freising S1
Pulling
Neufahrn
Eching
Lohhof
Unterschleissheim
Oberscheissheim
Feldmoching
Fasanerie
Moosach
Nannhofen S3
Malching
Maisach
Gernlinden
Esting
Olching
Gröbenzell
Lochhausen
Langwied
Altomünster
Karlsfeld
Allach
Ober-menzing
Pasing
Puchheim
Aubing
Leienfelsstr.
Neuaubing
Harthaus
Unterpfaffenhofen-Germering
Geisenbrunn
Gilching-Argelsried
Neugilching
Wessling
Steinebach
Seefeld-Hechendorf
Herrsching S5
Eichenau
Fürstenfeldbruck
Buchenau
Schöngeising
Grafrath
Türkenfeld
Geltendorf S4
Westkreuz
Lochham
Gräfelfing
Planegg
Stockdorf
Gauting
Mühlthal
Starnberg
Possenhofen
Feldafing
S6 Tutzing
Laimer Pl.
U4
U5
Westendstr.
Freiden-heimer Str.
Heimeranpl.
Messe-gelände
Holz-apfel-kreuth U6
Westpark
Partnachpl.
Harras
Mittersendling
Machtlfinger Str.
Forstenrieder Allee
U3
Aidenbachstr.
Obersendling
Siemenswerke
Thalkirchen
Solln
Grosshesselohe Isartalbahnhof
Pullach
Höllriegelskreuth
Buchenhain
Baierbrunn
Hohenschäftlarn
Ebenhausen-Schäftlarn
Icking
S7 Wolfratshausen
Olympiazentrum
U2 U3
Petuelring
Scheidplatz
Rotkreuzplatz
U1
Maillingerstr.
Stiglmaierplatz
Donnersberger-brücke
Laim
Hackerbr.
S1
Hohenzollern-platz
Josephsplatz
Theresienstrasse
Königspl.
Karlspl. (Stachus)
Hauptbahnhof
Theresienwiese
Bonner Platz
Implerstrasse
Brudermühlstrasse
Poccistrasse
Goetheplatz
U6 Kieferngarten
Freimann
Studentenstadt
Alte Heide
Nordfriedhof
Dietlindenstr.
Münchner Freiheit
Giselastrasse
Universität
Odeonsplatz
Lehel
Isartor
Marienplatz
Sendlinger Tor
Fraunhoferstr.
Kolumbuspl.
Silberhornstr.
Rosenheimerpl.
Untersberg-strasse
Arabellapark
U4
Richard-Strauss-Str.
Böhmerwaldplatz
Prinzrehentenplatz
Max-Weber-Platz
S3 Ismaning
Unterföhring
Johanneskirchen
Englschalking
Daglfing
Leuchtenbergring
S5 S7 Ostbahnhof
StMartinstrasse
Berg am Laim
U2
Innsbrucker Ring
Giesing
Karl-Preis-Platz
Perlach
Fasangarten
Michaelibad
Quiddestrasse
Neuperlach Zentrum
Therese-Giehse-Allee
Neuperlach Süd
U2 U5
Neuperlach Süd
Neubiberg
Ottobrunn
Hohenbrunn
Wächterhof
Höhenkirchen-Siegertsbrunn
Dürrnhaar
Aying
Peiss
Grosshelfendorf
S1 Kreuzstrasse
Fasangarten
Unterhaching
Taufkirchen-U
Furth
S27
Deisenhofen
Sauerlach
Otterfing
Holzkirchen S2
S6 Erding
Altenerding
Aufhausen
St Kolomann
Ottenhofen
Markt Schwaben
Poing
IM BAU
Grub
Heimstetten
Feldkirchen
Riem
Trudering
Gronsdorf
Haar
Vaterstetten
Baldham
Zorneding
Eglharting
Kirchseeon
Grafing Bahnhof
Grafing Stadt
S4 Ebersberg

ets. Spot-checks are common and carry an automatic fine of DM 60 if you're caught without a valid ticket (pleas of ignorance about the system won't do you any good, so save your breath). One final tip: Holders of a Eurail Pass, a Youth Pass, an Inter-Rail card, or a DB Tourist Card can travel free on all suburban railway trains.

By Taxi Munich's cream-color taxis are numerous. Hail them in the street, or telephone 089/21611 (there's an extra charge for the drive to the pickup point). Rates start at DM 2.90 for the first mile. There is an additional charge of 50 pfennig for each piece of luggage. Reckon on paying DM 7 to DM 10 for a short trip within the city.

By Bike Munich and its environs can easily be explored on two wheels. The city is threaded with a network of specially designated bike paths. A free map showing all bike trails and suggested biking tours is available at branches of the Bayerische Vereinsbank.

You can rent bicycles at the **Englischer Garten** (corner of Königstr. and Veterinärstr., tel. 089/397–016) for DM 5 per hour or DM 15 for the day (May–Oct., Sat. and Sun. in good weather); **Lothar Borucki** (Hans-Sachs Str. 7, tel. 089/266–506) hires them out for DM 60 per week. Bikes also can be rented from some S-Bahn and main-line stations around Munich, but not from the Hauptbahnhof. A list of stations that offer the service is available from the DB. The cost is DM 6–DM 8 (depending on type of bike) if you have a valid rail ticket; otherwise it's DM 10–DM 12.

Lodging

Munich can be an expensive place to lay your head down. There are plenty of hotels, but many of them are increasingly geared to the all-expenses-paid business traveler and have become prohibitively expensive for those on a fairly tight budget. Some of the big five-star hotels do offer significant weekend reductions, but even with these, prices can amount to DM 100-plus per person per night. The lodgings listed below may lack the luxuries and the facilities of a Sheraton or a Hilton, but they are clean and often friendlier than places with 500 beds. None of the pension-class lodgings have restaurants, but breakfast is automatically provided and is included in the price. Because Munich is both a major tourist destination and a trade-and-fairs center, rooms should be booked as far in advance as possible. Particularly busy times are the Oktoberfest (the last two weeks of September) and the international fashion fairs (usually held in March and early September).

The tourist office at Sendlingerstrasse 1, 8000 Munich 1, has a reservations department, but note that it will not accept telephone reservations. There's also a reservations office at the airport. The best bet for finding a room if you arrive without a reservation is the tourist office in the main train station, on the south side abutting Bayerstrasse (open daily 8 AM–10 PM, no telephone bookings). You'll be charged a small fee, but the operation is supremely well organized.

Highly recommended lodgings in each price category are indicated by a star ★.

Under DM 180

Adria. A modern and comfortable hotel, the Adria is located on the edge of Munich's museum quarter, in the attractive Lehel district, a short walk from the Isar River and the English Garden. There's no restaurant, but there is a large and bright breakfast room. *Liebigstr. 8, tel. 089/293–081. 51 rooms with bath. AE, DC, MC, V. Closed Dec. 24–Jan. 6.*

Brack. This modest but comfortable hotel on one of Munich's prettiest tree-lined streets is just south of the center and opposite the Poccistrasse subway station. The Brack has no restaurant but provides a good buffet breakfast to set you up for the day. *Lindwurmstr. 153, tel. 089/771–052. 50 rooms with bath. AE, DC, MC, V.*

Daniel. This is the place to stay if you value a downtown location; it's right on bustling Sonnenstrasse and the Stachus underground mall. The rooms are sleekly modern and comfortable. There's no restaurant. *Sonnenstr. 5, tel. 089/554–945. 80 rooms with bath. AE, DC, MC, V.*

★ **Gästehaus am Englischer Garten.** This converted 200-year-old mill, complete with ivy-clad walls and shutter-framed windows, stands on the edge of the English Garden, no more than a five-minute walk from the bars, shops, and restaurants of Schwabing (U-bahn stop: Münchener Freiheit). Rooms in the main building are more expensive but considerably more charming than those in the modern annex down the road. In summer, breakfast is served on the terrace. This hotel is a favorite, so book well in advance. *Liebergesellstr. 8, tel. 089/392–034. 27 rooms, most with bath or shower. No credit cards.*

Ibis. A comfortable modern hotel (built in 1988) in north Schwabing, 6½ kilometers (4 miles) north of the city center (U-bahn stop: Dietlindenstrasse), the Ibis stands adjacent to Ungererbad, a popular heated open-air swimming-pools complex, and is a 10-minute walk from the pavement cafés, trendy boutiques, bars, and discos of the fashionable Münchener Freiheit. *Ungererstr. 139, tel. 089/360–830. 140 rooms, most with bath. Facilities: restaurant. AE, DC, MC, V.*

Kraft. A functional postwar five-story hotel, it's a 10-minute walk south of the main train station and the same distance from the old city center, and it's close to the U-bahn and tram interchange at Sendlingertor-Platz. Rooms are plainly but neatly furnished. There is no restaurant, but snacks are available. *Schillerstr. 49, tel. 089/594–823. 37 rooms with bath. AE, DC, MC, V.*

Under DM 130

★ **Fürst.** Centrally located in a quiet street just off Odeonsplatz on the edge of the university quarter, this very basic, clean guest house is constantly busy. Book early. *Kardinal-Döpfner-str., tel. 089/281–043. 18 rooms, 4 with bath. No credit cards.*

Gröbner. It has a terrific central location—the Hofbräuhaus is just around the corner—and the appeal of a friendly, family-run hotel. American guests are especially welcome. The rooms are basically furnished but clean. Try for one on the second floor; they are especially large and airy. *Herrnstr. 44, tel. 089/293–939. 30 rooms, some with bath. No credit cards.*

Hotel Pension am Markt. Located in one of Munich's prettiest and quietest squares (U- and S-bahn stop: Marienplatz), this hotel is run almost like a private home. A grand piano stands in the lobby, to accompany the house canary. *Heiliggeiststr. 6, tel. 089/225–014. 30 rooms, most with bath. No credit cards.*

Kriemhild. If you're traveling with children, you'll appreciate the low rates at this pension in the western suburb of Nymphenburg, a 30-minute ride from downtown on the No. 12 tram. It's a few minutes' walk to the palace itself and to one of the city's best beer gardens, in Hirschgarten park. An extensive breakfast buffet is included in the room rate. *20 rooms, some with bath. Guntherstr. 16, tel. 089/170–077. Facilities: bar. MC, V.*

★ **Monopteros.** There are few better deals in Munich than this little hotel. It's located just south of the English Garden, with a tram stop (No. 20) for the 10-minute ride to downtown right by the door. The rooms may be basic, but the excellent service and warm welcome, added to the great location, more than compensate. There's no restaurant. *Oettingenstr. 35, tel. 089/292–348. 11 rooms, 3 with shower. No credit cards.*

Pension Beck. Frau Beck and her daughter run this friendly pension, which sprawls over several floors of a handsome Art Nouveau building in Lehel—on the No. 20 tram line and within easy walking distance of downtown. Frau Beck aims to provide two essentials: "A comfortable bed and a good cup of coffee." *Thierschstr. 36, tel. 089/225–768. 50 rooms, most with bath. No credit cards.*

Under DM 90

Jugend-Gästehaus. This excellently serviced modern lodging of the German Youth Hostels Association is five minutes by foot from the Thalkirchen U-bahn station, 15 minutes from the city center. Accommodations range from double rooms (DM 50, without bath) to three- and four-bed rooms to segregated dormitories, with shared bathrooms on each floor. *Miesingstr. 4, tel. 089/723–6550. 340 beds, 34 double rooms.*

Pension Agnes. This small and friendly family-run guest house, in the heart of the arty Schwabing district, lies midway between downtown and the Olympic center and is close to both the Josephsplatz subway stop and the No. 18 tram. Rooms are simply furnished. *Agnes-str. 58, tel. 089/129–3061. 35 beds, some double rooms; no private baths. No credit cards.*

Pension Amalien. This small lodging in the heart of the lively university quarter of Schwabing, two miles north of the main train station (underground stop: Universität), is surrounded by cafés and jazz bars. Some rooms are multibed. *Amalienstr. 71, tel. 089/283–971. No private baths. No credit cards.*

Pension Diana. Located in an 18th-century building in the jumble of winding old-town streets, the Diana is only a few steps from the pedestrianized city center (closest U-bahn/S-bahn station: Karlsplatz), with its many historic sights, including the twin-domed cathedral. It offers plainly furnished double and multibed rooms. *Altheimer Eck 15, tel. 089/2603107. No private baths. No credit cards.*

Camping. A big site with numerous services, including hot showers and a cafeteria, is located at Thalkirchen, near the zoo, 15 minutes by U-bahn south of the city center. *Zentralländstr. 49, tel. 089/723–1707.*

Adria, **19**
Bayerischer Hof, **7**
Brack, **3**
Camping, **5**
Daniel, **4**
Fürst, **11**
Gästehaus am Englischer Garten, **17**
Gröbner, **15**
Hotel Pension am Markt, **12**
Ibis, **13**
Jugend-Gästehaus, **6**
Kriemhild, **1**
Kraft, **2**
Monopteros, **18**
Pension Agnes, **9**
Pension Amalien, **10**
Pension Beck, **16**
Pension Diane, **8**
Splendid, **14**

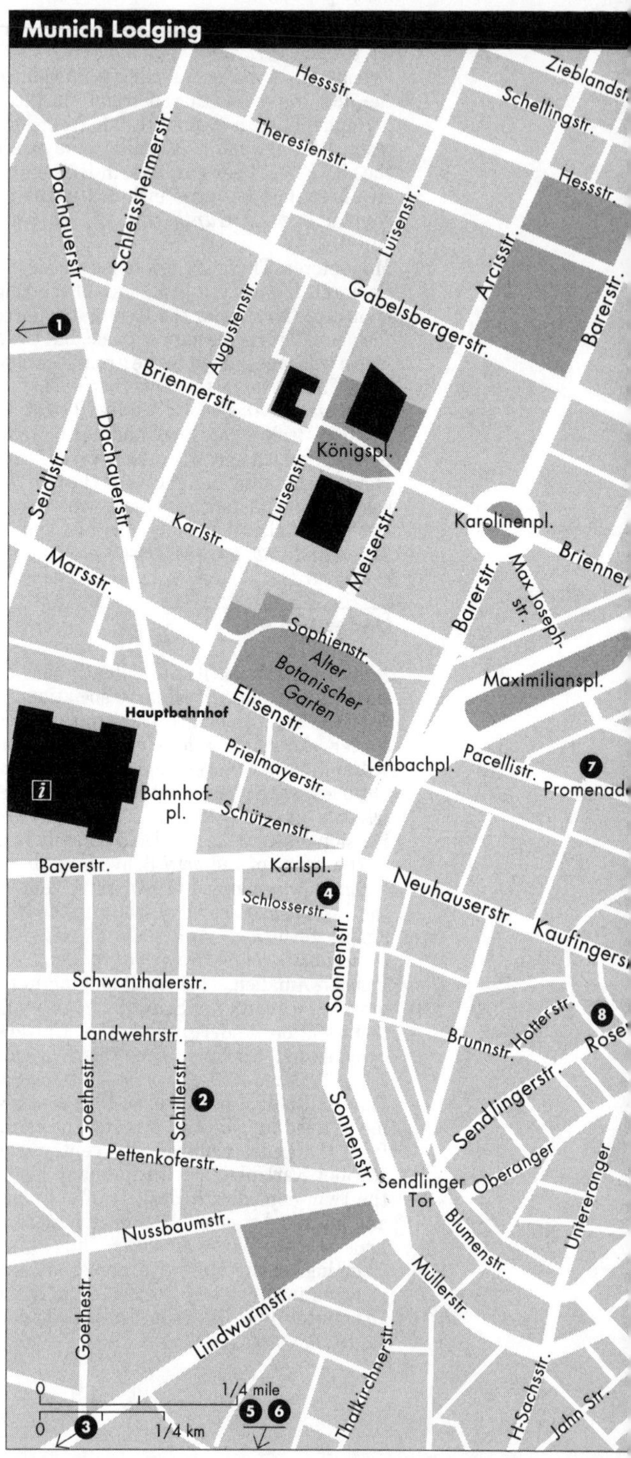

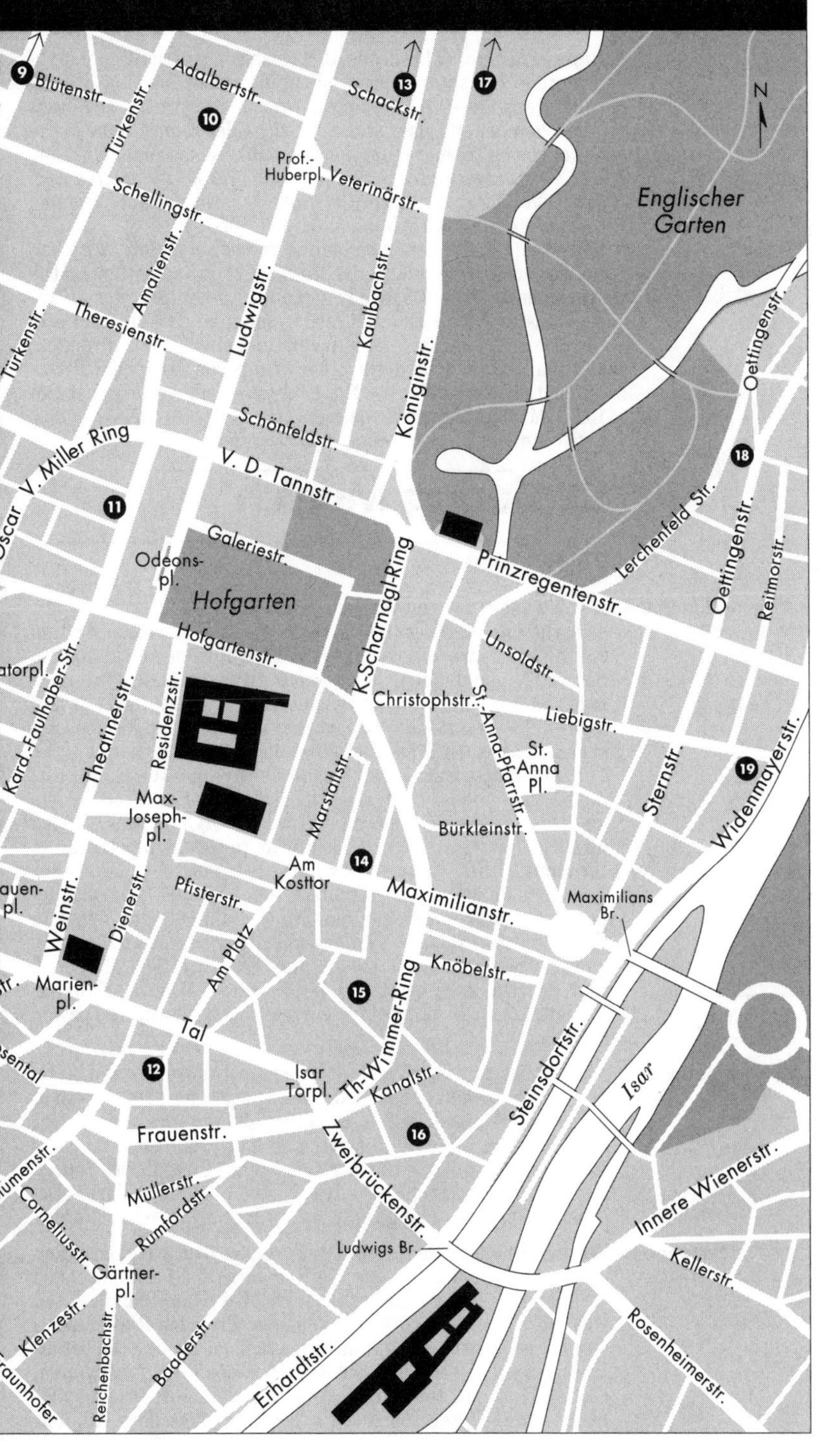

Blütenstr.
Adalbertstr.
Schackstr.
Türkenstr.
Prof.-Huberpl.
Veterinärstr.
Schellingstr.
Englischer Garten
Amalienstr.
Ludwigstr.
Kaulbachstr.
Theresienstr.
Königinstr.
Oettingenstr.
Türkenstr.
Schönfeldstr.
Oscar V. Miller Ring
V. D. Tannstr.
Lerchenfeld Str.
Galeriestr.
Odeons-pl.
K-Scharnagl-Ring
Prinzregentenstr.
Oettingenstr.
Reitmorstr.
Hofgarten
Hofgartenstr.
Unsoldstr.
Kard.-Faulhaber-Str.
Theatinerstr.
Residenzstr.
Christophstr.
St.-Anna-Pfarrstr.
Liebigstr.
St. Anna Pl.
Marstallstr.
Sternstr.
Widenmayerstr.
Max-Joseph-pl.
Bürkleinstr.
Am Kosttor
Maximilianstr.
Pfisterstr.
Maximilians Br.
Weinstr.
Dienerstr.
Am Platz
Knöbelstr.
Marien-pl.
Th.-Wimmer-Ring
Tal
Steinsdorfstr.
Isar
Isar Torpl.
Kanalstr.
Frauenstr.
Zweibrückenstr.
Innere Wienerstr.
Müllerstr.
Rumfordstr.
Corneliusstr.
Ludwigs Br.
Kellerstr.
Gärtner-pl.
Klenzestr.
Reichenbachstr.
Baaderstr.
Erhardtstr.
Rosenheimerstr.
Fraunhofer
N
9
10
11
12
13
14
15
16
17
18
19

Splurge

Bayerischer Hof. This is one of Munich's most traditional luxury hotels. It's set on a ritzy shopping street, and the No. 19 tram stops close to its imposing marble entrance. Old-fashioned comfort and class abound in the older rooms; some of the newer rooms are more functional. Double rooms go for DM 350–DM 470. *Promenadenpl. 2–6, tel. 089/21200. 440 rooms with bath. Facilities: 3 restaurants, nightclub, rooftop pool, garage, sauna, masseur, hairdresser. AE, DC, MC, V.*

★ **Splendid.** Chandelier-hung public rooms, complete with antiques and Oriental rugs, give this small hotel something of the atmosphere of a spaciously grand 19th-century inn. Have breakfast in the small courtyard in summer. The chic shops of the Maximilianstrasse are a five-minute stroll in one direction; an equally brief walk in the other brings you to the Isar River. The hotel is served by the No. 19 tram. Double rooms cost DM 130–DM 325. *Maximilianstr. 54, tel. 089/296–606. 37 rooms with bath and 4 apartments. Facilities: bar. AE, MC, V.*

Exploring Munich

Guided Tours

Orientation Tours If you want to take an organized tour of Munich to orient yourself, the one offering the best value is a daily afternoon trip lasting 2½ hours and costing DM 23; it includes a ride out to Schloss Nymphenburg. A one-hour city tour is also interesting, and it includes the arty Schwabing district, but it covers many of the central sights reachable on foot and at DM 13 is not such a good value. A DM 20 tour of the Olympiapark, site of the 1972 Olympics, includes a ride up the Olympic Tower, but it is no bargain unless you are especially interested in sports grounds. (If you are, you can explore the Olympiapark on your own by taking the U-2 or U-3 subway to the Olympiazentrum terminus.) All three tours are operated by Münchner Fremden-Rundfahrten (Arnulfstr. 8, tel. 089/591–504) and depart from outside the Hertie store on Bahnhofplatz, opposite the main train station. The one-hour tour departs daily at 10 and 2:30, and also at 11:30 AM June–August. The afternoon tour starts at 2:30, and the Olympic trip leaves twice daily, at 10 and 2:30. No bookings are necessary; just turn up and pay on the bus.

Walking and Bicycling Tours The Munich tourist office (*see* Important Addresses and Numbers, *above*) organizes guided walking tours for groups or individuals on demand, but no regular walking tours are offered. Tours can be tailored to suit individual requirements; costs vary accordingly. For the more energetic, **City Hopper Touren** (tel. 089/272–1131) offers daily escorted bike tours March–October. Advance bookings only, and start times are negotiable.

Excursions Bus excursions to the Alps, to Austria, to the royal palaces and castles of Bavaria, or along the Romantic Road can be booked through the tourist office or through **ABR** (Hauptbahnhof, tel. 089/591–315 or 089/59041). **Münchner Fremden-Rundfahrten** (*see above*) also organizes bus trips to most leading tourist attractions outside the city; the Royal Castles Tour, for example, costs DM 62. All tours leave from outside the Hertie department store. Other tours are offered by **Reisebüro Autobus**

Oberbayern (Lenbachpl. 1, tel. 089/558–061); offerings include a Late Riser's Excursion, which departs at 10 AM. All tours leave from Elisenstrasse, in front of the Botanischer Garten.

The Upper Bavarian Regional Tourist Office (*see* Important Addresses and Numbers, *above*) provides information and brochures for excursions and accommodations outside Munich.

The **S-bahn** can quickly take you to some of the most beautiful places in the countryside around Munich. Line S-6, for example, will whisk you lakeside to Starnberger See in half an hour; line S-4 runs to the depths of the Ebersberger Forest. You can bring along a bicycle on S-bahn trains.

Munich For Free—or Almost

As Munich becomes ever more expensive, it seems to offer more free, or nearly free, entertainment.

Street Entertainment

One of the best places for a low-cost evening out is the pedestrian stretch of the old city center between Karlsplatz and Marienplatz. On most dry evenings, except in the coldest of weather, you'll find a succession of street entertainers—some of them quite professional—from clowns and jugglers to classical violinists; there's even a semi-resident Bolivian musical quartet.

District **summer fests** are coming back into fashion. The liveliest of these is held in old Schwabing, usually in late-July, in the jumble of narrow streets off Münchener Freiheit. Traffic is barred for a day and the local pubs and cafés spread their tables and chairs into the streets. The musical flavor from half a dozen bands is traditional jazz.

Museums and Galleries

All **city-run museums** are free Sundays (though you still have to pay to see temporary exhibits). One of the best free evenings you'll ever have in Munich is a stroll along **Maximilianstrasse** (*see* Downtown Munich, *below*), site of many of the best private art galleries. On the first Thursday of every month, when many of the galleries open their new exhibits, you can wander in and out of them all, attending the first-night parties and picking up as much free liquor as you can hold.

The **Deutsches Museum** (German Museum of Science and Technology) stands on the Museuminsel (Museum Island) in the Neckar River, a 10-minute walk from downtown. Founded in 1903 and housed in its present monumental building since 1925, this is one of the most stimulating and innovative science museums in Europe. Twelve miles of corridors, six floors of exhibits, and 30 departments make up the immense collections. Set aside a full day if you plan to do justice to the entire museum. *Museumsinsel 1. Admission: DM 8 adults, DM 2.50 children. Open daily 9–5.*

Musical Events

Free **music** and **concerts** are a regular feature of the city. There are free brass-band concerts at the **Chinese Tower** beer garden in the Englischer Garten on Wednesday and weekend afternoons in summer. On Sunday mornings the **Waldwirtschaft** beer garden, by the Isar River in the Grosshesselohe district (Georg-Kalb-Str. 3), has free jazz concerts (mostly of traditional jazz). Similarly, some of the bigger bars in **Schwabing** have jazz bands Sunday mornings (known locally as Frühschoppen—when the beer is also often sold at a special low price). At least one Munich church will have a full sung **high mass** on Sunday mornings, often with an orchestra as well as a choir. But these events are not widely advertised in advance. Inquire at the tourist office for the latest information.

Walking, Biking, and Jogging Munich's biggest playground is the Englischer Garten (*see* Downtown Munich, *below*). Here you can take relaxing walks—or runs—among ancient trees or beside the River Isar. There are numerous children's playgrounds, several big beer gardens, including the one with the Chinese Tower, or Chinesischer Turm, and its brass-band music (the No. 54 bus from Münchener Freiheit drops you off beside the Tower); and a lake where for DM 7 two people can hire a rowboat for half an hour. During July, the city council organizes light entertainment on the giant meadow in front of the lake.

Markets The city's oldest market-fair, the week-long **Auerdult,** takes place three times a year—at the end of April, July, and October—on the square surrounding the church on Mariahilf-Platz, 3 kilometers (2 miles) south of downtown (catch the No. 25 tram from Sendlingertorplatz). The Auerdult is a mix of antiques show, flea market, and carnival, and it offers one of the biggest display of crockery and chinaware in Europe.

During most of December until Christmas Eve, Marienplatz and its neighboring streets are filled with festive stalls for the **Christkindlmarkt.** It's best seen at dusk, when all the fairy lights get switched on. Each evening around 5, a choir or band entertains from the balcony of the Rathaus beneath the Glockenspiel. You keep yourself warm as you wander between the avenues of stalls by sipping a DM 3 cup of Glühwein, a mixture of red wine and herbs and spices.

People-gazing One of finest places to watch the world go by—especially the chic and the trendy—while sipping a beer or a coffee is **Leopoldstrasse,** the busy, wide, tree-lined boulevard in Schwabing between the Münchener Freiheit and Giselastrasse subway stations on the U-3 and U-6 lines. The pavement cafés are open in good weather from midmorning till midnight.

Beery Activities On the little square called Am Platzl, near Marienplatz, is Munich's most famous beer hall, the **Hofbräuhaus.** *Hofbräu* means "royal brew," a term that aptly describes the golden beer that is served here in king-size liter mugs. Duke Wilhelm V founded the brewery in 1589, and although it still boasts royal patronage in its title, it's now state-owned. If the downstairs hall is too noisy for you, there's a quiet restaurant upstairs. And if there are too many tourists, return on a Saturday night to join the locals at the weekly hop in the upstairs ballroom.

The biggest free show of all—whether you drink beer or not—is the **Oktoberfest,** held on the giant Theresienwiese meadow 600 meters (1 mile) south of the Hauptbahnhof (*see* Outside the Center, *below*). Day and night through the last two weeks of September (it finishes on the first Sunday in October) you can wander among the huge beer tents, laid out in neat rows, of one of the biggest funfairs in Europe.

Highlights for First-time Visitors

Alte Pinakotek (*see* Downtown Munich)
Asamkirche (*see* Downtown Munich)
Englischer Garten (*see* Downtown Munich)

Frauenkirche (*see* Downtown Munich)
Marienplatz (*see* Downtown Munich)
Residenztheater (*see* Downtown Munich)
Schloss Nymphenburg (*see* Outside the Center)
Viktualienmarkt (*see* Downtown Munich)

Downtown Munich

Numbers in the margin correspond to points of interest on the Munich map.

1 Begin your tour of the city at the **Hauptbahnhof,** the main train station and site of the city tourist office, which is located on the corner of Bayerstrasse. Pick up a detailed city map here. Cross Bahnhofplatz, the square in front of the station, and walk toward Schützenstrasse. During the summer you'll see a blue-and-white maypole here—unless, that is, it's been stolen. A vigorous local custom, one that you'll find throughout Bavaria, holds that a neighboring town or city's maypole is fair game, and it will be returned only on payment of a suitable ransom, generally several barrels of beer. Notice the patterns painted on the pole; they represent the trades carried on in the city.

Schützenstrasse marks the start of Munich's pedestrian shopping mall, the Fussgängerzone, a mile and a half of traffic-free streets. Running virtually the length of Schützenstrasse is Mu-
2 nich's largest department store, **Hertie.** At the end of the street you descend via the pedestrian underpass into another shopping empire, a vast underground complex of boutiques and cafés. Above you stretches one of Europe's busiest traffic inter-
3 sections, **Karlsplatz,** known locally as *Stachus.* You'll emerge at one of Munich's most popular fountains, a circle of water jets that acts as a magnet on hot summer days for city shoppers and office workers seeking a cool corner. The semicircle of yellow-fronted buildings that back the fountain, with their high windows and delicate cast-iron balconies, gives the area a southern, almost Mediterranean air.

Ahead stands one of the city's oldest gates, the **Karlstor,** first mentioned in local records in 1302. Beyond it lies Munich's main shopping thoroughfare, Neuhauserstrasse and its extension, Kaufingerstrasse. On your left as you enter Neuhauserstrasse is another attractive Munich fountain, a jovial, late-19th-century figure of Bacchus. Neuhauserstrasse and Kaufingerstrasse are a jumble of ancient and modern buildings. This part of town was bombed almost to extinction in World War II and has been extensively rebuilt. Great efforts were made to ensure that these new buildings harmonized with the rest of the old city, though some of the newer structures are little more than functional. Still, even though this may not be one of the architectural high points of the city, there are at least some redeeming
4 features. **Haus Oberpollinger,** a department store hiding behind an imposing 19th-century facade, is one. Notice the weather vanes of old merchant ships on its high-gabled roof.

Shopping, however, is not the only attraction on these streets. Worldly department stores rub shoulders with two remarkable churches: Michaelskirche and the Bürgersaal. You come first to
5 the **Bürgersaal,** built in 1710. Beneath its modest roof are two contrasting levels. The upper level—the church proper—consists of a richly decorated Baroque oratory. Its elaborate stucco foliage and paintings of Bavarian places of pilgrimage

Alte Pinakothek, **25**
Alter Botanischer Garten, **32**
Alter Hof, **15**
Altes Rathaus, **11**
Antikensammlungen, **30**
Asamkirche, **13**
Bürgersaal, **5**
Englischer Garten, **24**
Feldherrnhalle, **21**
Frauenkirche, **8**
Glyptothek, **29**
Hauptbahnhof, **1**
Haus Oberpollinger, **4**
Hertie, **2**
Hofgarten, **20**
Hotel Vier Jahreszeiten, **17**
Jagd-und Fishereimuseum, **7**
Karlsplatz, **3**
Karolinenplatz, **27**
Königsplatz, **28**
Marienplatz, **9**
Maximilianstrasse, **16**
Michaelskirche, **6**
Nationaltheater, **18**
Neue Pinakothek, **26**
Neues Rathaus, **10**
Palace of Justice, **33**
Peterskirche, **14**
Residenz, **19**
Siegestor, **22**
Theatinerkirche, **23**
Viktualienmarkt, **12**
Wittelsbacher Fountain, **31**

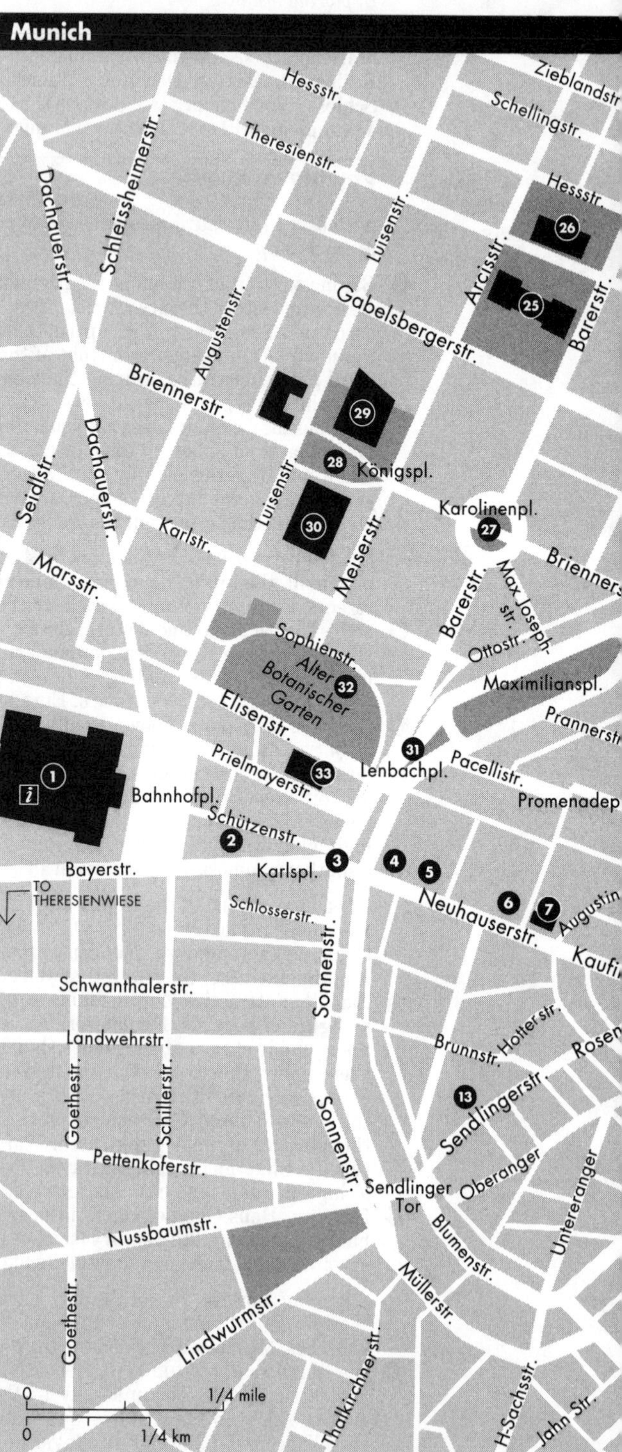

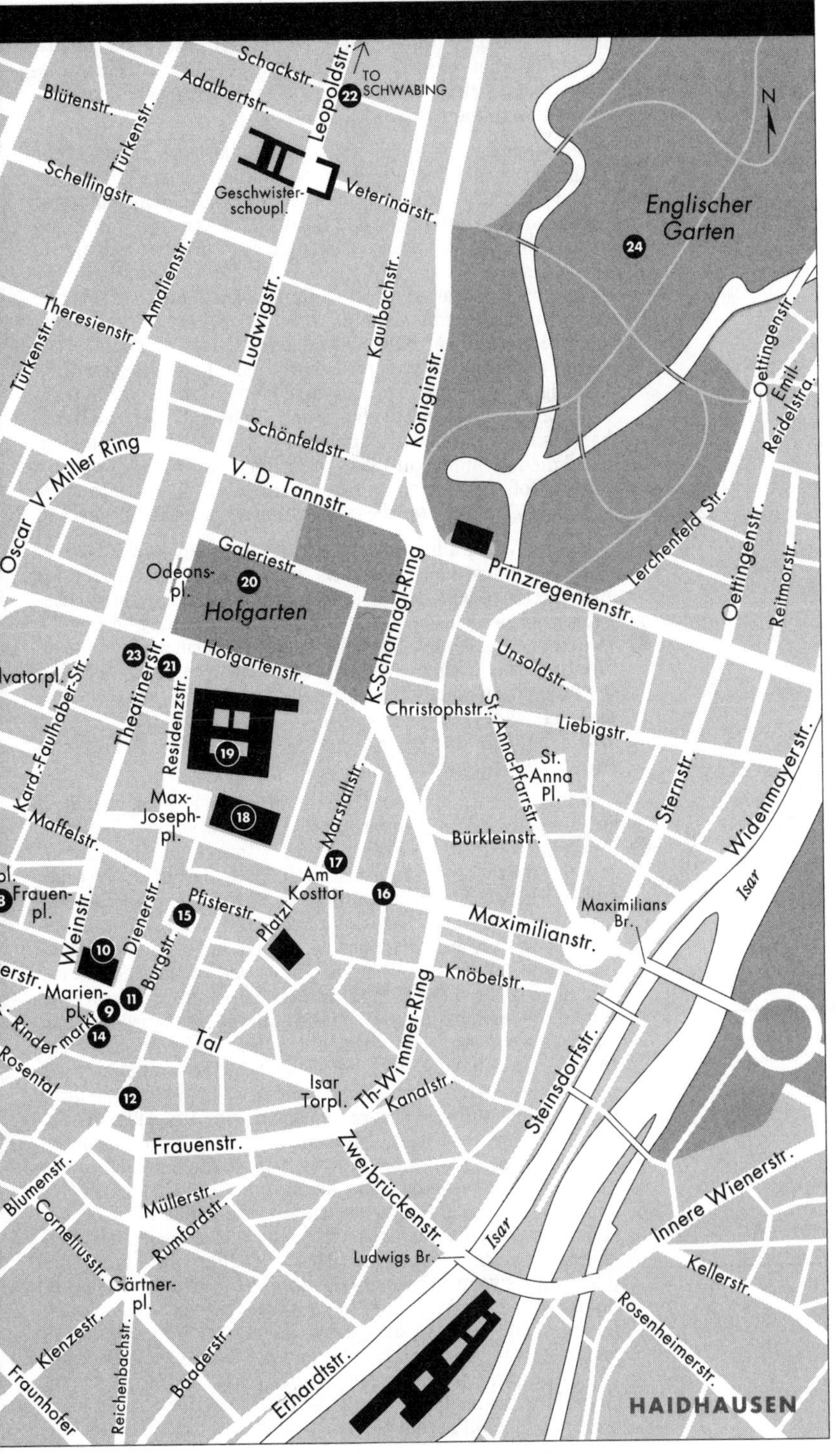

TO SCHWABING
N
Schackstr.
Adalbertstr.
Leopoldstr.
Blütenstr.
Türkenstr.
Schellingstr.
Geschwister-schoupl.
Veterinärstr.
Englischer Garten
Amalienstr.
Ludwigstr.
Kaulbachstr.
Theresienstr.
Türkenstr.
Königinstr.
Oettingenstr.
Emil-Reidelstra.
Schönfeldstr.
Oscar V. Miller Ring
V. D. Tannstr.
Lerchenfeld Str.
Oettingenstr.
Reitmorstr.
Galeriestr.
Odeons-pl.
Hofgarten
K-Scharnagl-Ring
Prinzregentenstr.
Hofgartenstr.
Unsoldstr.
lvatorpl.
Kard.-Faulhaber-Str.
Theatinerstr.
Residenzstr.
Christophstr.
St.-Anna-Pfarrstr.
Liebigstr.
St. Anna Pl.
Sternstr.
Widenmayerstr.
Max-Joseph-pl.
Marstallstr.
Bürkleinstr.
Maffelstr.
Am Kosttor
Maximilians Br.
Isar
pl.
Frauen-pl.
Weinstr.
Dienerstr.
Pfisterstr.
Platzl
Maximilianstr.
Burgstr.
Knöbelstr.
erstr.
Marien-pl.
Rindermarkt
Th.-Wimmer-Ring
Steinsdorfstr.
Tal
Rosental
Isar Torpl.
Kanalstr.
Frauenstr.
Zweibrückenstr.
Blumenstr.
Müllerstr.
Corneliusstr.
Rumfordstr.
Innere Wienerstr.
Isar
Ludwigs Br.
Kellerstr.
Gärtner-pl.
Klenzestr.
Reichenbachstr.
Baaderstr.
Rosenheimerstr.
Erhardtstr.
Fraunhofer
HAIDHAUSEN

project a distinctly different ambience from that of the lower level, reached by descending a double staircase. This gloomy, cryptlike chamber contains the tomb of Rupert Mayer, a famous Jesuit priest, renowned for his energetic and outspoken opposition to the Nazis.

A few steps farther is the restrained Renaissance facade of the
6 16th-century **Michaelskirche.** It was built by Duke Wilhelm V. Seven years after the start of construction the principal tower collapsed. The duke regarded the disaster as a sign from heaven that the church wasn't big enough, so he ordered a change in the plans—this time without a tower. Seven years later the church was completed, the first Renaissance church of this size in southern Germany. The duke is buried in the crypt, along with 40 members of Bavaria's famous Wittelsbach family (the ruling dynasty for seven centuries), including eccentric King Ludwig II. A severe neoclassical monument in the north transept contains the tomb of Napoléon's stepson, Eugene de Beauharnais, who married a daughter of Bavaria's King Maximilian I and died in Munich in 1824. You'll find the plain white stucco interior of the church and its slightly barnlike atmosphere soothingly simple after the lavish decoration of the Bürgersaal.

The massive building next to Michaelskirche was once one of Munich's oldest churches, built in the late-13th century for Benedictine monks. It was secularized in the early 19th century, served as a warehouse for some years, and today houses the
7 **Deutsches Jagd- und Fischereimuseum** (German Museum of Hunting and Fishing). Lovers of the thrill of the chase will find it a fascinating place. It also contains the world's largest collection of fishhooks. *Neuhauserstr. 53. Admission: DM 4 adults, DM 2 children and senior citizens. Open Tues., Wed., Fri.–Sun. 9:30–5; Mon. and Thurs. 9:30–9.*

Turn left on Augustinerstrasse and you will soon arrive in Frauenplatz, a quiet square with a shallow sunken fountain.
8 Towering over it is **Frauenkirche** (Church of Our Lady), Munich's cathedral. It's a distinctive late-Gothic brick structure with two enormous towers. Each is more than 300 feet high, and both are capped by very un-Gothic, onion-shape domes. The towers have become the symbol of Munich's skyline, some say because they look like overflowing beer mugs. The main body of the cathedral was completed in 20 years—a record time in those days—and the building was consecrated in 1494. The towers were added, almost as an afterthought, between 1524 and 1525. Jörg von Halspach, the Frauenkirche's original architect, is buried within the walls of the cathedral. The building suffered severe damage during the Allied bombing of Munich, as a series of photographs taken at the end of the war testifies. They show a gaunt, rubble-filled skeleton of a building. The cathedral was lovingly restored from 1947 to 1957. Today you'll find a church that combines most of von Halspach's original features with a stark, clean modernity and simplicity of line, emphasized by the slender white octagonal pillars that sweep up through the nave to the yellow-traced ceiling far above. There's a striking contrast between the pristine interior and the worn, shrapnel-studded redbrick exterior. As you enter the church, look on the stone floor for the dark imprint of a large footstep—the *Teufelstritt* (Devil's footprint). Local lore has many explanations for the phenomenon. One of the most fanciful is that the Devil challenged von Halspach to

build a nave without windows. Von Halspach wagered his soul and accepted the challenge, building a cathedral that is flooded with light from 66-foot-high windows that are invisible to anyone standing at the point marked by the Teufelstritt. Put the legend to the test and stand where the Devil is said to have been led by von Halspach: You'll see only the magnificent east windows in the apse. On your right, in the south aisle, is the elaborate, 15th-century black-marble memorial to Emperor Ludwig the Bavarian, guarded by four 16th-century armored knights. Two modern additions to the cathedral also seize the visitor's attention: the 1957 multicolored pulpit, and the huge 1954 crucifix that hangs over the chancel.

From the cathedral, follow any of the alleys heading east and
9 you'll reach the very heart of Munich, **Marienplatz,** which is
surrounded by shops, restaurants, and cafés. The square is named after the gilded statue of the Virgin Mary that has been watching over it for more than three centuries. It was erected in 1638 at the behest of elector Maximilian I as an act of thanksgiving for the survival of the city during the Thirty Years' War, the cataclysmic religious struggle that devastated vast regions of Germany. When the statue, which stands on a marble column, was taken down to be cleaned for a eucharistic world congress in 1960, workmen found a small casket in the base containing a splinter of wood that was said to have come from the cross of Christ.

10 Marienplatz is dominated by the 19th-century **Neues Rathaus**
(new town hall), built between 1867 and 1908 in the fussy, turreted, neogothic style so beloved by King Ludwig II. Architectural historians are divided over its merits, though its dramatic scale and lavish detailing are impressive. Perhaps the most serious criticism is that the Dutch and Flemish style of the building seems out of place amid the Baroque and Rococo of so much
11 of the rest of the city. The **Altes Rathaus** (old town hall), a medi-
eval building of assured charm, sits modestly, as if forgotten, in a corner of the square. Its great hall—destroyed in 1944 but now fully restored—was the work of the cathedral's chief architect, Jörg von Halspach.

In 1904, a glockenspiel (a chiming clock with mechanical figures) was added to the tower of the new town hall; it plays daily at 11 AM (also at 5 PM June–Sept.). As the chimes peal out over the square, doors flip open and brightly colored dancers and jousting knights go through their paces. They act out two events from Munich's past: a tournament held on Marienplatz in 1568, and the *Schäfflertanz* (Dance of the Coopers), which commemorated the end of the plague of 1517. When Munich was in ruins after the war, an American soldier contributed some paint to restore the battered figures, and he was rewarded with a ride on one of the jousters' horses, high above the cheering crowds. You can travel up there, too, by elevator. *Admission: DM 2 adults, DM 1 children. Open May–Oct., Mon.–Fri. 9–4; Nov.–Apr., Mon.–Fri. 9:30–4; closed Sat., Sun., and holidays.*

If you're thinking of lunch after the glockenspiel performance, cross the square, head through the old town-hall arcade, turn right, and join the crowds doing their day's shopping at the
12 **Viktualienmarkt,** the city's open-air food market (*Viktualien* is
an old German word for food). You'll find a wide range of produce available. German and international food, Bavarian beer,

and French wines make the market a feast for the eyes as well as for the stomach. It is also the realm of the garrulous, sturdy market women who run the stalls with dictatorial authority; one of them was reprimanded recently by Munich's leading newspaper for rudely warning an American tourist not to touch the fruit!

Somewhere beneath the tough exterior of the typical Munich market woman a sentimental heart must beat, for each morning fresh flowers are placed in the extended hand of a statue that stands along the edge of the market. The statue is of Munich's famous comedian Karl Valentin and is one of some half-dozen memorial fountains with statues of legendary Bavarian music-hall stars, singers, and comedians from the past that grace the market square.

In summer, take a chair at one of the tables of a lively beer garden set up beneath great chestnut trees and enjoy an alfresco lunch of Bavarian sausages and sauerkraut.

Various *Metzgereien* (butcher shops) in and around the market dispense different types of sausages and will make up sandwiches either to go or to be eaten on the premises. For *Thüringer Rostbratwurstl*—a slightly spicy, long thin sausage—or *Nürnberger Bratwurstl,* head for the Schlemmermeher Brotzeit Standl stall.

The market even sports a champagne bar where high-tone tidbits go along with the bubbly served by the glass.

From the market, follow Rosental into Sendlingerstrasse, one of the city's most interesting shopping streets, and head left toward Sendlinger Tor, a finely restored medieval brick gate. On your right as you head down Sendlingerstrasse is the remarkable 18th-century church of St. Johann Nepomuk, known as the
13 **Asamkirche** because of the two Asam brothers, Cosmas Damian and Egid Quirin, who built it. The exterior fits so snugly into the housefronts of the street (the Asam brothers lived next door) that you might easily overlook the church as you pass; yet the raw rock foundation of the facade, with its gigantic pilasters, announces the presence of something really unusual. Before you go in, have a look above the doorway at the statue of St. Nepomuk, a 14th-century Bohemian monk who drowned in the Danube; you'll see that angels are conducting him to heaven from a rocky riverbank. Inside you'll discover a prime example of true south-German, late-Baroque architecture. Red stucco and rosy marble cover the walls; there is an explosion of frescoes, statuary, and gilding. The little church overwhelms with its opulence and lavish detailing—take a look at the gilt skeletons in the little atrium—and creates a powerfully mystical atmosphere. This is a vision of paradise on earth that those who are more accustomed to the gaunt Gothic cathedrals of northern Europe may find disconcerting. It is a fine example, though, of the Bavarian taste for ornament and, possibly, overkill. Is it vulgar or a great work of architecture? You'll want to decide for yourself.

Return down Sendlingerstrasse toward the city center and turn right into the Rindermarkt (the former cattle market),
14 and you'll be beneath the soaring tower of **Peterskirche,** or Alter Peter (Old Peter), as Munich's oldest and smallest parish church is affectionately known. The church traces its origins to the 11th century and over the years has been restored in a vari-

ety of architectural styles. Today you'll find a rich Baroque interior with a magnificent late-Gothic high altar and aisle pillars decorated with exquisite 18th-century figures of the apostles. From the top of its 300-foot tower there's a fine view of the city and, in clear weather, the Alps. A notice at the entrance to the tower tells you whether the Alps can be seen, and it's worth the long climb to the top. *Admission to the tower: DM 2 adults, 50 pf children. Open daily in summer 9–7; in winter Mon.–Sat. 9–6; Sun. and holidays 10–6.*

From Peterskirche, cross the busy street called Tal (it means "valley," and was an early route into the old city) and step into
15 Burgstrasse. You'll soon find yourself in the quiet, airy **Alter Hof,** the inner courtyard of the original palace of the Wittelsbach rulers of Bavaria. They held court here starting in 1253, and something of the medieval flavor of those times has survived in this quiet corner of the otherwise busy downtown area. Don't pass through without turning to admire the medieval oriel (bay window) that hides modestly on the south wall, just around the corner as you enter the courtyard.

16 From the Hofbräuhaus, head north into **Maximilianstrasse,** Munich's most elegant shopping street, named after King Maximilian II, whose statue you'll see far down on the right. The king wanted to break away from the Greek-influenced classical style of city architecture favored by his father, Ludwig I, so he ingenuously asked his cabinet whether he could be allowed to create something original. Maximilianstrasse was the result. This broad boulevard, its central stretch lined with majestic buildings (now museums and government offices), culminates on a rise beyond the Isar River in the stately outlines of the Maximilianeum, a 19th-century palace now housing the Bavarian *Landtag* (parliament). Across Maximilianstrasse as you enter from the Hofbräuhaus stands another handsome city
17 palace: the **Hotel Vier Jahreszeiten,** a historic watering hole for princes, millionaires, and the expense-account jet set.

Turn left down Maximilianstrasse, away from the Maximilianeum, and you'll enter the square called Max-Joseph-Platz, dominated by the pillared portico of the 19th-century
18 **Nationaltheater,** home of the Bavarian State Opera Company. The statue in the center of the square is of Bavaria's first king, Max Joseph. Along the north side of this untidily arranged square (marred by the entrance to an underground parking lot)
19 is the lofty and austere south wall of the **Residenz,** the royal palace of Wittelsbach rulers for more than six centuries. It began as a small castle, to which the Wittelsbach dukes moved in the 14th century, when the Alter Hof became surrounded by the teeming tenements of an expanding Munich. In succeeding centuries, the royal residence developed parallel to the importance, requirements, and interests of its occupants. As the complex expanded, it came to include the **Königsbau** (on Max-JosefPlatz) and then (clockwise) the **Alte Residenz;** the **Festsaal** (Banquet Hall); the **Altes Residenztheater** (Cuvilliés Theater); **Allerheiligenhofkirche** (All Soul's Church, now ruined); the **Residenztheater;** and the **Nationaltheater.** Building began in 1385 with the Neuveste (New Fortress), which comprised the northeast section; it burned to the ground in 1750, but one of its finest rooms survived: the 16th-century **Antiquarium,** which was built for Duke Albrecht V's collection of antique statues (today it's used chiefly for state receptions). The throne room of

King Ludwig I, the **Neuer Herkulessaal,** is now a concert hall. The accumulated treasures of the Wittelsbachs can be seen in the **Schatzkammer,** or Treasury (one rich centerpiece is a small Renaissance statue of St. George, studded with 2,291 diamonds, 209 pearls, and 406 rubies), and a representative collection of paintings and tapestries is housed in the **Residenzmuseum.** Antique coins and Egyptian works of art are located in the two other museums of this vast palace. In the center of the complex, entered through an inner courtyard where chamber-music concerts are given in summer, is a small Rococo theater, built by François Cuvilliés from 1751 to 1755. The French-born Cuvilliés was a dwarf who was admitted to the Bavarian court as a decorative "bauble." Prince Max Emanuel recognized his latent artistic ability and had him trained as an architect. The prince's eye for talent gave Germany some of its richest Rococo treasures. *Admission to Treasury and Residenzmuseum: DM 3.50 adults. Open Tues.–Sun. 10–4:30. Admission to Staatliche Münzsammlung (coin collection): DM 2.50 adults, 50 pf children, free Sun. and holidays. Open Tues.–Sun. 10–4:30; in winter Sun. 10–1. Admission to Staatliche Sammlung Ägyptischer Kunst (Egyptian art): DM 3 adults, 50 pf children, free Sun. and holidays. Open Tues.–Sun. 10–5. Admission to Cuvilliés Theater: DM 1.50 adults, DM 1 children. Open Mon.– Sat. 2–5, Sun. 10–5.*

Directly north of the Residenz on Hofgartenstrasse lies the for-
20 mer royal garden, the **Hofgarten.** Two sides of the pretty, formal garden are bordered by arcades designed in the 19th century by the royal architect Leo von Klenze. On the east side of the garden, dominated for years by the bombed ruin of the Bavarian Army Museum, workers are busy on Munich's most controversial public-works project: the new State Chancellery. Opponents say the enormous bulk of the planned new building will disturb the harmony of the Hofgarten and its historic surroundings.

In front of the ruins of the Army Museum stands one of Europe's most unusual—some say most effective—war memorials. Instead of looking up at the monument you are led down to it: It is a sunken crypt, covered by a massive granite block. In the crypt lies a German soldier from World War I.

You can be forgiven for any confusion about your whereabouts ("Can this really be Germany?") when you step from the Hofgarten onto Odeonsplatz. To your left is the 19th-century
21 **Feldherrnhalle,** a local hall of fame modeled on the 14th-century Loggia dei Lanzi in Florence. In the '30s and '40s it was the site of a key Nazi shrine, marking the place where Hitler's abortive rising, or *Putsch,* took place in 1923. All who passed it had to give the Nazi salute.

Looking north up Ludwigstrasse, the arrow-straight avenue
22 that ends at the Feldherrnhalle, you'll see the **Siegestor,** or victory arch, which marks the beginning of Ludwigstrasse. The Siegestor also boasts Italian origins; it was modeled on the Arch of Constantine in Rome. It was built to honor the achievements of the Bavarian army during the Wars of Liberation (1813–1815).

Completing this impressively Italianate panorama is the great yellow bulk of the former royal church of St. Kajetan, the
23 **Theatinerkirche,** a sturdily imposing Baroque building. Its

lofty towers frame a restrained facade, capped by a massive dome. The church owes its Italian appearance to its founder, the Princess Henriette Adelaide, who commissioned it as an act of thanksgiving for the birth of her son and heir, Max Emanuel, in 1663. A native of Turin, the princess distrusted Bavarian architects and builders and thus summoned a master builder from Bologna, Agostino Barelli, to construct her church. He took as his model the Roman mother church of the newly formed Theatine order of Catholicism. Barelli worked on the building for 11 years but was dismissed before the project was completed. It was not for another 100 years that the Theatinerkirche was finished. Step inside to admire its austere, stucco interior.

Now head north up Ludwigstrasse. The first stretch of the street was designed by court architect von Klenze. Much as Baron Haussmann was later to demolish many of the old streets and buildings in Paris, replacing them with stately boulevards, so von Klenze swept aside the small dwellings and alleys that stood here to build his great avenue. His high-windowed and formal buildings have never quite been accepted by Müncheners, and indeed there's still a sense that Ludwigstrasse is an intruder. Most visitors either love it or hate it. Von Klenze's buildings end just before Ludwigstrasse becomes Leopoldstrasse, and it is easy to see where he handed construction over to another leading architect, von Gärtner. The severe neoclassical buildings that line southern Ludwigstrasse—including the Bayerische Staatsbibliothek (Bavarian State Library) and the Universität (University)—fragment into the lighter styles of Leopoldstrasse. The more delicate structures are echoed by the busy street life you'll find here in summer. Once the hub of the legendary artists' district of Schwabing, Leopoldstrasse still throbs with life from spring to fall, exuding the atmosphere of a Mediterranean boulevard, with cafés, wine terraces, and artists' stalls. In comparison, Ludwigstrasse is inhabited by the ghosts of the past.

At the south end of Leopoldstrasse, beyond the Siegestor, lies the great open quadrangle of the university, Geschwister-Scholl-Platz, named after the founders of the student Weisse Rose (White Rose) movement, a group of anti-Nazi campaigners who fell victim to the Gestapo in the '30s. At its north end, Leopoldstrasse leads into Schwabing itself, once Munich's Bohemian quarter but now distinctly upscale. Explore the streets of old Schwabing around Wedekindplatz to get the feel of the place. (Those in search of the young-at-heart mood that once animated Schwabing should make for Haidhausen, on the other side of the Isar.)

24 Bordering the east side of Schwabing is the **Englischer Garten.** Three miles long and more than a mile wide, it's Germany's largest city park, stretching from the central avenue of Prinzregentenstrasse to the city's northern boundary. It was designed for the Bavarian Prince Karl Theodor by a refugee from the American War of Independence, Count Rumford. While Count Rumford was of English descent, it was the open, informal nature of the park—reminiscent of the rolling parklands with which the English aristocracy of the 18th century liked to surround their country homes—that determined its name. It has an appealing boating lake, four beer gardens, and a series of curious decorative and monumental constructions, including

a Greek temple, the Monopteros, designed by von Klenze for King Ludwig I and built on an artificial hill in the southern section of the park. In the center of one of the park's most popular beer gardens is a Chinese pagoda, erected in 1789, destroyed during the war, and then reconstructed. The Chinese Tower beer garden is world-famous, but the park has prettier places in which to down a beer: the Aumeister, for example, along the northern perimeter. The Aumeister's restaurant is in an early 19th-century hunting lodge.

The Englischer Garten is a paradise for joggers, cyclists, and, in winter, cross-country skiers. The Munich Cricket Club grounds are in the southern section—proof perhaps that even that most British of games is not invulnerable to the single-minded Germans—and spectators are welcome. The park also has specially designated areas for nude sunbathing—the Germans have a positively pagan attitude toward the sun—so don't be surprised to see naked bodies bordering the flower beds and paths.

On the southern fringe of Schwabing are Munich's two leading art galleries, the Alte Pinakothek and the Neue Pinakothek, located next to each other on Barerstrasse. They are as complementary as their buildings are contrasting. The Alte Pinakothek (old picture gallery) was built by Leo von Klenze between 1826 and 1836 to exhibit the collection of old masters begun by Duke Wilhelm IV in the 16th century, while the Neue Pinakothek (new picture gallery), a low brick structure, was opened in 1981 to house the royal collection of modern art left homeless when its former building was destroyed in the war.

25 The **Alte Pinakothek** is among the great picture galleries of the world. For many, a visit here will serve as the highlight of a Munich stay. The bulk of the works is northern European, though Italians and Spaniards—notably Giotto—are reasonably well represented. Nevertheless, the works of such painters as Van Eyck, Cranach the Elder, Dürer, Rembrandt, and Rubens constitute the star attractions. Among the richly filled rooms, seek out Altdorfer's *Alexanderschlacht*, centerpiece of the duke's original collection. The writer and critic Friedrich von Schlegel (1772–1829), seeing the painting, declared: "If Munich has any other paintings of this quality, then artists should make pilgrimages there as well as to Rome or Paris." Munich has many such paintings . . . and many such pilgrims. *Barerstr. 27. Admission: DM 4 adults, 50 pf children, free Sun. and holidays. Admission to both the Alte Pinakothek and Neue Pinakothek: DM 7 adults. Open Tues.–Sun. 9–4:30, also Tues. and Thurs. 7 PM–9 PM.*

26 Across a sculpture-studded stretch of lawn is the **Neue Pinakothek.** It's a low brick building that combines high-tech and Italianate influences in equal measure. From outside, the museum does not seem to measure up to the standards set by so many of Munich's other great public buildings. On the other hand, the interior offers a magnificent environment for picture gazing, not the least as a result of the superb natural light flooding in from the skylights. The highlights of the collection are probably the Impressionist and other French 19th-century works—Monet, Degas, and Manet are all well represented. But there's also a substantial collection of 19th-century German and Scandinavian paintings—misty landscapes predominate—that are only now coming to be recognized as admirable

and worthy products of their time. *Barerstr. 29. Admission: DM 4 adults, 50 pf children, free Sun. and holidays. Open Tues.–Sun. 9–4:30, also Tues. 7 PM–9 PM.*

Back on Barerstrasse, walk south toward the city center (turn right from the old gallery or left from the new gallery). Before
27 you stretches the circular **Karolinenplatz,** with its central obelisk; it's a memorial, unveiled in 1812, to those Bavarians killed fighting Napoléon. Turn right onto Briennerstrasse. Opening
28 up ahead is the massive **Königsplatz,** lined on three sides with the monumental Grecian-style buildings by von Klenze that gave Munich the nickname "Athens on the Isar." In the '30s the great parklike square was laid with granite slabs, which resounded with the thud of jackboots as the Nazis commandeered the area for their rallies. Only recently were the slabs torn up; since then the square has returned to something like the green and peaceful appearance originally intended by Ludwig I. The two templelike buildings he had constructed there are muse-
29 ums: The **Glyptothek** features a permanent exhibition of Greek
30 and Roman sculptures; and the **Antikensammlungen** (Antiquities Collection) has a fine group of smaller sculptures, Etruscan art, Greek vases, gold, and glass. *Glyptothek: Königspl. 3. Admission: DM 3.50 adults, 50 pf children, free Sun. and holidays. Open Tues., Wed., and Fri.–Sun. 10–4:30, Thurs. noon–8:30. Antiquities Collection: Königspl. 1. Admission: DM 3.50 adults, 50 pf children, free Sun. and holidays. Open Tues. and Thurs.–Sun. 10–4:30, Wed. noon–8:30.*

Return to Karolinenplatz and head south along Barerstrasse. You'll come to Lenbachplatz, a busy square scarred by road intersections and tramlines, and overlooked by a series of handsome turn-of-the-century buildings. At the point where Lenbachplatz meets Maximiliansplatz you'll see one of Munich's most impressive fountains: the monumental late-19th-
31 century **Wittelsbacher Fountain.**

At the southwest corner of Lenbachplatz is the arched entrance
32 to the park that was once the city's botanical garden, the **Alter Botanischer Garten.** A huge glass palace was built here in 1853 for Germany's first industrial exhibition. In 1931 the immense structure burned down; six years later the garden was redesigned as a public park. Two features from the '30s remain: a small, square exhibition hall, still used for art shows; and the 1933 Neptune Fountain, an enormous work in the heavy, monumental style of the prewar years. At the international electricity exhibition of 1882, the world's first high-tension electricity cable was run from the park to a Bavarian village 30 miles away.

Opposite the southern exit of the park loom the freshly cleaned
33 and ornate contours of the 1897 law courts, the **Palace of Justice.** Just around the corner is the **Hauptbahnhof** (main railway station)—and the end of our tour.

Outside the Center

The site of Munich's annual beer festival—the renowned Oktoberfest—is only a 10-minute walk from the main train station; alternatively, ride the U-5 subway one stop. The festival site is Munich's enormous exhibition ground, the **Theresienwiese,** named after a young woman whose engagement party gave rise to the Oktoberfest. The party celebrated the betrothal in 1810 of Princess Therese von Sachsen-Hildburghausen to the Bavarian crown prince Ludwig, later Ludwig I. It was such a success, attended by nearly the entire population of Munich, that it became an annual affair. Beer was served then as now, but what began as a night out for the locals has become a 16-day international bonanza, attracting more than 6 million people. In enormous wooden pavilions that heave and pulsate to the combined racket of brass bands, drinking songs, and thousands of dry throats demanding more, they knock back around 5 million liters of beer. Like most of life's questionable pleasures, it has to be experienced once. Only the brave return for more.

The site is overlooked by a 19th-century hall of fame—one of the last works of Ludwig I—and a monumental bronze statue of the maiden **Bavaria,** more than 100 feet high. The statue is hollow, and 130 steps take you up into the braided head for a view of Munich through Bavaria's eyes.

The major attraction away from the downtown area is **Schloss Nymphenburg,** a glorious Baroque and Rococo palace that was a summer home to five generations of Bavarian royalty. It's located in the northwest suburb. To reach it, take a number 12 streetcar or a number 41 bus. Nymphenburg is the largest palace of its kind in Germany, stretching more than half a mile from one wing to the other. The palace grew in size and scope over a period of more than 200 years, beginning as a summer residence built on land given by Prince Ferdinand Maria to his beloved wife, Henriette Adelaide, on the birth of their son and heir, Max Emanuel, in 1663. As mentioned earlier, she had the Theatinerkirche built as a personal expression of thanks for the birth. The Italian architect Agostino Barelli, brought from Bologna for that project, was instructed to build the palace. It was completed in 1675 by his successor, Enrico Zuccalli. Within that original building, now the central axis of the palace complex, is a magnificent hall, the Steinerner Saal, extending over two floors and richly decorated with stucco and swirling frescoes. In the summer, chamber-music concerts are given here. The decoration of the Steinerner Saal spills over into the surrounding royal chambers, in one of which is the famous Schönheitengalerie (Gallery of Beauties). The walls are hung from floor to ceiling with portraits of women who caught the roving eye of Ludwig I, among them a butcher's daughter and an English duchess. The most famous portrait is of Lola Montez, a sultry beauty and high-class courtesan who, after a time as mistress of Franz Liszt and later Alexandre Dumas, captivated Ludwig I to such an extent that he gave up his throne for her.

The palace is set in a fine park, laid out in formal French style, with low hedges and gravel walks, extending into woodland. Tucked away among the ancient trees are three fascinating structures built as Nymphenburg expanded and changed occupants. Don't miss the **Amalienburg,** or hunting lodge. It's a Rococo gem, built by François Cuvilliés, architect of the Residenztheater. The silver-and-blue stucco of the little Amalienburg creates an atmosphere of courtly high life that makes it clear that the pleasures of the chase here did not always take place out-of-doors. In the lavishly appointed kennels you'll see that even the dogs lived in luxury. For royal tea parties, another building was constructed, the **Pagodenburg.** It has an elegant French exterior that disguises a suitably Oriental interior in which exotic teas from India and China were served. Swimming parties were held in the **Badenburg,** Europe's first post-Roman heated pool.

Nymphenburg contains so much of interest that a day hardly provides enough time for it all. Don't leave without visiting the former royal stables, the **Marstallmuseum,** or Museum of Royal Carriages. It houses a fleet of vehicles, including an elaborately decorated sleigh in which King Ludwig II once glided through the Bavarian twilight, postilion torches lighting the way. On the floor above are fine examples of Nymphenburg porcelain, produced here between 1747 and the 1920s. *Admission to the entire Schloss Nymphenburg complex: DM 5 adults, children accompanied by an adult go free. Open Tues.–Sun. 9–12:30 and 1:30–5 (4 PM in winter). Pagodenburg and Badenburg are closed Oct.–Mar. Marstallmuseum and Nymphenburg porcelain exhibition are open Apr.–Sept., Tues.–Sun. 9–noon and 1–5; Oct.–Mar., Tues.–Sun. 10–noon and 1–4. (Munich's botanic garden with its interesting tree collection and tropical greenhouses is adjacent to the palace grounds.)*

Of all the controversial buildings that mark Munich's skyline, none outdoes the circus-tent-like roofs of the **Olympiapark.** Built for the 1972 Olympics, the park, with its undulating, transparent tile roofs and modern housing blocks, represented a revolutionary marriage of technology and visual daring when first unveiled. Today, though still striking, it seems almost dated, a state of affairs not helped by the dingy gray of the faded tiles, or indeed by the fact that many of them are given to falling off. Take the elevator up the 960-foot Olympia Tower for a view of the city and the Alps; there's also a revolving restaurant near the top. *Admission to stadium: DM 1 adults, 50 pf children. Open daily 8:30–6. Admission to Olympia Tower: DM 5 adults, DM 2.50 children. Open daily 8 PM–midnight. Restaurant open daily 11–5:30 and 6:30 PM–10:30 PM; tel. 089/308–1039 for reservations.*

Day Trips from Munich

Ammersee. A large lake 40 kilometers (25 miles) south of Munich, the Ammersee is a popular spot for biking and water sports. It's about 40 minutes from Munich on the suburban S-5 line. *See* Chapter 3.

Andechs. The Benedictine monastery is the attraction here, and part of the lure is the monks' excellent beer and cheese. Getting there entails a trip on the suburban S-5 line, and then a bus ride or a hike. *See* Chapter 3.

Augsburg. This ancient city (founded in 15 BC) offers a wealth of architectural treasures. It's 30 minutes by train from Munich. *See* Chapter 3.

Berchtesgaden. An enchanting Alpine town nestled among high peaks beside one of southern Germany's prettiest lakes, the Königsee, this town is famous as the site of Adolf Hitler's mountaintop lair, the Eagle's Nest. But it's a long day trip: the scenic rail journey from Munich can take more than two hours. *See* Tour 3 in Chapter 4.

Chiemsee. Here, on an island in a big lake an hour or so southeast of Munich, stands one of Mad King Ludwig's fantasy castles, the Schloss Herrenchiemsee. *See* Chapter 3.

Dachau. The concentration camp site makes for a somber visit, but the town itself, with its 18th-century castle, is also well worth a stroll. It's 20 minutes from Munich on the suburban S-2 line. *See* Chapter 3.

Garmisch-Partenkirchen. A pretty Alpine town at the foot of Germany's highest mountain, the Zugspitze, Garmisch serves both as a winter sports center and a base for summer hiking. Trains leave hourly from Munich; the trip takes about 1½ hours. (If you are planning to scale the Zugspitze, ask for the special train ticket that includes a ride on a narrow gauge cog railway to the 2,966-meter/9,731-foot summit.) *See* Tour 1 in Chapter 4.

Landshut. This colorful, historic town, 40 minutes north of Munich, is home to two of the prettiest cobbled streets in Germany. *See* Chapter 3.

Lindau. An island in the Bodensee, Lindau has an Old Town full of architectural gems. It's 2½ hours from Munich by train. *See* Chapter 3.

Oberammergau. Although the famous Passion Play takes place only once a decade (the next is not until the year 2000), Oberammergau is itself a popular attraction owing to its many woodcarving shops. The old, ornately decorated village is set amid hills at the end of a slow but scenic 1½-hour rail trip from Munich. *See* Tour 1 in Chapter 4.

Passau. Two hours southeast of Munich, Passau has the distinction of standing on the confluence of three rivers. It's full of Baroque structures (and older buildings with Baroque facades). *See* Chapter 3.

Regensburg. Because it escaped the worst of the bombing during World War II, this is one of Germany's best-preserved medieval towns. It's a 90-minute train ride northeast of Munich. *See* Chapter 3.

Starnbergersee. This lovely lake—where Mad King Ludwig drowned—lies a little more than half an hour from Munich on the S-6 suburban line. A two-hour boat trip stops at several pretty villages. *See* Chapter 3.

Wasserburg. A well-preserved, if sleepy, town, Wasserburg offers a jumble of architectural styles in a tangle of ancient streets. It's 90 minutes from Munich, either by train or on the suburban S-4 line. *See* Chapter 3.

Shopping

Shopping Districts

Munich has an immense central shopping area, a mile and a half of pedestrian streets stretching from the train station to Marienplatz and north to Odeonsplatz. There's talk, too, of extending it still farther. The two main streets here are **Neuhauserstrasse** and **Kaufingerstrasse.** This is where most of the major department stores are located (*see* Department Stores, *below*). The most competitively priced shops lie in the slightly dingy side streets to the immediate south of the main train station, across Bayerstrasse. For good buys on such souvenirs as pewter-lidded beer mugs, explore the major department stores along the main pedestrianized street. The streets to avoid—except for window-shopping—are Maximilianstrasse, Residenzstrasse, and Theatinerstrasse, where prices are mind-boggling. Schwabing, located north of the university, boasts two of the city's most intriguing and offbeat shopping streets: **Schellingstrasse** and **Hohenzollernstrasse.** A delightful little open-air market is nearby at Elisabethplatz.

Department Stores

Hertie, occupying an entire city block between the train station and Karlsplatz, is the largest and, some claim, the best department store in the city. **Ludwig Beck** (Marienpl. 11) is great any-time, but comes into its own as Christmas approaches. A series of booths, each delicately and lovingly decorated, contains craftsmen turning out traditional German toys.

Specialty Stores

Antiques Bavarian antiques can be found in the many small shops around the Viktualienmarkt. Also try the area north of the university; Türkenstrasse, Theresienstrasse, and Barerstrasse are all filled with stores selling antiques. Munich's biggest antiques outlet is the **Palais Bernheimer** (Ottostr. 4–8); the range of goods is immense and encompasses everything from simple and inexpensive pieces of pewter to old-master paintings.

Folk Costumes Those with a fancy to deck themselves out in lederhosen or a dirndl or to sport a green loden coat and little pointed hat with feathers should head for **Loden-Frey** (Maffeistr. 7–9).

Food Markets Munich's **Viktualienmarkt** is *the* place. Located just south of Marienplatz, it's home to an array of colorful stands that sell everything from cheese to sausages, flowers to wine. A visit here is more than just an excuse to buy picnic makings: It's central to an understanding of the easy-come–easy-go nature of Müncheners.

Gift Ideas

Munich is a city of beer, and beer mugs and coasters make obvious choices for souvenirs and gifts. There are several specialty shops downtown. The best is **Ludwig Mory,** in the city hall on Marienplatz. Munich is also the home of the famous **Nymphenburg porcelain** factory. There's a factory outlet on Odeonsplatz, just north of Marienplatz; otherwise you can buy direct from the factory, on the grounds of Schloss Nymphenburg (Nördliches Schlossrondell 8). Other German porcelain manufacturers also have outlets in the city. For Dresden and Meissen ware, go to **Kunstring Meissen** (Briennerstr. 4 and Karlspl. 5). For Bavarian arts and crafts, the **Bayerischer Kunstgewerberein** (Pacellistr. 7) is unbeatable. For wood carvings, pewter, painted glass, and molded candles, try **A. Kaiser** and **Sebastian Weseley** (Rindermarkt 1), or **Otto Kellnberger's Holzhandlung** and the neighboring **Geschenk Alm** (Heiliggeiststr. 7–8). All four are near the Viktualienmarkt. For the best chocolates, try **Confiserie Rottenhöfer** (Residenzstr. 26) or the **Café Schöne Münchnerin,** opposite the Haus der Kunst.

Dining

Eating is a serious business in Munich, where the locals seem to be nibbling all day long—usually from snack stands called *Imbisse* or cafés specializing in take-out. The traditional fast-food nibbles, cheap but quite substantial, are the many varieties of *Wurst*, or sausage, but hamburgers and pizza slices seem to be gaining ground.

The most popular on-the-hoof traditional snacks come with a *Semmel* (roll) or a pretzel. They include *Fleischflanzerl*, a deep-fried meatball, and *Leberkäs*, a kind of meatloaf which, despite its name, does not have liver or cheese among its ingredients. The most common local sausage is grilled *Bratwurst*.

Most sausages are made with pork or beef; the exception is *Weisswurst*, or white sausage, made from veal and herbs. Weisswurst is not to everyone's taste, but it's a local specialty and well worth sampling. Legend has it that it was invented in 1857 by a butcher who had a hangover and mixed the wrong ingredients. A plaque on a wall in Marienplatz marks the spot where the "mistake" was made. The claim is that the genuine article is available only in and around Munich, served between midnight and noon and at no other time. For the biggest selection of take-out snacks in the city center, visit **Vinzenz Murr** (Rosenstr. off Marienplatz; closed from 6:30 PM and all day Sun.), or try any of the stalls in the outdoor food market called the **Viktualienmarkt** (open all day Mon.–Fri. and until 2 PM Sat.), a few minutes' walk from Marienplatz. At Vinzenz Murr you can also buy sliced meat and cheese, salad mixes, and rolls for a picnic in the little beer garden in the center of the Viktualienmarkt. You may eat your own food at any of the wooden tables that do not have tablecloths. The central concourse of the main train station has a string of snack stalls, too (open daily from early morning until around midnight).

More substantial repasts include *Tellerfleisch*, boiled beef with freshly grated horseradish and boiled potatoes on the side, served on wooden plates.

Among roasts, *sauerbraten* (beef) and *Schweinsbraten* (pork) are accompanied by dumplings and red cabbage.

Haxn refers to ham hocks roasted over a beech fire for hours, until they're crisp on the outside, juicy on the inside. They are served with sauerkraut and potato purée.

You'll also find soups, salads, fish and fowl, cutlets, game in season, casseroles, hearty stews, desserts, and what may well be the greatest variety and highest quality of baked goods in Europe, including pretzels.

Old Munich restaurants, called *Gaststätten*, feature what's referred to as *gutbürgerliche Küche*, loosely translated as good regional fare, and include brewery restaurants, beer halls, beer gardens, rustic cellar establishments, and *Weinstuben* (wine houses). More than a hundred such places brighten the scene. Most of them are open all day long, usually from 10 or 11 AM until midnight. In the city center, some beer restaurants serve hot meals all day through, but you can also just pop in for a beer or coffee.

Price estimates are per person for a two-course meal, including local taxes but excluding drinks. Highly recommended restaurants are indicated by a star ★.

Under DM 40

Franziskaner. Vaulted archways, cavernous rooms, bold blue frescoes, long wood tables, and a sort of spic-and-span medieval atmosphere—the look without the dirt—set the mood at this restaurant close by the State Opera. This is the place for an early morning Weisswurst and a beer. *Peruastr. 5, tel. 089/231–8120. No reservations. No credit cards.*

Goldene Stadt. Named for the "Golden City" of Prague, this is the place to find authentic Bohemian specialties. Try the roast duck or goose with dumplings. *Oberanger 44, tel. 089/264–382. Reservations advised. AE, DC, MC. Closed Sun.*

Kay's Bistro. The elegant vine-hung facade disguises one of the most bizarrely decorated restaurants in the city. The decor changes weekly, embracing styles as disparate as Caribbean and Chinese. The menu is similarly varied. This is the place for a chic and fun night out. *Utzschneiderstr. 1, tel. 089/260–3584. Reservations required. MC.*

★ **Piroschka Csarda.** This big, colorful venue is decorated Hungarian gypsy-style and tucked into a corner of the Haus der Kunst art gallery. The menu features classics such as Hungarian fish soup and *Fiaker* (coachman) goulash. There's gypsy violin music, too. *Prinzregentenstr. 1, tel. 089/295–425. AE, DC, MC, V. Open evenings only, until 1:30 AM. Closed Sun.*

Sangam. A rich selection of Indian dishes is prepared here by Indian cooks; you dine to the accompaniment of Indian music and, on some evenings, a belly dancer. The nearest U-bahn station (U-3/U-6, southbound) is Poccistrasse. *Ehrengutstr. 27, tel. 089/725–7184. Reservations recommended. AE, DC, MC, V.*

Spatenhaus. A view of the opera house and the royal palace complements the Bavarian mood of the wood-paneled and wood-beamed Spatenhaus. The menu is international, featuring everything from artichokes to *zuppa Romana. Residenzstr. 12, tel. 089/227–841. Reservations advised. DC, MC, V.*

Under DM 30

Donisl. This rough-and-ready place ranks high among the beer restaurants of Munich. It's located just off Marienplatz, and in summer its tables spill out onto the sidewalk. But the real action, night and day, is in the large central hall, with its painted and carved booths and garlands of dried flowers. *Weinstr. 1, tel. 089/220–184. No reservations. AE, DC, MC, V.*

Dürnbräu. A fountain plays outside this traditional Bavarian inn. Inside, it's crowded and noisy. Expect to share a table; your fellow diners will range from millionaires to students. *Dürnbräugasse 2, tel. 089/222–195. Reservations advised. AE, DC, MC, V.*

Grigoris. Traditional and off-beat Greek dishes highlight the menu at this little Schwabing venue. Lamb is served daily with a changing range of sauces. Vegetarians can choose from five different dishes. *Tengstr. 31, tel. 089/271–5625. Reservations advised. No credit cards. Closed Sun.*

Haxnbauer. This is among the most sophisticated of the beer restaurants. It has the usual sturdy/pretty Bavarian decor, but here there's a much greater emphasis on the food. Try the *Leberkäs*, a meat loaf of pork and beef, or *Schweinshaxe*, pork shanks. *Munzstr. 2, tel. 089/221–922. Reservations advised. MC, V.*

Hofbräuhaus. The heavy stone vaults of the Hofbräuhaus contain the most famous of the city's beer restaurants. It's just north of Marienplatz. Crowds of singing, shouting, swaying beer drinkers; hefty waitresses bearing frothing steins—some people love it; others deplore the touristy commercialism. *Am Platzl, tel. 089/221–676. No reservations. No credit cards.*

Hundskugel. This is Munich's oldest tavern, dating back to 1640; history drips from its crooked walls. The food is simple Bavarian fare at its best. If *Spanferkel*—roast suckling pig—is on the menu, make a point of ordering it. *Hotterstr. 18, tel. 089/264–272. Reservations advised. No credit cards.*

Max Emanuel Bräuerei. Folk music and theater are featured in this time-honored Munich institution, next to the university. The clientele is predominantly young, the atmosphere lively. In summer you can eat in the delightful little beer garden. The food is wholesomely Bavarian, with some Greek and French touches. *Adalbertstr. 33, tel. 089/271–5158. DC, MC.*

Pfälzer Weinprobierstube. A warren of stone-vaulted rooms, wood tables, flickering candles, dirndl-clad waitresses, and a vast range of wines add up to an experience as close to everyone's image of timeless Germany as you're likely to get. The food is reliable rather than spectacular. *Residenzstr. 1, tel. 089/225–628. No reservations. No credit cards.*

Ratskeller. Munich's Ratskeller is one of the few city-hall cellar restaurants to offer vegetarian dishes alongside the normal array of hearty and filling traditional fare. The decor is much as you would expect, with vaulted stone ceilings and flickering candles. *Marienpl. 8, tel. 089/220–313. Reservations advised. AE, MC, V.*

Weinhaus Neuner. Munich's oldest wine tavern serves good food—from nouvelle German to old-fashioned country fare—as well as superior wines in its three varied nooks and crannies: a wood-paneled restaurant, a wine tavern *(Weinstubl)*, and a small bistro. *Herzogspitalstr. 8, tel. 089/260–3954. Reservations advised. AE, DC, MC. Closed Sun.*

Under DM 20

Bella Italia. This chain of high-value, low-priced restaurants serves Italian dishes ranging from bowls of spaghetti to veal escalope. The best of them (where you can sit outside in a bustling square on sunny days) is at Hohenzollernplatz 8, Schwabing (beside the U-2 subway station and No. 18 tram). The others in the chain are at Sendlingerstr. 66 (near Karlsplatz in the city center), Türkenstr. 50 (near the university), and Passing Bahnhofplatz 3. *Open daily 11–11. No reservations. No credit cards.*

Dampfnud'l. One of the few places in the old city center open early for breakfast, this friendly café-restaurant caters to a wide variety of people. You can get anything from coffee and cake to beer and pretzels (there's a tiny beer garden at the back); at lunchtime, there are daily specials. *Altheimer Eck 12 (behind Neuhauserstr. and the big Karstadt store), tel. 089/260–3310. No reservations. No credit cards. Open 7–7; closed Sun.*

Franziskaner Poststuberl. This small beer restaurant, tucked away in a corner just off the Max Joseph Platz, serves traditional Munich fare (grilled sausages, sauerkraut, Leberkäs) from midmorning on. There's also a take-out counter. *Residenzstr. 10, tel. 089/231–8120. Reservations possible. No credit cards.*

Heng Long. A popular Beijing-style restaurant in the university quarter, the Heng serves three-course lunches for around DM 10 and can get very crowded with students. Early evening is calmer. *Amalienstr. 96, tel. 089/523–4389. Reservations advisable. No credit cards.*

Quinoa. Not everybody in Munich loves sausages and sauerkraut, as owner Heike Schwarzer found out when she opened this vegetarian bistro in the city center. You can choose a soup and a snack or a solid cooked meal from the big blackboard menu. *Sendlingerstr. 30. No reservations. No credit cards. Open midmorning–10 PM weekdays, till 4 PM Sat. Closed Sun.*

★ **Straubinger Hof.** Show up early if you want a table at this famous old establishment across the road from the Viktualienmarkt. The Weisswurst is served fresh 9 AM on. In summer, the little beer garden outside is the place to be. *Blumenstr. 5, tel. 089/260–8444. No reservations. No credit cards. Closed Sat. evenings, Sun., and Aug. 25–Sept. 10.*

Splurge

★ **Austernkeller.** This elegant and softly lit vaulted-cellar restaurant concentrates on delicate shellfish specialties. Expect to pay around DM 40 per person for a two-course meal. *Dinner only. Stollbergstr. 11, tel. 089/298–787. Reservations advised. Jacket and tie required. AE, DC, MC, V. Closed Mon. and Christmas.*

★ **Preysing Keller.** Devotees of food that's light and sophisticated but with recognizably Teutonic touches will love this converted 16th-century cellar. Entrées start at DM 30; try the fixed-price seven-course menu—a bargain at DM 100 per person—for best value and a fine sampling. *Innere-Wiener-Str. 6, tel. 089/481–015. Reservations required. Jacket and tie required. No credit cards. Closed Sun. and Dec. 23–Jan. 7.*

The Arts and Nightlife

The Arts

Most of Munich's major theaters and concert halls—the State Theater and Gasteig complex in particular—are extremely expensive, and tickets for major operatic events at the State Theater can be hard to obtain. You might be able to buy reduced-price tickets if you're in town for a preview night. And if you're willing to stand at the back of the State Theater, a limited number of *Stehplätze* (standing room) tickets are sold nightly for a fraction of what seats cost.

Some student performances at the Hochschule für Musik (*see below*) are free. Most of the main jazz haunts (*see below*) have free jam sessions on Sunday evenings.

The Munich International Filmfest, during the last week of June, gives you the opportunity to see a big variety of films (in various languages, including English) at lower-than-normal prices—if you buy a block of tickets. The Fest is centered on the Gasteig (*see below*).

Details of concerts and theater performances are listed in *Voschau* and *Monatsprogramm*, booklets available at most hotel reception desks, newsstands, and tourist offices. Some hotels will make ticket reservations; otherwise use one of the ticket agencies in the city center, such as **A-Z Schalterhalle** (Sendlingerstr. 79, tel. 089/267-024), **Residenz Bucherstube** (concert tickets only; Theatinerstr., tel. 089/220-868), or **Hieber Max** (Liebefrauenstr. 1, tel. 089/226-571).

Theater Munich has scores of theaters and variety-show haunts, although most productions will be largely impenetrable if your German is shaky. (An English-speaking troupe, the **Company,** presents about four productions a year; tel. 089/343-827). Listed here are the better-known theaters, as well as some of the smaller and more progressive spots. Note that most theaters are closed during July and August.

Bayerisches Staatsschauspiel/Neues Residenztheater (Bavarian State Theater/New Residence Theater) (Max-Joseph-Pl.; the box office is at Maximilianstr. 11, tel. 089/221-316). Open Mon.-Fri. 10-1 and 3:30-5:30, Sat. 10-12:30, and one hour before the performance.

Cuvilliés-Theater/Altes Residenztheater (Old Residence Theater) (Max-Joseph-Pl.; entrance on Residenzstr.). The box office, at Maximilianstrasse 11 (tel. 089/221-1316), is open Mon.-Fri. 10-1 and 3:30-5:30, Sat. 10-12:30, and one hour before the performance.

Deutsches Theater (Schwanthalerstr. 13, tel. 089/593-427). The box office is open Mon.-Fri. noon-6, Sat. 10-1:30.

Gasteig (Rosenheimerstr. 5, tel. 089/4809-8614). This modern cultural complex includes two theaters—the Carl-Orff Saal and the Black Box—where plays in English are occasionally performed. The box office is open Mon.-Fri. 10:30-2 and 3-6, Sat. 10:30-2.

Kleine Komödie (Bayerischer Hof Hotel, Promenadepl., tel. 089/292-810; Max-II-Denkmal, Maximilianstr., tel. 089/221-859). The box office at Bayerischer Hof is open Mon.-Sat. 11-8, Sun. and holidays 3-8. The box office at Max-II-Denkmal is open Tues.-Sat. 11-8, Mon. 11-7, Sun. and holidays 3-8.

Platzl am Platzl (Munzstr. 8-9, tel. 089/237-03711). Daily show (except Sunday) with typical Bavarian humor, yodeling, and *Schuhplattler* (the slapping of Bavarian leather shorts in time to the oompah music).

Prinzregententheater (Prinzregentenpl. 12, tel. 089/225-754). The box office is open Mon.-Fri. 10-1 and 3:30-5:30, Sat. 10-12:30, and one hour before the performance.

Theater der Jugend (Franz-Joseph-Str. 47, tel. 089/237-21365). The box office is open Tues.-Sat. 1:30-5:30.

Theater Kleine Freiheit (Maximilianstr. 31, tel. 089/221-123). The box office is open Mon.-Sat. from 11, Sun. from 2.

Concerts Munich's glossiest cultural center, built in 1984, is the **Gasteig,** just across the River Isar from the Deutsches Museum (take any S-bahn subway train to Rosenheimer Platz station). It's the permanent home of the Munich Philharmonic Orchestra, which regularly performs in its Philharmonic Hall. In addition to the Philharmonic, the city has three other orchestras: the Bavarian State Orchestra, based at the National Theater; the Bavarian Radio Orchestra, which gives Sunday concerts at the Gasteig; and the Kurt Graunke Symphony Orchestra, which generally puts on operettas at the Gartnerplatz theater. The leading choral ensembles are the Munich Bach Choir, the Munich Motettenchor, and Musica Viva, the latter specializing in contemporary music. (*See above* for information on where to buy tickets.)

Bayerischer Rundfunk (Rundfunkpl. 1, tel. 089/558–080). The box office is open Monday–Friday 9–noon and 1–5.
Galerie im Lenbachhaus (Luisenstr. 33, tel. 089/521–041). Though this is primarily an art gallery, chamber-music concerts are sometimes held here.
Gasteig Kulturzentrum (Rosenheimerstr. 5, tel. 089/480–980). The box office is open Mon.–Fri. 10:30–2 and 3–6, Sat. 10:30–2.
Herkulessaal in der Residenz (Hofgarten, tel. 089/224–641). The box office opens one hour before performances.
Hochscule für Musik (Arcisstr. 12, tel. 089/559–101). Concerts featuring music students are given free of charge.
Kongressaal des Deutscher Museums (Museumsinsel 1, tel. 089/221–790). The box office opens one hour before performances.
Olympiahalle (tel. 089/306–13577). The box office is open Mon.–Thurs. 8–5, Fri. 8–2. Pop concerts are held here.

Nightlife

Munich's nighttime attractions vary with the seasons. The year starts with the abandon of *Fasching,* the Bavarian carnival time, when every night is party night. No sooner has Lent brought the sackcloth curtain down on Fasching than the local weather office is being asked to predict when the spring sunshine will be warm enough to allow the city's 50 beer gardens to open. From then until late fall the beer garden dictates the style and pace of Munich's nightlife. When it rains, the indoor beer halls and taverns absorb the thirsty like blotting paper.

The beer gardens and beer halls close at midnight, but there's no need to go home to bed then: Some bars and nightclubs are open until 3 AM, and a few have all-night licenses. A word of caution about some of those bars, however: Most are honestly run and prices are only slightly higher than normal, but a few may be unscrupulous. The seedier are near the main train station. If you want to keep costs down, stick to beer or wine, and pay as you go.

For a city with such a free-and-easy reputation, Munich lacks the raunchy, no-holds-barred forthrightness of Hamburg's Reeperbahn. There are no live sex shows or wholesale sex-for-sale arrangements as in some other German cities. For striptease shows, explore the region south of the main railway station (Schillerstrasse, for example) or the neighborhood of the famous Hofbräuhaus (am Platzl).

Discos Schwabing is discoland. There are three in a 50-yard stretch of Occamstrasse: **Albatros, California New,** and **Circo Valentino. Peaches,** on the neighboring Feilitzstrasse, and **Meddos,** on Marktstrasse, are also young and fun. Across town, the **Lenbach Palast** (Lenbachpl. 3) features live bands nightly. The noisiest disco in town is **Crash** (Lindwurmstr. 88). The youngsters love it, despite the risk of ruptured eardrums. It is closed on Sunday.

Jazz Munich likes to think it's Germany's jazz capital, and to reinforce the claim some beer gardens have taken to replacing their brass bands with funky combos. Purists don't like it, but jazz enthusiasts are happy. The combination certainly works at **Waldwirtshaft Grosshesselohe** (Georg Kalb-Str. 3), in the southern suburb of Grosshesselohe. Sundays are set aside for jazz, and if it's a fine day the excursion is much recommended. Some city pubs also set aside Sunday midday for jazz: Try **Doktor Flotte** (Occamstr. 8). The best of the jazz clubs are **Allotria** (Turkenstr. 33); **Nachtcafé** (Maximilianpl. 5, open until 5 AM); **Schwabinger Podium** (Wagnerstr. 1); **Unterfahrt** (Kirchenstr. 96); and **Jenny's Place in the Blue Note,** Moosacherstr. 24, near the Olympiazentrum (tel. 089/351–0520), new live-jazz venue of a vivacious English actress and singer who has a great voice and a warm welcome for visitors from the United States and Britain.

3 Excursions from Munich

Including Augsburg, Konstanz, Lindau, Passau, and Regensburg

After a few days of city touring you may find yourself yearning for an interlude in a smaller, quieter place—and Munich's heart-of-Bavaria location makes it an ideal base for side trips to the region's towns and lakes. The dozen we suggest offer everything from Regensburg's medieval and Passau's Baroque architecture to the mountains of Garmisch-Partenkirchen, the water sports at the Ammersee, and the heavenly dark beer at the monastery in Andechs.

All but one of the following excursions are—technically—doable as day trips (the exception is Konstanz). Several of these sites, such as Dachau and the Starnbergersee, can be easily reached on Munich's suburban train system; but you may want to think twice before embarking on a two-hour rail journey to, say, Lindau or Passau, cramming a couple of days' worth of sightseeing into a few hours, and then rushing back to the station and enduring the long return trip. And since hotels in these areas are usually cheaper than those in Munich, it may save you money to make these excursions as overnights. On the other hand, if you're happily settled in city accommodations—or if you don't feel like lugging your bags along—you may find the notion of a day trip more appealing.

For Ammersee, Andechs, Chiemsee, Starnbergersee, and Wasserburg, *see* the Bavarian Alps map in Chapter 4.

In dining and lodging reviews throughout the chapter, highly recommended establishments are indicated by a star ★.

Ammersee

*The journey takes about 40 minutes from the Hauptbahnhof; trains usually run twice an hour. (*See *Starnbergersee*, below, *for information on the all-inclusive DM 35 Weissblau KombiKarte ticket from Munich, which is also valid for Amersee.)*

The Ammersee is one of two big lakes lying side by side about 40 kilometers (25 miles) south of Munich. (For the other, the Starnbergersee, *see below.*) The scenic 19-kilometer-by-6-kilometer (12-mile-by-4-mile) Ammersee is a popular venue for sailing and windsurfing, and cycle paths follow most of the shoreline. Bikes can be hired from the train station at Herrsching (tel. 08152/3426), a pretty little town on the east side of the lake and terminus of the S-5 line from Munich. Herrsching has a lakeside promenade with waterside restaurants and cafés. Boat tours depart daily at regular intervals from a small pier.

Andechs

Take the S-5 line from Munich to its terminus at Herrsching.

The sole attraction in this otherwise sleepy village 6 kilometers (4 miles) south of Herrsching is a **Benedictine monastery,** which is a place of pilgrimage for both students of religious artifacts and beer lovers. A rich dark beer brewed by the monks is served in a boisterous hall where you can also sample monastery-made cheese. The hilltop church dates from the 15th century but has noteworthy Rococo additions, and it contains relics said to have come from the Middle East at the time of the Crusades. You can cycle or walk to the monastery through beech woods (allow 1½ hours on foot) or take the No. 956 bus from the Herrsching train station. (If you don't have time to go out to Andechs, you can try the monastery beer in the Gasthof zur Post tavern opposite the Herrsching station.)

Augsburg

Frequent trains run from Munich's Hauptbahnhof; the fastest journey time, by InterCity, is 30 minutes. Tourist office: Verkehrsverein, Bahnhofstr. 7, tel. 0821/502–070.

Numbers in the margin correspond to points of interest on the Augsburg map.

Augsburg was established by Drusus, son of the Emperor Augustus (Drusus named the town Augusta), in 15 BC as a Roman military settlement. It's a city of architectural treasures, many of which owe their existence to the wealthy merchants of the Fugger family.

The local tourist department has created three color-coded walking tours of the city's historic heart. Start by picking up a color-coded pamphlet at the tourist office, which adjoins the main train station. Follow the blue route first to one of
1 Augsburg's many historic churches, **St. Annakirche.** This former Carmelite monastery dates from the 14th century. Visitors can wander through its quiet cloisters and view the chapel used by the Fugger family until the Reformation. In 1318, Martin Luther stayed in the monastery during his meetings with

Deutsche Barockgalerie, **4**
Dom St. Maria, **10**
Fuggerei, **8**
Maximilian-Museum, **2**
Mercury Fountain, **3**
Mozarthaus, **11**
Oblatter Wall, **12**
Rathaus, **9**
Rotes Tor, **6**
St. Annakirche, **1**
Sts. Ulrich and Afra, **5**
Vogeltor, **7**

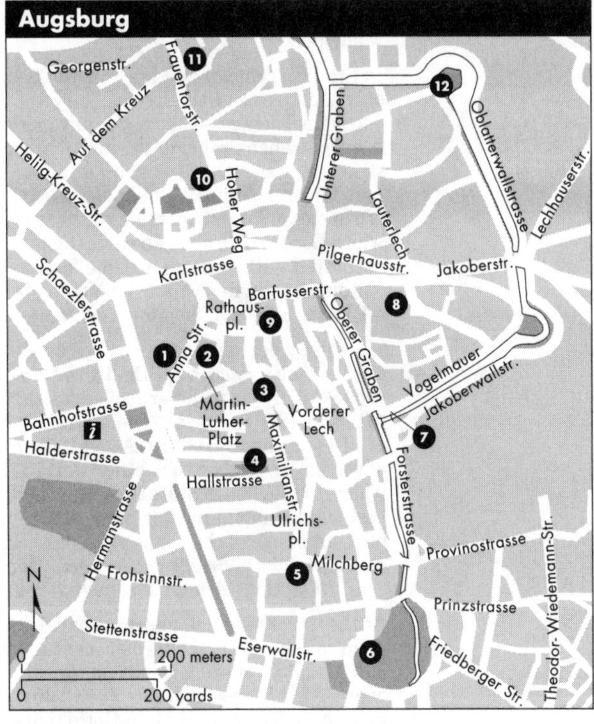

Cardinal Cajetanus, the papal legate sent from Rome to persuade the reformist to renounce his heretical views. Luther refused, and the place where he publicly declared his rejection of papal pressure is marked with a plaque on Augsburg's main street, the Maximilianstrasse.

Outside St. Annakirche, follow the green route southward,
2 along Martin-Luther-Platz, past the **Maximilian-Museum,** a permanent exhibition of Augsburg arts and crafts. *Phillipine-Welser-Str. 24. Admission free. Open Tues.–Sun. 10–4.*

At the end of the square in front of you is Maximilianstrasse; here you'll notice one of the three monumental and elaborate fountains that splash amid the buzz of traffic on this historic old
3 street. The **Mercury fountain,** 1599, by the Dutch master Adriaen de Vries (after a Florentine sculpture by Giovanni da Bologna), shows winged Mercury in his classic pose. Farther up Maximilianstrasse is another de Vries fountain: a bronze Hercules struggling to defeat the many-headed Hydra. The lantern-lined street was once the scene of a wine market; today the high-gabled, pastel facades of the 16th-century merchant houses assert themselves against encroaching postwar shops. On the right, as you walk up the slight incline of the street, stands a 16th-century building, the former home and business quarters of the Fuggers. The 16th-century building now houses a restaurant in its cellar and offices on the upper floors. In the ground-floor entrance are busts of two of Augsburg's most industrious Fuggers, Raymund and Anton. The busts are tributes from a grateful city to the wealth these merchants brought the community. Beyond a modern glass door is a quiet

courtyard with colonnades, originally reserved for the Fugger womenfolk.

In the 18th century another wealthy family built a rival palace only a few paces up the street. The von Liebenhofens wanted to outdo the Fuggers—but not at any price. Thus, to save money in an age when property was taxed according to the size of the street frontage, they constructed a long, narrow building running far back from Maximilianstrasse. The palace is composed of a series of interconnecting rooms that lead into a green-and-white Rococo ballroom: an extravagant, two-story hall heavily decorated with mirrors, chandeliers, and wall sconces. Marie Antoinette, on her way from Vienna to Paris to marry Louis XVI, was a guest of honor at the inauguration ball in 1770.

The family bequeathed the palace to the city after the war; to-
4 day its rooms contain the **Deutsche Barockgalerie** (German Baroque Gallery), a major art collection that features works of the 17th and 18th centuries. The palace adjoins the former church of a Dominican monastery. A steel door behind the banquet hall of the palace leads into another world of high vaulted ceilings, where the Bavarian State Collection highlights an exhibition of early Swabian old master paintings. Among them is a Dürer portrait of one of the Fuggers. *Maximilianstr. 46. Admission free, but donations are encouraged. Open May–Sept., Tues.–Sun. 10–5; Oct.–Apr., Tues.–Sun. 10–4.*

At the top of Maximilianstrasse on Ulrichsplatz, at the highest
5 point of the city, is the former monastery church of **Sts. Ulrich and Afra,** two churches built on the site of a Roman cemetery where St. Afra was martyred in AD 304. The original, Catholic building was begun as a late-Gothic construction in 1467; a Baroque-style preaching hall was added in 1710 as the Protestant church of St. Ulrich. St. Afra is buried in the crypt, near the tomb of St. Ulrich, a 10th-century bishop credited with helping to stop a Hungarian army at the doors of Augsburg in the battle of the Lech River. The remains of a third patron of the church, St. Simpert, are preserved in one of the church's most elaborate side chapels. From the steps of the magnificent altar, look back along the high nave to the finely carved Baroque wrought-iron and wood railing that borders the entrance. As you leave, pause to look into the separate but adjacent Protestant church of St. Ulrich, the former monastery assembly hall that was taken over and reconstructed by the Lutherans after the Reformation.

Turning to the color-coded tour guides, follow the green route south for a few hundred yards and you'll reach the city's ancient fortifications and its most important medieval entrance gate,
6 the **Rotes Tor** (Red Gate), which once straddled the main trading road to Italy. From here you can follow the traces of the early city fortifications northward and back to the city center,
7 passing the Gothic **Vogeltor** (Bird Gate) on Eserwell-Strasse and, on the street called Vorderer Lech, the rebuilt 16th-century home of Hans Holbein the Elder, one of Augsburg's most famous sons (the homes of two others, Leopold Mozart and Bertolt Brecht, are also on our route). The Holbein house is now a city art gallery with a regularly changing program of exhibitions. *Vorderer Lech 20. Open May–Oct., Tues.–Sun. 10–5; Nov.–Apr., Tues.–Sun. 10–4.*

At the end of Vorderer Lech, make a sharp right and follow the
green route over a small stream into the tranquillity of the
8 **Fuggerei.** This is the world's oldest social housing scheme, established by the Fugger family to accommodate the city's de-
serving poor. The 147 homes still serve the same purpose; the
annual rent of "one Rheinish Guilder" (DM 1.72) hasn't
changed, either. Understandably, there's quite a demand to
take up residence in this peaceful, leafy estate. There are four
requirements: Residents must be Augsburg citizens, Catholic,
and destitute through no fault of their own, and they must pray
daily for their original benefactors, the Fugger family.

From the Fuggerei, follow the green route back into the city center, stopping at the **Brecht** family home, a modest artisan's house and the birthplace of Bertolt Brecht, author of *The Threepenny Opera*. Today the house serves as a memorial center dedicated to Brecht's life and work. *Auf dem Rain 7. Admission: DM 2 adults, DM 1 children. Open May–Oct., Tues.–Sun. 10–5; Nov.–Apr., Tues.–Sun. 10–4.*

Two left turns will bring you to Rathausplatz, the center of
Augsburg, dominated by the 258-foot-high **Perlachturm** (open
Apr.–Sept., daily 10–6) and the adjacent massive, square
9 **Rathaus** (Town Hall). The great building, Germany's largest
city hall when it was built in the early 17th century, is one of the
finest Renaissance structures north of the Alps. (The Rathaus
can be visited between 10 and 6 on days when no official functions are taking place.)

From the great square in front of the Rathaus (its 16th-century
fountain commemorates the 1,600th anniversary of the founding of Augsburg), turn north again along the shopping streets
10 of Karolinenstrasse and Hoher Weg to the **Dom St. Maria** (Cathedral of the Virgin Mary); its square Gothic towers will signal
the way. The heavy bronze doors on the south portal date from
the 11th century; 11th-century windows on the south side of the
nave depict the prophets Jonah, Daniel, Hosea, Moses, and
David, to form the oldest cycle of stained glass in central Europe. Five altarpieces by Hans Holbein the Elder are among
the cathedral's other treasures.

A short walk from the cathedral, still following the green route, will take you to the quiet courtyards and small raised garden of the former Episcopal residence, a series of fine 18th-century buildings in Baroque and Rococo styles that now serve as the offices of the Swabian regional government. Although less than 40 miles from the capital of Bavaria, we're now firmly in Swabia, once such a powerful dukedom under the Hohenstaufens that its territory covered virtually all of present-day Switzerland. Today Swabia has become an administrative district of Bavaria, and Augsburg has yielded the position it once held to the younger city of Munich.

11 Head north again, along Frauentorstrasse, to the **Mozarthaus,** birthplace of Leopold Mozart, father of Wolfgang Amadeus Mozart and an accomplished composer and musician in his own right. A comfortable 17th-century home, it now serves as a Mozart memorial and museum, with some fascinating contemporary documents on the Mozart family. The last Augsburg family connection died just a few years ago. *Frauentorstr. 30. Admission free. Open Mon., Wed., Thurs. 10–noon and 2–5; Fri. 10–noon and 1–4; Sat. and Sun. 10–noon.*

Retrace your steps to the city center. If you have time and energy, you can continue your tour with a walk along the remains of the city's ancient north and east defenses. For part of the way a pleasant walk follows the moat, which was once part of the fortifications. 12 At the **Oblatter Wall** you can rent a boat and row between the green, leafy banks—a welcome break and a fine way to say farewell to Augsburg.

Lodging
Under DM 130

Dom Hotel. Just across the street from Augsburg's cathedral, this is a snug, comfortable establishment with a personal touch. Ask for one of the attic rooms, where you'll sleep under beam ceilings and wake to a rooftop view of the city. *Frauentorstr. 8, tel. 0821/153–031. 43 rooms with bath or shower. MC, V.*

Hotel Post. Centrally located on a tree-lined avenue, this hotel offers modern, comfortable accommodations. The breakfast room, decked out in crisp blue-and-white checks, makes for a good start to the day. *Fuggerstr. 5/7 (Am Konigspl.), tel. 0821/36044. 50 rooms, most with bath or shower. AE, DC, MC, V. Closed Christmas and New Year's Day.*

Dining
Under DM 20

Fuggerkeller. The vaulted cellars of the former Fugger home are now a bright and comfortable restaurant, owned and run by the luxurious Drei Mohren Hotel above it. The midday specials are a particularly good value; prices for dinner are higher. *Maximilianstr. 40, tel. 0821/510–031. Reservations advised. AE, DC, MC, V. Closed Sun. dinner and first 3 weeks of Aug.*

7-Schwaben-Stuben. This colorful old-town tavern, half a mile from the train station, offers a complete tour of Swabian cooking. Here you'll find excellent *Maultaschen* (a kind of ravioli) and *Spätzle*, the region's own pasta, often served with cheese and onion. *Bürgermeister-Fischerstr. 12, near Königsplatz, tel. 0821/314–563. AE, V.*

Chiemsee

Regular trains connect Munich with the lakeside town of Prien. Ask for the DM 35 three-in-one ticket (half-price for children), which includes the one-hour rail journey to Prien, a trip on a veteran steam train to the village of Stock, and a round-trip boat ride that takes in the two most important islands.

One of the biggest lakes in Germany, the Chiemsee has been a favorite Bavarian playground since "Mad" King Ludwig II built a fantasy palace on one of the lake's three islands. The **Schloss Herrenchiemsee** was based on Louis XIV's great palace at Versailles. But this was the result of more than simple admiration of Versailles on Ludwig's part: With his name being the German for Louis, he was keen to establish that he, too, possessed the absolute authority of his namesake, the Sun King. As with most of Ludwig's projects, the building was never completed, and Ludwig was never able to stay in its state rooms. Nonetheless, what remains is impressive—and ostentatious. The single most spectacular attraction in the palace is the Hall of Mirrors, a dazzling gallery (modeled on that at Versailles) where candle-lit concerts are held in the summer. Also of interest are the ornate bedroom Ludwig planned and the stately formal gardens. The south wing houses a museum containing Ludwig's christening robe and death mask, as well as other artifacts of his life. *Palace and museum admission: DM 5* *adults, DM 2.50 children. Open Apr.–Sept., daily 9–5; Oct.–Mar., daily 10–4. Guided tours offered May–Sept.*

Dachau

The town is only a 20-minute ride on the S-2 line of Munich's suburban train system, from either Marienplatz or the Hauptbahnhof.

The first Nazi concentration camp was built just outside this town, 20 kilometers (12 miles) northwest of Munich. To get to the camp memorial site, take the No. 722 bus from outside Dachau station. *Admission to camp grounds and museum free. Open Tues.–Sun. 9–5. A documentary film in English is shown daily at 11:30 and 3:30.*

If time permits, it's worth strolling around town. Head for the early 18th-century **castle,** where weekend summer concerts are held and the town's own beer is still brewed. (The castle brewery hosts a beer festival in early August.)

Dining The **Bräustüberl,** 50 yards from the castle, has a shady beer garden for summer lunches. In the town center, the **Helferwirt** has a secluded garden and a cozy restaurant serving Bavarian fare. Next to the ivy-covered town hall, on Freisingerstrasse, is the solid, historic **Zieglerbräu,** once a 17th-century brewer's home, now a wood-paneled restaurant.

Konstanz

You can do trip by rail and ferry or entirely by rail. Express trains leave Munich's Hauptbahnhof every two hours; it takes 2 hours 15 minutes to get to Lindau, and from there you can catch a ferry for Konstanz (a one-way boat ticket costs DM 14.80) from the harbor adjacent to the station. Or you can stay on the train for the scenic ride round the Bodensee; the line skirts the entire western shoreline. Because of the lake, the train journey from Munich is a long one—four hours or more, depending on the type of train and whether you have to change en route. The long travel time makes Konstanz more appropriate for an overnight stay than a day trip from Munich. Tourist office: Tourist-information Konstanz, Bahnhofplatz 13, 7750 Konstanz, tel. 07531/284–376.

Konstanz is a compact town, which can be explored comfortably on foot. Cyclists can hire **bikes** at the train station (tel. 07531/23955). This ancient town straddles the German border with Switzerland (the Swiss call their part of the conurbation Kreuzlingen) on the southern shores of the lake across the water from Lindau.

The **Bodensee** (Lake Constance) is the largest lake in the German-speaking world, 424 kilometers square, 339 kilometers around (163 miles square, 210 miles around), and bordered by Germany, Switzerland, and Austria. It's called a lake, but actually it's a vast swelling of the Rhine, gouged out by a massive glacier in the Ice Age and flooded by the river as the ice receded. The Rhine flows into its southeast corner, where Switzerland and Austria meet, and leaves at its west end.

This is one of the warmest areas of Germany, the result not so much of its southern location as of the warming influence of the lake, which gathers heat in the summer and releases it in the winter like a massive radiator. There are corners of the Bodensee that enjoy a near-tropical climate, where lemons, bougainvillaea, and hibiscus flourish and where vines grow in abundance. The lake itself practically never freezes (it has done so only once this century and twice in the last).

Because it's practically in Switzerland, Konstanz suffered no wartime bombing—the Allies were unwilling to risk inadvertent bombing of neutral Switzerland—with the result that Konstanz is among the best-preserved major medieval towns in Germany. It's said to have been founded in the 3rd century; by the 6th century it had become a bishopric; in 1192, it was made a Free Imperial City. But what really put Konstanz on the map was the Council of Konstanz, held between 1414 and 1417 and probably one of the most remarkable gatherings of the medieval world. Upwards of 100,000 people are said to have descended on the city during the great council. It was an assembly whose profound consequences are still felt today. The council was convened to settle the Great Schism, the rift in the church brought about in the 14th century when the papacy moved from Rome to Avignon in the south of France. With the move, a rival pope declared himself in Rome. The council provided a kind of summit for the various religious-political forces of the day: the religious leadership from Rome; the German Holy Roman Emperor, who controlled much of Europe in a loose pact with Rome; and religious rebels campaigning for change.

For all its vivid history, though, Konstanz is also a town to be enjoyed for its more worldly pleasures—its elegant Alstadt (Old Town), trips on the lake, walks along the promenade, the classy shops, the restaurants, the views. The heart of the city is the **Gondelhafen,** the harbor, with the simple bulk of the Konzilgebäude looming behind it. Put up in 1388 as a warehouse, the building is now a concert hall.

Walk around the council building and take the street called Marktstatte. It leads to the **Rosgarten Museum,** the museum of local history. If you want to learn more about the Council of Konstanz, step inside. *Rosgartenstr. 3–5. Admission: DM 2.50 adults, children free. Open Tues.–Sun. 10–5.*

Continue up Marktstatte to the **Altes Rathaus** (Old Town Hall), built in the Renaissance and painted with boldly vivid frescoes—swags of flowers and fruits, shields, architectural details, sturdy knights wielding immense swords. Walk into the courtyard to admire its Renaissance restraint.

Turn right down Wessenbergstrasse, the main street of the Old Town. It leads to **St. Stephanskirche,** an austere late-Gothic church with a very un-Gothic Rococo chancel. It stands in a little square surrounded by fine half-timbered houses. Look at the **Haus zur Katz** (on the right as you walk into the square). It was the headquarters of one of the city's trade guilds in the Middle Ages; now it houses the city archives.

Now walk through to the **Münster** (cathedral), built on the site of the original Roman fortress. Building on the cathedral continued from the 10th century through the 19th, resulting in today's oddly eclectic structure. The twin-towered facade, for example, is sturdily Romanesque, blunt and heavy-looking; the elegant and airy chapels along the aisles are full-blown 15th-century Gothic; the complex nave vaulting is Renaissance; the choir is severely neoclassical. Make a point of seeing the Holy Sepulchre tomb in the Mauritius Chapel at the far end of the church behind the altar. It's a richly worked 13th-century Gothic structure, 12 feet high, still with some of its original, vivid coloring and gilding, and studded with statues of the Apostles and figures from the childhood of Jesus.

Finally, you should walk up to the Rhine, through the **Niederburg,** the oldest part of Konstanz, a tangle of old, twisting streets. Once at the river, take a look at the two city towers here, the **Rheintor**—it's the one nearer the lake—and the aptly named **Pulverturm** (Powder Tower), the former city arsenal.

From Konstanz, numerous boat trips fan out to different parts of the lake. They are run by the Weisse Flotte (White Fleet) Line, which operates from a pretty little stone harbor beside the town's train station. Boat trips can last just an hour or take all day. Some sail up the Rhine to the spectacular waterfalls (Europe's largest) at Schaffhausen. For details, contact the tourist office. If you plan to use the ferries extensively, buy a **Bodensee Pass.** It gives 15 days' unlimited travel on all ferries, as well as on many trains, buses, and some local mountain railways. Cost is DM 70 (DM 35 for children 6 to 16). Contact **Bodensee-Schiffsbetriebe der Deutschen Bundesbahn** (Hafenstr. 6, 7750 Konstanz, tel. 07531/281–398).

One of the easiest boat trips is the half-hour ride to the beautiful island of **Mainau,** also known as the Island of Flowers. Not many people visit Germany expecting to find banana plantations, let alone such exotic flora as bougainvillea and hibiscus. But on Mainau these (and hundreds of more commonplace species) flourish, nurtured by the freakishly warm and moist climate. Visit in the spring and you'll find over a million tulips, hyacinths, and narcissi in bloom; rhododendrons and roses flower in May and June; dahlias dominate the late-summer display.

Travelers interested in the history of flight will appreciate a side trip from Konstanz across the lake to **Friedrichshafen.** It was here that the Zeppelin airships—and later the Dornier flying boats—were invented and developed. In both cases, it was the broad, smooth waters of the lake that made Friedrichshafen attractive to the pioneer airmen: The zeppelins were built in enormous, floating hangars on the lake; the Dorniers were tested on its calm surface. At the **Zeppelin-und-Bodensee-museum,** the whole unlikely tale is told in detail, complete with models—one 26 feet long—plans, photographs, and documents. *Adenauerpl. 1. Admission: DM 3. Open May–Oct., Thurs.–Tues. 10–5, Wed. 10–7; Nov.–Apr., Tues.–Sun. 10–noon and 2–5.*

From the museum, it's a short walk along the lakeside promenade to Friedrichshafen's **Schloss Hofen,** a small palace that served as the summer residence of the kings of Württemberg until 1918. The palace was formerly a priory—its foundations date to the 11th century—and the adjoining priory church is a splendid example of local Baroque architecture.

Lodging
Under DM 110

Buchner Hof. Elegant and well run, the small Buchner Hof is a 10-minute walk north of the old town just across the Rheinbrücke. It's a comfortable, quiet hotel, with spacious bedrooms featuring oak-veneer furniture (all of it new). *Buchnerstr. 6, tel. 07531/51035. 13 rooms with bath. Facilities:*

wine bar, sauna, solarium. AE, DC. Closed Christmas–Jan. 10.

Deutsches Haus. It's a modest but clean and friendly guest house in the heart of the old town, just a few hundred yards to the right of the train station. *Marktstätte 15, tel. 07531/27065. 42 rooms, half with shower. AE, DC, MC, V. Closed Dec. 15–Jan. 10.*

Dining
Under DM 20

Engstler's. Informal, friendly, and noisy, Engstler's stands across the street from the Council Building. The food is distinctly red-blooded, with game dishes heavily featured. Special children's menus are also available. In summer, eat in the beer garden. *Fischmarkt 1, tel. 07531/23126. AE, DC, MC, V. Closed Jan. and Feb.*

The Arts and Nightlife

You can enjoy high-quality musical evenings here at much lower prices than in the city. The region's own orchestra, founded in 1932, performs from October through April. Program details and bookings are available from **Bodensee Symphonie Orchester** (Spanierstr. 3, 7750 Konstanz, tel. 07531/52855). Konstanz has an annual summer music festival, from mid-June to mid-July, with a program of international events, including celebrated organ concerts in the cathedral. For program details and bookings, contact the Konstanz tourist office (tel. 07531/284–376). Performances are held in the Council Building.

The Bodensee **disco** scene is concentrated in Konstanz. **Flair** (Reichenauerstr. 212) is one of the biggest and best. Konstanz also has a **casino** (Seestr. 21, tel. 07531/63615), open 2–2 daily.

Landshut

Landshut is on the Plattling–Regensburg–Passau line, a 40-minute ride by express train from Munich.

This colorful and historic town, 65 kilometers (40 miles) north of Munich, is famous for the architecture on two of Germany's prettiest cobbled streets, Altstadt and Neustadt. Here you will find the first Italian Renaissance building constructed north of the Alps, the royal Wittelsbach family's 16th-century **Stadtresidenz.** Noteworthy, too, are the 13th-century **Trausnitz Castle,** on a hill overlooking the old town, and **St. Martin's Church.** The 16th-century church has the world's tallest ecclesiastical brick tower—133 meters (436 feet)—and possibly the world's most unusual stained-glass windows, which were fitted in 1946 and depict Hitler and other Nazi leaders in devilish poses.

Dining

There are several attractive Bavarian-style restaurants in Altstadt and Neustadt, most of them with charming beer gardens. The best are **Bräuereigasthof Ainmiller** (Altstadt 195), **Gasthaus Schwabl** (Neustadt 500), **Zum Hofreiter** (Neustadt 505), and the **Hotel Goldene Sonne** (Neustadt 520). The **Buddha** (Apothekergasse) serves a good, fixed-price Chinese lunch for around DM 10 per person.

Lindau

Express trains for Lindau leave Munich's Hauptbahnhof at two-hourly intervals throughout the day; the trip takes 2 hours 15 minutes. Trains take you right onto the island, adjacent to the harbor, where you can connect with ferries to other parts of the Bodensee. Tourist office: Am Hauptbahnhof, 8990 Lindau, tel. 08382/26000.

Old Lindau is an island town in the Bodensee, tethered to the shore by a 210-yard causeway. (For more on the Bodensee and on this area, *see* Konstanz, *above.*) As the island is just under a mile long and barely half a mile wide, it can easily be explored on foot or by bicycle. You can hire bikes at the train station (tel. 08382/4066).

It was originally three islands, on one of which the Romans built a military base. Under the Romans, the islands developed first as a fishing settlement, then as a trading center, a stage on the route connecting the rich lands of Swabia to the north with Italy. (It was a role that continued for hundreds of years. In the 18th and 19th centuries the Lindauer Bote, one of the most important stagecoach services between Germany and Italy, was based here. Goethe traveled on it on his first visit to Italy in 1786.) Commercial importance brought political power, and in 1275 little Lindau was made a Free Imperial City within the Holy Roman Empire. As the Empire crumbled toward the end of the 18th century, battered by Napoléon's revolutionary armies, so Lindau fell victim to competing political groups. It was ruled (briefly) by the Austrian Empire before passing into Bavarian rule in 1805.

The proud symbol of Bavaria, a **seated lion,** is one of the most striking landmarks you'll see in Lindau. The lion in question, 20 feet high and carved from Bavarian marble, stares out across the lake from a massive plinth at the end of one of the harbor walls. At the end of the facing wall there's a lighthouse, the **Neuer Leuchtturm.** You can climb up to its viewing platform for a look out over the waters. On a clear day you'll see the Three Sisters, three peaks in Liechtenstein. *Admission: DM 1 adults, 40 pf children. Open daily 9:30–6.*

The **Alter Leuchtturm,** or old lighthouse, stands at the edge of the inner harbor on the weathered remains of the original 13th-century city walls.

From the harbor, plunge into the maze of ancient streets that make up the Altstadt (the Old Town). They all lead eventually to the **Altes Rathaus** (Old Town Hall), the finest of Lindau's handsome historical buildings. It was constructed between 1422 and 1436 in the midst of what was then a vineyard (now a busy thoroughfare) and given a Renaissance face-lift 150 years later, though the original stepped gables were retained. The Emperor Maximilian I held an imperial council here in 1496; a fresco on the south facade depicts a scene from this high point of local history. The building was not always used for such noble purposes: Part of it served as the town prison. An ancient inscription, enjoining the townsfolk "to turn aside from evil and learn to do good," identifies it.

Face away from the town hall and walk down to the **Barfüsserkirche,** the Church of the Barefoot Pilgrims. Built from 1241 to 1270, it has for many years been Lindau's principal theater. The Gothic choir is a memorable location for concerts, especially of church music. The tourist office on Bahnhofplatz can provide details of performances.

Continue along Ludwigstrasse to Fischergasse, where you'll find a watchtower, once part of the original city walls. Pause in the little park behind it, the **Stadtgarten.** If it's early evening, you'll see the first gamblers of the night making for the neighboring casino.

Lindau's market square, Marktplatz, is just around the corner. A series of sturdily attractive old buildings line it, among them the 18th-century **Haus zum Cavazzen,** richly decorated with stucco and frescoes. Today it's the municipal art gallery and local history museum. *Am Marktpl. Admission: DM 2 adults, DM 1 children. Open Apr.–Nov., Tues.–Sat. 9–noon and 2–5, Sun. 10–noon. Closed Mon.*

Two contrasting churches also stand on Marktplatz: the simple, sparely decorated Gothic Stephanskirche and the more elaborate, Baroque Marienkirche. Both have charm—the Stephanskirche for its simplicity, the Marienkirche for its exuberance.

From Marktplatz, walk along pedestrians-only **Maximilianstrasse,** the main street of the old town, distinguished by half-timbered and gabled old houses. Turn right off Maximilianstrasse down cobbled Schafsgasse to reach the **Peterskirche** on Schrannenplatz. It's a solid Romanesque building, constructed in the 10th century and reputedly the oldest church in the Bodensee region. Step inside to see the frescoes by Hans Holbein the Elder (1465–1524). A number depict scenes from the life of St. Peter, the patron saint of fishermen and thus an important figure to the inhabitants of Lindau.

Lodging
Under DM 110

Brugger. This plain, modern guest house, in the Old Town at the mainland end of the island, is a 10-minute walk from the train station, or a couple of minutes by taxi (DM 6). *Bei der Heidenhammer 1, tel. 08382/6086. 28 rooms, 6 with shower. AE, DC, MC, V.*

Schachen-Schlössle. This turreted 15th-century manor house, set amid peaceful gardens close to the waterfront in the mainland town, is a remarkably good value, with rooms decorated in authentic rustic style. Book well in advance. *Enzisweilerstr. 5, tel. 08383/5060. 8 rooms, plus suites in adjoining building. Facilities: restaurant, bar. AE, DC, MC, V. Closed Jan.–Mar.*

Dining

Fish specialties predominate around the Bodensee. There are 35 different types of fish in the lake, with *Renken* and *Felchen* the most highly prized. Renken is a meaty white fish. Felchen belongs to the salmon family and is best eaten *blau* (poached) in rosemary sauce or baked in almonds (*Müllerin*). *Pfannkuchen* and *Spätzle* are common specialties. Both are flour-and-egg dishes. Pfannkuchen, or pancakes, are generally filled with meat, cheese, jam, or sultanas, or chopped into fine strips and scattered in a clear consommé known as *Flädlesuppe*. Spätzle, tiny, golden-roasted, dumplinglike noodles, are the usual accompaniment for a Sunday roast-beef lunch of *Rinderbraten*.

Under DM 20

Gasthaus zum Sünfzen. Located in the heart of the Old Town, this is an appealing old inn with little leaded windows and a simple, wood-paneled interior. The menu, which changes daily and seasonally, features such regional specialties as venison and lake fish, and sausages from the restaurant's own butcher shop. *Maximilianstr. 1, tel. 08382/5865. Reservations advised. AE, DC, MC, V. Closed Feb.*

★ **Historische Bräugaststätte zum Schlechterbräu.** This is where the locals come for *Frühschoppen*, a traditional Sunday brunch of two fat sausages with sauerkraut and a tall glass of beer. The interior is authentically Teutonic, with oak booths and colorful stained-glass lamps. The restaurant is located in the Old Town, on the island, near the Peterskirche. *In der Grub 28, tel. 08382/5842. No credit cards. Closed late Feb. and mid-Nov.*

Nightlife Lindau's evening entertainment ranges from traditional folk music and dancing to more modern fare such as jazz and pop concerts. Many resort hotels also organize regular *Heimatabende* (folk-music evenings) or *Gästeabende* (guest evenings). The tourist office has details.

In summer you can dance on the water—on one of the evening cruises organized by the Bodensee **Weisse Flotte** operators. The boats pick dancers and revelers up every Saturday night from May through September in Konstanz and Lindau. For further details and bookings, contact the **Bodensee-Schiffsbetriebe der Deutschen Bundesbahn** (Hafenstr. 6, 7750 Konstanz, tel. 07531/281–398).

Passau

It's a bit far from Munich—193 kilometers (120 miles) to the southeast, a two-hour train trip. The two best trains for a comfortable day trip—both of them are direct—leave the Hauptbahnhof at 7:48 AM and 9:48 AM. Tourist office: Fremdenverkehrsverein, Am Rathausplatz, 8390 Passau, tel. 0851/33421.

Numbers in the margin correspond to points of interest on the Passau map.

A pretty cathedral town much older than its Baroque facade, Passau is built on the confluence of three rivers against a backdrop of steep wooded hills. The old town is a jumble of cobbled streets lined with churches that testify to its former importance as a seat of medieval prince-bishops whose power and influence extended as far as Hungary.

A short walk to your right from the Passau station will bring you to a junction at Ludwigsplatz and the heart of the old town. Turn right into Neuburgerstrasse, and in 100 yards you'll come
1 to the **Nibelungenhalle** (and, beside it, the tourist office). This oddball piece of architecture may have an ancient name, but the structure is Nazi-era—a mass rally hall for 8,000 people.

Retrace your steps to the traffic-free zone around Ludwigsplatz. On Heilig-Geist-Gasse you'll find the 15th-century
2 **Spitalkirche Heiliger Geist,** or Infirmary Church of the Holy Ghost. It has some fine 16th-century stained glass and an exquisite 15th-century marble relief depicting the Way of the
3 Cross. Return to Ludwigstrasse and walk east to **Rindermarkt,** the old cattle market. On the way you'll pass the 17th-century Baroque **church of St. Paul** and walk through the medieval **Paulusbogen** (Paul's Arch), part of the original city walls. From Rindermarkt, turn right into narrow Luragogasse (named after one of the Italian builders who were busy in Passau in the 18th century) and continue on until you reach **Domplatz,** the expansive square fronting the cathedral. The statue you see in its center is of Bavarian King Maximilian Joseph I.

4 Now turn your attention to the **Dom,** the cathedral. A baptismal church stood here in the 6th century. Two hundred years later, when Passau became the seat of a bishop, the first basilica was built. It was dedicated to St. Stephan and became the

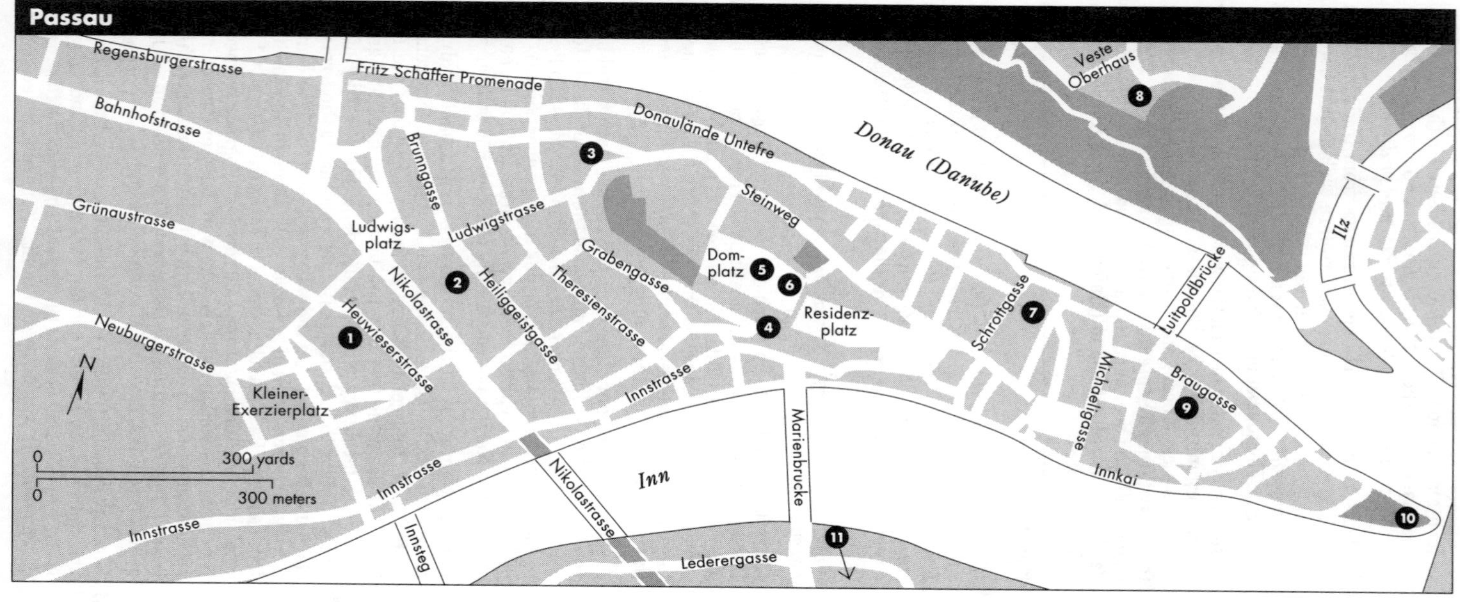

Alte Residenz, **5**
Dom, **4**
Dreiflusseck, **10**
Mariahilfberg, **11**
Neue Residenz, **6**
Nibelungenhalle, **1**
Niedernburg Abbey, **9**
Rathaus, **7**
Rindermarkt, **3**
Spitalkirche Heiliger Geist, **2**
Veste Oberhaus, **8**

original mother church of St. Stephan's Cathedral in Vienna. Little was left of the medieval basilica after a fire reduced it to smoking ruins in the 17th century. What you see today is an impressively heroic Baroque building, complete with dome and flanking towers. As you wander around its marble- and stucco-encrusted interior, you may feel as if you're in an Italian cathedral. There's little here to remind you of Germany and much that proclaims the exuberance of Rome. Beneath the octagonal dome is the largest church organ in the world. Built between 1924 and 1928, and enlarged from 1979 to 1980, it claims no less than 17,388 pipes and 231 stops. Lunchtime concerts (DM 3 adults, DM 1 children) are given daily on the monstrous instrument May through October at noon (except Sunday) and on Thursdays (DM 6 adults, DM 3 children) at 7:30 PM.

Bordering Domplatz are a number of sturdy 17th- and 18th-
5 century buildings, including the **Alte Residenz,** the former bish-
6 op's palace. Today it's a courthouse. The **Neue** (New) **Residenz**
is next door, though its main entrance faces Residenzplatz, one of the most gracious and quiet corners of the town. Step through the stately Baroque entrance of the palace to see the dazzling staircase, a scintillating study in marble, fresco, and stucco.

Outside again, turn into Schrottgasse and head toward the Danube. You'll soon find yourself staring at the bright Gothic
7 facade of Passau's 13th-century **Rathaus** (town hall). Originally
the home of a successful merchant, it was taken over after an uprising in 1298 and declared the seat of city government. Two assembly rooms of the Rathaus contain wall paintings depicting scenes from local history and lore. The Rathaus can be visited only on guided tours arranged by the tourist office. Half-hour boat rides offering panoramic views of Passau depart at regular intervals from the promenade on the Danube side of the town, close to the Rathaus.

Outside the Rathaus, face the Danube, cross the bridge on your
8 right—the Luitpoldbrücke—and climb to the **Veste Oberhaus,**
the powerful fortress commissioned by Bishop Ulrich II in 1219. Today the Veste Oberhaus is Passau's most important musuem, containing exhibits that illustrate the 2,000-year history of the city. It also commands a magnificent view of Passau and the three rivers that converge on it. A bus runs from Rathausplatz to the Veste Oberhaus from May though October, when the museum is open. *Museum admission: DM 3 adults, DM 1.50 children. Open Apr.–Oct., Tues.–Sun. 9–5; Nov.–Mar., Tues.–Sun. 10–4.*

Walk back across the Luitpoldbrücke and turn left to
9 **Niedernburg Abbey.** Founded in the 8th century as a convent, it
was destroyed by fire and rebuilt in the last century in a clumsy Romanesque style. Today it's a girls' school. In its church you can see the 11th-century tomb of a queen who was once abbess here—Gisela, sister of the Emperor Heinrich II and widow of Hungary's first and subsequently sainted king, Stephan, who became the patron of the Passau cathedral.

Head now to Passau's other major river, the Inn, a few steps away. Follow the river to the point where the Danube, Ilz, and
10 Inn meet—the **Dreiflusseck** (Corner of the Three Rivers). It's
the end of the journey for the Inn—which flows here from the mountains of Switzerland and through Austria—and the much

shorter Ilz, which rises in the Bavarian Forest; from here their waters are carried by the Danube to the Black Sea. The Inn's green water, the typical color of a mountain river, gives way slowly to the darker hues of the Danube, and the brownish Ilz add its small contributions to this colorful natural phenomenon.

Another place to take in the meeting of the three rivers is the
11 **Mariahilfberg,** site of a 17th-century monastery pilgrimage church. It is located on the other side of the Inn, in the so-called Innstadt, or Inn City. It was here that in 1974 archaeologists uncovered the site of the Roman citadel of Boiotro, a stout fortress with five defense towers and walls more than 12 feet thick. A Roman well was also found, its water still plentiful and fresh. A 15th-century merchant's home has been converted into a museum to house the items brought to light by the continuing excavations. *Römermuseum Kastell Boiotro, Am Severinstor. Admission: DM 2 adults, DM1 children. Open Mar.–Nov., Tues.–Sun. 10–noon and 3–5. Guided tour given 1st and 3rd Wed. of month at 5 PM.*

Lodging and Dining
Under DM 110

Dreiflüssehof. This modernized 19th-century villa offers double rooms for under DM 100 and, in its pine-paneled restaurant, solid Bavarian meals starting at DM 12. *Danzigerstr. 42, tel. 0851/51018. MC, DC, V.*

★ **Schloss Ort.** This restored 13th-century castle at the confluence of the three rivers offers some double rooms for around DM 85. The restaurant offers traditional Bavarian dishes and locally caught fish. *Am Dreiflusseck 11, tel. 0851/34072. Facilities: riverside terrace and garden, restaurant. AE, DC, MC, V. Closed Tues.*

Dining
Under DM 20

★ **Helig-Geist-Stiftsschenke.** This heavy-beamed cellar tavern—adjoining the Spitalkirche Heiliger Geist and operated by the church—serves reasonably priced three-course meals along with excellent wines from the church's Austrian vineyards, and it's got all the atmosphere you could ask for. *Heilig-Geist-Gasse 4, tel. 0851/2607. Reservations advised. AE, DC, MC. Closed Wed. and Jan. 10–Feb. 2.*

Regensburg

*Trains depart regularly from Munich's Hauptbahnhof; the journey takes a little more than 1½ hours. Although you can do the trip in one day, Regensburg has enough attractions to warrant staying overnight (*see below*). You might also visit the town as a stopover between Munich and Nürnberg. Tourist information: Altes Rathaus, 8400 Regensburg, tel. 0941/507-2141.*

For inexplicable reasons, few visitors to Bavaria venture as far as Regensburg, one of Germany's best-preserved medieval cities. (The town escaped serious damage in World War II.) Regensburg's story begins with the Celts in around 500 BC. They called their little settlement Radasbona. In AD 179, as an original marble inscription in the Museum der Stadt Regensburg proclaims, it became a Roman military post called Castra Regina. When Bavarian tribes migrated to the area in the 6th century, they occupied what remained of the Roman town and, apparently on the basis of its Latin name, called it Regensburg.

The Danube was the key to Regensburg's development. The settlement marked the river's northernmost navigable point, and thus it played a pivotal—and profitable—role in commerce across central Europe. Virtually all Regensburg's attractions are concentrated in the old town core, only a few minutes from the train station.

Numbers in the margin correspond to points of interest on the Regensburg map.

1 Begin your tour at the **Steinerne Brücke** (Stone Bridge). It leads south over the Danube to the almost-too-good-to-be-true
2 **Brückturm** (Bridge Tower): all tiny windows, weathered tiles, and pink plaster. (The brooding building with a massive roof to the left of the tower is an old salt warehouse.) The bridge is a central part of Regensburg history. Built in 1141, it was rightfully considered a miraculous piece of engineering at the time—and, as the only crossing point over the Danube for miles, effectively cemented Regensburg's control of trade in the region.

3 From the bridge, look up at the commanding towers of the **Dom St. Peter.** The cathedral, modeled on the airy, vertical lines of French Gothic architecture, is something of rarity this far south in Germany. It wouldn't look out of place in Köln or Bonn. Begun in the 13th century, it stands on the site of a much earlier Carolingian church. Construction dragged on for almost 600 years, and it was finally finished when Ludwig I of Bavaria, then the ruler of Regensburg, had the towers built. (These were replaced in the mid-1950s after their original soft limestone was found to be badly eroded.)

Walk under the Bridge Tower to Domplatz, the cathedral square. Before heading into the building, admire its intricate and frothy facade, embellished with delicate and skillful carving. A remarkable feature of the cathedral is its size: It can accommodate 7,000 people three times the population of Regensburg when construction began. Standouts of the austere interior are the glowing 14th-century stained glass in the choir and the exquisitely detailed statues of the Archangel Gabriel and the Virgin in the crossing (the meeting point of nave and choir). The **Domschatzmuseum** (Cathedral Museum) contains more valuable treasures. The entrance is in the nave. *Admission: DM 2.50. Open Apr.–Oct., Tues.–Sat. 10–5, Sun. 11:30–4; Dec.–Mar., Fri. and Sat. 10–4, Sun. 11:30–4.*

Complete your tour of the cathedral with a visit to the **cloisters,** reached by way of the garden. These contain a small octagonal chapel, the **Allerheiligenkapelle** (All Saint's Chapel), a typically solid Romanesque building, all sturdy grace and massive walls. You can barely make out the faded remains of stylized 11th-century frescoes on its ancient walls. The equally ancient shell of St. Stephan's church, the **Alter Dom** (Old Cathedral), can also be visited. *Admission: DM 2.50 Cloisters, chapel, and Alter Dom can be seen only on guided tours: mid-May–Oct., daily 10, 11, and 2; Oct.–Mar., daily 11 and noon; Apr.–mid-May, daily 11 and 2.*

To the south of the cathedral are the Neupfarrkirche and the church of St. Kassian. To the east lie the Niedermünster church, the Karmelitenkirche, and the Alte Kapelle. The
4 **Neupfarrkirche** (Neupfarrplatz), built between 1519 and 1540, is the only Protestant church in Regensburg, indeed one of a

Alte Kapelle, **6**
Altes Rathaus, **11**
Brückturm, **2**
Dom St. Peter, **3**
Karmelitenkirche, **7**
Museum der Stadt Regensburg, **10**
Neupfarrkirche, **4**
Niedermünster, **8**
Porta Praetoria, **9**
St. Emmeramus, **13**
St. Kassian, **5**
Schloss Thurn-und-Taxis, **12**
Steinerne Brücke, **1**

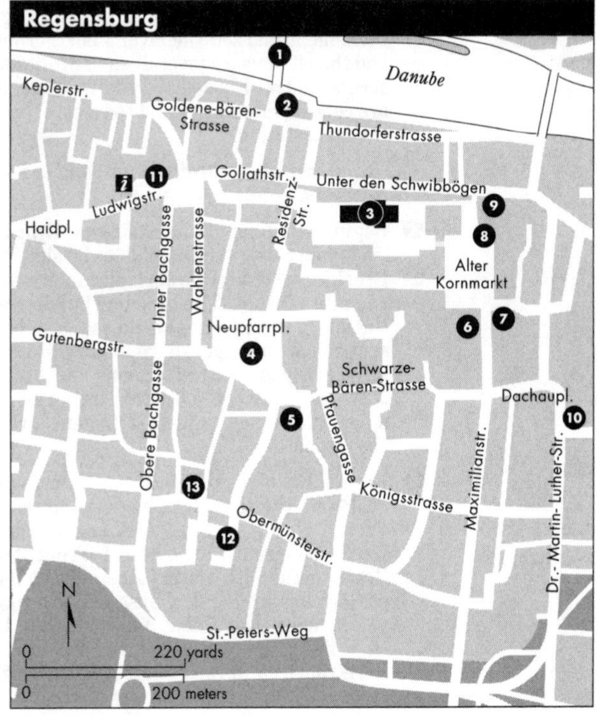

very few in Franconia. It's an imposing building, substantially less ornate than any other in the city. Some may find its restraint welcome after the exuberance of so many of the other
5 places of worship. **St. Kassian** is a much older building, the oldest church in the city, in fact, founded in the 8th century. Don't be fooled by its dour exterior; inside, the church has been endowed with delicate Rococo decoration.

From St. Kassian, turn right onto the pedestrians-only Schwarze Bären-Strasse, one of the best shopping streets in
6 the city. Turn left at the end. This will bring you to the **Alte Kapelle,** the Old Chapel. This, too, is a Carolingian structure, put up in the 9th century. As at St. Kassian, the dowdy exterior gives little hint of the joyous Rococo treasures within, extravagant concoctions of sinuous gilt stucco, rich marble, and giddy frescoes, the whole illuminated by light pouring in from the upper windows.

7 The adjoining **Karmelitenkirche** is Baroque from crypt to cupola. Finally, head north through the Alter Kornmarkt square to
8 the former parish church, the **Niedermünster,** another ancient structure (construction started in 1150) with a Baroque interior. Here in 1982 workmen discovered a Roman altar, dating from between AD 180 and 190, dedicated to the Emperor Commodus; a little stone plinth indicates that the altar was used for incense offerings. The site is open to the public.

A substantial Roman relic is located just round the corner from
9 the church (turn right as you leave it). This is the **Porta Praetoria,** one of the original city gates, a rough-hewn and

blocky structure. Look through the grille on its east side to see a section of the original Roman street, located about 10 feet below today's street.

From the Porta Praetoria, you can either backtrack through
10 Kornmarkt to the **Museum der Stadt Regensburg** or continue along Goldene-Bären-Strasse to the Fischmarkt and Altes Rathaus (Old Town Hall). For many, the museum is one of the highlights of a visit to the city, both for its unusual and beautiful setting—a former Gothic monastery—and for its wide-ranging collections, from Roman artifacts to Renaissance tapestries, all helping to tell the story of Regensburg. The most significant exhibits are the paintings by Albrecht Altdorfer (1480–1538), a native of Regensburg and, along with Cranach, Grünewald, and Dürer, one of the leading painters of the German Renaissance. *Dachaupl. 2–4. Admission: DM 3 adults, DM 1 children. Open Tues.–Sat. 10–4, Sun. and holidays 10–1.*

11 The **Altes Rathaus,** a picture-book complex of medieval buildings with half-timbering, windows large and small, and flowers in tubs, is among the best-preserved of its kind in the country, as well as one of the most historically important. It was here, in the imposting Gothic **Reichsaal** (Imperial Hall), that the "everlasting Imperial Diet" met from 1663 to 1805. This could be considered a forerunner of the German parliament, where representatives from every part of the Holy Roman Empire—plus the emperor and the prince-electors—assembled to discuss and determine the affairs of the far-reaching German lands. The hall is sumptuously appointed with tapestries, flags, and heraldic designs. Note especially the wood ceiling, built in 1408. If you have kids in tow, they'll want to see the adjoining torture chamber, the **Fragstatt,** and execution room, the **Armesünderstübchen.** Medieval notions of justice can be gauged by the fact that any prisoner who withstood three days of "questioning" here without confessing was released. *Rathauspl. Admission: DM 3 adults, DM 1.50 children. Open for guided tours only, Apr.–Oct., Mon.–Sat. 9:30, 10, 10:30, 11, noon, 1:30, 2, 2:30, and 4, and Sun. 10, 11, and noon.*

12 There's one more major sight in the downtown area, the **Schloss Thurn-und-Taxis.** To reach it from the Rathaus, head down Bachgasse for 500 yards. Members of the Thurn-und-Taxis family still live in this enormous structure, originally the Benedictine monastery of St. Emmeram. The Thurn-und-Taxis were not only the leading family of Regensburg from around 1600 onward but one of the most influential in Germany; their fortune came from running the German postal system, a monopoly they enjoyed until 1867. The former abbey cloisters are probably the architectural treasure of the palace itself, with their elegant and attenuated late-Gothic carving. As for the rest of the building, much of which was extensively rebuilt at the end of the 19th century, opinions remain divided. Some consider it the most vulgar and ponderously overdecorated specimen of its kind in Germany. Others admire its Victorian bombast and confidence. You can also visit the **Marstallmuseum** (Transport Museum) in the palace if you have a weakness for 18th- and 19th-century carriages and sleighs. *Admission to palace and cloisters: DM 3. Open for guided tours only, Mon.–Fri. 2:15 and 3:30, Sun. and holidays 10:15 and 11:30. Admission to Marstallmuseum: DM 3.50. Open for guided tours only, Mon.–Fri. 2, 2:40, and 3:15, and Sun 10, 10:40, and 11:15.*

13 Next to the palace there's one more church to be visited, **St. Emmeramus.** It's the work of the Asam brothers and is decorated in their customary and full-blown late-Baroque manner.

From Regensburg you can take a boat trip on the Danube to the beautiful Baroque monastery church at **Weltenburg,** built in the early 18th century by the noted Assam brothers and set among cliffs on a magnificent stretch of the river. *Tel. 09441/5858 for times. Round-trip fare: DM 7 adults, DM 4.50 children.*

Lodging and Dining
Under DM 110

Bischofshof. This small historic inn, in the heart of the old town between the Dom and the Altes Rathaus, was once a bishop's residence. It houses a reasonably priced restaurant and a beer garden. *Krautermarkt 3, tel. 0941/59086. 42 double rooms, some under DM 110. AE, DC, MC, V.*

Dining
Under DM 15
★

Historische Wurstküche. This rowdy, fun-filled place—the oldest sausage restaurant in town—has meals that start as low as DM 7. *Thundorferstr. 3, tel. 0941/59098. No credit cards.*

Starnbergersee

The S-6 suburban line runs from Munich's central Marienplatz to Starnberg and three other towns on the lake's west bank: Possenhofen, Feldafing, and Tutzing. The journey from Marienplatz to Starnberg takes 35 minutes. The east bank of the lake can be reached by bus from the town of Wolfratshausen, the end of the S-7 suburban line. The all-inclusive DM 35 Weissblau KombiKarte ticket—covering all public transport in Munich, from Munich to Starnberg, and the lake cruise, and valid all day for two adults and three children—is an excellent buy.

The biggest of two romantic lakes south of Munich (the other is the Ammersee; *see above*), this is where "Mad" Ludwig II of Bavaria drowned, on June 13, 1886. His body, with that of his doctor, was found in the lake shortly after the Bavarian government had placed him under house arrest in nearby Berg Castle on grounds of insanity. The state treasury had been almost drained by the King's extravagant building schemes; today, ironically, tourism has made such fantasy palaces as Neuschwanstein enormous moneymakers. There's a **memorial chapel** to Ludwig II on the bank opposite the spot where he drowned. **Berg** is the first of half a dozen pretty little villages on a delightful two-hour boat trip around the lake; you can break your cruise as often as you like. It runs May–October; the starting point is a two-minute walk from the Starnbergersee train station.

Wasserburg

Take either the suburban line S-4 to Ebersberg and change to a local train to Wasserburg, or the Salzburg express, changing at Grafing Bahnhof to the local line. Both trips take 90 minutes.

Now a sleepy town on the banks of the romantic River Danube 54 kilometers (34 miles) southwest of Munich, Wasserburg was an important trading center in the days when river transport was the chief means of communication. The well-preserved old town is a delightful jumble of Gothic, Renaissance, and Baroque architecture; noteworthy sights include the Gothic **town**

hall in the main square, Marienplatz, and the 15th-century **St. Jakob's Church.**

Dining
Under DM 20

Gasthaus zum Löwen. This wood-paneled restaurant serves up simple and traditional Bavarian fare. In summer the tables spill out onto the sidewalk. *Marienpl. 10, tel. 08071/7400. No credit cards.*

Herrenhaus. With its centuries-old wine cellar, it offers the most compelling atmosphere for dining in town. *Herrengasse 17, tel. 08071/7400. AE, MC. Closed Sat. and Mon.*

4 The Bavarian Alps

Including Garmisch, Oberammergau, Neuschwanstein Castle, and Berchtesgaden

The German Alpine region stretches 485 kilometers (300 miles) from the huge Bodensee (Lake Constance) in the west to Berchtesgaden in the east. It embraces rolling meadowland, a string of enchanting lakes, castles, and remote, rugged peaks where the snow remains for most of the year. As varied as Germany is (more so than ever since reunification), this is the area that down through the years has given us the popular picture of "German-ness." Stock images from tourist office posters—the fairy-tale castles you've seen in countless ads, those picture-book villages of too-good-to-be-true wood homes with brightly frescoed facades and window boxes filled with flowers in summer, sloping roofs heavy with snow in winter—are brought to life here. To complete the picture, onion-dome church spires rise out of the mist against the backdrop of the mighty Alps. Even the people sometimes appear to be actors completing a carefully staged scene.The entire area is laced with possibilities for delightful excursions. Here you will find a wide range of resorts at which to spend a weekend or week, to use either as bases for further explorations or as places to relax and take advantage of sporting opportunities. Sports possibilities are legion: downhill and cross-country skiing and ice-skating in winter; swimming, sailing, golf, and, above all, hiking in summer.

This chapter suggests three tour bases from which virtually all the region's major attractions can be reached by public transport: Garmisch-Partenkirchen, Bad Tölz, and Berchtesgaden. Rail routes penetrate deep into the German Alps—almost to the mountainous Austrian border—but most lines operate on a

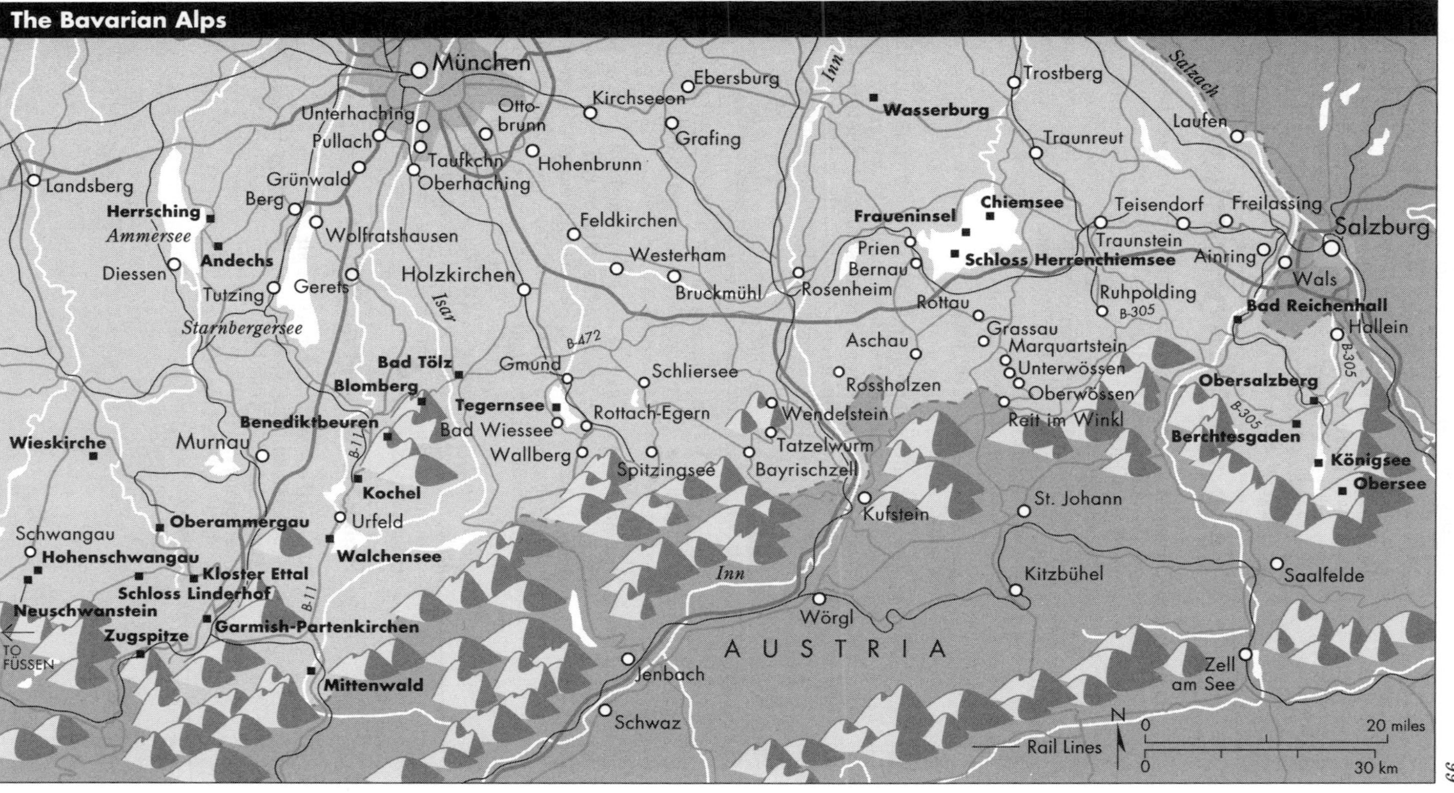

The Bavarian Alps
München
Unterhaching
Pullach
Otto-brunn
Taufkchn
Oberhaching
Hohenbrunn
Kirchseeon
Ebersburg
Grafing
Inn
Wasserburg
Trostberg
Salzach
Traunreut
Laufen
Landsberg
Grünwald
Berg
Herrsching
Ammersee
Andechs
Diessen
Tutzing
Gerets
Wolfratshausen
Starnbergersee
Holzkirchen
Isar
Feldkirchen
Westerham
Bruckmühl
Rosenheim
Fraueninsel
Chiemsee
Prien
Bernau
Schloss Herrenchiemsee
Rottau
Teisendorf
Freilassing
Traunstein
Ainring
Salzburg
Wals
Ruhpolding
B-305
Bad Reichenhall
Hallein
B-472
Bad Tölz
Gmund
Schliersee
Aschau
Grassau
Marquartstein
Unterwössen
Oberwössen
Rossholzen
Blomberg
Tegernsee
Rottach-Egern
Wendelstein
Reit im Winkl
Obersalzberg
Benediktbeuren
Bad Wiessee
Wallberg
Tatzelwurm
Bayrischzell
Spitzingsee
Berchtesgaden
Wieskirche
Murnau
B-11
Kochel
Königsee
Obersee
Kufstein
St. Johann
Oberammergau
Urfeld
Schwangau
Hohenschwangau
Walchensee
Kloster Ettal
Schloss Linderhof
Neuschwanstein
Kitzbühel
Saalfelde
Garmish-Partenkirchen
Zugspitze
TO FÜSSEN
Wörgl
A U S T R I A
Jenbach
Mittenwald
Zell am See
Schwaz
Rail Lines
N
0
20 miles
0
30 km

radial system fanning out from Munich. However, a good system of buses, most of them operated by the Deutsches Bundesbahn, links nearly all the places mentioned on this tour, should you prefer to travel, say, across the Alps from Garmisch to Berchtesgaden. *For a complete bus timetable, contact the Fremdenverkehrsverband (Bavarian regional tourist office), Oberbayern, Sonnenstr. 10, 8000 Munich 2, tel. 089/597–347.*

Essential Information

Lodging and Dining Despite the enormous year-round popularity of the Alps, the region offers plenty of high-quality inexpensive inns and restaurants. Outside the main centers it's still possible to find friendly and cozy bed-and-breakfasts for around DM 20–DM 25 per person. These inexpensive lodgings can often be spotted by the simple green *Zimmerfrei* (room available) or *Fremdenzimmer* (guest room) sign in a cottage window. They are usually approved by the local tourist office.

Highly recommended establishments are indicated by a star ★.

Hiking The Alps offer enormous possibilities for hiking; you will find hundreds of marked, numbered routes with signs giving distances (in kilometers) or average estimated times to reach various destinations. But a word of caution: the weather can change suddenly, so always carry a small rucksack with extra warm clothing and rain gear. *For a general guide to hiking in the Alps, plus some suggested routes, contact the Deutscher Alpenverein, Praterinsel 5, 8000 Munich 22, tel. 089/235–0900.*

Biking Bicycles can be hired for around DM 6 per day at the following train stations: Garmisch, Oberammergau, Kochel, Bad Tölz, Tegernsee, and Berchtesgaden.

Boating Passenger boats operate on all the major Bavarian lakes. They're mostly excursion boats and many run only in the summer. However, there's an important year-round service on Chiemsee that links the mainland with the islands of Herreninsel and Fraueninsel. Eight boats operate year-round on the Tegernsee, connecting Tegernsee town, Rottach-Egern, and Bad Wiessee. A fleet of 21 silent, electrically driven boats glides through the waters of the Königsee near Berchtesgaden to the most remote of Bavaria's lakes, the Obersee. All ferry rides are inexpensive.

Highlights for First-time Visitors

Benediktbeuren Monastery (*see* Tour 2)
Kehlsteinhaus (Eagle's Nest) near Berchtesgaden (*see* Tour 3)
Kloster Ettal (*see* Tour 1)
Oberammergau (*see* Tour 1)
Schloss Linderhof (*see* Tour 1)
Tegernsee (*see* Tour 2)
Zugspitze (*see* Tour 1)

Tour 1: Garmisch-Partenkirchen

Garmisch-Partenkirchen is an ideal base from which to explore the western area of the Bavarian Alps. From this pretty town at the foot of Germany's highest mountain, you can visit the Passion Play village of Oberammergau; Schloss Linderhof, one of "Mad" King Ludwig's castles; the 14th-century Benedictine abbey of Ettal, which still brews its own beer; and the old town of Mittenwald on the Austrian border. Buses provide the best way of getting around here, although regular train service links Garmisch with Mittenwald via a 30-minute climb, which on clear days offers views of the Zugspitze and other peaks.

From Munich
By Train An hourly service connects Munich's main train station (Hauptbahnhof) with Garmisch. The scenic journey, which skirts the northern edge of the Alpine region for much of the way, takes 1½ hours.

By Car Autobahn E-6, following a route similar to the train's, connects Munich with Garmisch. The distance is 95 kilometers (60 miles).

Garmisch-Partenkirchen

Tourist office: Bahnhofstr. 34, 8100 Garmisch-Partenkirchen, tel. 08821/18022.

Once two separate communities, Garmisch and Partenkirchen were fused in 1936 to accommodate the winter Olympics. But while winter sports do rank high on the agenda here, Garmisch—as the town is commonly known—isn't all skiing, skating, and hiking. The 18th-century parish church of St. Martin, off the Marienplatz, contains some significant stucco work by the Wessobrunn artists Schmuzer, Schmidt, and Bader. Across the Loisach River on Pfarehausweg stands another, older St. Martin's, whose Gothic wall paintings include a larger-than-life-size figure of St. Christopher. Nearby, in Frühlingstrasse, are some beautiful examples of Upper Bavarian houses; at the end of Zöppritzstrasse lies the villa of composer Richard Strauss, who lived there until his death in 1949.

But the number-one attraction in Garmisch is the **Zugspitze,** the highest mountain (9,731 feet) in Germany. There are two ways up the mountain: a leisurely 75-minute ride on a cog railway, or a 10-minute hoist by cable car. The railway journey starts from the train station in the center of town; the cable car begins its giddy ascent from the Eibsee, just outside town on the road to Austria. The round-trip fare for both is DM 50 adults, DM 26 children aged 4–16; there are sizable discounts for families. All fares include a day's ski pass. You can ride up on one route and down on the other.

If DM 50 stretches the vacation budget too much, take a cable car to one of the lesser peaks. The round-trip fare to the top of the **Alpspitze,** some 2,000 feet lower than the Zugspitze, is DM 27 adults, DM 16 children aged 4–16; to the top of the **Wank** and back costs DM 19 (you ride in four-seat cable cars). Both mountains can be tackled on foot, providing you're properly shod and physically fit.

Two interesting hikes out of Garmisch, which will take you through striking *Klammen,* or gorges. The **Höllentalklamm** route starts at the Zugspitze mountain railway terminal in town and ends at the top of the mountain (you'll want to turn back before reaching the summit unless you have mountaineering experience). The **Partnachklamm** route is even more challenging; if you attempt all of it, you'll have to stay overnight in one of the mountain huts along the way. It starts at the Olympic ice stadium in town and takes you through a series of **tunnels** and **galleries,** past a pretty little mountain lake, and far up the Zugspitze. An easier way to tackle this route is to ride part of the way up in the Eckbauer cable car that sets out from the Olympic ice stadium. There's a handy inn at the top where you can gather the strength for the hour-long walk back down to the cable-car station.

Lodging
Under DM 150

Hilleprandt. Bavarian country house–style decor—light pine wood, cheerful patterned furnishings—gives this little hotel, just a couple of blocks behind the train station, a homey atmosphere. *Riffelstr. 17, tel. 08821/2861. 16 rooms, 8 with shower. Facilities: sun terrace, sauna, restaurant, children's playroom, bar, bicycles. MC, V.*

Hotel Garmischer Hof. Situated in the town center, within easy reach of the train and cable-car stations, the swimming pool, and the spa park, the Garmischer Hof is a comfortable, traditional hotel, with an appealing garden and fine views. *Bahnhofstr. 53, tel. 08821/51091. 43 rooms with bath or shower. AE, DC, MC, V.*

Rheinischer Hof. This small, friendly, modern lodging looks onto the Zugspitze. It's a 10-minute walk from the train station, or a short trip by taxi. *Zugspitzestr. 76, tel. 08821/72024. 26 rooms, 19 with bath or shower. Facilities: restaurant, outdoor pool, garden, sauna, solarium. No credit cards. Closed mid-Nov.–mid-Dec.*

Under DM 110

Bavaria. Take a short walk left from the train station entrance to this simple but comfortable hotel nestled in its own pleasant gardens. *Partnachstr. 51, tel. 08821/3466. 30 rooms, 5 with bath. Facilities: restaurant, for hotel guests only. AE. Closed Nov.–early Dec.*

Roter Hahn. A modern bed-and-breakfast with functional furnishings, this inn stands only a few strides to the left of the Garmisch terminal's main entrance. *Bahnhofstr. 44, tel. 08821/54065. 28 rooms, 24 with shower or bath. Facilities: indoor pool and sauna. No credit cards.*

Zugspitz. All the rooms in this elegant lodging—which, despite its name, does not offer views of the mountain—were renovated in 1986 and have bath or shower. It's located two blocks behind the train station, close to the departure point of the Zugspitze cog railway. *Klammstr. 19, tel. 08821/1081. 35 rooms. Facilities: restaurant, indoor pool, sun terrace, wine bar. AE, MC, V.*

Under DM 70

Fraundorfer. A traditional Bavarian beer tavern since the early 19th century, this lodging serves up heaps of homey comforts. Its rustic pine woodwork and richly patterned red and green fabrics are typical of this part of the world. *Ludwigstr. 24, tel. 08821/2176. 24 rooms, 6 with bath. Facilities: restaurant. MC, V. Closed 1st week of Apr. and most of Nov.*

Gästehaus Kornmüller. American visitors are particularly fond of the Kornmüller, a traditional Bavarian guest house on the outskirts of town. *Höllentalstr. 36, tel. 08821/3557. 32 rooms, 8 apartments; 4 suites, most with bath, in adjoining house. AE, MC, V.*

Camping. There is a well-equipped camping site beside a small lake in the village of Grainau, literally at the foot of the Zugspitze, about 8 kilometers (5 miles) from Garmisch. *Campingplatz Zugspitze, 8104 Grainau, tel. 08821/3180.*

Dining

Under DM 30

Alte Poststube. This gnarled old tavern is to be found in one of the town's ritziest hotels, the Posthotel Partenkirchen, but it offers a good selection of traditional Bavarian fare at reasonable prices. Ask if fish from the Walchensee lake is available. *Ludwigstr. 49, tel. 08821/51067. Reservations advisable in the evening. AE, DC, MC, V.*

Under DM 20

Fraundorfer. This traditional Bavarian inn has been in operation since 1820. Live country music and yodeling are a regular dinner accompaniment, and folk dances are held from time to time. Guest rooms are also available. *Ludwigstr. 24, tel. 08821/2176. No reservations. MC, V. Closed Tues., Apr. 1–10 and Nov. 6–Dec. 6.*

Under DM 15

Stahls Badstubn. This place is part of Garmisch's Alpspitz swimming lido and has made a big splash among the locals. Order from a menu that's nearly as long as the Olympic-size pool. *Klammstr. 47, tel. 08821/58700. Reservations advised. No credit cards.*

Splurge

Posthotel Partenkirchen. Wood paneling encloses you in the rustic elegance of a 500-year-old vaulted cellar setting. Traditional Bavarian dishes share the menu with Swiss, French, and vegetarian specialties. Entrées cost DM 18–DM 48; three-course menus range DM 26–DM 75 per person. *Ludwigstr. 49, tel. 08821/51067. Reservations advised. Jacket and tie optional. AE, DC, MC, V.*

The Arts and Nightlife

Bavarian folk music and dancing are performed on Saturday evenings during the summer in the **Bayernhalle** (Brauhausstr. 19). Concerts of classical and popular music are presented Saturday through Thursday, mid-May through September, in the resort park bandstand in Garmisch, and on Friday in the Partenkirchen resort park.

Garmisch-Partenkirchen's folklore theater, the **Bauerntheater,** is entertaining, but it helps to have some knowledge of German. The theater is in the Rassensaal (Ludwigstr. 45). Program details can be obtained from the tourist office (*see above*).

Garmisch is home to one of three state-run casinos (Bahnhofstr. 74, tel. 08821/53099) located in the region. It's open daily from 3 PM until 3 AM. You'll need a passport to get in; men also need a jacket and tie.

Kloster Ettal

This 14th-century monastery lies 15 kilometers (9 miles) from Garmisch and close to Oberammergau. The regular Garmisch-Oberammergau bus service (which links the two towns' train stations) passes through Ettal. Tourist office: Ammergauerstr. 8, tel. 08822/534.

The great monastery was founded in 1330 by Holy Roman Emperor Ludwig der Bayer (Ludwig the Bavarian) for a group of knights and a community of Benedictine monks. The abbey was replaced with new buildings in the 18th century and now serves as a school. However, the original 10-sided church was brilliantly redecorated in 1744–1753, becoming one of the foremost examples of Bavarian Rococo. It is open to visitors. The church's chief treasure is its enormous dome fresco (83 feet wide), painted by Jacob Zeiller, circa 1751–52.

A liqueur with legendary health-giving properties, made from a centuries-old recipe, is still distilled at the monastery by the monks. It's made with more than 70 mountain herbs. You can't get the recipe, but you can buy bottles of the libation (DM 19 each) from the small stall outside the monastery. The monks also brew their own beer, which is on sale in the tavern opposite the monastery.

Lodging and Dining
Under DM 110
★

Hotel Ludwig der Bayer. If the hotel's Bräustuberl is full, try its neighboring Klosterstube; there should be a pillared, paneled corner where you can enjoy a plate of pork knuckle, Bavarian dumplings, and a mug of monastery-brewed beer for under DM 20. The hotel itself, run by the Benedictines from across the road, is large and comfortable. *Kaiser Ludwig Pl. 10, tel. 08822/6601. 65 rooms with bath or shower. Facilities: indoor pool, sauna, solarium, tennis court, bowling alleys, sun terrace, fitness room. Restaurant reservations advised. No credit cards. Restaurant closed Nov. 9–Dec. 22.*

Oberammergau

A regular bus service departs from the Garmisch-Partenkirchen train station. Tourist office: Verkehrsamt, Eugen-Papst-str. 9a, 8103 Oberammergau, tel. 08822/1021.

Oberammergau is magnificently situated above an Alpine valley. Its main streets are lined with beautifully frescoed houses, occupied for the most part by families whose men are engaged in the highly skilled wood-carving craft, which has flourished here for nearly four centuries.

However, Oberammergau is best known not for its wood carving but for its Passion Play, which is performed, in faithful accordance to a solemn vow, once every decade in years ending with zero. The play started as an offering of thanks, commemorating the fact that in 1633 the Black Plague stopped just short of the village as though by miracle. The Passion Play was first performed in 1634 and has been presented every 10 years since 1680.

The 16-act, 5½-hour play depicts the final days of Christ, from the Last Supper through the Crucifixion and Resurrection. It is presented on a partly open-air stage against a mountain backdrop every day from late-May to late-September each Passion Play Year (the next will be held in the year 2000). Locals count on seeing a half million visitors or more in summers when the Passion Play is presented. The entire village is swept up by the play, with some 1,500 residents directly involved in its preparation and presentation, which begins several years beforehand.

If you visit Oberammergau in a non-play year you can still visit the theater, the Oberammergau Passionspielhaus, and explore backstage. Tours of the huge building, with its 5,200-seat auditorium, and vast stage open to the mountain air, are given by guides who will demonstrate the remarkable acoustics by reciting Shakespearean soliloquies. *Passionweise. Admission with guided tour: DM 4 adults, DM 2.50 children. Open daily 10–noon and 1:30–4:30.*

Oberammergau's shop windows are crammed with the creations of the wood-carvers. From June through September, a workshop is open free to the public at the Pilatushaus (Verlegergasse); potters and traditional painters can also be seen at work.

Historic examples of the skill of Oberammergau craftsmen are on view at the Heimatmuseum, which also includes one of Germany's finest collections of Christmas crèches, dating from the mid-18th century. *Dorfstr. 8. Admission: DM 2.50 adults, 50 pf children. Open May 10–Oct. 10, Tues.–Sat. afternoons only.*

Many of the exteriors of Oberammergau's homes, such as the 1784 Pilatushaus on Ludwig-Thoma-Strasse, are decorated with stunning frescoes. In summer, geraniums pour from every window box, and the village explodes with color.

Oberammergau's 18th-century **St. Peter and St. Paul church** is regarded as the finest work of Rococo architect Josef Schmuzer and has striking frescoes by Matthäus Günther.

Lodging
Under DM 150

Hotel Turm Wirt. Rich wood paneling reaches from floor to ceiling in this popular and historic old hotel, located in the shadow of Oberammergau's mountain, the Kofel. The hotel's own band presents regular Bavarian folk evenings. *Ettalerstr. 2, tel. 08822/3091. 22 rooms with bath. Facilities: children's playroom, games room, restaurant. AE, DC, MC, V. Closed most of Jan. and mid-Oct.–mid-Dec.*

★ **Hotel Wolf.** Blue shutters punctuate this attractive old hotel's white walls; the steeply gabled upper stories bloom with flowers. *Dorfstr. 1, tel. 08822/6971. 31 rooms with bath. Facilities: outdoor pool, sauna, solarium, beer tavern, sun terrace, restaurant. AE, DC, MC, V.*

Under DM 110

Alte Post. A historic coaching inn on the main street, the Alte Post is decorated in Bavarian country house–style with an abundance of light pine woodwork. Rooms are cozy but not luxurious. *Dorfstr. 19, tel. 08822/1091. 27 rooms, 15 with bath. Facilities: restaurant, beer garden, bowling alley. AE, MC, V. Closed Nov.–mid-Dec.*

Hotel-Gasthof Zur Rose. The Rose offers good value and great views. In addition to rooms in the main building, it has 10 apartments in two annexes. *Dedlerstr. 9, tel. 08822/3071. 29 rooms, most with bath. Facilities: restaurant. AE, DC, MC, V. Closed Nov. 1–Dec. 15.*

Dining
Under DM 30

Ammergauer Stubn. A homey beer tavern, the Stubn, located in the Wittelsbach hotel, offers a comprehensive menu that combines Bavarian specialties with international dishes. *Dorfstr. 21, tel. 08822/1011. Reservations advised. AE, DC, MC. Closed Tues. and Nov. 7–Dec. 20.*

Hotel Wolf. The hotel's restaurant serves regional dishes in a traditional Bavarian ambience. Try the venison when it's in season, or the fat mountain trout at any time of the year. *Dorfstr. 1, tel. 08822/6971. Reservations advised. AE, DC, MC.*

Under DM 20 **Alte Post.** You can enjoy carefully prepared local cuisine on the original pine tables in this 350-year-old inn. There's a special children's menu, and in summer, meals are also served in the beer garden. *Dorfstr. 19, tel. 08822/1091. AE, MC, V.*

Schloss Linderhof

*Remotely located 10 kilometers (6 miles) west of Ettal along a narrow mountain valley road, Schloss Linderhof can be reached by bus from Oberammergau, but the service is infrequent and varies according to the season. Obtain transport information from the Oberammergau tourist office (*see above*).*

Schloss Linderhof is the only one of Ludwig II's royal residences to have been completed during the monarch's short life, and the only one in which he spent much time. It was built on the grounds of his father's hunting lodge between 1874 and 1878.

Linderhof was the smallest of the so-called Dream King's castles. Set in grandiose sylvan seclusion, this charming French-style Rococo confection is said to have been inspired by the Petit Trianon of Versailles. From an architectural standpoint, it could well be considered a disaster, a mish-mash of conflicting styles, lavish on the outside, vulgarly overdecorated on the inside. Ludwig's bedroom is filled with brilliantly colored and gilded ornaments; the Hall of Mirrors is a shimmering dreamworld; and the dining room boasts a fine piece of 19th-century engineering—a table that rises and descends from and to the kitchens below. The formal gardens contain further touches of Ludwig's love of fantasy: There's a Moorish Pavilion—bought wholesale from the 1867 Paris Universal Exposition—and a grotto, said to have been modeled on Capri's Blue Grotto but with a rock that slides back at the touch of a button.

According to legend, while staying at Linderhof the eccentric king would dress up as Lohengrin to be rowed in a swan boat on the grotto pond; in winter, he took off on midnight sleigh rides behind six plumed horses and a platoon of outriders holding flaring torches. *Admission: DM 6 adults, DM 3 children. Open Apr.–Sept., 9–12:15 and 12:45–5:30, Oct.–Mar., 10–12:15 and 12:45–4.*

Mittenwald

Mittenwald, 20 kilometers (12 miles) southeast of Garmisch and snugly set beneath the towering peaks of the Karwendel range, straddles the German-Austrian border en route to Innsbruck. The town is easily reached by train from Garmisch; the scenic 30-minute ride climbs to Klais—at almost 3,000 feet the highest main-line train station in Germany—before descending into Mittenwald. Tourist office: Kurverwaltung, Dammkarstr. 3, 8102 Mittenwald, tel. 08823/33981.

Many regard Mittenwald as the most beautiful town in the Bavarian Alps. It is situated on the spine of an important north–south trade route dating back to Roman times. In the Middle Ages, Mittenwald became the staging point for goods shipped up from Verona by way of the Brenner Pass and Innsbruck. From there, goods were transferred to rafts, which carried them down the Isar to Munich. As might be expected, Mittenwald grew rich on this traffic; its early prosperity is reflected to this day in the splendidly decorated houses with ornately carved gables and brilliantly painted facades that line its main street. In the mid-17th century, however, the international trade route was moved to a different pass, and the fortunes of Mittenwald went into swift decline.

Prosperity returned to Mittenwald in 1684, when a farmer's son, Matthias Klotz, returned from a 20-year stay in Cremona as a master violin maker. In Cremona, Klotz had studied with Nicolo Amati, who gave the violin its present form. Klotz brought his master's pioneering ideas back to Mittenwald. He taught the art to his brothers and friends; before long, half the men in the village were making violins. With the ideal woods for violins coming from neighboring forests, the trade flourished. Mittenwald soon became known as "The Village of a Thousand Violins," and stringed instruments—violins, violas, and cellos—made in Mittenwald were shipped around the world. Klotz's craft is still carried on in Mittenwald, and the town has a fascinating museum, the **Geigenbau und Heimatmuseum,** devoted to it. *Obermarkt 4, tel. 08823/8561. Admission: DM 2 adults, 50 pf children. Open Mon.–Fri. 10–11:45 and 2–4:45, weekends and public holidays 10–11:45.*

The museum is next to Mittenwald's 18th-century **St. Peter and St. Paul church.** Check the back of the altar and you'll find Klotz's name, carved there by the violin maker himself. In front of the church is a monument to Klotz. The church itself, with its elaborate and joyful stucco work, which coils and curls its way around the interior, is one of the most important Rococo structures in Bavaria. Note its Gothic choir loft, incorporated into the church in the 18th century. The bold frescoes on its exterior are characteristic of *Luftlmalerei,* an art form that reached its height in Mittenwald. You can see other fine examples of it on the facades of three famous houses: the Goethehaus, the Pilgerhaus, and the Pichlerhaus.

Lodging

Under DM 110

Alpenhotel Erdt. In the center of town, a five-minute walk from the train station, the small, family-run Erdt offers convenience as well as comfort. Furnishings are modern, but each room is warmly decorated. *Albert-Schottstr. 7, tel. 08823/2001. 37 rooms, 6 with bath. Facilities: garden, sun terrace, bar. No restaurant. AE, DC, MC, V. Closed Nov.–mid-Dec. and Apr.*

Franziska. An excellent value, this Bavarian country-style guest house, with spacious grounds and mountain views as well as numerous facilities (but no restaurant), stands at the southern end of town, about 10 minutes by foot from the train station. *Innsbruckerstr. 24, tel. 08823/5051. 19 rooms, 14 with bath or shower. Facilities: garden, sun terrace, billiards, library, fitness room, café, wine bar, sauna, solarium. AE, MC, V. Closed Nov.–mid-Dec.*

Under DM 70

Gasthof Hornsteiner. It's a friendly, family-run tavern with rooms offering terrific views over the town and beyond to the Karwendelgebirge peaks. Rooms are simply furnished; ask for a front-facing one with a balcony. The Hornsteiner is a 15-minute walk from the train station. *Schwibbacherweg 2, tel. 08823/1382. 11 rooms, 8 with shower. No credit cards.*

Wipfelder. You'll find this family-run guest house on the southern edge of town beside the River Isar. The rooms, gaily decorated with crisp linen and colorful fabrics, have a homey atmosphere. *Riedkopfstr. 2, tel. 08823/1057. 11 rooms, 8 with* *bath. Facilities: garden, sun terrace. No credit cards. Closed Oct. 20–Dec. 20.*

Dining
Under DM 30
★
Alpenrose. Drop in during the fall for the best venison you'll taste in these parts: The entire month of October is devoted to venison dishes. Hearty Bavarian fare is offered year-round. *Obermarkt 1, tel. 08823/5055. Reservations advised.*

Under DM 20
Gasthof Hornsteiner. On a summer's day, a table on the sun terrace of this comfortable tavern overlooking both town and mountains offers just about the best view in the neighborhood. You can expect generous portions of traditional Bavarian fare; the schnitzels are an excellent value. *Schwibbacherweg 2, tel. 08823/1382. No reservations. No credit cards. Closed Mon.*

Wieskirche, Neuschwanstein Castle, and Füssen

Bus No. 1084 will take you to these destinations and back in one (long) day. Two morning buses depart from the Garmisch train station, at 8 and 12:10. The direct trip to Füssen takes two hours. For Neuschwanstein, get off at Hohenschwangau, next to Schwangau. Tourist office: Kurverwaltung, Augsburger Torplatz 1, Füssen, tel. 08362/7077.

The **Wieskirche** (Church of the Meadow) stands in an alpine meadow near Steingaden, its yellow and white walls and steep red roof set off by the dark backdrop of the Trauchgauer mountains. The architect Dominicus Zimmermann was commissioned in 1745 to build the church on this spot, where, six years earlier, a local woman claimed to have seen tears running down the face of a picture of Christ. Although the church was dedicated as the Pilgrimage Church of the Scourged Christ, it is now known as the Wieskirche. Visit it on a fine day, when alpine light streaming through its high windows displays the full glory of the glittering interior. This is Bavarian Rococo at its scintillating best. Together with the pilgrimage church of Vierzehnheiligen in north Bavaria (*see* Chapter 6), the Wieskirche represents the culmination of German Rococo ecclesiastical architecture. As at Vierzehnheiligen, the simple exterior gives little hint of the ravishing interior. A complex oval plan is animated by a series of brilliantly colored stuccos, statues, and gilt. A luminous ceiling fresco completes the decoration. Note the beautifully detailed choir and organ loft. Concerts are presented in the church in the summer. Contact the Städtische Musikschule Schongau (tel. 08861/7216) for details.

The bus continues another 22 kilometers (13 miles) to **Schwangau,** a lakeside resort town and an ideal center from which to explore the surrounding mountains. Schwangau is where you encounter the heritage of Bavaria's famous 19th-century king, Ludwig II. Both his childhood home and the most spectacular of his exotic castles are at the town's doorstep. Ludwig spent much of his youth at Schloss Hohenschwangau; it is said that its neo-Gothic atmosphere provided the primary influences that shaped the construction of the wildly romantic Schloss Neuschwanstein, the fairy-tale castle Ludwig built across the valley after he became king.

Hohenschwangau palace was built by the knights of Schwangau in the 12th century. Later it was remodeled by Ludwig's father, the Bavarian crown prince (and later king) Maximilian, between 1832 and 1836. It was here that the young Ludwig met the composer Richard Wagner. Their friendship shaped and deepened the future king's interest in theater, music, and German mythology—the mythology upon which Wagner drew for his *Ring* cycle of operas. Wagner saw the impressionable Ludwig principally as a potential source of financing for his extravagant operas rather than as a kindred spirit. For all his lofty idealism, the composer was hardly a man to let scruples interfere with his self-aggrandizement.

Ludwig's love of the theater and fantasy ran so deep that when he came to build **Neuschwanstein,** he employed a set designer instead of an architect. The castle soars from its mountainside like a stage creation—it should hardly come as a surprise that Walt Disney took it as the model for his castle in the movie *Sleeping Beauty* and later for the Disneyland castle itself.

The king's bedroom in this fantasy castle is tomblike, dominated by a great Gothic-style bed. The throne room is without a throne; Ludwig died before one could be installed. Corridors are outfitted as a ghostly grotto, reminiscent of Wagner's *Tannhäuser*. During the 17 years from the start of construction until his death, the king spent only 102 days in this country residence. Chamber concerts are held at the beginning of September in the gaily decorated minstrels' hall, one room at least that was completed as Ludwig conceived it. (Program details are available from the Verkehrsamt, Schwangau, tel. 08362/81051.) There are some spectacular walks around the castle. Make for the **Marienbrücke** (Mary's Bridge), spun like a medieval maiden's hair across a deep, narrow gorge. From this vantage point, there are giddy views of the castle and the great Upper Bavarian plain beyond. *Admission to Schloss Hohenschwangau, including a guided tour: DM 8 adults, DM 4 children under 14 and senior citizens. Open Apr.–Sept., daily 8:30–5:30; Oct.–Mar., daily 10–4. Admission to Schloss Neuschwanstein, including a guided tour: DM 8 adults, DM 4 children under 14. Open Apr.–Sept., daily 8:30–5:30; Oct.–Mar., daily 10–4. The two castles are ½ mi from each other and about 1 mi from the center of Schwangau. Cars and buses are barred from the approach roads, but the 1-mi journey to Neuschwanstein can be made by horse-drawn carriages, which stop in the village of Hohenschwangau. A bus from the village takes a back route to the Aussichtspunkt Jugend; from there, it's only a 10-minute walk to the castle. The Schloss Hohenschwangau is a 15-minute walk from the village.*

Bear in mind that more than 1 million people pass through the two castles every year. If you visit in the summer, get there early. The best time to see either castle without waiting for up to two hours in line is a weekday in January, February, or early March. The prettiest time, however, is the fall.

The castles are only 5 kilometers (3 miles) from **Füssen,** a picture-postcard town at the foot of the mountains that separate Bavaria from the Austrian Tyrol. Füssen also has a notable castle, the **Hohes Schloss,** one of the best-preserved late-Gothic castles in Germany. It was built on the site of the Roman fortress that once guarded this Alpine section of the Via Claudia, the trading route from Rome to the Danube. It has a spectacular 16th-century Rittersaal (Knights' Hall) with a fine carved ceiling, and a princes' chamber with a Gothic tiled heating oven. *Magnuspl. 10. Admission: DM 4 adults, DM 2 children. Open daily 2–4.*

Lodging
Under DM 110

Fürstenhof. A five-minute walk from the Füssen station and the town center, this quiet lodging nestles against the forest. *Kemptenerstr. 23, Füssen, tel. 08362/7006. 15 rooms with bath. No restaurant. AE, MC.*

Dining
Under DM 15

Gasthaus zum Schwanen. This modest establishment offers good regional cooking with no frills at low prices. The Swabian *Maultaschen*—a kind of local ravioli—are made on the premises and are excellent. *Brotmarkt 4, tel. 08362/6174. No credit cards. Closed Sun. evening, Mon., and Nov.*

Lodging and Dining
Under DM 110

Coloman. This friendly, traditional Schwangau inn serves a range of dishes for under DM 20, from pork and dumplings to duck and game. There's a beer garden for sunny summer days. *Kröb 2, tel. 08362/8288. 14 rooms, 5 with bath. AE, V.*

Tour 2: Bad Tölz

Bad Tölz is a good base from which to explore some of the main attractions of the central Bavarian Alps: the Benediktbeuren monastery, lakes Tegernsee, Kochelsee, and Walchensee, and the mountain scenery. The most practical way to get around is by bus—or bike. Bicycles can be hired from the Bad Tölz train station (tel. 08041/4404).

From Munich
By Train

Bad Tölz is easily reached by a regular train service from Munich's Hauptbahnhof. The journey takes one hour.

By Car

Take either Autobahn A-8 to Holzkirchen and then proceed cross-country via the B-318 and B-472; or follow the slower but more scenic B-11 direct from Munich. The distance is 53 kilometers (33 miles).

Bad Tölz

Tourist office: Kurverwaltung, Ludwigstr. 11, 8170 Bad Tölz, tel. 08041/70071.

The main street of this old market town on the River Isar fills up with colorful stalls every Wednesday—as it has for centuries. The town is divided into "old" and "new" halves. The so-called new quarter dates back to the mid-19th century, when the discovery of iodine springs brought the town a health spa—allowing plain old Tölz to add *Bad* (German for "bath") to its name—and a new prosperity. You can take the waters, enjoy a full course of health treatment at any of the many specially equipped hotels, or just splash around in Bad Tölz's large lido, the **Alpamare,** where one of its indoor pools is disguised as a South Sea beach, complete with surf. *Ludwigstr. 13. Admission: 3-hour ticket DM 19 (weekends DM 22) adults, DM 14 children. Open daily 8AM–9PM.*

Bad Tölz clings to its ancient customs and traditions more tightly than does any other Bavarian community. Folk costumes, for example, are not only preserved but are regularly worn. The town is also famous for its painted furniture, particularly farmhouse cupboards and chests. You can admire samples of painted furniture, as well as folk costumes and other historic crafts, in the **Heimatmuseum,** housed in the Altes Rathaus (Old Town

Hall). *Marktpl. Admission: free. Open Tues.–Sat. 10–noon and 2–4, Thurs. 10–noon and 2–6, Sun. 10–1.*

If you're in Bad Tölz on November 6, you'll witness one of the most colorful traditions of the Bavarian Alpine area: the Leonhardi-Ritt equestrian procession, which marks the feast day of St. Leonhard, the patron saint of horses. The procession ends north of the town at an 18th-century chapel on the Kalvarienberg, above the Isar River.

Lodging
Under DM 150
★

Bellaria. An excellent value and an elegant lodging, the style here, both inside and out, is ornate baroque. It's a taxi ride from the train station, in the "new money" half of town—the section built to cater to the early 19th-century flood of health-spa visitors. *Ludwigstr. 22, tel. 08041/70071. 24 rooms with bath. Facilities: garden, sun terrace, sauna, solarium, massage. No restaurant. AE, DC, MC, V.*

Under DM 110

Am Wald. This family-run inn on the "old" side of the river features well-worn comforts and a friendly atmosphere. *Austr. 39, tel. 08041/9014. 35 rooms, 30 with bath. Facilities: indoor pool, sauna, restaurant (closed Tues.). AE, DC, M. Closed Nov.*

Tannenberg. A well-equipped modern lodging catering particularly to those seeking the spa waters, the Tannenberg is situated in the "new" district, a short walk to the town center but a DM 9 taxi ride from the train station. *Tannenbergstr. 1, tel. 08041/2868. 16 rooms, 14 with bath. Facilities: restaurant, in-house doctor, health baths, masseur, indoor pool, sauna, solarium, gardens. No credit cards.*

Under DM 70

Zollhaus. It's a 150-year-old beer tavern, beyond the spa district on the edge of town. If you're arriving by train you'll need a taxi, but once you're settled in it's a straight walk along elegant Ludwigstrasse to the town center. *Benediktbeurerstr. 7, tel. 08041/9749. 12 rooms, 6 with bath. Facilities: restaurant. No credit cards.*

Splurge
★

Hotel Jodquellenhof. *Jodquellen* are the iodine springs that have made Bad Tölz wealthy. You can take advantage of these revitalizing waters at this imposing 19th-century spa hotel, where the emphasis is on fitness. Doubles go for between DM 215 and DM 300; the least expensive rooms are singles, at DM 120. *Ludwigstr. 15, tel. 08041/5090. 81 rooms with bath. Facilities: outdoor pool, indoor thermal baths, sauna, solarium, restaurant. AE, DC, MC, V.*

Dining
Under DM 20

Kolbergarten. This 19th-century hotel has been catering to generations of visitors to the spa waters—and indulging them with delicious afternoon teas of cream cakes and Apfelstrudel. You can eat on a sun terrace overlooking neatly kept gardens or in the hotel's separate beer garden. *Fröhlichgasse 5, tel. 08041/1501. No credit cards.*

Zantl. Located on one of Bad Tölz's oldest streets, this comfortable Bavarian tavern has a welcoming beer garden for warm summer days and solid dishes like *Schweinebraten und Knödeln* (roast pork and dumplings) and pan-fried schnitzel, which you can wash down with locally brewed beer. *Salzstr. 31, tel. 08041/9794. No reservations necessary. AE. Closed Fri.–Sat. evenings.*

Benediktbeuren

Take the Kochel bus (times vary according to season—check at the tourist office or the train station) from the Bad Tölz station 13 kilometers (8 miles) to this delightful village.

Founded in the mid-8th century, the monastery of Benediktbeuren is thought to be the oldest Benedictine institution north of the Alps. It was a flourishing cultural center in the Middle Ages; paradoxically, it also gave birth to one of the most profane musical works of those times, the *Carmina Burana*. The 1936 orchestration by Bavarian composer Carl Orff of the work is regularly performed in the monastery courtyard, the place where the original piece was first heard in the 12th century. The father of the Asam brothers, whose church-building and artistic decoration made them famous far beyond the borders of 18th-century Bavaria, painted the frescoes of the 17th-century monastery church. Cosmas Damian Asam, the eldest son, was born at Benediktbeuren.

Kochel

Catch a local train from the tiny station beside the Benediktbeuren monastery in order to continue to the lake and village of Kochel.

Kochel's excellent all-weather lido includes a collection of indoor and outdoor pools, water slides, and enough other games to keep a family amused the whole day long. *Trimini, Kochel. Admission: 3-hour ticket DM 7.50 adults, DM 4 children; all-day family ticket DM 25. Open daily 9–8:30.*

In good weather, a little ferry chugs its way round the lake. The area is also good for walking; the lakeside terrain is flat and there are several inviting taverns dotting the shore. Two mountains overlooking the lake—the **Benediktenwand** (1,646 meters/5,400 feet) and the **Herzogstand** (1,615 meters/5,300 feet)—are also relatively easy to climb, but you need to allow up to five hours to scale them. The latter is best reached from the Walchensee, a much bigger lake adjoining the Kochelsee. **Urfeld,** a pretty hamlet beside the Walchensee, is a 15-minute bus ride from the Kochelsee train station.

Lodging and Dining
Under DM 110

Alpenhotel Schmied von Kochel. The Schmied von Kochel (Blacksmith of Kochel) was a local folk hero, and the use of his name is one of several traditional touches that distinguish this 100-year-old Alpine-style hotel. A zither player can be heard most evenings in the intimate restaurant. *Schlehdorferstr. 6, tel. 08851/216. 34 rooms with bath or shower. Facilities: solarium, sauna, bowling alley. MC, V.*

Tegernsee

Both rail and bus lines connect Bad Tölz and Tegernsee. To get here by rail, take the Munich train a couple of stops to Schaftlach, then change for the scenic local train, which runs alongside the lake into the town. Buses connect the Bad Tölz and Tegernsee train stations, but they depart only a few times daily. Tourist office: Kuramt, Hauptstr. 2, 8180 Tegernsee, tel. 08022/180140.

About 17 kilometers (10 miles) east of Bad Tölz on B-472 is one of the loveliest of the Alpine lakes, the Tegernsee, which is dotted with sails in summer and ice skaters in winter. Its wooded shores are lined with flowers in late spring; in fall, its trees provide a colorful contrast to the dark, snowcapped mountains. Elbowing each other for room on the banks of this heavenly stretch of water are expensive health clinics, hotels, and a former Benedictine monastery. The monastery, set in parklike grounds on the southeast shore of the lake, was founded in the 8th century. The late-Gothic monastery church was refurbished in Italian Baroque style in the 18th century, with frescoes by Hans Georg Asam, whose work also adorns the monastery of Benediktbeuren.

Dining
Under DM 20

Seehotel Zur Post. This lakeside hotel-restaurant with a fine winter garden and terrace offers excellent fresh lake fish, but chef Hartmut Münchof would also like you to try some of his special creations, such as avocado salad. *Seestr. 3, tel. 08022/3951. Reservations advised. DC, MC, V. Closed early Jan.–Feb. 15.*

Under DM 15
★

Herzogliches Bräustuberl. Once a monastery, then a royal retreat, the Bräustuberl is now a beer hall popular with locals. Only snacks are served in this atmospheric and often crowded place, but the adjoining Keller offers hearty Bavarian meals. The beer is brewed on the premises. In summer, quaff it beneath the huge chestnuts and admire the lake and mountains over the rim of your glass. *Schlosspl. 1, tel. 08022/4141. No credit cards.*

Tour 3: Berchtesgaden

This tour covers the eastern section of the Bavarian Alps. The scenery here is much more rugged, and you should get local advice on weather conditions—even in the middle of summer—before venturing on any hikes to high altitudes. Apart from Berchtesgaden itself, an increasingly popular attraction is the Kehlsteinhaus (also called the Eagle's Nest), the mountaintop hideaway of Adolf Hitler and his Nazi hierarchy. Bavaria's least spoiled—some would say most beautiful—lake, the Königsee, is in this region, too. And no visit would be complete without a trip down the cavernous salt mines just outside Berchtesgaden.

From Munich
By Train

As the crow flies, Berchtesgaden lies about 75 kilometers (47 miles) from Munich, but because of the town's location deep inside the folds of the Alps, the distance by rail or road is more than doubled. Trains depart regularly from Munich's Hauptbahnhof. The trip can take up to 2½ hours; express services are quicker.

By Car

Take the Autobahn Salzberg, E-11, and turn off at Siegsdorf onto the B-306.

Berchtesgaden

Tourist office: Kurdirektion, Königseerstr. 2, 8240 Berchtesgaden, tel. 08652/5011.

Berchtesgaden is an ancient market town set in the noblest section of the Bavarian Alps. While as a high-altitude ski station it may not have quite the charm or cachet of Garmisch-

Partenkirchen, in summer it serves as one of the region's most popular (and crowded) resorts, with top-rated attractions in a heavenly setting. Unfortunately, its name is indelibly linked to that of Adolf Hitler—it was Der Führer's favorite mountain retreat. High on the slopes of Obersalzberg he built a luxurious headquarters hideaway, where many top-level Nazi staff meetings were held during World War II.

Salt—or "white gold," as it was known in medieval times—was the basis of Berchtesgaden's wealth. In the 12th century Emperor Barbarossa gave mining rights to a Benedictine abbey that had been founded here a century earlier. The abbey was secularized early in the 19th century, when it was taken over by the Wittelsbach rulers. The last royal resident, Crown Prince Rupprecht, who died here in 1955, furnished it with rare family treasures that now form the basis of a permanent collection.

The **Königliches Schloss Berchtesgaden** now serves as a museum. Fine Renaissance rooms provide the principal exhibition spaces for the prince's collection of sacred art, which is particularly rich in wood sculptures by such great late-Gothic artists as Tilman Riemanschneider and Veit Stoss. You can also visit the abbey's original, cavernous 13th-century dormitory and cool cloisters, which still convey something of the quiet and orderly life led by medieval monks. *Admission: DM 5 adults, DM 2 children. Open Easter–Sept., Sun.–Fri. 10–1 and 2–5; Oct.–Easter, Mon.–Fri. 10–1 and 2–5. No admission after 4 PM, when last tour starts.*

Examples of Berchtesgaden wood carvings and other local crafts are on display at one of the most interesting museums of its kind in the Alps, the **Heimatmuseum.** *Schroffenbergerallee 6. Admission: DM 3 adults, DM 1 children. Open Mon.–Fri. 9–12 and 2–5, Sat. 9–1; guided tours 10 AM and 3 PM Mon.–Fri. only.*

For many travelers, the pièce de résistance of a Berchtesgaden stay might well be a visit to its salt mine, the Salzbergwerk. In the days when the mine was owned by Berchtesgaden's princely rulers, only selected guests were allowed to see how the source of the city's wealth was won from the earth. Dressed in traditional miner's clothing, visitors sit astride a miniature train that transports them nearly half a mile into the mountain to an enormous chamber where the salt is mined. A couple of rides down wood chutes used by the miners to get from one level to another, and a boat ride on an underground saline lake the size of a football field are included in the 1½-hour tour. *Admission: DM 12.50 adults, DM 6.50 children under 11. Open May–mid-Oct., daily 8:30–5; mid-Oct.–Apr., Mon.–Sat. 12:30–3:30.*

For an experience of a different kind, in summer a bus takes visitors up to **Obersalzberg,** site of Hitler's luxurious mountain retreat on the north slope of the Hoher Goll. (Most of the Nazi complex was destroyed in 1945, as was Hitler's chalet; only a few basement walls remain.) The hairpin bends of Germany's highest road lead to the base of the 6,000-foot peak on which sat the so-called Adlerhorst or Eagle's Nest, the Kehlsteinhaus. Hitler had the road built in 1937–39. It climbs more than 2,000 feet in less than 4 miles and comes to an end at a lot that clings to the mountain about 500 feet below the Kehlsteinhaus. A tunnel in the mountain brings you to an elevator that whisks you up to the Kehlsteinhaus—and what appears to be the top of the world. There are refreshment rooms and a restaurant where you can steel yourself for the giddy descent to Berchtesgaden. The round-trip (Berchtesgaden post office to Eagle's Nest and back) costs DM 24, half price for children. By car you can travel only as far as the Obersalzberg bus station. The return fare from there is DM 18. *Open mid-May–mid-Oct.*

The view from the Kehlsteinhaus is stunning: The jagged Watzmann slumbers above two mountain lakes, the Obersee and the Königsee. Both lakes lie within the Berchtesgaden National Park, 210 square kilometers (82 square miles) of wild mountain country where flora and fauna have been left to develop as nature intended. The park is modeled on the United States' Yellowstone National Park; no roads penetrate the area. The park administration organizes guided tours of the area from June till September (contact the Nationalparkverwaltung, Doktorberg 6, 8240 Berchtesgaden, tel. 08652/61068).

One less strenuous way into the National Park is by boat. A fleet of 21 excursion boats, electrically driven so that no noise disturbs the peace of the lake, operates on the **Königsee.** Only the skipper of the boat is allowed to shatter the silence with a trumpet fanfare to demonstrate the lake's remarkable echo. The notes from the trumpet bounce back and forth from the almost vertical cliffs that plunge into the dark green water. A cross on a rocky promontory marks the spot where a boatload of pilgrims hit the cliffs 100 years ago and sank. The voyagers, most of whom drowned, were on their way to the tiny twin-towered Baroque chapel of St. Bartholomä, built in the 17th century on a peninsula where an early Gothic church once stood.

Another lake, the much smaller **Obersee,** can be reached by a 15-minute walk from the second stop on the boat tour. The Obersee rivals the larger lake for sheer beauty. Its backdrop of jagged mountains and precipitous cliffs is broken by a waterfall, the Rothbachfall, that plunges more than 1,000 feet to the valley floor. *Boat service on the Königsee runs year-round (except when the lake freezes over). Round trips can be interrupted at St. Bartholomä and Salletalm, the landing stage for the Obersee. Full round-trip fare: DM 15 adults, DM 7.50 children.*

Lodging
Under DM 110

Hotel-Café Grassl. Centrally located, the Grassl commands fine views. All the rooms are large and traditionally furnished, but ask for one away from the main street, which can be noisy. There's no restaurant, but the in-house café serves excellent pastries from its own bakery. *Maximilianstr. 15, tel. 08652/4071. 32 rooms, some with bath or shower. AE, DC, MC, V.*

Hotel Watzmann. The USAAF Director of Operations in Berchtesgaden awarded the Hotel Watzmann a special certificate of appreciation for its hospitality to American servicemen. They, in turn, appreciate its cozy Bavarian style and good restaurant. *Franziskanerpl., tel. 08652/2055. 37 rooms, half with shower. Facilities: heated garden-terrace, restaurant. AE, MC, V. Closed Nov. 3–Dec. 18.*

Under DM 70

Hotel zum Türken. The 10-minute journey from Berchtesgaden is worth it for the view. Confiscated by the Nazis, it's located at the foot of the road up to Hitler's mountaintop retreat. Remains of their wartime bunkers adjoin the hotel. *8240 Obersalzberg-Berchtesgaden, tel. 08652/2428. 17 rooms, half with bath or shower. AE, DC, MC, V. Closed Nov. 1–Dec. 20.*

Dining
Under DM 30

Alpenhotel Denninglehen. The mountain hotel's restaurant (which includes a nonsmoking room) is 3,000 feet up in the resort area of Oberau, just outside Berchtesgaden, and its terrace offers magnificent views. *8240 Berchtesgaden-Oberau, tel. 08652/5085. Reservations advised. MC. Closed Dec. 1–20.*

Hotel Post. This is a centrally located and solidly reliable hostelry with a well-presented international menu. Try fish from the nearby Königsee if it's offered. In summer you can eat in the beer garden. *Maximilianstr. 2, tel. 08652/5067. Reservations advised. Jacket and tie optional. AE, DC, MC, V.*

Under DM 15

Fischer. You can pop into this farmhouse-style eatery for *Apfelstrudel* and coffee or for something more substantial from a frequently changing international and local menu. It's a short walk across the bridge from the railway station. *Königsseerstr. 51, tel. 08652/4044. Reservations advised in July and Aug. AE. Closed Nov. 1–Dec. 18.*

Shopping

Berchtesgaden, like Oberammergau, has a **wood-carving** tradition that dates back centuries; there's a central selling point at **Schloss Adelsheim** (Schroffenbergallee). The town is famous for its *Spanschachtel*, delicate, finely constructed wood boxes made to contain everything from pins and needles to top hats. You'll find modern versions in every souvenir shop and, if you're lucky, you might even come across a 100-year-old example in one of the town's antiques shops.

Bad Reichenhall

Take the train back down from Berchtesgaden—or take one of the slower but perhaps more scenic buses, which depart from outside the Berchtesgaden train station. Tourist office: Kurgastzentrum, Wittelsbadcherstr. 15, 8230 Bad Reichenhall, tel. 08651/3003.

Although Berchtesgaden is more famous, Bad Reichenhall is older and claims a more interesting history, thanks to the saline springs that made the town rich. The springs, which form Europe's largest saline source, were first tapped in pre-Christian times; the salt they provided in the Middle Ages supported the economies of cities as far away as Munich and Passau. In the early 19th century King Ludwig I built an elaborate salt works and spa house here—the **Alte Saline** and **Quellenhaus**—in vaulted, pseudomedieval style. Their pump installations are astonishing examples of 19th-century engineering. *Admission: DM 3 adults, DM 1.50 children. Open daily 10–11:30 and 2–4.*

Bad Reichenhall even possesses a 19th-century "saline" chapel, part of the spa's facilities and built in exotic Byzantine style at the behest of Ludwig I. Salt is so much a part of the town that you can practically taste it in the air. Not surprisingly, most of the more expensive hotels offer special spa treatments based on the health-giving properties of the saline springs. The waters can also be taken in the attractive spa gardens throughout the year (open Mon.–Sat. 8–12:15 and 3–5, Sun. and holidays 10–12:15). Bad Reichenhall's own symphony orchestra performs five days a week during the summer season and four days a week in winter. Like most resorts in the area, this one also has a casino (tel. 08651/4091); it's open daily 3 PM–3 AM. You'll need to show your passport and be dressed respectably (which translates as jacket and tie for men).

It's ironic that Bad Reichenhall, which flourishes on the riches of its underground springs, has a 12th-century basilica dedicated to **St. Zeno,** patron saint of those imperiled by floods and the dangers of the deep. Much of this ancient church was remodeled in the 16th and 17th centuries, but some of the original cloisters remain.

Lodging
Under DM 70

Kurfürst. Centrally located and with a reasonably priced restaurant (guests only at lunchtime), this hotel is plain but popular. *Kufürstenstr. 11, tel. 08651/2710. 12 rooms. Facilities: gardens. AE, DC, MC, V. Closed Dec. 15–Jan. 15.*

5 The Black Forest

Including Freiburg and Baden-Baden

The Black Forest—*Schwarzwald* in German—is a name that conjures up images of a wild, isolated place where time passes so slowly it can be measured by the number of rings on the trunks of felled trees. And this southwest corner of Germany is indeed a rural region where dense woodland stretches away to the horizon; but it is neither inaccessible nor a backwater. The first recorded holidaymakers checked in here 19 centuries ago, when the Roman emperor Caracalla and his army rested and soothed their battle wounds in the natural-spring waters of what later became Baden-Baden. But it wasn't until the early 19th century that Baden-Baden attained its renown as an elegant spa town, attracting virtually the entire nobility of Europe. The Black Forest (and not Switzerland) gave the world its first cuckoo clock, and the first downhill skier hurtled down a Black Forest slope in 1891. The world's first ski lift opened at Schollach in 1907.

Mark Twain put the Black Forest on the tourist map for Americans. In his 1880 book *A Tramp Abroad,* he waxed poetic on the beauties of this forest.

Despite the extravagant wealth of Baden-Baden (which still draws millionaires like bees to a summer garden) and the hustle and bustle of Freiburg, the Black Forest means countryside—a hikers' and bikers' paradise of thick woodland, empty trails, and wayside inns.

We suggest that you make Freiburg your base. From this ancient cathedral city, you can explore in several directions.

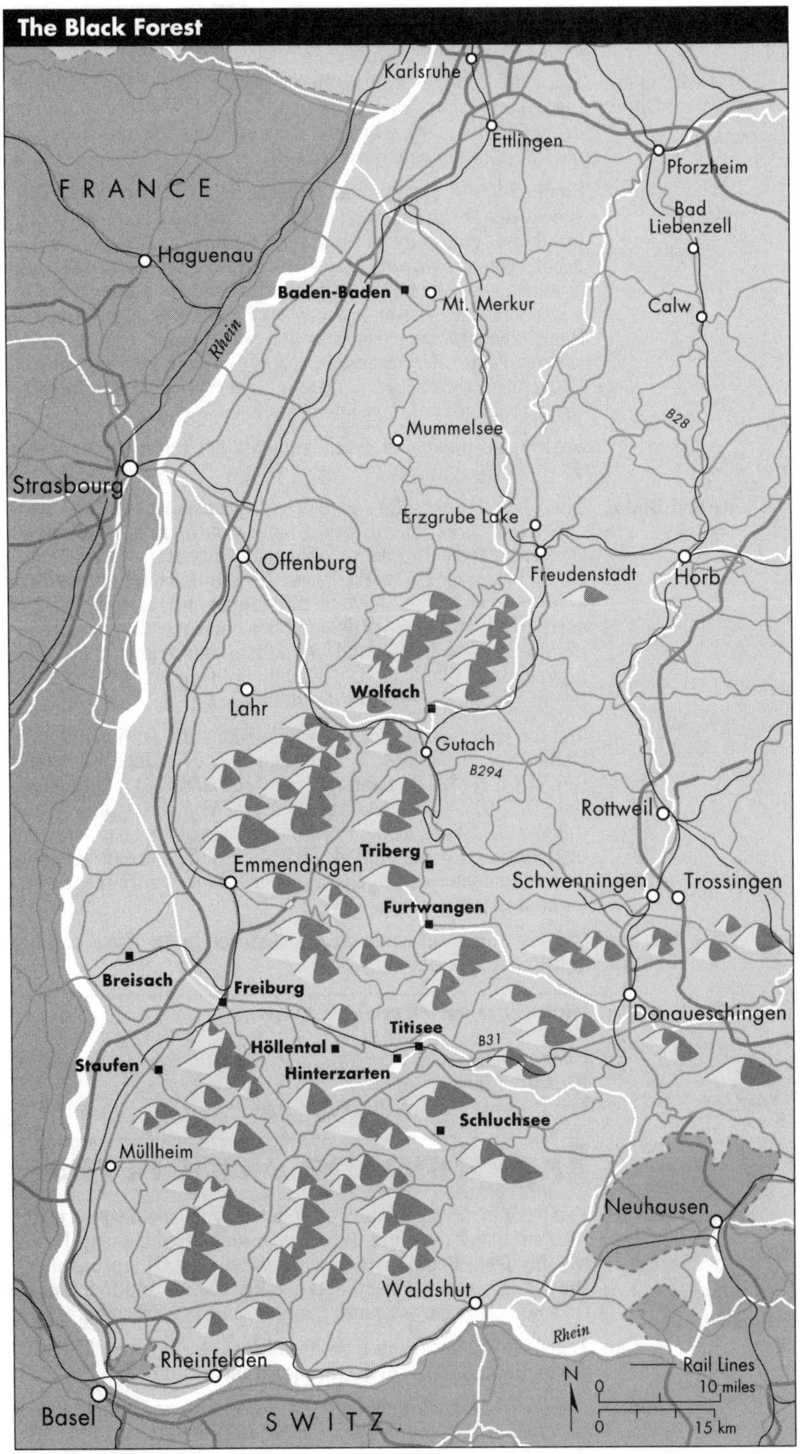
The Black Forest
Karlsruhe
Ettlingen
Pforzheim
FRANCE
Bad Liebenzell
Haguenau
Baden-Baden
Mt. Merkur
Calw
Rhein
B28
Mummelsee
Strasbourg
Erzgrube Lake
Offenburg
Freudenstadt
Horb
Wolfach
Lahr
Gutach
B294
Rottweil
Triberg
Emmendingen
Schwenningen
Trossingen
Furtwangen
Breisach
Freiburg
Donaueschingen
Titisee
Höllental
B31
Staufen
Hinterzarten
Schluchsee
Müllheim
Neuhausen
Waldshut
Rhein
Rheinfelden
Rail Lines
0
10 miles
0
15 km
N
Basel
SWITZ.

Essential Information

Lodging and Dining Reasonable prices are the rule in Freiburg and the surrounding countryside. Baden-Baden is worth visiting to splash around in the thermal baths or to peep inside the luxurious casino, but it's an expensive place to stay.

Smoked hams, cherry cake, and cherry *Schnaps* are the chief specialties of the region. Try *z'Nuni,* the local farmers' second breakfast, generally eaten around 9 AM. It consists of smoked bacon, called *Schwarzwaldgeräuchertes*—the most authentic is smoked over fir cones—a hunk of bread, and a glass of chilled white wine. No visitor to the Black Forest will want to pass up the chance to try *Schwarzwalderkirschtorte,* Black Forest cherry cake. *Kirschwasser,* locally called *Chriesewässerle* (from the French *cerise,* meaning cherry), is cherry brandy, the most famous of the region's excellent schnapps.

Highly recommended establishments are indicated by a star ★.

Hiking and Biking The Black Forest offers a wealth of signposted walking routes as well as three long-distance north-south trails, the longest stretching from Pforzheim to the Swiss city of Basel, 280 kilometers (175 miles) away. Walks vary in length from a few hours to a full weekend. The **Clock-carriers' Road,** following the path of early Black Forest clock dealers, is a perennial favorite. Three nights' lodging in bed-and-breakfasts plus transport of your luggage is available for DM 175 and up. Contact the tourist office in Freiburg (*see below*) for details.

You can rent bicycles from the following train stations: **Baden-Baden** (tel. 07221/61445), **Breisach** (tel. 07667/209), **Freiburg** (tel. 0761/214–337), **Hinterzarten** (tel. 07652/331), **Schluchsee** (tel. 07656/227), **Titisee** (tel. 07651/8298), and **Wolfach** (tel. 07834/215). Check at the Freiburg tourist office (*see below*) for information about guided bike tours. They're reasonably priced, and your luggage is transported for you from one overnight stop to the next.

The Arts and Nightlife Culture and entertainment are centered in Freiburg and Baden-Baden (*see below*).

Highlights for First-time Visitors

Baden-Baden
Freiburg Münster
The Höllental (Hell Valley) train ride

Exploring the Black Forest

From Frankfurt *By Train* Freiburg is 275 kilometers (170 miles) from the nearest major German city, Frankfurt. InterCity trains depart hourly during the day from Frankfurt's main train station (Hauptbahnhof); the 275-kilometer (175-mile) trip takes 2 hours and 15 minutes. On some services, you must change trains in Karlsruhe.

By Car Take the A-5 autobahn from Frankfurt to Freiburg. The 275-kilometer (172-mile) drive takes two and a half hours.

From Munich *By Train* Freiburg lies 410 kilometers (260 miles) west of Munich. InterCity trains from Munich take 3 hours and 20 minutes.

By Car Driving time on the 410-kilometer (260-mile) route is four hours.

Guided Tours

The Freiburg tourist office (*see below*) organizes one-day bus tours of the Black Forest at reasonable prices, from DM 40 upward. You can beat the cost of several separate train trips by joining a tour that visits several places; moreover, some tours visit sites that are hard to reach via public transport. We especially recommend the tour that takes in the **Uhrenmuseum** in **Furtwangen** (a clock museum where the cuckoo takes pride of place); the **Triberg waterfall;** and **die Wolfacher Glashütte,** the traditional glassblowing factory at **Wolfach.** All three places are otherwise difficult to reach without a car.

Freiburg im Breisgau

Tourist office: Verkehrsamt, Rotteckring 14, tel. 0761/368-9090.

Numbers in the margin correspond to points of interest on the Freiburg map.

Freiburg, or Freiburg in Breisgau, to give the town its full name, is a compact place of 180,000 people, and the visitor can comfortably explore it on foot or bicycle. The train station (Hauptbahnhof) is in the city center, close to lodgings and the main attractions.

The town was founded in the 12th century. Despite extensive wartime bomb damage, skillful restoration has helped re-create the original and compelling medieval atmosphere of one of the most appealing historic towns in Germany. For Americans, Freiburg has particular significance: The 16th-century geographer Martin Waldseemüller, who first put the name America on a map, in 1507, was born here.

Towering over the rebuilt medieval streets of the city is its most
1 famous landmark, the **Münster,** Freiburg's cathedral. The pioneering 19th-century Swiss art historian Jacob Burckhardt described its delicately perforated 370-foot spire as the finest in Europe. The cathedral took three centuries to build, from around 1200 to 1515. You can easily trace the progress of generations of builders through the changing architectural styles, from the fat columns and solid, rounded arches of the Romanesque period to the lofty Gothic windows and airy interior of the choir, the last parts of the building to be completed. Of particular interest are the luminous 13th-century stained-glass windows; a 16th-century triptych (three-panel painting) by Hans Baldung-Grien; and paintings by Holbein the Younger and Lucas Cranach the Elder. If you can summon the energy, climb the tower; the reward is a magnificent view of the city and the Black Forest beyond. Go on a Friday and you'll see the colorfully striped awnings of the market stalls spread out below, a fitting accompaniment to the 16th-century market house, the
2 **Kaufhaus.** The four statues you see on the fine facade beneath its steeply pitched roof are of Hapsburg monarchs.

3 The city's other main square is **Rathaus Platz,** where Frei-
4 burg's famous **Rathaus** (Town Hall) stands, constructed from two 16th-century patrician houses joined together. Among its

Kaufhaus, **2**
Münster, **1**
Rathaus, **4**
Rathaus Platz, **3**

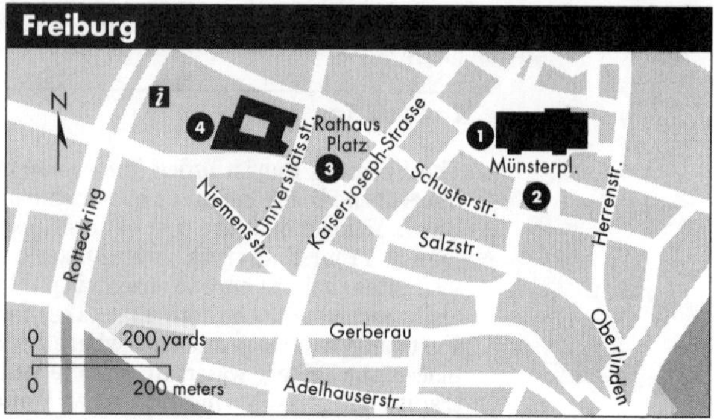

attractive Renaissance features is an oriel, or bay window, clinging to a corner and bearing a bas-relief of the romantic medieval legend of the Maiden and the Unicorn.

Lodging
Under DM 110

Rappen. Located in the heart of the pedestrian-only old town, this hotel features brightly painted farmhouse-style rooms. The appealing rustic theme extends to the excellent restaurant. Wine lovers will appreciate the wide choice—more than 200—of regional vintages. *Münsterpl. 13, tel. 0761/31353. 20 rooms with bath. AE, DC, MC, V.*

Under DM 70

DJH Jugendherberge. A youth hostel in the suburb of Ebnet, 5 kilometers (3 miles) from the train station (take the No. L-1 or B-18 bus), it offers dormitory and family-room accommodations for DM 12–DM 25 per person. *Kartäuserstr. 151, tel. 0761/67656. 70 beds, plus four 4-bed family rooms.*

Gasthaus Paradies. Less than a mile's walk (or ride, on the No. L-3 or L-4 bus) from the train station, this small, family-run guest house is not to be confused with the much more expensive Hotel Paradies. None of the rooms have a private shower or bath, but there is a small restaurant. *11 Friedrich-Ebert-Platz, tel. 0761/273–700. No credit cards.*

Goldener Sternen. This friendly neighborhood beer restaurant/inn lies north of the old town, less than a mile from the train station. To get there, take the No. L-3 or L-4 bus from the station. *Emmendingerstr. 1, tel. 0761/278–373. 9 rooms, 3 with bath. Facilities: restaurant. No credit cards.*

Hotel Schützen. This brightly painted old inn stands 2½ kilometers (1½ miles) from the train station. The Waldsee bus, No. L-1, which you can pick up at the station, stops outside. *Schützenallee 12, tel. 0761/72021. 14 rooms, 4 with bath; multibed rooms available. Facilities: restaurant. No credit cards.*

Camping. There are five camping sites, catering to tents, caravans, and camper vans, in and around Freiburg. The Freiburg tourist office (*see above*) will provide you with addresses and details.

Splurge

Park Hotel Post. A hotel since the turn of the century, with good old-fashioned service to match, the Park Hotel Post is right next to the train station. The Jugendstil facade with stone balconies and central copper-dome tower has earned the building protected status. Double rooms range from DM 165 to DM 190, depending on size; the cheapest singles cost DM 118.

Eisenbahnstr. 35, tel. 0761/31683. 41 rooms, most with bath. AE, DC, MC, V.

Dining
Under DM 30

Alte Weinstube zur Traube. This cozy old wine tavern offers a rich and varied selection of classic French and Swabian dishes. *Zander* (pike) roulade with crab sauce and braised pork with lentils are especially recommended. *Schusterstr. 17, tel. 0761/32190. Reservations advised on weekends and in Aug. AE, DC, MC, V. Closed Sun., Mon. lunch, and July 15–30.*

★ **Zum Roten Bären.** The Red Bear has a history dating from 1120 and is said to have been an inn since 1311, making it the oldest in Germany. True or not, it's the archetypal German history-book inn; it also offers lodging. Fixed-price meals start at DM 25 per person; the best deals are on the *Tageskarte* (menu of the day). Spätzle comes with most dishes. *Oberlinden 12, tel. 0761/36913. Reservations advised. AE, DC, MC, V.*

Under DM 20

Oberkirchs Weinstuben. The landlord of this Old Town tavern in a small hotel personally bags some of the game that ends up in the kitchen. Fresh trout is another specialty. In summer, the dark oak dining tables spill onto a garden terrace. *Münsterpl. 22, tel. 0761/31011. V. Closed Sun., public holidays, and Christmas Eve–Jan. 22.*

Ratskeller. For typical Black Forest ambience, make for this restaurant in the shadow of the cathedral on Münsterplatz. The dark interior, with wood paneling and exposed beams, is complemented by the time-honored dishes, with roast meats and rich sauces predominating. *Münsterpl. 11, tel. 0761/37530. Reservations advised. Closed Sun. evening and Mon.*

Schwär's Löwen. It's well worth the trip to the suburb of Littenweiler (5 kilometers/3 miles on the No. L-1 or B-17 bus) to enjoy this tavern's rich and varied offerings, from fresh trout to fresh game. The three-course lunch menu is a bargain, and on summer days you can choose between a sun terrace and a beer garden. A few rooms under DM 70 are also available. *Kapplerstr. 120, tel. 0761/63041. No credit cards. Closed Mon.*

Shopping

Cuckoo clocks and locally made glassware can be costly, but if you shop around it's possible to find reasonably priced items. In Freiburg, you'll find the biggest range of clocks—in terms of size, style, and price—at **Hansen's** (Münsterpl. 6). For glassware, head for the big chain department stores—**Hertie** and **Kauhof,** both on the pedestrianized Josephstrasse.

The Arts and Nightlife

Freiburg's annual **Zeltmusick** festival is a musical jamboree held June and July in tents—*Zelt* is German for tents—that sprout on the city outskirts. The accent is on jazz, but most types of music are featured, including classical. The city also has a Philharmonic orchestra; it gives concerts year-round in the city theater. Chamber-music concerts are presented in the summer in the courtyard of the ancient Kufhaus, opposite the Münster. For program details and tickets for all the above, contact **Freiburg Verkehrsamt** (Rotteckring 14, tel. 0761/216-3289). For jazz, make for the **Jazz Haus** (Schnewlinstr. 1), where live music is featured nightly.

Freiburg has an annual summer **theater** festival. Performances are given in the city's theater complex and spill out onto the streets and squares as well. Street theater is also featured in the annual **Schlossberg** festival, held in August, a popular and informal carnival-like event centering on the castle.

English-language **movies** are shown at Freiburg's **German-American Institute** (Kaiser-Joseph-Str. 266, tel. 0761/31645).

Nightlife in Freiburg revolves around the city's wine bars and wine cellars. **Oberkirchs Weinstuben** and **Die Zwiebel,** both located on Münsterplatz, are typically atmospheric; you can also look for night spots on any of the streets around the cathedral. The top discos are **El PI** (Schiffstr. 16) and **Lord Nelson** (Bertoldtstr. 26). **Sam's Dance Palace** (Humboldtstr. 2) is fun if you don't mind crowds.

Breisach

Trains run frequently (except during the late morning) from Freiburg. The trip takes 30 minutes. Tourist office: Verkehrsamt, Werd 9, tel. 07667/83227.

Twenty kilometers (12 miles) northwest of Freiburg on B-31 is the town of Breisach. It stands by the Rhine River; everything you see to the west on the opposite bank is in France. Towering high above the town and the surrounding vineyards is the **Stephansmünster,** the cathedral of St. Stephen, built between 1200 and 1500 (and almost entirely rebuilt after World War II). As at Freiburg, the transition from sturdy Romanesque styles to airy and vertical Gothic styles is easy to see. North of the town rises the **Kaiserstuhl,** or Emperor's Chair, a volcanic outcrop clothed in vineyards that produce high-quality wines.

Lodging and Dining
Under DM 30

Kapuzinergarten. Local wines complement quality regional cooking in a picture-postcard setting. The sun terrace offers views of the town. Rooms for under DM 110 are also available. *Kapuzinergasse 26, tel. 07667/1055. AE. Closed Feb.*

The Höllental and Hinterzarten

The region's most scenic train route passes through the rugged country dubbed Hell Valley (Höllental) *by the 19th-century engineers and workers who laid the track. Trains run every 30 minutes, chugging up from Freiburg toward Titisee and Schluchsee lakes via the town of Hinterzarten. The trip to Schluchsee takes only 50 minutes. Take one train to Hinterzarten (35 minutes), and then resume the journey on a later one. Tourist office: Freiburgerstr. 3, Hinterzarten, tel. 07652/1501.*

The lovely 800-year-old town of Hinterzarten is the most important resort in the southern Black Forest. Some buildings date to the 12th century, among them **St. Oswald's** church, built in 1146. Hinterzarten's oldest inn, **Weisses Rossle,** has been in business since 1347. The **Park Hotel Adler,** established in 1446, has been under the same family management for 14 generations, although the original building was burned down during the Thirty Years' War and the inn where Marie Antoinette and her retinue put up in 1770 has been considerably altered since her visit. In winter Hinterzarten is one of Germany's most popular centers for *Langlauf* (cross-country skiing).

Lodging and Dining
Under DM 110

Cafe Imbery. You'll find this comfortable country guest house in the center of town. The good, solid meals are under DM 20. *Rathausstr. 14, tel. 07652/1092. No credit cards. Closed 3 weeks in Apr.; restaurant also closed Thurs.*

Splurge **Park Hotel Adler.** It may be too expensive for a meal (a two-course lunch costs DM 40–DM 60 per person; a four-course dinner, DM 55–DM 90), but if you've got something to celebrate or are just feeling ritzy, take afternoon tea here (DM 27). The Adler, one of Germany's finest hotels, stands on nearly 2 acres of grounds. Marie Antoinette once ate here, and the highest standards are kept up in the French restaurant and a paneled 17th-century dining room. An orchestra accompanies dinner and later moves to the bar to play for dancing. The cost of the sumptuously appointed double rooms runs from DM 280 to DM 470. *Adlerpl., tel. 07652/1270. 42 rooms and 32 suites with bath. Facilities: indoor pool, sauna, solarium, indoor and outdoor tennis, table tennis, golf range. AE, DC, MC, V.*

Titisee and Schluchsee Lakes

For train information, see *The Höllental and Hinterzarten,* above. *Tourist offices: Kurverwaltung Titisee, am Kurhaus, Titisee, tel. 07651/8101; Kurverwaltung, Haus des Gastes, Schluchsee, tel. 07656/7732.*

The **Titisee,** a jewel among lakes, is a star attraction. Set in a mighty forest, the 1½-mile-long lake is invariably crowded in summer with boats and windsurfers. Boats and boards can be rented at several points along the shore.

But the biggest lake in the Black Forest, and the Hell Valley train's final destination, is the **Schluchsee,** next to the 4,500-foot **Feldberg,** the region's highest mountain. Here you can swim, sailboard (you'll find boards for hire at a couple of shops on the shore, five minutes from the train station), or set out on any of numerous well-marked hikes.

Lodging
Under DM 70
Pension Ketterer. Close to the lakeside and only a few strides from the train station, this family house offers double rooms for as low as DM 40, including breakfast. *Jägerstr. 3, Titisee, tel. 07651/8297. 5 rooms without bath. No credit cards.*

Lodging and Dining
Under DM 70
Cafe Pension alte Schmiede. Both the solid meals and the comfortable rooms are bargains here. *Faulenfürsterstr. 3, Schluchsee, tel. 07656/846. 6 rooms, 3 with bath. No credit cards.*

Staufen

Frequent trains link Freiburg with Staufen. The journey takes 30 or 50 minutes, depending on whether you get a through train or have to change at Bad Krozingen. Tourist office: Verkehrsamt, Rathaus, tel. 07633/80536.

Staufen is the town where Dr. Faustus is reputed to have made his pact with the Devil. The legend of Faustus is remembered today chiefly because of Goethe's drama *Faust,* published in the early 19th century. The play depicts the doctor as a man driven to make a pact with the Devil; in return for immortality, Faustus sells his soul. In fact, the original Faustus was an alchemist, an early scientist, in the 16th century. He made a pact not with the Devil but with a local baron who was convinced Faustus could make his fortune by discovering the secret of how to make gold from base metals. In his attempts Dr. Faustus died in an explosion that produced such noise and sulphurous stink that the townspeople were convinced the Devil had carried him off. You can visit the ancient inn, the **Gasthaus Löwen,** on the market square, Marktplatz, where Faustus lived and died. The frescoes on its walls tell his story in vivid detail.

Lodging and Dining
Under DM 70

Kreuz Post. This old inn stands conveniently close to the train station. The menu offers country fare, from schnitzel with egg noodles to locally caught trout. *Hauptstr. 65, tel. 07633/5240. 11 rooms, 3 with bath. No credit cards. Closed Jan.; restaurant also closed Wed. dinner and Thurs.*

Baden-Baden

Trains run frequently from Freiburg; the journey takes just under an hour. Tourist office: Kurverwaltung, Augustaplatz 8, tel. 07221/275–200.

This is millionaires' territory, but worth a look to see how rich and cultured Europeans live (or spend their holidays). If you're traveling to or from Freiburg by train via Frankfurt and Karlruhe, you could stop off here for a few hours; or you can make a day trip during your Freiburg stay.

Baden-Baden, set in a wooded valley of the northern Black Forest, sits atop the extensive underground hot springs that gave the city its name. The Roman legions of the Emperor Caracalla discovered the springs when they settled here in the 1st century and named the place Aquae. The leisure classes of the 19th century rediscovered the bubbling waters, establishing Baden-Baden as the unofficial summer residence of many of Europe's royal families, who left their imprint on the city in the palatial homes and stately villas that still grace its tree-lined avenues.

As Germany's ultimate high-fashion resort, it lives unashamedly on leisure and pleasure. Here the splendor of the Belle Epoch lives on to a remarkable extent. Some claim that one out of five residents is a millionaire. In the evening, Baden-Baden is a soft-music-and-champagne-in-a-silver-bucket kind of place, and in the daytime, it follows the horseback-riding-along-the-bridle-paths tradition. It features a crowded season of ballet performances, theater, concerts, and recitals, along with exciting horse racing and high-stakes action at its renowned casino.

Baden-Baden claims that the casino, Germany's first, is the most beautiful in the world, a boast that not even the French can challenge, for it was a Parisian, Jacques Bénazet, who persuaded the sleepy little Black Forest spa to build gambling rooms to enliven its evenings. In 1853, his son Edouard Bénazet commissioned Charles Séchan, a stage designer associated with the Paris opera house, to come up with a design along the lines of the greatest French imperial palaces. The result was a series of richly decorated gaming rooms in which even an emperor could feel at home—and did. Kaiser Wilhelm I was a regular visitor, as was his chancellor, Bismarck. Visitors as disparate as Dostoevsky, the Aga Khan, and Marlene Dietrich have all been patrons.

Few people visit Baden-Baden to go sightseeing (though those who feel the urge might want to see the **Neues Schloss,** or New Castle, a 19th-century fortress that was rebuilt in the Renaissance style for the grand dukes of Baden; today it's a museum of local history). Above all, you'll want to stroll around this supremely elegant resort and sample the gracious, Old-World atmosphere of a place that, more than almost anywhere else in Europe, retains the feeling of a more unhurried, leisured age.

The most lavish swimming pool in the region is the **Caracalla** complex. Opened in 1985, it has five indoor pools and two outdoor pools, a sauna, a solarium, and Jacuzzis, plus thermal water-therapy treatment courses. *Römerpl. 11, tel. 07221/275-940. Admission: DM 14 for 2 hours. Open daily 8 AM–10 PM.*

The **Friedrichsbad** swimming pool offers mixed nude bathing. *Römerpl. 1, tel. 07221/275–920. Admission: DM 25; children under 16 not admitted. Open Mon. and Wed.–Sat. 8 AM–10 PM, Tues. 8–4.*

Dining
Under DM 30

Bratwurstglöckle. Hunt out the large bronze bell—the *Glöckle*—that hangs outside this traditional beer and wine tavern. It signals good food and drink at reasonable prices. *Steinstr. 7, tel. 07221/2968. No credit cards.*

Löwenbräukeller. This Bavarian-style restaurant with a small, tree-shaded beer garden serves only one beer—Munich's famous Löwenbräu—along with a wide selection of Baden wines. The food is simple and filling, with regional specialties predominating. *Gernsbacherstr. 9, tel. 07221/22311. No reservations. No credit cards.*

Splurge

Allee. This large restaurant in the noble Europäischer Hof hotel mixes international and regional dishes, with the emphasis on classic French cooking. The buffet lunch is particularly good value. A two-course lunch costs DM 38–DM 55 per person; a three-course dinner, DM 50. The hotel offers 64 double rooms costing from DM 200 to DM 400. *Kaiserallee 2, tel. 07223/23561. Reservations advised. Jacket and tie required. AE, DC, MC, V.*

Lodging and Dining
Under DM 70

Gasthof Kühler Krug. At this neighborhood inn, a DM 8 taxi ride from the train station, you can eat and sleep in expensive Baden-Baden without blowing a hole in your pocket. *Beuernerstr. 115, tel. 72338. 10 rooms without bath. No credit cards.*

Splurge

Europäischer Hof. The large **Allee** restaurant in this noble hotel mixes international and regional dishes, with the emphasis on classic French cooking. A two-course lunch costs DM 38–DM 55 per person (the buffet lunch is particularly good rahue); a three-course dinner, DM 50. The hotel offers 64 double rooms costing from DM 200 to DM 400. *Kaiserallee 2, tel. 07223/23561. Reservations advised. Jacket and tie required. AE, DC, MC, V.*

The Arts and Nightlife

There's plenty of culture in Baden-Baden, but you're liable to have to pay big-city prices and more to see a decent concert. The best-value performances are given by Baden-Baden's orchestra at the **Kurhaus** (Werderstr.). The orchestra also presents an annual two-week summer festival, the **Musikalische Sommer.** For program details and tickets, call 07221/275–2500.

Baden-Baden's **Theater am Goetheplatz** presents a regular program of drama, opera, and ballet. Tickets costs DM 35–DM 55 per person. Call 07221/275–268 for program details and tickets.

The glittering **casino** charges only DM 5 to get in; you'll need your passport as ID, and men must wear a jacket and tie. You'll have to sign a form guaranteeing that you can meet any debts you run up (minimum stake is DM 5—maximum, DM 20,000).

6 Franconia

Including Nürnberg, Bayreuth, Würzburg, and Bamberg

The ancient kingdom of the Franks is known today as Franconia or, in German, Franken. Although mainly rural, its castles and its architecturally rich towns provide a solid reminder of the region's past importance in the Holy Roman Empire. It was only in the early 19th century, following Napoleon's conquest of what is now southern Germany, that the area was incorporated into northern Bavaria. Modern Franconia stretches from the Bohemian Forest on the Czechoslovak border in the east to the outskirts of Frankfurt in the west. But its heart—and the focal point of this tour—is an area known as the Frankisches Schweiz, bounded by Nürnberg on the south, Bamberg on the west, and the cultural center of Bayreuth on the east.

Despite its beauty and history, Franconia is not a mainstream tourist destination; many Germans simply drive straight through on the way south. But the region rates high with epicures in search of authentic German regional cuisine. It is also noted for its liquid refreshments, from both the grape and the grain. Franconian white wine, often sold in distinctive stubby bottles called *Bocksbeutel*, is renowned as one of the driest in Germany. And the region has the biggest concentration of village breweries in the world, producing a wide range of styles, the most distinctive of which is *Rauchbier*, a dark and heady smoked brew.

We suggest Bamberg and Nürnberg as tour bases. From Bamberg you can explore the surrounding unspoiled countryside of the Steigerwald and the Frankisches Schweiz and visit several towns to the north, including the princely seat of Coburg (home of Albert, husband of England's Queen Victoria), and

Kulmbach (which produces the strongest beer in the world). From Nürnberg you can reach the Wagnerian town of Bayreuth and the magnificent, castle-dominated Würzburg.

Franconia has an excellent rail network, but bus services are not so good. The main regional **tourist information office** is Fremdenvekehrsverband Franken, Am Plärrer 14, 8500 Nürnberg 81, tel. 0911/264–202.

Essential Information

Lodging Franconia is one of the bargain areas of Germany, probably because it's a region people travel through rather than to. Small towns and villages offer excellent low-cost accommodation; even in more touristy Bamberg, lodging costs are comparably favorable. Prices in Nürnberg, however, can be in the big-city class.

Highly recommended hotels are indicated by a star ★.

Dining Small-town and country pubs serve up farmer's wife–size portions of such solid south German dishes such as *Schweinshaxe* (pork knuckle) and *Knödel* (dumplings), often for around DM 10, accompanied by a half liter (almost a pint) of guaranteed-high-quality local beer for about DM 2—something like half of big-city prices.

Highly recommended restaurants are indicated by a star ★.

Shopping Handwoven baskets, hand-blown glass, and various kinds of gingerbead cookies (*Lebkuchen*)—inexpensive items useful as keepsakes or gifts—are specialties of this region. *See* the listings under each town, *below*, for particulars.

Hiking and Biking The area between Bamberg and Bayreuth is particularly well-suited for those who enjoy getting away under their own steam. There are countless marked walking and biking trails along quiet lanes and through forests. Bicycles can be hired at the following train stations: **Bamberg** (tel. 0951/832–325), **Bayreuth** (tel. 0921/282–360), **Coburg** (tel. 09561/7721), **Forcheim** (tel. 09191/1707), **Kulmbach** (tel. 09221/2705), **Staffelstein** (tel. 09573/266), and **Würzburg** (tel. 0931/34321).

If you are visiting in midsummer, it's advisable to reserve bikes in advance. You can usually collect your bike at one station and drop it off at any other station.

Festivals For lovers of opera, and especially of Wagner, a visit to Franconia in July, when the annual Wagner Festival takes place in Bayreuth, is a major event (*see* Bayreuth, *below*). But a word of warning: Tickets to performances are hard to come by, and they can be astronomically expensive.

Highlights for First-time Visitors

Altes Rathaus, Bamberg (*see* Tour 2)
The *Bamberg Rider* statue, Bamberg (*see* Tour 2)
Dürer's House, Nürnberg (*see* Tour 1)
The Markgräfliche's Opera House, Bayreuth (*see* Tour 1)
Medieval town center, Rothenburg-ob-der-Tauber (*see* Tour 1)
Residenz, Würzburg (*see* Tour 1)
Vierzehnheiligen Pilgrimage Church (*see* Tour 2)

Franconia

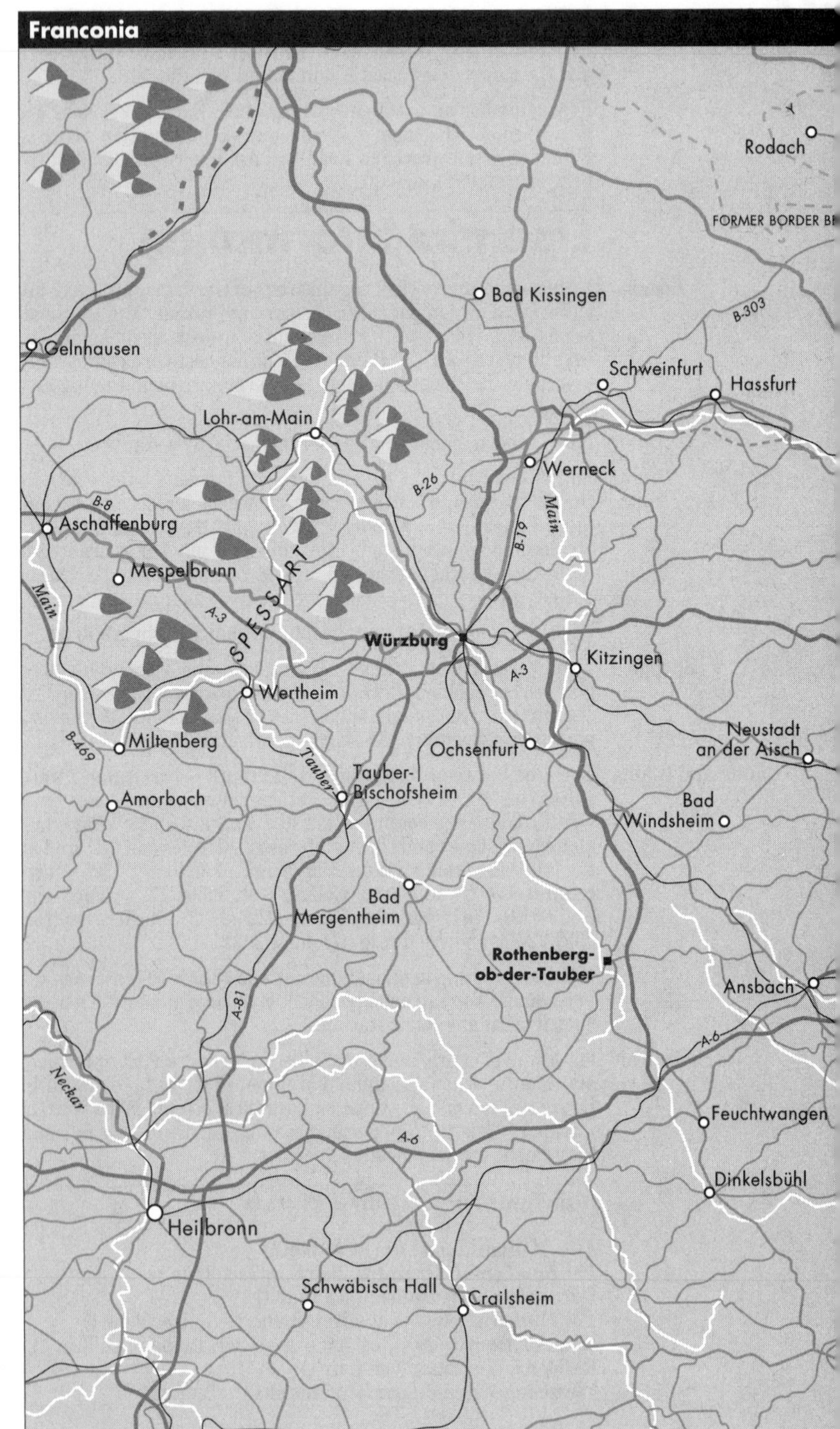

Rodach
FORMER BORDER B
Bad Kissingen
B-303
Gelnhausen
Schweinfurt
Hassfurt
Lohr-am-Main
Werneck
B-26
Main
B-8
Aschaffenburg
B-19
SPESSART
Mespelbrunn
Main
A-3
Würzburg
Kitzingen
A-3
Wertheim
Neustadt
an der Aisch
B-469
Miltenberg
Ochsenfurt
Tauber
Tauber-
Bischofsheim
Amorbach
Bad
Windsheim
Bad
Mergentheim
Rothenberg-
ob-der-Tauber
Ansbach
A-81
A-6
Neckar
Feuchtwangen
A-6
Dinkelsbühl
Heilbronn
Schwäbisch Hall
Crailsheim

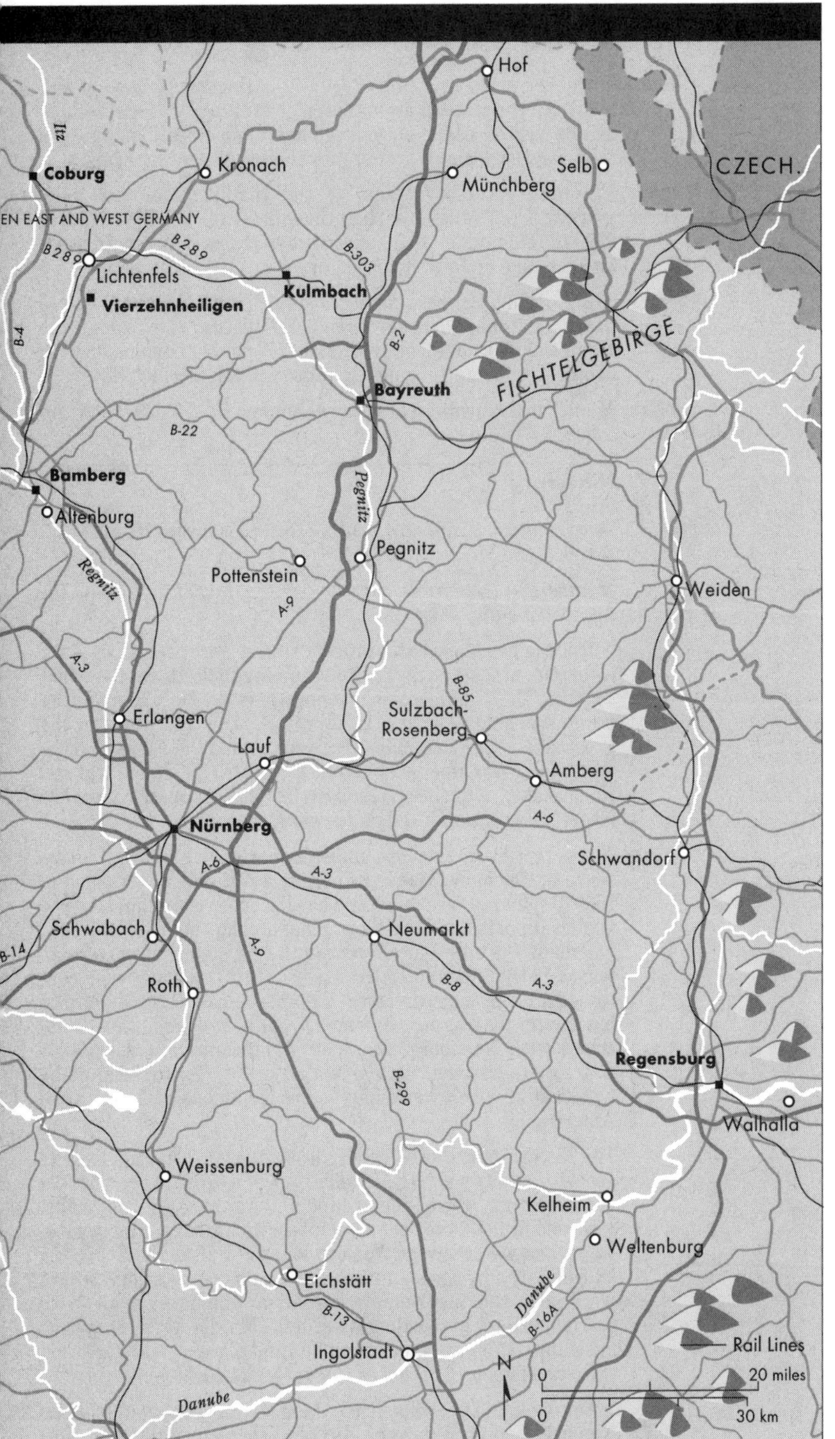
Hof
Coburg
Kronach
Selb
CZECH.
Münchberg
EN EAST AND WEST GERMANY
B289
B289
B-303
Lichtenfels
Kulmbach
Vierzehnheiligen
B-4
B-2
FICHTELGEBIRGE
Bayreuth
B-22
Bamberg
Altenburg
Pegnitz
Regnitz
Pegnitz
Pottenstein
A-9
Weiden
A-3
B-85
Sulzbach-Rosenberg
Erlangen
Lauf
Amberg
A-6
Nürnberg
Schwandorf
A-6
A-3
Schwabach
Neumarkt
B-14
A-9
B-8
A-3
Roth
Regensburg
B-299
Walhalla
Weissenburg
Kelheim
Weltenburg
Eichstätt
Danube
B-13
B-16A
Rail Lines
Ingolstadt
N
0
20 miles
0
30 km
Danube

Tour 1: Nürnberg

Nürnberg is the second largest city in Bavaria (following Munich). All the attractions in this city tour are close together and can be visited easily on foot; good train connections link you with Bayreuth and Würzburg for the suggested day trips.

From Munich
By Train Frequent InterCity trains do the 165-kilometer (103-mile) journey from Munich's Hauptbahnhof (tel. 089/239–1256 or 239–1257) in under two hours. Other trains make more stops and can take up to an hour longer.

By Bus A Europabus Express connects Munich with Nürnberg once a day. The bus leaves from Arnulfstrasse, beside the Hauptbahnhof, and the trip takes 2½ hours. For information contact Deutsche Touring, Arnulfstr. 3, tel. 089/591–824.

By Car Munich and Nürnberg are directly linked by the A-9 (E-45) autobahn.

Nürnberg

Tourist office: Frauentorgraben 3, 8500 Nürnberg 70, tel. 0911/ 23360.

Numbers in the margin correspond to points of interest on the Nürnberg map.

Nürnberg has played a significant role in German history since its origin, at least as far back as the year 1040. It was here that the first "diet," or meeting of rulers, of every Holy Roman Emperor was held. And it was here, too, that Hitler staged the greatest and most grandiose Nazi rallies and the Allies held the war trials. Wartime bombing destroyed much of medieval and Renaissance Nürnberg, though faithful reconstruction has largely re-created the city's prewar atmosphere.

Albrecht Dürer, the first indisputable genius of the Renaissance in Germany, was born here in 1471, and he returned in 1509 to spend the rest of his life here. Earlier the minnesingers, medieval poets and musicians, chief among them Tannhäuser, had made the city a focal point in the development of German music. In the 15th and 16th centuries their traditions were continued by the meistersingers. Both groups were celebrated much later by Wagner. Among a great host of inventions associated with Nürnberg, the most significant were the pocket watch, gun casting, the clarinet, and the geographical globe (the first of which was made before Columbus discovered the Americas).

The historic heart of Nürnberg is compact; all principal sights are within easy walking distance. To get a sense of the city, begin your tour by walking around all or part of the **city walls.** Finished in 1452, they come complete with moats, sturdy gate-
1 ways, and watchtowers. You can join the wall at the **Königstor** (Royal Gate), by the Hauptbahnhof (main train station), where you'll also see the **Handwerkerhof,** a "medieval mall" with craftsmen busy pretending it's still the Middle Ages. They turn out puppets, baskets, pewter mugs and plates, glassware, and the city's famous *Lebkuchen* (gingerbread cookies).

After walking the walls, leave them at Königstor and head up
2 Königstrasse to **St. Lorenz Kirche.** This beautiful church was

Albrecht-Dürer-Haus, **11**
Alt-Stadt-Museum, **9**
Altes Rathaus, **7**
Frauenkirche, **5**
Gansemännchen-brunnen, **8**
Germanisches Nationalmuseum, **13**
Helig-Geist-Spital, **3**
Kaiserburg, **10**
Königstor, **1**
St. Lorenz Kirche, **2**
St. Sebaldus Kirche, **6**
Schöner Brunnen, **4**
Spielzeug Museum, **12**
Verkehrsmuseum, **14**

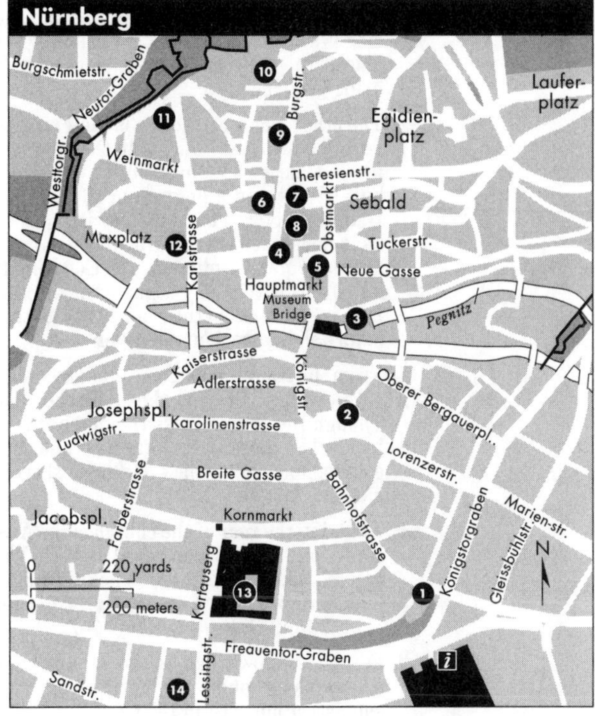

begun around 1220 and completed about 1475. It's a sizable church; two towers flank the main entrance, which is covered with a forest of carving. In the lofty interior, note the works by sculptors Adam Kraft and Veit Stoss: Kraft's great stone tabernacle to the left of the altar and Stoss's *Annunciation* at the east end of the nave are considered their finest works. There are many other carvings throughout the building, a fitting testimonial to the artistic richness of late-medieval Nürnberg.

From the church, walk up to the Hauptmarkt, crossing the little museum bridge over the Pegnitz River. To your right, set on
3 graceful arcades over the river, is the **Helig-Geist-Spital** (Holy
Ghost Hospital), begun in 1381. It's worth looking into the courtyard to admire its elegant wood balconies and spacious arcades. Continue the few paces to the **Hauptmarkt** (Main Market). Like Munich's Viktualienmarkt, Nürnberg's market is more than just a place to do the shopping. Its colorful stands, piled high with produce and shaded by striped awnings, are a central part of the city. The red-armed market women are a formidable-looking bunch, dispensing flowers, fruit, and abuse in about equal measure. It's here that the Christkindlmarkt is held in December.

There are two principal sights in the market. One is the
4 **Schöner Brunnen** ("Beautiful Fountain"). It's an elegant, 60-
foot-high Gothic fountain carved around the year 1400, looking for all the world as though it should be on the summit of some lofty Gothic cathedral. Thirty figures arranged in tiers stand sentinel on it. They include prophets, saints, local noblemen, sundry electors of the Holy Roman Empire, and one or two

strays, such as Julius Caesar and Alexander the Great. A gold ring is set into the railing surrounding the fountain, reputedly placed there by an apprentice carver. Stroking it is said to bring good luck.

5 The other major attraction is the **Frauenkirche** (Church of Our Lady), which was built, with the approval of Holy Roman Emperor Charles IV, in 1350 on the site of a synagogue that burned down in a pogrom in 1349. (The area covered by the Hauptmarkt was once the Jewish quarter of the city.) These days, most visitors are drawn not so much by the church itself as by the **Männleinlaufen,** a clock dating from 1500 that's set in its facade. Every day at noon the electors of the Holy Roman Empire glide out of the clock to bow to the Emperor Charles IV before sliding back under cover.

From the Hauptmarkt, continue the short distance north to the
6 13th-century **St. Sebaldus Kirche,** on Sebaldkircheplatz. Though the church lacks the number of art treasures boasted by rival St. Lorenz, its lofty nave and choir are among the purest examples of Gothic ecclesiastical architecture in Germany: elegant, tall, and airy.

7 Abutting the rear of the church is the **Altes Rathaus** (Old Town Hall), built in 1332, destroyed in World War II, and subsequently painstakingly restored. Visit its dungeons, hacked from the underground rock. *Rathauspl. Admission: DM 2. Open May–Sept., Mon.–Sat. 10–4, Sun. 10–1.*

8 Facing the town hall is the bronze **Gansemännchenbrunnen** (Gooseman's Fountain). It's an elegant work of great technical sophistication, cast in 1550.

Walk north from the Altes Rathaus along Burgstrasse. On your
9 left you'll pass the Fembohaus, now the **Alt-Stadt-Museum** (Old City Museum). It's one of the finest Renaissance mansions in Nürnberg, a dignified, patrician dwelling completed in 1598. The story of the city is told in its museum. *Burgstr. Admission: DM 2. Open year-round, Tues.–Fri. and Sun. 10–5, Sat. 10–1.*

At the end of Burgstrasse you'll reach Nürnberg's number-one
10 sight, the **Kaiserburg** (the Imperial Castle). This immense cluster of buildings, standing just inside the city walls, was the residence of the Holy Roman Emperors. Impressive rather than beautiful, the complex comprises three separate groups of buildings. The oldest, dating from around 1050, is the **Burggrafenburg,** the Burgrave's Castle, with a craggy, ruined seven-sided tower and bailiff's house. It stands in the center of the complex. To the east is the **Kaiserstallung** (Imperial Stables). These were built in the 15th century as a granary, then converted into a youth hostel after the war. The real interest, however, centers on the Imperial Castle itself, the westernmost part of the fortress. The standout feature here is the Renaissance **Doppelkappelle** (Double Chapel). The lower part of the chapel was used by the castle minions and is accordingly austere, befitting their lowly status. The adjoining upper part, correspondingly richer, larger, and more ornate, was where the emperor and his family worshipped. Visit also the **Rittersaal** (Knight's Hall) and the **Kaisersaal** (Throne Room). Their heavy oak beams, painted ceilings, and sparse interiors have changed little since they were built in the 15th century.

Descending from the west part of the castle, walk across the
11 cobbled square to the **Albrecht-Dürer-Haus,** located opposite the Tiergärtner gate. This was the home of the great German painter from 1509 to his death in 1528. It is also about the best-preserved late-medieval house in the city, typical of the prosperous merchants' homes that once filled Nürnberg. *Albrecht-Dürer-Str. 39. Admission: DM 3.50 adults, DM 2 children and senior citizens. Open Mar.–Oct. and Christkindlmarkt, Tues. and Thurs.–Sun. 10–5, Wed. 9–5; Nov.–Feb., Tues., Thurs., and Fri. 10–5, Wed. 9–1.*

12 The **Spielzeug Museum** (Toy Museum) is located on Sigmundstrasse. To reach it, walk down the street that runs past Dürer's house. One or two exhibits date from the Renaissance; most, however, are from the 19th century. Simple dolls vie with mechanical toys of extraordinary complexity. There's even a little Ferris wheel. *Sigmundstr. 220. Admission: DM 3 adults, DM 1.50 children. Open Tues. and Thurs.–Sun. 10–5, Wed. 10–9.*

13 A final sight in the historic area is the **Germanisches Nationalmuseum** (Germanic National Museum), located close by the Hauptbahnhof. It is the largest of its kind in Germany, and about the best-arranged. The setting gets everything off to a flying start; the museum is located in what was once a Carthusian monastery, complete with cloisters and monastic outbuildings. Few aspects of German culture, from the Stone Age to the 19th century, are not covered here, and quantity and quality are evenly matched. *Kornmarkt. Admission: DM 3 adults, DM 1 children. Open Tues., Wed., and Fri.–Sun. 9–5, Thurs. 8 AM–9:30 PM.*

14 Children love the **Verkehrsmuseum** (Transportation Museum), located just south of the National Museum outside the city walls. It houses original 19th- and early 20th-century trains and stagecoaches, along with some 40,000-odd stamps in the extensive exhibits on the German postage system. *Lessingstr. 6. Admission: DM 4 adults, DM 2 children. Open Apr.–Sept., Mon.–Sat. 10–5, Sun. 10–4; Oct.–Mar., daily 10–4.*

Lodging
Under DM 180

Deutscher Hof. A short walk to the left of the main train station on the fringes of the old town, this comfortable modern hotel is ideally located for a short visit. *Frauentorgraben 29, tel. 0911/203–821. 48 rooms, 35 with bath. Facilities: 2 restaurants. AE, DC, MC, V.*

Under DM 130

Am Josephsplatz. This lodging in the heart of the old town has been accommodating visitors for more than 150 years. It was completely renovated in 1987, and now the rooms are stylishly modern. *Josephsplatz 30, tel. 0911/241–156. 35 rooms with bath. AE, DC, MC.*

Steichele. An old wine tavern owned and managed by the same family for three generations, the Steichele is centrally located a short walk from the train station just off Jakobsplatz. Rooms have a warm Old World air. *Knorrstr. 2, tel. 0911/204–377. 52 rooms, 40 with bath. Facilities: restaurant. AE, DC, MC, V.*

Under DM 90

Alte Messehalle. This is a small, modest but pleasant hotel overlooking a park and only a short walk from the old town. *Am Stadtpark 5, tel. 0911/533–366. 57 room. AE, DC, MC, V.*

Burg-Hotel Kleines Haus. Standing under the shadow of the castle, this bargain lodging offers the comforts of a private home while providing some upscale facilities. *Schildgasse 16,* *tel. 0911/203–040. 22 rooms, 18 with bath. Facilities: indoor pool, sauna, solarium. AE, DC, MC, V.*

Pfälzer Hof. A comfortable little guest house inside the old city walls, just a short walk from the main train station, the Pfälzer adjoins the German National Museum. *Am Gräslein 10, tel. 0911/221–411. 20 rooms, 8 with bath. No credit cards. Closed Christmas–mid-Jan.*

Dining

Under DM 40

Nassauer Keller. The exposed-beam-and-plaster decor complements the resolutely traditional cooking. The restaurant has a memorable location in the cellar of a 12th-century tower by the church of St. Lorenz. *Karolinenstr. 2–4, tel. 0911/225–967. Reservations advised. Jacket and tie required. AE, DC, MC.*

Under DM 30

Böhms Herrenkeller. A colorful and historic old-town wine tavern serving traditional Franconian dishes of fresh river fish and game (in season), it's in a building that dates from the late-15th century. *Theatergasse 19, tel. 0911/224–465. DC, MC, V. Closed Sat.*

Königshof. One of Franconia's oldest wine taverns, dating from 1560, and now under the protection of a building preservation law, this restaurant offers a big selection of Franconian dishes, but the best value is the *Mittagsmenüs*, three-course lunch specials. *Zirkelschmiedsgasse 28, tel. 0911/227–678. AE, DC. Closed Mon.*

Under DM 20

Bratwurstglöcklein. Handily located in the Handwerkerhof, opposite the main train station, at the start of our Nürnberg tour, this restaurant keeps prices on main-course meals under DM 12.50. In summer you can sit outside in the beer garden. *Handwerkerhof am Königstor, tel. 0911/227–625. No credit cards. Open till 9 PM. Closed Sun., public holidays, Christmas–Mar. 21.*

Bratwurst Haüsle. There are few better places to try Nürnberg's famous grilled sausages than this dark, wood-paneled old inn. The mood is noisy and cheerful. *Rathauspl. 1, tel. 0911/227–695. No credit cards. Closed Sun.*

★ **Helig-Geist-Spital.** Heavy wood furnishings and a choice of more than 100 wines makes this authentic and picturesque wine tavern a popular spot for visitors. It may be touristy, but it's the real thing for all that. *Spitalgasse 16, tel. 0911/221–761. AE, DC, MC, V.*

Zur Schranke. This ancient beer tavern beside the old town wall has just about the cheapest menu in town—a big list of basic Bavarian dishes. *Beim Tiergärtnertor 3, tel. 0911/225–474. No credit cards. Closed Sun., Oct., Christmas.*

Splurge

★ **Romantik-Restaurant Rottner.** Located in the Grossreuth-Schweinau suburb, southwest of the city center, the gingerbread-house exterior is a foretaste of the delights in this family-run inn. The nouvelle style prevails here, even in regional dishes. Expect to pay up to DM 50 per person for three courses without drinks. *Winterstr. 15, tel. 0911/612032. MC. Closed Sat. lunch, Sun., and Dec. 27–Jan. 31.*

Shopping

Across from the main train station is the famous **Handwerkerhof** (Handicraft Court). It has many shops where engravers, glassblowers, silversmiths, goldsmiths, and other artisans make their wares. You can watch them work and buy examples of their art. (The market is closed Christmas–March 20.) For a wide range of souvenirs, try **Elsässer** (Königstr.).

Department stores and bakeries sell Nürnberg's famous *Lebkuchen* (gingerbread cookies).

Bayreuth

A regular train service connects Nürnberg with this music-festival town. The trip, a little more than an hour, meanders through some of Franconia's finest countryside. Tourist office: Luitpoldplatz 7–9, 8580 Bayreuth, tel. 0921/88588.

Bayreuth (pronounced By-roit) is the small town where Richard Wagner finally settled after a lifetime of rootless shifting through Europe, and here he built his great theater, the Festspielhaus, as a suitable setting for his grandiose and heroic operas. The annual Wagner Festival, first held in 1876, brings the town to a halt as hordes of Wagner lovers descend on Bayreuth, pushing prices sky-high and filling hotels to bursting. The festival is usually held in July, so unless you plan to visit the town specifically for it, this is the time to stay away. Likewise, those whose tastes do not include opera and the theater will find little here to divert them.

Wagner and his wife Cosima, daughter of the composer Franz Liszt, lie buried in the garden of the **Wahnfried,** the home Wagner constructed for them in 1874. Today the austere neoclassical building, just south of the town center, is a museum. At 10, noon, and 2, excerpts from Wagner's operas are played in the living room. *Richard-Wagner-Str. 48. Admission: DM 2.50 adults (DM 3.50 in July and Aug.), DM 1 children. Open daily 9–5.*

From the museum, you are close to the **Neues Schloss** (New Palace). If Wagner is the man most closely associated with Bayreuth, then it's well to remember that had it not been for the woman who built this glamorous 18th-century palace, he would never have come here in the first place. The Margravina Wilhelmina, sister of Frederick the Great of Prussia, devoured books; wrote plays and operas (which she directed and, of course, acted in); and built, transforming much of the town and bringing it near bankruptcy. Her distinctive touch is much in evidence in the wild flights of Rococo decoration. *Ludwigstr. 21. Admission: DM 3 adults, DM 1.50 children. Open Apr.–Sept., daily 10–noon and 1:30–4:30; Oct.–Mar., daily 1:30–3:30.*

Wilhelmina's other great architectural legacy is the **Markgräfliche's Opernhaus** (Margravina's Opera House), just a step or two from the New Palace. Built between 1745 and 1748, it is a Rococo jewel, sumptuously decorated in red, gold, and blue. Apollo and the nine Muses cavort across the frescoed ceiling. *Admission: DM 2 adults, DM 1.50 children. Open Apr.–Sept., daily 9–11:30 and 1:30–4:30; Oct.–Mar., daily 10–11:30 and 1:30–3.*

The **Festspielhaus** stands a mile or so north of the downtown area at the head of Bürgerreutherstrasse. This plain, almost intimidating building is the high temple of Wagner—who conceived, planned, and financed the building specifically as a setting for his monumental operas. Today it is very much the focus of the annual Wagner festival, still masterminded by descendants of the composer. The spartan look is partly explained by Wagner's near-permanent financial crises, partly by his desire to achieve perfect acoustics. For this reason, the wood seats have no upholstering, and the walls are bare of all ornament. *Auf dem Grünen Hügel. Admission: DM 2 adults, DM 1.50 children. Open Jan.–mid-June, Sept., and Nov.–Dec., Tues.–Sun. 10–11:30 and 1:30–3. Closed mid-June–Aug. and in Oct.*

If you want festival tickets (prices are steep, with DM 230 the most expensive seat), write to **Theaterkasse** (Luitpoldpl. 9, 8580 Bayreuth) no later than September preceding the year in which you plan to attend. Then hope for the best—a computer decides (though the more applications you make, the better your chances). If you get tickets, make hotel reservations at once. If you don't get them, you can console yourself with visits to the Markgräfliche's Opernhaus (*see above*); performances are given most nights in July and August. Check with the tourist office for details.

Lodging
Under DM 110

Zum Lohmüle. This friendly old country-style inn with an imposing half-timbered facade stands in the center of town, a short walk from the train station. *Badstr. 37, tel. 0921/63031. 42 rooms, half with bath or shower. Facilities: restaurant. AE, DC, MC. Closed Sept. 1–15.*

Under DM 70

Gasthof Vogel. Centrally located near the Stadthalle, the Vogel offers basic, well-run comfort. There's a noisy beer restaurant and a tree-shaded courtyard. *Friedrichstr. 13, tel. 0921/68268. 8 rooms with bath. restaurant. No credit cards.*

Dining
Under DM 20

Weihenstephan. Long wood tables, copious regional specialties, and beer from the oldest brewery in Germany make this a perennial favorite with tourists and locals. In summer, the flower-strewn and crowded terrace is the place to be. *Bahnhofstr. 5, tel. 0921/82288. Reservations advised. No credit cards.*

Wolffenzacher. The rowdy atmosphere, the city-center location, and the local specialties—this is a great place to try *Schweinshaxe*—make this traditional haunt a good bet. *Badstr. 1, tel. 0921/64522. Reservations advised. MC.*

Würzburg

It takes about 1¼ hours by train to cover the 110 kilometers (69 miles) from Nürnberg to Würzburg. Tourist office: Fremdenverkehrsamt, Haus zum Falken, Marktplatz, tel. 0931/37398.

Würzburg was all but obliterated during World War II in a saturation bombing raid. The date was March 16, 1945—seven weeks before Germany capitulated. Although the bombing lasted no more than 20 minutes, 87% of Würzburg was wiped off the map, with some 4,000 buildings destroyed and at least that many people killed.

Much of what you'll see was rebuilt after the war, and painstaking reconstruction has returned most of the city's famous sights to their former splendor, in many cases using original stones from the bombed-out structures.

The train station stands on the fringes of the rebuilt old town (there's an information office opposite the main entrance on Bismarckstrasse). It's less than a mile along Kaiserstrasse and Theaterstrasse to the **Residenz,** the first and most impressive stop on an easy walking tour of Würzburg. Construction of the Residenz started in 1719 under the brilliant direction of Balthasar Neumann, the German architectural genius of his age. Most of the interior decoration was entrusted to the Italian stuccoist Antonio Bossi and the Venetian painter Giovanni Battista Tiepolo. But the man whose spirit infuses the Residenz is von Schönborn, who unfortunately did not live to see the completion of what has come to be considered the most beautiful palace of Germany's Baroque era and one of Europe's most sumptuous buildings, frequently referred to as the "Palace of Palaces."

Anyone harboring doubts as to whether the prince-bishops of 18th-century Würzburg were bishops first and princes only incidentally will have them swept aside in a hurry. The Residenz is irrefutable evidence of the worldly power of these glamorous rulers and men of God.

From the moment you enter the building, the splendor of the Residenz is evident, as the largest Baroque staircase in the country, the **Treppenhaus,** stretches away from you into the heights. Halfway to the second floor, the stairway splits and peels away at 180 degrees to the left and right.

Dominating the upper reaches of this vast space is Tiepolo's giant fresco of **The Four Continents,** a gorgeous exercise in blue and pink with allegorical figures at the corners representing the continents (only four were known of at the time).

Next, make your way to the **Weissersaal** (the White Room) and then beyond to the grandest of the state rooms, the **Kaisersaal** (Throne Room). The Baroque/Rococo ideal of *Gesamtkunstwerk*—the fusion of the arts—is illustrated to perfection here. Architecture melts into stucco, stucco invades the frescoes, the frescoes extend the real space of the room into their fantasy world. Nothing is quite what it seems, and no expense was spared to make it so. Tiepolo's frescoes show the visit of the Emperor Frederick Barbarossa to Würzburg in the 12th century to claim his bride. The fact that the characters all wear 16th-century Venetian dress hardly seems to matter. Few interiors anywhere use such startling opulence to similar effect. The room is airy, magical, intoxicating. You'll find more of this same expansive spirit in the **Hofkirche,** the chapel, which offers further proof that the prince-bishops experienced little or no conflict between their love of ostentation and their service to God. Among the lavish marbles, rich gilding, and delicate stuccowork, note the Tiepolo altarpieces, ethereal visions of *The Fall of the Angels* and *The Assumption of the Virgin*. Finally, tour the palace garden, the **Hofgarten;** the entrance is next to the chapel. This 18th-century formal garden, with its stately gushing fountains and trim, ankle-high shrubs outlining geometrical flower beds and gravel walks, is the equal of any in the country. *Admission, including guided tour: DM 3.50 adults, DM 2.50 students over 14 and senior citizens, DM 1.50 children. Open Apr.–Sept., Tues.–Sun. 9–5; Oct.–Mar., Tues.–Sun. 10–4.*

To the left is Würzburg's attractive pedestrian shopping area, Schönbornstrasse, named after the bishop who commissioned Neumann to build the Residenz. On the left as you enter the street is another example of Neumann's work, the distinctive Baroque **Augustinerkirche** (Church of St. Augustine). The church was a 13th-century Dominican chapel; Neumann's additions date from the early 18th century. At the end of Schönbornstrasse is Würzburg's Romanesque cathedral, the **Dom,** begun in 1045. Step inside and you'll find yourself, somewhat disconcertingly, in a shimmering Rococo treasure house. This is, perhaps, only fitting: Prince-Bishop von Schönborn, who came up with the concept of the Residenz, is buried here.

Alongside the cathedral is the **Neumünster,** built above the grave of the early Irish martyr St. Kilian, who brought Christianity to Würzburg and, with two companions, was put to death here in 689. Their missionary zeal bore fruit, however, for 17 years after their death, a church was consecrated in their memory. By 742, Würzburg had become a diocese; over the following centuries 39 churches flourished throughout the city. Once an abbey church, the Neumünster's former cloistered churchyard contains the grave of Walther von der Vogelweide, the most famous minstrel in German history.

Across the pedestrian zone toward the river lies Würzburg's market square, the **Markt,** with shady trees and a framework of historic old facades. At one end, flanked by a Rococo mansion, are the soaring late-Gothic windows of the 14th- to 15th-century **Marienkapelle** (St. Mary's Chapel), where architect Balthasar Neumann lies buried. Pause beneath its finely carved portal and inspect the striking figures of Adam and Eve; you shouldn't have great difficulty recognizing the style of Tilman Riemenschneider. The original statues are in Würzburg's museum, the Mainfränkische Museum, on the Marienberg, across the river; the ones in the portal of the Marienkapelle are copies.

On your explorations along the edge of the pedestrian zone and market square note the exquisite "house Madonnas," small statues of the Virgin set into corner niches on the second level of many old homes. So many of these lovely representations of the city's patron saint can be seen that Würzburg is frequently referred to as "the town of Madonnas."

On the way to the **Marienburg Fortress,** you'll cross the Old Main Bridge, already standing before Columbus sighted America. Among the city's glories are the twin rows of infinitely graceful statues of saints that line the bridge. Note particularly the *Patronna Franconiae (Weeping Madonna)*. There's also a great view of the fortress from the bridge.

To reach the Marienburg, you can make the fairly stiff climb on foot or take the bus from the Old Main Bridge. It runs every half hour starting at 9:45 AM.

The Marienburg was the original home of the prince-bishops, beginning in the 13th century. The oldest buildings—note especially the **Marienkirche,** the core of the complex—date from even earlier, around 700. In addition to the rough-hewn medieval fortifications, there are a number of fine Renaissance and Baroque apartments. The highlight of a visit to the Marienburg is the **Mainfränkische Museum** (the Main-Franconian Museum). The rich and varied history of Würzburg is brought alive by this remarkable collection of art treasures. The standout is the gallery devoted to Würzburg-born Renaissance sculptor Tilman Riemenschneider, including the originals of the great Adam and Eve statues, copies of which adorn the portal of the Marienkapelle. You'll also be exposed to fine paintings by Tiepolo and Cranach the Elder, and to exhibits of porcelain, firearms, antique toys, and ancient Greek and Roman art. *Admission to Marienburg Fortress: DM 2 adults, DM 1 students* *over 14 and senior citizens. Open Apr.–Sept., Tues.–Sun. 9–noon and 1–5; Oct.–Mar., Tues.–Sun. 10–noon and 1–5. Admission to Mainfränkische Museum: DM 2.80 adults, DM 2 students over 14. Open Apr.–Oct., daily 10–5; Nov.–Mar., daily 10–4.*

Lodging
Under DM 130

Franziskaner. This comfortable and friendly family-run hotel is centrally located; it's only a two-minute walk from the city's pedestrian shopping area. *Franziskanerpl. 2, tel. 0931/15001. 47 rooms, most with bath or shower. AE, DC, MC, V.*

Dining
Under DM 30

Juliusspital Weinstuben. The food here—predominantly hearty Franconian specialties—takes second billing to the excellent wine from the tavern's own vineyard. *Juliuspromenade 19, tel. 0931/54080. Reservations advised. No credit cards. Closed Wed. and Feb.*

Under DM 20

Backofele. More than 400 years of tradition sustain this historic old tavern. You can dine well on oxtail in Burgundy sauce or homemade rissoles in wild mushroom sauce. *Ursulinergasse 2, tel. 0931/59059. Reservations advised. No credit cards.*

Stadt Mainz. Recipes from the original proprietor's own cookbook, dated 1850, form the basis of the imaginative fish-dominated menu of the Stadt Mainz hotel's restaurant. *Semmelstr. 39, tel. 0931/53155. Reservations advised on weekends. No credit cards. Closed Sun. dinner and Mon., and Dec. 20–Jan. 20.*

Lodging and Dining
Under DM 130

Strauss. Close to the river and the pedestrians-only center, this lodging has been run by the same family for more than 100 years. The emphasis is on clean, simple comforts. The restaurant, which is in the Under DM 40 range, specializes in Franconian cuisine. *Juliuspromenade 5, tel. 0931/42085. 77 rooms, many with shower. AE, DC, MC, V. Closed Dec. 20–Feb. 1.*

The Arts

Every June Würzburg hosts a Mozart festival on the grounds of the Residenz. Contact the tourist office (*see above*) for details. Würzburg's music school orchestra gives regular performances; call 0931/37436 for details and tickets.

Rothenburg-ob-der-Tauber

This stunning medieval town is 95 minutes from Nürnberg by train; change at Steinach. Trains run every 90 minutes or so, but it's best to check the schedule in advance. Tourist office: Rathaus, Marktplatz 2, tel. 09861/40492.

Numbers in the margin correspond to points of interest on the Rothenburg-ob-der-Touber map.

Rothenburg-ob-der-Tauber (literally, "the red castle on the River Tauber") is the kind of gemlike medieval town that even Walt Disney might have thought too good to be true, with gingerbread architecture galore and a wealth of fountains and flowers against a backdrop of towers and turrets. Rothenburg was a small but thriving 17th-century town that had grown up around the ruins of two 12th-century churches. Then it was laid low by the havoc of the Thirty Years' War, the cataclysmic religious struggle that all but destroyed Germany in the 17th century. Its economic base was devastated, and the town slumbered until modern tourism rediscovered it. Nowadays it milks its "best-preserved-medieval-town-in-Europe" image to the full, undoubtedly something of a tourist trap, but genuine enough for all that.

1 Begin your visit by walking around the **city walls,** more than a
mile long. Stairs every 200 or 300 yards provide ready access.
There are great views of the tangle of pointed and tiled roofs,
2 and of the rolling country beyond. Then make for the **Rathaus**
(Town Hall), the logical place to begin an exploration of Rothenburg itself. Half the building is Gothic, begun in 1240, the other half classical, begun in 1572. A fire in 1501 destroyed part of the structure, hence the newer, Renaissance section, which faces the main square. Go inside to see the **Historiengewölbe,** a museum housed in the vaults below the building that charts Rothenburg's role in the Thirty Years' War. Great prominence is given to the Meistertrunk (Master Drink). This event will follow you around Rothenburg. It came about when the Protestant town was captured by Catholic forces. During the victory celebrations, so the story goes, the conquering general was embarrassed to find himself unable to drink a six-pint tankard of wine in one go, as his manhood demanded. He volunteered to spare the town further destruction if any of the city councillors could drain the mighty draught. The mayor, a man by the name of Nusch, took up the challenge and succeeded, and Rothenburg was preserved. The tankard itself is on display at the Reichsstadtmuseum (*see below*). On the north side of the main square is a mechanical figure that acts out the epic Master Drink daily at 11 AM and 3 PM; and the town holds an annual pageant celebrating the feat, with townsfolk parading the streets dressed in 17th-century garb. *Rathauspl. Admission: DM 2 adults, DM 1 children. Open mid-Mar.–Oct., daily 9–6.*

3 Just north of the town hall is the **Stadtpfarrkirche St. Jakob** (parish church of St. James), the repository of further works by Tilman Riemenschneider, including the famous Heiliges Blut (Holy Blood) altar. Above the altar a crystal capsule is said to contain drops of Christ's blood. The church has other items of interest, including three fine stained-glass windows in the choir dating from the 14th and 15th centuries and the famous Herlin-Altar, with its 15th-century painted panels. *Open Easter–Oct., daily 9–5; Nov.–Easter, daily 10–noon and 2–4.*

4 Another of Rothenburg's churches, **St. Wolfgang's,** is built into the defenses of the town. From within the town it looks like a peaceful parish church; from outside it blends into the forbidding city wall. Through an underground passage you can reach the sentry walk above and follow the wall for almost its entire length.

5 Two museums you won't want to miss are the **Mittelalterliches**
6 **Kriminalmuseum** and the **Puppen und Spielzeugmuseum.** The
former sets out to document the history of German legal processes in the Middle Ages and contains an impressive array of instruments of torture. The latter is an enchanting doll and toy museum housed in a 15th-century building near the Rathaus. There are 300 dolls, the oldest dating from 1780, the newest from 1940. *Mittelalterliches Kriminalmuseum: Burggasse 3. Admission: DM 3.50 adults, DM 2 children. Open Apr.–Oct., daily 10–6; Nov.–Mar., daily 2–4. Puppen und Spielzeugmuseum: Hofronnengasse 13. Admission: DM 3.50 adults, DM 1.50 children. Open Mar.–Dec., daily 10–6; Jan.–Feb., daily 11–5.*

City Walls, **1**
Herterlichbrunnen, **8**
Mittelalterliches Kriminalmuseum, **5**
Puppen und Spielzeugmuseum, **6**
Rathaus, **2**
Reichsstadt-museum, **7**
St. Wolfgang's, **4**
Stadtpfarrkirche St. Jakob, **3**

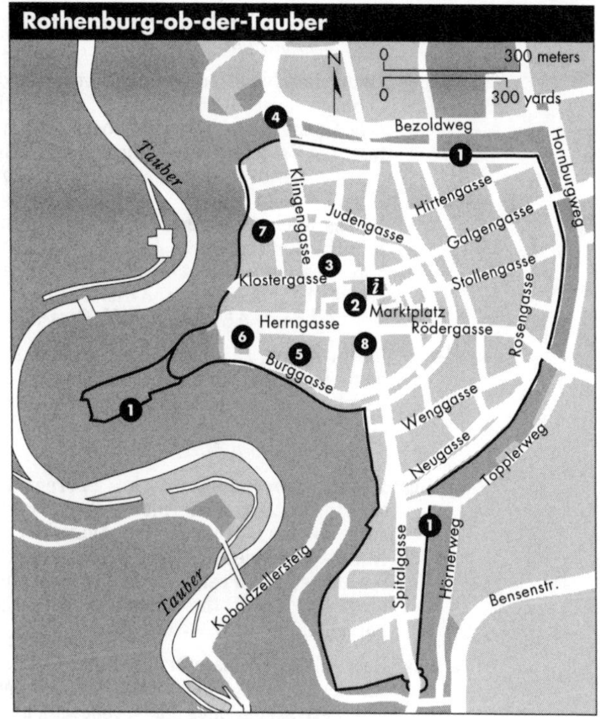

7 The **Reichsstadtmuseum** (Imperial City Museum) turns out to be two attractions in one. It's the city museum and contains artifacts that illustrate Rothenburg and its history. Among them is the great tankard, or *Pokal*, of the Meistertrunk. The setting of the museum is the other attraction; it's a former convent, the oldest parts of which date from the 13th century. Tour the building to see the cloister, the kitchens, and the dormitory, then see the collections. *Hofronnengasse 13. Admission: DM 3.50 adults, DM 1.50 children. Open Mar.–Dec., daily 10:00–6; Jan.–Feb., daily 11–5.*

8 Cobbled Hofronnengasse runs into the Marktplatz (Market Square), site of an ornate Renaissance fountain, the **Herterlichbrunnen.** To celebrate some momentous event—the end of a war, say, or the passing of an epidemic—the *Schäfertanz* (Shepherds' Dance) was performed around the fountain. The dance is still done, though for the benefit of tourists rather than to commemorate the end of a threat to Rothenburg. It takes place in front of the Rathaus several times a year, chiefly at Easter, in late May, and throughout June and July.

Lodging
Under DM 130

Klosterstüble. Nestling in the shadow of a church and dating from the 16th century, this attractive historic house was renovated recently to include late-20th-century comforts. *Heringsbronnengasse 5, tel. 09861/6774. 14 rooms with bath. Facilities: restaurant. DC, MC, V.*

Zum Rappen. Close to one of the town's gates, the Würzburger Tor, this long-established tavern offers modest comforts but central location at reasonable prices. *Würzburger Tor 6, tel.*

09861/6071. 70 rooms, some with shower. Facilities: restaurant, beer garden, wine bar. AE, DC, MC, V. Closed Jan.

Dining
Under DM 30
★

Baumeisterhaus. In summer, you can dine in one of Rothenburg's loveliest courtyards; if the weather's cooler, move inside to the paneled dining room. The menu, changed daily, features Bavarian and Franconian specialties. *Obere Schmiedgasse 3, tel. 09861/3404. Reservations advised. AE, DC, MC, V.*

Reichs-Küchenmeister. Master chefs in the service of the Holy Roman Emperor were the inspiration for the name of this hotel-restaurant. Test the skills of the present chef by ordering any of the game dishes. *Kirchpl. 8, tel. 09861/2046. Reservations advised. AE, DC, MC, V. Closed Tues. Nov.–Mar.*

Under DM 20

Markusturm. This old hostelry close to the Rathaus takes its name from the ruins of the town's first defensive walls, along which the inn is built. You'll find traditional Franconian dishes and freshwater fish. *Rödergasse 1, tel. 09861/2370. AE, V. Closed Feb.–mid-Mar.*

Shopping

Hummel **porcelain** figures are a perennial favorite among visitors to this area of Germany. Prices vary dramatically, so be sure to shop around. Try **Unger's** (Herrngasse) and the **Kunstwerke Friese** (Grüner Markt, near the Rathaus). The latter also stocks a selection of the beautifully crafted porcelain birds made by the Hummel manufacturers, the Goebel Porzellanfabrik.

The Arts

Rothenburg's Meistertrunk drama festival, in June, celebrates the town's log-ago deliverance from conquest and destruction. The festival combines plays, concerts, and carnival-like attractions.

Tour 2: Bamberg

Bamberg, one of Germany's most historic cities, was already a seat of the Holy Roman Empire in the early 11th century. Today a number of architectural memorials recall this imperial past. The centerpiece is the huge Romanesque cathedral on its commanding hill, but equally fascinating is the jumble of medieval streets and the later architectural jewels clustered below them. This compact city, which once boasted it had more breweries than church towers (it still has 10), lies in the heart of Franconia. It's an ideal base from which to visit the nearby towns of Kulmbach and Coburg and the magnificent Rococo church known as Vierzehnheiligen.

From Munich
By Train

Direct service throughout the day links Munich with Bamberg, but some trains can be slow, with the 240-kilometer (150-mile) journey lasting almost three hours. A faster alternative is to take an InterCity express train to Nürnberg and then switch to a local for the remaining 70 kilometers (44 miles).

By Car

Autobahns cover the entire 230-kilometer (145-mile) journey. Take the A-9 (E-45) to Nürnberg, and then the A-73.

Bamberg

Tourist office: Hauptwachestr. 16, 8600 Bamberg, tel. 0951/21040.

With all its chief attractions inside a one-mile square, this is an ideal town for exploring on foot or by bicycle (*see* Hiking and Biking, *above*), although some of the imperial buildings, including the cathedral, are situated on a steep hill. The train station is in the 19th-century part of the town, a mile and a half from the historic heart. Much of old Bamberg stands on an island in the River Pegnitz, and it's among this jumble of streets that you'll find the **tourist office** (Hauptwachestr. 16)—a good place to start your tour. Stroll through the pedestrian Gr̈ner Markt to reach the ancient sandstone bridge, on which stands the **Altes Rathaus** (Old Town Hall), a highly colorful rickety Gothic building dressed extravagantly in Rococo. It's best seen from the adjacent bridge upstream, where it appears to be practically in danger of being swept off by the river.

Across the bridge the towers of the **Dom** beckon you up the hill. It's one of the most important of Germany's cathedrals, a building that tells not only Bamberg's story but that of much of Germany as well. The first building here was begun by Heinrich II in 1003, and it was in this partially completed cathedral that he was crowned Holy Roman Emperor in 1012. In 1237 it was mostly destroyed by fire, and the present late-Romanesque/early Gothic building was begun. From the outside, the dominant features are the massive towers at each corner. Heading into the dark interior, you'll find one of the most striking collections of monuments and art treasures of any European church. The most famous is the *Bamberger Reiter* (Bamberger Rider), an equestrian statue, carved—no one knows by whom—around 1230 and thought to be an allegory of knightly virtue. The larger-than-life-size figure is an extraordinarily realistic work for the period, more like a Renaissance statue than a Gothic piece. Compare it to the mass of carved figures huddled in the tympana, the semicircular spaces above the doorways of the church; while these are stylized and obviously Gothic, the *Bamberg Rider* is poised and calm. In the center of the nave you'll find another great sculptural work, the massive tomb of Heinrich and his wife, Kunigunde. It's the work of Tilman Riemenschneider, Germany's greatest Renaissance sculptor. Pope Clement II is also buried in the cathedral, in an imposing tomb under the high altar; he is the only pope to be buried north of the Alps.

After you've toured the cathedral, go next door to see the **Diözesanmuseum** (Cathedral Museum). In addition to a rich collection of silver and other ecclesiastical objects, the museum contains a splinter of wood and the *heilige Nagel*, or holy nail, both reputedly from the cross of Jesus. A more macabre exhibit is Heinrich's and Kunigunde's skulls, mounted in elaborate metal supports. The building itself was designed by Balthasar Neumann, the architect of Vierzehnheiligen church, and constructed between 1730 and 1733. *Dompl. 5. Admission: DM 2.50 adults, DM 1.50 children. Open Apr.–Sept., daily 9–noon and 1:30–5; Oct.–Mar., daily 9–noon and 1:30–4.*

Keep your ticket for the cathedral museum to visit the adjoining **Neue Residenz** (Dompl. 8; open same hours). This immense Baroque palace was the home of the prince-electors. Their wealth and prestige can easily be imagined as you tour the glittering interior. Most memorable is the **Kaisersaal** (Throne Room), complete with impressive ceiling frescoes and elaborate stucco work. You'll also be able to visit the rose garden in back of the building, which offers a fine view of the Benedictine abbey church of St. Michael.

The palace also houses the **Staatsbibliothek** (State Library). Among the thousands of books and illuminated manuscripts are the original prayer books belonging to Heinrich and his wife, a 5th-century manuscript by the Roman historian Livy, and handwritten manuscripts by the 16th-century painters Dürer and Cranach. *Open Mon.–Fri. 9–5:30, Sat. 9–noon.*

Back down the hill, stroll through the narrow, sinuous streets of old Bamberg, past half-timbered and gabled houses and formal 18th-century mansions. Peek into cobbled, flower-filled courtyards or take time out in a waterside café, watching the little steamers as they chug past the colorful row of fishermen's houses that comprise Klein Venedig (Little Venice).

On Schillerplatz you'll find **Hoffmann-Haus.** E.T.A. Hoffmann, the Romantic writer, composer, and illustrator, lived in this little house between 1809 and 1813. The house has been preserved much as it was when Hoffmann lived here—complete with the hole in the floor of his upstairs study through which he talked to his wife below. *Schillerpl. 26. Admission: DM 1 adults, 50 pf children. Open May–Oct., Tues.–Fri. 9:30–5:30, Sat. and Sun. 9:30–1.*

Lodging
Under DM 110
★

Barock Hotel am Dom. Standing close by the cathedral in the heart of the old town, this hotel offers a stylish combination of Old-World elegance and discreet modern luxury. *Vorderer Bach 4, tel. 0951/54031. 19 rooms. AE, DC, MC. Closed Jan. 6–31.*

Under DM 70

Café und Gasthaus Graupner. This hotel offers simple accommodations at low prices in the heart of the old town. There's no restaurant; the café provides hearty breakfasts. A modern, 10-room annex without noticeable charm houses overflow guests. *Langestr. 5, tel. 0951/25132. 28 rooms, most with bath. AE, MC.*

Dining
Under DM 20

Brauereiausschank Schlenkerla. A centuries-old monastery turned beer tavern, this place offers *Rauchbier*, a strong malty brew with a smoky aftertaste, as well as smoked meats and other Franconian specialties. *Dominikanerstr. 6, tel. 0951/56060. No credit cards.*

Under DM 15

Gasthof Keesmann. The Keesmann serves its own brand of beer along with a range of simple Franconian dishes, ranging in price from DM 7.50 to DM 15. *Wunderburg 5, tel. 0951/26646. No credit cards. Open daily from 9 AM.*

Greifenklau. If you want to work up an appetite and view the Rococo Laurenzikirche church, walk up the street named Kaulberg to this picturesque inn, which serves some of the best pork dishes in town. *Laurenziplatz 20, tel. 0951/53219. No credit cards. Closed Sun. from 2 PM.*

Lodging and Dining
Under DM 110

Alt Ringlein. Built in 1302, this inn in Bamberg's medieval center has functioned as such since the 17th century. Its Scandinavian modern interior is a startling contrast, but the restaurant—which serves local cuisine in the Under DM 30 range—has the heavy beams, stone floor, and paneled walls that define "rustic" in southern Germany. *Dominikanerstr. 9, tel. 0951/54098. 54 rooms with bath. AE, DC, MC, V.*

Gasthof Weierich. Located alongside the walls of the towering cathedral, the Weierich offers lodging at moderate prices. The three charming restaurants—all in the Under DM 30 range—offer game (in season), fish, and other Franconian specialties. Lugbank 5, tel. 0951/54004. 23 rooms, 10 with bath. *Reservations advised. No credit cards.*

Under DM 70 **Gasthof Fässla.** This is one of Bamberg's 10 small home-brewery taverns, several of which offer lodging. The Fässla was fully renovated in 1990, and all rooms now have modern bathrooms. *Obere Königstr. 21, tel. 0951/2298. 21 rooms. No credit cards.*

Gasthof Spezial. This is another little brewery pub, directly across the street from the Fässla (*see above*), providing inexpensive food and lodging. The rooms are simple but cozy; breakfast is served in the tavern. *Obere Königstr. 10, tel. 0951/24304. 7 rooms without bath. No credit cards.*

Shopping Bamberg's main shopping area runs along Hauptwachstrasse. Across from the tourist information center is **Pappenberg's,** a shop selling candles, pewter, and wood carvings. An excellent place to shop for pottery is **Der Topferladen** (Untere Brücke 1), near the Altes Rathaus. The shop sells decorative plates, mugs, and bowls from more than 70 potters. On Saturday there's a small **flea market** on the Untere Brücke.

Kulmbach

Frequent trains from Bamberg take a little less than an hour. Tourist office: Stadthalle, Sutte 2, 8650 Kulmbach, tel. 09221/802–216.

In a country where the brewing and drinking of beer breaks all records, this town produces more per capita than anywhere else in Germany: 9,000 pints per man, woman, and child. A quarter of the work force in Kulmbach earns a living directly or indirectly from beer. One of Kulmbach's five breweries also produces the strongest beer in the world—the *Doppelbock* Kulminator 28—which takes nine months to brew and has an alcohol content of more than 11%. Tours of the **Erste Kulmbacher Union (EKU) brewery** (EKU-str. 1, tel. 09221/820), where Kulminator 28 is made, are given Monday through Thursday, but on a reservation-only basis. Another special local brew is *Eisbock*, which is frozen as part of the brewing process to make it stronger. The locals claim it's the sparklingly clear spring water from the nearby Fichtelgebirge hills that makes their beer so special. Kulmbach celebrates its beer every year in a nine-day festival that starts on the last Saturday in July. The main festival site, a mammoth tent, is called the Festspulhaus, or, literally, "festival swallowing house," a none-too-subtle dig at nearby Bayreuth and its Festspielhaus, where Wagner's operas are performed.

It would be unfair to pretend that Kulmbach is nothing but beer, beer, and more beer. The old town contains a warren of narrow streets that merit exploration. Likewise, no visitor here will want to miss the **Plassenburg,** symbol of the town and the most important Renaissance castle in the country. It's located a 20-minute hike from the old town on a rise overlooking Kulmbach. The first building here, begun in the mid-12th century, was torched by marauding Bavarians, who were anxious to put a stop to the ambitions of Duke Albrecht Alcibiades, a man who seems to have had few scruples when it came to self-advancement and who spent several years murdering, plundering, and pillaging his way through Franconia. His successors built today's castle starting in about 1560. Externally, there's little to suggest the graceful Renaissance interior, but as you enter the main courtyard the scene changes abruptly. The tiered space of the courtyard is covered with precisely carved figures, medallions, and other intricate ornaments, the whole comprising one of the most remarkable and delicate architectural ensembles in Europe. Inside, you may want to see the **Deutsches Zinnfigurenmuseum** (Tin Figures Museum), with more than 300,000 ministatuettes, the largest collection of its kind in the world. *Admission: DM 2 adults, DM 1 children. Open Apr.–Sept., daily 10–4:30; Oct.–Mar., daily 10–3:30.*

Dining
Under DM 20

EKU Inn. If you're here for the beer, this hostelry is an ideal place to try Kulminator 28, the world's strongest—or at least to buy a bottle as a souvenir. The EKU Inn also serves weaker brands, as well as a range of hearty Franconian dishes. It's handily located in the center of the old town, close to the Marktplatz. *Klostergasse 7, tel. 09221/5788. No credit cards.*

Lodging and Dining
Under DM 110

Gasthof Schweizerhof. At this traditional inn a mile east of the train station and the town center, you'll find neat but plain rooms. The restaurant serves solid Bavarian food (in the Under DM 20 range), plus beer from its own brewery. *Ziegelhüttenerstr. 38, tel. 09221/3985. 8 rooms, 4 with bath. No credit cards.*

Shopping

If you've enjoyed a visit to the Plassenburg museum, visit **Wanderer und Ranning** (Obere Stadt 34) and buy some tin figures to take home. The shop boasts more than 1,000, in all shapes and sizes. Traditional *Trachtenschmuck* silver jewelry is sold in three shops in town: **Brückner** and **Juwelier Hubschmann** (both on Langgasse), and **Giorgio Canola** (Kressinsteinerstr. 11).

Coburg

A 40-minute train trip will bring you from Bamberg to this little-known but pretty old town with its strong connection to the British monarchy. Tourist office: Herrngasse 4, 8630 Coburg, tel. 09561/74180.

Coburg was founded in the 11th century and remained in the possession of the dukes of Saxe-Coburg-Gotha until 1918; the present duke still lives there. In fact, it's as the home of the Saxe-Coburgs, as they are generally known, that the town is most famous. They were a remarkable family, providing a seemingly inexhaustible supply of blue-blooded marriage partners to ruling houses the length and breadth of Europe. The most famous of these royal mates was Prince Albert, husband of Queen Victoria.

The Marktplatz, ringed with gracious Renaissance and Baroque buildings, is the place to start your tour. The **Rathaus** (Town Hall), begun in 1500, is the most imposing structure. A forest of ornate gables and spires projects from its well-proportioned facade. Look at the statue of the **Bratwurstmännla** on the building; the staff he carries is claimed to be the official length against which the town's famous bratwurst sausages are measured.

Just off the square, on Schlossplatz, you'll find **Schloss Ehrenburg,** the ducal palace. Built in the mid-16th century, it has been greatly altered over the years, principally following a fire in the early 19th century. It was in this dark and imposing heap that Prince Albert spent much of his childhood. The throne room; the Hall of Giants, named for its larger-than-life frescoes; and the Baroque-style chapel can all be visited. *Schlosspl. Admission: DM 4 adults, children (with parents) free. Tours Apr.–Sept., daily at 10, 11, 1:30, 2:30, 3:30, and 4:30; and Oct.–Mar., daily at 10, 11, 1:30, and 2:30.*

The major attraction in Coburg, however, is the **Veste Coburg** (the fortress), one of the largest and most impressive in the country. To reach it, you pass through the **Hofgarten** (Palace Gardens), today the site of the **Naturwissenschaftliches Museum** (Natural History Museum). It's the country's leading museum of its kind, with more than 8,000 exhibits of flora and fauna, as well as geological, ethnological, and mineralogical specimens. *Admission: DM 2. Open Apr.–Oct., daily 9–6; Nov.–Mar., daily 9–5.*

The brooding bulk of the castle lies beyond the garden on a small hill above the town. The first buildings were constructed around 1055, but with progressive rebuilding and remodeling through the centuries, today's predominantly late-Gothic/early Renaissance edifice bears little resemblance to the original rude fortress. It contains a number of museums (all open the same hours as the castle). See the **Fürstenbau,** or Palace of the Princes, where Martin Luther was sheltered for six months in 1530. Among the main treasures are paintings by Cranach. Dürer, Rembrandt, and Cranach (again) are all represented at the **Kunstsammlungen,** the art museum in the fortress, as are many examples of German silver, porcelain, arms and armor, and furniture. Finally, there's the **Herzoginbau,** the duchess's building, a sort of 18th-century transportation museum, with carriages and ornate sledges for speeding in style through the winter snows. *Admission to Veste Coburg: DM 2.50 adults, children (with parents) free. Open Apr.–Oct., Tues.–Sun. 9–noon and 2–4; Nov.–Mar., Tues.–Sun. 9–noon and 2–3:30.*

Lodging
Under DM 110

Goldene Traube. High levels of comfort plus an excellent central location are provided by this sturdy favorite. Some of the cheaper rooms are plain, however. *Am Viktoriabrunnen 2, tel. 09561/9833. Facilities: sauna, restaurant, parking. AE, DC, MC, V.*

Dining
Under DM 20

★ **Goldenes Kreuz.** In business since 1477, this restaurant boasts all the rustic decor you'll ever want and large portions of Franconian food. Not for lovers of nouvelle cuisine. *Herrngasse 1, tel. 09561/90473. Reservations advised. No credit cards.*

Ratskeller. The stone vaults of this establishment make it the sort of emphatically Teutonic place where local specialties always taste better. *Markt 1, tel. 09561/92400. Reservations advised. No credit cards.*

Under DM 15

Coburger Markthalle. A corner of the indoor market hall adjacent to the Rathaus (town hall) accommodates several fast food stalls, where you can pick from a tasty range of dishes and snacks, from Franconian sausages to Turkish kebabs and rice. *Markthalle, Marktplatz, tel. 09561/75490. No credit cards. Closed Sat. evening and all day Sun.*

Shopping

Head for **Grossmann's** (Ketchinggasse 20–24) for delicious smoked hams, gingerbread, and an almond cake known as *Elizenkuchen.* Off the market square, you'll find **Kaufmann's** (Judengasse). Run by a husband-and-wife team, it has fine hand-blown glass and homemade jewelry.

Lichtenfels, southeast of Coburg, is the place for baskets; there's even a state-run basket-weaving school here. The best selection is at **Es Körbla** (Stadtknechtgasse), just off the market square.

Vierzehnheiligen Church

This remarkable religious monument is difficult to reach by public transport, but worth the effort if you fancy combining a visit with a bike ride. Take the train to Staffelstein, 20 minutes up the line, where you can hire bicycles (tel. 09573/266) for the 16-kilometer (10-mile) round-trip.

Vierzehnheiligen is probably the single most ornate Rococo church in Europe, although you might not know it just from looking at the exterior. There are the onion-dome towers, the lively curving facade, but little to suggest the almost explosive array of paintings, stucco, gilt, statuary, and rich rosy marble inside. The church was built by Balthasar Neumann (architect of the Residenz at Würzburg; *see above*) between 1743 and 1772 to commemorate a vision of Christ and 14 saints—*Vierzehnheiligen* means "14 saints"—that appeared to a shepherd back in 1445. Your first impression will be of the richness of the decoration and the brilliance of the coloring, the whole more like some fantastic pleasure palace than a place of worship. Notice the way the entire building seems to be in motion—almost all the walls are curved—and how the walls and ceiling are alive with delicate stucco. In much the same way the builders of Gothic cathedrals aimed to overwhelm through scale and verticality, Neumann wanted to startle worshipers through light, color, and movement. Anyone who has seen the gaunt Romanesque cathedrals of Protestant north Germany will have little difficulty understanding why the Reformation was never able to gain more than a toehold in Catholic south Germany. There are few more uplifting buildings in Europe.

There is a simple café on the grounds of the church complex.

7 The Rhineland Palatinate

Including Mainz, Worms, Speyer, and the Wine Road

For most travelers—even seasoned ones—the Rhineland means the spectacular stretch between Bingen (where the river leaves the Rheingau region and swings north) and the ancient city of Koblenz (at the mouth of the Mosel). Each bend of the river brings the familiar calendar vistas. But there's another part of the Rhineland where vineyards climb slopes crowned by ancient castles. This is the Rhineland Palatinate. It lacks the grandeur of the river above Bingen, the elegance of the resorts of Boppard and Koblenz, and the cachet of the wines of the Rheingau. But for that reason the crowds are smaller, the prices lower, and the pace slower. And there are attractions here you won't find in the more popular stretch of the river farther north, including the warmest climate in Germany. The south-facing folds of the Palatinate hills shelter communities where lemons, figs, and sweet chestnuts grow alongside vines. It's a region where few autobahns penetrate and where most other roads lead to truly off-the-beaten-track territory. One of these roads is Germany's first specially designated Weinstrasse (Wine Road), a winding, often narrow route with temptations—vineyards and farmsteads that beckon the traveler to sample the current vintage. If you're covering the route by car, take along a nondrinker as co-driver, or split the driving between you. And take your time.

At the northern end of the Wine Road beckon three of Germany's oldest cities: Mainz, Worms, and Speyer. They are among the Rhineland's great imperial centers, where emperors and princes met and where the three greatest Romanesque cathedrals in Europe still stand.

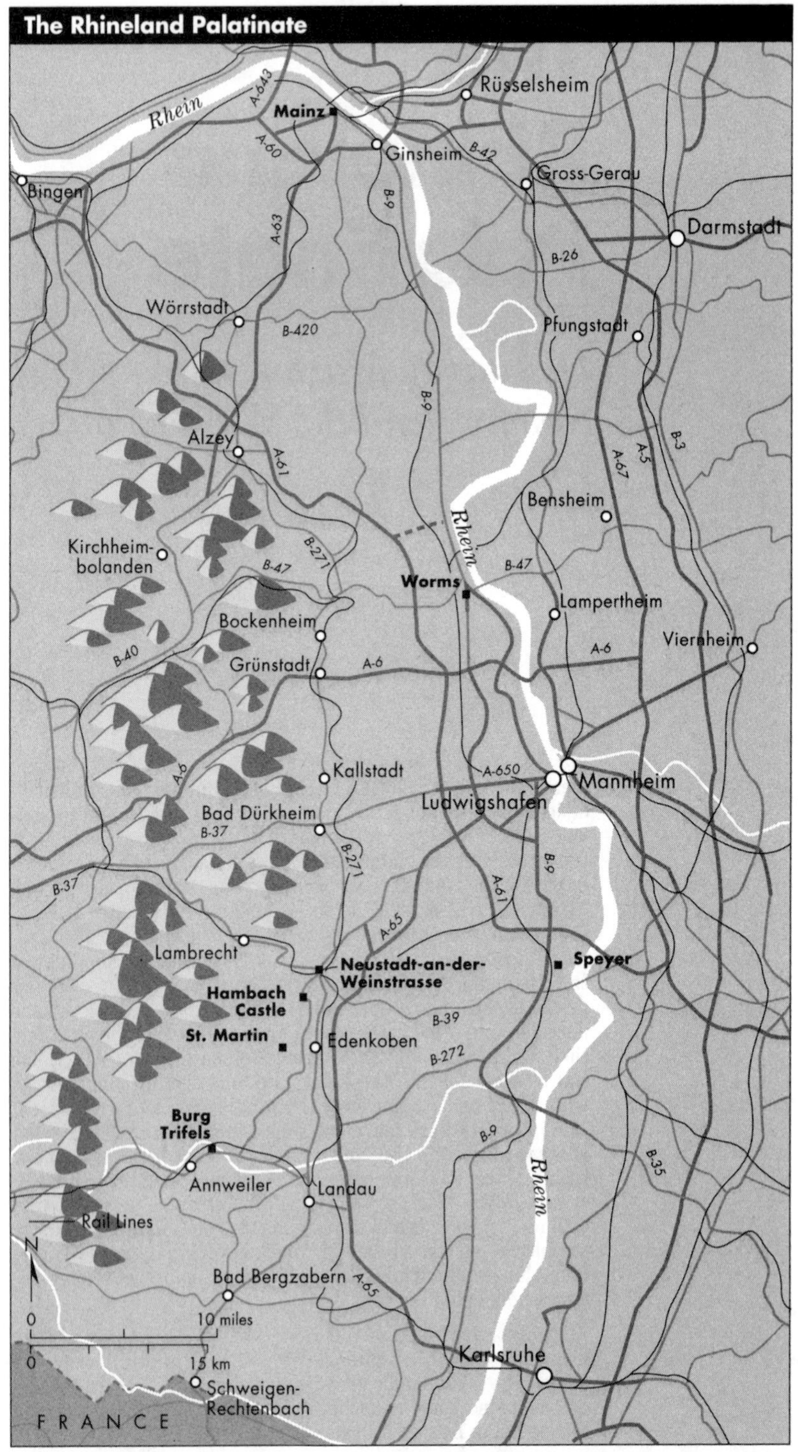
The Rhineland Palatinate
Rhein
Mainz
Rüsselsheim
Ginsheim
Gross-Gerau
Bingen
Darmstadt
Wörrstadt
Pfungstadt
Alzey
Bensheim
Kirchheim-bolanden
Worms
Lampertheim
Bockenheim
Viernheim
Grünstadt
Kallstadt
Mannheim
Ludwigshafen
Bad Dürkheim
Lambrecht
Neustadt-an-der-Weinstrasse
Speyer
Hambach Castle
St. Martin
Edenkoben
Burg Trifels
Annweiler
Landau
Rail Lines
Bad Bergzabern
Karlsruhe
Schweigen-Rechtenbach
FRANCE
N
0
10 miles
0
15 km
A-643
A-60
A-63
B-9
B-42
B-26
B-420
A-61
B-271
B-47
B-40
A-6
B-37
A-650
A-65
B-39
B-272
B-35
A-67
A-5
B-3

Essential Information

Lodging Accommodations are plentiful, with those along the Wine Road mostly simple and inexpensive inns. The region has many bed-and-breakfasts; keep an eye open for signs reading *Zimmer Frei,* meaning "rooms available." Accommodation prices in Mainz are higher, and if you plan to visit during the famous Mainz Karnival in February, it's essential to book ahead. The same applies if you're visiting the area during any of the wine festivals during late summer or fall. Expect higher prices then, too.

Highly recommended establishments are indicated by a star ★.

Dining Though Mainz can offer more elegant dining, in most of the towns and villages of the Rhineland Palatinate you'll eat local specialties in local inns. Sausages are more popular here than in almost any other area of the country, with the herb-flavored *Pfalzer* a favorite. *Hase im Topf,* a highly flavored rabbit pâté made with port, Madeira, brandy, and red wine, is another specialty to look for. The Rhineland Palatinate, though not geographically the largest wine-producing area in the country, nonetheless produces more wine than does any other region in Germany, and all restaurants will have a range of wines to offer.

Highly recommended restaurants are indicated by a star ★.

Biking The vineyard-lined country roads on either side of the Wine Road are a cyclist's dream. You can rent bikes at any of the main train stations for DM 10 a day (DM 12 for a bike with gears)—half that if you have a valid train ticket. A pamphlet issued free at railway stations, *Radeln mit der Bahn,* describes bike tours in the immediate area.

Hiking You can cover the entire Wine Road on foot, along a clearly marked trail that winds its way between the vineyards covering the slopes of the Palatinate forest. Maps and information can be obtained from the **Fremdenverkehrsverband** (Bezirkstelle Pfalz, Exterstr. 4, 6730 Neustadt an der Weinstrasse). The **Wasgau nature park** on the edge of the Palatinate forest is also fine walking country, and the tourist office at Dahn offers a vacation package that includes not only overnight stops but a walking stick and a bottle of locally made schnapps to help you cover the distance between them. Contact the **Fremdenverkehrsbüro Dahn** (Schulstr. 29, 6783 Dahn, tel. 06391/5811).

The Arts and Nightlife Mainz is the cultural center of the region, with a resident orchestra, opera, and theater. Its annual cathedral music festival lasts through the summer. All three of the region's great Romanesque cathedrals—at Mainz, Worms, and Speyer—have regular organ recitals and chamber-music concerts.

Festivals The wine festivals of the towns and villages of the Wine Road are numerous enough to take up several vacations. From late May through October, the entire area seems to be caught up in one long celebration. The most important festivals include the **Weinlesefest** in Neustadt an der Weinstrasse (with the coronation of the local Wine Queen), in the first week of October, and the **Mainzer Weinmarkt** in Mainz's Volkspark, the last weekend of August and the first weekend of September.

Mainz is also the focus of the Rhineland **carnival** celebrations; the entire city changes into fancy dress on one wild day, the Monday before Lent. In mid-June there's the **Mainzer Johannisnacht,** a weekend of festivities commemorating the pioneer printer Johannes Gutenberg.

Highlights for First-time Visitors

Burg Trifels (*see* Tour 2)
Cathedrals of Mainz, Worms, and Speyer (*see* Tour 1)
Gutenberg Museum, Mainz (*see* Tour 1)
Synagogue, Worms (*see* Tour 1)
Village of St. Martin (*see* Tour 2)

Tour 1: Mainz, Worms, and Speyer

The three great Romanesque basilicas of the Rhineland together constitute one of the architectural wonders of Germany. They lie along the western bank of the Rhine in a nearly straight line that stretches some 90 kilometers (54 miles), from Mainz at the north end to Speyer in the south, with Worms at the halfway mark. The three cities are linked by a picturesque vineyard road, the Liebfrauenstrasse, named after the region's most famous wine.

From Frankfurt
By Train Mainz is 20 minutes from Frankfurt by the speedy InterCity or EuroCity express; a slower service takes double the time. Trains depart about every half-hour. A half-hourly service also links Mainz and Worms; this leg of the journey takes about 45 minutes. To reach Speyer, take the train from Mainz to Ludwigshafen (one leaves every hour and the trip takes 40 minutes), change for the 10-minute trip to Schifferstadt, and then change again for the 10-minute run to Speyer.

By Bus The **Europabus** company (tel. 069/790–3240) operates a twice-daily service to Mainz, leaving Frankfurt's main railway station forecourt at 7 AM and 3:30 PM. The journey takes an hour. Infrequent regional buses link Mainz and Worms and Worms and Speyer; they're marginally cheaper than trains, but the trains are faster, more frequent, and considerably more convenient.

By Car Mainz is 20 minutes west of Frankfurt on the A-67 and A-60 autobahns. Worms lies about 50 kilometers (30 miles) south of Mainz on Route 9. To reach Speyer, join the A-61 Autobahn 6 kilometers (4 miles) southwest of Worms and follow the Heilbronn signs for 30 kilometers (18½ miles), exiting at the Speyer junction.

Mainz

Tourist office: Verkehrsverein Mainz, Bahnhofstr. 15 (follow Bahnhofstrasse from the main railway station for 100 yards; it's on the left), tel. 06131/233–741.

Mainz is a bustling, businesslike but friendly Rhine-side city, with a brilliantly planned central pedestrian zone that makes touring on foot a breeze. All streets lead to the spacious market square, flattened in the war but since rebuilt with its medieval flavor intact. Watching over the square with the dignity of age is the sturdy, turreted **cathedral.** Step inside and silence falls about you like a cloak. One thousand years of history accompany you through the aisles and chapels. The first cathedral here—dedicated to Sts. Martin and Stephan—was built at the end of the 10th century. In 1002, Heinrich I, the last Saxon emperor of the Holy Roman Empire, was crowned in the still-far-from-complete building. In 1009, on the very day of its consecration, the cathedral burned to the ground. Rebuilding began almost immediately. The cathedral you see today was largely finished at the end of the 11th century. Substantial sections were rebuilt at the end of World War II. Before that, in the 18th century, an imposing Baroque spire was constructed; similarly, in the Gothic period, rebuilding and remodeling did much to alter the Romanesque purity of the original. With all these additions and modifications, can the cathedral really be considered Romanesque? The answer has to be yes, if only because its ground plan links it so firmly to the cathedrals at Speyer and Mainz. Notice the towers at each end and the spires that rise between them; one may be Baroque, but its positioning and something of its bold impact produce an effect that is nothing if not Romanesque. Inside, though pointed arches proliferate, the walls have the same grim, fortresslike massiveness of Speyer. True, there's more stained glass—more light generally—but the weight of masonry is full-fledged Romanesque. The **Dom und Diozesän Museum** (Cathedral Treasury and Museum) contains a series of rich ecclesiastical objects that will appeal to anyone with a taste for the intricate skills of medieval and Renaissance craftsmen. *Admission free. Open Mon.–Sat. 9–noon and 2–5.*

Opposite the east end of the cathedral on Liebfrauenplatz is one of the most popular attractions in the Rhineland, the **Gutenburg Museum.** It charts the life and times of Mainz's most famous—and unquestionably most influential—son, Johannes Gutenburg (1390–1468). It was in Mainz, in 1456, that Gutenburg built the first machine that could print from movable type. The significance of his invention was immense, leading to an explosion in the availability of information. This wasn't actually the building in which Gutenburg worked; that's long since disappeared, but a vivid sense of his original workshop is conveyed. There's a fine reconstruction of his printing machine, as well as exhibits charting the development of printing and bookbinding. But the highlight must be the copy of the Gutenburg Bible, one of only 47 extant, not only one of the most historically significant books in the world but surely one of the most beautiful. *Liebfrauenpl. 5. Admission free. Open Tues.–Sat. 10–5, Sun. 10–1.*

From the Gutenburg Museum, return to the 20th century by crossing Rheinstrasse to the **Rathaus** (Town Hall). This is no ancient structure but an unashamedly modern glass-and-concrete building put up in the 1970s. Opinions have been divided over its merits for as long as the building's been here.

For another example of modern Mainz, take a look at the church of **St. Stephan.** It's on Willigisplatz, a half mile south of the Rathaus. You'll walk through the rebuilt old town on your way there, an example of sensitive reconstruction following near-total destruction in the war. The church itself is one of the oldest single-nave Gothic buildings in this part of the Rhineland.

But look at the stained glass in the choir; it was designed by Russian-born painter Marc Chagall in the 1970s. Its vivid coloring is a strangely beautiful complement to the austere Gothic design of the rest of the church.

Mainz claims to put on the wildest pre-Lent carnival in Germany. Be here in early February if you want to put that boast to the test. The city erupts in a Rhineland riot of revelry, the high point of which is the procession through the old town.

Lodging
Under DM 180

Hammer. The Hammer is a basic, few-frills hotel downtown by the train station. Rooms are modern and comfortable—and soundproof. *Bahnhofpl. 6, tel. 06131/611–061. 40 rooms with bath. Facilities: sauna, solarium. AE, DC, MC, V.*

Ibis. A few strides from the Rhine and a short walk from the cathedral, this recently built hotel offers comfortable but plainly decorated rooms. *Holzhofstr. 2, tel. 06131/2470. 144 rooms with bath. Facilities: restaurant, bar. AE, MC, V.*

Under DM 130

Am Hechenberg. If you value coziness over convenience, head for this edge-of-town hotel. Its main deficiency is the absence of a restaurant. *Am Schinnergraben 82, tel. 06131/507001. 42 rooms with bath. Facilities: sauna, solarium, games room, gardens. AE, DC, MC, V.*

Under DM 90

Hotel Pfeil-Continental. Located in the same central building as the tourist office, on a busy street (so ask for a room at the back), this hotel has 31 simply furnished but clean rooms, all of them with bath. There's no restaurant, but a breakfast buffet is included in the room rate. *Bahnhofstr. 15, tel. 06131/232–179. AE, DC, MC, V. Closed mid-Dec.–early Jan.*

Zum Schildknecht. Climb the stairs to the cozy bedrooms in a charming, medieval, cottagelike home in the center of the old town. There's a wine tavern on the ground floor (serving wine from its own vineyard), so expect some noise at night, even though the streets all around are traffic-free. *Heiliggrabstr. 6, tel. 06131/225–755. 11 rooms, most with bath/shower. No credit cards.*

Dining
Under DM 40

Drei Lilien. An authentic Roman altar stone stands at the entrance of this leading Mainz restaurant—and indeed its cuisine is the subject of some local worship. A visit to the restaurant would have to be counted as a splurge. Much cheaper, but boasting the same high standards, is the bistro beneath. *Ballpatz 2, tel. 06131/225–068. AE, DC, MC, V. Closed Tues.*

Under DM 30

Kartauser Hof. If the weather allows it, take a table in the walled courtyard, a pretty sun-trap smothered in flowers in the summer. The menu often includes locally caught fish. *Kartauserstr. 14, tel. 06131/222–956. AE, DC, MC, V.*

★ **Rats- und Zunftstuben Heilig Geist.** Parts of the building date from Roman times, but most of it is Gothic, with vaulted ceilings and stone floors. The menu features Bavarian specialties with nouvelle touches. *Rentengasse 2, tel. 06131/225–757. Reservations advised. AE, DC, MC. Closed Sun. dinner and Mon.*

Zum Augustiner. Once a week, the Augustiner gets deliveries of fresh fish and vegetables from France, and on any morning you can find chef Michael Muller at the city market buying whatever he can't get from his French suppliers. The outstanding results are described on his daily handwritten menu. Prices are surprisingly reasonable. *Augustinerstr. 8, tel. 06131/231–737. AE, MC.*

Shopping Mainz's pedestrian zone makes shopping a delight. The streets around the central market square are packed with shops selling Rhineland mementos. (We particularly recommend **Augustenstrasse.**) Church and commerce are closely linked here, and there's a leading wine shop attached to the cathedral. In Christina Kronberger's **Weinkabinett** you'll find what the region's vineyards have to offer, as well as some attractive accessories. On the other side of the market square is **Korb-Schneider,** a basketware shop packed floor to ceiling with everything from wine baskets to rocking chairs. The square itself is the scene of a lively **market** on Tuesday, Thursday, and Saturday. Mainz also has a famous **flea market,** the Krempelmarkt, held along the banks of the Rhine every third Saturday of the month (except Apr. and Oct.).

The Arts and Nightlife Mainz has an annual **cathedral music festival** that lasts through the summer. Organ recitals are given in the cathedral every Saturday at noon from mid-August to mid-September. Classical-music concerts are also given regularly at the **Kurfürstliches Schloss** (Diether-von-Isenburg-Str., tel. 06131/228–729).

Night owls make for the Altstadt, the old town. The central Marktplatz is the scene from May through September of a nightly program of open-air pop music, jazz, and street cabaret.

Worms

Tourist office: Verkehrsverein der Stadt Worms, Neumarkt 14 (on the central "new" market square), tel. 06241/853–560.

Numbers in the margin correspond to points of interest on the Worms map.

Worms is one of the most important wine centers in Germany. There's some industry on the outskirts of the city, but the rebuilt old town is compact and easy to explore.

Worms is the site of another Romanesque cathedral, a great, gaunt structure of craggy magnificence. The city, which was devastated in World War II, is among the most ancient cities in Germany, founded as far back perhaps as 5,000 years ago, settled by the Romans, and later one of the major centers of the Holy Roman Empire. More than 100 diets of the empire were held here, including the one in 1521 before which Martin Luther came to plead his "heretical" case.

It was the Romans who made Worms important, but it was a Burgundian tribe, established in Worms from the 5th century, who gave the city its most compelling legend—the Nibelungen. The story, written probably in the 12th century and considerably elaborated throughout the years, is complex and sprawling, telling of love, betrayal, greed, war, and death. It ends when the Nibelungen—the Burgundians—are defeated by Attila the Hun, their court destroyed, their treasure lost, their heroes dead. (One of the most famous incidents tells how Hagen, treacherous and scheming, hurls the court riches into the Rhine; by the Nibelungen bridge there's a bronze statue of him, caught in the act.)

The Nibelungen may be legend, but the story is based on historical fact. For instance, it's known that a Burgundian tribe was defeated, in present-day Hungary, by Attila the Hun in 437. Not until Charlemagne resettled Worms almost 400 years later, making it one of the major cities of his empire, did the city prosper again. Worms wasn't just an administrative and commercial center, but a great ecclesiastical city as well. The first expression of this religious importance was the original cathedral, consecrated in 1018. In 1171 a new cathedral was started. This is the one you come to Worms to see.

When you visit Speyer Cathedral (*see below*), you'll quickly re-
1 alize that **Worms Cathedral,** by contrast, contains many Gothic elements. In part this is simply a matter of chronology. Speyer Cathedral was completed more than 100 years before the one at Worms was even begun, long before the lighter, more vertical lines of the Gothic style were developed. But there's another reason. Once built, Speyer Cathedral was left largely unaltered; at Worms, the cathedral was remodeled frequently as new styles in architecture and new values developed. Nonetheless, as you walk around the building, you'll find that same muscular confidence, that same blocky massiveness that you'll note at Speyer. The ground plans of the churches are similar, with two towers at each end, a prominent apse at the east end, and short transepts (the "arms" of the church). The Gothic influence here is most obvious inside, especially in the great rose window at the west end (over the main entrance). It could almost be in a French church and presents a striking contrast to the tiny, round-headed windows high up in the nave. Notice, too, how a number of the main arches in the nave are pointed, a key characteristic of the Gothic style. It wasn't only in the Gothic period that the cathedral was altered, however. As you near the main altar you'll see the lavish Baroque screen of columns supporting an opulent gold crown that towers above the altar. This is the Baroque at its most potent. The choir stalls, installed in 1760, are equally opposed in spirit to the body of the church. Intricately carved and gilded, they proclaim the courtly and sophisticated glamour of the Rococo.

Outside the cathedral, cross the square to see the simple
2 **Dreifaltigkeit Church** (Church of the Holy Trinity). Remodeling of the church in the 19th century produced today's austere building (the facade and tower are still joyfully Baroque). It's a Lutheran church and as good a place as any in the city to recall Luther's appearance in 1521 before the Holy Roman Emperor and massed ranks of Catholic theologians to defend his heretical beliefs. Luther ended his impassioned plea against the corruption of the church and for its reform (hence Reformation) with the ringing declaration, "Here I stand, I can do no different. God help me. Amen!" He was duly excommunicated. From the church, walk back past the cathedral to see the
3 **Lutherdenkmal,** a 19th-century group of statues of Luther and other figures from the Reformation. It's on the little area of grass next to the street called, appropriately enough, Lutherring.

Worms was also one of the most important Jewish cities in Germany, a role that came to a brutal end with the rise of the Nazis. From the Luther monument you can walk along
4 Lutherring to see the rebuilt **synagogue,** the oldest in the country. It was founded in the 11th century; in 1938, it was entirely destroyed. In 1961, the synagogue was rebuilt, using as much of the original masonry as had survived. The ancient Jewish

Cathedral, **1**
Dreifaltigkeit Church, **2**
Judenfriedhof, **5**
Liebfrauenkirche, **7**
Lutherdenkmal, **3**
Städtisches Museum, **6**
Synagogue, **4**

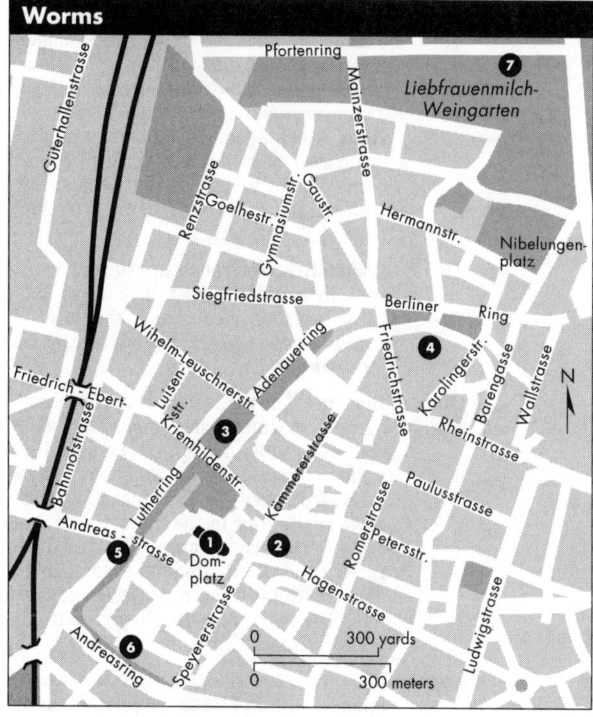

5 cemetery, the **Judenfriedhof,** can also be visited. *Admission free. Open daily 10–noon and 2–4.*

6 To bone up on the history of the city, visit the **Städtisches Museum** (Municipal Museum). It's housed in the cloisters of a former Romanesque church. *Weckerlingpl. Admission: DM 2.50 adults, DM 1 children. Open May.–Sept., Tues.–Sun. 9–noon and 2–5; Oct.–Apr., Tues.–Sun. 10–noon and 2–4.*

If you visit the city in late August or early September, you'll find it embroiled in its carnival, the improbably named Backfischfest, or Baked Fish Festival. The highlight is the **Fischerstechen,** a kind of water-borne jousting in which contestants spar with long poles while balancing on the wobbly decks of flat-bottom boats. The winner is crowned King of the River; the losers get a dunking. Baked fish is the culinary highlight of the festival, of course. The wine is never in short supply.

Don't leave Worms without visiting the vineyard that gave birth to Germany's most famous export wine, Liebfraumilch (Our Lady's Milk). The vineyard encircles the Gothic pilgrim-
7 age church of the **Liebfrauen** convent, the **Liebfrauenkirche,** an easy 20-minute walk north from the old town. Buy a bottle or two from the shop at the vineyard.

Lodging
Under DM 180

Dom Hotel. This modern and centrally located hotel offers little more than functional comfort, but it's still the best in town. The Bacchus restaurant (*see below*) is a plus. *Obermarkt 10, tel. 06241/6913. 66 rooms with bath. AE, DC, MC, V.*

Under DM 130 **Central.** Although a few miles southwest of Worms, in Frankenthal, this well-equipped hotel makes a good base. *Karolinenstr. 6, tel. 06233/8780. 80 rooms with bath. Facilities: indoor pool, sauna, squash courts, bowling alley, hairdresser, 2 restaurants, bar. AE, DC, MC, V.*

Hotel Nibelungen. This downtown hotel is a fine old building, renovated to a high standard of comfort ten years ago. The management estimates that 60% of the guests come from the United States. *Martinsgasse 16, tel. 06241/6977. 46 rooms with bath. AE, DC, MC, V.*

Under DM 90 **Lortze-Eck.** Ten rooms are tucked away above a tavern restaurant in a quiet corner of central Worms. They are simply furnished but clean, and the location couldn't be better. *Schlossergasse 10–12, tel. 06241/24561. 10 rooms without bath. No credit cards.*

Dining

Under DM 40 **Bacchus.** The name here is apt: This is the place to drink some of the best wine in the region. The food is ample, with local specialties predominating. *Obermarkt 10, tel. 06241/6913. Reservations advised. Jacket and tie required. AE, DC, MC, V.*

Le Bistro Leger. Don't be put off by the chi-chi name; French it certainly is, but in the down-to-earth manner of the best bistros of provincial France. The menu, which changes daily, features fresh local produce plus such exotic dishes as tender shark cutlets. Oysters, in season, are the specialty, and the wine list is impressive. *Siegfriedstr. 2, tel. 06241/46277. AE, MC, V. Closed Tues.*

Shopping This wine town is the place to shop for wine glasses, bottle openers (some of them elaborately carved from local wood), and wine coolers. The tourist office (Neumarkt 14) sells the most original wine cooler, a terra-cotta replica of a Roman example unearthed by archaeologists. Also try the **Winzergenossenschaft** at Edenkoben (Weinstr. 130, open daily). **Studio Rhodt** (Theresienstr. 111) has an interesting selection of handmade ceramics for sale.

Antiques hunters report two shops worth digging through: **Antik–Markt** (Hochheimerstr. 76) and **Antik Schimmel** (Kammererstr. 48). The city also has a **flea market;** it's held Saturday in March, June, September, and December in the city's main parking lot, near the Rhine.

The Arts and Nightlife The cathedral offers a regular program of organ and chamber-music concerts. There's also a city theater, the **Städtisches Spiel und Festhaus,** where concerts and dramas are staged. For program details and tickets, contact the box office on Rathenaustrasse or call tel. 06241/22525.

Worms has a square-dance club, **The Crackers,** which welcomes guests. Call tel. 06241/23400 if you'd like to join in. The city's discotheques and bars are concentrated around Judengasse.

Speyer

Tourist office: Verkehrsamt der Stadt Speyer, Maximilianstr. 11 (opposite the main railway station), tel. 06232/14395.

Speyer was probably founded in Celtic times and became one of the great cities of the Holy Roman Empire. Between 1294 and 1570, no fewer than 50 full diets (meetings of the rulers of the empire) were convened here. The focus of your visit will be the imperial cathedral, the **Kaiserdom,** one of the largest medieval churches in Europe, certainly one of the finest Romanesque cathedrals, and a building that more than any other in Germany conveys the pomp and majesty of the early Holy Roman emperors. It was built in only 30 years, between 1030 and 1060, by the emperors Konrad II, Heinrich III, and Heinrich IV. A four-year restoration program in the 1950s returned the building to almost exactly its condition when first completed.

There's an understandable tendency to dismiss most Romanesque architecture as little more than a cruder version of Gothic, the style that followed it and that many consider the supreme architectural achievement of the Middle Ages. Where the Gothic is seen as delicate, soaring, and noble, the Romanesque by contrast seems lumpy and earthbound, more fortress-like than divine. It's true that even the most successful Romanesque buildings are ponderously massive, but they possess a severe confidence and potency that can be overwhelming. What's more, look carefully at the decorative details and you'll see vivid and often delicate craftsmanship.

See as much of the building from the outside as you can before you venture inside. You can walk most of the way around it, and there's a fine view from the east end from the park by the Rhine. If you've seen Köln Cathedral, the finest Gothic cathedral in Germany, you'll be struck at once by how much more massive Speyer Cathedral is in comparison. The few windows are small, as if crushed by the surrounding masonry. Notice, too, their round tops, a key characteristic of the style. The position of the space-rocket-like towers, four in all (two at either end), and the immense, smoothly sloping dome at the east end give the building a distinctive, animated profile; it has a barely suppressed energy and dynamism. Notice, too, how much of a piece it is; having been built all in one go, the church remains faithful to a single vision. Inside, the cathedral is dimly mysterious, stretching to the high altar in the distance. In contrast to Gothic cathedrals, whose walls are supported externally by flying buttresses, allowing the interior the minimum of masonry and the maximum of light, at Speyer the columns supporting the roof are massive. Their bulk naturally disguises the side aisles, drawing your eye to the altar. Look up at the roof; it's a shallow stone vault, the earliest such vaulted roof in Europe. Look, too, at the richly carved capitals of the columns, filled with naturalistic details—foliage, dogs, birds, faces.

No fewer than eight Holy Roman emperors are buried in the cathedral, including, fittingly enough, the three who built it. They lie in the crypt. This, too, should be visited to see its simple beauty, uninterrupted by anything save the barest minimum of decorative detail. The entrance is in the south aisle. *Kaiserdom. Admission to crypt: 50 pf. For guided tours, tel. 06232/102–259. Cost is DM 1 adults, 50 pf children. Open Apr.–Sept., weekdays 9–5:30, Sat. 9–4, Sun. 1:30–3; Oct.–Mar., weekdays 9–11:30 and 2–4:30, Sat. 9–11:30 and 1:30–4, Sun. 1:30–4:30.*

Treasures from the cathedral and the imperial tombs are kept in the city's excellent museum, the **Historisches Museum der Pfalz,** on nearby Grosses Pfaffengasse. Beneath its ornate, turreted roof there's also one of the region's most comprehensive **wine museums.** The museum re-opened in 1990 following renovations. *Open Apr.–Nov., Mon.–Sat. 9–5.*

Lodging
Under DM 130

Goldener Engel. The "Golden Angel" has been in business since 1701 and offers both atmosphere and modern comfort. There's no restaurant, but it adjoins Wirstschaft zum Alten Engel (*see below*). *Mühlturmstr. 1a, tel. 06232/76732. 42 rooms and 2 suites with bath. AE, DC, MC, V.*

Hotel Kurpfalz. This is a turn-of-the-century villa, fully renovated and given a convincing Old World atmosphere. It's small and family-run. *Mühlturmstr. 5, tel. 06232/24168. 10 rooms and 1 suite, all with bath. AE, DC, MC.*

Dining
Under DM 30
★

Wirstschaft zum Alten Engel. Regional dishes from the Palatinate and the French Alsace region dominate the menu in this historic cellar tavern in the heart of the city. *Mühlturmstr. 1a, tel. 06232/76732. Reservations advised. AE, DC, MC. Closed lunch, Sat. and Aug.*

Shopping Speyer's shopping streets can be found west of the cathedral and around the central market square.

The Arts As in Mainz and Worms, the cathedral is the site of regular **organ and chamber-music concerts.** The city's commitment to music grew with the celebrations in 1990 marking the town's 2,000th anniversary. Concerts are scheduled for early fall. The city's theater is the **Stadthalle** (Obere Langgasse). Contact the local tourist office, the Verkehrsamt (Maximilianstr. 11) for concert and theater tickets.

Tour 2: Along the Wine Road

If you're driving—or if you're an energetic cyclist—the best way to cover the Wine Road is to set out from either end of the 100-kilometer (60-mile) route: Schweigen-Rechtenbach, on the French border, or Bockenheim, convenient to Mainz and Frankfurt. Otherwise, base yourself in the town of Neustadt an der Weinstrasse, the center not only of the region but of the route itself. From there, regular train and bus services will get you to all the worthwhile sights and wine villages.

From Frankfurt
By Train

Half-hourly services connect Frankfurt and Mainz; change trains in Mainz for Ludwigshafen and in Ludwigshafen for the 25-minute run to Neustadt. The entire journey takes between two and three hours, depending on connections.

By Bus The bus trip from Frankfurt to Neustadt involves several changes and is not recommended.

By Car The most direct route from Frankfurt (120 kilometers/70 miles) is the southerly Autobahn A-5, joining the A-67 just beyond Darmstadt and branching onto the westerly A-6 shortly before Mannheim. After 30 kilometers (18 miles) on the A-6, watch for the Wine Road exit (signposted Bad Dürkheim and Neustadt an der Weinstrasse).

Neustadt an der Weinstrasse

Tourist office: Verkehrsamt, Exterstr. 4 (between the main railway station and the central market), tel. 06321/855–329.

The biggest, most bustling town on the Wine Road is Neustadt an der Weinstrasse. It's wine that makes Neustadt tick, and practically every shop seems linked with the wine trade. A remarkable 5,000 acres of vineyards lie within the official town limits.

The narrow streets of the old town center still following the medieval street plan. If you need to get your sightseeing fix, make for central Marktplatz to see the Gothic **Stiftskirche** (Collegiate Church). It's an austere Gothic building, constructed in the 14th century for the elector of the Rhineland Palatinate. Inside, a wall divides the church in two, a striking reminder of former religious strife. The church, indeed the whole region, became Protestant in the Reformation during the 16th century. At the beginning of the 18th century, the Catholic population of the town petitioned successfully to be allowed a share of the church. The choir (the area around the altar) was accordingly designated the Catholic half of the church, while the nave, the main body of the church, was reserved for the Protestants. To keep the squabbling communities apart, the wall was built inside the church. Is it an instance of religious tolerance or intolerance? And who got the better deal? As you wander round the church—be sure to look at the intricate 15th-century choir stalls and the little figures, monkeys, and vine leaves carved into the capitals of the nave columns—you can ponder these matters.

Lodging
Under DM 150

Hotel Garni Tenner. Located in the Haardt district, this hotel has its own small park of rare and exotic trees and shrubs. Rooms are modern and functional, but comfort is assured. *Mandelring 216, Neustadt-Haardt, tel. 06321/6541. 40 rooms with bath. Facilities: indoor pool, sauna, solarium, terrace. AE, DC, MC. Closed Christmas Day.*

Pfalzgraf. Centrally located in the pedestrian zone, no more than a minute's walk from the train station, this hotel is in a tastefully modernized turn-of-the-century building. Ask for a mansard room; they're small but cozy. *Friedrichstr. 2, tel. 06321/2185. 40 rooms with bath. Facilities: restaurant, café. AE, DC, MC, V.*

Under DM 110

Burckshof. Its conical turrets and high gables make this elegant little palace of a hotel easy to spot among the vineyards beyond Neustadt. (It's between the villages of Gimmeldingen and Konigsbach). Sample a local wine on the balustraded terrace or in the hotel's charming garden. *6730 Neustadt 15, tel. 06321/66016. 23 rooms, most with shower. No credit cards.*

Under DM 70

Gästehaus Gisela. Located on the ouskirts of Neustadt in the Mussbach district, the Gisela pension is especially recommended for families. Children will immediately feel at home in Gunter Walcher's friendly, comfortable house. For the grown-ups, Herr Walcher organizes wine tastings. There are riding stables nearby. *Kleingasse 6, tel. 06321/69503. 9 rooms, 5 with bath. No credit cards.*

Dining
Under DM 30

Herberge aus der Zunftzeit. Dating from the 14th century, this is one of the oldest taverns on the Wine Road. Take a place at one of the ancient oak tables and order from a wine list as long as your arm. The Pfalzer sausage and *Zwiebelkuchen* (onion tart) are made on the premises and are unbeatable. *Mittelgasse 14, tel. 06321/7688. MC. Closed Mon.*

Ratsherrenstuben. This half-timbered building with a quiet courtyard, where every Monday for centuries the local vintners have been meeting to discuss business, offers local wines and full-bodied local specialties. *Marktpl. 10–12, tel. 06321/2070. Reservations advised. DC, MC, V. Closed Wed.*

Zur Festwiese. You'll find above-average local and regional cuisine in this hotel restaurant in a pleasant town-center location. *Festplatzstr. 6, tel. 06321/32506. AE, DC, MC, V. Closed Sun. dinner.*

Under DM 20 **Weinstube Eselsburg.** The tavern's jovial landlord finds time between serving creative Palatinate dishes to sketch and paint. He sings, too. The tavern is in the Musbach area of Neustadt, a 10-minute drive from the town center. *Kurpfalzstr. 62, Neustadt-Mussbach, tel. 06321/66984. No credit cards.*

Shopping Shopping along the Wine Road means, naturally, **wine.** Plenty of vineyards along the roadside invite you in to pass judgment on the year's vintage. In Neustadt, **Karl Sauter** (118 Hampstr.) is a walking encyclopedia of knowledge, and his shop is one of the best places to pick up a gift box of the area's best.

Nightlife If you tire of the wine taverns on the Wine Road, try the exotic **Bahama Club** (Landauerstr. 65). Neustadt has surprisingly upbeat nightlife; **Madison** (am Kartoffelmarkt 2) is the "in" place.

St. Martin and Hambach Castle

Trains leave Neustadt about once every hour for the five-minute run to Maikammer; from there, a quiet country road leads 3 kilometers (2 miles) to St. Martin—a pleasant half-hour stroll. Buses for Hambach run regularly from Neustadt.

St. Martin, 10 kilometers (6 miles) south of Neustadt, may be the loveliest village not only on the Wine Road but in the whole area—a reputation it nurtures by encouraging the surrounding vineyards to encroach on its narrow streets. You'll find vines clinging everywhere, linking the ancient houses with curling green garlands. Visit the little 15th-century church to see the imposing Renaissance tomb of the Dalberg family. Their castle, now romantically ruined, stands guard over the village.

There's another castle hereabouts you can visit, especially if your blood is stirred by tales of German nationalism and the overthrow of tyranny. It's **Hambach Castle,** standing about a half mile outside the village of Hambach, itself about 8 kilometers (5 miles) north of St. Martin. It's not the castle, built in the 11th century and largely ruined in the 17th, that's the attraction. Rather, you'll visit to honor an event that happened here in May 1832. Fired by the revolutionary turmoil that was sweeping across Europe and groaning under the repressive yoke, as they saw it, of a distant and aristocratic government, 30,000 stalwart Germans assembled at the castle demanding democracy, the overthrow of the Bavarian ruling house of Wittelsbach, and a united Germany. The symbol of their heroic demands was a flag, striped red, black, and yellow, which they flew from the castle. The old order proved rather more robust than these proto-democrats had reckoned on; the crowd was rapidly dispersed with some loss of life. The new flag was banned. It was not until 1919 that the monarchy was ousted and a united Germany became fully democratic. Fittingly, the flag flown from Hambach nearly 90 years earlier was adopted as that of the new German nation. (It was a short-lived triumph:

Hitler did away with both democracy and the flag when he came to power in 1932, and it was not until 1949, with the creation of the Federal Republic of Germany, that both were restored.) The castle remains a focus of the democratic aspirations of the Germans. Exhibits chart the progress of democracy in Germany. *Admission: DM 2.50 adults, DM 1 children. Open Mar.–Nov., daily 9–5.*

Burg Trifels

Trains leave Neustadt hourly for Landau, where you change for the 20-minute run to Annweiler.

Burg Trifels, standing sentinel over the village of Annweiler, is one of the most romantic buildings in the country, its drama only slightly spoiled by the fact that what you see today is a rather free reconstruction of the original Romanesque castle, rebuilt in 1937 (a period when a lot of Germans were keen on reestablishing what they saw as the glories of their "race"). The original castle was constructed in the mid-12th century by the Emperor Barbarossa, whose favorite castle it was said to have become. In 1193, English King Richard the Lion-Hearted, captured by Barbarossa on one of Richard's endless forays across Europe, was held for ransom here (the English grudgingly paid the immense sum). Of more lasting significance was the fact that from 1126 to 1273 Burg Trifels housed the imperial crown jewels. That's what's said to have led to the legend that Burg Trifels was the site of the Holy Grail, the bowl used by Christ at the Last Supper. In the Middle Ages, the Holy Grail was the object of numerous knightly quests, the purpose of which was not so much to find the Grail as to prove one's steadfastness and Christian virtue by embarking on an impossible task. *Admission: DM 3 adults, DM 1.50 children under 14. Open Apr.–Sept., Tues.–Sun. 9–1 and 2–6; Oct.–Mar., Tues.–Sun. 10–1 and 2–5.*

If you visit Burg Trifels, you'll pass the ruins of two neighboring castles as you head up the hill. These are the castles of **Scharfenberg** and **Anebos.** Their craggy, overgrown silhouettes add greatly to the romance of a visit to Burg Trifels.

8 Heidelberg and the Neckar Valley

Including Mannheim and Heilbronn

Heidelberg claims to be Germany's number one tourist destination. It's a claim that's obviously challenged by Munich and Berlin, but on a comparative, visitor-per-capita basis, Heidelberg is up there near the top, if not at the summit. For many, it *is* the summit of a visit to Germany, an indispensable part of any itinerary—a judgment shared by the scores of writers, composers, and historical figures who have visited the university city over the centuries and fallen under its spell.

If you visit in summer, when the city is so packed you can hardly move down some of the narrower streets, you might wish you could be transported to a more leisurely century. Transport yourself instead to one of the nearby Neckar River towns, where accommodation is cheaper and more easily available and access to Heidelberg is still easy. Or consider staying 15 kilometers (10 miles) east in Mannheim, an industrial city with surprising charm. The Neckar Valley beyond Heidelberg has its own charm. It's a favored holiday route, snaking a scenic way east, then south, between the river and the wooded slopes of the Odenwald Forest, before hitting the rolling, vine-covered countryside around Heilbronn. This is not off-the-beaten-track territory, but there are plenty of opportunities along the way to escape into quiet side valleys and to visit little towns that sleep in leafy peace. You'll find just as much to charm you here as along the Romantic Road, but little of the tourist hype. Scarcely one of these towns is without its guardian castle, standing in stern splendor above medieval streets. This is a region that can delight—and sometimes surprise—even the most hardened traveler.

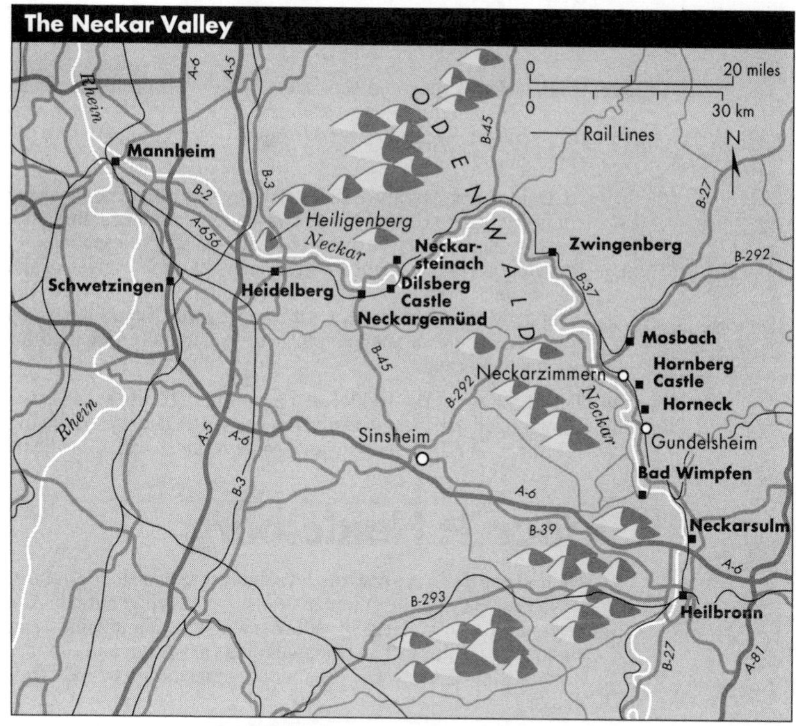

Essential Information

Lodging If you plan to visit Heidelberg or Mannheim in summer, make reservations well in advance and expect to pay top rates. To get away from the crowds, consider staying out of town—at Neckargemünd, say—and taking the bus into the city. Staying in a castle hotel can be fun. This area is second only to the Rhine for baronial-style castle hotels studding the hilltops. Most have terrific views as well as stone-passageways-and-four-poster-bed atmosphere.

Highly recommended establishments are indicated by a star ★.

Dining In Heidelberg you'll be dining with tradition at your table: There are few restaurants in the city that don't have decor to match the stage-set atmosphere of the town. Elsewhere, you'll find atmosphere and frequently excellent food in the restaurants of the castle hotels along the Neckar. In smaller towns along the valley, simple inns, dark and timbered, are the norm. Outside Heidelberg and Mannheim, prices can be low. Specialties in the Neckar Valley are much the same as along the Wine Road, with sausages and local wines figuring prominently.

Highly recommended restaurants are indicated by a star ★.

Biking The Neckar Valley is ideal for biking—although the Odenwald hills on the northern bank call for a machine with plenty of gears. If you follow the river, keep to the south bank, where traffic is lighter than on the other side. Bikes can be hired from any of the train stations en route for DM 12 per day—half that if you have a valid train ticket.

Hiking The Neckar Valley and the Odenwald Forest on its northern bank are splendid hiking territory. Try any of the small valleys—known by the locals as *Klingen*—that cut north into the Odenwald.

In Heidelberg, escape the crowds by crossing the Theodor Heuss Bridge to the north bank of the Neckar and climbing the heights above the river along the path called **Philosophenweg.** Many painters have captured the views the route gives of the city below. Strike off into the woodland above toward the summit of the **Heiligenberg.** On the way you'll pass a curious Nazi-era relic—an open amphitheater originally intended for woodland festivals.

The Arts and Nightlife The highlight of the Heidelberg arts-and-nightlife scene is the annual open-air **theater festival** in the castle courtyard during August. For information and reservations, call tel. 06221/58976.

Tour 1: Heidelberg

Heidelberg deserves several days, but as we mentioned before, if you're visiting in summer, consider staying outside the city—in a nearby Neckar Valley town or in Mannheim—and commuting in daily. The transport links are good, and the cost is more than offset by the cheaper accommodation outside Heidelberg.

From Frankfurt

By Train The most direct service to Heidelberg leaves Frankfurt every 90 minutes; journey time is just over one hour. A more frequent InterCity service involves a change at Mannheim, and the ticket is more expensive.

By Bus The **Europabus** No. 1018 from Frankfurt to Paris calls at Heidelberg. The bus leaves Frankfurt's main train station daily at 10 PM and gets to Heidelberg one hour later.

By Car From Frankfurt, take the Autobahn A-5 (European Autobahn E-4) due south for 70 kilometers (43 miles), exiting at Heidelberg.

Tourist office: Verkehrsverein Heidelberg, Friedrich-Ebert-Anlage 2, 6900 Heidelberg, tel. 06221/21341.

Exploring If any city in Germany can be said to encapsulate the spirit of the country, it must be Heidelberg. Scores of poets and composers—virtually the entire 19th-century German Romantic movement—have sung its praises. And others, too. Goethe and Mark Twain both fell in love here: the German writer with a beautiful young woman, the American with the city itself. Sigmund Romberg set his operetta *The Student Prince* in the city; Carl Maria von Weber wrote his lushly Romantic opera *Der Freischütz (The Marksman)* here. Composer Robert Schumann was a student at the university. It was the university, the oldest in the country, that gave impetus to the artistic movement that claimed Heidelberg as its own, but the natural beauty of the city—embraced by mountains, forests, vineyards, and the Neckar River, and crowned by its ruined castle—provided the materials of their trade. The campaign they waged on behalf of the town has been astoundingly successful. Heidelberg's fame is out of all proportion to its size; over 2.5 million visitors crowd its streets every year. If you want to find the *feine Heidelberg* ("fine Heidelberg") of poet Viktor von Scheffel's day, avoid visiting in summer. Late fall, when the vines turn a faded gold, or early spring, with the first green shoots of the year appearing, can both be captivating. Best of all, visit in the depths of winter, when hoary river mists creep through the narrow streets of the old town and awaken the ghosts of a romantic past.

The city was the political center of the Rhineland Palatinate. At the end of the Thirty Years' War (1618–1648), the Elector Carl Ludwig married his daughter to the brother of Louis XIV in hopes of bringing peace to the Rhineland. But when the elector's son died without an heir, Louis XIV used the marriage alliance as an excuse to claim Heidelberg, and, in 1689, the town was sacked and laid to waste. Four years later, he sacked the town again. From its ashes arose the town you see today: a Baroque town built on Gothic foundations, with narrow, twisting streets and alleyways. The new Heidelberg changed under the influence of industrial development stretching into the suburbs, but the old heart of the city remains intact, exuding the spirit of romantic Germany.

Extending west to east through the old town is **Hauptstrasse,** an elegant pedestrian mall that runs straight as an arrow for a half mile to the main square, **Marktplatz.** This tour will take you down Hauptstrasse, where you can explore the attractions along it and on its narrow side streets, before going on to the number-one sight, the castle. You can then visit the rest of the town around Marktplatz.

Numbers in the margin correspond to points of interest on the Heidelberg map.

1 As you walk down Hauptstrasse, the **university**—or part of it anyway; there are four separate university complexes in the town—enfolds you almost immediately. On Brunnengasse, a lane to your left, is the anatomy wing, a former monastery taken over by the university in 1801. What had been a chapel became a dissecting laboratory; the sacristy became a morgue.

Out on Hauptstrasse again, pause in front of the **Haus zum Riesen** (the Giant's House), so called because the local worthy who built it in 1707 (using stone from the destroyed castle) put up the larger-than-life statue of himself that you see over the front door. Wander down Hauptstrasse. On your right you'll pass the Protestant **Providence Church** (built by the Elector Carl Ludwig in the mid-16th century) and the richly ornate
2 doorway of the **Wormser Hof,** former Heidelberg seat of the bishops of Worms. Look at its lead-paned Renaissance oriel window (bay window) on the second floor: It's one of the finest in the city.

Opposite, on the left, is Heidelberg's leading museum, the
3 **Kurpfälzisches Museum** (Electoral Palatinate Museum), housed in a Baroque palace. Its collections chart the history of Heidelberg. Among the exhibits are two contrasting standouts. One is a replica of the jaw of Heidelberg Man, a key link in the evolutionary chain and thought to date from half a million years ago; the original was unearthed near the city in 1907. You'll need rare powers of imagination to get much of a sense of this early ancestor from just his (or her) jaw, however. The oth-

Alte Brücke, **16**
Castle, **10**
Heiliggeistkirche, **14**
Hotel zum Ritter, **15**
Königstuhl, **12**
Königstuhl funicular, **9**
Kurpfälzisches Museum, **3**
Molkenkur, **11**
New University, **6**
Old University, **4**
Rathaus, **13**
St. Peter, **8**
Studentenkarzer, **5**
Universitätsbibliothek, **7**
University, **1**
Wormser Hof, **2**

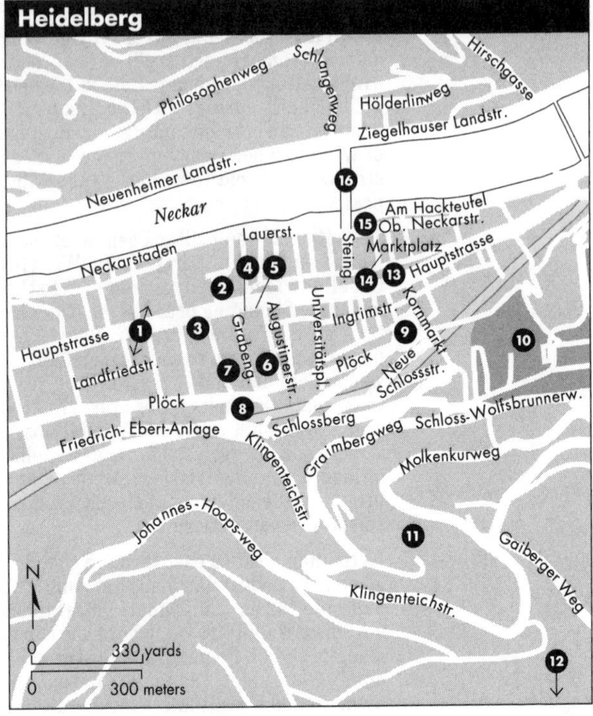

er presents no such problems. It's the *Twelve Apostles Altarpiece,* one of the largest and finest works of early Renaissance sculptor Tilman Riemenschneider. Its exquisite detailing and technical sophistication are matched by the simple faith that radiates from the faces of the Apostles. On the top floor of the museum there's a rich range of 19th-century German paintings and drawings, many of Heidelberg. *Hauptstr. 97. Admission: DM 2 adults, children free. Open Tues.–Sun. 10–5 (Thurs. 10–9).*

4 From the museum, you're two blocks from the **Old University,** founded in 1386 and rebuilt in the early 18th century for the Elector Johann Wilhelm. Behind it, in Augustinerstrasse, is
5 the former students' prison, the **Studentenkarzer,** where, from 1712 to 1914, unruly students were incarcerated (tradition dictated that students couldn't be thrown into the town jail). The students could be held for up to 14 days; they were left to subsist on bread and water for the first three but thereafter were allowed to attend lectures, receive guests, and have food brought in from the outside. A stay in the jail became as coveted as a scar inflicted in the university's fencing clubs. There's bravado, even poetic flair, to be deciphered in the graffiti of two centuries that cover the walls and ceiling of the narrow cell. *Admission: DM 1 adults, 70 pf children. Open Mon.–Sat. 9–5.*

6 Across Universitätsplatz (University Square) is the **New University,** built between 1930 and 1932 with funds raised in the United States by a former American student at the university, the U.S. Ambassador to Germany, J. G. Schurman. The ancient section you see incorporated in the new building is all that

remains of the old city walls. It's the **Hexenturm,** the Witches' Tower, where witches were locked up in the Middle Ages.

Opposite the New University, at the end of the street called
7 Plöck, is the university library, the **Universitätsbibliothek.** Its
1.5 million volumes include the 14th-century *Manesse Codex*, a
collection of medieval songs and poetry once performed in the
courts of Germany by the Minnesänger. *Plöck 107–109. Admission free. Open Mon.–Fri. 8:30 AM–10 PM, Sat. 9–5.*

Opposite the library is the city's oldest parish church, the
8 Gothic church of **St. Peter.** Linger in its graveyard; the graves
of many leading citizens are here, some dating back 500 and
more years. The Baroque building you see immediately east of
the church, originally a Jesuit seminary, later a lunatic asylum,
is a students' dormitory.

9 From here, continue along Plöck to the **Königstuhl funicular,**
which hoists visitors to the Königstuhl heights, 1,860 feet
10 above Heidelberg, stopping at the ruined **castle** on the way.
The two-minute ride to the castle costs DM 2 (DM 1.30 for children); the 17-minute ride to the top costs DM 4 (DM 2.40 for children). The funicular leaves every 20 minutes in the morning and every 10 minutes in the afternoon. The funicular may be the quickest way to get to the castle, but you can also take the winding road up, following in the footsteps of generations of earlier visitors. (You can always walk down from the castle if you want to pretend to be Mark Twain but don't fancy the hike up.)

The castle was already in ruins when Germany's 19th-century Romantics fell under its spell, drawn by the mystery of its Gothic turrets and Renaissance walls etched against the verdant background of the thick woodland above Heidelberg. The oldest parts still standing date from the 15th century, though most of the great complex was built in the Renaissance and Baroque styles of the 16th and 17th centuries, when the castle was the seat and power base of the Palatinate Electors. What's most striking is the architectural variety of the building, vivid proof of changing tastes (and uses) down the years. There's even an "English wing," built in 1610 by the Elector Friedrich V for his teenage Scottish bride, Elizabeth Stuart; its plain square-windowed facade appears positively foreign in comparison to the more opulent styles of the rest of the castle. (The enamored Friedrich also had a charming garden laid out for his young bride; its imposing arched entryway, the Elisabethentor, was put up overnight to surprise her on her 19th birthday.) The architectural highlight, however, remains the Renaissance courtyard—harmonious, graceful, and ornate.

Allow at least two hours to tour the complex—and expect long lines in summer (up to 30 minutes is usual). On no account miss the **Heidelberger Fass** or the fascinating **Apothekenmuseum.** The Heidelberger Fass is an enormous wine barrel in the cellars, made from 130 oak trees and capable of holding 49,000 gallons. It was used to hold wines paid as tax by wine growers in the Palatinate. In the rule of the Elector Carl Philip, the barrel was guarded by the court jester, a Tyrolean dwarf called Perkeo. Legend has it that, small or not, he could consume frighteningly large quantities of wine—he was said to have been the most prodigious drinker in Germany—and that he died when he drank a glass of water by mistake. A statue of

Perkeo stands opposite the massive barrel. The Apothekenmuseum is a delight, filled with containers (each with a carefully painted enamel label), beautifully made scales, little drawers, shelves, a marvelous reconstruction of an 18th-century apothecary's shop, dried beetles and toads, and a mummy with a full head of hair. *Castle admission: DM 4 adults, DM 2 children (this qualifies you for the tour and for entry to the Heidelberger Fass). Open Apr.–Oct., daily 9–7; Nov.–Mar. 9–6. Guided tours from 9–noon and 1:30–4. Apothekenmuseum admission: DM 2 adults, DM 1 children. Open Apr.–Oct., daily 10–5; Nov.–Mar., Sat. and Sun. only 11–5.*

The castle is floodlit in the summer, and in June and September fireworks displays are given from the terraces. In August, the castle is the setting for an open-air theater festival. Performances of *The Student Prince* figure prominently.

There are fine views of the old town from the castle terraces, but for an even better view, ride the funicular up to either of the
11 12 next two stops, **Molkenkur** and, at the summit, **Königstuhl.** If the weather's clear, you can see south as far as the Black Forest, and west to the Vosges Mountains of France.

Back in town, walk toward the river from the funicular station to **Kornmarkt.** It's one of the oldest squares in Heidelberg, graced with a fine Baroque statue of the Virgin Mary. The impressive building on the corner of Mittelgasse was once Heidelberg's foremost hostelry, the Prinz Karl, where Mark Twain stayed in 1874. A few years earlier it had been used as a barracks by Bismarck's triumphant Prussian army as they swept through the Rhineland forcibly uniting Germany. The young Prince Wilhelm von Preussen, later Kaiser Wilhelm I, was among the soldiers stationed there; prudently, he brought
13 along his own camp bed. The **Rathaus** (Town Hall), a stately Baroque building dating from 1701, faces you now. Be here at 7 PM to hear the melodious chimes that ring out from the building. The west side of the Rathaus fronts Heidelberg's market square, the Marktplatz. It was here, in the towering shadow of
14 the 14th-century **Heiliggeistkirche** (Church of the Holy Ghost) that criminals were tortured and decapitated and witches were burned. The church itself, dominating the west side of the square, fell victim to the plundering General Tilly, leader of the Catholic League, during the Thirty Years' War. Tilly loaded the church's greatest treasure, the *Biblioteka Palatina*, at the time the largest library in Germany, onto 500 carts and trundled it off to Rome, where he presented it to the pope. Few of the volumes found their way back to Heidelberg. At the end of the 17th century, French troops plundered the church again, destroying the family tombs of the Palatinate electors; only the 15th-century tomb of Elector Ruprecht III and his wife Elisabeth von Hohenzollern remain today.

Opposite the church, on Hauptstrasse, you'll see the elaborate
15 Renaissance facade of the **Hotel zum Ritter,** all curlicues, columns, and gables. It takes its name from the statue of a Roman knight ("Ritter") atop one of the many gables. Its builder, Carolus Belier, had the Latin inscription *Persta Invicta Venus* added to the facade in gold letters—"Beauty, Remain Unconquerable." It was an injunction that seems to have had the desired effect: This was the only Renaissance building in the city to have been spared the attentions of the invading French in 1689 and 1693. Between 1695 and 1705 it was used as Heidel-

berg's town hall; later it became an inn. Today it's the most atmospheric hotel in town (*see* Lodging and Dining, *below*). Skirt the cathedral, cross the former fish market, the Fischmarkt, and turn down picturesque Steingasse. Within a few steps
16 you'll have reached the river and the romantically turreted **Alte Brücke** (Old Bridge). It's the fifth bridge to be built here since medieval times, its predecessors having suffered various unhappy fates (one was destroyed by ice floes). The Elector Carl Theodor, who built it in 1786–88, must have been confident that it would last: He had a statue of himself put on it, the plinth decorated with Neckar nymphs (river maidens). Just to be on the safe side, he also put up a statue of the saint appointed to guard over it, St. John Nepomuk. You can walk onto the bridge from the old town under a portcullis spanned by two Baroque towers, each capped with a *Spitzhelm* spire. In the left (west) tower are three dank dungeons that once held common criminals. Between the towers, above the gate, were more salubrious lockups, with views of the river and the castle; these were reserved for debtors. Above the portcullis you'll see a memorial plaque that pays warm tribute to the Austrian forces who helped Heidelberg beat back a French attempt to capture the bridge in 1799. Walk onto the bridge and turn to soak up one of the finest views in Heidelberg, across the river to the old town and the castle above. There are equally good views from the road that runs along the far side of the river. For the best view of all, climb up **Schlangenweg**—it means Snake Path—to **Philosophenweg,** a path through the woods above the river. Be here as the sun sets, turning the castle to gold, for a vision to cherish for a lifetime.

Lodging

Under DM 180

Neckar Hotel. You're assured a river view at this friendly modern hotel. The location is ideal, halfway between the train station and the old town. *Bismarckstr. 19, tel. 06221/10814. 25 rooms with bath. AE, MC, V.*

Under DM 130

Central. This establishment provides a simple bed and breakfast on the castle side of the Neckar River, beneath the Königstuhl. *Kaiserstr. 75, tel. 06221/20672. 51 rooms with bath. AE, MC, V.*

Hotel Seipel. Leimen is a pleasant wine village 6½ kilometers (4 miles) south of Heidelberg, and the Seipel—a modern hotel on the edge of a sports park and woodland—offers an alternative to the expensive places in the nearby city. *Am Sportpark, Leimen, tel. 06224/7040. 30 rooms with bath. MC.*

Parkhotel Haarlaas. A room overlooking the Neckar costs more, but how can you visit Heidelberg and shun a room with a view? The hotel is on the outskirts of town, but a regular bus service stops nearby. *In der Neckarhelle 162–164, tel. 06221/45021. 100 rooms, 95 with bath. AE, DC.*

Dining

Under DM 40

Merian Stuben. Ornate 19th-century decor, high ceilings, and deferential uniformed waiters combine to give an unmistakably Victorian air to this restaurant. The large menu, ranging from local specialties to international dishes, is very correct, too. The Merian adjoins the Stadthalle beside the river. *Neckarstaden 24, tel. 06221/27381. AE, DC, MC, V. Closed Mon. and Jan.*

Perkeo. Ask for a table in the atmospheric Schlosstube, and, if suckling pig is on the menu, ask for that, too. You'll then be dining in the style for which this historic old restaurant has been known for close to three centuries. *Hauptstr. 75, tel. 06221/160613. Reservations advised. AE, DC, MC, V.*

★ **Zur Herrenmühle.** You'll sample delicately prepared classic French cuisine from pewter plates at rough-hewn tables at this atmospheric 17th-century tavern in the old town. Fish is the specialty here, and the desserts are noteworthy. *Hauptstr. 237, tel. 06221/12909. Reservations advised. AE, DC, MC. Closed lunch.*

Under DM 30 **Schnookelooch.** This picturesque and lively old tavern dates back to 1407 and is inextricably linked with Heidelberg's history and its university. Most evenings a piano player joins the fun. *Haspelgasse 8, tel. 06221/22733. Reservations required. No credit cards.*

★ **Zum Roten Ochsen.** Bismarck and Mark Twain ate here; so, too, many years later, did John Foster Dulles. It's been run by the Spengel family for more than a century, and they jealously guard the rough-hewn, half-timbered atmosphere. The mood is festive and noisy, with rowdy singing most nights. *Hauptstr. 217, tel. 06221/20977. Reservations required. No credit cards. Closed Sun., public holidays, and mid-Dec.–mid-Jan.*

Lodging and Dining
Under DM 130

Gutsschänke Grenzhof. This small farmhouse-turned-hotel, on the rural fringes of Heidelberg in the district of Grenzhof, has maintained some of its former atmosphere. It's set in expansive gardens, and walking trails skirt the front door. *Grenzhof No. 9, tel. 06202/3604. 10 rooms with bath. Facilities: restaurant (dinner only), café, beer garden. AE, MC.*

Intercity Arcade. This modern (1986) lodging adjoining Heidelberg's railway station, a mile or two from the old town district, aims to be family-friendly. Functional rooms in the 8-story building are soundproofed against traffic noise. *Lessingstr. 3, tel. 06221/9130. 99 rooms with bath. Facilities: restaurant with special children's menu, bar, children's playroom. AE, DC, MC, V.*

Splurge ★ **Romantik Hotel zum Ritter St. Georg.** The only Renaissance building in Heidelberg offers atmosphere by the barrel-load. One dining room flourishes rough plaster walls, arched doorways, exposed beams, and a suit of armor; in another, the food is served on pewter dishes. Meals run from DM 18 to DM 58. The comfortable bedrooms—some traditional, some more modern—average DM 200 for a double. *Hauptstr. 178, tel. 06221/24272. 31 rooms with bath. AE, DC, MC, V.*

Shopping

The Neckar Valley is famous for its **glass** and **crystal.** You can buy directly from the factory at Neckarzimmern or from such Heidelberg shops as **Crystal** (Hauptstr. 135) and **König** (Universitätspl.). Both are in the excellent pedestrian shopping zone, which stretches for more than a half mile through the ancient heart of the city. You can find interesting (and, often, reasonably priced) **antiques** at **Spiess & Walther** (Friedrich-Ebert-Anlage 23a).

Heidelberg has two tempting **markets.** On Wednesday and Sunday mornings, make for the central market square, Marktplatz; on Tuesday and Friday mornings, make for Friedrich-Ebert-Platz. Sunday's is a flea market; the others are a mixture of flea and green markets. There's another **flea market** in the Dehner suburb every second Saturday.

The Arts

Information on all upcoming events is listed in Heidelberg's monthly *Ketchup* magazine (which costs DM 3); the monthly

Konzerte im Heidelberger Stern (available free—pick it up at the tourist office); and *Heidelberg Aktuell* (also free and available from the tourist office).

Heidelberg has a thriving theater scene. The **Theater der Stadt** (Friedrichstr. 5) is the best-known theater in town; others include the **Zimmer Theater** (Hauptstr. 118, tel. 06221/21069) and the **Theater in Augustinum** (Jasperstr. 2, tel. 06221/3881). Theater tickets are available from **Theaterkasse** (Theaterstr. 4, tel. 06221/20519). For information on performances at the castle during the annual **Schloss-Spiele festival,** call 06221/58976.

Nightlife Heidelberg's nightlife is concentrated around the Heiliggeistkirche (Church of the Holy Ghost), in the Old Town. For a fun night out, try the **Hard Rock Café** (Hauptstr.); it's not exactly Student Prince territory, but it's a good place for videos and burgers. For blues, jazz, and funk, try **Hookemann** (Fischmarkt 3); admission is free. Germany's oldest jazz cellar is **Cave 54** (Krämergasse 2). The **Goldener Reichsapfel** nearby is always crowded after 10 PM; the mood is smokey and loud. **Club 1900** (Hauptstr.) is a well-established disco. The fanciest bars, along with many trendy cafés, are along the main pedestrian street, Haupstrasse. For most, however, nightlife in Heidelberg means a visit to one of the student taverns to drink wine and beer, lock arms, and sing. There are no better places to try than **Zum Roten Ochsen** and **Schnookelooch,** both in business for several centuries and both offering low-beamed Teutonic fun and games. They can, however, get overrun with tourists in midsummer, so try the numerous drinking haunts, along Unterestrasse, where students spill out onto the street.

Tour 2: Mannheim and Schwetzingen

Mannheim

An hourly InterCity train connects Heidelberg with Mannheim. The journey takes 12 minutes. Tourist office: Bahnhofplatz 1, 6800 Mannheim 1, tel. 0621/101–011.

The Neckar and the Rhine meet at Mannheim, a major industrial center and the second-largest river port in Europe. Inside its industrial sprawl lurks an elegant old town, carefully rebuilt after wartime bomb damage. Mannheim is unusual among the cities of the Rhine for having been founded only in 1606, but it's even more unusual for having been laid out on a grid pattern. It was the forward-looking Palatinate Elector Friedrich IV who built the city, imposing on it the rigid street plan that forms the heart of the old town, or Quadratstadt (literally, "squared town"). Streets running northeast-southwest—from one river to the other—are labeled A through U; those running northwest-southeast are numbered 1 through 7. So, if you're looking for the central Marktplatz, it's G-1 on your map. Rationalism rules. The only exception to this system is Kurpfalzstrasse, which cuts through the heart of the town, leading southwest from the Neckar to the Schloss (palace). There's a terrific view down it from the main staircase of the palace.

Though it was the Elector Friedrich IV who built Mannheim, his court was at Heidelberg. In 1720, the Elector Carl Philip went one stage further, moving the court to Mannheim rather than rebuilding what remained of his castle at Heidelberg after it had been sacked by Louis XIV's French troops in 1689 and again in 1693. (What, ironically, helped prompt his decision was the desire to build a palace modeled on the absolutist, classical lines of Louis XIV's great palace at Versailles; like many 18th-century German rulers, Carl Philip eagerly seized the example provided by Louis XIV to reinforce his own absolute right to rule.) The palace was 40 years in the building, completed only in 1768. Five separate architects were employed, their combined efforts producing one of the largest buildings in Europe, a vast, relentlessly symmetrical edifice containing more than 400 rooms and 2,000 windows, and with a frontage more than a quarter-mile long. The palace was reduced to a smoking ruin in World War II, and rebuilt in the '50s. Today it belongs to Mannheim University. The great hall and some of the state rooms can be visited; they're impressive, but strangely lifeless now. *Furfürstlichtes Schloss. Admission: DM 2 adults, DM 1 children. Open Apr.–Oct., Tues.–Sun. 10–noon and 3–5; Nov.–Mar., Sat. and Sun. only 10–noon and 3–5. Tours daily Apr.–Oct.*

From the palace, you can either head off to the right to visit the Städtische Kunsthalle (City Art Museum) or make a left to see the Jesuitenkirche (Jesuit Church) three blocks away at A-4. The **Jesuitenkirche** is the largest and most important Baroque church in Germany, its immense, rigorously classical facade flanked by graceful domed spires (known as *Spitzhelm,* after their resemblance to old-time German helmets) and topped by a massive dome. It was begun in 1733, commissioned by the Elector Carl Philip to commemorate his family's return to Catholicism. The church, too, was severely bombed during the war, and most of the internal decorations were lost (including what were probably the most lavish ceiling and dome paintings in the country). But, though plainer now, the airy grandeur of the interior suggests something of its former magnificence. Pause as you go in to look at the ornate wrought-iron gates at the entrance.

The **city art museum** is located at Friedrichsplatz, at the east fringe of the Quadratstadt, a 10-minute walk from the Jesuit Church. The building itself is a prime example of Jugendstil (Art Nouveau) architecture, constructed in 1907. Provocative and large-scale modern sculptures stand outside. Inside, you'll find one of the largest and best collections of modern art in Germany. All the big names are here, from Manet to Warhol. *Moltkestr. 9. Admission free. Open Tues.–Sun. 10–5 (Thurs. 10–8).*

Lodging
Under DM 130

Hotel am Bismarck. The Iron Chancellor's statue stands guard over this centrally located hotel. It's family-run, with individually furnished, homey rooms. The room rate includes a substantial buffet breakfast. *Bismarckpl. 9–11, tel. 0621/403–096. 50 rooms with bath. AE, MC, V.*

Dining
Under DM 30

Alte Munz. For old German atmosphere, local specialties, and a wide range of beers, the Alte Munz is hard to beat. Try the suckling pig if it's available. *P–7 1, tel. 0621/28262. Reservations advised. AE, MC, V.*

Goldene Gans. Freshly made local dishes (Pfälzer liver-dumpling and home-cured sausage are two to try) and wines from the tavern's own vineyards combine with surprisingly low prices to make this a terrific, low-cost bet. *Tattersallstr. 19, tel. 0621/105–277. No credit cards. Closed Sun. and Dec. 24–Jan. 6.*

Under DM 20 **Eichbaum Brauhaus.** You can dine here well for DM 10, washing the large portions of Rhineland fare down with beer brewed on the premises. In summer, a large beer garden beckons. *Kafertalerstr. 168, tel. 0621/372–735. AE, MC.*

Lodging and Dining
Under DM 130 **Löwen-Seckenheim.** This modest but comfortable modern hotel in the Seckenheim district has a popular tavern-style restaurant and in summer a beer garden. *Hauptstr. 159, tel. 0621/48080. 65 rooms, most with bath. Facilities: restaurant, bar. AE, MC. Closed Dec. 23–Jan. 7.*

Under DM 90 **Zum Ochsen.** This picturesque old tavern in the Feudenheim district has been in business since 1632. Bedrooms are on the small side, but comfortably and individually furnished. In the paneled dining rooms you'll find fine Sauerbraten and a wide choice of local wines. *Hauptstr. 70, Feudenheim, tel. 0621/792–065. AE, MC, V.*

Schwetzingen

Trains leave every half-hour from Mannheim station for the 15-minute ride to Schwetzingen.

Schwetzingen is worth visiting for its impressive palace, a formal 18th-century building constructed as a summer residence by the Palatinate electors. It's a noble, rose-colored building, imposing and harmonious, but the real interest centers on the park, a blend of formal French and informal English styles, with neatly bordered gravel walks trailing off into the dark woodland. The 18th-century planners of this delightful park had fun with the construction of an exotic mosque, complete with minarets and a shimmering pool. Somewhere along the line they got more than a little muddled, however, and gave the building a very German Baroque portal. Be sure to see the charming Rococo theater, the scene each June of an international music festival. Another rare pleasure awaits you if you're in Schwetzingen in June: The town is Germany's asparagus center, and fresh asparagus dishes dominate the menu of every local restaurant.

Tour 3: Along the Burgenstrasse

The Burgenstrasse—named after the castles (*Burgen*) that mark the route like milestones—runs from Mannheim to Nürnberg, but the stretch we'll be following snakes through the Neckar Valley between Heidelberg and Heilbronn. You can visit the villages individually, basing yourself in Heidelberg or Heilbronn; or you can cover the route easily in a day trip. Local buses and trains connect the villages, and a daily Europabus service covers the entire route.

This is wine country, and there are numerous vineyards along the Neckar Valley road (B-27) between Heidelberg and Heilbronn. Those around **Gundelsheim** are judged to be the best, but for sheer historical worth you can't beat a bottle from the **Hornberg Castle** estate (*see* Mosbach, *below*).

Neckargemünd

Trains leave Heidelberg's main railway station about every half-hour for the 12-minute ride to Neckargemünd and continue on to Neckarsteinach, five mintues farther along. The Europabus leaves Heidelberg station daily at 8 AM *and stops in Neckargemünd 15 minutes later.*

An hour's walk from Heidelberg along the river bank (or a short train or bus ride) brings you to a collection of Neckar valley castles. Neckargemünd, on the south bank of the river, was once a bustling river town; today it's a sleepy sort of place, though it can make a good base from which to see Heidelberg if you want to avoid the summertime crowds there. Eight kilometers (5 miles) farther, perched impregnably on a hill, is **Dilsberg Castle,** one of the few hereabouts to have withstood General Tilly's otherwise all-conquering forces in the Thirty Years' War. Until the students' jail in Heidelberg was built, its dungeons were used to accommodate the university's more unruly students. To reach the castle, take the train from Neckargemünd to Neckarsteinach; it's a pleasant two-mile walk, over a bridge across a bend in the river. The view from the castle's battlements over the valley and the green expanse of the Odenwald forest beyond is worth the walk and the climb.

Neckarsteinach is known as the **Vierburgenstadt** (Town of the Four Castles), for the fairly obvious reason that there are four castles here. They form one large complex—the **Schadeck**—most of which dates from the 12th century. Today it's mostly ruined, but those sections still intact are the baronial residence of an aristocratic German family.

Lodging
Under DM 180

Hotel zum Ritter. If you can't get the accommodation you're looking for in Heidelberg, this half-timbered, 16th-century alternative, with exposed beams and creaking passages, can't fail to impress. It overlooks the Neckar, so ask for a room with a view. *Neckarstr. 40, tel. 06223/7035. 40 rooms with bath. AE, MC, V.*

Dining
Under DM 20

Waibels Gasthaus Neckartal. The terrace commands a fine view of the river, but even on rainy days you'll receive a warm welcome—and excellent traditional cuisine—in the cozy dining room. The venison stew, an autumn dish, is famous hereabouts. *Ortsstr. 9, Rainbach, tel. 06223/2455. AE, MC. Closed Mon.–Tues. and Jan.*

Lodging and Dining
Under DM 150

Zum Schwanen. This fine old country-house hotel sits right on the Neckar and offers splendid, uninterrupted views. The smaller double rooms go for less than DM 150. The restaurant has a French accent, and if you choose with care you can keep costs under DM 30. *Uferstr. 16, tel. 06223/7070. 11 rooms and one apartment with bath. AE, DC, MC, V.*

Under DM 110

Zum Röss'l. It's been catering to travelers for nearly 350 years. The wood-paneled restaurant, where you can dine for under DM 30, serves fish from the nearby river, meat from the Röss'l's own butcher shop, and an excellent brandy from its own distillery. The small but comfortably furnished rooms on the upper floors cost less than DM 90 for a double. *Heidelberger Str. 15, tel. 06223/2665. 13 rooms, 6 with bath. MC.*

Zwingenberg

Trains leave Heidelberg approximately once an hour for the 40-minute run to Zwingenberg. The daily Europabus service, leaving Heidelberg at 8 AM, covers the route directly in 48 minutes.

In Zwingenberg you'll find what many believe to be the most romantic castle of the Burgenstrasse, its medieval towers thrusting through the dark woodland. Some say it's the most romantic along the Neckar (the one at Heidelberg excepted). It's owned by the margraves of Baden and is open limited times only, but if you happen along when the castle is open, stop in to admire the frescoed 15th-century chapel and the collection of hunting trophies. *Admission: DM 3. Open May–Sept., Tues., Fri., and Sun. only 2–4.*

Mosbach

You have to change at Neckarelz on the hour-long ride from Heidelberg to Mosbach. Trains leave approximately once an hour from Heidelberg's main railway station.

The little town of Mosbach is one of the most charming towns on the Neckar, and its ancient market square, Marktplatz, contains one of Germany's most exquisite half-timbered buildings. It's the early 17th-century **Palmsches Haus,** its upper stories smothered with intricate timbering. The **Rathaus,** built 50 years earlier, is a modest affair in comparison.

A 5-kilometer (3-mile) riverside stroll east from Mosbach brings you to the massive circular bulk of **Hornberg Castle** rising above the woods that drop to the riverbank. The road up to the castle leads through vineyards that have been providing excellent dry white wines for centuries. Today the castle is part hotel and restaurant (*see below*) and part museum. In the 16th century it was home to the larger-than-life knight Götz von Berlichingen (1480–1562). When this remarkable fellow lost his right arm fighting in a petty dynastic squabble, the Landshut War of Succession, in 1504, he had a blacksmith fashion an iron one for him. The original designs for this fearsome artificial limb are on view in the castle, as is a suit of armor that belonged to him. For most Germans, the rambunctious knight is best remembered for a remark he delivered to the Palatinate elector (which was faithfully reproduced by Goethe in his play *Götz von Berlichingen).* Responding to a reprimand from the elector, von Berlichingen told him, more or less, to "kiss my ass" (the original German is substantially more earthy). To this day, the polite version of this insult is known as a "Götz von Berlichingen." *Admission: DM 2.50 adults, DM 1 children. Open Apr.–Nov., daily 9–5.*

During the Peasants' War (1525), Götz von Berlichingen and his troops destroyed the fine medieval castle of **Horneck,** 5 kilometers (3 miles) upriver. It was subsequently rebuilt and stands in all its medieval glory. Once it was owned by the Teutonic Order of Knights; today it has a more mundane role as the retirement home of a German charity.

Lodging and Dining
Splurge
★

Burg Hornberg. Some complain that it hasn't much panache for an 11th-century castle, but rooms (doubles cost between DM 120 and DM 190) are comfortable, and some have great views over the hotel's own vineyards to the river. The restaurant features venison (in season) and fresh fish; a meal there will cost about DM 70—more if you order a bottle of the castle estate's own excellent wine. *6951 Neckarzimmern, tel. 06261/4064. 27 rooms and 1 suite with bath. Facilities: garden, sun terrace, minigolf. MC, V.*

Bad Wimpfen

Trains leave Heidelberg hourly for Bad Wimpfen. The journey takes 70 minutes.

Rich in history and beauty, Bad Wimpfen was founded by the Romans, who built a fortress here and a bridge across the Neckar in the 1st century AD. By the early Middle Ages, Bad Wimpfen had become an imperial center; the 12th-century Emperor Barbarossa built his largest palace here. Much of what remains of it can be visited, including the imperial living quarters with their stately pillared windows, from which the royal inhabitants enjoyed fine views of the river below. *Kaiserpl. Admission: DM 2. Open Apr.–Sept., Tues.–Sun. 9–noon and 2–5.*

After you've seen the fortress, you'll want to explore the small, winding streets of the historic center, a picture-postcard jumble of Gothic and Renaissance buildings. **Klostergasse,** a stage set of a street, is the standout. If you want to see the town in more detail, follow the marked walking tour; it begins at the Rathaus and is marked by signs bearing the town arms, an eagle with a key in its beak. Highlights of the tour are two churches: the early Gothic **Ritterstiftskirche** (Knights' Church) **of Sts. Peter and Paul;** and the **parish church** on the market square, Marktplatz. Sts. Peter and Paul stands on a charming square, shaded by gnarled chestnut trees. The rough-hewn Romanesque facade is the oldest part of the church, left standing when the town ran out of money after rebuilding the remainder of the church in Gothic style during the 13th century. The outline of the walls of this original building are clearly visible on the floor inside. The cloisters are delightful, an example of German Gothic at its most uncluttered and pure. In the parish church, be sure to see the 13th-century stained glass; it's among the oldest in the country.

Heilbronn

Trains leave Heidelberg for Heilbronn about once an hour. Journey time is just over an hour, longer if you have to change at Neckarelz. The Europabus leaving Heidelberg main railway station daily at 8 AM takes one hour and 40 minutes.

Heilbronn owes its name to a "holy well," or Heiligen Brunnen, a little fountain that bubbles up out of the ground by the church of St. Kilian; it owes its fame to the Romantic German classic *Kätchen von Heilbronn*, by early 19th-century writer Heinrich von Kleist. He modeled the virtuous, put-upon Kätchen on the daughter of Heilbronn's lord mayor, and the family home still stands on the west side of the central square, Marktplatz. Its ornate oriel window, decorated with figures of four of the prophets, makes it easy to spot.

Most of the leading sights in Heilbronn are grouped in and around Marktplatz, dominated by the sturdy **Rathaus,** built in the Gothic style in 1417 and remodeled in the Renaissance. Set into its clean-lined Renaissance facade beneath the steeply eaved red roof is a magnificently ornate 16th-century **clock.** It's divided into four distinct parts. The lowest is an astronomical clock, showing the day of the week, the month, and the year. Above it is the main clock; note how its hour hand is larger than the minute hand, a convention common in the 16th century. Above this there's a smaller dial that shows the phases of the sun and the moon. Then, at the topmost level, suspended from a delicate stone surround, there's a bell, struck alternately by the two angels that stand on either side of it. Be here at noon, when the whole elaborate mechanism swings into action. As the hour strikes, an angel at the base of the clock sounds a trumpet; another turns an hour glass and counts the hours with a scepter. Simultaneously, the twin golden rams between them charge each other and lock horns while a cockerel spreads its wings and crows.

Behind the market square is Heilbronn's most famous church, the **Kilianskirche** (Church of St. Kilian), dedicated to the Irish monk who brought Christianity to the Rhineland in the Dark Ages and who lies buried in Würzburg. Its lofty Gothic tower was capped in the early 16th century with a fussy, lanternlike structure that ranks as the first major Renaissance work north of the Alps. At its summit there's a soldier carrying a banner decorated with the city arms. Walk around the church to the south side (the side opposite the main entrance) to see the well that gave the city its name.

Lodging
Under DM 180

Arcade. The centrally located Arcade Hotel opened in 1989 and offers up-to-date comfort and service at a reasonable price. Rooms are small but adequately furnished (although double rooms have twin beds). *Weinsbergerstr. 29, tel. 07131/10888. AE, DC, MC, V.*

Park-Villa. This beautifully converted fin-de-siècle villa stands in its own park—hence the very apt name. Rooms are elegantly comfortable and quiet, with restful parkland views. *Gutenbergstr. 30, Am Lerchenberg, tel. 07131/72028. 23 rooms with bath. AE, DC, MC, V.*

Dining
Under DM 40

Festhalle Harmonie. Eat on the terrace in summer to enjoy the view of the city park. Inside, the decor fuses traditional and modern styles. For best value, try one of the fixed-price menus. *Friedrich-Weber-Allee 28, tel. 07131/86890. Reservations required. Jacket and tie required. No credit cards. Closed most of Aug.*

Under DM 30
★

Ratskeller. For sturdy and dependable regional specialties—try Swabian *Maultaschen*, a kind of local ravioli—and as much Teutonic atmosphere as you'll ever want, you won't go wrong in this, the basement restaurant of the town hall. *Marktpl. 7, tel. 07131/84628. Reservations advised. No credit cards. Closed Sun. dinner.*

Shopping

Wine is the chief product of the Neckar region, and Heilbronn is the place to buy it. The city has an internationally renowned wine festival in the second week of September, the "Weindorf," where more than 200 wines from the Heilbronn region alone are offered. Outside festival time, you'll find numerous shops stocking wine in Heilbronn's central shopping zone, and you can also buy directly from vineyards. A good one to try is the **Amalienhof** (Lukas-Cranach-Weg 5). If you're in the market for **antiques,** take time to comb **Monika Finkbeiner's** well-stocked shop (Allee 38).

The Arts The city tourist office (tel. 07131/562–270) publishes a free monthly magazine, *Heilbronn Today & Tomorrow,* which lists upcoming events. The **Stadttheater** (Berliner Pl. 1, tel. 07131/563–001) is the city's leading theater. You can buy tickets from the tourist office. In summer, **classical concerts** are given in the gardens behind the Festhalle; contact the tourist office for details of performances and tickets.

Neckarsulm

Trains leave Heilbronn about every half-hour for the 10-minute run to Neckarsulm.

The busy little industrial city of Neckarsulm is the home of the German automobile manufacturer Audi and the site of the **Deutsches Zweirad Museum** (German Motorcycle Museum). It's located close by the NSU factory, where motorbikes were first manufactured in Germany. Among its 180 exhibits are the world's first mass-produced machine (the Hildebrand and Wolfmüller), a number of famous racing machines, and a rare Daimler machine, the first one made by that legendary name. The museum also has an exhibit of old bicycles, the oldest dating back to 1817, and early automobiles. All are arranged over four floors in a handsome 400-year-old building that belonged to the Teutonic Order of Knights until 1806. *Urbanstr. 11. Admission: DM 5 adults, DM 3 children, DM 10 for a family ticket. Open daily 9–noon and 1:30–5.*

9 Frankfurt

With Walking Tours of the Old Town

Frankfurt, home of the second-biggest airport in Europe (after London's Heathrow), is the gateway to Germany for most air travelers. Although it's only the sixth-largest German city, its post–World War II role as the country's financial capital has given it an ultramodern, metropolitan atmosphere. A Hamburg banker described it this way: "It's more aggressive and competitive than other German cities, but also more open and hospitable. Frankfurt is more American in temperament than the average German city." It's certainly gone all-out to give itself a late-20th-century face. While bigger cities, such as Munich, have attempted with considerable success to reclaim the physical character of their past, Frankfurt has developed a New York–style skyline. Not for nothing is this city of 625,000 people nicknamed "Mainhattan"—after the River Main on which it stands.

So why come to Frankfurt? Partly because it's a deeply historic city, one of the joint capitals of Charlemagne's empire, the city where no fewer than 30 Holy Roman Emperors were elected and crowned, the city where Gutenburg set up his print shop, the city where Goethe was born, the city where the first German parliament met. There may be only faint shadows of this original Frankfurt for you to see today, but they are here nonetheless and, this being Germany, beautifully cared for, too.

Frankfurt's commercial clout has its historic side as well. The city was a major trading center as early as the 12th century. Its first international Autumn Fair was held in 1240; in 1330 its Spring Fair was inaugurated. Both are still going strong today.

The stock exchange, one of the half dozen most important in the world, was established back in 1595. The Rothschilds opened their first bank here, in 1798.

Essential Information

Important Addresses and Numbers

Tourist Information For advance information, write to the **Verkehrsamt Frankfurt/ Main** (Gutleutstr. 7–9, tel. 069/2123–8800). The main tourist office is at Römerberg 27 (tel. 069/2123–8708) in the heart of the old town. It's open Monday through Friday from 9 AM to 7 PM and Saturday through Sunday from 9:30 AM to 6 PM. A secondary information office is at the main train station (Hauptbahnhof) opposite track 23 (tel. 069/2123–8849). This location is open Monday through Saturday from 8 AM to 10 PM and Sunday from 9:30 AM to 8 PM. Both offices can help you find accommodations.

Consulates **U.S. Consulate General,** Seismayerstrasse 21, tel. 069/75304.

British Consulate General, Bockenheimer Landstrasse 51–53, tel. 069/720406.

Emergencies **Police:** tel. 110. **Fire:** tel. 112. **Medical Emergencies:** tel. 069/ 792–0200.

Pharmacies: tel. 069/11500. **Dental Emergencies:** tel. 069/660–727.

English-language Bookstores **British Bookshop,** Börsenstrasse 17, tel. 069/280–492.
American Book Center (ABC), Jahnstr. 36, tel. 069/552816.
America Haus (library, newspapers, cultural events), Staufenstrasse 1, tel. 069/722–860.

Travel Agencies **American Express International,** Steinweg 5, tel. 069/210–548.
Thomas Cook, Kaiserstrasse 11, tel. 069/13470.
D.E.R. Deutsches Reisebüro, Eschersheimer Landstrasse 25–27, tel. 069/156–6289.
Hapag-Lloyd Reisebüro, Rossmarkt 21, tel. 069/216–2286.

Lost and Found **Fundbüro Stadt,** Mainzer Landstrasse 323, tel. 069/750–02403;
Fundbüro Bahn, at the train station, tel. 069/265–5831;
Fundbüro Flughafen, at the airport, tel. 069/960–2413.

Where to Change Money Banks are generally open from 8:30 AM until 4 PM; some close for lunch between 1 and 2. Bank offices at the airport and the main train station keep longer hours. **Airport:** Arrival Hall (Ankunfthalle) B8, 6:15 AM–9:30 PM; Arrival Hall B6, 7:30 AM–9 PM; Departure Hall (Abflughalle) B, 7 AM–9:30 PM. **Train station:** Deutsche Verkehrs-Kredit Bank office at the south entrance, 6:30 AM–10 PM; in the shopping passage (Einkaufspassage), 8–8.

Arriving and Departing by Plane

Frankfurt airport lies 10 kilometers (6 miles) southwest of the downtown area, on the Köln–Munich Autobahn.

Between the Airport and Downtown Getting into Frankfurt from the airport is easy. There are two S-Bahn lines (suburban trains) that run from the airport to downtown Frankfurt. One line, S-14, goes to Hauptwache square in the heart of Frankfurt. Trains run every 20 minutes;

the trip takes about 15 minutes. The other line, S-15, goes to the Hauptbahnhof (main train station), just west of the downtown area. Trains run every 10 minutes; the trip takes 11 minutes. One-way fare for both services is DM 3.30 (DM 4.40 during rush hours). InterCity express trains to and from most major western German cities also stop at the airport. There are hourly services to Köln, Hamburg, and Munich, for example. City bus No. 61 also serves the airport, running between it and the Südbahnhof train station in Sachsenhausen, south of the downtown area. The trip takes about 30 minutes.

Arriving and Departing by Train and Bus

By Train Euro-city and InterCity trains connect Frankfurt with all German cities and many major European cities. The new InterCity Express (ICE) line links Frankfurt with Hamburg and Munich. All long-distance trains arrive at and depart from the Hauptbahnhof. For information, call **Deutsche Bundesbahn** (German Railways), tel. 069/19419, or ask at the information office in the station.

By Bus More than 200 European cities—including all major West German cities—have bus links with Frankfurt. Buses arrive and depart from the south side of the Hauptbahnhof. For information and tickets, contact **Deutsche Touring,** Am Römerhof 17, tel. 069/79030.

Getting Around

On Foot Downtown Frankfurt is compact and easily explored on foot. There are fewer pedestrians-only streets in the downtown area than in some other major German cities; the most important radiate from Hauptwache square. The Römer complex, south of Hauptwache, is also pedestrianized. From here, you can easily cross the river on the Eisener Steg (Iron Bridge) to Sachsenhausen, most of whose tangle of small streets are best explored on foot.

By Public Transportation Frankfurt lays claim to a smooth-running, well-integrated public transportation system, consisting of the U-bahn (subway), S-bahn (suburban railway), and Strassenbahn (streetcars). Fares for the entire system are uniform, though based on a complex zone system that can be hard to figure out. A basic one-way ticket for a ride in the inner zone costs DM 1.70 (DM 2.20 during rush hours). For rides of just a stop or two, buy a **Kurzstrecken Karte;** cost is DM 1.20. The best buy of all is a 24-hour ticket, a **24-Stunden.** It costs DM 7 and allows unlimited travel in the inner zone for any 24-hour period. For information and assistance, call tel. 1368–2694.

By Taxi Fares start at DM 3.60 and increase by DM 1.80 per kilometer. There is an extra charge of 50 pfennigs per piece of baggage. You can hail taxis in the street or call them at tel. 069/250–001, tel. 069/230–033, or tel. 069/545–011. Note that there's an extra charge for the driver coming to the pickup point.

By Bike In summer, you can rent bikes at the **Goetheturm** (Goethe Tower) at the edge of the Frankfurt Stadtwald (tel. 069/49111).

Lodging

Frankfurt is not only a major financial center; it is an important trade-fair venue attracting thousands of business visitors throughout the year. Consequently, accommodation is plentiful but expensive. Room rates can leap by up to 50% during major fair weeks. Dates in 1992 to try to avoid are: Jan. 25–29 (The Premiere); April 8–12 (Fur Show); August 22–26 (International Autumn Fair); September 8–13 (International Automechanika Show); and September 30–Oct. 5 (International Book Fair). These dates may change, so it's best to confirm them with the German-American Chamber of Commerce (tel. 212/974–8830; in London 071/734–0543).

Most of the bigger—and most costly—hotels are located in the downtown area between the main train station and the Messegelände (trades fair exhibition center). There are several lower-priced lodgings in the central area, but most are scattered through the suburbs, although they are generally accessible by public transport. Unless otherwise stated, all lodgings include breakfast, however modest, in the room price.

Highly recommended establishments are indicated by a star ★.

Under DM 180

Am Zoo. As the name suggests, this hotel is close to the zoo. It offers above-average lodging for the price. The kitchen makes its own cakes for the coffee shop; the restaurant's ornate windows will keep you preoccupied while you wait for dinner. *Alfred-Brehm Platz 6, tel. 069/490–771. 85 rooms with bath. AE, DC, MC, V. Closed Dec. 20–Jan. 5.*

Liebig. A comfortable, family-run hotel, this establishment has spacious, high-ceilinged rooms and a friendly feel. Ask for a room at the back—it's much quieter. Try the Weinstube restaurant for excellent Hessen wine. *Liebigstr. 45, tel. 069/727–551. 20 rooms with bath. MC, DC, V.*

Maingau. This excellent-value hotel is within easy reach of the downtown area, close to the lively Sachsenhausen quarter, Rooms are basic but clean and comfortable, some with TVs. Families are welcome. *Schifferstr. 38–40, tel. 069/617–001. 100 rooms with bath. Facilities: restaurant. AE, MC.*

Neue Kräme. This distinctly basic hotel in the heart of the old town is on a pedestrian street, meaning that traffic noise is minimal. There's no restaurant, but drinks and snacks are available. *Neue Kräme 23, tel. 069/284–046. 21 rooms with bath. AE, DC, MC, V.*

Under DM 130

Attache. This simple but comfortable downtown hotel has no restaurant, but a buffet breakfast provides a hearty start to the day. *Kölnerstr. 10, tel. 069/730282. Facilities: bar. AE, DC.*

★ **Hotel Pension West.** For home comforts, a handy location (close to the university), and good value, try this family-run pension. It's in an older building and scores highly for old-fashioned appeal. *Gräfstr. 81, tel. 069/778–011. 20 rooms with bath. MC. Closed Christmas.*

Motel Frankfurt. Though modern and plain, this motel has private facilities in all rooms. It's accessible to public transport, standing just a few hundred yards from the Dornbusch subway station on the northbound U-1, U-2, and U-3 lines, and it adjoins a quiet park. Children under 12 sharing rooms with their parents stay free. *Escherheimer Landstr. 204, tel. 069/568-011. 54 rooms with bath. AE.*

Waldhotel Hensels Felsenkeller. It's off the beaten track—south of the river, in the Oberrad district, a short walk from the Stadtwald and a 10-minute walk from an S-bahn station. The hotel offers terrific value and, though basically furnished, is spotlessly clean and efficiently run. *Buchrainstr. 95, tel. 069/652–086. 21 rooms, most with bath. Facilities: restaurant, café, indoor pool. No credit cards.*

Under DM 90

Hotel Atlas. For those planning to visit one of Frankfurt's big trade fairs, the Atlas is conveniently located close to the exhibition center and less than a mile's walk north from the main train station. The pension's seven rooms are modest, and bathroom facilities are shared. *Zimmerweg 1, tel. 069/723–946. AE.*

Hotel Kolpinghaus. This excellently located lodging stands only a few blocks from St. Bartholomew's Cathedral (the *Dom*), one of the chief attractions of the old center. The subway station at Konstablerwache is a few blocks away. *Am Allerheiligentor, tel. 069/288–541. 25 rooms, 8 with bath or shower. Facilities: restaurant. AE, DC.*

Hotel Weisses Haus. Located just north of the old center, this modest accommodation, with a friendly and helpful management, stands about a mile from the main attractions of the historic quarter. *Jahnstr. 18, tel. 069/554–605. 20 rooms, 7 with shower. Facilities: restaurant. AE, V.*

Pension Erika. No double room in this little guest house near the main train station costs more than DM 60 per night, but bathroom facilities are shared. The Erika is a block away from the U-6/U-7 Westend subway station. *Mendelssohnstr. 92, tel. 069/747–900. 12 rooms. No restaurant. No credit cards.*

Pension Uebe. This modest but comfortable 11-room guest house is right beside a subway station (Grüneburgweg) two stops up the line from the Hauptwache station, the start of our city walking tour. *Grüneburgweg 3, tel. 069/591–209. 11 rooms, including 3 doubles (at DM 116) with bath. No restaurant. No credit cards.*

Youth Hostel **Haus der Jugend.** It's a short walk from this youth hostel, pleasantly positioned on the south bank of the River Main, to the nightlife of Sachsenhausen or to the Museumufer, where many of Frankfurt's best museums and art galleries are concentrated. Beds cost DM 20–DM 25 per person. *Deutschherrnufer 12, tel. 069/619–058. Dormitories and 4-bedded rooms.*

Splurge

★ **Steigenberger Frankfurter Hof.** The atmosphere throughout this imposing 19th-century building, ideally located in the Old Town, is of old-fashioned, formal elegance, with burnished woods, fresh flowers, and thick-carpeted hush. Double-room prices are steep—DM 360–DM 520—but out of season the hotel sometimes offers discount weekend rates. The Restaurant Français is among the gourmet high spots of Germany; four-

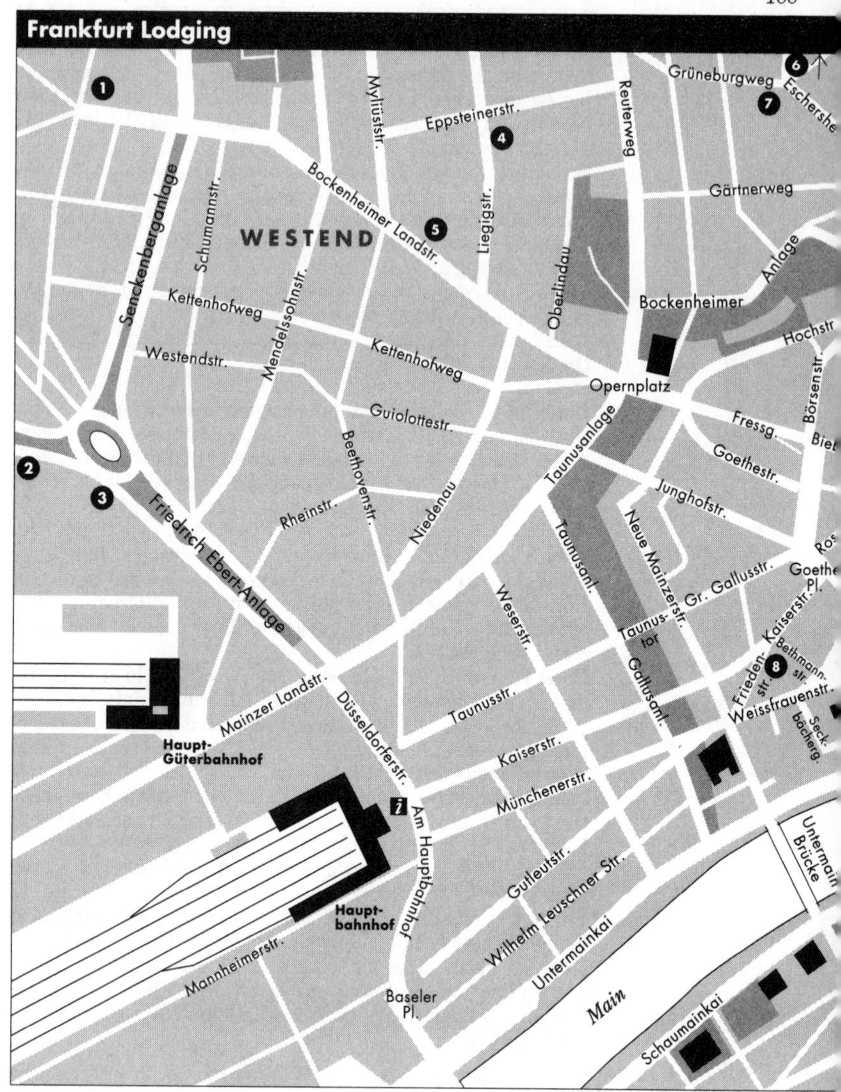

Am Zoo, **13**
Attache, **3**
Haus der Jugend, **14**
Hotel Atlas, **2**
Hotel Kolpinghaus, **12**
Hotel Pension West, **1**
Hotel Weisses Haus, **9**
Liebig, **4**
Maingau, **11**
Motel Frankfurt, **6**
Neue Kräme, **10**
Pension Erika, **5**
Pension Uebe, **7**
Steigenberger Frankfurter Hof, **8**
Waldhotel Hensels Felsenkeller, **15**

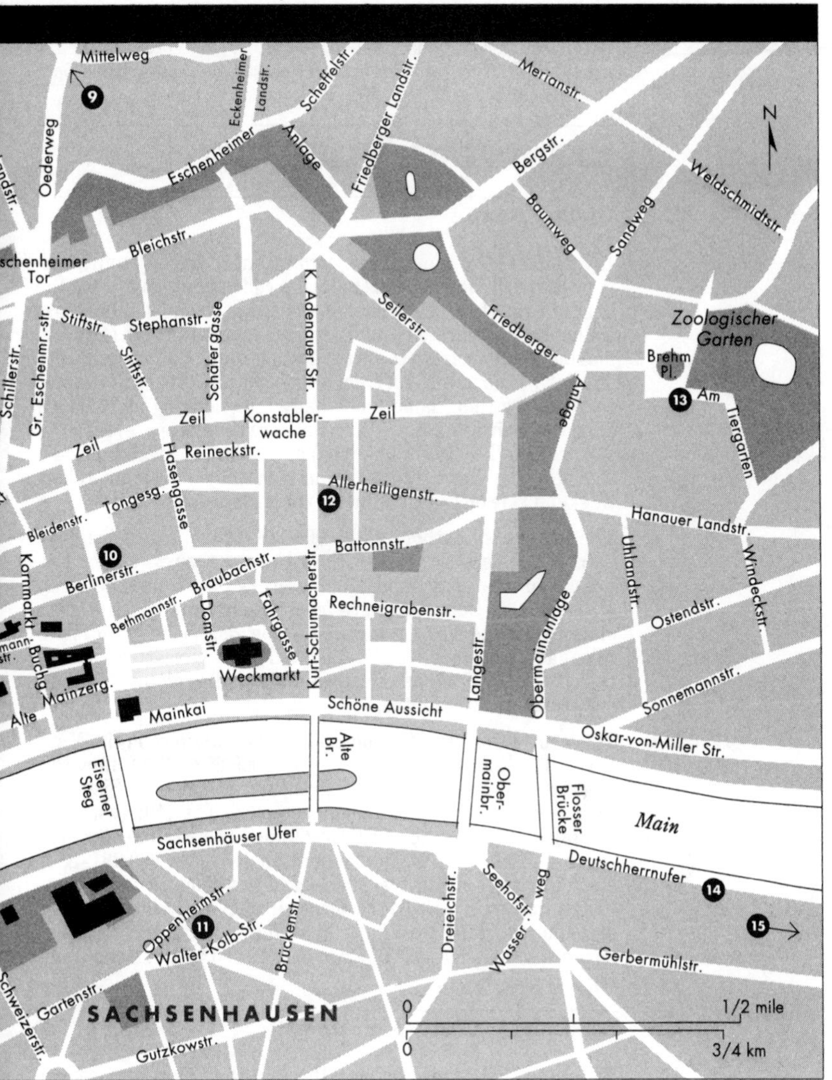
Mittelweg
Eschenheimer
Landstr.
Scheffelstr.
Friedberger Landstr.
Merianstr.
Oederweg
Eschenheimer
Anlage
Bergstr.
Weldschmidtstr.
Baumweg
Sandweg
Bleichstr.
Eschenheimer Tor
K. Adenauer Str.
Seilerstr.
Friedberger
Zoologischer Garten
Brehm Pl.
Am Tiergarten
Stiftstr.
Stephanstr.
Schäfergasse
Gr. Eschenmr.-str.
Schillerstr.
Zeil
Konstablerwache
Anlage
Reineckstr.
Hasengasse
Tongesg.
Allerheiligenstr.
Hanauer Landstr.
Bleidenstr.
Battonnstr.
Uhlandstr.
Windeckstr.
Kornmarkt
Berlinerstr.
Braubachstr.
Bethmannstr.
Domstr.
Fahrgasse
Kurt-Schumacherstr.
Rechneigrabenstr.
Obermainanlage
Ostendstr.
Langestr.
Buchg.
Mainzerg.
Weckmarkt
Sonnemannstr.
Alte
Mainkai
Schöne Aussicht
Oskar-von-Miller Str.
Eiserner Steg
Alte Br.
Obermainbr.
Flosser Brücke
Main
Sachsenhäuser Ufer
Deutschherrnufer
Dreieichstr.
Seehofstr.
Wasserweg
Oppenheimstr.
Walter-Kolb-Str.
Brückenstr.
Gerbermühlstr.
Schweizerstr.
Gartenstr.
SACHSENHAUSEN
Gutzkowstr.
0
1/2 mile
0
3/4 km

course menus start at DM 70 per person. The bar is a classy late-night rendezvous. *Am Kaiserpl. 17, tel. 069/21502. 330 rooms and 30 suites with bath. Facilities: 4 restaurants, bar, shopping mall. AE, DC, MC, V.*

Exploring Frankfurt

Guided Tours

If you don't have a lot of time, joining one of the city tourist office's **English-language bus tours** is a convenient way to see the best of Frankfurt in the shortest possible time. The tours last 2½ hours and operate twice daily from March through October, leaving at 10 AM from the train station tourist office (opposite Track 23), and at 2:15 PM from Römerberg 27. From November to February there is only one daily tour, leaving at 10:30 AM from the train station. If you have more time to spare, save the DM 28 fare (DM 14 for children) and follow our walking tour. The best combination is to do your own thing on foot and take a weekend ride on the Ebbelwei Express (*see below*).

The city transit authority (tel. 069/136–82425) runs a brightly painted old-time streetcar—the **Ebbelwei Express** (Cider Express)—on Saturday and Sunday every 30 minutes between 1:30 and 5:30. Departures are from the Ostbahnhof (east train station) and the fare—it includes a free glass of cider (or apple juice) and a pretzel—is DM 4.50. All the major attractions in the city are covered as the streetcar trundles along. The ride lasts just over 30 minutes.

Boat Trips There are a variety of round-trips and excursions on the Main River. The **Köln-Dusseldorfer** line (tel. 069/2088–288) offers the most trips; they leave from the Frankfurt Mainkai am Eisernen Steg, just south of the Römer complex. The **Fahrgastschiff Wikinger** company (tel. 069/293960) and the **Frankfurter Personenschiffahrt Anton Nauheimer Company** (tel. 069/281–884) also offer trips along the Main and excursions to the Rhine. Prices vary from DM 15 for a one-hour round-trip along the city shoreline to DM 48 for a half-day or full-day cruise. Combined boat trips and wine-tasting trips are offered by **Deutsche Touring** (tel. 069/79030).

Frankfurt for Free—or Almost

You can spend hours roaming through the **city-run museums** and not have to spend a cent—they don't charge admission except for special exhibitions. *Strandgut* magazine, available for free in many of Frankfurt's *Kneipen* (pubs) and at most movie theaters, is your best bet for finding out about free or low-cost events in Frankfurt. Movie and theater programs, as well as live music and other events are listed here. Look for *Eintritt Frei* (admission free) alongside the listings.

Live jazz concerts are held every Sunday morning in the **Historic Museum on Römerberg.** These concerts are very popular and tend to get rather crowded, but the atmosphere is always lively and friendly and the music enjoyable.

Check out the **Kleinmarkthalle** close to Liebfrauenberg for a taste of a real old Frankfurt institution. This covered market hall is a feast for the eyes as well as the stomach, with everything from fresh fruits and vegetables and butchers selling homemade Hessian sausages to brilliantly colored flowers. The gallery upstairs is reserved for more exotic products from such foreign countries as Turkey and Lebanon. It's open from 8 AM to 6 PM on weekdays, Saturday from 8 AM to 1 PM.

On Sunday morning, wander through the Sachsenhausen flea market at the **Schlachthof** (Abbatoir) on Seehoferstrasse, where antiques and art works can be found among the second-hand offerings.

All you'll need to invest is energy when you climb the **Goetheturm** (Goethe Tower) on the Sachsenhäuser Berg hill. Climbing the many steps up to the top of the 141 meter tower yields a sweeping view of all of Frankfurt and its environs, and on a clear day, as far as the Taunus.

The old quarter of **Höchst** is Frankfurt's most western suburb. Located on the Main River, during the Middle Ages it was a town in its own right, governed by Mainz until it was engulfed by the spread of Frankfurt. Unlike Frankfurt, however, Höchst was not devastated by wartime bombing and still possesses many of its original historic buildings. It's worth taking the time to explore the picturesque Altstadt (Old Town), with its attractive market and half-timbered houses.

Höchst was once a porcelain manufacturing town to rival Dresden and Vienna. Production ceased in the late-18th century, but was revived by an enterprising businessman in 1965. Today you can tour the factory of **Höchster Porzellan Manufaktur** (Bolongarostr. 186, tel. 069/300–9020). You must call to arrange for a guided tour of the works. You can also see a fine exhibit of porcelain at the **Bolongaropalast** (Bolongaro Palace), a magnificent residence facing the river. It was built in the late 18th century by an Italian snuff manufacturer. Its facade—almost the size of a football field—is nothing to sneeze at. Also on Bolongaro Strasse is the **Höchster Schloss.** Built in 1360, this castle was originally the seat and customs house of the Archbishop of Mainz. Destroyed and rebuilt several times, it now houses the **local history museum.** Höchst can be reached via the S-1, S-2, and S-3 suburban trains from the main train station, or Konstablerwache station. *Admission free. Open daily 10–4.*

The major attraction to the southwest of the city is the **Stadtwald** (City Forest), which is threaded with lovely paths and trails, as well as containing one of Germany's most impressive sports stadiums. Of particular interest is the Waldehrpfad—a trail leading past a series of rare trees, each identified by a small sign. The Stadtwald was the first place in Europe where trees were planted from seed (they were oaks, sown in 1398), and there are still many extremely old trees in evidence. In addition to bird sanctuaries and wild-animal enclosures, the forest also boasts a number of good restaurants and is a pleasant place in which to eat and linger. *Take bus No. 36 from Konstablerwache to Hainer Weg.*

Near Börneplatz you can visit the **old Jewish quarter.** The **Alte Jüdische Friedhof** (Old Jewish Cemetery) is located on the east side of the square. Partly vandalized in the Nazi era, it is nearly all that remains of prewar Jewish life in Frankfurt. The cemetery can be visited by prior arrangement only. *Corner of Kurt-Schumacher-Str. and Battonstr., tel. 069/740–2125.*

During excavation, a Jewish **ritual bath,** or *Mikwe*, was uncovered. Citizens' groups went to work to make sure that it was preserved, and it remains, incorporated into the office block, dwarfed by modern buildings. *Eckenheimer Landstr.*

The Old Town

Numbers in the margin correspond to points of interest on the Frankfurt map.

Start your tour of Frankfurt in the reconstructed old town, at
1 the square called **Hauptwache,** hub of the city transportation
network. The Hauptwache is a handsome 18th-century building a single story high under a steeply sloping roof. It was built
as the city's guardhouse and prison; today it serves as a café.

2 To the south of the square is the **Katerinenkirche** (Church of St. Katherine), the most important Protestant church in the city. What you see today is a simplified version of the second church on the site, put up after the war. It was in the original church here that the first Protestant sermon was preached in Frankfurt, in 1522. Step inside to see the simple, postwar stained glass. *Open daily 10–5.*

Head south from the church along Berlinerstrasse to the circu-
3 lar bulk of the **Paulskirche** (Church of St. Paul's), a handsome,
mostly 18th-century building that, church or not, is more interesting for its political than for its religious significance. It was here that the short-lived German parliament met in May 1848. The parliament was hardly a success—it was disbanded within a year, having achieved little more than offering the Prussian king the crown of Germany, but it remains a focus for the democratic aspirations of the German people. The building you see today, modeled loosely on the original, was rebuilt after the war in the expectation that it would become the home of the new German parliament. The German Book Dealers' annual Peace Prize is awarded in the hall, as is the Goethe Prize. *Open daily 10–3.*

Walk along the pedestrian street called Neue Krame and over Braubachstrasse. On your left you'll pass the Gothic turrets and crenellations of the **Steinernes Haus** (Stone House), originally built in 1464, destroyed in World War II, and rebuilt from 1957 to 1960 with an altered interior. Today it is the home of the Frankfurt Kunstverein (Arts Association). *Markt 44. Admission: DM 6. Open Tues.–Sat. 11–6.*

You are now entering the historic heart of Frankfurt, the an-
4 cient **Römerberg Square,** which has been the center of civic life
for centuries. Immediately on your right and occupying most of
5 the square is the city hall, called the **Römer.** It's a modest-look-
ing building compared with many of Germany's city halls, though it has a certain charm. Its gabled Gothic facade with ornate balcony is widely known as the city's official emblem. Three individual patrician buildings make up the Römer. From left to right they are the Alt-Limpurg, the Zum Römer (from which the entire structure takes its name), and the Lowenstein. The mercantile-minded Frankfurt burghers used the complex not only for political and ceremonial purposes, but also for trade fairs and other commercial ventures.

The most important events to take place in the Römer were the banquets held to celebrate the coronations of the Holy Roman

Emperors. These were mounted in the glittering and aptly named **Kaisersaal** (Imperial Hall), starting in 1562, last used in 1792 to celebrate the election of the Emperor Francis II, who would later be forced by Napoléon to abdicate.

The most vivid description of the ceremony was by Germany's leading poet, Goethe, in his "Dichtung und Wahrheit" ("Poetry and Truth"). It is said that the young Goethe, as a 16-year-old, smuggled himself into the banquet celebrating the coronation of Emperor Joseph II by posing as a waiter to get a firsthand impression of the festivities.

Today visitors can see the impressive full-length 19th-century portraits of the 52 emperors of the Holy Roman Empire that line the walls of the banqueting hall. *Admission: DM 1 adults, 50 pf children. Open Mon.–Sat. 9–6, Sun. 10–4.*

In the center of the square stands the fine 16th-century **Fountain of Justitia** (Justice). At the coronation of Emperor Matthias in 1612, wine instead of water flowed from the fountain. The crush of thirsty citizens was so great, however, that they had to be restrained to prevent damage from being done to the stonework. This event has recently been revived by the city fathers, but only for special festive occasions, when oxen are roasted as well.

6 On the south side of the Römerberg is the **Nikolaikirche** (Church of St. Nicholas). It was built in the late-13th century as the court chapel for the Holy Roman Emperors, and it's worth trying to time your visit to coincide with the chimes of the glockenspiel carillon, which ring out three times a day. It's a wonderful sound. *Carillon chimes daily at 9 AM, noon, and 5 PM. Nikolaikirche open Mon.–Sat. 10–5.*

7 Beside the Nikolaikirche is the **Historisches Museum** (History Museum), where you can see a perfect scale model of the old town, complete with every street, house, and church. There is also an astonishing display of silver, exhibits covering all aspects of the city's life from the 16th to the 20th century, and a children's museum. *Saalgasse 19. Admission free. Open Tues.–Fri. 10–1; children's museum 1–5.*

Behind the church, on the east side of the square, is a row of painstakingly restored half-timbered houses, dating from the 15th and 16th centuries. They are an excellent example of how the people of Frankfurt have begun, albeit belatedly, to take seriously the reconstruction of their historic buildings.

Leaving the square, walk the short distance to the Main River. At Mainkai, the busy street that runs parallel to the tree-lined river, you will see on your left the **Rententurm,** one of the city's medieval gates, with its pinnacled towers at the base of the main spire extending out over the walls. To your right and in
8 front is the **Eiserner Steg,** an iron bridge built as a pedestrian walkway to connect central Frankfurt with the old district of Sachsenhausen. From here river trips and boat excursions start, as well as the old steam train. (For details, *see* Tours and Excursions, *above.*)

9 Stroll along Mainkai, past the Eiserner Steg, to **Leonardskirche** (St. Leonard's Church), which is a magnificently preserved 15th- and 16th-century building, with a fine 13th-century porch. Its main treasure is the beautifully carved Bavarian altar, circa 1500.

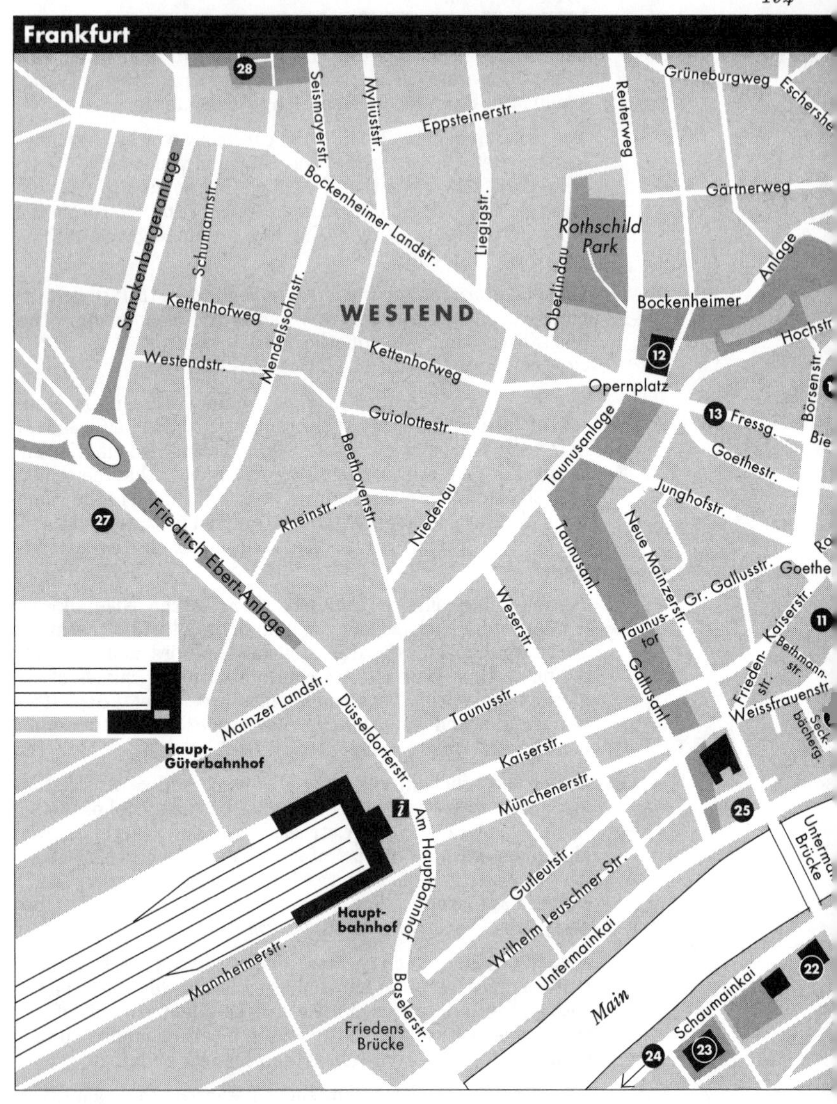

Alte Oper, **12**
Börse, **14**
Deutsches Architektur-museum, **21**
Deutsches Filmmuseum, **22**
Dom St. Bartholomäus, **18**
Eiserner Steg, **8**
Fressgasse, **13**
Goethehaus und Goethemuseum, **11**
Hauptwache, **1**
Historisches Museum, **7**
Jüdisches Museum, **25**
Karmeliterkirche, **10**
Katerinenkirche, **2**
Kuhhirtenturm, **19**
Leonardskirche, **9**
Liebfrauenkirche, **16**
Messe, **27**
Museum für Kunsthandwerk, **20**
Nikolaikirche, **6**
Palmengarten/ Botanischer Garten, **28**
Paulskirche, **3**
Römer, **5**
Römerberg Square, **4**
Schweizer Platz, **26**
Städelsches Kunstinstitut und Städtische Galerie, **23**
Städtische Galerie Liebieghaus, **24**
Staufenmauer, **17**
Zoologischer Garten, **15**

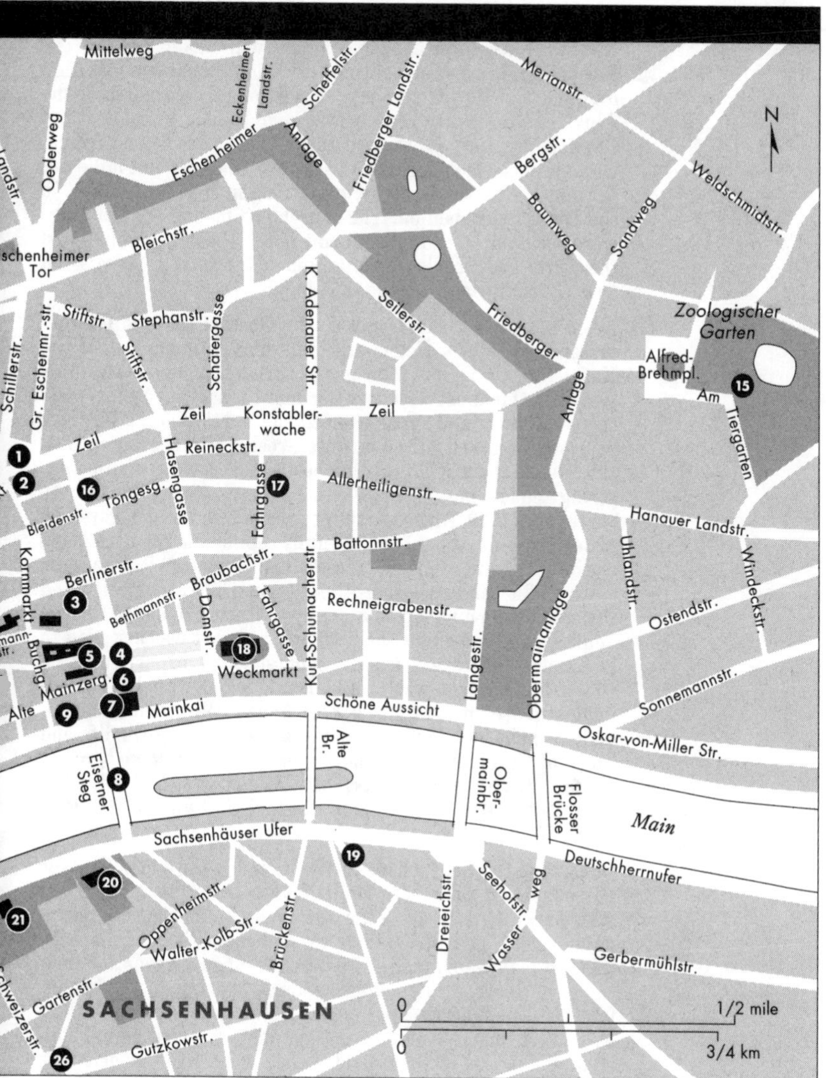
Mittelweg
Eckenheimer Landstr.
Scheffelstr.
Friedberger Landstr.
Merianstr.
Oederweg
Eschenheimer Anlage
Bergstr.
Weldschmidtstr.
Baumweg
Sandweg
Eschenheimer Tor
Bleichstr.
K. Adenauer Str.
Seilerstr.
Friedberger Anlage
Zoologischer Garten
Stiftstr.
Stephanstr.
Schäfergasse
Alfred-Brehmpl.
Schillerstr.
Gr. Eschenmr.-str.
Zeil
Konstablerwache
Am Tiergarten
Reineckstr.
Töngesg.
Fahrgasse
Allerheiligenstr.
Bleidenstr.
Hasengasse
Hanauer Landstr.
Battonnstr.
Kornmarkt
Berlinerstr.
Braubachstr.
Uhlandstr.
Windeckstr.
Bethmannstr.
Domstr.
Rechneigrabenstr.
Ostendstr.
Buchg.
Weckmarkt
Kurt-Schumacherstr.
Langestr.
Obermainanlage
Mainzerg.
Sonnemannstr.
Alte
Mainkai
Schöne Aussicht
Oskar-von-Miller Str.
Eiserner Steg
Alte Br.
Obermainbr.
Flosser Brücke
Main
Sachsenhäuser Ufer
Deutschherrnufer
Dreieichstr.
Seehofstr.
Wasserweg
Oppenheimstr.
Walter-Kolb-Str.
Brückenstr.
Gerbermühlstr.
Gartenstr.
SACHSENHAUSEN
Gutzkowstr.
0
1/2 mile
3/4 km

Continue a short way along Mainkai, then turn right into the
narrow Karmeliter Gasse, which will take you to the
10 **Karmeliterkirche** (Carmelite Church and Monastery). Within
its quiet cloisters is the largest religious fresco north of the
Alps, a 16th-century representation of the birth and death of
Christ. Jörg Ratgeb, the creator of this 262-foot-long fresco,
was one of the most important artists of his time, but it did not
prevent his brutal death by quartering in 1526 for his part in
the Peasants' Rebellion. The church and monastery buildings
were secularized in 1803 and now house the city archives and
the Early and Prehistory Museum. *Münzgasse 4. Admission
free. Cloisters open weekdays 8–4.*

11 From here it's a short way to the **Goethehaus und Goethemuseum** (Goethe's House and Museum). Coming out of the Karmeliterkirche into Münzgasse, turn left and go to the junction of Bethmannstrasse and Berliner Strasse. Use the pedestrian walkway and cross over to the north side of Berliner Strasse, then turn left again onto Grosser Hirschgraben. Outside No. 23 there will probably be a small crowd of visitors entering and leaving. This is where Johann Wolfgang von Goethe was born in 1749. Although the original house was destroyed by Allied bombing, it has been carefully rebuilt and restored in every detail as the young Goethe would have known it. The room in which Goethe was born has been turned into a memorial, and the one in which he wrote is set up as it used to be. In Goethe Senior's study, look for the little window that was installed so he could keep an eye on the street outside and, in particular, on young Johann, who was well known to wander afield. The adjoining museum contains a permanent collection of manuscripts, paintings, and memorabilia documenting the life and times of Germany's outstanding poet. *Grosser Hirschgraben 23, tel. 069/282–824. Admission: DM 3 adults, DM 1.50 children. Open Apr.–Sept., Mon.–Sat. 9–6, Sun. 10–1; Oct.–Mar., Mon.–Sat. 9–4. Sun. 10–1.*

On leaving the Goethehaus turn left, and at the end of Grosser
Hirschgraben bear left again and retrace your steps up
Rossmarkt. Cross over to the Gutenberg Memorial and continue along the pedestrian zone to Rathenau-Platz. From here
take a window-shopping stroll past the elegant shops and boutiques of Goethestrasse, which ends at Opernplatz and Frank-
12 furt's reconstructed opera house, the **Alte Oper.** Wealthy
Frankfurt businessmen gave generously for its original construction in the 1870s, provided they were given priority for
the best seats. Kaiser Wilhelm II traveled all the way from
Berlin for the gala opening in 1880. Destroyed by incendiary
bombs in 1944, the opera house remained in ruins for many
years while controversy raged over its reconstruction. The new
building, in the classical proportions and style of the original,
was finally opened in 1981, and now houses modern facilities for
opera, ballet, concerts, and conferences.

The steps of the opera house, or the Rothschild Park opposite, are a good spot from which to take in the impressive sight of Frankfurt's modern architecture. In this part of the new town you are close to the financial center (the West End), and if you look down Taunusanlage and Mainzer Landstrasse, the view both to the right and left is dominated by gleaming skyscrapers that house the headquarters of West Germany's biggest and richest banks. More than 365 international banks also have offices here, confirming Frankfurt's position as the country's financial capital. If you have a camera, take a photo, especially in the early evening, when the setting sun is mirrored in the glass and metal facades.

Return to the beginning of the pedestrian zone. This is the site of Bockenheimer Tor, one of the gateways in the old walled city. Wander at leisure down Bockenheimer Strasse, known lo-
13 cally as **Fressgasse** ("Food Street"). It's a gourmet shopper's paradise and one of Frankfurt's liveliest streets.

Next, cross over onto Biebergasse, a continuation of the main
14 shopping center. Just around the corner is the Frankfurt **Börse** (Stock Exchange), Germany's leading stock exchange and financial powerhouse. The Börse was founded by Frankfurt merchants in 1558 to establish some order in their often chaotic dealings, but the present building dates from the 1870s. In the past, the trading on the dealers' floor was hectic. These days, computerized networks and international telephone systems have removed some of the drama, but it is still an exciting scene to watch. There is a visitors' gallery. *Admission free. Open weekdays Mon.–Fri. 11:30–1:30.*

From here there is a choice of two routes. You can continue along Biebergasse, past the Hauptwache, and walk east along the **Zeil,** the city's largest pedestrian zone and main shopping street. It is lined with department stores selling every conceivable type of consumer goods and can get very crowded. The far end of the Zeil brings you to Alfred-Brehm Platz and the en-
15 trance to the **Zoologischer Garten** (Zoological Garden). This is one of Frankfurt's chief attractions, ranking among the best zoos in Europe. Its remarkable collection includes some 5,000 animals of 600 different species, a Bears' Castle, an Exotarium (aquarium plus reptiles), and an aviary, reputedly the largest in Europe. Many of the birds can be seen in a natural setting. The zoo is an ideal place for a family outing, as it also has a restaurant and a café, along with afternoon concerts in summer. *Zoo admission: DM 7 adults, DM 3 children. Exotarium admission: DM 3.50 adults, DM 1.50 children. Combined ticket price: DM 8.50 adults, DM 4 children. Open mid-Mar.–Sept., daily 8–7; mid-Nov.–mid-Feb., daily 8–5; between seasons open daily 8–6.*

Alternatively, if you don't want to go all the way down the Zeil, just after the Hauptwache turn right down Liebfrauenstrasse. Here, in more peaceful surroundings, you will come to the
16 **Liebfrauenkirche** (Church of Our Lady), a late-Gothic church dating from the end of the 14th century. Among its few surviving features of interest are the fine tympanum relief over the south door, the ornate Rococo furnishings, the 16th-century choir, and the frieze work around the pointed arches. Outside, there is also a delightful Rococo fountain.

Turn off onto Töngesgasse and walk to Fahrgasse. Follow the
17 signs to the **Staufenmauer,** which is one of the few surviving stretches of the old city wall. The Staufenmauer and the Saalhofkapelle (Chapel) (near the Eiserner Steg bridge) are the two oldest parts of the medieval city in evidence today. *Admission free. Saalhofkapelle. Open Tues. and Thurs.–Sat. 10–5, Wed. 10–8, Sun. 10–5.*

Continue down Fahrgasse, cross Berliner Strasse at a convenient point, bear left along Braubachstrasse for a few yards,

18 and then turn right onto Domstrasse. You are now at the **Dom St. Bartholomäus** (Cathedral of St. Bartholomew) or Kaiserdom (Imperial Cathedral), as it is more popularly known. This grand Gothic structure dates from 1290 and was used primarily for imperial coronations, hence the name. It was built to replace an earlier church established by Charlemagne's son, Ludwig the Pious, on the present site of the Römerberg. The cathedral suffered little damage during World War II and still contains most of its original treasures, including a life-size crucifixion group and a fine 15th-century altar. Its most impressive exterior feature is its tall, red sandstone tower (almost 300 feet high), which was added between 1415 and 1514. Excavations in front of the main entrance in 1953 revealed the remains of a Roman settlement and the foundations of a Carolingian imperial palace. *Admission free. Open Mar.–Oct., daily 9–noon and 3–6; Nov.–Feb., daily 9–noon and 3–5.*

Walk on now, down the lane called Zum Pfarrturm, and head toward the river. On the Mainkai, cross to **Sachsenhausen** over the Alte Brücke. Formerly a village separate from Frankfurt, Sachsenhausen is said to have been established by Charlemagne, who arrived here with a group of Saxon families in the 8th century and formed a settlement on the banks of the Main. It was an important bridgehead for the crusader Knights of the Teutonic Order and, in 1318, officially became part of Frankfurt. After crossing the bridge, look along the bank to your left
19 and you'll see the 15th-century **Kuhhirtenturm** (Shepherd's Tower), the only remaining part of Sachsenhausen's original fortifications. The composer Paul Hindemith lived in the tower from 1923 to 1927 while working at the Frankfurt Opera.

Sachsenhausen is now largely residential but is also renowned for its collection of museums, most of which are threaded along the riverbank. The district has a distinctly medieval air, with narrow back alleys, quaint little inns, and quiet squares that have escaped the destructive tread of the modern developer. There is much of authentic historical interest here. For Frankfurters and visitors alike, it is where you'll also find the best city nightlife—from clubs and discos to traditional taverns and restaurants, tucked in among the half-timbered houses.

No fewer than seven top-ranking museums line the Sachsenhausen side of the Main, on Schaumainkai, known locally as the Museumsufer (Museum Riverbank). These range from exhibitions of art, crafts, and architecture to the German Film Museum.

20 One of Frankfurt's newest museums is the **Museum für Kunsthandwerk** (Museum of Applied Arts), which was opened in 1985. This award-winning building, designed by the American architect Richard Meier, contains a vast collection of European and Asian handicrafts, including furniture, glassware, and porcelain. *Schaumainkai 17. Admission free. Open Tues. and Thurs.–Sun. 10–5, Wed. 10–8.*

21 A little farther along is the **Deutsches Architekturmuseum** (Museum of German Architecture), currently Frankfurt's most popular museum. Created by German architect Oswald Mathias Ungers, it is housed within a period villa, though the interior is entirely modern. There are five floors of drawings, models, and audiovisual displays that chart the progress of German architecture through the ages, as well as many special

exhibits. *Schaumainkai 43. Admission free. Open Tues. and Thurs.–Sun. 10–5, Wed. 10–8.*

Next door is Germany's first museum devoted exclusively to the
22 cinema, **Deutsches Filmmuseum** (German Film Museum). The
exhibits include an imaginative collection of film artifacts. The
museum has its own movie theater. *Schaumainkai 41. Admis-*
sion free. Open Tues. and Thurs.–Sun. 10–5, Wed. 10–8.

23 Farther on you will come to the **Städelsches Kunstinstitut und Städtische Galerie** (Städel Art Institute and Municipal Gallery). This building houses one of the most significant art collections in Germany, with fine examples of Flemish, Dutch, German, and Italian old masters, plus a sprinkling of French Impressionists. *Schaumainkai 63. Admission: DM 2. Open Tues. and Thurs.–Sun. 10–5, Wed. 10–8.*

24 Finally, it's worth stopping at the **Städtische Galerie Liebieghaus** (Liebieg Municipal Museum of Sculpture). Here, in this charming 17th-century villa, is housed the city's internationally famous collection of classical, medieval, and Renaissance sculpture. Some pieces are exhibited in the lovely gardens surrounding the house. *Schaumainkai 71. Admission free. Open Tues. and Thurs.–Sun. 10–5, Wed. 10–8.*

From there you can backtrack along the Schaumainkai to the
Untermain Brücke, cross the bridge to the other side of the river, turn left into Untermainkai, and at number 14–15 come to
25 the recently opened **Jüdisches Museum** (Jewish Museum),
housed in the former Rothschild Palais. Designed by the architect Ante von Kostelac, the museum focuses on Frankfurt's
centuries-old Jewish community, the second largest in Germany after Berlin prior to the Hitler years. The museum contains
extensive archives of Jewish history and culture, including a library of 5,000 books, large photographic collection, and docu-
mentation center. *Untermainkai 14–15. Admission free. Open*
Tues. and Thurs.–Sun. 10–5, Wed. 10–8.

If you have time and energy, there is more to explore in Sachsenhausen. It's very much the up-and-coming district—take a
26 short detour down to **Schweizer Platz;** you'll find it full of new
shops, boutiques, cafés, and bars thronging with people and activity.

Retrace your steps back to Schaumainkai and return to the north bank of the river by way of Friedens Brücke, which will take you, via Baseler Strasse, to the main train station, in Frankfurt's West End.

From here, three avenues lead to the center of town: Kaiserstrasse, Münchenerstrasse, and Taunusstrasse. They are lined with fast-food joints, shops, strip clubs, cinemas, and restaurants, and at night, with neon lights flashing and rock music blaring, have a rather seedy atmosphere.

Continue past the main train station and wander north along
27 Friedrich-Ebert-Anlage to the **Messe,** a vast complex of exhibition halls where some of the world's greatest trade fairs are
held annually. In addition to the two major fairs in spring and
fall, among the more important smaller ones are the Automobile Show in March, the Fur Fair at Easter, and the International Book Fair in early fall.

Farther north still, along Senckenbergeranlage, is the delightful **Palmengarten und Botanischer Garten** (Tropical Garden and Botanical Garden). The large greenhouses enclose a variety of lush tropical and subtropical flora, including 800 species of cactus, while the surrounding park offers numerous leisure facilities. During most of the year there are flower shows and exhibitions; in summer, concerts are held in an outdoor bandshell. Situated between the Palmengarten and the adjoining Grüneburgpark, the botanical gardens contain a wide assortment of wild, ornamental, and rare plants from around the world. *Entrance at Siesmayerstr. 61. Admission: DM 4.50 adults, DM 1.50 children. Open Apr.–Sept., daily 9–6; Oct.–Mar., daily 9–dusk.*

28

Day Trips from Frankfurt

Frankfurt's central location makes a large number of day trips possible. But tempting as it may be to use the city as a base for your visit to Germany, remember that it's an expensive place to stay for any extended period.

Bad Homburg. *See* Excursions from Frankfurt, *below.*

Hanau. *See* Excursions from Frankfurt, *below.*

Heidelberg. The city that inspired Germany's Romantic movement is set among dark green vine-covered hills, on one of which towers its famous red sandstone castle. The train trip from Frankfurt takes 70 minutes (you may have to change at Mannheim); some InterCity trains can do the journey in less than an hour. *See* Chapter 8.

Koblenz. Founded by the Romans in AD 9 at the confluence of the Mosel and Rhine rivers, Koblenz is a colorful city with a long and noble past. Evidence of its strategic importance down the ages is the Festung Ehrenbreitstein—Europe's biggest fortress. An hourly train from Frankfurt Hauptbahnhof takes 80 minutes. *See* Chapter 10.

Limburg. *See* Excursions from Frankfurt, *below.*

Mainz. Here you'll find one of the finest Romanesque cathedrals in the Rhine region. InterCity trains leave every hour from Frankfurt's main train station and take 20 minutes; the journey takes 40 minutes by slower trains. *See* Chapter 7.

Marburg. *See* Excursions from Frankfurt, *below.*

Steinau and Fulda. If you set out early enough, you can visit both these towns at the southern end of the Fairy-tale Road in one day. Picture-postcard Steinau was the home of the Brothers Grimm during their schoolboy years. Fulda, 45 kilometers (28 miles) farther along, boasts some of the best Baroque architecture in central Germany. Hourly trains from Frankfurt's Hauptbahnhof take 55 minutes to reach Steinau and another 30 minutes to Fulda. (Some express trains can get you to Fulda in one hour.) *See* Chapter 11.

Wiesbaden. Although it's one of the oldest cities in Germany—founded by the Romans, who discovered hot springs there—Wiesbaden's fame and fortune are rooted in the 19th century, when it became a popular spa for Europe's upper crust. This Rhine River town has one of the Continent's best-preserved 19th-century streets, the elegant Wilhelmstrasse. Frequent trains from Frankfurt's Hauptbahnhof will get you there in less than an hour.

Shopping

The heart of Frankfurt's shopping district is the ritzy pedestrian street called **Zeil,** running east from Hauptwache square. It is one of the busiest shopping streets in the country—the so-called "shopping mile"—turning over more than 1 billion Deutsche Marks' worth of business every year. The streets running off Zeil and the Hauptwache are home to a series of upscale fashion shops. There's another elegant shopping mall, extending over three stories, in the **BfG building** on the corner of Theaterplatz and Neue-Mainzer-Strasse.

Extending west from the Hauptwache is **Grosse Bockheimer Strasse** (or Fressgasse to the locals). Cafés, restaurants, and above all, food shops are the draw here. This is the place for fish (fresh or smoked), cheeses, and a wide range of local specialties, including frankfurters.

In **Niederrad,** also just over the river adjacent to Sachsenhausen, visit Steinmetzbetrieb Ferdinand Stang (Hahnstr. 18) for an amazing selection of art objects made from all types of stone.

Typical—and inexpensive—Frankfurt specialties to look for as gifts include several local delicacies. **Apfelwein,** or apple wine, can be purchased in most supermarkets and in the taverns in Sachsenhausen, south of the river. Look, too, for **Bethmännchen und Brenten** (marzipan cookies) and **Frankfurter Kranz** (a sort of creamy cake) in local bakeries and sweetshops. **Jewelry** designed and made by local craftsmen is an unusual gift to take home. **La Galleria** (Berlinerstr.) and **Luise Schloze** (Kaiserstr.) both have good selections. A **Struwwelpeter** puppet or doll, named after the character in the famous children's book by Heinrich Hoffmann, also makes a good gift to take home.

Frankfurt is also home to the largest range of **Meissen porcelain** outside the famous china-pottery town (near Dresden) itself. You'll find the best selection, including reasonably priced small pieces, in the Japanese-owned **Mitsukoshi** department store on Kaiserstrasse.

In Sachsenhausen, a **flea market** is held Saturday between 8 and 2 at the **Schlachthof** (Seehoferstrasse). Get there early if you're looking for bargains. There's a wide range of goods on display, a lot of it pretty junky, though you can sometimes find better-quality goods, too. In any event, it's a colorful and vivid place to explore.

Dining

The world has heard of the Frankfurter sausage; otherwise this corner of Germany has little to offer in the way of original culinary delights. Business-account dining has spawned many exotic and expensive "international" restaurants, but the ones we list here offer mainly the traditional solid German fare of pork in its various forms, with dumplings or fried potatoes or *Spätzle,* a form of egg noodle. Do keep an eye out for *grüne*

Sosse (green sauce), a mixture of seven herbs said to have been a favorite at Goethe's table.

Sachsenhausen is the home of the famous *Ebbelwei* (apple-wine or cider) taverns. Look for a green pine wreath over the entrance to tell passersby that a freshly pressed—and alcoholic—apple juice is on tap. You can eat well in these small inns, too, though the menu might need some explanation. For example, *Handkas mit Musik* does not promise music at your table. The *Musik* means that the cheese, or *Kas* (from Käse) will be served with raw onions, oil, vinegar, and bread and butter. Most traditional apple-wine taverns serve this specialty without a fork, and those who ask for one give themselves away as strangers. There are about 15 of these taverns; two of the best-known are **Zum Gemalten Haus** (Schweizerstr. 67), and **Lorsbacher Tal** (Grosse Rittergasse 49).

Also seek out two local pastry delicacies: *Frankfurter Kranz*, a triple-layer cake filled with butter cream, cherries, and pistachio nuts; and *Bethmännchen* (pronounced BET-men-shen), a small cake filled with a local variety of marzipan.

Highly recommended restaurants are indicated by a star ★.

Under DM 40

Bistrot 77. Specialties from Alsace are served at this subtly chic and light French restaurant in Sachsenhausen. Working owners Guy and Dominique Mosbach are always happy to advise. *Ziegelhüttenweg 1–3, tel. 069/614–040. Reservations advised. AE, DC, MC, V. Closed Sat. lunch, Sun., and mid-June–mid-July.*

★ **Börsenkeller.** The dark, rather masculine atmosphere of this restaurant reflects its favored status among businessmen from the nearby stock exchange. The food is traditional and substantial, though always prepared with some style. *Schillerstr. 11, tel. 069/281–115. Reservations advised. Jacket and tie required. AE, DC, MC, V. Closed Sun.*

Die Gans. The name means "goose," which is one of the many game dishes on chef Uwe Stolzenberger's menu. *Schweizerstr. 70. tel. 069/622625. Reservations advised. AE, DC, MC, V. Closed lunch.*

Gildenstuben. This is a lusty Bohemian beer tavern with a spacious beer garden overlooking a park. It offers Czech dishes and genuine Pilsener Urquell and Budvar beers. *Bleichstr. 38, tel. 069/283–228. No credit cards.*

Lunico. The delicate-looking decor contrasts with robust Italian dishes. The restaurant is on the edge of the business district and is open until 4 AM during trade-fair weeks. *Tanus-str. 47, tel. 069/251010. Reservations necessary. AE, DC, MC, V. Open daily 12–12.*

Under DM 30

Maredo. If you're tired of pork and dumplings, head here for plain old-fashioned grilled beef. The steaks are fresh and cooked over charcoal. There's a choice of 16 salads. The restaurant is northwest of the old center; take a subway on the U-6 and U-7 lines to Alte Oper station. *Grosse Bockenheimer Landstr. 24, tel. 069/288–054.* There's a sister restaurant of the same name at *Taunus-Anlage 12, 069/724–0795 (S-bahn sta-*

tion Taunus-Anlage, between Hauptbahnhof and Hauptwache). AE, V.

Steinernes Haus. An unpretentious historic inn, it was salvaged from the wreckage of World War II along with the cathedral and town hall around the corner. The traditional fare is popular with locals. *Braubachstr. 35, tel. 069/283491. No credit cards.*

Zur Eulenburg. Take the subway or a streetcar out to Seckbacher Landstrasse, in the district of Bornheim, a mile northeast of the old town, to eat in this popular apple-wine tavern. Portions are huge. *Eulengasse 46, tel. 069/451–203. No credit cards. Closed lunch, Mon., and Tues.*

Under DM 20

Dippegucker. This bright and cheerful fast-food eatery serves a wide selection of German dishes, from the bulky soup-in-a-meal *Eintopf* to roasts and grills. Take subway U-1 or U-3 to Eschenheimer Tor. *Eschenheimer Anlage 40, tel. 069/551–945. No credit cards.*

Fabrik. A large apple-wine tavern in Sachsenhausen, ideal for an outdoor supper on a warm summer evening (there are 300 seats in the garden alone), the Fabrik offers a wide range of tasty dishes, from the local *Handkäs* to grills. *Mittlerer Hasenpfad 1, tel. 069/624–406. No credit cards. Open from 6 PM. Closed Mon. in winter and all Jan.*

Wieland Stubb. Locals say cook-owner Hedi makes the best fried potatoes (*Bratkartoffeln*) in Frankfurt; they accompany her schnitzels. Portions are big and prices are low—they start at DM 8.50. Try Hedi's homemade *grüne Sosse* (green sauce; *see above*). Take subway U-5 to Glauburgstrasse station, walk back down Eckenheimer Landstrasse two blocks, and Wielandstrasse is on your left. *Wielandstr. 1, tel. 069/558–551. No reservations. No credit cards. Closed weekends.*

Zum Bären. This is the place to dine if you're visiting Höchst. A 200-year-old hostelry favored by Goethe, it serves hearty, inexpensive three-course lunches of solid German fare. The tavern, located on the Schlossplatz (castle square) in the old town quarter, also has a roomy beer garden—a delight on a warm summer's day. *Schlossplatz 8, tel. 069/301–524. Reservations possible. AE. Closed Mon. lunch, mid-Feb.*

★ **Zum Gemalten Haus.** This is the real thing—a traditional apple-wine tavern in the heart of Sachsenhausen. Its name means "At the Painted House," a reference to the frescoes that cover the walls inside and out. If there isn't room when you arrive, order a glass of apple wine and hang around until someone leaves. The traditional cider-tavern dishes include excellent smoked meats. *Schweizerstr. 67, tel. 069/614–559. No credit cards. Closed Mon. and Tues.*

Splurge

★ **Weinhaus Brückenkeller.** This establishment offers magnificent German specialties in the sort of time-honored arched cellar that would have brought a lump to Bismarck's throat. Though the food may be unmistakably Teutonic, it's light and delicate. The wine cellars—don't be shy about asking to see them—hold around 85,000 bottles. A two-course dinner costs DM 38–DM 50; for a four-course feast, expect to pay around DM 100. *Schutzenstr. 6, tel. 069/284–238. Reservations ad-*

vised. Jacket and tie required. AE, DC, MC, V. Closed lunch, Sun., and 3 weeks in July.

The Arts and Nightlife

The Arts

Frankfurt is a flourishing cultural center—it has the biggest city arts budget in Germany. But tickets for top-class concerts are both hard to obtain and expensive. The **Städtische Bühnen**—the municipal theaters—are the leading venues, but Frankfurt also has about the most lavish opera house in the country. Pick up a copy of the twice-monthly listings magazine *Frankfurter Wochenschau* from any tourist office. For information about concerts, call tel. 069/11517.

Tickets for theaters can be purchased from the tourist office at Römerberg 27 and from all theaters. Alternatively, try the **Ludwig Schäfer** agency in Sachsenhausen (Schweizer-Str. 28a, tel. 069/623–779), or **Kartenkiosk Sandrock** (Hauptwache Passage, tel. 069/20115). For **English-language productions,** try either the **Café-Theater** (Hamburger Allee 45, tel. 069/777–466) or the **Playhouse** (Hansaallee 152, tel. 069/151–8326).

The most glamorous venue for classical music concerts is the **Alte Oper,** or Old Opera House (Opernpl. tel. 069/134–0400), a magnificently ornate heap that was rebuilt and reopened in 1981 after near-total destruction in the war. Paradoxically, only light operettas are performed there today. The main hall, a restrained, elegant auditorium, seats 2,500. The rear of the auditorium can be sealed off to form a 500-seat theater. Below, there's another auditorium, Hindemith Hall, with seating for 340. Even if you don't take in a performance, it's worth having a look at the ponderous and ornate lobby, an example of 19th-century classicism at its most self-confident. Both the city's respected opera company and highly regarded Frankfurt Ballet perform at the **Städtische Bühnen** (Theaterpl., tel. 069/256–2434).

The **Festhalle** (tel. 069/75750) at the trade-fair building is the scene for many rock concerts and other large-scale spectaculars. Frankfurt's new cultural center, the **Künstlerhaus Mouson Turm** (Waldschmidtstr. 4, tel. 069/405–8950) hosts a regular series of concerts of all kinds, as well as plays and exhibits.

Nightlife

Frankfurt's "Left Bank" is across the river in **Sachsenhausen.** It's hardly the quaint old Bohemian quarter it likes to bill itself as, but for bars, discos, clubs, and beer and wine restaurants this is about the best place to try. If you're in search of a rowdy night out, check out the **Apfelwein** (cider) taverns—they're touristy but fun. A green wreath over the door identifies them. If the area doesn't agree with you, try the ever-more-fashionable district of **Bornheim,** northeast of downtown. It has an almost equal number of bars, clubs, and the like, but the atmosphere is less forced, more authentic.

For a beer tour of Germany, visit the **Frankfurter Bierhaus** for a choice of 44 different brews served in vaulted cellars with regional tidbits (Schutzenstr. 10).

Jazz **Der Frankfurter Jazzkeller** (Kleine Bockenheimer Str. 18a) is the oldest jazz cellar in Germany, founded by legendary trumpeter Carlo Bohländer. It offers hot, modern, free jazz. **Jazz Kneipe** (Berlinstr. 70) is a reliable bet for swing jazz and is open until 4 AM. **Schlachthof** (Deutschhernufer 36) is the place for Dixieland jazz, beer by the barrelful, and apple wine; the mood is rowdy and fun. **Sinkkasten** (Brönnerstr. 9) features jazz, rock, pop, and African music; it's sometimes hard to get into but worth the effort for serious fans (open 8 PM–1 AM, weekend 8 PM–2 AM).

Excursions from Frankfurt

Bad Homburg

Homburg is easily reached in 25 minutes by S-bahn train S-5 from Konstablerwache station in the city center. Tourist office: Verkehrsamt, Louisenstr. 58, tel. 06172/121.

Just a few miles north of Frankfurt, Bad Homburg lies at the foot of the **Taunus** hills. The Bad Homburg spa was first known to the Romans but was rediscovered and made famous in the 19th century. Illustrious visitors included the Prince of Wales, the son of Queen Victoria, and Tsar Nicholas II. And here in 1841, the world's first casino was founded. Today the sights in Bad Homburg include a 17th-century castle, the picturesque Altstadt (Old Town), and the enchanting Kurpark.

The most historically noteworthy sight in the city is the 17th-century **Schloss.** The 172-foot **Weisser Turm** (White Tower) is all that remains of the medieval castle that once stood here. The Schloss that stands here today was built between 1680 and 1685 by Friedrich II of Hesse-Homburg, and a few alterations were made during the 19th century. The state apartments are exquisitely furnished, and the Spiegelkabinett (Hall of Mirrors) is especially worth a visit. *Schlosspl. Admission: DM 2 adults, DM 1 children. Open Mar.–Oct., Tues.–Sun. 10–5; Nov.–Feb., Tues.–Sun. 10–4.*

Also within the town, and certainly its greatest attraction over the centuries, is the **Kurpark,** with its more than 31 fountains. In the park you'll find not only the popular, highly saline Elisabethenbrunnen spring but also a Siamese temple and a Russian chapel, mementos left by two distinguished guests—King Chulalongkorn of Siam and Tsar Nicholas II.

Only 6 kilometers (4 miles) from Bad Homburg, and accessible by direct bus service, is the **Saalburg Limes** fort, the best-preserved Roman fort in Germany. Built in AD 120, the fort could accommodate a cohort (500 men) and was part of the fortifications along the 342-mile-long Limes Wall. The fort has been rebuilt as the Romans originally left it, with wells, armories, parade grounds, and catapults, as well as shops, houses, baths, and temples.

Dining
Under DM 20

Zum Adler. This simple restaurant serves traditional Hessian fare. *Neu Anspach. AE, DC, MC, V.*

Hanau

Hanau is easily reached in less than a half-hour by frequent S-7 and S-8 suburban trains from Frankfurt's Hauptbahnhof. Tourist office: Verkehrsbüro, Altstädter Markt 1, 6450 Hanau, tel. 06181/252–400.

Jacob Grimm was born in Hanau in 1785, his brother Wilhelm a year later. A bronze memorial to the pair, erected in 1898, stands on Neustädter Marktplatz. Behind the statue is the solid bulk of Hanau's 18th-century **Rathaus** (Town Hall). Every day at noon its bells play a tribute to another of the city's famous sons, the composer Paul Hindemith (1895–1963), by chiming out one of his canons. At 10 AM the carillon plays a choral composition; at 2 PM a minuet; and at 4 a piece entitled *Guten Abend* (Good Evening) rings out for the crowds hurrying across the Marktplatz to complete their shopping before returning home.

Hanau was almost completely obliterated by wartime bombing raids, and there's little of the Altstadt (Old Town) that the Grimm brothers would recognize now. Behind the Rathaus, however, is a corner that has been faithfully reconstructed. It's dominated by the **Altes Rathaus** (Old Town Hall), a handsome 16th-century Renaissance building, its two half-timbered upper stories weighted down by a steep slate roof. Today it's the home of the German goldsmiths' craft. Known as the **Deutsches Goldschmiedehaus** (German Goldsmiths House), it contains a permanent exhibit and regular national and international displays of goldsmiths' and silversmiths' crafts. *Altstädter Markt 6. Admission charge depends on exhibit. Open Tues.–Sun. 10–noon and 2–5.*

You'll find various memorials and museums devoted to the brothers Grimm all along the Fairy-tale Road. For the first memorial, however, you have to head in another direction—to **Schloss Philippsruhe,** a palace on the banks of the Main River in the suburb of Kesselstadt (a No. 1 or No. 10 bus will take you there from Neustädter Marktplatz in 10 minutes). Schloss Philippsruhe has much more than Grimm exhibits to offer: It's the oldest French-style Baroque palace east of the Rhine. Philippsruhe may remind you of Versailles, although its French-trained architect, Julius Ludwig Rothweil, planned it along the lines of another palace in the Paris area, the much smaller Clagny palace. Philippsruhe—as its name, "Philipp's Rest," suggests—was built for Count Philipp Reinhard von Hanau. He didn't enjoy its riverside peace for long, however: He died less than three months after moving in. After the French builder Jacques Girard completed work on the palace, creating its very French appearance, the invading French confiscated it in 1803. Later Napoléon gave it as a present to his sister Pauline Borghese, who then put it up for sale. American forces took over Philippsruhe as a military quarters for a time in 1945, and until the postwar reconstruction of Hanau was complete it served as the town hall. Every year on the first weekend of September, the palace grounds are invaded again—this time by the people of Hanau, for a great party to commemorate the rebuilding of their war-ravaged town. *Schloss Philippsruhe, Kesselstadt. Admission free. Open Tues.–Sun. 10–5.*

There's a café on the grounds of the palace, overlooking the River Main; it has the same hours as the palace.

Limburg

Limburg is about an hour's train ride north from Frankfurt's main train station. Tourist office: Verkehrsamt, Hospitalstr. 2, tel. 06431/203.

This pretty and ancient town, dating back to the 8th century, has a splendid seven-spired cathedral and ecclesiastical art treasures along with it; there's also an appealing castle.

The **Stifts-und Pfarrkirche St. Georg und Nikolaus** towers above the Lahn River. Construction of the cathedral began in 1220, and evident in the building is the transition from Romanesque to Gothic style; each side presents a new perspective. Extensive restoration recently uncovered the original medieval coloring and bright frescoes from the 13th century.

Treasures from the cathedral are on display in the **Diözesanmuseum** in the **Schloss,** next door to the cathedral. It houses ecclesiastical art treasures from the bishopric of Limburg. Be sure to see the Byzantine cross reliquary that was stolen from the palace church in Constantinople in 1204 and the Patri-Stab (Peter's Staff), set with precious stones and adorned with gold.

The **Schloss** adjacent to the cathedral dates to the 7th or 8th century, although the castle's current building only goes back to the 13th century. The group of residences, the chapel, and other buildings added in the 14th to 16th centuries serve as an architectural counterbalance to the cathedral. *Admission to Schloss and museum: DM 2 adults, DM 1 children. Open mid-Mar.–mid-Nov., Tues.–Sat. 9:30–12:30 and 2–5; Sun. 11–5.*

Dining
Under DM 30

St. Georgs-Stuben. In the Stadthalle, only a few minutes' walk from the center of Limburg, this pleasant restaurant serves local and international dishes. *Hospitalstr. 4, tel. 06431/26027. AE, DC, MC, V.*

Marburg

Regular trains from Frankfurt's Hauptbahnhof do the 110-kilometer (69-mile) journey to Marburg in about an hour. Tourist office: Neue Kasselerstr. 1 (at the main train station), tel. 06421/201–249.

A center of religious change in the days of Martin Luther, Marburg became, in 1527, the home of Europe's first non-Catholic university. Centuries later, this university was the base from which the brothers Jacob and Wilhelm Grimm began collecting their fund of folktales. This quiet town has an old quarter huddled round a hilltop castle, **Schloss Marburg,** which makes an ideal day's outing. Other attractions include the twin-spired Gothic **Elizabethkirche** church and, for fans of the Brothers Grimm, the **Brüder-Grimm-Stube** (Markt 23; open Tues.–Sun. 11–1 and 3–6), an exhibition on their life in Marburg. A free walking tour, in English, of Marburg's old town (Apr.–Oct., 3 PM daily) departs from the main entrance of the Elizabethkirche and lasts about two hours.

10 The Rhineland

Including Koblenz, Trier, Bonn, Köln, and Aachen

The Rhine is so inextricably a part of German history, folklore, and culture, so bound up with romantic imagery, that the first-time visitor to its banks may be forgiven a sense of disappointment. For much of its length, industrial development has pushed down to the water's edge. Choked highways and railway lines leave little room for cyclists and hikers. Tourist-packed pleasure boats and coal-blackened barges nudge each other noisily aside.

For most of the way, the Rhine isn't even a spectacular river. It creeps almost reluctantly into Germany from its source in Switzerland and leaves the country again with broad disdain in the flat northwest, sweeping on into the Netherlands and to the sea. Less than a tenth of this 1,355-kilometer (840-mile) journey matches the picture-postcard image that is summed up by the very word "Rhine." This section became Germany's top tourist site all of 200 years ago. Around 1790 a spearhead of adventurous travelers from various parts of Europe arrived by horse-drawn carriages to explore the sector of the river between Bingen and Koblenz, now known as the Middle Rhine Valley. They were overwhelmed by the dramatic and romantic scenery, which exists nowhere else on the Continent. It didn't take long for the word to spread. Other travelers followed in their coach tracks, and soon thereafter the first sightseeing cruises went into operation.

Today the passage through the Rhine Valley still makes for one of Europe's most memorable journeys. The Mittel Rhein (Middle Rhine) could be considered an obligatory day trip out of Frankfurt—it's quite possibly Germany's number-one, not-to-be-missed excursion. But there's far more to the Rhine as it wends its way north to Köln.

This chapter divides the Rhineland into five tours. The first covers the Rheingau, source of Germany's finest wines. The second tour covers the most famous stretch of the river, the 60 kilometers (36 miles) from Rüdesheim to Koblenz. Mention the Rhineland to most visitors, and this is the magical stretch they'll assume you mean. It's a land of steep and thickly wooded hills, of terraced vineyards rising step by step above the riverbanks, of massive hilltop castles, and of tiny wine villages hugging river shores.

The most famous tributary of the Rhine is the Mosel, which flows into the river at Koblenz. The third tour covers its snaking passage through another great wine-producing area, with scenery almost as striking as that found along the Rhine. At its west end, almost on the French border, is Trier, once one of the greatest cities in the Roman Empire.

The fourth tour covers Bonn, a sleepy university town that unexpectedly became the capital of West Germany, and Köln (Cologne), the greatest of the Rhine cities, a vibrant and bustling metropolis boasting the largest and most dramatic Gothic cathedral in the country. The fifth tour is a side trip to Aachen, capital of Charlemagne's Holy Roman Empire in the 9th century and site of the most important Carolingian (pre-Romanesque) cathedral in Europe.

If you plan to make any trip through the Rhineland, remember that this is one of Germany's major tourist areas, drawing visitors from around the world. As a result, prices here in summer are high, often substantially above those found elsewhere in the country. Make reservations well in advance, and don't expect to have the place to yourself.

Essential Information

Lodging There's a vast selection of places to lay your head. The most romantic are the old riverside inns and hotels and the castle-hotels, some of which are enormously luxurious. In the cities of the Rhineland, there's a similarly large choice. Modern high rises are common. A great many hotels close for the winter; most are also booked well in advance, especially for the wine festivals in the fall and during important trade fairs. Whenever possible, make reservations long before you visit. Prices are, in general, surprisingly moderate, and you can save considerably by settling for a hotel or pension without a Rhine view.

Highly recommended establishments are indicated by a star ★.

Dining If you come to the Rhine hoping to eat fish, you'll be disappointed: The polluted waters have destroyed all but a few of the fish that once thrived. However, there are numerous local specialties that are hearty rather than sophisticated: *Himmel und Erde*, a mixture of potatoes, onions, and apples; *Hämmchen*, or pork knuckle; *Hunsrücker Festessen*, sauerkraut with potatoes, horseradish, and ham. Many small inns and restaurants offer these and other regional dishes at extremely affordable prices.

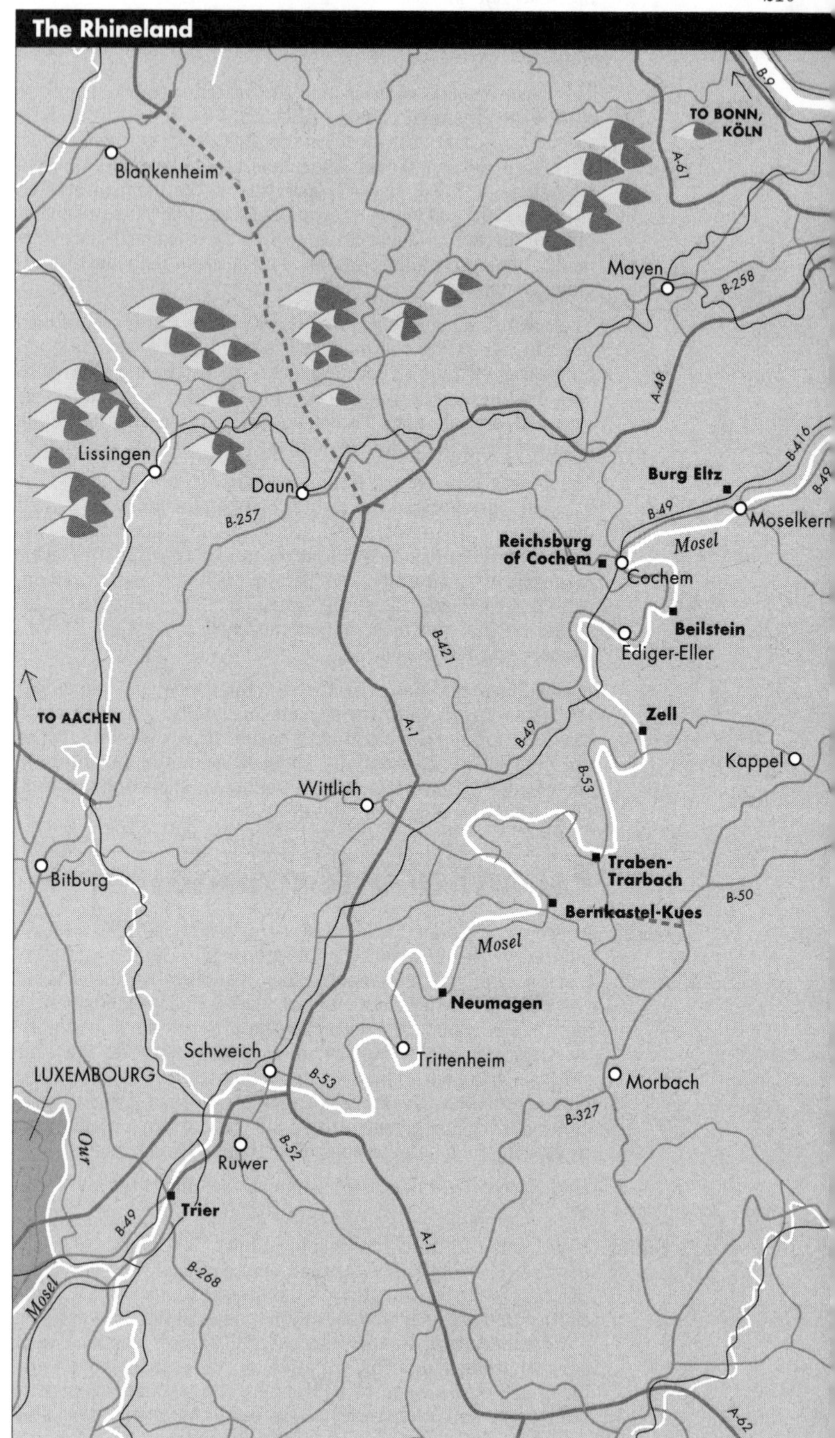
The Rhineland
TO BONN, KÖLN
B-9
A-61
Blankenheim
Mayen
B-258
A-48
Lissingen
Daun
B-257
B-416
Burg Eltz
B-49
B-49
Moselkern
Mosel
Reichsburg of Cochem
Cochem
Beilstein
Ediger-Eller
B-421
TO AACHEN
A-1
B-49
Zell
Kappel
B-53
Wittlich
Bitburg
Traben-Trarbach
B-50
Bernkastel-Kues
Mosel
Neumagen
Schweich
Trittenheim
LUXEMBOURG
B-53
Morbach
B-327
Our
B-52
Ruwer
Trier
B-49
A-1
B-268
Mosel
A-62

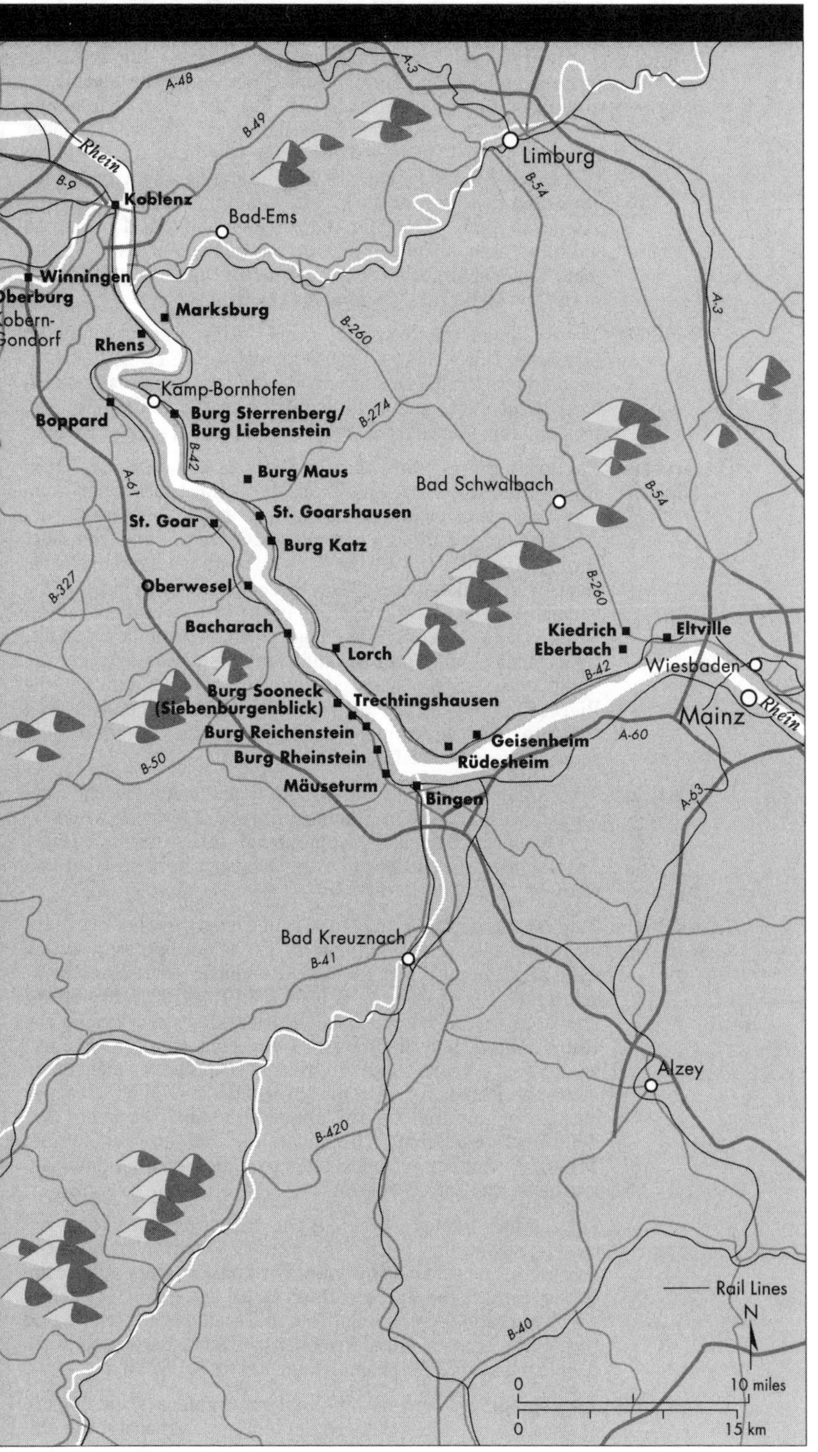
A-48
A-3
B-49
Rhein
Limburg
B-54
B-9
Koblenz
Bad-Ems
Winningen
Oberburg
Kobern-
Gondorf
Marksburg
A-3
Rhens
B-260
Kamp-Bornhofen
Boppard
Burg Sterrenberg/
Burg Liebenstein
B-274
B-42
Burg Maus
Bad Schwalbach
A-61
B-54
St. Goarshausen
St. Goar
Burg Katz
B-327
Oberwesel
B-260
Bacharach
Kiedrich
Eltville
Lorch
Eberbach
Wiesbaden
B-42
Burg Sooneck
(Siebenburgenblick)
Trechtingshausen
Mainz
Rhein
Burg Reichenstein
Geisenheim
A-60
B-50
Burg Rheinstein
Rüdesheim
Mäuseturm
Bingen
A-63
Bad Kreuznach
B-41
Alzey
B-420
Rail Lines
N
B-40
0
10 miles
0
15 km

Highly recommended restaurants are indicated by a star ★.

Biking There are bicycle paths along both banks of the Rhine and along large stretches of the Mosel. (Sometimes they come uncomfortably close to the busy roads that hug the river.) Rhine and Mosel ferries accept bikes, so cyclists can criss-cross the river at will. The vine-covered slopes of the Rheingau and Mosel are just gentle enough for cyclists, but the steeper, heavily wooded Rhine gorge is only for the fittest. Rent bikes from any railway station along the rivers; for DM 10 a day (half that if you have a valid rail ticket) you can pick up a bike from one station and hand it over at any other. It's much better than being tied to one of the few bike-rental shops along the Rhine.

Hiking The Rheingau, the Rhine gorge, and the Mosel are great hiking territory. Don't choose a route alongside the river, however; head up into the hills on either side and take a top road—you'll have great views and you'll leave the traffic behind. You can pick up hiking maps from any of the Rhineland tourist offices.

The Arts and Nightlife The leading music and theater festivals are concentrated in Bonn, Köln, Koblenz, and Trier. In Bonn, the Bonner Sommer—a continuous program of folklore, music, and street theater, much of it outdoors and most of it free—runs from May through October. In 1992 the city also hosts the Beethoven Festival, which takes place every three years. In Köln there's a summer season of organ recitals in the city's great cathedral, while Trier's cathedral is the magnificent setting for organ festivals in May, June, August, and September. Köln is where the nightlife is. The city has a complex of taverns and discos, the Bierdorf Colon, at Breitestrasse 29. Koblenz, however, can compete, with a complete wine village, the Weindorf, just south of the city's Pfaffendorfer bridge.

Festivals The Rhineland literally bursts into flame in August and September with a **Rhein in Flammen** fireworks festival, while every town and village along Rhine and Mosel has its annual wine festival after the vineyard harvest, usually in September and October.

Guided Tours

Boat Trips Trips along the Rhine and Mosel range from a few hours to days or even a week or more in length. The major operator, with a fleet of 25 boats, is the **Köln-Düsseldorfer Deutsche Rheinschiffahrt** (Frankenwerft 15, 5000 Köln 1, tel. 0221/208–8288), known as the **K-D** Rhine line. It offers daily services on the Rhine, Mosel, and Main rivers from April through October, as well as a year-round program of excursions, principally along the Rhine. K-D day drips run DM 25–DM 50. Cheaper outings are offered by the **Bingen-Rüdesheimer Fähr- und Schiffahrtsgesellschaft** (Rheinkai 10, Bingen, tel. 06721/14140). A Rhine trip from Bingen to Rüdesheim, on the opposite bank, and back costs DM 8.

For the best values, check out the K-D's combined river-rail tickets, which allow you to break your river trip at any place the boats stop and continue by train. For further sailings along the Rhine, contact the **Boppard-Basel Hebel** line (tel. 06742/2420), which operates from March through December; for trips along the Mosel, contact **Mosel-Personenschiffahrt Bernkastel-Kues** (Goldbachstr. 52, Bernkastel-Kues, tel. 06531/8222).

Two shipping companies in Koblenz organize short "castle cruises" from Easter through September. Two boats, the *Un-*

dine and the *Marksburg*, ply the Rhine between Koblenz and Boppard, passing 10 castles during the 75-minute, one-way voyage. Details and reservations are available from **Personenschiffahrt Merkelbach** (Emserstr. 87, 5400 Koblenz-Pfaffendorf, tel. 0261/76810); and **Personenschiffahrt Wolfgang Vomfell** (Koblenzerstr. 64, 5401 Spay/Rhein, tel. 02628/2431). Another Koblenz operator, **Rhein und Moselschiffahrt Gerhard Collee-Holzenbein** (Rheinzollstr. 4, tel. 0261/37744), runs day cruises as far as Rüdesheim on the Rhine and Cochem on the Mosel.

From Köln, three shipping companies operate boat tours on the Rhine: The **Köln-Düsseldorfer** line (Frankenwerft 15, tel. 0221/2088288) has hourly trips starting at 10:30, daily, April through September; the **Rhein-Mosel Schiffahrt** (Konrad Adenauer-Ufer, tel. 0221/121714) has daily departures every 45 minutes starting at 10, April through September; and the **Dampfschiffahrt Colonia** (Lintgasse 18, tel. 0221/211325) has daily departures every 45 minutes beginning at 10, May through September. All tours leave from the landing stages near the Hohenzollern Brücke, a short walk from the cathedral.

Bus Tours **Deutsche Touring** (Am Römerhof 17, tel. 069/790–3253) has a daily bus trip from Frankfurt along the "Riesling Route" that encompasses the vineyards of the Rhineland between Frankfurt and Rüdesheim. The tour includes a wine tasting (by candlelight) and a trip along the Rhine to the wine village of St. Goar. The cost is DM 80.

A bus tour from Koblenz or Bingen costs DM 20–DM 30.

Bus trips into the countryside around Köln (to the Eifel Hills, the Ahr Valley, and the Westerwald) are organized by several city travel agencies. Three leading tour operators are: **Globus Reisen** (Hohenzollernring 86, tel. 0221/160260), **Univers-Reisen** (am Rinkenpfuhl 57, tel. 0221/209020), and **Küppers-Reiseburo-Etrav** company (Longericher-Strasse 183, tel. 0221/210966).

City Tours **Bus tours** of Köln leave from outside the tourist office (opposite the main entrance to the cathedral) at 10 and 2, May through October, and at 11 only November through April. The tour lasts two and a half hours and costs DM 14 adults, DM 7 children; English-speaking guides are available. **"Köln by Night"** bus tours are offered Friday and Saturday in July and August. These trips leave the tourist office at 8 PM and feature a tour of the city, a boat ride on the Rhine, a cold supper, and visits to a wine tavern and the Köln TV tower; the cost is DM 40. A two-hour **walking tour** of the city, with an English-speaking guide, is also available. Tours leave from outside the tourist office daily at 4:30, May through September; the cost is DM 7. Most central hotels offer a special tourist package, the **"Kölner Knüller,"** which includes a sightseeing tour voucher, a pass for all the city's museums, and other reductions. The package costs DM 26.

Highlights for First-time Visitors

Aachen Cathedral (*see* Tour 5)
Beethovenhaus, Bonn (*see* Tour 4)
Burg Eltz (*see* Tour 3)
Drosselgasse, Rüdesheim (*see* Tour 1)

Köln Cathedral (*see* Tour 4)
Porta Nigra, Trier (*see* Tour 3)
Römische Palastula, Trier (*see* Tour 3)
Trier Cathedral (*see* Tour 3)
View from Siebenburgenblick (*see* Tour 2)

Tour 1: The Rheingau

The Rheingau, the sunny, south-facing stretch of the Rhine that produces Germany's finest wines, extends only 25 kilometers (15 miles), so you can base yourself in any of the small towns and villages that lie between the vineyards and the river. Rüdesheim and Eltville have the greatest selection of accommodations. *Tourist office: Städtisches Verkehrsamt, Rheinstr. 16 (running parallel to the Rhine), 6200 Rüdesheim, tel. 06722/2962.*

From Frankfurt
By Train Fast, frequent trains run from Frankfurt to Wiesbaden and Mainz, where you'll have to change to local services for the Rheingau villages. The trip to Wiesbaden takes from 30 to 50 minutes, depending on the train; to Mainz, 20 minutes on the InterCity train.

By Bus There is no direct bus service from Frankfurt to either Eltville or Rüdesheim, but once you're there, local bus services connect the individual villages and towns.

By Car Follow Autobahn A-66 40 kilometers to Wiesbaden and pick up route No. 42 from there to Eltville. The journey takes a half hour or so, depending on traffic conditions.

Eltville

Eltville is the geographic heart of the Rheingau, though Rüdesheim, 15 kilometers (9 miles) west, enjoys greater fame. Eltville's half-timbered buildings crowd narrow streets that date to Roman times. Though the Romans imported wine to Germany, they never made it here. It was Charlemagne, so the story goes, who in the 9th century first realized that the sunny slopes of the Rheingau could be used to produce wines. Eltville's vineyards may not go that far back, but some, including **Hanach** and **Rheinberg,** have been in use since the 12th century. Today the town is best known for the production of Sekt, sparkling German wine (champagne by any other name, though the French ensured that it could not legally be called that by including a stipulation in the Treaty of Versailles in 1919). Sekt cellars rest coolly beneath the town's winding streets. Those of the **Matheus Muller** company are several miles long and hold up to 15 million bottles. While the cellars are not open to the public, you can amble through the courtyards of some formidable old vineyard buildings, including the white-walled, slate-roofed **Eltzerhof,** one of the more beautiful. Eltville also has its own **castle,** commissioned by the Archbishop of Trier in 1330. In it is a museum devoted to **Johannes Gutenberg,** father of the modern printing press. The Prince-Archbishop of Mainz admitted Gutenberg to the court in Eltville, thereby saving the inventor from financial ruin. *Admission: DM 1.50 adults, 50 pf children. Open May–Sept., Sun. only, 2–5.*

In Eltville, the Gothic parish church of **Sts. Peter and Paul** has some fine 14th-century stained glass and ceiling frescoes; its walls are lined with the tombstones and monuments of noble families who rose to prominence on the prestige of the local wine.

To see one of Germany's oldest church organs, dating from around 1500, head inland for 5 kilometers (3 miles) to the village of **Kiedrich** (well sign-posted from Eltville). It's a pleasant, uphill walk, along a small stream rich in trout; or you take a bus—the tourist office in Rüdesheim (*see above*) will give you details on bus service. The medieval organ in the village church was rescued from disrepair by a 19th-century English nobleman who called here during a Rhineland tour and was so enchanted that he stayed, becoming a benefactor who saved not only the organ but the entire village from poverty.

Two miles farther on (the bus service from Eltville also covers this upland route, but it's infrequent) is the great monastery of **Eberbach,** where *The Name of the Rose* was filmed. The two huge dormitories, each nearly 100 yards long, are among the most impressive medieval structures in Germany. The monastery's vineyards still produce some of the Rhineland's finest wines, and it is now the headquarters of the region's wine-growing industry. There are tastings every weekend in the monastery cellars (the DM 5 cost includes three wines and the glass itself). You have to book ahead, by mail or phone. *Kloster Eberbach, Postfach 6228, Eltville, tel. 06723/4228. Open Apr.–Sept., daily 10–6; Oct.–Mar., weekdays 10–4, weekends 11–4.*

Eight kilometers (5 miles) west of Eltville (there's a regular bus service) is the village of **Geisenheim,** a name inextricably linked with Rheingau wines at their finest. "Rhineland is wineland" is a saying in this part of the world, and indeed, you'll see a checkerboard of terraced vineyards stretching from the Rhine's riverside villages all the way back to a protective line of forests at the base of the Taunus Mountains. Geisenheim has some of the most renowned vineyards in the area, with grapes that create wines on a par with those from the Loire Valley and Burgundy.

Overlooking Geisenheim from a spur of the Rheingau hills is the 18th-century **Schloss Johannisberg,** built on the site of a 12th-century abbey and still owned by the von Metternich family. Schloss Johannisberg produces what is generally regarded as one of the very best Rheingau wines, along with a renowned Sekt. On the castle terrace you can order the elegant estate-bottled golden wine by the glass. As you leave the castle, you can buy a bottle or two of the excellent wine at a shop just outside the walls.

Dining
Under DM 30

Restaurant zur Rebe. Portions are enormous at this friendly Rhine-side tavern and restaurant. If it's autumn, try any of the game dishes, and of course the new wine. *Hauptstr. 19, Eltville, tel. 06723/3013. No credit cards. Closed Wed.*

Lodging and Dining
Under DM 150

Hotel und Weinhaus "Zum Krug." This beautifully renovated 18th-century farmhouse and vintner's home, about 3 kilometers (2 miles) from Eltville in Hattenheim, is now a flower-smothered family-run hotel. Owner Josef Laufer runs a restaurant serving excellent local cuisine and wines from his own vineyard. *Hauptstr. 34, Hattenheim, tel. 06723/2812. 9 rooms with bath. Reservations advised. MC, V.*

Rüdesheim

Eltville is for those who value peace and quiet; Rüdesheim is boisterous and touristy (which means that accommodation is more plentiful and generally cheaper). It's arguably the Rhine Valley's prettiest and most popular wine town. Set along the river's edge, it is a picturesque place of half-timbered and gabled medieval houses.

Angling up from the river toward the romantic old town is the region's most famous Weingasse (wine alley), the extraordinary **Drosselgasse** (Thrush Lane). This narrow, 200-yard-long cobbled lane is lined with cozy wine taverns and rustic restaurants. At night, voices raised in song and brass bands create a cacophony, shattering whatever peace the town may have known by day.

Above Rüdesheim, at an elevation of 1,000 feet, stands the **Niederwald-Denkmal,** a colossal stone statue of Germania, the heroically proportioned woman who symbolizes the 1871 unification of the German Empire. The giant figure was built between 1876 and 1883 on the orders of Bismarck. Niederwald can be reached by car or chair lift, or you can climb to the statue's steep perch. Whichever way you choose, the ascent offers splendid views, including one of the little island in the middle of the Rhine where the *Mäuseturm* (Mouse Tower) is situated (*see* Tour 2, *below*). The chair-lift station to the monument is located a short walk from the Drosselgasse. It operates continuously every day from late-March to early November; round-trip fare is DM 7 adults, DM 3.50 children.

Schloss Brömserburg, one of the oldest castles on the Rhine, was built more than 1,000 years ago by the Knights of Rüdesheim on the site of a Roman fortress. Inside its stout walls are wine presses, drinking vessels, and collections related to viticulture from prehistoric times to the present. *Weinmuseum in der Brömserburg, Rheinstr. 2. Admission: DM 3 adults, DM 2 children. Open Apr.–Oct., daily 9–12:30 and 1:30–6.*

Lodging and Dining

Under DM 150

Rüdesheimer Hof. For a taste of Rheingau hospitality, try this typical inn. There's a terrace for summer dining on excellent local specialties, which you can enjoy along with any of the many wines offered. *Geisenheimerstr. 1, tel. 06722/2011. 42 rooms with bath. AE, MC, DC, V. Closed mid-Nov.–mid-Feb.*

Under DM 110

Altes Haus. The restaurant of this historic Rhineland house in the neighboring village of Assmannshausen is prized for its wine-based dishes. The hotel is popular with bus tours, but the prices are correspondingly lower than in quieter establishments: A small double room without bath is less than DM 60. *Lorcher Str. 8, Assmannshausen, tel. 06722/2051. 28 rooms, some with bath. Reservations advised. No credit cards.*

Gasthof Trapp. Tucked in behind the central market square is a popular family-run restaurant/hotel where good food is combined with a high standard of comfort. *Kirchstr. 7, tel. 0672/3640. 34 rooms, 18 with bath. AE, MC, V. Closed mid-Nov.–mid-Mar.*

Krone. Insist on a room overlooking the Rhine—those at the back of this otherwise excellent small hotel look onto a busy railway line and can be noisy. There's a very attractive Rhine-side terrace where wines from the Krone's own copious cellars are served. *Rheinstr. 30, tel. 06722/3068. 55 rooms with bath. AE, DC, MC, V. Closed mid-Nov.–mid-Mar.*

Under DM 70 **Landgut Ebertal.** This traditional Rhineland homestead in the woods above Rüdesheim is particularly recommended for families. There are ponies for hire and various other farm animals, which young visitors are encouraged to feed and tend. *Aulhausen 1, tel. 06722/2518. 15 rooms, 2 with bath. No credit cards.*

Shopping **Wine** is, of course the chief product of the Rheingau. Combine your shopping with a wine tasting at any of the vineyards you'll find hugging the road between Eltville and Rüdesheim, or make the trip to the Eberbach monastery or the Schloss Johannisberg above Rüdesheim for a really classy label. If you don't have room for a bottle of wine, search the wine shops of Eltville's town center or Rüdesheim's Drosselgasse for a corkscrew carved from a vine-stock or a pottery wine-jug.

Tour 2: The Rhine Gorge between Rüdesheim and Koblenz

After sweeping west past Rüdesheim, the Rhine swings north again, passing between steep, wooded banks on which you'll see the castles that give this section of the river its romantic image. This 60-kilometer (36-mile) stretch is where the Lorelei cliff stands ominous sentinel; where the Mouse Tower clings like driftwood to a rock isolated by perilous currents; and where the promenades of Bacharach and Koblenz wind along the shore. You can cycle the length of the gorge in a day or cover the distance at leisure by train and bus, crossing the river by ferry whenever it suits you. The train and bus routes follow each bank, and most of the towns en route are served by the K-D boats that ply the river (*see* Guided Tours, *above*), and often by local ferries. Make Rüdesheim or Koblenz your base and follow the river either north or south.

The Rhine Gorge

If you start out from Rüdesheim, cross by ferry to Bingen and take a boat ride from there to the romantic **Castle of Burg Rheinstein.** It was Prince Friedrich von Preussen, a cousin of Emperor Wilhelm I, who acquired the original medieval castle in 1825 and transformed it into the picture-book castle you see high above the Rhine today. The prince is buried in the castle's fanciful Gothic chapel.

The ride to **Burg Rheinstein** takes you past one of the most famous sights on the Rhine, the **Mäuseturm** (Mouse Tower), a 13th-century edifice clinging to a rock in the river. According to legend, it was constructed by an avaricious bishop as a customs post to exact taxes from passing river traffic. The story suggests that the greedy bishop grew so unpopular that he was forced to hole up in the tower, where he was eventually devoured by mice.

Beyond the Mäuseturm there are two other medieval castles you can visit: **Burg Reichenstein,** which towers high above the picturesque wine town of **Trechtingshausen;** and **Burg Sooneck,** which in the 12th century was the most feared stronghold in the Rhineland. Reichenstein castle is now a luxurious hotel where you can enjoy lunch in an excellent restaurant with a sensational view. Sooneck, towering above the Rhine on a rocky outcrop, was destroyed several times during its colorful history and rebuilt in its present form in 1840 by the Prussian King Friedrich Wilhelm IV. From the castle you can follow a path through vineyards to one of the most spectacular vantage points of the entire Rhineland: the **Siebenburgenblick** (Seven-Castle View).

Two miles north of Burg Sooneck, at the village of **Niederheimbach,** take the ferry back across the Rhine to the historic little wine town of **Lorch,** whose ancient walls mark the northernmost limit of the Rhinegau. Its parish church of **St. Martin** has a Gothic high altar and 13th-century carved choir stalls.

Northward from Lorch, both banks of the river offer competing attractions. The only way anyone could get to see them all would be to zigzag back and forth across the river by ferry. Fortunately, at most points between here and Koblenz, crossing the Rhine is easy via small ferries that run frequently.

Downstream from Lorch, on the west bank, lies busy **Bacharach,** whose long association with wine is indicated by its name, which comes from the Latin "*Bacchi ara,*" meaning "altar of Bacchus," the Roman god of wine. The town was a thriving center of Rhine wine trade in the Middle Ages. Something of its medieval atmosphere can still be found in the narrow streets within its 14th-century defensive walls and towers.

Oberwesel, 8 kilometers (5 miles) north of Bacharach, also retains its medieval look. Sixteen of the original 21 towers that studded the town walls still stand; one does double duty as the bell tower of the 14th-century church of **St. Martin.** Towering above the town are the remains of the 1,000-year-old **Burg Schönburg,** whose massive walls, nearly 20 feet thick in places, were not strong enough to prevent its destruction by rampaging French troops in 1689. Part of the castle has been restored and today houses a comfortable hotel.

The ruins of another medieval castle, **Burg Rheinfels,** stand at the outskirts of the next stop along the road, the town of **St. Goar,** named after an early missionary who became the patron saint of Rhine boatmen and tavern keepers. The Rhine here narrows dramatically, funneling its waters into a treacherous maelstrom of fast-flowing currents and eddies. These rushing torrents are what gave rise to the legend of the Lorelei, a grim, 400-foot-high rock that protrudes from the river just outside **St. Goarshausen.** So many boats were wrecked on it that people began to say a bewitching water nymph with golden tresses inhabited the rock, and lured sailors to watery graves by her beauty and strange songs.

These days, in season, the Lorelei's siren song can serve as a trap for tourists rather than sailors. Excursion boats leave regularly from Koblenz and Bingen on Lorelei cruises, and as these overcrowded vessels pass within sight of the famed cliffs, each and every one plays a taped version of the Lorelei song (a Heinrich Heine poem set to music), blasting the creation above the roar of the river.

You can see a statue of the Lorelei in St. Goarshausen. To get there, take the ferry from St. Goar. North and south of St. Goarshausen are two castles whose 14th-century owners feuded so unrelentingly that the fortresses came to be known as Katz (cat) and Maus (mouse). **Burg Katz,** just north of St. Goarshausen, was built in 1371 by Count Wilhelm II von Katzenelnbogen (literally, cat's elbow). It was he who dubbed the rival castle south of St. Goarshausen **Burg Maus.** The rivalry, however, was a serious matter. There was constant competition between many of the castle-bound nobles of the Rhine to establish who would extract tolls from passing river traffic, a lucrative and vicious business. Napoléon, not one to respect medieval traditions, put an end to the fighting in 1806 when he destroyed Burg Katz. It was later reconstructed using the original medieval plans. Neither castle is open to the public.

If you visit this area in September, stay for the **Rhein in Flammen** (Rhine in Flames) festival, a pyrotechnic orgy of rockets and flares that lights up the towns of St. Goar and St. Goarshausen and their surrounding vineyards.

Rivalry between neighboring castles was common even when the keepers were members of the same family. At **Kamp-Bornhofen,** 12 kilometers (8 miles) north of St. Goar, are **Burg Sterrenberg** and **Burg Liebenstein,** once owned by two brothers. When their relations deteriorated over a river-toll feud, they built a wall between them. Today the castles keep the rivalry going by running competing wine taverns.

Across from Kamp-Bornhofen is the mile-long promenade of elegant **Boppard,** usually lined with excursion and pleasure boats. Luxurious hotels, restaurants, and spa facilities are Boppard's hallmarks. There are also wine taverns of every caliber. The old quarter is part of a walking tour marked by signs from the 14th-century **Carmelite church** on Karmeliterstrasse. (Inside the church, grotesque carved figures peer from the choir stalls.) There are substantial ruins from a 4th-century Roman fort in Boppard. Take the chair lift up **Gideonseck** to view this stretch of the Rhine from on high.

At Boppard, the river swings east and then north to **Rhens,** a town that traces its origins back some 1,300 years. A vital center of the Holy Roman Empire, Rhens was where German kings and emperors were elected and then presented to the people. The monumental site where the ceremonies took place, the **Königstuhl,** is on a hilltop just outside Rhens, on the road to Waldesch. It was here, in 1388, that the rift between the Holy Roman Empire and the papacy (to which the emperor was nominally subject) proved final. The six German prince-electors who nominated the emperor declared that henceforward their decisions were final and need no longer be given papal sanction.

Marksburg, the final castle on this fortress-studded stretch of the Rhine, is located on the opposite bank of the river, 500 feet above the town of **Braubach.** Marksburg was built in the 12th century to protect silver and lead mines in the area; so successful were its medieval builders that the castle proved impregnable—it is the only one in the entire Middle Rhine Valley to have survived the centuries intact. Within its massive walls is a collection of weapons and manuscripts, a medieval botanical garden, and a restaurant.

Koblenz

Tourist office: Fremdenverkehrsamt der Stadt Koblenz, Verkehrspavillon, 5400 Koblenz, tel. 0261/31304.

Numbers in the margin correspond to points of interest on the Koblenz map.

Located at a geographical nexus known as the **Deutsches Eck** (corner of Germany), Koblenz is the heart of the Middle Rhine region. Rivers and mountains converge here, where the Mosel flows into the Rhine on one side and the Lahn flows in on the other. Three mountain ridges intersect at Koblenz as well.

Koblenz serves as the cultural, administrative, and business center of the Middle Rhine. Its position at the confluence of two rivers bustling with steamers, barges, tugs, and every other kind of river boat makes it one of the most important traffic points on the Rhine.

The heart of historic Koblenz is close to the point where the Rhine and Mosel meet. Koblenz was founded by the Romans in AD 9. Its Roman name, Castrum ad Confluentes (the camp at the confluence), was later corrupted to Koblenz. It became a powerful city in the Middle Ages, when it controlled trade on both rivers. The city suffered severe bomb damage from air raids during the last world war (85% of its buildings were destroyed), but extensive restoration has done much to re-create the atmosphere of old Koblenz. An English-speaking guide leads a walking tour of the old town every Saturday at 2:30, June–October.

Koblenz is centered on the west bank of the Rhine, but begin
1 your tour on the opposite side, at **Festung Ehrenbreitstein,** Europe's largest fortress. Set 400 feet above the river, it offers a commanding view of the old town (the view alone justifies a visit). Ride the cable car (the Sesselbahn) up if the walk is too daunting. The earliest buildings date from about 1100, but the bulk of the fortress was constructed in the 16th century. In 1801, Napoléon's forces partially destroyed Festung Ehrenbreitstein; the French then occupied Koblenz for 18 years, a fact that some claim accounts for the Gallic joie de vivre of the city. More concrete evidence of French occupation can be seen in the shape of the fortress's 16th-century **Vogel Greif cannon.** The French absconded with it after they first penetrated the city in 1794; the Germans took it back in 1940; and the French commandeered it again in 1945. The 15-ton cannon was peaceably returned in 1984 by French President François Mitterrand. It is on view at the **Staatliche Sammlung Technischer Kulturdenkmäler Museum,** one of several museums in the fortress. The others include the **Rheinmuseum,** which charts the history of the Rhineland, and the **Museum für Vorgeschichte und Volkskunde,** the museum of prehistory and ethnography. If you can schedule your visit to Koblenz for August, you'll catch one of the most spectacular fireworks displays in Europe at the fortress on the second Saturday of the month. *Fortress and museum: Admission free. Open Easter–Oct., daily 9–5.*

2 The place to begin a tour of the **old town** is the **Pfaffendorfer Brücke.** Three competing attractions stand at its west end. The

Deutsches Eck, **6**
Festung Ehrenbreitstein, **1**
Liebfrauenkirche, **9**
Moselanlangen, **8**
Pfaffendorfer Brücke, **2**
Residenzschloss, **3**
Rheinanlagen, **5**
St. Kastor Kirche, **7**
Schängelbrunnen, **10**
Weindorf, **4**

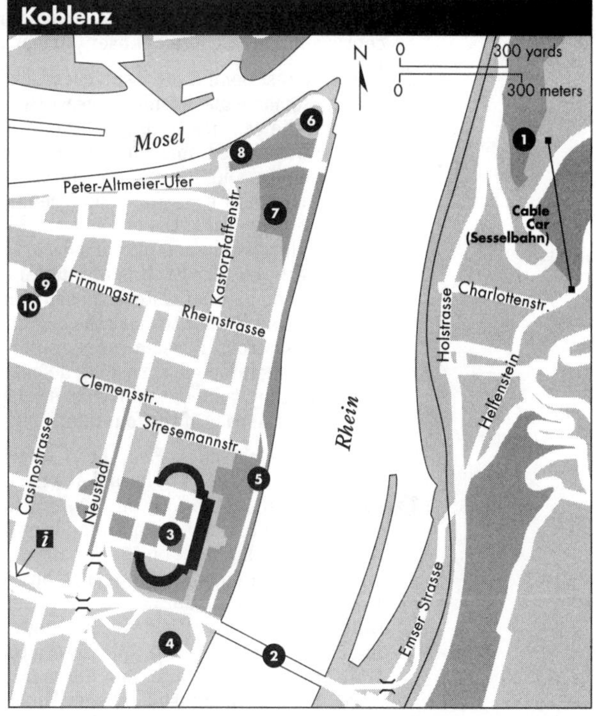

3 most conspicuous is the gracious **Residenzschloss,** the prince-
elector's palace. It was built in 1786 by Prince-Elector Clemens
Wenzeslaus as an elegant replacement for the grim
Ehrenbreitstein fortress. The popular prince, who also built
the city's still-thriving theater, cemented his popularity by
throwing a three-day party when he moved in. He lived there
for only three years, however; in 1791 he was forced to flee to
Augsburg when the French stormed the city. Today the palace
is home to the city government. To the left of the palace is the
4 **Weindorf,** a self-contained wine "village," constructed for a
mammoth exhibition of German wine in 1925. It is now one of
the city's prime tourist attractions.

The third attraction here is the 10-kilometer-long (6-mile-long)
5 riverside promenade, the **Rheinanlagen,** the longest in the
Rhineland. If you want to cover it all, rent a bike. When the
weather's good, it can be fun to while away an hour or so pedal-
ing along the Rhine.

From the bridge, you can either head straight into the old town
6 or stroll along to the **Deutsches Eck.** You'll have seen this curious structure from the fortress; if you have a taste for the more
unusual manifestations of Germany's nationalism, it's worth a
closer look. The sharply pointed piece of land juts into the river
like the prow of some early ironclad warship. It's a historic site,
first settled and named by the German Order of Knights in
1216. In 1897 a statue of Kaiser Wilhelm I, the first emperor of
the newly united Germany, was erected on the Deutsches Eck.
It was destroyed at the end of World War II, however, and replaced by the ponderous altarlike monument to German unity

you see today. The monument was again in the spotlight recently amid the excitement over German reunification.

7 Standing just behind the Deutsches Eck is **St. Kastor Kirche,** a sturdy Romanesque basilica consecrated in 836 and remodeled through the centuries. It was here in 843 that the Treaty of Verdun was signed, formalizing the division of Charlemagne's great empire and leading to the creation of Germany and France as separate states. Inside, compare the squat columns in the nave, typical of the muscular architecture of the Romanesque style with the complex and decorative fan vaulting of the Gothic sections. The **St. Kastor fountain** outside the church is an intriguing piece of historical oneupmanship. It was built by the occupying French to mark the beginning of Napoléon's ultimately disastrous Russian campaign of 1812. When the Russians, having inflicted a crushing defeat on Napoléon, reached Koblenz, they added the ironic inscription "Seen and approved" to the base of the fountain.

8 From the Deutsches Eck, head along the **Moselanlangen**
(Mosel Promenade) to the old town. The focus is the little
9 square called **Am Plan.** On one side of it is the **Liebfrauenkirche**
(Church of Our Lady), which stands on Roman foundations at
the old town's highest point. The bulk of the church is of austere
and weighty Romanesque design, but its choir is one of the
Rhineland's finest and most ornate examples of 15th-century
Gothic architecture. Rising incongruously above the west front
are two 17th-century Baroque towers topped by onion domes.
Walk around to the rear of the church to reach the 17th-century
town hall, a former Jesuit college. You'll be drawn to the little
10 statue of a street urchin, the **Schängelbrunnen** (literally "scala-
wag fountain") in the square—every three minutes he spouts
water at unwary passersby.

Lodging
Under DM 180

Hohenstaufen. The recently renovated Hohenstaufen is centrally located, a 10-minute walk from both the Mosel and the Rhine. There's a grand-hotel spaciousness to the modern interior, and many of the comfortably furnished rooms have been enlarged. *Emil-Schuller-Str. 41–43, tel. 0261/32303. 68 rooms with bath. Facilities: bar, restaurant. AE, DC, MC, V.*

Under DM 130

Kleiner Riesen. It's an older hotel offering basic, no-nonsense value for the money, but it's comfortable and well-run, and the riverside location is a big plus. *Kaiserin-Augusta-Anlagen 18, tel. 0261/32077. 27 rooms with bath. Facilities: parking. AE, DC, MC, V.*

Zum Schwarzen Baren. Koblenz's Black Bear is a historic Rhineland hostelry, comfortably renovated and family-run. Ask for a room at the rear of the building—the front looks out on a busy main road. The hotel's tavern/restaurant draws regulars from far and wide. *Koblenzer Str. 35, tel. 0261/44074. 13 rooms, 8 with bath. AE, DC, MC, V.*

Dining
Under DM 40

Weinhaus Hubertus. The flower-laden, half-timbered 17th-century exterior gives a good idea of the country-style mood inside. Antiques and dark wood predominate. The food is ample and cooked with gusto. *Florinsmarkt. 54, tel. 0261/31177. Reservations advised. No credit cards. Closed lunch.*

Under DM 30

Fährhaus am Stausee. The garden terrace where you can dine on warm sunny days extends to the banks of the Mosel. A range of dishes, predominantly fish, fill the menu of this old established restaurant. *An der Fähre 3, Metternich, tel. 0261/2093. MC.*

Wacht am Rhein. Here you can eat well and watch the river traffic pass, either at a table at one of the picture windows or on the terrace. Freshly caught river fish feature prominently. *Adenauer-Ufer 6, tel. 0261/15313. AE, MC, V.*

Shopping Koblenz has two flea markets held each Saturday in summer at **Peter-Almeier-Ufer** and at **Florinsmarkt.** For antiques and handicrafts, prowl the old city around the cathedral or make for the **Weindorf** (wine village), where more than just wine is offered.

The Arts The **Rheinische Philharmonie** orchestra plays regularly in the **Rhein-Mosel-Halle** (Julius-Wegeler-Str). **Organ recitals** are frequently given in two fine churches: the **Christuskirche,** and the **Florinskirche.** Koblenz has a theatrical tradition dating back to the 18th-century rule of the Prince-Elector Clemens Wenzeslaus. The gracious neoclassical theater he built in 1787 is still in regular use; tel. 0261/34629 for program details and tickets.

Nightlife Koblenz's **Weindorf** (wine village) has the greatest concentration of taverns in the Rhineland, and they come to life at night. The mood is merry, the wine is inexpensive (and good), and sometimes there are live bands. Singles make for the **Tanzcafé Besselink** (opposite the main train station)—it's open until 3 AM. Disco fans favor the **Apropos** (Schulgasse 9) and the **Metro Club** in Koblenz-Hochheim (Alte Heerstr. 130). The nightclub scene is dominated by the **Mocambo** (Poststr. 2a) and the **Petit Fleur** (Rheinstr. 30), while the best jazz can reportedly be heard at the **Lampenputzer** (Gemüsegasse 4).

Tour 3: Along the Mosel to Trier

While a tour along the meandering Mosel River to the historic city of Trier could be considered a side trip from the Rhine, it's actually an excursion endowed with a magic and charm all its own. In fact, Trier could easily qualify as the best-kept secret when it comes to German cities. You can cover this stretch easily by bike, or hop from village to village on the bus or rail lines that follow the river bank. Base yourself in Koblenz or Trier—or stay at any of the charming inns or pensions that stand invitingly between the vineyards and the river.

Along the Mosel

You don't have to travel far up the Mosel Valley to be reminded that wine plays every bit as important a role here as it does along the Rhine. The river's zigzag course passes between steep, terraced slopes where grapes have been grown since Roman times.

The Mosel is one of the most hauntingly beautiful river valleys on earth: turreted castles look down from its leafy perches, its hilltops are crowned with bell towers, and throughout its expanse, skinny church spires stand against the sky. For more than 100 miles, the silvery Mosel River meanders past a string of storybook medieval wine villages, each more attractive than the other. The first village you'll reach, **Winningen,** 15 kilometers (10 miles) from Koblenz, is the center of the valley's largest vineyards. Stop off to admire Germany's oldest half-timbered house in **Kirchenstrasse** (No. 1); it was built in 1320. On the slopes above Winningen's narrow medieval streets is a mile-long path reached by driving up Fährstrasse to Am Rosenhang. Once there, high above the Mosel, you'll get a bird's-eye view of the **Uhlen, Röttgen, Bruckstück, Hamm,** and **Domgarten** vineyards.

For an even finer view of the river and its rich valley, follow the road for 8 kilometers (5 miles) to **Kobern-Gondorf,** on the north bank of the river, and turn off into the idyllic little Mühlental Valley. Here you can climb up through the steep vineyards to the remains of **Oberburg** castle, built in the 12th century by the powerful Knights of Leyen. On the way, you'll pass a 13th-century Romanesque chapel, **St. Matthew's.**

The Mosel bristles with almost as many castles as the Rhine. Among them is what many deem the most impressive in the country, **Burg Eltz.** It's located above the village of Moselkern, Fifteen kilometers (10 miles) from Koben-Gondorf. The only way to reach the castle from Moselkern is to walk 3 kilometers (2 miles) along a gentle footpath that winds through the wild valley. It's worth the trek to see what may well be the most perfectly proportioned medieval castle in Germany. Perched on the spine of an isolated, rocky outcrop, bristling with towers and pinnacles, it at first looks unreal—like an image suspended in time and space. Upon closer exposure, Burg Eltz turns out to be the apotheosis of all one expects of a medieval castle: It's easily as impressive in its own special way as "Mad" King Ludwig's fantasy creation, Neuschwanstein. But Burg Eltz is the real thing: an 800-year-old castle, with modifications from the 16th century. It's a mystery why Burg Eltz is not better known, or more visited. There are few sites in Germany where the sense of the centuries unfolding is as vivid. The magic continues in the interior, which is decorated with heavy Gothic furnishings. There is also an interesting collection of old weapons. *Admission: DM 5.50 adults, DM 3.50 children. Open Apr.–Oct., Mon.–Sat. 9–5:30, Sun. 10–5:30.*

Destruction was the fate suffered by the next castle along the valley, the famous **Reichsburg** (Imperial Fortress) **of Cochem,** 15 kilometers (10 miles) from Berg Eltz. The 900-year-old castle was rebuilt in the 19th century after Louis XIV stormed it in 1689. Today it stands majestically over Cochem. *Admission: DM 3.50 adults, DM 1.50 children. Open daily 9–6.*

Cochem itself is one of the most attractive towns of the Mosel Valley, with a riverside promenade to rival any along the Rhine. If you're traveling by train, just south of Cochem you'll be plunged into Germany's longest railway tunnel, the Kaiser-Wilhelm, an astonishing 4-kilometer-long (2½-mile-long) example of 19th-century engineering that saves travelers a 21-kilometer (13-mile) detour along one of the Mosel's great loops.

By car, follow the loop of the river for 8 kilometers (5 miles) past Cochem and you'll reach the little town of **Beilstein.** It has a mixture of all the picture-pretty features of a German river and wine town in this romantic area of the country. Take a look at the marketplace carved into the rocky slope.

At the village of **Ediger-Eller,** 10 kilometers (6 miles) from Beilstein, stop by the roadside vineyard of **Freiherr von Landenberg** (Moselstr. 60). Sample a glass of wine from the Baron's vines and visit his private viticulture museum.

Zell, 12 kilometers (8 miles) upriver, on another great loop, is a typical Mosel River town, much like Cochem. Located about midway between Koblenz and Trier, this small, historic town is made up of picturesque red-roofed homes and age-old fortifications falling into ruin. A scenic backdrop is provided by the vineyards that produce the famous Schwarze Katz (Black Cat) wine, which is rated as one of Germany's very best whites. Stroll the town's medieval arc along the river. On your way you'll notice a small, twin-towered castle, Schloss Zell, dating from the 14th century. After considerable restoration, the castle evolved into an elegant hotel furnished with exquisite antiques. Its restaurant serves regional cuisine and wine from the owner's own Black Cat vineyards.

Straddling the Mosel 18 kilometers (11 miles) farther along is **Traben-Trarbach,** a two-town combination that serves as headquarters of the regional wine trade and offers a popular wine festival in summer. Visit the ruins of **Mont Royal** high above Traben on the east bank. This enormous fortress was built around 1687 by Louis XIV of France, only to be dismantled 10 years later under the terms of the Treaty of Rijswijk. Partially restored by the Nazis, the fortress retains some of its original forbidding mass.

Bernkastel-Kues is 27 kilometers (17 miles) away by road, but if you're in the mood for some exercise, you can reach it on foot from Traben-Trarbach in about an hour by taking the path that cuts across the tongue of land formed by the exaggerated loop of the river. The road, following the river, practically doubles back on itself as it winds leisurely along. Bernkastel, on the north bank of the river, and Kues, on the south, were officially linked early this century. **Marktplatz,** the heart of Bernkastel, meets all the requirements for the ideal small-town German market square. Most of the buildings are late-Gothic/early Renaissance, with facades covered with intricate carvings and sharp gables stabbing the sky. In the center of the square is **Michaelsbrunnen** (Michael's fountain), a graceful 17th-century work. Wine used to flow from it on special occasions in bygone years. Today, although wine flows freely in the town—especially during the local wine festival in the first week of September—only water ever comes from the fountain. There's a fortress here, too: **Burg Landshut,** a 13th-century castle glowering above the town. Visit it for some amazing views of the river either from its ramparts or from the terrace of the restaurant within its old walls, and to wander around its flower-strewn remains. In summer, a bus makes the trip up to the castle every hour from the parking lot by the river. The town's most famous wine is known as Bernkasteler Doktor. According to a story, the wine got its unusual name when it saved the life of the prince-bishop of Trier, who lay dying in the castle. After all other medicinal treatment had failed to cure him, he was offered a glass of the local wine—which miraculously put him back on his feet. Try a glass of it yourself at the castle (or buy a bottle from the vineyard bordering the street called Hinterm Graben).

The town's remaining attraction owes its existence to Cardinal Nikolaus Cusanus, a 15th-century philosopher and pioneer of German humanist thought. He founded a religious and charitable institution, complete with a vineyard, on the riverbank in Kues. The vineyard is still going strong, and tastings are held daily at 3 in the St. Niklaus-Hospital (Cusanusstr. 2). The buildings here comprise the largest Gothic ensemble on the Mosel. Among them is the Mosel-Weinmuseum. *Admission: DM 2 adults, DM 1 children. Open May–Oct., daily 10–5; Nov.–Apr., daily 2–5.*

From Bernkastel-Kues to Trier is a farther 66 kilometers (41 miles) of twisting river road. Endless vineyards and little river towns punctuate the snaking path of the Mosel. Among them is **Neumagen,** settled by the Romans in the 4th century. In its main square, there's a modern copy of the famous carved relief of a Roman wine ship plying a choppy-looking Mosel. If you continue on to Trier, you can see the original in the Landesmuseum.

Trier

Tourist office: Tourist Information, An der Porta Nigra (adjoining Trier's great Roman gate), Postfach 3830, 5500 Trier, tel. 0651/48071.

Trier's claim to fame is not only that it's the oldest town in Germany, but it's also the first civilized settlement in Europe. It dates from 2,000 BC, when Prince Trebeta, son of an Assyrian queen, arrived here and set up residence on the banks of the Mosel; he named the place Treberis, after himself. An inscription on a historic old house on Trier's marketplace states: "*Ante Romam Treveris stetit annis mille trecentis*" ("1,300 years before Rome stood Trier").

Eventually the legions of Julius Caesar set up camp at this strategic point of the river, and Augusta Treverorum (the town of Emperor Augustus in the land of the Treveri) was founded in 16 BC. It was described as "*urbs opulentissima*"—as beautiful a city as existed beyond Rome itself.

Around AD 275, an Alemannic tribe stormed Augusta Treverorum and reduced it to rubble. But it was rebuilt in even grander style and renamed Treveris. Eventually it evolved into one of the leading cities of the empire and was promoted to *Roma Secunda,* a second Rome north of the Alps. As a powerful administrative capital, it was adorned with all the noble civic buildings of a major Roman settlement, plus public baths, palaces, barracks, an amphitheater, and temples. Roman emperors such as Diocletian (who made it one of the four joint capitals of the empire) and Constantine lived in Trier for years at a time.

Trier survived the collapse of Rome and became an important center of Christianity; it was later one of the most powerful archbishoprics in the Holy Roman Empire. The city thrived throughout the Renaissance and Baroque periods, taking full advantage of its location at the meeting point of major east-west and north-south trade routes, and growing fat on the commerce that passed through. It also became one of Germany's most important wine-exporting centers. A later claim to fame is as the birthplace of Karl Marx.

To do justice to the city, consider staying for at least two full days. A ticket good for all the Roman sights in Trier costs DM 6 adults, DM 3 children. Between May and October there are bus and walking tours of the city conducted by the local tourist board in English. Buses depart from the Porta Nigra gate at 10:30 and 2:30 daily. The two-hour tour costs DM 12 adults, DM 6 children. The walking tour leaves from the gate at 2. The cost is DM 6 adults, DM 3 children.

Numbers in the margin correspond to points of interest on the Trier map.

1 Begin your tour at the **Porta Nigra** (the Black Gate), located by the city's tourist office. This is by far the best-preserved Roman structure in Trier and one of the grandest Roman buildings in northern Europe. It's a city gate, built in the 4th century. Its name is misleading, however: The sandstone gate is not actually black, but dark gray. Those with an interest in Roman construction techniques should look for the holes left by the original iron clamps that held the entire structure together. This city gate also served as part of Trier's defenses and was proof of the sophistication of Roman military might and ruthlessness. Attackers were often lured into the two innocent-looking arches of the Porta Nigra only to find themselves enclosed in a courtyard—and at the mercy of the defending forces. *Admission: DM 2 adults, DM 1 children and senior citizens. Open Apr.–Oct., daily 9–1 and 2–5; Nov. and Dec., daily 10–4; Jan.–Mar., Tues.–Sun. 9–1 and 2–5.*

To the side are the remains of the Romanesque Simeonskirche,
2 today the **Städtisches Museum Simeonstift** (open Tues.–Fri.
9–5, Sat. and Sun. 10–1). The church was built in the 11th century by Archbishop Poppo in honor of the early medieval hermit Simeon, who, for seven years, shut himself up in the east tower of the Porta Nigra. Collections of art and artifacts produced in Trier from the Middle Ages to the present now commemorate Simeon's feat. Simeon also has one of Trier's main streets named after him: Simeonstrasse. It leads directly to
3 **Hauptmarkt,** the main square of old Trier. A 1,000-year-old
market cross and a richly ornate 16th-century fountain stand in the square.

From Hauptmarkt, turn left (east) down Stirnstrasse to see Trier's great **Dom** (cathedral). Before you go in, take a look at
4 the adjoining 13th-century **Liebfrauenkirche** (Church of Our
Lady). It's one of the oldest purely Gothic churches in the country. The interior is elegantly attenuated.

5 If you want a condensed history of Trier, visit the **Dom:** There is almost no period of the city's past that is not represented here. It stands on the site of the Palace of Helen of Constantine, mother of the Emperor Constantine, who knocked the palace down in AD 326 and put up a large church in its place. The church burned down in 336 and a second, even larger one was built. Parts of the foundations of this third building can be seen in the east end of the current structure (begun in about 1035). The cathedral you see today is a weighty and sturdy edifice with small, round-headed windows, rough stonework, and asymmetrical towers, as much a fortress as a church. Inside, Gothic styles predominate—the result of remodeling in the 13th century—though there are also many Baroque tombs, altars, and confessionals. This architectural jumble of Roman-

Amphitheater, **11**
Barbarathermen, **10**
Bischöfliches Museum, **6**
Dom, **5**
Hauptmarkt, **3**
Kaiserthermen, **9**
Karl-Marx-Haus, **12**
Liebfrauenkirche, **4**
Porta Nigra, **1**
Rheinisches Landesmuseum, **8**
Römische Palastaula, **7**
Städtisches Museum Simeonstift, **2**
Weininformation Mosel-Saar-Ruwer, **13**

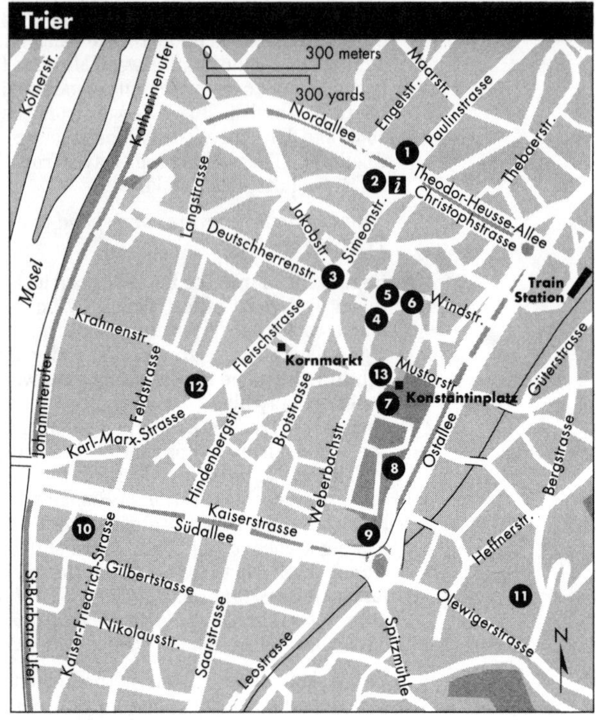

esque, Gothic, and Baroque styles gives the place the air of a vast antiques shop. Make sure you visit the Baroque **Domschatzmuseum** in the treasury, site of two extraordinary objects. One is the 10th-century **Andreas Tragalter** (St. Andrews's Portable Altar), made of gold by local craftsmen. It is smaller than the Dom's main altar, but it is no lightweight. The other treasure is the **Holy Robe,** the garment supposedly worn by Christ at the time of his trial before Pontius Pilate and gambled for by Roman soldiers. The story goes that it was brought to Trier by Helen of Constantine, a tireless collector of holy relics. It is so delicate and old that it is displayed only every 30 years (you'll have to come back in 2019 if you want to see it); the rest of the time it lies under a faded piece of 9th-century Byzantine silk. *Domschatzmuseum admission: DM 1 adults, 50 pf children. Open Mon.–Sat. 10–12, 2–5, Sun. 2–4.*

Excavations around the cathedral have unearthed a series of
6 antiquities, most of which are housed in the **Bischöfliches Museum** (Episcopal Museum) in Windstrasse, just behind the cathedral. The exhibits include a 4th-century ceiling painting believed to have adorned the Emperor Constantine's palace. *Windstr. 6–8. Admission: DM 1 adults, 50 pf children. Open Mon.–Sat. 9–1 and 2–5, Sun. 1–5.*

Just south of the cathedral complex—take Konstantinstrasse—is another impressive reminder of Trier's Roman
7 past: the **Römische Palastaula** (Roman Basilica). Today, this is the major protestant church of Trier. When first built by the Emperor Constantine around AD 300, it was the Imperial Throne Room of the palace. At 239 feet long, 93 feet wide, and

108 feet high, it demonstrates the astounding ambition of its Roman builders and the sophistication of their building techniques. It is the second-largest Roman interior in existence—only the Pantheon in Rome is larger. Look up at the deeply coffered ceiling: More than any other part of the building, it conveys the opulence of the original structure. *Konstantinstr. Open Apr.–Oct., Mon.–Sat. 9–1 and 2–6, Sun. 11–1 and 2–6; Nov.–Mar., Tues.–Sat. 11–noon and 3–4, Sun. 11–noon.*

From the Palastaula, turn south. To your left, facing the
8 grounds of the prince-elector's palace, is the **Rheinisches Landesmuseum** (Rhineland Archaeological Museum), which houses the largest collection of Roman antiquities in Germany. Pride of place goes to the 3rd-century stone relief of a Roman ship transporting immense barrels of wine up the river. If you stopped off in Neumagen on the way to Trier, you probably saw the copy of it in the town square. *Ostallee 44. Admission free. Open Mon.–Fri. 9:30–4, Sat. 9:30–1, Sun. 9–1.*

9 From the museum, walk down to the ruins of the **Kaiserthermen** (imperial baths), just 200 yards away. Begun by Constantine in the 4th century, these were once the third-largest public baths in the Roman Empire, exceeded only by Diocletian's baths in Yugoslavia and the baths of Caracalla in Rome. They covered an area 270 yards long and 164 yards wide. Today only the weed-strewn fragments of the **Calderium** (hot baths) are left, but they are enough to give a fair idea of the original splendor and size of the complex. When the Romans pulled out, the baths were turned into a fortress (one window of the huge complex served as a city gate for much of the Middle Ages), then a church, and then a fortress again. Don't confuse them
10 with the much smaller **Barbarathermen** (open same hours) in Kaiser-Friedrich-Str. *Admission: Open Jan.–Mar. and Nov., Tues.–Sun. 9–1 and 2–5; Apr.–Sept., daily 9–1 and 2–6; Oct., daily 9–1 and 2–5; closed Dec.*

Just east of the Kaiserthermen are the remains of the
11 **Amphitheater** built around AD 100, the oldest Roman building in Trier. In its heyday it seated 20,000 people. You can climb down to the cellars beneath the arena to see the machines that were used to change the scenery and the cells where lions and other wild animals were kept before being unleashed to devour maidens and do battle with gladiators. *Olewigerstr. See Porta Nigra for hours and admission.*

After this profusion of antiquities, you may want to shift gears
12 and see the **Karl-Marx-Haus** on Karl-Marx-Strasse, south of Kornmarkt in the old town. It was here that Marx was born in 1818. Serious social historians will feel at home in the little house, which has been converted into a museum charting Marx's life and the development of socialism around the world. A signed first edition of *Das Kapital*, the tome in which Marx sought to prove the inevitable decline of capitalism, may prove a highlight for some. *Admission: DM 2 adults, DM 1 children. Open Apr.–Oct., Tues.–Sun. 10–6, Mon. 1–6; Nov.–Mar., Tues.–Sun. 10–1 and 3–6, Mon. 3–6.*

Trier is, of course, also a city of wine, and beneath its streets are cellars capable of storing nearly 8 million gallons. To get to know the wines of the region, drop in at the tavern run by the
13 **Weininformation Mosel-Saar-Ruwer** (Konstantinpl. 11, tel. 0651/73690). The city also has a wine trail, a picturesque 1½-

mile walk studded with information plaques that lead to the wine-growing suburb of **Olewig.**

Lodging
Under DM 180
★ **Petrisberg.** The building is unimposing externally, but inside features striking antiques and rooms with superb views over vineyards, forests, and parklands. For all that, it's no more than a 10-minute walk from the old town. There's a moody *Weinstube* (wine bar) in the basement, but no restaurant. *Sickingenstr. 11, tel. 0651/41181. 26 rooms and 3 suites with bath. Facilities: parking. No credit cards.*

Dining
Under DM 30
Ratskeller zur Steipe. Buried in the vaults beneath the town hall, the Ratskeller offers Teutonic mood and fare. In summer, you can move upstairs and eat on the terrace. *Hauptmarkt 14, tel. 0651/75052. Reservations advised. AE, DC, V. Closed Mon. and Jan.–Easter.*

★ **Zum Domstein.** Centrally located, and built above a Roman cellar, it takes its history seriously—not only keeping its wines well stored within its ancient walls, as the Romans did, but serving authentic Roman dishes in the restaurant above. Many of them are the staples of today's Italian cuisine. *Hauptmarkt 5, tel. 0651/74490. AE, DC, V. Closed Christmas.*

Lodging and Dining
Under DM 180
Eurener Hof. This family-run hotel offers homey comforts combined with faultless service. It stands on a busy main road outside the city center but is still within walking distance of most of the sights. (Ask for one of the quieter rooms at the back.) The cozy restaurant has a log-fire grill, and there are separate beer and wine taverns. *Eurenerstr. 171, tel. 0651/88077. 57 rooms with bath. AE, MC.*

Under DM 130
Gasthaus Klosterschencke Pfalzel. A Roman official's home once stood here, and then a convent and a monastery; and in 1824 a small guest house opened within the cloistered walls. You eat beneath vaulted ceilings or in the wine cellar, where the estate's own wines are served. *Klosterstr. 10, tel. 0651/6089. 9 rooms, 5 with bath. AE, DC, MC, V.*

Hotel-Cafe Astoria. This beautifully renovated 19th-century city villa is ideally located between the Mosel River and the old town. The rooms on the first floor are larger, but all rooms are cozy and comfortably furnished. *Bruchhausenstr. 4, tel. 0651/73890. 25 rooms with shower. Facilities: bar, café, courtyard terrace. AE, MC, V.*

Shopping
Trier's best shopping is to be found along the pedestrian streets in the **old town:** Simeonstrasse, Fleischstrasse, Nagelstrasse, Palatstrasse, and Hauptmarkt. For local handicrafts, glassware, ceramics, and fabrics, make for **Kunsthandwerkerhof** (Simeonstiftpl.).

The Arts
Trier's **cathedral** is the magnificent setting for much of the sacred music to be heard in the city; there are **organ recital festivals** in May, June, August, and September.

Tour 4: Bonn and Köln

The Rhine cities of Bonn and Köln are each worth special attention but are close enough together for travelers to manage in one tour. Base yourself in either place. There's a larger choice of accommodations, and much more to see and experience, in Köln.

From Frankfurt
By Train There are hourly InterCity services from Frankfurt to both Bonn and Köln. The journey time to Bonn is about two hours; to Köln, 2½ hours.

By Bus **Deutsche Touring** (tel. 069/79030) operates a daily nonstop service between Frankfurt and Köln. Buses leave Frankfurt at 3 PM and Köln at 11 AM. The Frankfurt–Köln run takes three hours; the Köln–Frankfurt journey, 2¼ hours.

By Car The quickest route from Frankfurt to Bonn (160 kilometers/100 miles) and Köln (188 kilometers/116 miles) is the A-3 Autobahn, which cuts through the Westerwald. Travel time to Bonn is 80 minutes; to Köln, two hours. For the most spectacular route, however, leave the A-3 after Limburg and follow the A-48 to Koblenz—which will add about 20 kilometers (12 miles) and 20 minutes to your drive.

Bonn

Tourist office: Tourist Information Cassius-Bastel, Münsterstr. 20 (100 yards from the main railway station), 5300 Bonn, tel. 0228/773–466.

Numbers in the margin correspond to points of interest on the Bonn map.

Bonn, a quiet university town on the Rhine, became the capital of the Federal Republic in 1949, after the postwar political division of Germany. The choice was something of a stopgap: Many people think this small city was picked over more weighty contenders, such as Frankfurt and Munich, to preserve Berlin's chance of regaining its pre–World War II status when reunification finally came. And in a parliamentary vote on June 20, 1991, the politicians indeed decided (by a narrow margin) to move the seat of government back to Berlin. The move will take some 12 years; it will be costly—some estimates go as high as $30 billion—and it will involve tens of thousands of civil servants and their families.

Some suggest that Bonn's greatest asset is its surrounding countryside: the legendary **Siebengebirge** (Seven Hills) and the **Kölner Bucht Valley.** In the capital's streets, old markets, stores, pedestrian malls, parks, and the handsome Südstadt residential area, life is unhurried and unsophisticated by larger city standards. *Guided tours of Bonn start from the tourist office (*see above*): May–Oct., Mon.–Sat. at 10 and 2; Sun. and Apr. at 10; Nov.–Mar., Sat. at 11. The two-hour tour costs DM 14 adults, DM 7 children.*

Bonn's status may be new, but its roots are ancient. The Romans settled this part of the Rhineland 2,000 years ago, calling
1 it Castra Bonnensia. Bonn's cathedral, the **Münster,** stands where two Roman soldiers were executed in AD 253 for Christian beliefs. **Münsterplatz,** site of the cathedral and a short walk from the tourist office in Münsterstrasse 20, is the logical place to begin your tour. The 900-year-old cathedral is vintage late-Romanesque, with a massive octagonal main tower and a soaring spire. It was chosen by two Holy Roman Emperors for their coronations (in 1314 and 1346), and was one of the Rhineland's most important ecclesiastical centers in the Middle Ages. The bronze 17th-century figure of St. Helen and the ornate Rococo pulpit are highlights of the interior. *Open daily 7AM–7PM.*

Alter Friedhof, **5**
Beethovenhaus, **7**
Government Buildings, **8**
Kurfürstliches Schloss, **2**
Münster, **1**
Poppelsdorfer Schloss, **3**
Rathaus, **6**
Rheinisches Landesmuseum, **4**

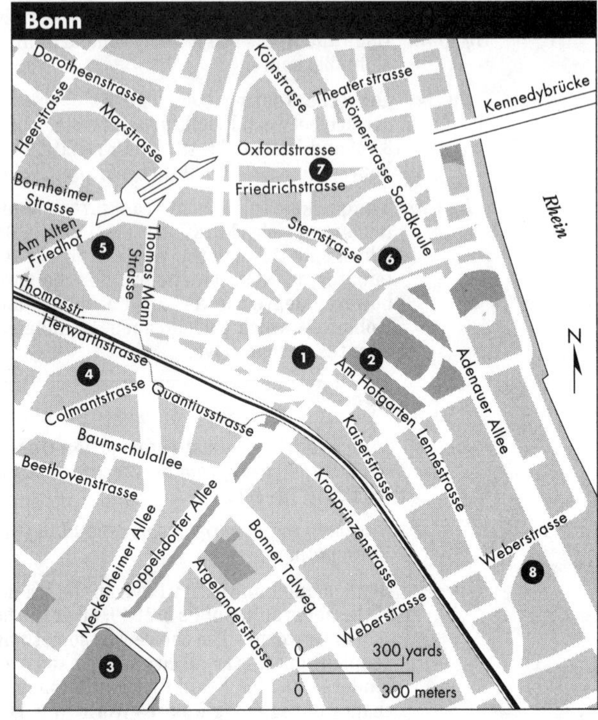

2 Facing the Münster is the grand **Kurfürstliches Schloss,** built in the 18th century by the prince-electors of Köln; today it houses a university. If it's a fine day, stroll through the Hofgarten (Palace Gardens), or follow the chestnut tree avenue called Poppelsdorfer Allee southward to another electors' palace, the
3 smaller **Poppelsdorfer Schloss,** built in Baroque style between 1715 and 1753. The palace has a beautiful botanical garden with an impressive display of tropical plants. *Meckenheimer Allee. Admission free. Open May–Sept., Mon.–Fri. 9–6, Sun. and holidays 9–1; Oct.–Apr., Mon.–Fri. 9–6.*

On your way back to the old town, take Meckenheimer Allee
4 and then Colmanstrasse, to see the **Rheinisches Landesmuseum** (the walk is about a quarter-mile long). The museum, one of the largest in the Rhineland, charts the history, art, and culture of the Rhine Valley from Roman times to the present day. The main draw is the skull of a Neanderthal man, regarded by anthropologists as a vital link in the evolutionary chain. The skull was put together from fragments found in the Neander Valley near Düsseldorf in 1856. *Colmanstrasse 14–16. Admission: DM 4 adults, DM 2 children. Open Tues. and Thurs. 9–5, Wed. 9–8, Fri. 9–4, and Sat.–Sun. 11–5.*

At the end of Colmanstrasse, take the underpass below the rail-
5 road line and follow Thomasstrasse for 300 yards to the **Alter Friedhof** (the Old Cemetery). This ornate graveyard is the resting place of many of the country's most celebrated sons and daughters. Look for the tomb of composer Robert Schumann and his wife Clara. *Am Alten Friedhof. Open Mar.–Aug., dai-*

ly 7 AM–8 PM; Sept.–Feb., daily 8–6. Guided tours May–Sept. at 3 on Tues. and Thurs.

From the Alter Friedhof, follow Sternstrasse into the old town center and proceed to the **Markt** (market), where you'll find an
6 18th-century **Rathaus** (Town Hall) that looks like a pink doll's house.

7 Just north of the town hall are Bonngasse and the **Beethovenhaus.** The latter has been imaginatively converted into a museum celebrating the life of the great composer. Here you'll find scores, paintings, a grand piano (his last, in fact), and an ear trumpet or two. Perhaps the most impressive exhibit is the room in which Beethoven was born—empty save for a bust of the composer. *Bonngasse 20. Admission: DM 5 adults, DM 1.50 children. Open Apr.–Sept., Mon.–Sat. 9–1, 2–5, Sun. 10–1; Oct.–Mar., Mon.–Sat. 10:30–4, Sun. 10–1.*

A tour of Bonn would not be complete without some mention of
8 the **government buildings,** which will continue as such until the government's move to Berlin is completed, and which are located in a complex about a mile south of downtown. Strung along the Rhine, in spacious, leafy grounds between Adenauerallee and the river, are the offices of the **Federal President,** the high-tech **Chancellery,** and the **Federal Parliament;** the '60s high rise you see contains the offices of members of parliament.

Lodging
Under DM 180

Rheinhotel Dreesen. The Rhine rolls by a stone's throw from your room at this turn-of-the-century villa in Bonn's Bad Godesberg suburb (there are fast, frequent bus and suburban train services to town). The hotel's leafy park and glass-roofed garden entice the visitor to linger. *Rheinstr. 45–49, Bad Godesberg, tel. 0228/82020. 67 rooms with bath. AE, DC, MC, V.*

Rheinland Bonn. This modest lodging has the advantage of being a short walk from the center of the old town. Rooms are comfortable, and a good buffet breakfast greets the day. *Berliner Freiheit 11, tel. 0228/658096. 31 rooms with bath. AE.*

Sternhotel. For good value, solid comfort, and a central location, the family-run Stern is tops. Rooms can be small, but all are pleasantly furnished. Snacks are available at the bar. *Markt 8, tel. 0228/654–455. 70 rooms with bath. AE, DC, MC, V.*

Dining
Under DM 40

Das Haus Daufenbach. The stark white exterior disguises one of the most distinctive restaurants in Bonn. The mood is rustic, with simple wood furniture and antlers on the walls. The wines are from the restaurant's own vineyards. *Brüderfasse 6, tel. 0228/637–9944. Reservations recommended. AE, DC, MC, V. Closed Sun. dinner.*

Under DM 30

Em Hottche. Travelers have been given sustenance at this tavern since the late-14th century, and today it offers one of the best-value lunches in town. The interior is rustic, the food stout and hearty. *Markt 4, tel. 0228/658–596. AE, DC, MC, V. Closed last 2 weeks in Dec.*

Im Stiefel. A great student hangout, it's noisy and nearly always full, but it comes complete with basic wood tables, pewter plates, and dark wood paneling. *Bonngasse 30, tel. 0228/634–806. V. Closed Sun. and holidays.*

Shopping

You'll find **Beethoven mementos** everywhere—from portrait busts to special recorded editions of the composer's works. The main shopping street is traffic-free **Poststrasse,** which runs from central Münsterplatz. The international comings and goings in the city keep **antiques** dealers busy. Two to visit are **Paul Schweitzer** (Löbestr. 1) in the Bad Godesberg suburb, and **Kunsthaus Brucke** (Gangolfstr. 9).

Bonn is a city of **markets,** with two open daily: the **Wochenmarkt** on Marktplatz and the **Blumenmarkt,** a flower market, on Remigiusplatz. There's a **flea market** from April through October on the third Saturday of each month at **Rheinaue** (Ludwig-Erhard-Str.). If you're in the Bonn area on the second weekend of September, don't miss the **Pützchens Markt,** a huge country fair.

The Arts Don't come to Bonn looking for bargain tickets; music and theater tend to be expensive here. Every three years the city hosts a **Beethoven Festival.** The next one takes place in 1992, from September 11 to October 4. Contact the Bonn tourist office (tel. 0228/773466) for programs and ticket information. The Bonn **Symphony Orchestra** opens its winter season in grand style every September with a concert on the market square, in front of City Hall. Otherwise, concerts are given in the Beethovenhalle (they're free on Sunday morning). From May through October, the **Bonner Sommer** festival offers a colorful program of folklore, music, and street theater, much of it outdoors and most of it free. Chamber-music concerts are given regularly at the **Schumannhaus** (tel. 0228/773–6666). In May and June, concerts are held on Sunday evening in the **Bad Godesberg Redoute;** admission is free. In July and August, **organ recitals** are given Wednesday evening at 8 in the **Church of the Holy Cross** (Kaiserpl.). Contemporary composers edge out Beethoven and the classics in a summer **"Festival of New Music."**

Bonn hosts a famous dance festival, the **International Dance Workshop,** in July and August. For program details and tickets, tel. 0228/11517. Opera, ballet, and musicals are also staged regularly at the **Oper der Stadt Bonn** (Am Böselagerhof 1, tel. 0228/773–666), which is popularly known as "La Scala of the Rhineland."

Nightlife Nightlife in Bonn? There's the story of the visitor who asked where he could find some action in Bonn. "She's taken the night off to visit her aunt in Köln," was the reply. Things have changed, considering the number of bars in the Altstadt; low-priced taverns and discos are clustered in the streets around the central market square. Locals, though, tend to head for nearby Köln for a night out.

Köln

Tourist office: Verkehrsamt der Stadt Köln, Untere Fettenhennen 19 (across the square from the cathedral), 5000 Köln 1, tel. 0221/221–3340.

Köln (Cologne), 27 kilometers (17 miles) north of Bonn, is the largest city on the Rhine (the fourth largest in Germany) and one of the most interesting. While not as old as Trier, it has been a dominant power in the Rhineland since Roman times. Known throughout the world for its scented toilet water, eau de cologne (first produced here in 1705 from an Italian formula), the city is today a major commercial, intellectual, and ecclesiastical center. Many business travelers are attracted to its numerous trade fairs, held in the two massive convention centers located on the Deutzer side of the Rhine.

Köln is a vibrant, bustling city, with something of the same sparkling spirit that makes Munich so memorable. It claims to have more bars than any other German city and a host of excellent eating places. It also puts on a wild carnival every February, with three days of orgiastic revelry, bands, parades, and parties that last all night.

Köln was first settled by the Romans in 38 BC. For nearly a century it grew slowly, in the shadow of imperial Trier, until a locally born noblewoman, Julia Agrippina, daughter of the Roman general Germanicus, married the Roman Emperor Claudius. Her hometown was elevated to the rank of a Roman city and given the name Colonia Claudia Ara Agrippinensium. For the next 300 years, Colonia (hence Cologne, or Köln) flourished. Proof of the richness of the Roman city is provided today by the **Römisch-Germanisches Museum** (Roman-German Museum; *see below*)—one place you won't want to miss if you have any interest in Roman heritage. When the Romans left, Köln was ruled first by the Franks, then by the Merovingians. In the 9th century, Charlemagne, the towering figure who united the sprawling German lands (and ruled much of present-day France) and was the first Holy Roman Emperor, restored Köln's fortunes and elevated it to its preeminent role in the Rhineland. Charlemagne also appointed the first archbishop of Köln. The ecclesiastical heritage of Köln forms one of the most striking characteristics of the city, which has no fewer than 12 Romanesque churches. Its Gothic cathedral is the largest and the finest in Germany.

Köln eventually became the largest city north of the Alps and, in time, evolved into a place of pilgrimage second only to Rome.

In the Middle Ages, it was a member of the powerful Hanseatic League, occupying a position of greater importance in European commerce than did either London or Paris.

Köln entered modern times as the number-one city of the Rhineland. Then, in World War II, bombings destroyed 90% of it. Only the cathedral remained relatively unscathed. Almost everything else had to be rebuilt more or less from the ground up, including all of the glorious Romanesque churches.

Early reconstruction was accomplished in a big rush—and in what might seem something of a slapdash manner. A good part of the former old town along the Hohe Strasse (old Roman High Road) was turned into a pedestrian shopping mall, one of the first in Germany. Though the mall won accolades in the press when it opened, it is pretty much without charm or grace.

The same could be said for the totally re-created facades of the old-town dwellings facing the river—they emerged looking like Disneyland kitsch, nothing to be taken seriously. Add the fact that six-lane expressways wind their way along the rim of the city center—barely yards from the cathedral—and the heart of Köln turns out to be something of a mishmash of bad and beautiful, a mixed blessing.

On the plus side, much of the Altstadt (old town), ringed by streets that follow the line of medieval city walls, is closed to traffic. Most major sights are within this orbit, easily reached on foot. Here, too, you'll find the best shops.

Numbers in the margin correspond to points of interest on the Köln map.

Towering over the old town is the extraordinary Gothic cathe-
1 dral, the **Kölner Dom,** dedicated to Sts. Peter and Mary. It's comparable to the best French cathedrals; a visit to it may prove a highlight of your trip to Germany. What you'll see is one of the purest expressions of the Gothic spirit in Europe. Here, the desire to pay homage to God took the form of building as large and as lavish a church as possible, a tangible expression of God's kingdom on earth. Its spires soar heavenward and its immense interior is illuminated by light filtering through acres of stained glass. Spend some time admiring the outside of the building (you can walk almost all the way around it). Notice how there are practically no major horizontal lines—all the accents of the building are vertical. It may come as a disappointment to learn that the cathedral, begun in 1248, was not completed until 1880. Console yourself with the knowledge that it was still built to original plans. At 515 feet high, the two west towers of the cathedral were by far the tallest structures in the world when they were finished (they are still the tallest in a church). The length of the building is 470 feet; the width of the nave is 147 feet; and the highest part of the interior is 140 feet.

The cathedral was built to house what was believed to be the relics of the Magi, the three kings or wise men who paid homage to the infant Jesus (the trade in holy mementos was big business in the Middle Ages, and not always too scrupulous). Since Köln was by then a major commercial and political center, it was felt that someplace special had to be constructed to house the relics. Anxious to surpass the great cathedrals then being built in France, the masons set to work. The size of the building was not simply an example of self-aggrandizement on the part of the people of Köln, however; it was a response to the vast numbers of pilgrims who arrived to see the relics. The ambulatory, the passage that curves around the back of the altar, is unusually large, allowing cathedral authorities to funnel large numbers of visitors up to the crossing (where the nave and transepts meet, and where the relics were originally displayed), around the back of the altar, and out again. Today the relics are kept just behind the altar, in the same enormous gold-and-silver **reliquary** in which they were originally displayed. The other great treasure of the cathedral is the **Gero Cross,** a monumental oak crucifixion dating from 975. Impressive for its simple grace, it's in the last chapel on the left as you face the altar.

Other highlights to admire are the stained-glass windows, some of which date from the 13th century; the 15th-century altar painting; and the early 14th-century high altar with its surrounding arcades of glistening white figures and its intricate choir screens. The choir stalls, carved from oak around 1310, are the largest in Germany, seating 104 people. There are more treasures to be seen in the **Dom Schatzkammer,** the cathedral treasury, including the silver shrine of Archbishop Engelbert, who was stabbed to death in 1225. *Admission: DM 2 adults, DM 1 children. Open Mon.–Sat. 9–5:30, Sun. 12:30–4:30.*

Back down at street level, you have the choice of either more
2 culture or commerce. Köln's **shopping district** begins at nearby **Wallrafplatz,** and a recommended shopping tour will take you down Hohe Strasse, Schildergasse, Neumarkt, Mittel-

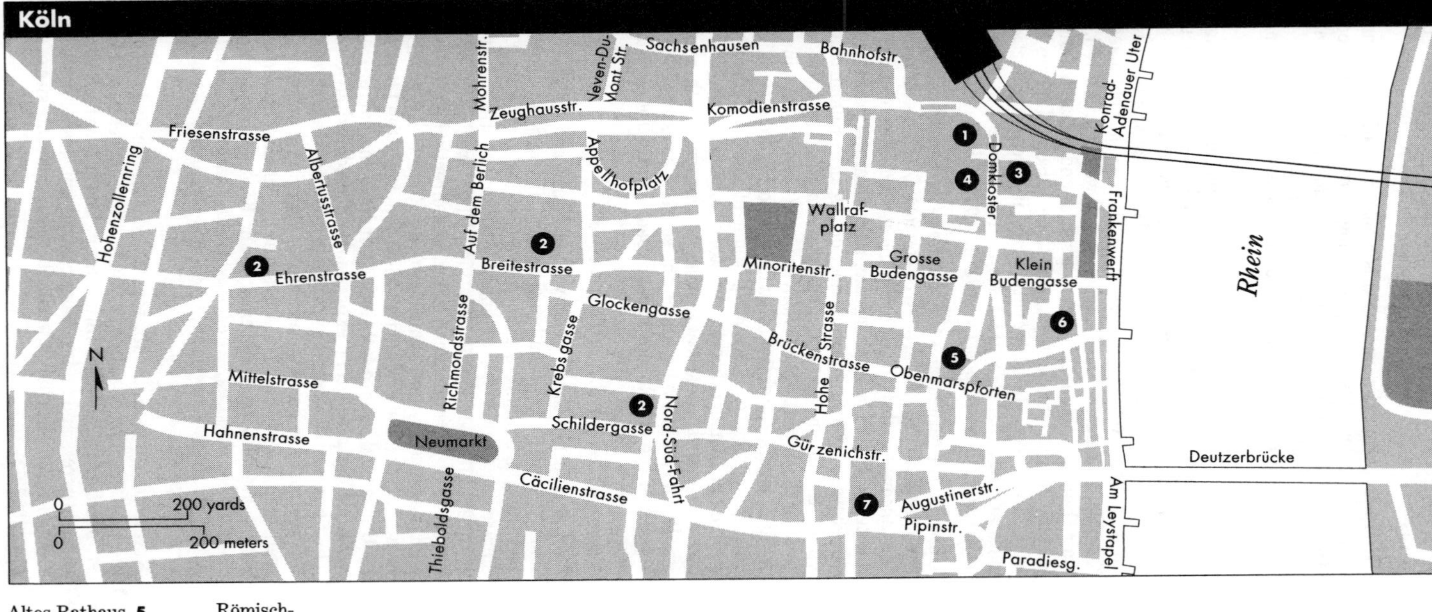

Altes Rathaus, **5**
Gross St. Martin, **6**
Gürzenich, **7**
Kölner Dom, **1**
Römisch-Germanisches Museum, **4**
Shopping District, **2**
Wallraf-Richartz-Museum, **3**

strasse, Hohenzollernring, Ehrenstrasse, Breitestrasse, Tunisstrasse, Minoritenstrasse, and then back to Wallrafplatz.

Grouped around the cathedral is a collection of superb museums. If your priority is painting, try the ultramodern
3 **Wallraf-Richartz-Museum** and Museum Ludwig complex (which includes the Philharmonic concert hall beneath its vast roof). Together, they form the largest art collection in the Rhineland.

The Wallraf-Richartz-Museum contains pictures spanning the years 1300 to 1900, with Dutch and Flemish schools particularly well represented (Rubens, who spent his youth in Köln, has a place of honor, but there are also outstanding works by Rembrandt, Van Dyck, and Frans Hals). Of the other old masters, Tiepolo, Canaletto, and Boucher are all well represented. Renoir, Bonnard, Monet, Sisley, Pissarro, and Cézanne number among the more modern painters. The **Museum Ludwig** is devoted exclusively to 20th-century art; its Picasso collection is outstanding. *Bischofsgartenstr. 1. Admission: DM 3 adults, DM 1.50 children. Open Tues.–Sun. 10–5, Thurs. 10–8.*

4 Opposite the cathedral is the **Römisch-Germanisches Museum,** built from 1970 to 1974 around the famous Dionysus mosaic that was uncovered at the site during the construction of an air-raid shelter in 1941. The huge mosaic, more than 100 yards square, once covered the dining-room floor of a wealthy Roman trader's villa. Its millions of tiny earthenware and glass tiles depict some of the adventures of Dionysus, the Greek god of wine and, to the Romans, the object of a widespread and sinister religious cult. The pillared 1st-century tomb of Lucius Publicius, a prominent Roman officer, some stone Roman coffins, and a series of memorial tablets are among the museum's other exhibits. Bordering the museum on the south is a restored 90-yard stretch of the old Roman harbor road. *Roncallipl. 4. Admission: DM 3 adults, DM 1.50 children. Open Tues.–Fri. and weekends 10–5, Wed. and Thurs. 10–8.*

5 Now head south to the nearby **Alter Markt** and its **Altes Rathaus,** the oldest town hall in Germany (if you don't count the fact that the building was entirely rebuilt after the war). The square has a handsome assembly of buildings—the oldest dating from 1135—in a range of styles. There was a seat of local government here in Roman times, and directly below the current Rathaus are the remains of the Roman city governor's headquarters, the Praetorium. Go inside to see the 14th-century **Hansa Saal,** whose tall Gothic windows and barrel-vaulted wood ceiling are potent expressions of medieval civic pride. The figures of the prophets, standing on pedestals at one end, are all from the early 15th century. Ranging along the south wall are nine additional statues, the so-called *Nine Good Heroes,* carved in 1360. Charlemagne and King Arthur are among them. *Altes Rathaus, Alter Markt. Admission: DM 2 adults, DM 1 children. Open Mon.–Fri. 8:30–4:45, Sat. 10–2. Praetorium open Tues.–Sun. 10–5.*

Now head across Unter Käster toward the river and one of the
6 most outstanding of Köln's 12 Romanesque churches, the **Gross St. Martin.** Its massive 13th-century tower, with distinctive corner turrets and an imposing central spire, is another landmark of Köln. The church was built on the riverside site of a Roman granary.

Gross St. Martin is the parish church of Köln's colorful old city, the **Martinsviertel**, an attractive combination of reconstructed, high-gabled medieval buildings, winding alleys, and tastefully designed modern apartments and business quarters. Head here at night—the place comes to vibrant life at sunset.

At the south end of the district, in Gürzenichstrasse, you'll find one of Germany's most attractive cultural centers, the
7 **Gürzenich.** This Gothic structure, all but demolished in the war but carefully reconstructed, takes its name from a medieval knight (von Gürzenich), from whom the city acquired a quantity of valuable real estate in 1437. The official reception and festival hall built on the site has played a central role in the city's civic life through the centuries. A concert here can be a memorable experience. Part of the complex consists of the remains of the 10th-century Gothic church of **St. Alban,** left ruined after the war as a memorial to the city's war victims. On what's left of the church's floor (made of slate from the nearby Eifel Hills and Rhine cobblestones), you can see a sculpture of a couple kneeling in prayer. It's an oddly moving work, a fitting memorial to the ravages of war.

Lodging
Under DM 130

★ **Altstadt.** Located close by the river in the old town, this is the place for charm. All the rooms are individually decorated, and the service is impeccable—both welcoming and efficient. *Salzgasse 7, tel. 0221/234–187. 28 rooms with bath. Facilities: sauna. AE, DC, MC, V. Closed Christmas.*

Im Stapelhäuschen. Try for the top room, tucked under the steep eaves of this lovingly preserved 13th-century house in Köln's riverside fish market. The ground-floor tavern-style restaurant serves more than 300 Rhine wines. *Fischmarkt 1–3, tel. 0221/213–043. 32 rooms without bath. MC, V.*

Landhaus Gut Keuchhof. This converted farmhouse, now on a list of specially protected Rhineland buildings, is on the western edge of the city in the suburb of Loevenich, but there are frequent buses to the city center. Behind the rustic brick facade are rooms of up-to-date comfort, some of them still of farmhouse size. There are a very pleasant garden and an excellent restaurant. *Braugasse 14, Loevenich, tel. 02234/76033. 43 rooms with bath. MC.*

Weinhaus Lenz. The main railway station and the cathedral are both a short walk away from this friendly, comfortable hotel, built above and around a popular wine tavern. The rustic decor of the tavern is in stark contrast to the late-20th-century decor of the bedrooms, but they're light and airy and the beds are comfortable. *Ursulaplatz 9–11, tel. 0221/120–055. 104 rooms with bath. AE, DC, MC, V.*

Dining
Under DM 40

Ratskeller. Köln's city hall cellar restaurant is one of the Rhineland's best. Fish comes fresh from the Ratskeller tank, but the meat, especially the *Sauerbraten* (marinated beef), is also highly recommended. *Rathausplatz 1 (Alter Markt entrance), tel. 0221/218–301. MC.*

Under DM 30

Gaststätte Früh am Dom. For real down-home German food, there are few places to compare with this time-honored former brewery. Bold frescoes on the vaulted ceilings establish the mood. The beer garden is delightful for summer dining. *Am Hof 12–14, tel. 0221/236–618. Reservations advised. No credit cards.*

★ **Weinhaus im Waldfisch.** The black-and-white gabled facade of this 400-year-old restaurant signals that here, too, you'll come face-to-face with traditional specialties in a time-honored atmosphere. The restaurant is tucked away between the Heumarkt (Haymarket) and the river. *Salzgasse 13, tel. 0221/219–575. Reservations advised. DC, MC. Closed weekends and holidays.*

Under DM 20 **Gasthof Paeffgen.** The Paeffgen brewery is one of Köln's last family-run establishments. The Koelsch is served by aproned waiters at typical taproom tables, where you can also feast on substantial portions of Rhineland fare. *Friesenstr. 64–66, tel. 0221/135–461. No credit cards.*

Shopping The center of Köln, south of the cathedral, is one huge pedestrian shopping zone. It'll take you about half an hour to stroll through it all. From the cathedral, head south along Hohe Strasse to Schildergasse, then to Neumarkt, Mittelstrasse, Hohenzollernring, Ehrenstrasse, Breitestrasse, Tunisstrasse, Minoritenstrasse, and back to the starting point, Wallrafplatz. Between Mittelstrasse and Ehrenstrasse is a glass-roofed bazaar where dozens of shops share space. Hohe Strasse is the best place to look for Köln's most celebrated product: **eau de cologne.** In nearby Glockengasse (No. 4711, of course) you can visit the house where the 18th-century Italian chemist Giovanni-Maria Farina first concocted it. Köln is also known for delicious **Ludwig chocolate.** You'll have no difficulty finding it in any of the delicatessens along the route. **Lintgasse** is the place for antiques; flea markets are held every third Saturday at the **Alter Markt** in the old town, and every fourth Sunday at **Nippes** (Wilhelmpl.). The best department stores are **Kaufhof** (Hohestr.), **Hertie** (Neumarkt), and **Karstadt** (Breitestr.).

The Arts Cheap tickets for concerts and opera are as difficult to obtain in Köln as they are in Bonn. The evening cash desk, which normally opens an hour before performances, sometimes has spare tickets in the lower price range.

Köln's **Westdeutsche Rundfunk Orchestra** performs regularly in the city's excellent concert hall, the **Philharmonie** (Bischofsgarten 1, tel. 0221/2040820). The smaller **Gürzenich Orchestra** also gives regular concerts in the Philharmonie, but the natural setting for its music is the restored **Gürzenich,** medieval Köln's official reception mansion. Year-round **organ recitals** in Köln's cathedral are supplemented from June through August with a summer season of organ music. Organ recitals and chamber concerts are also presented in the churches of St. Maria Himmelfahrt (Marzellenstr. 26), St. Aposteln (Neumarkt 30), and Trinitätskirche (Filzengraben 4). For details on all church concerts, tel. 0221/534–856.

Köln's opera company, the **Oper der Stadt Köln** (Schauspielhaus, Offenbachpl. 1) is known for exciting classical and contemporary productions. The city's small ballet company, the **Kölner Tanzforum,** hosts an international festival, the **Internationale Sommerakademie des Tanzes,** every July.

Köln's two principal theaters are the **Schauspielhaus** (Offenbachpl. 1) and the smaller **Kammerspiele** (Ubierring 45). Telephone 0221/2218400 for program details and tickets for both. Of the 20 or so private theaters in the city, **Der Keller** (Kleingedankstr. 6, tel. 0221/318–059) is the best-known venue for contemporary drama.

Nightlife Köln's nightlife is found in three distinct areas: around the **Friesenplatz** S-bahn (suburban railway) station, in **Zulpicherstrasse,** and between the **Alter Markt** and **Neumarkt** in the Altstadt, or old city. This latter area offers the lowest prices. While this is not Hamburg, virtually all tastes are catered to. For the last word in disco experience, make for the **Hauptbahnhof** on Friday or Saturday night. The old waiting room has been turned into a concert hall and disco, enabling Köln's boppers to get down on ancient polished parquet and check their style in original mahogany-framed mirrors. Friday night is "Trad Jazz" night at **Dr. Flotte's** (corner of Roon and Hochstadenstr). Two other worthwhile jazz clubs are **Duke's** (Hohenzollernring 92), and, a little farther afield, **Initiative Kölner Jazz haus** (Mozartstr. 60), which features international musicians.

Tour 5: Aachen

Trains leave Köln's main railway station every half-hour for Aachen; journey time is 50 minutes (40 minutes by InterCity Express). A daily Europabus service runs between the two cities; journey time is one hour.

It's not in the Rhineland proper, but **Aachen,** 70 kilometers (45 miles) from Köln, less than an hour away by car, bus, or train, is an essential excursion for anyone staying in Köln. It's an essential excursion, too, if you have any interest in German history, for as the city of Charlemagne, Aachen bears the stamp of this most famous Holy Roman Emperor as no other place in Germany does. Aachen is also known by two other names: Bad Aachen, because of the hot springs that give it health-resort status; and Aix-la-Chapelle, because of the eight-sided chapel built by Charlemagne in the late-8th century that now serves as the core of the city's imposing cathedral.

Charlemagne's father, Pippin, had settled in Aachen because of the healthy sulfur springs emanating from the nearby Eifel Mountains (Roman legions earlier pitched camp here because of these same healing waters). After his coronation in Rome in 800, Charlemagne spent more and more time in Aachen, building his spectacular palace and ruling his vast empire from within its walls.

The **Dom** (cathedral) remains the single greatest storehouse of Carolingian architecture in Europe. Built over the course of 1,000 years, it features a mixture of styles ranging from the imperial chapel at its heart to its 19th-century bell tower. In the cathedral's cool, august interior, you'll find Charlemagne's sturdy marble throne, a battered but still impressive monument. It's just one of many extraordinary treasures here: The **Domschatzkammer** (cathedral treasury) is about the richest in Europe. Though Charlemagne had to journey all the way to Rome for his coronation, the next 32 Holy Roman Emperors were crowned here in Aachen. The coronations were almost invariably accompanied by the presentation of a lavish gift to the cathedral. In the 12th century, Barbarossa gave the great chandelier you'll find hanging in the center of the imperial chapel; his grandson, Emperor Friedrich II, donated the glistening, richly ornamented golden shrine in which the remains of Charlemagne are kept. Emperor Karl IV, son of the king of Bohemia, journeyed from Prague in the late 14th century with the sole purpose of commissioning a bust of Charlemagne for the cathedral. The bust, on view in the treasury, contains a piece of bone from Charlemagne's skull. The Ottonian Emperor Otto III gave the cathedral its fine 10th-century altar painting, while the 11th-century emperor Heinrich II donated its fine copper pulpit. *Dom open 7–7. Domschatzkammer admission: DM 3 adults, DM 2 children and senior citizens. Open Apr.–Sept., Mon. 10–2, Tues., Wed., Fri., Sat. 10–6, Thurs. 10–8, Sun. 10:30–5; Oct.–Mar., Tues.–Sat. 10–5, Sun. 10:30–5, Mon. 10–2.*

Opposite the cathedral, across Katschhof Square, is the **Rathaus** (Town Hall). It was built starting in the early 14th century on the site of the Aula, or great hall, of Charlemagne's palace.

Its first major official function was the coronation banquet of the Emperor Karl IV in 1349, held in the great Gothic hall you'll find there today. The austere, vaulted hall, with its archways decorated with lightly drawn emblems and its rough stone walls bearing the 20th-century equivalent of medieval torches, was largely rebuilt after the war. On the north wall of the building are statues of 50 Holy Roman Emperors. The greatest of the mall, Charlemagne, stands in bronze atop a graceful fountain, the Kaiserbrunnen, in the center of the square. *Rathaus. Admission: DM 1 adults, 50 pf children. Open Mon.–Fri. 8–1 and 2–5, Sat.–Sun. 10–1 and 2–5.*

The hot springs that drew the Romans and Charlemagne's father to Aachen can still be enjoyed by the visitor. Just south of the cathedral is the arcaded, neoclassical **Elisenbrunnen.** Experts agree that the spa waters here—the hottest north of the Alps—are effective in helping to cure a wide range of ailments. Drinking the sulfurous water in the approved manner, however, can be an unpleasant business. Still, if you want to emulate the great and the good who have, through the centuries, dutifully swallowed their medicine—Dürer, Frederick the Great, and Charlemagne himself, among them—hold your nose as you drink it. There are three pools in the city where you can sit in the waters, too. In Dürer's time, the baths were enjoyed for more than their health-giving properties, and there were regular crackdowns on the orgylike goings-on. Today modesty reigns in the hot pools of Aachen.

Like all German spas, Aachen also has its **Spielbank** (casino). It's housed in the porticoed former **Kurhaus,** in the parklike grounds fronting Monheimsallee (facing the Kurbad Quellenhof). The casino is open daily 3 PM–3 AM.

Lodging
Under DM 130

Benelux. Small and family-run, the centrally located Benelux has comfortable modern rooms and a smattering of antiques in the public areas. *Franzstr. 21, tel. 0241/22343. 33 rooms with bath. Facilities: parking. AE, DC, MC, V.*

Dining
Under DM 20

Os Oche. For simple, filling meals served on long wood tables, beer from the barrel, and informal, friendly service, this is a place that's hard to beat. The Os Oche likes to claim the best stews in Germany. *Alexanderstr. 109, tel. 0241/39909. DC, V.*

Zum Schiffgen. This is a traditional inn where the pot roasts and stews are justly voted tops by the locals. Dishes change with the seasons. *Hühnermarkt 21, tel. 0241/33529. AE, DC, MC, V. Closed Sun., and Mon. dinner.*

11 The Fairy-tale Road

With Excursions to Eisenach, Erfurt, and Weimar

The Fairy-tale Road is, like the Romantic and Wine roads, an invention of the tourist industry. Its 600-kilometer (375-mile) length extends far beyond the territory traversed by the first fairy-tale travelers, Jacob and Wilhelm Grimm. These brothers, whose collection of colorful stories have thrilled generations of children, did virtually all their research in the area between Frankfurt and Göttingen, where they studied as students and, later, traveled on business as academics and administrators. The official Fairy-tale Road winds from Hanau (outside Frankfurt), where the brothers were born in the late-18th century, to Bremerhaven, on the North Sea coast. This chapter doesn't cover the whole exhausting route. Instead we suggest you base yourself in Kassel, where the brothers worked as librarians, and take leisurely trips into the surrounding villages and enchanting countryside, where you can still imagine bumping into Little Red Riding Hood, Snow White and her seven dwarfs, Rapunzel, or Rumpelstiltskin.

The heart of Fairy-tale country lies in central Germany between Frankfurt (to the south) and Hannover (to the north). One of the main north-south InterCity railroad routes, linking Munich, Frankfurt, and Hamburg, cuts through the region, with a stop at Kassel. From Kassel, all our suggested trips can be made by rail (with the exception of Sleeping Beauty's castle at Sababurg, which is a bike ride from Münden). Note that there are two train stations in Kassel: the Hauptbahnhof, in the city center, and Wilhelmshöhe Bahnhof, near the palace. Some trains leave Kassel from Wilhelmshöhe only; check with the

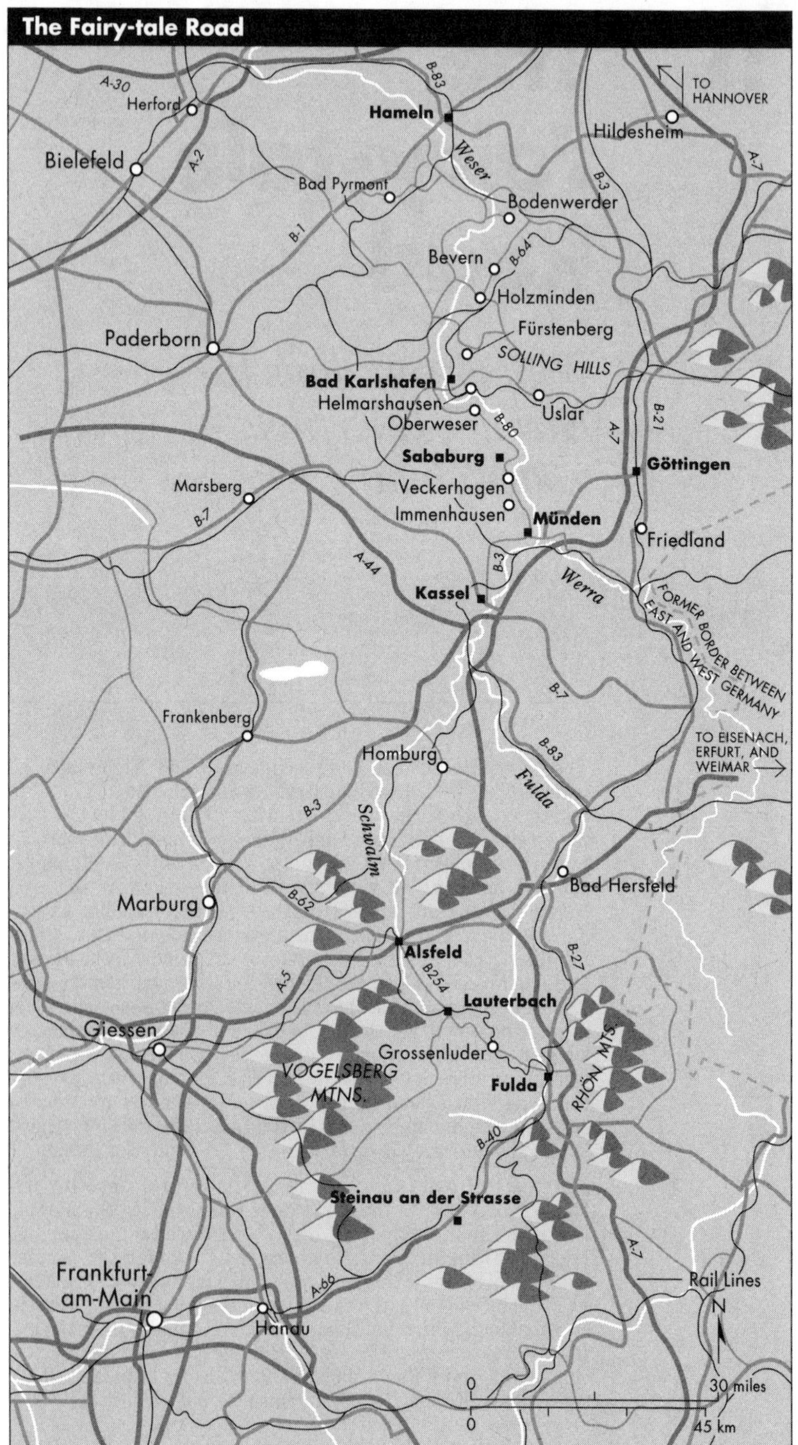
The Fairy-tale Road
TO HANNOVER
A-30
Herford
Hameln
B-83
Hildesheim
Bielefeld
A-2
Weser
Bad Pyrmont
B-3
A-7
Bodenwerder
B-1
Bevern
B-64
Holzminden
Fürstenberg
Paderborn
SOLLING HILLS
Bad Karlshafen
Helmarshausen
Uslar
Oberweser
B-80
B-21
A-7
Sababurg
Göttingen
Veckerhagen
Marsberg
Immenhausen
Münden
B-7
Friedland
A-44
B-3
Werra
Kassel
FORMER BORDER BETWEEN EAST AND WEST GERMANY
B-7
Frankenberg
B-83
TO EISENACH, ERFURT, AND WEIMAR
Homburg
Fulda
B-3
Schwalm
Bad Hersfeld
B-62
Marburg
Alsfeld
B-27
A-5
B254
Lauterbach
Giessen
Grossenluder
VOGELSBERG MTNS.
Fulda
RHÖN MTS.
B-40
Steinau an der Strasse
A-7
Frankfurt-am-Main
Rail Lines
A-66
N
Hanau
0
30 miles
0
45 km

train-information office in the Hauptbahnhof (tel. 0561/324-156).

We also suggest overnight trips from your base in Kassel to three historic towns outside the Fairy-tale country, in what used to be East Germany. Eisenach, Erfurt, and Weimar, in the new state of Thüringia, are more accessible by public transport from this side of the now-vanished Iron Curtain than from, say, Berlin.

Essential Information

Lodging and Dining Accommodation and food in this part of Germany are generally cheaper than in more touristy areas. You'll come across lots of inviting inns offering rooms and meals in small towns and villages throughout Fairy-tale country.

If you are in the western area of the region, try Westphalian ham, famous for more than 2,000 years. The hams can weigh as much as 33 pounds and are considered particularly good for breakfast, when a huge slice is served on a wood board with rich, dark pumpernickel bread baked for some 20 hours. If you're keen to do as the locals do, you'll wash it down with a glass of strong, clear Steinhäger schnapps. A favorite main course is *Pfefferpothast*, a sort of heavily browned goulash with lots of pepper. The "hast" at the end of the name is from the old German word *Harst*, meaning "roasting pan." Rivers and streams filled with trout and eels are common around Hameln. Göttinger *Speckkuchen* is a heavy and filling onion tart.

Highly recommended establishments are indicated by a star ★.

Shopping Locally made pottery, porcelain, and glassware abound in this region, and it's possible to find bargains if you shop around. Germany's oldest **porcelain** factory is at Fürstenberg, high above the Weser River, halfway between Kassel and Hameln. The crowned gothic letter *F* that serves as its trademark is world-famous. You'll find Fürstenberg porcelain in shops throughout the area. Be sure to get the 14% sales-tax rebate available to overseas visitors.

There are some excellent small, privately run **potteries** and **glassworks** in the area. In Bad Karlshafen, you can watch the craftsmen and craftswomen at work in a studio in the Baroque Rathaus and buy goods directly from them. In the village of Immenhausen, just north of Kassel, you can visit a local glass foundry (the **Glashütte Süssmuth**) and watch glassblowers create fine works that are also for sale (shop hours: Mon.–Fri. 9–5, Sat. 9–1). A good selection of **garden gnomes** featuring Grimm fairy-tale characters is available at the Heissner Shop (Schlitzerstr. 24) in Lauterbach.

Kassel, Fulda, Göttingen, and Hameln all have attractive central pedestrian areas where it's a pleasure to shop for all manner of gift items.

Biking and Hiking Bicycles can be rented at the following train stations: **Bad Karlshafen** (tel. 05762/1009), **Hanau** (tel. 06181/31010), and **Fulda** (tel. 0661/73081). Cycling can be linked with a boat trip along the River Weser, too (*see* Boat Trips, *below*).

For hikers, every tourist office in the region provides details of signposted local routes. Of particular interest for sturdy walkers is a long-distance path stretching more than 100 kilometers (62 miles) northwest from Münden along the River Weser through a nature park. For details, contact Fremdenverkehrsverband Weserbergland-Mittelweser (3250 Hameln, tel. 05151/202–517).

Boat Trips The reasonably priced boat services on the River Weser take you by spectacular scenery and allow you to visit a few out-of-the-way places—Bad Karlshafen, for example (*see below*). The best-value trip sails out of Kassel. From April through October, an excursion boat makes a four-hour trip daily up the Fulda River from Kassel. It leaves the Altmarkt pier at 2 and returns at 6. The trip costs DM 16 adults, DM 9 children.

From May through September two companies—**Oberweser-Dampfschiffahrt** and **Weisse Flotte Warnecke** (each with a fleet of six ships)—operate daily services on the Weser River between Hameln, Bodenwerder, and Bad Karlshafen. On Monday, Wednesday, Friday, and Saturday, the Oberweser-Dampfschiffahrt boats sail as far as Münden, and on Tuesday, Thursday, Saturday, and Sunday, from Münden to Hameln. On the days when there is no service between Bad Karlshafen and Münden, a bus service ferries boat passengers between the two towns. You can also go one way by boat (the trip takes four hours) and return by bus. For further information and bookings, contact **Oberweser-Dampfschiffahrt** (Inselstr. 3, 3250 Hameln, tel. 05151/22016) or **Weisse Flotte Warnecke** (Hauptstr. 39, 3250 Hameln, tel. 05151/3975, and on Weserstr., Bodenwerder, tel. 05533/4864).

The Arts Tickets for concerts and theater are considerably cheaper in this part of Germany, although theater will be just as impenetrable as it is elsewhere if you do not understand German. **Kassel** is hosting a 100-day arts festival in summer 1992 (*see* Kassel, *below*).

In **Fulda,** chamber-music concerts are given regularly from September through May in the chandelier-hung splendor of the bishops' palace; call tel. 0661/102–326 for program details and tickets. **Göttingen's** symphony orchestra presents about 20 concerts a year. In addition, the city has a nationally known boys' choir and an annual Handel music festival in June. Call tel. 0551/56700 for program details and tickets for all three.

As for theater, one wing of the magnificent bishops' palace in **Fulda** is now the city's main theater; call tel. 0661/102–326 for program details and tickets. **Göttingen's** two theater companies—the 100-year-old Deutsches Theater and the Junge Theater—are known throughout Germany; call tel. 0551/496–911 for program details and tickets. **Hameln's** main theater, the Weserbergland Festhalle (Rathauspl. tel. 0515/3747), has a regular program of drama, concerts, opera, and ballet from September through June; call for program details and tickets. **Kassel** has no fewer than 35 theater companies. The principal venues are the Schauspielhaus, the Tif-Theater, the Stadthalle, and the Komödie. Call tel. 0561/158–523 for program details and tickets for all.

Highlights for First-time Visitors

Alsfeld's Altes Rathaus (*see* Tour 1)
Eisenach Castle (*see* Tour 2)
Hameln (Hamlin) (*see* Tour 1)
Kassel's Staatliche Kunstsammlungen (*see* Tour 1)
Münden (*see* Tour 1)
The Sababurg (*see* Tour 1)
Steinau Castle and **Amtshaus** (*see* Tour 1)
Weimar old town (*see* Tour 2)

Tour 1: The Fairy-tale Road

From Frankfurt
By Train Speedy Frankfurt–Hamburg InterCity trains stop at Kassel every half hour during the day. The journey takes 85 minutes.

By Car It's autobahn all the way (175 kilometers/109 miles) from Frankfurt to Kassel. Take the A-5 autobahn and switch to the A-7.

Kassel

Tourist office: Obere Koünigestr. 8, tel. 0561/787–8002.

The Brothers Grimm not only lived and worked as librarians in this town but also used it as a base from which to explore the countryside, looking for tales. In the center of Kassel, the **Brüder Grimm Museum** occupies five rooms of the Palais Bellevue, where the brothers once lived and worked. Exhibits include furniture, memorabilia, letters, manuscripts, and editions of their books, as well as paintings, aquarelles, etchings, and drawings by Ludwig Emil Grimm, a third brother and a graphic artist of note. *Palais Bellevue, Schöne Aussicht 2. Admission free. Open daily 10–5.*

Although seldom included on tourist itineraries in the past, Kassel turns out to be one of the unexpectedly delightful cities of western Germany, full of contrasts and surprises. Much of its center was destroyed in World War II, and Kassel subsequently became the first German city to construct a traffic-free pedestrian downtown. The city has an unusually spacious and airy feel, due in large part to the expansive parks and gardens along the banks of the Fulda River. Today it is a major cultural center, with a vibrant theater and an internationally known art festival, Dokumenta, held every five years and scheduled for June–September 1992 (*see* The Arts, *below*).

Kassel's leading art gallery, the **Staatliche Kunstsammlungen** (State Art Collection), is one of Germany's best. It houses 17 Rembrandts, along with outstanding works by Rubens, Hals, Jordaens, Van Dyck, Dürer, Altdorfer, Cranach, and Baldung Grien. *Schloss Wilhelmshöhe. Admission free. Open Tues.–Sun. 10–5.*

The art gallery is located in part of the 18th-century **Wilhelmshöhe Palace,** which served as a royal residence from 1807 to 1813, when Jerome, Napoléon's brother, was king of Westphalia. Later it became the summer residence of the German Emperor Wilhelm II. The great palace stands at the end of the 5-kilometer-long (3-mile-long) Wilhelmshöher Allee, an avenue that runs straight as an arrow from one side of the city to the other. Beyond the palace, the Wilhelmshöhe heights are crowned by an astonishing monument, a red-stone octagon bearing a giant statue of **Hercules,** built at the beginning of the 18th century. You can climb inside the octagon to the base of the Hercules statue. *Admission: DM 2 adults, DM 1 children. Open mid-Mar. to mid-Nov., Tues.–Sun. 10–4.*

From there, the view of Kassel spreads below you, bisected by the straight line of the Wilhelmshöher Allee. But that's only for starters: At 3:30 PM on Sunday and Wednesday from mid-May through September, water gushes from a fountain beneath the Hercules statue, rushes down a series of cascades to the foot of the hill, and ends its precipitous journey on a 175-foot-high jet of water. It's a natural phenomenon, with no pumps. It takes so long to accumulate enough water that the sight can be experienced only on those two special days, on holidays, and, during the summer, on the first Saturday of each month, when the cascades are also floodlit. The No. 1 bus runs from the city to the Wilhelmshöhe. The No. 23 climbs the heights to the octagon and the Hercules statue. A café lies a short walk from the statue, and there are several restaurants in the area.

The Wilhelmshöhe was laid out as a Baroque park, its elegant lawns separating the city from the thick woods of the Habichtswald (Hawk Forest). It comes as something of a surprise to see the turrets of a romantic medieval castle, the **Löwenburg** (Lion Fortress), breaking the harmony. There are more surprises, for this is no true medieval castle but a fanciful, stylized copy of a Scottish castle, built 70 years after the Hercules statue that towers above it. The architect was a Kassel ruler who displayed an early touch of the mania later seen in the castle-building excesses of Bavaria's eccentric Ludwig II. The Löwenburg contains a collection of medieval armor and weapons, tapestries, and furniture. *Admission, including guided tour: DM 2 adults, DM 1 children. Open Tues.–Sun. 10–4.*

One other museum has to be included in this tour of Kassel. It's the **Deutsches Tapeten Museum,** the world's most comprehensive museum of tapestry, with more than 600 exhibits tracing the history of the art through the centuries. *Brüder-Grimm-Pl. 5. Admission free. Open Tues.–Fri. 10–5, Sat.–Sun. 10–1.*

Lodging
Under DM 150

Schlosshotel Wilhelmshöhe. Set in the beautiful Baroque Wilhelmshöhe Park, this is no ancient palace but a modern hotel with its own sports center. *Schlosspark 2, tel. 0561/30880. 100 rooms with bath. Facilities: restaurant, café, bar, indoor pool, whirlpool, sauna, solarium. AE, DC, MC, V.*

Under DM 110

Seidel. This modern, functional hotel offers clean and basic bed-and-breakfast accommodation a 10-minute walk (or a DM 7 taxi ride) from the train station. *Holländischestr. 27, tel. 0561/86047. 40 rooms, some with bath. Facilities: café. AE, DC, MC, V.*

Under DM 70

Gasthof Friedenschänke. At this small, comfortable lodging in the center of town, you can also enjoy a beer and home-style cooking. *Friedenstr. 15, tel. 0561/23348. 7 rooms, half with bath. No credit cards.*

Hamburger Hof. This quiet, family-run lodging—pleasant, if a little threadbare—is barely 100 yards from the front entrance of the train station. *Werner-Hilpertstr. 18, tel. 0561/16002. 20 rooms, some with shower. No credit cards.*

Dining
Under DM 30
Die Pfeffermühle. The "Peppermill" is in Kassel's Gude Hotel. The menu is truly international: Indian and Russian dishes share space with traditional German fare. *Frankfurterstr. 299, tel. 0561/48050. Reservations advised. AE, DC, MC, V. Closed Sun. evening.*

Under DM 20
Weinhaus Boos. If you're visiting Kassel's Wilhelmshöhe Palace, the streetcar from Untere Königsstrasse in the town center stops outside this popular wine tavern (get off at Querallee). Try a white wine from Franconia with a plate of Westphalian ham. *Wilhelmshöhe Allee 97, tel. 0561/22209. AE. No lunch weekdays.*

Under DM 15
Henkel im Bahnhof. You can pop into this popular train-station eatery from 9:30 AM until 10 PM for breakfast, lunch, or supper. The big menu includes specialty game dishes in season but also caters to vegetarians and diabetics. *Hauptbahnhof. AE.*

Ratskeller. You eat here within the embracing surroundings of cellar vaults. If you're lucky, you'll call when owner-chef Robert Kuhn is holding one of his "specialty" weeks. *Obere Königstr. 8, tel. 0561/15928. Reservations advised. AE, DC, MC, V.*

The Arts
Kassel holds free **outdoor concerts** in Wilhelmshöhe Park every Wednesday, Saturday, and Sunday afternoon from May through September. Ask the local tourist office for program details.

In 1992 the city hosts a major modern-art exhibition known as the **Documenta.** Held only once every five years, the exhibition runs June 13–September 20. International celebrities usually participate, and there are daily events. If you are planning to stay for several days, a three-day pass, costing DM 30, allows unlimited admission to all events.

Nightlife
Kassel is disco city. The **Jet Set** (Untere Königstr.) and **Jenseits von Eden** (Untere Königstr.) are two to try. **Club 21** (Friedrich-Ebert-Str. 61a) is another favorite.

Münden

Trains run throughout the day from Kassel to Münden (also known as Hannoversch Münden). The trip takes just under 30 minutes. Tourist office: Verkehrsbüro Naturpark Münden, Hannover, tel. 05541/75313.

Back in the 18th century the German scientist and explorer Alexander von Humboldt included Münden in his short list of the world's most beautiful towns. You just may agree with him when you get here.

A 650-year-old bridge crosses the Weser River to lead into this old walled settlement, which appears untouched by recent history—frozen in the dim and distant past, you might think. You'll have to travel a long way through Germany to find a grouping of half-timbered houses as harmonious as that in this beautiful old town, surrounded by forests and the Fulda and Werra rivers, which join and flow as the Weser River to Bremen and the North Sea.

Take your camera with you on a stroll down Langenstrasse; No. 34 is where the famous Dr. Eisenbarth died, in November 1727. The extraordinary doctor won a place for himself in German folk history as a result of his success both as a physician and as a marketplace orator; a quack who delivered what he promised! A dramatization of his life is presented in the summer in front of the medieval Rathaus. Contact the tourist office (*see above*) for details.

If you're traveling by car or are feeling energetic enough to hire a bicycle (from the Münden train station), head north on the B-64; 10 kilometers (6 miles) north of Münden in the village of Veckerhagen, take a left turn to the signposted **Sababurg.** You're now on the road to Dornröschen's, or **Sleeping Beauty's castle.** The castle—which is not accessible by public transport—stands just as the Grimm fairy tale tells us it did, in the depths of the densely wooded Reinhardswald, still inhabited by deer and wild boar. Sababurg was built as a 14th-century fortress by the archbishop of Mainz to protect a nearby pilgrimage chapel. Later it was destroyed and then rebuilt as a turreted hunting lodge for the counts of Hessen. Today it is a fairly luxurious hotel. Even if you don't stay the night, a trip to the castle (it has an excellent restaurant) will be a highlight of any stay in this region.

Lodging and Dining
Under DM 110

Berghotel Eberberg. It's worth crossing the River Fulda by the Pionierbrücke bridge from the old town and making the short walk up the forested hill to this hotel-restaurant and former castle, if only to see the view over Münden. The restaurant serves traditional dishes for under DM 20. Some rooms are under DM 110. *Tillyschanzenweg 14, tel. 05541/5088. 27 rooms with bath. AE, DC, MC, V. Restaurant closed Sun.*

Göttingen

The hourly Kassel–Hannover train service stops at Göttingen. The journey takes 20 minutes. Tourist office: Fremdenverkehrsverein, Altes Rathaus, tel. 0551/54000.

Göttingen, where the Brothers Grimm worked for seven years beginning in 1830, is one of Germany's ancient seats of learning. The university appears to dominate every aspect of life here, and there's scarcely a house more than a century old that doesn't bear a plaque linking it with a famous person who once studied or taught here. In one of the towers of the city's old defense wall, Otto von Bismarck, the "Iron Chancellor" and founder of the 19th-century German Empire, pored over his books as a 17-year-old law student. It looks like a romantic student's den now (the tower is open to visitors), but Bismarck was a reluctant tenant—he was banned from living within the city center because of "riotous behavior" and his fondness for wine. The taverns where Bismarck and his cronies drank are still there, all of them associated with Göttingen luminaries.

The strong link between the students and their university city is symbolized by a statue in the central market square. There stands the **Gänseliesel,** the little Goose Girl of German folklore, carrying her geese and smiling shyly into the waters of a fountain. Above her pretty head is a charming wrought-iron *Jugendstil* (Art Nouveau) bower of entwined vines. The students of Göttingen contributed money toward the erection of the bronze statue and fountain in 1901, and they have given it a central role in a custom that has grown up around the university: Graduates who earn a doctorate traditionally give Gänseliesel a kiss of thanks. Göttingen says she's the most kissed girl in the world.

Directly behind the Gänseliesel is the **Rathaus** (town hall). It was begun in the 13th century but never completely finished. The result is the part-medieval, part-Renaissance building you see today. The bronze lion's-head knocker on the main door dates from early in the 13th century and is the oldest of its type in Germany. Step through the door, and in the lobby striking murals tell the city's story. The medieval council chamber served for centuries as the center of civic life. Within its painted walls and beneath its heavily beamed ceiling, the council met, courts sat in judgment, visiting dignitaries were officially received, receptions and festivities were held, and traveling theater groups performed.

In the streets around the town hall you'll find magnificent examples of Renaissance architecture. Many of these half-timbered, low-gabled buildings house businesses that have been there for centuries. The **Ratsapotheke** (pharmacy) across from the town hall is one; medicines have been doled out there since 1322.

A short stroll up the street on your left, Weenderstrasse, will bring you to the most appealing shopfront you're likely to find in all Germany: the 16th-century Schrödersches Haus. On the way, you'll pass the ancient student tavern Zum Szültenbürger. Another tavern, Zum Altdeutschen, is around the corner on Prinzenstrasse (the street is named after three English princes, sons of King George III, who lived in a house here during their studies in Göttingen from 1786 to 1791). Don't be shy about stepping into either of these taverns, or any of the others that catch your eye: The food and drink are inexpensive, and the welcome invariably warm and friendly.

Behind Weenderstrasse, on Ritterplan, is Göttingen's only noble home, a 16th-century palace that is now the **Städtisches Museum** (City Museum). It has an instructive exhibition charting the architectural styles you'll come across in this part of Germany, as well as a valuable collection of antique toys and a reconstructed apothecary's shop. *Ritterplan. Admission free. Open Tues.–Fri. 10–1 and 3–5, Sat. and Sun. 10–1.*

Lodging
Under DM 110

Zur Sonne. In the heart of the pedestrianized old town, a stone's throw from the Rathaus, this small family-run hotel provides simple, modern rooms. The train station is only a few hundred yards away, along Goetheallee. *Paulinerstr. 10, tel. 0551/56738. 40 rooms without bath. Facilities: restaurant. DC, MC, V.*

Dining
Under DM 15

Junkenschänke. This has been a haunt of university students for centuries. A 15th-century inn of dark, gnarled beams, it offers hearty meals and beer at down-to-earth prices. *Barfüsserstr. 5, tel. 0551/57320. No credit cards.*

★ **Zum Schwarzen Bären.** The "Black Bear" is one of Göttingen's oldest tavern-restaurants, a 16th-century half-timbered house that breathes history and hospitality. The specialty of the house is *Bärenpfanne*, a generous portion of local meats. *Kurzestr. 12, tel. 0551/58284. Reservations advised. AE, DC, MC. Closed Mon.*

Nightlife

The ancient student taverns that crowd the downtown area are the focus of local nightlife, but for something more sophisticated try the **Malibu** (Lange Geismar 33).

Fulda

Trains running every 40 minutes link Kassel with Fulda. The journey takes 40 minutes. Tourist office: Städtische Verkehrsbüro im Stadtschloss, tel. 0661/102345.

Fulda is a treasure trove of Baroque architecture. Its grandest example is the immense **bishops' palace,** on Schlossstrasse, crowning the heights of the city. The great collection of buildings began as a Renaissance palace in the early 17th century and was transformed into its present Baroque splendor a century later by Johann Dientzenhofer. Much of the palace is now used as municipal offices, but you can visit several of the former public rooms. The Fürstensaal (Princes' Hall) on the second floor provides a breathtaking display of Baroque decorative artistry, with ceiling paintings by the 18th-century Bavarian artist Melchior Steidl. Concerts are regularly held within its fabric-clad walls (contact the city tourist office in the palace for program details; tel. 0661/102–345). The palace also has permanent displays of the faience ceramics for which Fulda was once famous, as well as some fine local glassware. *Schlossstr. Admission: DM 2 adults, DM 1 children. Open Mon.–Thurs. 10–12:30 and 2:30–5, Fri. 2:30–4:30, Sat.–Sun. 10–12:30.*

Pause at the windows of the great Fürstensaal to take in the view across the palace park to the **Orangery.** If you have time after your palace tour, stroll over for a visit. There's a pleasant café on the first floor.

Across the broad boulevard that borders the park you'll see the tall twin spires of the **Dom,** Fulda's 18th-century cathedral. The Dom was built by Dientzenhofer on the site of an 8th-century basilica, which at the time was the largest church north of the Alps. The basilica had to be big enough to accommodate the ever-growing number of pilgrims from all parts of Europe who converged on Fulda to pray at the grave of the martyred St. Boniface, the "Apostle of the Germans." A black alabaster bas-relief depicting his death marks the martyr's grave in the crypt. The cathedral museum contains a document bearing his writing, along with several other treasures, including a fine 16th-century painting by Lucas Cranach the Elder of Christ and the adulteress (who looks very comely in her velvet Renaissance costume). *Dom Museum, Dompl. Admission: DM 2 adults, DM 1.50 children. Open Apr.–Oct., Mon.–Fri. 10–5:30, Sat. 10–2, Sun. and holidays 12:30–5:30; Nov.–Mar., Mon.–Fri. 10–noon and 1:30–4, Sat. 10–2, Sun. and holidays 12:30–4. Closed Jan.*

To one side of the cathedral you'll see one of Germany's oldest churches, the **Michaelskirche,** or Church of St. Michael, built in the 9th century along the lines of the Church of the Holy Sepulchre in Jerusalem. It has a harmony and dignity that match the majesty of the Baroque facade of the neighboring Dom.

From the Dom, head into the center of town, passing on your right the former guardhouse of the bishops' palace and on your left the 18th-century city parish church. Your goal is the Rathaus, about the finest Renaissance half-timbered town hall in this part of the country. The half-timbering, separating the arcaded first floor from the steep roof and its incongruous but charming battery of small steeples, is particularly delicate.

Lodging
Under DM 110

Zum Kurfürsten. In the heart of the old town, this lodging is itself part of Fulda's Baroque face. But behind the venerable facade guests are assured of modern facilities. *Schloss-str. 2, tel. 0661/70001. 68 rooms with bath. Facilities: sauna, restaurant. AE, DC, MC, V.*

Splurge
★

Romantik Hotel Goldener Karpfen. The hotel dates from the Baroque era but has a later facade. Inside, it has been renovated to a high standard of comfort. Afternoon coffee (DM 5.50 per two-cup pot) in the comfortable, tapestry-upholstered chairs of the hotel's lounge is one of Fulda's delights. Double rooms run DM 200–DM 380. *Simpliciuspl. 1, tel. 0661/70044. 50 rooms and 4 suites with bath or shower. Facilities: restaurant, sauna, fitness room. AE, DC, MC, V.*

Dining
Under DM 20

Zum Ritter. This rustic tavern a few strides from the palace makes an ideal stopover for lunch. Watch for the *Pfefferposthast* (hashbrowns) and *Forellen* (river trout). *Kanalstr. 18, tel. 0661/8165. MC, V.*

Lauterbach and Alsfeld

Both towns, closely associated with famous Grimm fairy tales, are on the same train route, 25 and 45 minutes, respectively, from Fulda. The service from Fulda runs every hour on the half-hour; the trip from Kassel to Alsfeld takes 105 minutes. Tourist offices: Verkehrsverein, Rathaus, Marktplatz 14, Lauterbach, tel. 06641/18412; Verkehrsbüro, Rittergasse 5, Alsfeld, tel. 06631/182165.

Lauterbach, a resort town of many medieval half-timbered houses, has not just one castle but two—the Riedesel and the Eisenbach. The town is the setting of one of the Grimm fairy tales, the one in which the Little Scallywag loses his sock. Lauterbach's other claim to fame is its garden gnomes, turned out here by the thousands and exported all over the world. These ornaments are made in all shapes and sizes, from three inches to three feet tall, by the firm of Heissner Keramik. Several shops in Lauterbach sell the gnomes if you'd like to take one home with you.

Alsfeld claims to be the source of the Red Riding Hood story, and you'll find a statue to the young lady in the center of town. The half-timbered houses of the medieval town center lean out almost far enough to touch each other across the narrow, winding cobbled streets. Seek out Kirchplatz, a small square behind the late-Gothic Walpurgiskirche church off the main square. The rightward lurch of No. 12 seems to defy gravity. But the jewel of Alsfeld is the **Altes Rathaus** (old town hall), built in 1512. It looks more like the handiwork of Walt Disney than of 16th-century craftsmen, and its combination of stone-colonnaded ground floor, half-timbered middle, and steep slate roof, punctured by two towers as round and pointed as witches' hats, seems to defy gravity. If you want to get a full photograph of this unusual building (which is not open to the public), try to avoid Tuesdays and Fridays, when market stalls selling everything from pots and pans to cabbages clutter the square—and the view—until late afternoon.

Lodging and Dining
Under DM 70

Hessischer Hof. This is an 18th-century inn with a half-timbered facade on a cobbled street. The rooms are simply but appealingly furnished, and the bar serves a broad range of meals, from solid schnitzels to salads and fish dishes. The locally brewed beer is delicious. *Hintergasse 18, Lauterbach, tel. 06641/2704. 10 rooms, most with shower. No credit cards.*

Zur Alten Schmiede. The exterior of this 17th-century inn in the old town center has changed little over the centuries. The rooms are simple and do not have private facilities. You'll find good local food in the popular bar/restaurant. *Untergasse 12, Alsfeld, tel. 06631/2465. No credit cards.*

Steinau an der Strasse

To reach Steinau, take the train from Kassel and change at Fulda. The hourly service (at 10 minutes past the hour) from Fulda to Steinau takes 25 minutes. Tourist office: Verkehrsamt, tel. 06663/5655.

Although born in Hanau, near Frankfurt, the Grimm brothers spent much of their childhood in this charming town, complete with its own towering castle. Their father was the local magistrate.

Steinau dates from the 13th century. At the top of the town stands a castle straight out of a Grimm fairy tale. Originally an early medieval fortress, it was rebuilt in Renaissance style between 1525 and 1558 and used by the counts of Hanau as their summer residence and later to guard the increasingly important trade route between Frankfurt and Leipzig. It's not difficult to imagine the young Grimm boys playing in the shadow of its great gray walls, perhaps venturing into the encircling dry moat.

The fine, half-timbered, turreted house where the family resided is only a few hundred yards from the castle. Officially called the **Amthaus,** it now contains the tourist office and a museum of exhibits from the childhood of the brothers Grimm. *Open Mon.–Fri. 8–noon and 1–5. There's another, larger Grimm museum in the castle itself, the Grimm Museum im Schloss. Admission: DM 2 adults, DM 1 children. Open Mar.–Oct., Tues.–Sun. 10–11:30 and 1–4:30; Nov.–Feb., Tues.–Sun. 10–11 and 1–3.*

In front of the castle, in Steinau's ancient market square, Am Kumpen, is the Gothic church of **St. Catherine,** where the Grimm brothers' grandfather, Friedrich, was parson. Across the square, in the former stables of the castle, is a small puppet theater, **Die Holzkuppe,** where presentations of the Grimm fairy tales are staged. *Die Holzkuppe Marionettentheater. Call tel. 06663/245 for program details.*

In the center of the square is a **Grimm memorial fountain.** It was built only in 1985, but its timeless design blends perfectly with the background provided by Steinau's 16th-century **Rathaus** (Town Hall). The six bronze figures you see on the white stucco facade of the Rathaus represent a cross section of 16th-century Steinau's population—from the builder who helped construct the town to the mother and child who continue its traditions.

Lodging and Dining
Under DM 110

Burgmannenhaus. Located next to the Grimm tales' puppethouse near the town square, this crooked gingerbread hostelry dates from 1589. Distorted walls, oak beams, and a carved stone fireplace testify to the inn's antiquity. On warm summer days you can sit in the chestnut-shaded garden with a beer or a pot of coffee. *Brüder-Grimmstr. 49, tel. 06663/6539. 8 rooms with shower. No credit cards.*

Under DM 70 **Weisses Ross.** This may be a simple inn, but you can sleep within its gnarled walls in the knowledge that the Grimm brothers overnighted here almost 200 years ago. *Brüder-Grimmstr. 48, tel. 06663/5804. 6 rooms, most with bath. Facilities: restaurant. No credit cards.*

Bad Karlshafen

*It takes a little over two hours by train to reach Bad Karlshafen from Kassel, but if you can travel on Tuesday, Thursday, Saturday, or Sunday, you can take the train as far as Münden (only 30 minutes from Kassel) and join the Weser River boat for a scenic ride to Bad Karlshafen (*see *Boat Trips*, above*). Tourist office: Kurverwaltung, Rathaus, tel. 05672/1022.*

It was from the inland harbor of Bad Karlshafen that German troops embarked to join the English Hanoverian forces in the American War of Independence. George III, the English king who presided over the loss of the American colonies, was a Hanoverian—his grandfather, George I, spoke only German when he became king of England in 1715—and it was only natural that the people of Hanover should rally to the English cause in times of crisis. Flat barges took the troops down the Weser to Bremen, where they were shipped across the North Sea for the long voyage west. Many American families can trace their heritage to this small spa and the surrounding countryside.

Viewed from one of the benches overlooking the harbor, there's scarcely a building that's not in the imposing Baroque style. The grand Rathaus behind you is the best example. Bad Karlshafen stands out in solitary splendor amid its neighboring Weser Valley towns, whose half-timbered architecture has given rise to the expression "Weser Renaissance"—the style you see wherever else you travel in this area, from Münden to Hameln.

Dining
Under DM 20 **Gaststätte-Hotel Weserdampfschiff.** You can step right from the deck of a Weser pleasure boat into the welcoming garden of this popular riverside hotel-tavern. Fish from the river land right in the tavern's frying pan. *Weserstr. 25, tel. 05672/2425. No credit cards.*

Hameln

*From Kassel, the train journey to Hameln, via Altenbeken, takes two hours and 30 minutes; you can also reach Hameln on the riverboat/bus service from Münden, but the 100-kilometer (62-mile) water trip takes nine hours and is expensive (*see *Boat Trips*, above*). Tourist office: Verkehrsverein, Deisterallee am Bürgergarten, tel. 05151/202–517.*

The story of the Pied Piper of Hameln had its origins in an actual event. In the 13th century an inordinate number of young men in Hameln were being conscripted to fight in an unpopular war in Bohemia and Moravia, so that citizens became convinced that they were being spirited away by the Devil playing his flute. In later stories the Devil was changed to a gaudily attired rat catcher who rid the town of rodents by playing seductive melodies on his flute so that the rodents followed him willingly, waltzing their way right into the Weser. However, when the town defaulted on its contract with the piper and refused to pay up, the piper settled the score by playing his merry tune to lead Hameln's children on the same route he had taken the rats. As the children reached the river, the Grimms wrote, "they disappeared forever."

This tale is included in the Grimms' other book, *German Legends*. A variation of the story appears on the plaque of a 17th-century house at No. 28 Osterstrasse, fixing the date of the event as June 26, 1284. In more recent times, the Pied Piper tale has been immortalized via an ultramodern sculpture group set above a reflecting pool in a pedestrian area of town. Today you'll find Hameln tied to its Pied Piper myth every bit as much, say, as the little Bavarian village of Oberammergau is dominated by its Passion Play. There are even rat-shaped pastries in the windows of Hameln's bakeries. The house that bears the Pied Piper plaque—a brilliant example of Weser Renaissance—is known as the Rattenfängerhaus, the rat catcher's house, despite the fact that it was built some time after the sorry story is said to have occurred. To this day, no music is played and no revelry of any kind takes place in the street that runs beside the house, the street along which the children of Hameln are said to have followed the piper.

The Rattenfängerhaus is one of several beautiful half-timbered houses on the central Osterstrasse. At one end is the Hochzeitshaus (Wedding House), now occupied by city government offices and a tourist information center. Every Sunday from mid-May to mid-September the story of the Pied Piper is played out at noon by actors and children of the town on the terrace in front of the building. The half-hour performance is free: Get there early to ensure a good place. The carillon of the Hochzeitshaus plays a "Pied Piper song" every day at 8:35 and 11:05, and mechanical figures enacting the story appear on the west gable of the building at 1:05, 3:35, and 5:35.

Lodging
Under DM 110

Christinenhof. This protected, half-timbered, 17th-century landmark was converted into a small hotel in 1989. It's tastefully decorated in dark cherry wood and marble. *Alte Markstr. 18, tel. 05151/7168. 18 rooms, half with bath. Facilities: sauna, indoor pool, bar. AE, MC, V.*

Hotel zur Börse. A long-established, family-run property in the old town, this hotel offers comfortable accommodations and friendly service. Its attractive winter garden is a pleasant retreat. *Osterstr. 41 (entrance on Kopmanshof), tel. 05151/7080. 34 rooms with shower. AE, DC, V. Closed Christmas and New Year's Day.*

Dining
Under DM 20

★ **Rattenfängerhaus.** This is Hameln's most famous building, reputedly the place where the Pied Piper stayed during his rat-removing assignment. Rats are all over the menu, from "Rat-remover cocktail" to a "Rat-tail dessert." But don't be put off: The traditional dishes are excellent, and the restaurant is guaranteed to be rodent-free. *Osterstr. 28, tel. 05151/3888. Reservations advised. AE, DC, MC, V.*

Tour 2: Eisenach, Erfurt, and Weimar

These three towns lie outside Fairy-tale country proper, but with the Iron Curtain now removed they make a handy train trip from Kassel. It's a three-hour journey to Weimar, best undertaken as an overnight excursion. If you have time and don't mind getting up early, you can take a day to get there, stopping along the way to visit Eisenach and Erfurt (to do this, you need to catch the 6:30 AM train from Kassel Hauptbahnhof).

Eisenach

Stand in the ancient market square, ringed by half-timbered houses, and it's difficult to imagine that this town was until recently a center of the East German auto industry and home of the now-shunned Wartburg automobile. The noisy little family car was named after the famous castle that broods over Eisenach. Begun in 1067, the **Wartburg** gave shelter to the German minstrels Walther von der Vogelweide and Wolfram von Eschenbach, the Protestant reformer Martin Luther, Richard Wagner, and Goethe himself. Johann Sebastian Bach was born in Eisenach and must have climbed the hill to the castle that was already centuries old when he was a boy. It's said that Walther von der Vogelweide, Germany's most famous minstrel, won a celebrated song contest here, an event immortalized by the Romantic writer Novalis and by Wagner in *Tannhäuser*. Luther sought shelter from papal proscription within its stout walls, and from May 1521 until March 1522 worked on the translation of the New Testament that paved the way to the Protestant Reformation. The study in which Luther worked is open to the public.

There's much of interest in this fascinatng castle, including a portrait of Luther and his wife, by Lucas Cranach the Elder, and a moving sculpture, the *Kneeling Angel*, by the great 15th-century artist Tilman Riemenschneider. The 13th-century Great Hall is breathtaking—it's here that the minstrels are said to have sung for courtly favors. Don't leave without climbing the Belvedere for a panoramic view of the distant Harz Mountains and Thüringen Forest, and be sure to bask in the medieval atmosphere of the half-timbered, cottage-style interior courtyards of the castle. *Admission free (at press time). Open Nov.–Feb., daily 9–5; Mar.–Oct., daily 8:30–5:30.*

The castle is an easy stroll from the center of town along Friedrich-Engels-Strasse and Reuterweg. On the way, you'll pass the **Reuter-Wagner Museum,** which has a comprehensive exhibition on Wagner's life and work (Reuterweg 2; open Mon.–Fri. 9–12:30 and 2–5; Sun. 9–4; closed Sat.). The town also has museums devoted to Luther and Bach: the **Lutherhaus** (Lutherplatz 8; open Mon.–Sat. 9–1 and 2–5; Sun. 2–5) and the **Bachhaus** (Frauenplan 21; open weekdays except Wed. 9–5, weekends 9–12:30 and 1–5; closed Wed.).

Lodging
Under DM 110

Wartburghotel. Where else can you sleep under a roof that once sheltered Luther, Goethe, and Wagner? You'll need to book well in advance, particularly for one of the few rooms with a sweeping view of Eisenach and the surrounding countryside.

The standard of comfort is above-average for a German castle-hotel, with antiques and Oriental rugs offsetting modern but (for eastern Germany) stylish furnishings. *Auf der Wartburg, tel. 0623/5111. 30 rooms and apartments, most with bath. Facilities: restaurant, shuttle bus to town center. No credit cards.*

Dining
Under DM 15

Gastmahl des Meeres. You're always well served at a Gastmahl des Meeres fish restaurant in eastern Germany, and Eisenach's is among the best of the popular chain. It's a large, friendly place, smothered in flowers as fresh as the fish from the restaurant's tanks. *Auf der Esplanade, tel. 030/3885. No reservations. No credit cards. Closed weekends.*

Erfurt

Erfurt emerged relatively unscathed from World War II, most of its medieval buildings beautifully intact. Today it is Europe's largest producer of flower and vegetable seeds—a field pioneered by a local botanist, Christian Reichart, in the 18th century. The city's outskirts are full of greenhouses and plantations.

Erfurt is dominated by its magnificent cathedral, the 12th-century **Dom,** which you reach by a broad staircase from the expansive cathedral square. Its Romanesque origins are most evident in the choir, where you'll find splendid stained-glass windows and some of the most beautifully carved choir stalls in Germany. (They have a mundane motif—the history of the vintner's trade.) Nearby, look for a remarkable group of figures—a man flanked by two women. The man is the 13th-century Count von Gleichen. But the women? There are two stories: One has it that they are the count's first and second wives; the other, possibly older story identifies them as his wife and his mistress, a Saracen beauty who saved his life under mysterious circumstances during the Crusades. The cathedral's biggest bell, the Gloriosa, is the largest free-swinging bell in the world. It took three painstaking years to lift it—inch by inch with wooden wedges—into the bell tower. Today the authorities aren't taking chances with such a heavy treasure, and the bell is rung only on special occasions. *Open May–Sept., daily 9–5; Oct.–Apr., daily 9–11:30 and 12:30–4.*

Next to the cathedral and connected to it by a long open staircase is the Gothic **Church of St. Severus.** Step inside to admire the extraordinary font, a masterpiece of intricately carved sandstone, which reaches practically to the roof of the church.

The cathedral square is bordered by attractive houses dating back to the 16th century. Behind the predominantly neo-Gothic Rathaus (city hall), you'll find Erfurt's outstanding attraction, the **Krämerbrücke** (Shopkeepers' Bridge), spanning the Gera River. You'd have to travel to Florence to find anything like this Renaissance bridge incorporating shops and homes. For centuries goldsmiths, artisans, and merchants plied their wares here. Today antiques shops predominate, but the bridge is still a fun place to search for bargains. The surrounding area is known as Klein Venedig (Little Venice), not for any real resemblance but for the regular flooding caused by the nearby river. It's crisscrossed with ancient streets, lined with picturesque and often crumbling homes.

On the way back from the Krämerbrücke to the center of town, follow Gotthardstrasse and you'll pass the **St. Augustine Cloisters,** where the young Martin Luther spent his formative years. Today it's still a seminary. In nearby Leninstrasse you'll find the interesting **Stadtmuseum Erfurt,** the local history museum, housed in a beautiful late-Renaissance house, Zum Stockfisch. *Leninstr. 169. Open Sun.–Thurs. 10–6.*

Dining
Under DM 15

Vital. Good-size portions of typical Thüringen fare (lots of local sausage) are served here in simple but pleasant surroundings. *Domplatz 3, tel. 061/24317. No credit cards.*

Weimar

Tourist office: Weimar-Information, Marktstrasse 4, tel. 0621/2173.

Weimar, a pretty town on the River Ilm between the Ettersberg and Vogtland hills, has a place in German political and cultural history out of all proportion to its size (population 63,000). It's not even a particularly old city by German standards: Its civic history dates from about 1410. But by the early 19th century it had become one of Europe's cultural centers, where Lucas Cranach and his son painted, where Goethe and Schiller lived as neighbors, where Johann Sebastian Bach played the organ for his royal Saxon patrons, and where Carl Maria von Weber wrote some of his best music. Walter Gropius founded his Staatlich Bauhaus school of architecture here in 1919, and in the same year, behind the classical pillars of the National Theater, the German National Assembly drew up the constitution of the Weimar Republic. After the collapse of the ill-fated Weimar government, Adolf Hitler chose this unsuspecting city as the site of the first national congress of his new Nazi Party. On the outskirts of Weimar, the Nazis built—or forced prisoners to build—the infamous Buchenwald concentration camp. "Seldom in history did German greatness and German megalomania exist so close together," a native journalist has written.

Weimar owes much of its greatness to the widowed Duchess Anna Amalia, who in the late-18th century went talent-spotting for cultural figures to decorate the glittering court that her Saxon forebears had set up in the town. Goethe was among her finds, and he served the countess as a counselor, advising on financial matters and town design. Schiller followed, and the two became valued visitors to the countess's home. Their statues stand today before the **National Theater,** Goethe with a patronizing hand on the shoulder of the younger Schiller. The theater, sadly, isn't the one where Goethe and Schiller produced their leading works; the Baroque building became too small to admit the increasing numbers of visitors, and it was demolished in 1907, to be replaced by a larger building with better technical facilities. This second theater was bombed in the war and rebuilt in its present form in 1948, the first of many ruined theaters to arise from the rubble of postwar East Germany. It reopened with a performance of Goethe's *Faust.*

Adjacent to the National Theater, on Theaterplatz, you'll see the surprisingly modest home of the Duchess Anna Amalia, the **Wittumspalais,** an exquisite Baroque house exuding a warmth that must have worked like a magnet on Goethe and Schiller. The drawing room where they met—complete with the cherrywood table at which the company sat—can be visited, and the east wing of the house contains a small museum that is a fascinating memorial to those cultural gatherings. *Admission: DM 1.50 adults, 50 pf children. Open Wed.–Sun. 9–noon and 1–5.*

Goethe spent 57 years in Weimar, 47 of them in the **Goethe Haus,** which has become a shrine for millions of visitors from all over the world. It stands at the entrance of the street called Frauenplan, two blocks south of Theaterplatz. Now a museum, it holds a collection of writings illustrating not only the great man's literary might but also his interest in the sciences (particularly medicine) and his administrative skill (and frustrations) as Weimar's exchequer. You'll see the desk at which he stood to write and the modest bed in which he died. *Frauenplan 1. Admission: DM 1.50 adults, 50 pf children. Open Mar.–Oct., daily 9–1 and 2–5; Nov.–Feb., daily 9–1 and 2–4.*

Around the corner from Goethe's home, on a tree-shaded square, is the **Schillerhaus,** the sturdy green-shuttered home in which Schiller and his family lived for three years. Schiller's study, a cozy room dominated by his desk, was tucked under the mansard roof. The collection of books and much of the remaining furniture were added later, although they all date from around Schiller's time. *Neugasse. Admission: DM 1.50 adults, 50 pf children. Open Mar.–Oct., daily 9–noon and 1–5; Nov.–Feb., daily 9–noon and 1–4.*

On the nearby central town square, at No. 12 Marktplatz, you'll find another historic Weimar house, the Renaissance **home of Lucas Cranach the Elder,** its long, imposing front richly decorated and bearing the coat of arms of the painter's family. It now houses a modern-art gallery.

A short walk south, past the Goethe Haus and across Wieland Platz, brings you to the **Historischer Friedhof** (Historic Cemetery). Virtually every gravestone in this leafy, peaceful cemetery commemorates a famous citizen of Weimar. Goethe and Schiller lie entombed in a vault in the classical chapel. *Admission free. Goethe-Schiller vault open daily (except Tues.) 9–1 and 2–5.*

On the other side of the River Ilm, amid meadowlike parkland, you'll find Goethe's beloved **Gartenhaus** (Garden House), where he spent many happy hours and where he began his masterly *Iphigenie auf Tauris*. Goethe is said to have felt close to nature here; you can soak up the same bucolic atmosphere on footpaths along the peaceful river, where time seems to have stood still. Just across the river is a generous German tribute to another literary giant: William Shakespeare, commemorated in 1904 with a statue that shows him on a marble plinth, remarkably at ease in his foreign surroundings. *Goethe Gartenhaus. Admission free. Open daily 9–noon and 1–5.*

In the Ettersberg hills just north of Weimar is a blighted patch of land—**Buchenwald**—that contrasts cruelly with the rich countryside that so inspired Goethe. This was one of the most infamous Nazi concentration camps, where 35,000 men, women, and children from 35 countries met their deaths. Each victim is commemorated today by a small stone placed on the outlines of the barracks (which have long since disappeared), and by a massive memorial tower built in a style that some critics find reminiscent of the Nazi megalomania it seeks to condemn. The tower stands on the highest point of Buchenwald and is approached by a long, broad flight of steps; at its base is a sculpture representing the victims of the camp. *Admission free. Open Tues.–Sun. 9:45–4:30. Bus tours are organized by Weimar's tourist office (*see above).

Lodging
Under DM 110

Hospiz. In 1991 this Evangelical Church pension was being modernized and expanded. Bathrooms were being added to many of the rooms, elderly furnishings were being replaced, and other work was bringing this old established pension up to standard. Prices will rise accordingly, but in 1992 the centrally located Hospiz could be an insider's tip for visitors. *Amalienstr. 2, tel. 0621/2711. 21 rooms, most with bath. Facilities: restaurant, parking. No credit cards.*

Splurge

Elephant. Goethe, Schiller, Liszt—and Hitler: The guestbook of this centrally located 17th-century hotel contains names of the famous and the infamous. For that reason it's one of Germany's best-known hotels, so early reservations are essential. Recent renovation has added many modern facilities while leaving the Old World charm largely untouched. Double rooms, some under DM 150, are unusually large and comfortable. *Am Markt 19, tel. 0621/61471. 116 rooms and suites. Facilities: 4 restaurants, bar, nightclub, sauna, garage. AE, DC, MC, V.*

Dining
Under DM 20

Elephantenkeller. In the ancient vaulted cellar restaurant of the centrally located Elephant Hotel, you'll eat well in surroundings that haven't changed much since Goethe's day. Only the functional '50s style of some of the furnishings disturbs the picture. *Am Markt 19, tel. 0621/61471. No credit cards.*

Zum Weissen Schwan. Both Goethe and Schiller are said to have dined here—and they probably did, since the tavern that preceded this fine old restaurant was already more than two centuries old when the two poets came to town. Goethe's home, in fact, was right next door. The food is wholesome Thüringen but is not cheap, and it's essential to reserve a table. *Frauenstorstr. 23, tel. 0621/61715. Jacket and tie advised. AE, DC, MC, V.*

12 Hamburg

With Excursions to Bremen and Lübeck

Despite its reputation as an impatient business and trading center, Hamburg offers a big welcome to visitors, and it ranks just after Berlin and Munich in popularity with foreign tourists. And yet Hamburg still has something of an image problem. Mention of the city invariably triggers thoughts of the gaudy night world of the Reeperbahn, that sleazy strip of clip joints, sex shows, and wholesale prostitution. But to those who know Hamburg, the Reeperbahn's presence could be considered an indication of the city's prevailing live-and-let-live attitude, part and parcel of the dramatic diversity and apparently irreconcilable contradictions that make up this fascinating port.

Hamburg is both a city and a state. Its official title—the Free and Hanseatic City of Hamburg—refers to its status as an international trading post dating from the Middle Ages. For hundreds of years Hamburg ranked as Europe's leading port, yet it is situated 100 kilometers (62 miles) from the sea.

Hamburg gained world renown as the kingpin of the Hanseatic League, that medieval mafia of north German merchant cities that banded together to dominate shipping in the Baltic and the North Sea, with trading satellites set up in Bergen, Visby, Danzig, Riga, Novgorod, and other points of the compass. But it was only after the demise of the Hansa that Hamburg arrived at the crest of its power.

During the 19th century the largest shipping fleets on the seas, with some of the fastest ships afloat, were based here; tentacles of shipping lanes reached to the far corners of the earth. Ties to

New York, Buenos Aires, and Rio de Janeiro were stronger than those to Berlin or Frankfurt. During the four decades leading up to World War I, Hamburg became one of the world's richest cities. Its aura of wealth and power was projected right up to the outbreak of World War II, and even today it shows.

The miracle of present-day Hamburg is that in spite of having been virtually wiped off the map by the 1940–1944 bombing raids, it now stands as a remarkably faithful replica of that glittering prewar city. In what surely must rank as the most successful reconstruction of any major German city, Hamburg is once again a place of enormous style, verve, and elegance.

The distinguishing feature of downtown Hamburg is the Alster. Once an insignificant waterway, it was dammed during the 18th century to form an artificial lake. Divided at its south end, it is known as the Binnenalster (Inner Alster) and the Aussenalster (Outer Alster), the two separated by a pair of graceful bridges, the Lombard Brücke and the John F. Kennedy Brücke. The Inner Alster is lined with stately hotels, department stores, fine shops, cafés; the Outer Alster is framed by the spacious greenery of parks and gardens against a backdrop of private mansions.

From late spring into fall, sailboats and board-surfers skim across the surface of the Outer Alster. White passenger steamers zip back and forth. The view from one of these vessels (or from the shore of the Outer Alster) is of the stunning skyline of six spiny spires (five churches and the Rathaus) that is Hamburg's identifying feature.

Sometimes called a "Venice of the North," the city is threaded with countless canals and waterways, spanned by some 1,000 bridges, more even than you'll find in Venice. Swans glide on the canals. Arcaded passageways run along the waterways. In front of the Renaissance-style Rathaus is a square that resembles the Piazza San Marco.

But what truly distinguishes Hamburg from most other cities is the extent of greenery at its heart. Almost half of its area is devoted to either agriculture or parkland. This fondness for growing things has been a dominant treasure of Hamburg for centuries: In the 16th century anyone caught chopping down a tree was sentenced to death.

Hamburg is endowed with considerable architectural diversity. Of particular interest are the 14th-century houses of Deichstrasse—the oldest residential area in Hamburg—and the Kontorhausviertel (literally, "Business House Quarter"). The latter contains some unique clinker-brick buildings from the '20s. A variety of turn-of-the-century *Jugendstil* (Art Nouveau) buildings can also be found in various parts of the city.

Anyone accustomed to the *Gemütlichkeit* (conviviality) and jolly camaraderie of Munich should be advised that Hamburg on initial exposure presents a more somber face. Hamburgers are staunchly conservative in dress and demeanor and liberal in politics. Members of the merchant elite are extremely status-conscious, yet not inclined to put on airs. People here are reputed to be notoriously frugal on the one hand, generous hosts on the other, with a penchant for indulging their tastes for the most refined delicacies. In a city that vibrates with energy, the people work hard and play hard, and turn out to be friendlier than they may appear at first.

Essential Information

Important Addresses and Numbers

Tourist Information The main branch of the tourist office is the **Tourismus Zentrale Hamburg** (Burchardstr. 14, tel. 040/300–510). It's open Monday–Friday 7:30 AM–6 PM, Saturday 7:30 AM–3 PM. In addition to its comprehensive hotel guide, the tourist office also publishes a monthly program of events in the city, *Hamburg Vorschau*, available for DM 2.30, which details upcoming shows, plays, movies, and exhibits. The illustrated magazine *Hamburg Tips* is issued quarterly and details major seasonal events; it's free of charge.

Other tourist offices include **Tourist Information im Bieberhaus** (Hachmannplatz, tel. 040/3005–1245. Open Monday–Friday 7:30 AM–6 PM, Saturday 8 AM–3 PM). It's located just outside the main train station. There's also a tourist office in the **station** (tel. 040/300–51230); it's open daily 7 AM–11 PM. The **airport tourist office** (tel. 040/300–51240) is open 8 AM–11 PM. At the harbor, there's an office at the **St. Pauli Landungsbrücken** (boat landings); it's open daily 9–6 (tel. 040/300–51200). There's also an office in the **Hanse Viertel** shopping mall, open weekdays 10–6:30 (Thursday 10–9), Saturday 10–3 (10–6 on the first Saturday of the month), Sunday 11–3 (tel. 040/300–51220).

All offices can help with accommodations, and there's a central booking office for telephone callers (tel. 040/19412). A DM 5 fee is charged for every room reserved; the cost is then deducted when you pay the hotel.

Consulates **U.S. Consulate General,** Alsterufer 28, tel. 040/441–710. **British Consulate General,** Harvestehuder Weg 8a, tel. 040/446–071.

Emergencies **Police:** tel. 110. **Ambulance** and **Fire Department:** tel. 112. **Medical Emergencies:** tel. 040/228–022. **Dentist:** tel. 040/468–3260 or 040/11500.

English-language Bookstore **Frensche** (Spitalerstrasse 26e, tel. 040/327–585) stocks books and newspapers.

Travel Agency **American Express,** Rathausmarkt 5, tel. 040/331–141.

Car Rental **Avis,** Drehbahn 15–25, tel. 040/341–651. **Hertz,** Amsinckstrasse. 45, tel. 040/230–045.

Where to Change Money The **Deutsche-Verkehrs-Kredit Bank** in the main foyer (south entrance) of the main railway station, the Hauptbahnhof, is open daily 7:30 AM–10 PM.

Arriving and Departing by Plane

Hamburg's international airport, **Fuhlsbüttel,** is 11 kilometers (7 miles) northwest of the city. All major U.S. airlines fly to Hamburg; there are also regular flights from Britain. There are frequent flights from other major German cities.

Between the Airport and Downtown The most convvenient, cheapest, and often quickest way to get from the airport to the city center is to catch the **Airport-City-Bus,** which runs between the airport and Hamburg's Hauptbahnhof (main train station) daily at 20-minute intervals. Along the way, buses stop at the hotels Reichshof, Atlantic, and Hamburg-Plaza, the central bus station at Adenauerallee 78, and at the fairgrounds. Buses run from 6:30 AM to 10:30 PM. Tickets are DM 3.20 adults, DM 1.10 children. The **Airport-Express** (bus No. 110) runs every 10 minutes between the airport and the Ohlsdorf U- and S-bahn station, a 17-minute ride from the main train station. The fare is the same as above.

If you're picking up a rental car at the airport, follow the signs to *Stadtmitte* (downtown).

Arriving and Departing by Train and Bus

By Train EuroCity and InterCity trains connect Hamburg with all German cities and many major European cities. Two new InterCity Express lines link Hamburg with Frankfurt and Munich, and Würzburg and Munich, respectively. There are two principal stations: the centrally located **Hauptbahnhof,** and **Hamburg-Altona,** located west of the downtown area. For information, call 040/19419 for the main station, and 040/391–82850 for Hamburg-Altona.

By Bus The **ZOB,** or Zentral-Omnibus-Bahnhof, Hamburg's bus station, is located right behind the Hauptbahnhof (Adenauerallee 78). For information call 040/247–575, or contact the **Deutsche Touring-Gesellschaft** in Frankfurt (Am Römerhof 17, tel. 069/7931).

Getting Around

On Foot The historic center of Hamburg can be explored easily on foot. The downtown area's Binnenalster and Jungfernstieg, many shopping streets and shopping galleries, and harbor are all close enough to make walking easy.

By Public Transportation The HVV, Hamburg's public-transportation system, includes the **U-bahn** (subway), the **S-bahn** (suburban train), and **buses.** A one-way fare is DM 3.20 adults, DM 1.10 children, and tickets are available on all buses and at the automatic machines in all stations and at most bus stops. An **all-day ticket** (Tageskarte) valid from 9 AM to 1 AM costs DM 6.20 for unlimited rides on the HVV system. If you're traveling with family or friends, a **group or family ticket** (Gruppen- od. Familienkarte) is a good value; a group of up to four adults and three children can travel around for the entire day for only DM 11. It's not necessary to present the exact change when buying a ticket. Ticket-vending machines also return change.

In the north of Hamburg, the HVV system connects with the **A-bahn** (Alsternordbahn), a suburban train system that extends into Schleswig-Holstein.

Night buses (Nos. 600–640) serve the downtown area all night, leaving the Rathausmarkt and Hauptbahnhof every hour.

Information on the HVV system can be obtained directly from the **Hamburg Passenger Transport Board** by calling 040/322–911 (open daily 7 AM–8 PM).

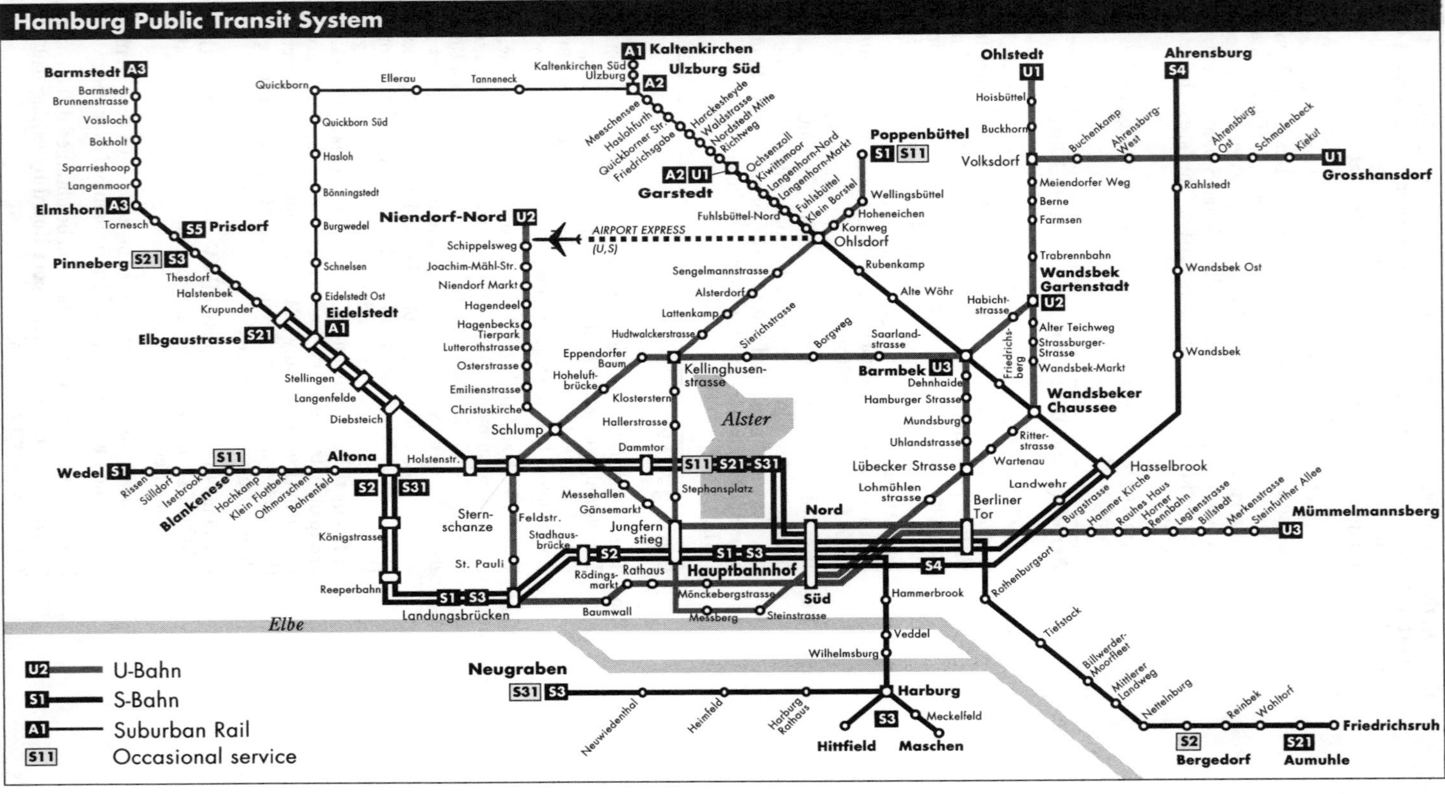
Hamburg Public Transit System
Barmstedt A3
Barmstedt Brunnenstrasse
Vossloch
Bokholt
Sparrieshoop
Langenmoor
Elmshorn A3
Tornesch
S5 Prisdorf
Pinneberg S21 S3
Thesdorf
Halstenbek
Krupunder
Elbgaustrasse S21
Stellingen
Langenfelde
Diebsteich
Quickborn
Ellerau
Tanneneck
Quickborn Süd
Hasloh
Bönningstedt
Burgwedel
Schnelsen
Eidelstedt Ost
Eidelstedt A1
A1 Kaltenkirchen
Kaltenkirchen Süd
Ulzburg
Ulzburg Süd A2
Meeschensee
Haslohfurth
Quickborner Str.
Friedrichsgabe
Harckesheyde
Waldstrasse
Nordstedt Mitte
Richtweg
A2 U1
Garstedt
Ochsenzoll
Kiwittsmoor
Langenhorn-Nord
Langenhorn-Markt
Fuhlsbüttel
Klein Borstel
Fuhlsbüttel-Nord
Poppenbüttel S1 S11
Wellingsbüttel
Hoheneichen
Kornweg
Ohlsdorf
Niendorf-Nord U2
AIRPORT EXPRESS (U,S)
Schippelsweg
Joachim-Mähl-Str.
Niendorf Markt
Hagendeel
Hagenbecks Tierpark
Lutterothstrasse
Osterstrasse
Emilienstrasse
Christuskirche
Schlump
Sengelmannstrasse
Alsterdorf
Lattenkamp
Hudtwalckerstrasse
Sierichstrasse
Borgweg
Saarlandstrasse
Eppendorfer Baum
Hoheluftbrücke
Kellinghusenstrasse
Klosterstern
Hallerstrasse
Alster
Rubenkamp
Alte Wöhr
Barmbek U3
Dehnhaide
Hamburger Strasse
Mundsburg
Uhlandstrasse
Lübecker Strasse
Lohmühlenstrasse
Berliner Tor
Habichtstrasse
Friedrichsberg
Ritterstrasse
Wartenau
Landwehr
Hasselbrook
Ohlstedt U1
Hoisbüttel
Buckhorn
Volksdorf
Meiendorfer Weg
Berne
Farmsen
Trabrennbahn
Wandsbek Gartenstadt U2
Alter Teichweg
Strassburger-Strasse
Wandsbek-Markt
Wandsbeker Chaussee
Buchenkamp
Ahrensburg-West
Ahrensburg S4
Ahrensburg-Ost
Schmalenbeck
Kiekut
U1 Grosshansdorf
Rahlstedt
Wandsbek Ost
Wandsbek
Wedel S1
Rissen
Sülldorf
Iserbrook
Blankenese
S11
Hochkamp
Klein Flottbek
Othmarschen
Bahrenfeld
Altona
S2
S31
Holstenstr.
Königstrasse
Reeperbahn
Sternschanze
Feldstr.
St. Pauli
S1 S3
Landungsbrücken
Dammtor
S11 S21 S31
Stephansplatz
Messehallen
Gänsemarkt
Jungfernstieg
Stadthausbrücke
S2
Rödingsmarkt
Rathaus
Baumwall
Hauptbahnhof
S1 S3
Nord
Süd
Mönckebergstrasse
Messberg
Steinstrasse
S4
Burgstrasse
Hammer Kirche
Rauhes Haus
Horner Rennbahn
Legienstrasse
Billstedt
Merkenstrasse
Steinfurther Allee
Mümmelmannsberg U3
Rothenburgsort
Tiefstack
Billwerder-Moorfleet
Mittlerer Landweg
Nettelnburg
S2 Bergedorf
Reinbek
Wohltorf
Friedrichsruh
S21 Aumuhle
Hammerbrook
Veddel
Wilhelmsburg
Elbe
Neugraben
S31 S3
Neuwiedenthal
Heimfeld
Harburg Rathaus
Harburg
S3
Meckelfeld
Hittfield
Maschen
U2 U-Bahn
S1 S-Bahn
A1 Suburban Rail
S11 Occasional service

By Taxi Taxi meters start at DM 3, and the fare is DM 1.60 per kilometer, plus 50 pfennigs for each piece of luggage. To order a taxi, call tel. 040/441–011.

By Bike Most major streets in Hamburg have paths reserved for bicyclists. From May through September, rent bikes at the tourist information office in Bieberhaus, outside the main train station. Prices range from DM 2 per hour to DM 20 for the whole weekend. For information, call tel. 040/300–51245.

Lodging

Hamburg is one of Germany's most expensive cities, with luxury hotels that charge for one night's stay what a small-town hostelry might demand for two weeks' full board. A full schedule of trade fairs and arts festivals keeps most rooms booked in advance. But it also leads many of the expensive hotels to offer lower rates on the weekends, when all those businesspeople have gone home. Some offer luxury accommodation on certain weekends for as low as DM 150 a night for a double room. You have to book well in advance (the tourist office will alert you to special offers and make bookings).

It's difficult to find a hotel room where you'll feel really at home for less than DM 100, although the farther out of Hamburg you venture, the more reasonable the room rates become. Within the city, the area immediately around the main railway station has several acceptable low-priced hotels. The east side of the Alster Lakes has more economical accommodations than the more upscale west side, and the views are the same. If you want to stay within walking distance of the city center, then choose accommodations between the main railway station and the Alster Lakes. The choice is wide and prices are reasonable. Cheap hotels in the famous (or infamous) St. Pauli (Reeperbahn) area are not recommended unless you plan to stay out late or are a heavy sleeper, since this is nightclub land (and some of the ostensible "hotels" have a dubious clientele).

All city tourist offices (*see* Essential Information, *above*) will book hotel accommodation, and there is a special telephone service (tel. 040/19412) for hotel bookings. There are also two agencies that will book private rooms: **Agentur Zimmer Frei,** Heimweg 3, Hamburg 13, tel. 040/412070; and **Agency Günter R. Kenne,** Ohbaumsfeld 15, 2105 Seevetal (a Hamburg suburb), tel. 04185/3481. A nominal fee of up to DM 10 is levied on hotel and private-accommodation bookings. Breakfast is usually included in the room rates of pensions and medium-price hotels. Double rooms far outnumber singles, and the rates given are usually for double occupancy. Rates for single rooms or for single occupancy of double rooms are usually around 20% cheaper than for doubles.

Highly recommended establishments are indicated by a star ★.

Under DM 180

Central (Main Railway Station) **Aussen Alster.** Only minutes from the train station and just 50 yards from the Alster Lakes, this small, discreet hotel is set in a gracious 19th-century town house. Try for a balcony room with a view of the lake. *Schmilinskystr. 11–13, tel. 040/241–*

Hamburg Lodging

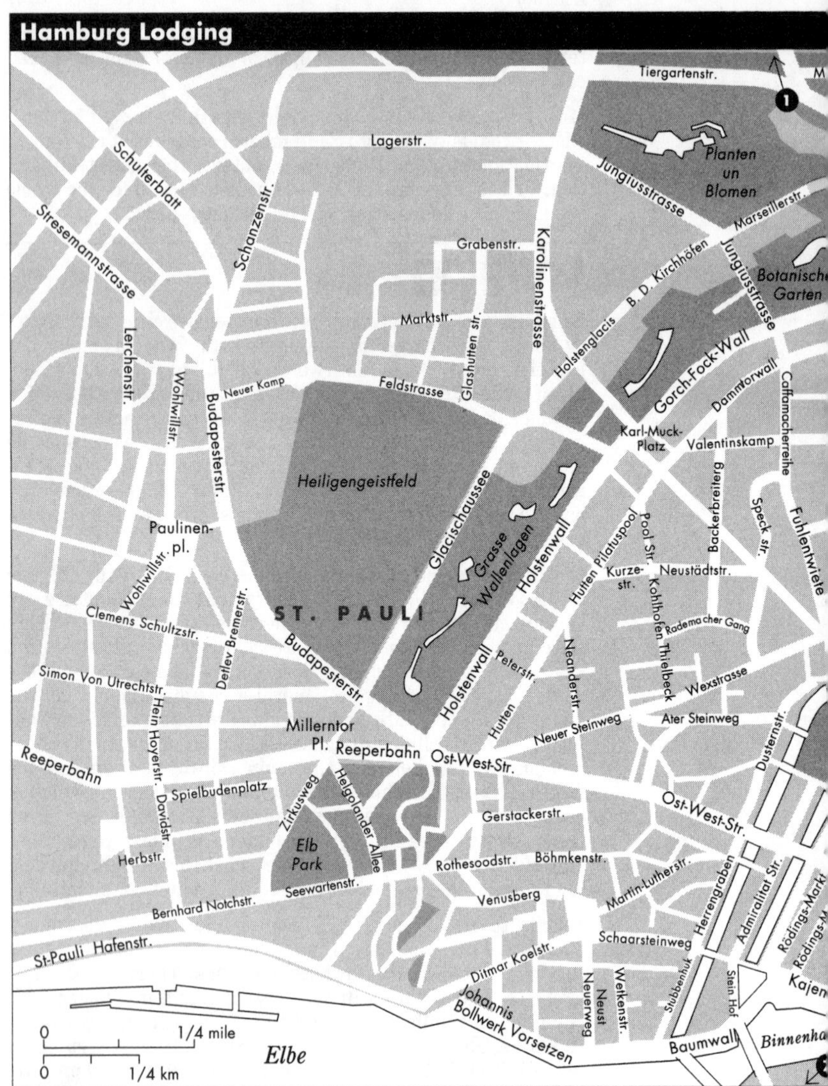

Alameda, **4**
Annenhof, **14**
Atlantic Hotel Kempinksi, **8**
Auf den Stintfang, **7**
Aussen Alster, **16**
Baseler Hof, **5**
Hotel Abtei, **2**
Hotel-Garni Mittelweg, **3**
Hotel Lilienhof, **11**
Hotel-Pension am Nonnenstieg, **1**
Hotel-Pension bei der Esplanade, **4**
Jugendgästehaus Horner Rennbahn, **13**
Kronprinz, **12**
Nippon Hotel, **17**
Pension Helga Schmidt, **9**
Steens Hotel, **10**
Vier Jahreszeiten, **6**
Wedina, **15**

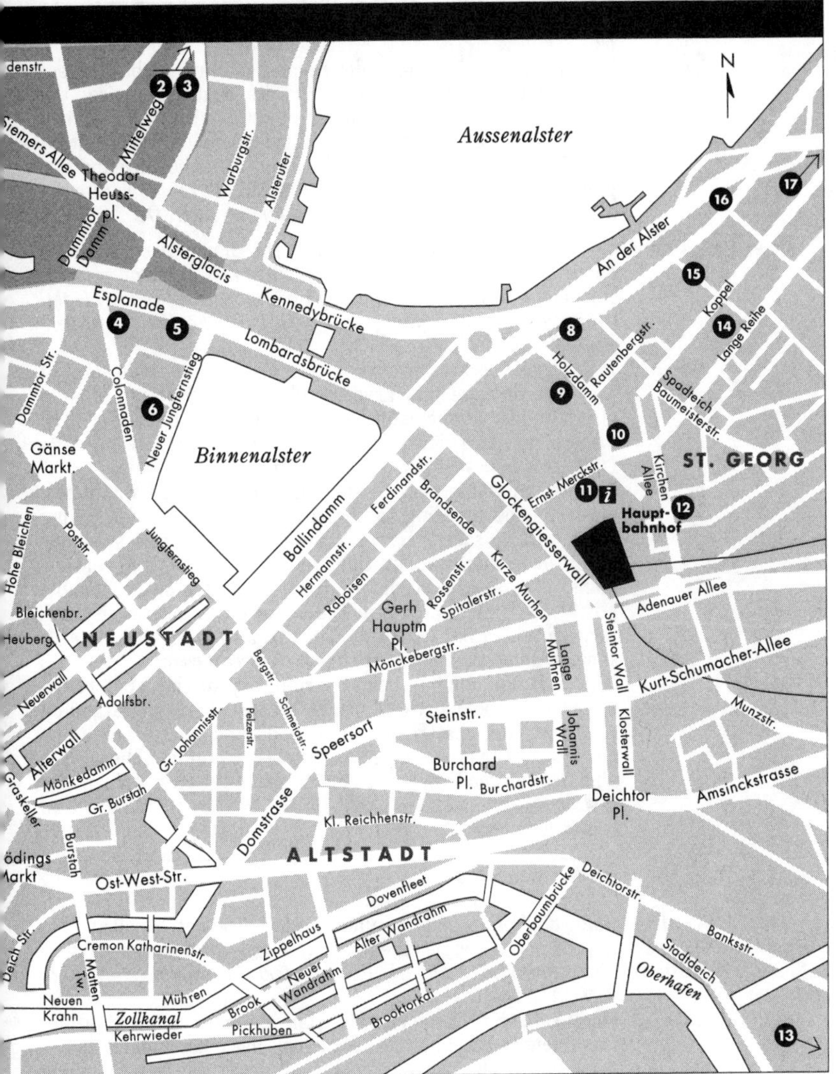
Aussenalster
Binnenalster
ST. GEORG
NEUSTADT
ALTSTADT
Hauptbahnhof
Mittelweg
Siemers Allee
Theodor Heuss-pl.
Dammtor Damm
Warburgstr.
Alsterufer
Alsterglacis
Kennedybrücke
Lombardsbrücke
An der Alster
Esplanade
Colonnaden
Neuer Jungfernstieg
Dammtor Str.
Gänse Markt.
Holzdamm
Rautenbergstr.
Koppel
Lange Reihe
Spadteich
Baumeisterstr.
Ernst-Merckstr.
Kirchen Allee
Glockengiesserwall
Ballindamm
Ferdinandstr.
Brandsende
Hermannstr.
Raboisen
Rossenstr.
Kurze Murhen
Spitalerstr.
Gerh Hauptm Pl.
Mönckebergstr.
Lange Murhren
Steintor Wall
Adenauer Allee
Kurt-Schumacher-Allee
Munzstr.
Jungfernstieg
Poststr.
Hohe Bleichen
Bleichenbr.
Heuberg
Neuerwall
Adolfsbr.
Alterwall
Bergstr.
Schmiedstr.
Pelzerstr.
Gr. Johannisstr.
Speersort
Steinstr.
Johannis Wall
Klosterwall
Burchard Pl.
Burchardstr.
Deichtor Pl.
Amsinckstrasse
Mönkedamm
Gr. Burstah
Graskeller
Domstrasse
Kl. Reichhenstr.
Burstah
Ödings Markt
Ost-West-Str.
Deichtorstr.
Dovenfleet
Oberbaumbrücke
Banksstr.
Stadtdeich
Oberhafen
Cremon
Katharinenstr.
Zippelhaus
Alter Wandrahm
Neuer Wandrahm
Deich Str.
Matten Tw.
Neuen Krahn
Mühren
Brook
Brooktorkai
Zollkanal
Kehrwieder
Pickhuben
N
2
3
4
5
6
8
9
10
11
12
13
14
15
16
17

1557. 27 rooms with bath. Facilities: sauna, solarium. AE, DC, MC, V.

Kronprinz. Considering its downscale position (on a busy street opposite the railway station) and its moderate price, the Kronprinz is a surprisingly attactive hotel, with a whiff of five-star flair. Rooms are individually styled—modern but homey. Try for No. 45, with its combination of mahogany and red plush. *Kirchenallee 46, tel. 040/243–258. 69 rooms with bath/shower. Facilities: restaurant, bar, terrace. AE, DC, MC, V.*

Alster Lakes Area

Baseler Hof. Centrally located near the Binnen Alster and the opera house, this hotel offers friendly and efficient service. Rooms are neatly if functionally furnished. *Esplanade 11, tel. 040/359–060. 150 rooms, most with bath. Facilities: restaurant. AE, DC, MC, V.*

Hotel Abtei. Located on a quiet, tree-lined street a mile north of the downtown area in Harvestehude, this elegant period hotel offers understated comfort and reliable levels of service. Try for a room with a view of the garden. *Abteistr. 14, tel. 040/442–2905. 12 rooms with bath. AE, DC, MC, V.*

Hotel-Garni Mittelweg. Chintz curtains, flowered wallpaper, old-fashioned dressing tables, a country house–style dining room which, sadly, serves only breakfast—there's a cozy small-town charm about this converted turn-of-the-century mansion in upscale Pöseldorf. It's well located on fashionable Mittelweg, a short walk from the Alster Lakes and the city center. *Mittelweg 59, tel. 040/414–1010. 30 rooms with bath or shower (showers slightly cheaper). No credit cards.*

Nippon Hotel. You'll be asked to remove your shoes before entering your room at this Japanese hotel. There are tatami on the floor, futon mattresses on the beds, and an attentive Japanese staff. By cutting some Western-style comforts, the hotel is able to offer good value in a smart area of the city. A Japanese restaurant was added in 1990. *Hofweg 75, tel. 040/227–1140. 42 rooms with bath. AE, DC, MC, V.*

Under DM 130

Central (Main Railway Station)

Alameda. For no-frills lodging, this is a good bet. Small and basic, the hotel occupies the first two floors of a downtown building. *Colonnaden 45, tel. 040/344–000. 18 rooms, some with bath. AE, DC, MC, V.*

Hotel Lilienhof. A short walk from the main railway station, this friendly little hotel offers clean, basic accommodation in small but newly furnished rooms, all with cable television and most with shower. The room rate includes a substantial breakfast buffet. *Ernst-Merck-Str. 4, tel. 040/241–087. 16 rooms. No credit cards.*

Hotel-Pension bei der Esplanade. Bei der Esplanade takes up the third and fourth floors of the building that houses the Alameda (there's no elevator). The rooms are basic but quiet, clean, and comfortable. *Colonnaden 45, tel. 040/342–961. 14 rooms, some with bath. No credit cards.*

Steens Hotel. Small and intimate, this hotel is decorated in light and airy Scandinavian style, with pale wood and modern furnishings. It's conveniently located close to the train station. Have breakfast in the garden when the weather's good. *Holzdamm 43, tel. 040/244–642. 11 rooms, most with bath. AE, DC, MC, V.*

Wedina. Centrally located and family-run, this establishment offers simple and reliable comforts that are more than adequate for an overnight stay. The little garden provides a leafy retreat; try for a room opening onto it. *Gurlittstr. 23, tel. 040/243–011. 23 rooms, most with bath. Facilities: pool, sauna, bar. AE, DC, MC, V. Closed mid-Dec.–mid-Feb.*

Alster Lakes Area **Hotel-Pension am Nonnenstieg.** The owner, Frau Hedermann, is friendly and helpful. Ask for a room with a kitchen alcove if you want to cook for yourself. Extra beds can be put in rooms at no extra charge to accommodate a family, and prices are lower for longer stays. *Nonnenstieg 11, tel. 040/473–869. 30 rooms with bath. No credit cards.*

Under DM 90

Central (Main Railway Station) **Annenhof.** You'll get basic but clean lodging at the centrally located Annenhof for as little as DM 50 for a double room. Bathrooms are shared. Breakfast is an extra DM 8. *Lange Reihe 23, tel 040/243–426. 12 rooms. No credit cards.*

Pension Helga Schmidt. Use of Frau Schmidt's kitchen is included in the very reasonable price of her comfortable rooms, all of which have shower, television, and radio. The pension is a short walk from the main railway station and the city center. *Holzdamm 14, tel. 040/280–2119. 14 rooms. No credit cards.*

Youth Hostels

Hamburg has two youth hostels, both of them open to members of the International Youth Hostel Federation (*see* Student and Youth Travel in Chapter 1):

Auf dem Stintfang. *Alfred-Wegener-Weg 5, tel. 040/313–488 (St. Pauli district—Reeperbahn subway station). More than 360 beds in dormitories. Overnight stay, including breakfast: DM 14–DM 18.*

Jugendgästehaus Horner Rennbahn. *Rennbahnstr. 100, tel. 040/651–1671 (eastern edge of town—Horner Rennbahn stop on the U-3 subway line). More than 260 beds in dormitories. Overnight stay, including breakfast: DM 18–DM 22.*

Splurge

★ **Atlantic Hotel Kempinski.** There are few more sumptuous hotels in Germany than this expansive and gracious Edwardian palace, located just north of the old town, close by the Aussenalster. The lobby is positively baronial, with an imposingly grand staircase and deep leather armchairs. The service is hushed and swift. The luxurious double rooms cost between DM 330 and DM 390, but there are occasional weekend reductions. *An der Alster 72, tel. 040/28880. 230 rooms and 13 suites, all with bath. Facilities: 2 restaurants, bar, nightclub, rooftop pool, sauna, masseur, airport check-in desk. AE, DC, MC, V.*

★ **Vier Jahreszeiten.** This hotel opened in 1897, and it's still owned and run by the Haerlin family. Antiques—the hotel has a set of near-priceless Gobelins tapestries—line the public rooms and stud the stylish bedrooms; forests of flowers stand in massive vases; rare oil paintings hang on the walls; and, of course, all the rooms (doubles start at DM 400) are individually decorated. *Neuer Jungfernstieg 9–14, tel. 040/34940. 175 rooms and 12 suites, all with bath. Facilities: 4 restaurants, 2 bars, tearoom, pastry shop, wine shop. AE, DC, MC, V.*

Exploring Hamburg

Guided Tours

Orientation Tours The tourist office organizes bus tours of the city, all with English-speaking guides (tel. 040/300–51244). The tours leave from Kirchenallee by the main train station, across from the Hotel Phoenix. A bus tour lasting 1 ¾ hours sets off at 11 and 3 daily and costs DM 18 adults, DM 9 children. A longer tour, lasting 2½ hours, starts at 10 and 2, costing DM 22 adults, DM 11 children. Combination bus tours of the city and boat tours of the harbor are conducted at irregular times, according to demand. They cost DM 24 adults, DM 12 children. City tours aboard the nostalgic *Hummelbahn*, converted railroad wagons pulled by a tractor, are offered on weekends only, starting at the Kirchenallee stop at 10, noon, 2, and 4. The DM 14 fare (DM 7 children) includes a *Rollmop* snack—a rolled and skewered pickled herring.

Walking Tours Tours of the downtown area are organized by the **Museum für Arbeit.** They are held weekends only, May through September. Call 040/298–42364 for information.

Boat Tours Water dominates Hamburg, and there are few better ways to get to know the city than by taking a trip around the massive harbor. During the summer months, excursion boats and barges leave the Landungsbrücken (piers) every half hour for tours of the harbor lasting up to 90 minutes. During the winter, departures are not as frequent, with operators usually waiting for a full boat before setting off. The boats leave from pier Nos. 2, 3, and 7, and the trips cost between DM 12 for adults (DM 6 for children under 14) and DM 16 (DM 8 for children). For information on harbor tours, call 040/376–80024 or 040/314–644. Boat trips around the Alster Lakes and through the canals leave from the Jungfernstieg in the center of the city.

During the summer they leave every half hour, less regularly in winter. Fares are from DM 10 (DM 5 for children under 14) to DM 23 for the complete three-hour tour (DM 11.50 for children).

From May through September, there's a romantic, night-time tour of the Alster Lakes leaving the Jungfernstieg every evening at 8 (the fare is DM 17). A nighttime tour of the harbor sets off every Saturday at 8 from pier No. 2 with a band aboard, and the DM 49 fare includes a cold buffet, as much beer as you can drink, and a (slightly uneven) dance floor. The **Störtebeker** line offers a six-course Baroque-style banquet during a four-hour tour of the harbor. You have to book in advance for that one (call tel. 040/220–2552 or 040/229–5250).

Hamburg for Free—or Almost

More than a third of Hamburg's area consists of lakes, canals, rivers, parks, and gardens, which can be enjoyed year-round. The **Alster Lakes**, which are dotted in summer with sailboats and windsurfers, can be just as much fun when they freeze over in winter; on the coldest weekends, gaily colored tents appear on the ice and mulled wine is ladled out from makeshift bars. The best parks are the **Planten un Blomen,** which connects the Aussenalster with the Elbe River (*see* Downtown Hamburg, *be-*

low), and the City Park, or **Stadtpark**, where you can hire an inexpensive rowboat and venture out of the park limits and into the canal system, which runs as far as the Elbe. (Warning: Keep track of your route to avoid getting lost.) Both parks are ideal for jogging and biking. From May through September you can hire bikes for DM 2 an hour, DM 10 a day, or DM 20 for the weekend.

Hamburg means ships—both big and small. At the **Schulauer Fährhaus,** the Elbe River ferryboat station in the suburb of Wedel, you can watch ships being saluted in traditional style as they arrive or depart. The ceremony is fascinating—each ship is greeted with its national flag and its national anthem—and is played out daily from sunrise to sunset. Afterward you can descend to a cellar **museum of ships in bottles.** It's open daily 10–6, admission is DM 2.50, and children are admitted free—an excellent deal for the kids, for whom the museum is a delight. *To reach the Schulauer Fährhaus take either the S-l suburban line (alight at the Wedel terminus) or the No. 189 bus.*

Music lovers head for Hamburg's **Musikhalle,** where the city's three leading orchestras perform, and the **Staatsoper,** one of the world's leading opera houses. Often you can get cheap tickets from the evening cash desk, which usually opens half an hour before performances begin. Standing room at the opera costs as little as DM 5. Many of Hamburg's churches offer excellent **organ recitals** for the cost of a voluntary contribution in the offertory box. Contact the Amt für Kirchenmusik, Uhlandstr. 49 (tel. 040/220–5131), for details.

A central Hamburg agency called the Last-Minute-Kartenshop (tel. 040/353–565) offers reductions of up to 50% on **theater and concert tickets.** It's located at the Poststrasse entrance to the Hanse-Viertel shopping area. The reduced-price tickets are for same-day performances. The agency also sells advance-reservation tickets, but for these you'll pay the normal price. *Open Mon.-Sat. 10–7, Sun. 11–7; for cheap tickets, daily 3–6:30.*

Hamburg has a magnificent open-air forum for street theater and music in its **Rathausmarkt,** the central market square in front of the city hall. Here you can sit at the base of the Heinrich Heine statue and join him in watching the daily program of Hamburg's buskers. It's also an ideal vantage point from which to soak up the bustle of city life.

The Rathausmarkt has a weekly market, but the city's real showpiece is the **Fischmarkt** at the Elbe River piers, the Landungsbrücken (*see* Downtown Hamburg, *below*). On Sunday morning the daily fish market grows into a sprawling flea market, where you'll come across everything from grandmother's attic treasures to the latest chic baubles. The market is for early risers only—it starts at 5 AM in summer and 7 in winter, and it's officially over at 10, though the fun continues in the surrounding bars. (You can enjoy a cheap breakast with free jazz in the auction hall, the Fischauktionshalle, Grosse Elbestrasse 9.) *To get to the Fischmarkt, take the S-1 or S-2 suburban railway line or the U-3 subway line and alight at Landungsbrücken.*

Orientation

The best way to get to know the center of Hamburg—the canal-crossed area between Binnenalster and the Elbe—is alone, on foot, with a guidebook in hand. (You'll find a useful sightseeing pamphlet, *Hamburg Tips*, at Tourist Information in Bieberhaus, the city's main tourist office, on the north side of the Hachmannplatz outside the main railway station.) But if you're venturing farther afield—to St. Pauli, the harbor, or the Speicherstadt—then take one of the tourist buses that leave at regular intervals from Kirchenallee (*see* Guided Tours, *above*).

Highlights for First-time Visitors

Alter Botanischer Garten (Old Botanical Gardens)
Fischmarkt (Fish Market)
The harbor
Hauptbahnhof
Michaeliskirche
Reeperbahn

Downtown Hamburg

Numbers in the margin correspond to points of interest on the Hamburg map.

1 Your tour begins at **Dammtor** train station, an elevated steel-and-glass Jugendstil structure built in 1903. Recently renovated, it is one of many Art Nouveau buildings you'll see during your stay in Hamburg. Pick up a detailed city map from the first-floor Booking Hall. Turn left out of the station and head toward the Congress Centrum Hamburg (CCH), a vast, modern conference-and-entertainment complex at the northeast
2 corner of **Planten un Blomen** park.

3 Planten un Blomen and the adjoining **Alter Botanischer Garten** (Old Botanical Gardens) lie within the remains of the 17th-century fortified wall that defended the city during the Thirty Years' War, the cataclysmic religious struggle that raged in Germany between 1618 and 1648. The remains of the old fortifications and moats have since been cleverly integrated into a huge, tranquil park on the edge of the city center.

The entire park area is known as **Wallringpark** and includes Planten un Blomen and the Alter Botanischer Garten, plus the Kleine and Grosse Wallanlagen parks to the south. You'll need to cover a lot of ground on foot to see everything Wallringpark has to offer, but a trip on the light railway—which crosses all four parks—will give you a taste of its many aspects. If you take the railway, aim to finish your journey at Stephansplatz.

The walking tour will take you through Planten un Blomen and the Alter Botanischer Garten. Past the Congress Centrum, bear left in a sweeping arc through the ornamental Planten un Blomen park. This park, opened in 1935, is famous all over Germany for its well-kept plant, flower, and water gardens, and offers many places to rest and admire the flora. If you visit on a summer's evening, you'll see the **Wasserballet,** an illuminated fountain "dance" in the lake set to organ music. Make sure you get to the lake in good time for the show—it begins at 10 PM each evening during the summer (at 9 PM in September).

Follow the signs to the Alter Botanischer Garten, an equally green and open park that specializes in rare and exotic plants. Tropical and subtropical species are grown under glass in hothouses, with specialty gardens—including herbal and medicinal—clustered around the old moat. The special appeal of the **Kleine** and **Grosse Wallanlagen** parks is their well-equipped leisure facilities, including a children's playground and theater, a model-boat pond, roller- and ice-skating rinks, and outdoor chess.

When you leave, make your way to the east entrance, to the Alter Botanischer Garten at Stephansplatz. Take the U-bahn
4 south for one stop to **Jungfernstieg,** the most elegant boulevard in downtown Hamburg. You'll emerge from the U-bahn station onto Jungfernstieg's wide promenade, looking out over one of the city's most memorable vistas—the Alster Lakes. It's these twin lakes that give downtown Hamburg its distinctive sense of openness and greenery.

Today's attractive Jungfernstieg promenade, laid out in 1665, used to be part of the muddy millrace that channeled water into the Elbe River. The two lakes meet at the 17th-century defense wall at Lombard Brücke, the first bridge visible across the water.

Hamburg's best-known café, the **Alsterpavillon** (Jungfernstieg 54), is an ideal vantage point from which to observe the constant activity on the Inner Alster. It's open daily 10 AM–11 PM. In summer, the boat landing below is the starting point for the *Alsterdampfer*, the flat-bottom passenger boats that teem on the lakes. Small sailboats and rowboats hired from yards on the shores of the Alster are very much a part of the summer scene. But in winter conditions can be severe enough to freeze both lakes (only 8 feet deep at their deepest point), and commuters take to their ice skates to get to work. *Alster Lake and canal tours, Jungfernstieg, tel. 040/341–141. Fare for lake tour: DM 10 adults, DM 5 children. Operates Apr.–Oct., departing daily every half hour 10–6. Fare for combination lake and canal tour: DM 15 adults, DM 7 children. Operates Apr.–Oct., departing daily every 40 min. 10–6.*

Every Hamburger dreams of living within sight of the Alster, but only the wealthiest can afford it. Hamburg has its fair share of millionaires, some of whom are lucky enough to own one of the magnificent garden properties around the Alster's perimeter (the locals call it "Millionaire's Coast"). But you don't have to own one of these estates to be able to enjoy the waterfront—the Alster shoreline offers 7 kilometers (4.6 miles) of tree-lined public pathways. Popular among joggers, these trails are a lovely place for a stroll.

It's hardly surprising that the area around Jungfernstieg contains some of Hamburg's most exclusive shops. Even the unpredictable nature of the north German weather isn't enough to deter Hamburgers from pursuing a favorite pastime: window-shopping. Hidden from view behind the sedate facade of Jungfernstieg is a network of nine covered arcades that together accounts for almost a mile of shops offering everything from cheap souvenirs to expensive haute couture. Many of the air-conditioned passages have sprung up in the last two decades (*see* Shopping, *below*), but some already existed in the 19th cen-

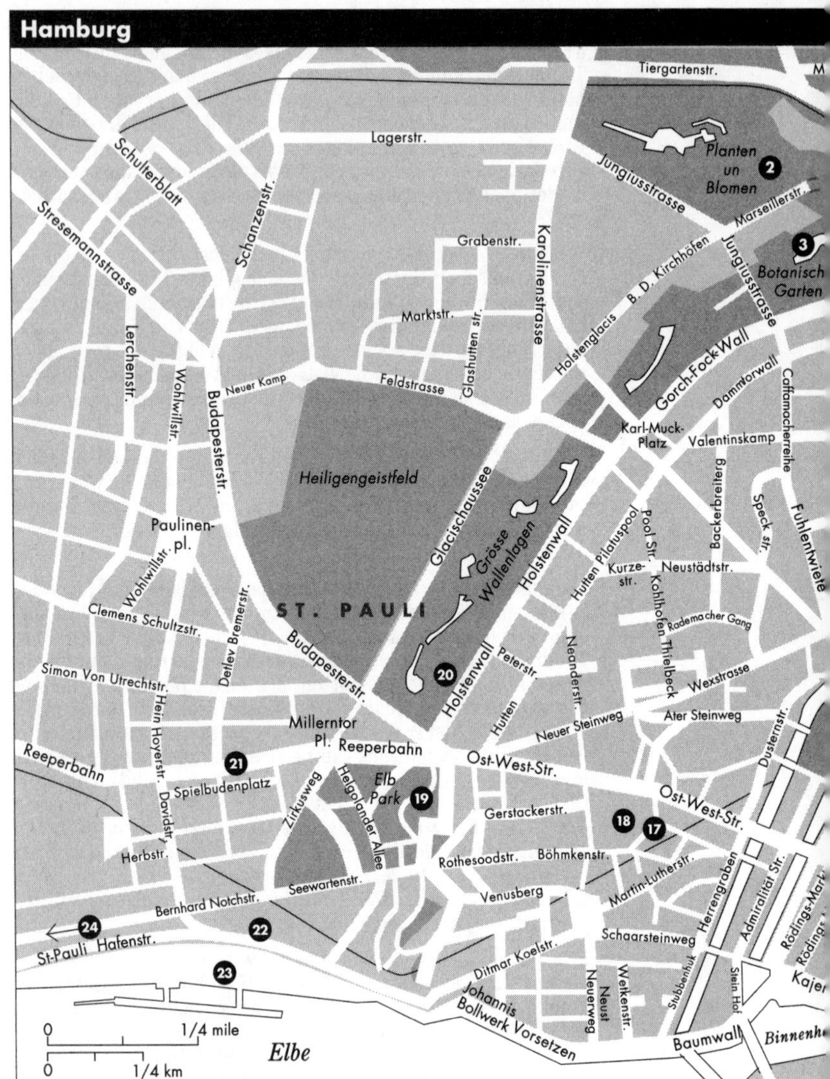

Alter Botanischer Garten, **3**
Bismarckdenkmal, **19**
Blankenese, **24**
Chilehaus, **12**
Dammtor, **1**
Deichstrasse, **15**
Fischmarkt, **22**
Hauptbahnhof, **7**
Jacobikirche, **10**
Jungfernstieg, **4**
Katherinenkirche, **13**
Kontorhausviertal, **11**
Krameramts-wohnungen, **17**
Kunsthalle, **8**
Landungsbrücken, **23**
Michaeliskirche, **18**
Mönckebergstrasse, **6**
Museum für Hamburgische Geschichte, **20**
Museum für Kunst und Gewerbe, **9**
Nikolaikirche, **16**
Planten un Blomen, **2**
Rathaus, **5**
Reeperbahn, **21**
Speicherstadt, **14**

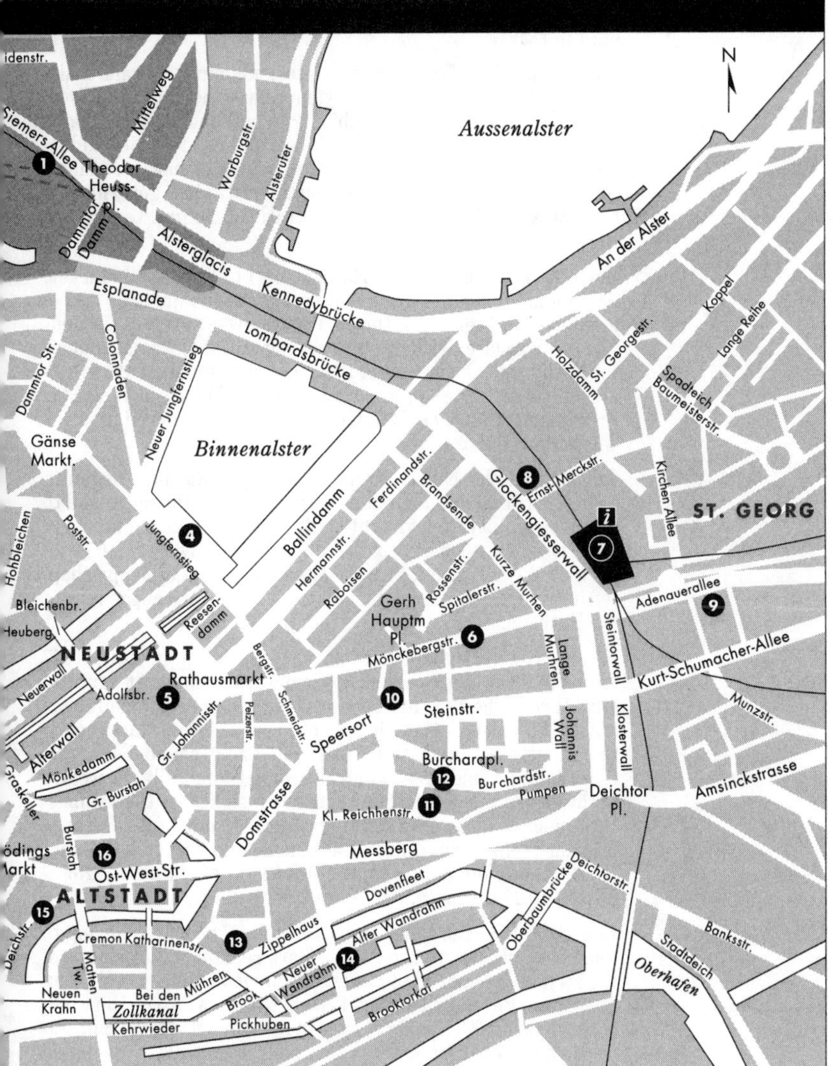
Aussenalster
Binnenalster
NEUSTADT
ALTSTADT
ST. GEORG
Siemers Allee
Theodor Heuss-pl.
Dammtor Damm
Mittelweg
Warburgstr.
Alsterufer
Alsterglacis
Esplanade
Kennedybrücke
Lombardsbrücke
An der Alster
Colonnaden
Dammtor Str.
Neuer Jungfernstieg
Gänse Markt.
Jungfernstieg
Ballindamm
Hermannstr.
Ferdinandstr.
Brandsende
Glockengiesserwall
Ernst-Merckstr.
Holzdamm
St. Georgestr.
Koppel
Lange Reihe
Spadreich
Baumeisterstr.
Kirchen Allee
Poststr.
Hohbleichen
Bleichenbr.
Heuberg
Reesen-damm
Raboisen
Rossenstr.
Spitalerstr.
Kurze Murhen
Gerh Hauptm Pl.
Mönckebergstr.
Adenauerallee
Steintorwall
Lange Murhren
Kurt-Schumacher-Allee
Rathausmarkt
Neuerwall
Adolfsbr.
Bergstr.
Schmeidstr.
Pelzerstr.
Gr. Johannisstr.
Steinstr.
Speersort
Johannis Wall
Klosterwall
Munzstr.
Alterwall
Mönkedamm
Graskeller
Gr. Burstah
Domstrasse
Burchardpl.
Burchardstr.
Pumpen
Deichtor Pl.
Amsinckstrasse
Kl. Reichhenstr.
Burstah
Messberg
Ost-West-Str.
Dovenfleet
Deichtorstr.
Oberbaumbrücke
Zippelhaus
Alter Wandrahm
Cremon
Katharinenstr.
Deichstr.
Matten Tw.
Neuer Wandrahm
Bei den Mühren
Brook
Neuen Krahn
Zollkanal
Kehrwieder
Pickhuben
Brooktorkai
Banksstr.
Stadtdeich
Oberhafen
1
4
5
6
7
8
9
10
11
12
13
14
15
16

tury (the first glass-covered arcade, called Sillem's Bazaar, was built in 1845).

Turn off the Jungfernstieg onto Reesendamm street and make
5 your way to the next stop on your tour—the **Rathaus** (Town
Hall). To most Hamburgers this large building is the symbolic heart of the city. As a city-state—an independent city and simultaneously one of the 15 federal states of newly reunited Germany—Hamburg has a city council and a state government, both of which have their administrative headquarters in the Rathaus.

Both the Rathaus and the Rathausmarkt (Town Hall Market) lie on marshy land—a fact that everyone in Hamburg was reminded of in 1962 when the entire area was severely flooded. The large square, with its surrounding arcades, was laid out after Hamburg's Great Fire of 1842. The architects set out to create an Italian-style square, drawing on St. Mark's in Venice for their inspiration. The rounded glass arcade bordered by trees was added in 1982.

Building on the Nordic Renaissance-style Rathaus began in 1866 when 4,000 wooden piles were sunk into the moist soil to provide stability for its mighty bulk. Building was completed in 1892, the year a cholera epidemic claimed the lives of 8,605 people in 71 days. A fountain and monument to that unhappy chapter in Hamburg's life can be found in a courtyard at the rear of the Rathaus.

No one is likely to claim that this immense building, with its 647 rooms and towering central clock tower, is the most graceful structure in the city, but for the sheer opulence of its interior, it's hard to beat. Although you get to see only the state rooms, the tapestries, huge staircases, glittering chandeliers, coffered ceilings, and grand portraits convey forcefully the wealth of the city in the last century and give insight into the bombastic municipal taste. The starting point for tours of the Rathaus interior is the ground-floor Rathausdiele, a vast pillared hall. *English-language tours: DM 1 adults, 50pf children. Mon.–Thurs. 10:15 and 3:15, Fri.–Sun. 10:15 and 1:15.*

Leave the Rathaus square by its east side, perhaps pausing to join other visitors to the city who are relaxing on the steps of
the striking memorial to the poet Heinrich Heine, a real Ham-
6 burg fan. Beyond lies **Mönckebergstrasse,** a broad, bustling
street of shops that ends at the Hauptbahnhof (main train station). Mönckebergstrasse is a relatively new street—it was laid out in 1908, when this part of the old town was redeveloped. Although the shops here are not quite as exclusive as those of Jungfernstieg, the department stores and shopping precincts on both sides of the street provide a wide selection of goods at more easily affordable prices. One word of warning to shoppers: If you want to go on a shopping spree on a Saturday, you will find that the shops close at 2 PM—unless it is the first Saturday of the month, when the shops are open from 9 to 6:30. This rather quirky rule applies to all of Hamburg's shopping centers and throughout most of Germany.

When you reach the end of Mönckebergstrasse, you'll meet the busy main road of Steintorwall, which was the easternmost link of the former defense wall encircling the old town in the 17th century. Rather than battling to cross against the fast-moving
7 traffic, take the subway to the **Hauptbahnhof.**

The Hauptbahnhof was built at the turn of the century and opened in 1906. Today it caters to a heavy volume of international, national, and suburban rail traffic. Despite the fact that it was badly damaged during the World War II and has been modernized many times over, its architectural impact remains intact. This enormous 394-foot-long, cast-iron-and-glass building is accentuated by a 460-foot-wide glazed roof that is supported only by pillars at each end. The largest structure of its kind in Europe, it is remarkably spacious and light inside.

Retrace your steps and leave the Hauptbahnhof by the entrance you came in. Turn right on Steintorwall, which continues as Glockengiesserwall Strasse, until you come to the
8 **Kunsthalle** (Art Gallery) on the corner of Ernst-Merckstrasse.

The Kunsthalle houses one of the most important art collections in West Germany. It comprises two linked buildings: The one facing you is known as the Kunsthaus, exhibiting mainly contemporary works; adjoining it on your left is the Renaissance-style Kunsthalle, built in 1868. The entrance to both, which are known collectively as the Kunsthalle, is via the Kunsthaus building.

The Kunsthalle's 3,000 paintings, 400 sculptures, and coin and medal collection present a remarkably diverse picture of European artistic life from the 14th century to the present. Masterpieces in the gallery's possession include the oldest known representation of the murder of Thomas à Becket, the head of the English church in the 14th century. This painting, called *Thomas Altar*, was painted by Meister Francke in 1424 and depicts Becket's death in Canterbury Cathedral.

One room of paintings shows works by local artists since the 16th century. There is also an outstanding collection of German Romantic paintings, including works by Runge, Friedrich, and Spitzweg. An exhibition of European art by such painters as Holbein, Rembrandt, Van Dyck, Tiepolo, and Canaletto is on display, as are examples of the late-19th-century Impressionist movement by artists from Leibl and Lieberman to Manet, Monet, and Renoir. *Glockengeisserwall 1, tel. 040/24862612. Admission: DM 4 adults, DM 1 children. Open Tues.–Sun. 10–6.*

A quite different but equally fascinating perspective on art is
9 offered by the nearby **Museum für Kunst und Gewerbe** (Museum of Arts and Crafts). To reach it, head in the direction from which you came until you see the major crossroads with Kurt-Schumacher-Allee on your left. Turn down this street, and you'll find the museum in the first block on your left.

The Museum für Kunst und Gewerbe was built in 1876 as a museum and school combined. Its founder, Justus Brinckmann, intended it to be a stronghold of the applied arts to counter what he saw as a decline in taste due to industrial mass production. A keen collector, Herr Brinckmann amassed a wealth of unusual objects, including a fine collection of ceramics from all over the world. The museum houses a wide range of exhibits from a collection of 15th- to 18th-century scientific instruments (ground floor) to an Art Nouveau room setting, complete with ornaments and furniture, all either original or faithfully reproduced (first floor). *Steintorpl. 1, tel. 040/248–62630. Admission: DM1. Open Tues.–Sat. 10–6.*

10 Return to the city center for a visit to the **Jacobikirche** (St. Jacob's Church), just off the Mönckebergstrasse. Turn right out of the museum onto Kurt-Schumacher-Allee, cross over Steintorwall by the subway and continue west along Steinstrasse to the Jacobikirche on your right—you'll recognize it by its needle spire.

This 13th-century church was almost completely destroyed during the Second World War. Only the furnishings, put into storage until restoration of the building was completed in 1962, survived. The interior is not to be missed—it houses such treasures as the vast Baroque organ on which J. S. Bach played in 1720 and three Gothic altars from the 15th and 16th centuries. *Steinstr. Open weekdays 10–4, Sun. 10–1.*

Upon leaving the Jacobikirche, cross over Steinstrasse and
head down Mohlenhofstrasse, bearing left at the end onto
Burchardstrasse. This area, south of the Jacobikirche between
11 Steinstrasse and Messberg, is known as the **Kontorhausviertal**
(Business-House Quarter). Its fascination lies in a series of imaginative clinker-brick buildings designed in the New Objec-
tivity style of 1920s civic architect Fritz Schumacher.

12 Of particular interest in this quarter is the **Chilehaus** at the corner of Burchardstrasse and Pumpen, a fantastical 10-story building that at first looks like a vast landlocked ship. The Chilehaus was commissioned by businessman Henry Sloman, who traded in saltpeter from Chile. This building is the most representative example of the north German clinker-brick architecture of the '20s.

Next, your tour will take you south toward the Freihafen (Free
Port) to see the 19th-century warehouse city of **Speicherstadt,**
13 with a visit to the restored **Katherinenkirche** (St. Catherine's
Church) en route. From the Messberg end of Pumpen Street,
cross the busy Ost-West-Strasse by Messberg station and con-
tinue down Dovenfleet, which runs alongside the Zoll Kanal
(Customs Canal). Continue until Dovenfleet turns into Bei den
Mühren, and you'll see the distinctive green copper spire of the
Katherinenkirche.

The church is dedicated to St. Catherine, a princess of Alexandria martyred at the beginning of the 4th century. Both the exterior and interior of the church were severely damaged during World War II, but it has since been carefully reconstructed according to the Baroque design. Almost none of the original interior furnishings escaped destruction. Only two 17th-century epitaphs (to Moller and von der Feehte) remain. *Bei den Mühren. Open daily in the summer 9–6, in winter 9–4.*

Continue for about 200 meters along Bei den Mühren with the
14 looming bulk of the **Speicherstadt** warehouses in view across
the canal. Cross the first bridge you come to—it leads to the
center of the warehouse district in the Free Port.

Hamburg's free-port status has existed since the 12th century, when Emperor Barbarossa, the Holy Roman Emperor Frederick I, granted the city special privileges, which included freedom from customs dues on the Elbe River. The original free port was situated at the point where the Alster meets the Elbe near Deichstrasse, but it was moved farther south as Hamburg's trade increased over the following centuries. The advent of steamships in the middle of the 19th century necessitated a total restructuring of the free port, and the Speicherstadt warehouses came into being.

The warehouses offer another aspect of Hamburg's extraordinary architectural diversity. A Gothic influence is apparent here, with a rich overlay of gables, turrets, and decorative outlines. These massive rust-brown warehouses are still used today to store and process every conceivable commodity, from coffee and spices to raw silks and handwoven Oriental carpets. Although you won't be able to go in, the nonstop comings and goings will give you a good sense of a port at work.

As you leave the Free Port over the bridge by which you entered, you pass through a customs control point, at which you
may be required to make a customs declaration. Turn left after
the bridge, where Bei den Mühren becomes Neuen Krahn.
15 Take your second right—onto **Deichstrasse,** which runs alongside Nikolaifleet, a former course of the Alster and one of
Hamburg's oldest canals.

You are now in one of the oldest residential areas of the Old Town of Hamburg, which dates to the 14th century. Many of the original houses on Deichstrasse were destroyed in the Great Fire of 1842, which broke out in No. 42 and left some 20,000 people homeless. The houses you see today date mostly from the 17th to 19th centuries, but a few of the early dwellings escaped the ravages of the fire.

Number 27 Deichstrasse, for example, built in 1780 as a warehouse, is the oldest of its kind in Hamburg. And farther along at No. 39 is the Baroque facade of a house built in 1700. Today Deichstrasse is a protected area of great historical interest. All the buildings in the area have been painstakingly restored—thanks largely to the efforts of public-spirited individuals. You may wish to make a small detour down one of the narrow alleys between the houses (Fleetgänge) to see the fronts of the houses facing the Nikolaifleet. After exploring this lovely area, take the Cremon Bridge at the north end of Deichstrasse. This angled pedestrian bridge spans Ost-West-Strasse.

The Cremon Bridge will take you to Hopfenmarkt square, just
16 a stone's throw from the ruins of the **Nikolaikirche** (St. Nicholas's Church). You won't need precise directions to find the
church, with its 476-foot tower—the second-highest in Germany. Only the tower and outside walls of the 19th-century neo-
Gothic church survived World War II. Unlike most of the other
war-torn churches in Hamburg, the Nikolai was not rebuilt. Instead, the tower was declared a monument to those killed and
persecuted during the war.

The Weinkeller unter St. Nikolai, a wine cellar and small wine museum located beneath the former church, is open for browsing and wine tasting as well as for the purchase of wine. *Ost-West-Str. between Hopfenmarkt and Neue Berg. Open weekdays 1–6, Sat. 9–1.*

Turn right onto Ost-West-Strasse and cross to the other side at
the Rödingsmarkt U-bahn station. Continue along Ost-West-
Strasse until you reach Krayenkamp, a side street to your left
17 that opens onto the historic **Kramerамtswohnungen** (Shop-
keepers-Guild Houses). The distance from the Nikolaikirche to
Krayenkamp is about half a mile.

This tightly packed group of courtyard houses was built between 1620 and 1626 for the widows of members of the shopkeepers' guild. They were used as homes for the elderly after 1866, when the freedom to practice trades was granted. The half-timbered, two-story dwellings were restored in the 1970s and are now protected buildings. Their unusual twisted chimneys and decorative brick facades have drawn more than curious visitors—an artists' colony has taken firm root here.

One of the houses, marked "C," is open to the public. A visit inside the furnished setting gives one a sense of life in one of these 17th-century dwellings. Some of the houses have been converted to suit modern-day commercial purposes—you'll find a gallery, shops, and a bar-cum-restaurant in the style of Old Hamburg. *Historic House "C," Krayenkamp 10. Admission free. Open Tues.–Sun. 10–5.*

The Krameramtswohnungen lie in the shadow of Hamburg's
18 best-loved and most famous landmark, **Michaeliskirche** (St.
Michael's Church), on the other side of Krayenkamp Road. Michaeliskirche, or "Michel," as it is called locally, is Hamburg's principal church and northern Germany's finest Baroque ecclesiastical building. Constructed on this site in the 17th century, it was razed when lightning struck almost a century later. It was rebuilt in the late 18th century in the decorative Nordic Baroque style, but fell victim in 1906 to a terrible fire, which destroyed much of the church. A replica was erected in 1912, but it suffered yet more bad luck during World War II. By 1952, it had once again been restored.

The Michel has a distinctive 433-foot brick and iron tower bearing the largest tower clock in Germany, 26 feet in diameter. Just above the clock is the viewing platform (accessible by an elevator or stairs), which affords a magnificent panaroma of the city, the Elbe River, and the Alster Lakes. Twice a day, at 10 AM and 9 PM (on Sundays at noon only), a watchman plays a trumpet solo from the tower platform, and during festivals an entire wind ensemble crowds onto the platform to perform. Traffic permitting, the music can be heard at street level. *Michaeliskirche: open daily 9–5. St. Michael's Tower: open in summer Mon.–Sat. 9–5:30, Sun. 11:30–5:30; in winter Mon., Tues., and Thurs.–Sat. 10–4, Sun. 11:30–4. Elevator fee: DM 3 adults, DM 1.80 children. Staircase fee (449 steps): DM 1.80.*

Return to the Krayenkamp entrance to the Michel and turn
right. Stay on this road for about 200 meters, until you reach a
19 park, the enormous **Bismarckdenkmal** (Bismarck Monument)
rising high above the greenery. Take the pathway leading to it, and as you climb you'll realize that part of its height is due to the sandy hill on which it stands. The colossal 111-foot granite monument, erected between 1903 and 1906, is a mounted statue of Chancellor Bismarck, the Prussian "Iron Chancellor" who was the force behind the unification of Germany. The plinth features bas-reliefs of various German tribes. Created by the sculptor Hugo Lederer, the statue symbolizes the German Reich's protection of Hamburg's international trade.

Leave the monument by the north exit onto Ost-West-Strasse.
Cross it and continue straight ahead up the street called
20 Holstenwall to the **Museum für Hamburgische Geschichte** (Museum of Hamburg History). Because Holstenwall is a fast-flow-

ing street, you may wish to cross by the St. Pauli U-bahn station on the traffic island.

A visit to this museum is highly recommended—it will give you an excellent overall perspective of the forces that have guided Hamburg's development over the centuries. The museum's vast and comprehensive collection of artifacts charts the history of Hamburg from its origins in the 9th century to the present day. The Hamburg Historical Society began building the collection in 1839—three years before the Great Fire—and salvaged a number of items for display in the museum. More material was acquired in 1883 when several street blocks were torn down to make way for the expansion of the free port, and these provide an excellent record of life at the time.

Of particular interest to American visitors is the record of German immigrants to the United States between 1850 and 1914. The Historic Emigration Office's microfilm file lists the names of almost 5 million people who left the Port of Hamburg for the promise of a better life in the New World. The first-floor office will research individual cases for visitors and provide information and documents. Allow an hour for this service, and expect to pay a fee of between $30 and $60.

Among the museum's many attractions are an exhibit that describes, through pictures and models, the development of the port and shipping between 1650 and 1860 and a 16th-century architectural model of Solomon's Temple measuring 11 feet square and made of five different types of wood.

Railway buffs will delight in the railway section and escape into past eras of train travel. The centerpiece of this section is a model layout of the Hamburg-to-Harburg rail link, complete with a puffing miniature steam locomotive. As a modern InterCity train is put through its paces, you may also see a 32:1 scale model of the legendary propeller-driven Reichsbahn *Zeppelin* of 1931 heading past in the opposite direction. Trains from every decade of the 20th century run strictly according to timetable on what is the largest model railway in Europe today. *Holstenwall 24, tel. 040/350–42360. Admission to the museum: DM 2 adults, 70 pf children. Open Tues.–Sun. 10–6. Historic Emigration office: open Tues.–Sat. 10–1 and 2–5.*

Return along Holstenwall to the St. Pauli U-bahn station—you are now at the start of a long, neon-lit street stretching nearly
21 half a mile as far as the eye can see. This is the **Reeperbahn**. The hottest spots in town are concentrated in the St. Pauli harbor area, on the Reeperbahn and on a little side street known as the Grosse Freiheit (or Great Freedom, and that's putting it mildly!). The shows are expensive and explicit, but to walk through this area is an experience in itself, and you can soak up the atmosphere without spending anything. It's *not* advisable, however, to travel through this part of the city alone at night.

St. Pauli is sometimes described as a "Babel of sin," but that's not entirely fair. It offers a broad menu of entertainment in addition to the striptease and sex shows. Among its other attractions are theaters, clubs, music pubs, discos, a bowling alley, and Panoptikum, the only waxworks museum in West Germany (located between the St. Pauli U-bahn and Davidstrasse). The Theater Schmidt on the Reeperbahn, a more recent arrival to the local scene, offers a repertoire of live music, vaudeville, chansons, and cabaret, while the St. Pauli Theater on Spielbudenplatz, a veteran of the age of velvet and plush, serves up a popular brand of lowbrow theater in Hamburger dialect.

It's no understatement to say that while some of the sex clubs may be relatively tame, a good many others are pornographic in the extreme. None gets going until about 10; all will accommodate you till the early hours. Order your own drinks rather than letting the hostess do it for you, pay for them as soon as they arrive, and be sure to check the price list again before handing over the money. If you order whiskey, for example, you can be sure you will not get an inexpensive brand.

Saturday night finds St. Pauli pulsating with people determined to have as much fun as possible. As the bright lights begin to fade sometime around daybreak, those who are made of
22 stern stuff continue their entertainment at the **Fischmarkt**
(Fish Market).

The Altona Fischmarkt swings into action every Sunday morning at 5 in the summer and two hours later in the winter. It is by far the most celebrated of Hamburg's many markets and is worth getting out of bed early for. If you're coming from the Reeperbahn, return to the St. Pauli U-bahn station and travel for one stop south to Landungsbrücken station. Turn right at the crossroads at the foot of the hill and walk beside the Elbe for about 200 meters, and you'll see the market stalls on the road to your left.

Sunday fish markets became a tradition in the 18th century, when fishermen used to sell their catch before church services began. Today freshly caught fish is only one of a compendium of wares on sale at the popular Fischmarkt in Altona. In fact, you can find almost anything—from live parrots and palm trees to armloads of flowers and bananas, valuable antiques to second-, third- and fourth-hand junk. You'll find plenty of bars and restaurants in the area where you can breakfast on strong coffee or even raw herring, and live jazz is played in the auction hall, the Fischauktionshalle, at Sunday morning jam sessions (Grosse Elbestrasse 9). *Fischmarkt: between Grosse Elbstr. and St. Pauli Landungsbrücken. Open Sun. 5–10 AM in summer and 7–10 AM in winter.*

A visit to the port is not complete without a tour of one of the
most modern and efficient harbors in the world. Hamburg is
Germany's largest seaport, with 33 individual docks and 500
berths lying within its 78 square kilometers (30 square miles).
Short round-trips by ferry leave from the nearby landings at
23 **Landungsbrücken.** To find the booking hall and departure
point, leave the Fischmarkt and return the way you came, but
instead of turning left up the hill to the U-bahn station, bear
right toward the long limestone building instantly recogniz-
able by its two towers. This is Landungsbrücken, the main passenger terminal for a whole range of ferry and barge rides,
both one-way and round-trip, along the waterways in, around,
and outside Hamburg. In the first-floor booking hall is the main
ticket office and information desk.

There's usually a fresh breeze, so do dress warmly enough for your trip, but don't expect rolling surf and salty air, as Hamburg's port is 56 nautical miles from the North Sea. The HADAG line and other companies organize round-trips in the port lasting about one hour and taking in several docks. *Harbor tours run year-round with frequent starting times. Fare for 1-*

hour trip: DM 12 adults, DM 6 children. In summer, the tours start at half-hourly intervals from Pier No. 2 at Landungsbrücken. In winter, tours start whenever a boat is full.

You can combine an evening trip around the harbor with a cold buffet dinner, as much beer as you can drink, and dancing on a "party ship." Book at the HADAG pavilion on Landungsbrücken (tel. 040/313–687). Fare: DM 49. Departures May 3–Dec. 6 at 8 PM.

One trip you should try to make is to the waterside village of
24 **Blankenese,** 14 kilometers (9 miles) west of Hamburg. Take a ferry from Landungsbrücken to get there. But you'll need plenty of energy when you arrive to tackle the 58 flights of steep and narrow lanes crisscrossing the hills and valleys of the village.

Blankenese is another of Hamburg's surprises—a city suburb with the character of a quaint fishing village. Some Germans like to compare it to the French and Italian Rivieras. Many of them consider it the most beautiful part of Hamburg. In the 14th century Blankenese was an important ferry point, but it wasn't until the late-18th and 19th centuries that it became a popular residential area.

You have a choice of transportation back to the city—by ferry, by S-bahn, or on foot. The celebrated Elbe River walk is long—about 8 miles (13 kilometers) from Blankenese to Landungsbrücken—but it's one of Hamburg's finest.

Shopping

Hamburg's bargain-shopping street is central **Mönckebergstrasse,** which is where you'll find the leading chain stores: **Kaufhof, Karstadt,** and **Hertie.** All three offer quality German-made clothing, household goods, china and glassware, and local souvenirs at moderate prices. The standard Hamburg souvenir is a *Buddelschiffe*—a ship in a bottle, a curiosity that Hamburg seems to lead the world in producing. Specimens are not particularly cheap, but you might find an affordable example at **Binikowski** (Lokstedterweg 68).

On the Jungfernstieg, the elegant boulevard bordering the Binnenalster, you'll find Hamburg's best but most expensive department store, the **Alsterhaus.** Stretching south and east of the Jungfernstieg is Europe's largest enclosed shopping area, a glittering collection of arcades that Hamburgers call this their "Quartier Satin." As you might expect from the nickname, the arcades don't offer much budget shopping, but you may turn up surprises in some of the smaller boutiques. Three of the best are to be found in the **Hansa Viertel,** the area of arcades at Grosse Bleiche 36. **Rügge** is excellent for glass and porcelain; the **Ramada-Shop** has a wide range of souvenirs; and **Candy and Company** is so proud of its fancy gift-wrapping that the shop promises you "won't want to give anything away." Just off central Gänsemarkt (lined by attractive shops and boutiques), you'll find, at 12 ABC-Strasse, an Aladdin's cave of novelty items (lamps shaped like bunches of bananas) and original gifts.

Food Markets and Flea Markets

There are more than 50 markets in Hamburg each week; check with the tourist office for a full listing. The most famous is the **St. Pauli Fischmarkt,** held on Sunday between 5 AM (7 AM in winter) and 10 AM. Fish is the main offering, some of it sold directly from fishing boats, but you can also find fruits and vegetables and a miscellaneous selection of bric-a-brac. It's a terrific place for early morning browsing. The market's also a traditional setting for a last beer after a night on the town. In the heart of **Blankenese,** there's a lively fruit and vegetable market on Tuesday (8 AM–2 PM), Friday (8 AM–6 PM), and Saturday (8 AM–1 PM) that offers real village charm. Take the S-Bahn to Blankenese to reach it. The **Isemarkt,** near the Hoheluftbrücke, is considered the most beautiful market in the city; it boasts around 300 stalls selling produce, fish, clothing, and toys. The market is held Tuesday and Friday 8:30 AM–2 PM.

Dining

Hamburg's basic specialty is fish in all its forms. For the most economical seafood, seek out any of the small restaurants in the port area. The most celebrated dish is probably *Aalsuppe,* eel soup, a tangy concoction not entirely unlike Marseilles's famous bouillabaisse. A must in summer is *Aalsuppe grün,* seasoned with dozens of herbs. Smoked eel, *Räucheraal,* is equally good. In fall, try *Bunte oder Gepflückte Finten,* a dish of green and white beans, carrots, and apples. Available any time of year is *Küken ragout,* a concoction of sweetbreads, spring chicken, tiny veal meatballs, asparagus, clams, and fresh peas cooked in a white sauce. Other Hamburg specialties include *Stubenküken* (chicken), *Vierländer Mastente* (duck), *Birnen, Bohnen und Speck* (pears, beans, and bacon), and the sailors' favorite, *Labskaus*—a stew made from pickled meat, potatoes, and (sometimes) herring, and garnished with a fried egg, sour pickles, and lots of beets.

Meat-eaters will appreciate both the **Block House** chain, which has no less than 15 steak restaurants in Hamburg, and the **Denver** chain, whose five restaurants present a larger selection of both meat and seafood. These restaurants aren't fancy, of course, but they're a step up from the hamburger chains. **Hopi** (Oberstr. 3) offers steaks for an unbeatable DM 11. **John Johnson** (Steindamm 43) features steaks "American-style"—large and accompanied by various relishes. One of Germany's most attractive **McDonald's** hamburger restaurants occupies a traditionally styled former guard-house on Mönckebergstrasse. Even the Chinese have a restaurant chain in Hamburg—there are four **King Du** restaurants, the most central at Colonnaden 15. All are reasonably priced and serve decent if unexceptional Chinese food. The ubiquitous German sausage costs just a couple of marks at stands on many street corners. If it's picnic weather, buy a carton of potato salad, a few slices of locally cured ham, and a corn roll or two from the food department of any of the chain stores on Mönckebergstrasse, and make for the banks of the Alster to enjoy a low-cost alfresco lunch.

Highly recommended restaurants are indicated by a star ★.

Under DM 40

Ahrberg. This restaurant on the river in Blankenese has a pleasant terrace for summer dining and a cozy, wood-paneled dining room for colder days. The menu features a range of traditional German dishes and seafood specialties. *Strandweg 33, tel. 040/860–438. Reservations advised. AE, DC, MC. Closed Sun.*

★ **Ratsweinkeller.** High stone and brick arches, with ship models suspended from them, and simple wood tables set the mood at this cavernous late-19th-century haunt under the town hall. You can order a fancy or a no-nonsense meal; the fixed-price menus at lunch are a bargain. *Grosse-Johannisstr. 2, tel. 040/364–153. Reservations advised. AE, DC, MC, V. Closed Sun. and holidays.*

Under DM 30

At Nali. This is one of Hamburg's oldest and most popular Turkish restaurants. It has the added advantage of staying open till 2 AM, handy for those hankering after a late-night kebab. *Rutschbahn 11, tel. 040/410–3810. Reservations advised. AE, DC, MC, V.*

Bei Max. This is one of Hamburg's liveliest beer taverns, serving excellent local brews and hot meals until 2 AM. Take a place at one of the heavy oak tables and dig into such local delights as pickled herring and Hamburg-style potato soup (spiced with smoked pork). *Colonnaden 9, tel. 040/346–435. No reservations. No credit cards.*

★ **Fischerhaus.** Always busy (expect to share a table) and plainly decorated, this establishment offers time-honored and ultra-reliable Hamburg fish specialties. This is a great place to try eel soup. The clientele matches the food. *Fischmarkt 14, tel. 040/314–053. No reservations. No credit cards. Closed Sun. and holidays.*

Sagres. Portuguese and Spanish restaurants are part of the city's seafaring tradition, and this is one of the best. You'll probably have to wait at the bar for a table. The mood is busy and cheerful, the decor simple. *Vorsetzen 46, tel. 040/371–201. AE.*

Weinstube Dorf. You'll be sharing a table, for this basement tavern is cozily cramped. The wines are excellent, and the small menu is packed with delicious things—the fish in particular. The walls are covered with photographs of Hamburg actors; this is a favorite haunt for the nearby Schauspielhaus. *Lange Reihe 39, tel. 040/245–614. MC.*

Under DM 20

Monte Bello. Giovanni d'Alba broke away from the family concern, La Luna, to open this lower-priced restaurant on Hamburg's Friedensallee. But d'Alba lost nothing of the family touch; mangel-wurzel leaves, for instance, are among the fresh produce and herbs that garnish the pasta. Lunches start as low as DM 8. *Friedensallee 245, tel. 040/881–0201. MC. Closed Sun.*

Shanghai. Authentic Shanghai dishes form the basis of the menu at this friendly, family-run restaurant in central Hamburg, a two-minute walk from the main railway station. Midday meals can be as cheap as DM 10. The decor is a bit gloomy, but the mood is cheerful. *Ernst-Merck-Str. 8. No reservations. MC.*

Vico. This is one of the city's better Greek restaurants. The Aphrodite-Platte is a generous combination at an unbeatable DM 16.50; scampi and octopus come a couple of marks higher. The decor is more German provincial than Greek. *Lubeckerstr. 133, tel. 040/250–3614. MC. Closed Mon.*

Splurge

★ **Fischereihafen-Restaurant Hamburg.** For the best fish in Hamburg, make for this big, upscale restaurant in Altona, just west of the downtown area and located right on the Elbe. The menu changes daily, according to what's available in the fish market that morning. Expect to pay around DM 50 per person. *Grosse Elbstr. 143, tel. 040/381–816. Reservations required. Jacket and tie required. AE, MC.*

The Arts and Nightlife

The Arts

The arts flourish in this elegant metropolis. The Hamburg city ballet is one of the finest in Europe—the Ballet Festival in July is a cultural high point. Full information on upcoming events is available in the magazine *Hamburger Vorschau*—pick it up in tourist offices and most hotels for DM 2.30—and the magazine *Szene Hamburg,* sold at newsstands throughout the city for DM 4.

A number of travel agencies sell tickets for plays, concerts, and the ballet, and ticket prices reflect the high standard of the productions. But there are possibilities for acquiring cheap tickets—try the *Abendkasse* (evening cash desk) half an hour before a performance starts. You might strike it lucky and be offered a bargain by somebody handing back an unwanted ticket. You can get reductions of up to 50% on same-day theater and concert tickets at a central Hamburg agency, the Last-Minute-Kartenshop (*see* "Hamburg for Free—or Almost," *above*). Other ticket agencies include **Theaterkasse im Alsterhaus** (Jungfernstieg 16, tel. 040/359–01323); **Theaterkasse Central** (Gerhart-Hauptmann-Pl., tel. 040/324–312); and the charming boutique **Garlic,** at Grosse-Bleichen 36 (tel. 040/342–742).

Theater The city has a full program of theater year-round, though you'll need to understand German well to get the most of the productions. Leading theaters include: **Deutsches Schauspielhaus** (Kirchenallee 39, tel. 040/248–713), probably the most beautiful theater in the city, lavishly restored to its full 19th-century opulence in the early 1980s and now the most important venue in Hamburg for classical and modern theater; **Thalia-Theater** (Alstertor, tel. 040/322–666), presenting a varied program of plays old and new; the newly reopened Flora Theater, where at press time *Phantom of the Opera* was heading for a long run (corner of Alsenstr. and Stresemannstr., tel. 040/2707–5270); and **Ohnsorg-Theater** (Grosse Bleichen 23, tel. 040/350–80321), presenting works in the local dialect, which even those who know German are likely to find largely incomprehensible. The **English Theater** (Lerchenfeld 14, tel. 040/225543) may provide the antidote: As the name suggests, all productions are in English.

Concerts The **Musikhalle** (Karl-Muck-Pl., tel. 040/346–920) is Hamburg's most important concert hall; both the Hamburg Philharmonic and the Hamburg Symphony Orchestra appear regularly. Visiting orchestras from overseas are also showcased here. The **Norddeutscher Rundfunk Studio 10** (Oberstr., tel. 040/413–2504) has regular concerts by the symphony orchestra and guest appearances by visiting musicians.

Opera and Ballet The **Hamburgische Staatsoper** (Dammtorstr. 28, tel. 040/351–721) is one of the most beautiful theaters in the country and the leading north German venue for top-class opera and ballet. The **Operettenhaus** (Spielbudenpl. 1, tel. 040/270–75270) puts on light opera and musicals.

Film Movie tickets cost around DM 9–DM 13; the seats closer to the screen are usually cheaper than the ones in back (though not by much.) Films in English are sometimes shown at various central cinemas and at the **British Film Club** (Rothenbaumchaussee 34, tel. 040/448–057).

Nightlife

The Reeperbahn Whether you think it sordid or sexy, the Reeperbahn in the St. Pauli district is as central to the Hamburg scene as are the classy shops along Jungfernstieg. A walk down the street leading off it called Grosse Freiheit (an appropriate name: It means "Great Freedom"), lined with windows behind which sit prostitutes, can be quite an eye-opener. (Women on their own shouldn't head down here unless they happen to have a black belt in karate.) **Colibri** at number 34, **Safari** at number 24, and **Salambo** at number 11 are the best-known clubs, and they cater to the package-tour trade as much as to those on the prowl by themselves. Don't expect much to happen here before 10 PM.

Prices are high. If you order anything to drink, ask to see the price list first (legally, it has to be on display), and pay as soon as you're served. You can do the Reeperbahn for DM 50 or so by avoiding places with cover charges, ordering beer and paying for it as it comes (usually with an obligatory schnapps), and doggedly refusing any invitation to buy a drink for the pretty girl who has just slipped onto the bar stool next to yours. (And resist any offer of free drinks in return for participation in the live sex act or S&M show at the Salambo.)

Jazz Clubs The jazz scene in Hamburg is thriving as never before. There are more than 100 venues and few nights when you won't have a wide selection from which to choose. Among the leading clubs are: **Birdland** (Gärtnerstr. 122, tel. 040/405–277), featuring everything from traditional New Orleans sounds to avant-garde electronic noises; **Cotton Club** (Alter Steinweg 10, tel. 040/343878), Hamburg's oldest jazz club; **Fabrik** (Bamerstr. 36, tel. 040/391–565), which offers Sunday-morning *Früschoppen* (brunch) concerts at 11 (they're always packed, so get here early); and **Pö'dingsmarkt/Riverkasematten** (Rödingsmarkt/Ost-West-Str., tel. 040/367–963), one of the oldest and biggest jazz cellars in Germany, presenting a wide range of concerts.

Excursions from Hamburg

Ahrensburg

Ahrensburg lies about 25 kilometers (16 miles) northwest of Hamburg. To get there, take the S-bahn line S-4 to Ahrensburg or the U-bahn line U-1 to Ahrensburg-Ost.

One of Schleswig-Holstein's major attractions is the romantic 16th-century **Schloss Ahrensburg** (Ahrensburg Castle). Ahrensburg itself is mainly a commuter town (population 27,000); the magnificent castle and nearby **Bredenbecker Teich** lake make it well worth a day's excursion.

Surrounded by lush parkland on the banks of the Hunnau, Schloss Ahrensburg, a whitewashed-brick, moated Renaissance castle, stands much as it did when it was constructed at the end of the 16th century. Originally built by Count Peter Rantzau, it changed hands in 1759 and was remodeled inside by its new owner. The interior was again altered in the mid-19th century and recently underwent renovation.

Inside are period furniture and paintings, fine porcelain, and exquisite crystal. On the grounds stands a simple 16th-century church erected at the same time as the castle, although the west tower was completed later and Baroque alterations were made in the 18th century. The church is nestled between two rows of 12 almshouses, or *Gottesbuden* (God's cottages). *Admission: DM 3. Open Tues.–Sun. 10–12:30 and 1:30–5.*

Altes Land

Ferries depart from the Landungsbrücken boat landing in the St. Pauli district of Hamburg every hour between 9 and 5 from May through September. Take the ferry to Cranz or Lühe; the trip lasts 50 minutes.

The marshy **Altes Land** extends 30 kilometers (19 miles) west from Hamburg along the south bank of the river Elbe to the town of Stade. This traditional fruit-growing region is dotted with huge half-timbered farmhouses and crisscrossed by canals. The fertile land is a popular hiking spot, especially in spring, when the apple and cherry trees are in blossom. Some of the prettiest walks take you along the dikes running next to the rivers Este and Lühe. Much of the territory is best covered on foot, so wear your walking shoes. You may want to bring a picnic lunch as well.

From the dock at Cranz, walk south into the suburb of **Neunfelde** and visit the Baroque St. Pancras Church, with its unusual painted barrel roof. The altar inside was built in 1688, and the organ, dating from the same period, was designed by Arp Schnitger, an organ builder and local farmer.

The village of **Jork** in Lower Saxony lies some 9 kilometers (5 miles) on foot to the west of Neunfelde, just beyond the confluence of the Este and Elbe rivers. Stroll through Jork and take in the early 18th-century church and decorative farmhouses. The old windmill in nearby **Borstel** is worth a short detour.

Lühe is the ferry docking point closest to the town of Stade, but be prepared to walk about 13 kilometers (8 miles) to reach it.

Stade lies on the west edge of the Altes Land on the river Schwinge and was once a member of the Hanseatic League of trading towns. Four times the size of Jork, with a population of 45,000, the town is notable for the ruins of a rampart wall around the Altstadt (Old Town); it also contains the obligatory half-timbered houses.

Bremen and Bremerhaven

Half-hourly InterCity trains connect Hamburg's three main stations—Altona, Dammtor, and Hauptbahnhof—with Bremen; journey time is one hour. For Bremerhaven, change at Bremen; trains depart every 40 minutes or so. This leg of the trip takes another 70 minutes.

Bremen plays a central role in the delightful fable of the Bremer Stadtmusikanten, or Bremen Town Musicians, a rooster, cat, dog, and donkey quartet that came to Bremen to seek its fortune. You'll find statues of this group in various parts of the city, the most famous being a handsome bronze of the four, one perched on the back of another, to form a pyramid of sorts. This statue stands alongside the northwest corner of the Rathaus on one of Europe's most impressive market squares, bordered by the Rathaus, an imposing 900-year-old Gothic cathedral, a 16th-century guild hall, and a modern glass and steel parliament building, with a high wall of gabled town houses as backdrop.

On the square stands the famous stone statue of the knight Roland, erected in 1400. Three times larger than life, the statue serves as Bremen's shrine, good-luck piece, and symbol of freedom and independence.

The ancient Rathaus is a structure of great interest, a Gothic building that acquired a Renaissance facade in the early 17th century. The two styles combine harmoniously in the magnificent, beamed banquet hall, where painted scenes from Bremen's 1,200-year history are complemented by model galleons and sailing ships that hang from the ceiling in vivid recollection of the place such vessels have in the story of the seafaring city. Bremen is Germany's oldest and second-largest port—only Hamburg is bigger—and it has close historical seafaring ties with North America. Forty-eight kilometers (30 miles) upriver, at **Bremerhaven,** is the country's largest and most fascinating maritime museum, the **Deutsches Schiffahrtsmuseum,** with a harbor containing seven genuine old trading ships. *Admission: DM 3 adults, DM 1.50 children. Open Apr.–Sept., Tues.–Sun. 10–6.*

Bremen, together with Lübeck and Hamburg, was an early member of the Hanseatic League, and its rivalry with the larger port on the Elbe is still tangible. Though Hamburg may still claim its historical title as Germany's "door to the world," Bremen likes to boast: "But we have the key."

Charlemagne established a diocese here in the 9th century, and a 15th-century statue of him, together with seven princes, adorns the Rathaus. In its massive vaulted cellars is further evidence of the riches accumulated by Bremen in its busiest years: barrels of fine, 17th-century Rhine wine. Other bounty from farther afield formed the foundation of one of the city's many fascinating museums, the **Übersee Museum,** a unique collection of items tracing the histories and cultures of the many peoples with whom the Bremen traders came into contact. One section is devoted to North America. *Bahnhofspl. 13. Admission: DM 2 adults, 50 pf children. Open Tues.–Sun. 10–6.*

Don't leave Bremen without strolling down Böttcherstrasse, a stretch of houses and shops reconstructed between 1924 and 1931 in historical exactitude at the initiative of a Bremen coffee millionaire, Ludwig Roselius. Walk, too, through the idyllic Schnoorviertel, a jumble of houses, taverns, and shops once occupied or frequented by fishermen and tradespeople.

Lübeck

Trains leave Hamburg almost hourly for the 40-minute journey to Lübeck. Tourist office: Verkehrsverein, Beckergrube 95, tel. 0451/1228109.

Until late 1989 Lübeck bordered the now-vanished Iron Curtain on the west. The historic core of this 12th-century port is like a moated castle; the River Trave feeds the encircling canals. You'll find the first canal just over half a mile from the train station. From there, the town can easily be explored on foot.

Lübeck has been an important strategic town since the Middle Ages, when it became a chief stronghold of the Hanseatic merchant princes, who controlled trade on the Baltic Sea. Today the town is close to every German's heart—or more precisely, hip pocket, since its most famous landmark, the **Holstentor** gate, is pictured on the DM 50 note. The ancient gate, built between 1464 and 1478, is flanked by two squat round towers, solid symbols of Lübeck's prosperity as a trade center. Pass through its yawning entranceway on Holstentor Platz on your way from the train station. A short walk along Holstenstrasse brings you to the strikingly colonnaded medieval **market square,** which looks like a Hollywood backdrop for a jousting tournament. The **Rathaus** (town hall), which has undergone several architectural face-lifts since it went up in 1240, is particularly noteworthy.

From the market square, walk into Breitestrasse, turn left, and head for the 18th-century Baroque **Buddenbrookhaus,** made famous in Thomas Mann's *Buddenbrooks*. Mann's family once lived in the house. Continue along Breitestrasse and turn right into Koberg. Here you'll find the **Heiligen-Geist Spital** (Holy Ghost Hospital), one of the oldest—and most beautiful—in the world. Built in the 14th century by the town's rich merchants, it's still caring for the sick today.

At the other end of the old-town island you'll find the **Dom** (cathedral), which is Lübeck's oldest building—its foundation stone was laid in 1173 by Prince Henry the Lion, who founded the town. The Gothic hall church, which incorporates late-Romanesque and Renaissance features, was bombed during World War II but rebuilt between 1958 and 1977. Guided tours of old Lübeck, lasting approximately 90 minutes, depart daily from mid-April to mid-October and weekends from mid-October to mid-April, from outside Lübeck's smaller tourist information office on the market square. Call 0451/72339 for departure times and details.

Harbor and coastal cruises also operate out of Lübeck. Check with the Lübeck tourist office (*see above*) for details.

Lodging
Under DM 110

Altstadt. Behind the protected facade of this old building stands a hotel that opened in 1984. The Altstadt offers modern but not luxurious comforts. The studios, fitted with small kitchens, are an excellent value for those planning to stay a few days. *Fischergrube 52, tel. 0451/72083. 19 rooms with bath, 9 studios. AE, MC.*

Dining
Under DM 20

Ratskeller. In bad weather, you eat in the ancient stone cellars; when the sun shines, there's an outdoor terrace on the market square. The specialty is Baltic Sea fish, particularly flounder and baked eel. *Am Markt 13, tel. 0451/72044. No credit cards.*

Under DM 15

Niederegger. This famous café in the heart of the old town, close to the Rathaus, has been making cakes and marzipan concoctions since 1806. A range of cooked dishes, priced from DM 8, is available, too. It's open daily until 6. *Breitestr. 89, tel. 0451/53007. No credit cards.*

13 Berlin

With Walking Tours of West and East

Berlin is settling back into its role as Germany's major city: not just the nation's cultural capital but—with the historic vote by the German parliament on June 20, 1991, to return the seat of the government to its historic home—once again its political capital, too. For nearly 40 years it was a city split in two by a 10-foot-high concrete wall, with its larger western half an island of capitalist democracy, surrounded by an East Germany run by hard-line Stalinist Communists. Built in 1961 at the height of the Cold War, the Berlin Wall symbolized the separation of two distinctly different political and economic systems. Ironically, though, it also became a major tourist attraction, where viewing platforms along the western side enabled visitors to see the battlefront-like No Man's Land, guarded by soldiers and peppered with deadly mines and booby traps. The Wall's demolition cast it once more as a symbol: this time, though, a symbol of the change sweeping over former Iron Curtain countries. Two large chunks of the Wall have been left standing as reminders of the grim past.

Berlin actually began as two cities, more than 750 years ago. Museum Island, on the Spree River, was once called Cölln, while the mainland city was always known as Berlin. As early as the 1300s, Berlin prospered from its location at the crossroads of important trade routes, and it became filled with merchants and artisans of every description. After the ravages of the Thirty Years' War (1618–48), Berlin rose to power as the seat of the Brandenburg dynasty, and 200 years later when the Brandenburgian and Prussian realms united under the Hohenzollerns, Berlin was the chosen capital. The 1701 coronation of the enlightened ruler King Friedrich II—also known as Frederick the Great—set off a renaissance in the city, especially in the construction of academic institutions such as the Academy of Arts and the Academy of Sciences.

The Prussian empire, especially under Count Bismarck in the late-19th century, proved to be the dominant force in unifying the many independent German principalities. Berlin maintained its status as the German capital throughout the German Empire (1871–1918), the post–World War I Weimar Republic (1919–33), and Hitler's Third Reich (1933–45). In the 1920s and early '30s the city also served as an important European social and cultural capital, tinged with a reputation for decadence. But during World War II, acting as the Nazi headquarters, it was bombed to smithereens—at the end of hostilities there was more rubble in Berlin than in all other German cities combined. Most of what you see there today has been built, or rebuilt, since 1945.

With the division of Germany after World War II, Berlin also was partitioned, with American, British, and French troops in the districts to the west, the Soviet Union's forces to the east.

After the Potsdam Agreement in 1945, the three western zones of occupation gradually merged into one, becoming West Berlin, while the Soviet-controlled eastern zone defiantly remained separate. In 1948, in an attempt to force the Western Allies to relinquish their stake in the city, the U.S.S.R. set up a blockade cutting off all overland supply routes from the West. The Western Allies countered by mounting the Berlin Airlift, during which some 750,000 flights delivering 2 million tons of goods kept Berlin alive for most of a fateful year, until the Soviets finally lifted the blockade. As peace conferences repeatedly failed to resolve the question of Germany's division, the Soviets in 1949 established East Berlin as the capital of its new puppet state in East Germany.

West Berlin was not technically part of the West German republic, though it was clearly tied to its legal and economic system. The division of the city was emphasized even more in 1961 when the East Germans constructed the infamous Berlin Wall. With the Wall now on the junk pile of history, access is easy to the eastern part of the city, where visitors can at last appreciate the qualities that mark the city as a whole. Its particular charm always lay in its spaciousness, its trees and greenery, its racy atmosphere, and the ease with which you could reach the lakes and forests within its perimeter. It is a vast city, laid out on an epic scale—West Berlin alone is four times the size of Paris. Whole towns and villages are inlaid into the countryside beyond the downtown area. The really stunning parts of the pre-war capital are in the eastern sector, with its grand boulevards and monumental buildings, the classical Brandenburg Gate, and the stately tree-lined avenue of Unter den Linden.

What really makes Berlin special, however, are the intangibles—the spirit and bounce of the city. Here is life in a pressure cooker, life on the edge—literally and figuratively. Berliners of whatever age are survivors; they have lived with adversity all their lives, and have managed to do so with a mordant wit and cynical acceptance of life as it is rather than the way one hopes it might be.

Berliners are brash, no-nonsense types, who speak German with their own racy dialect. Their high-voltage energy is invariably attributed to the bracing Berlin air, the renowned *Berliner Luft.* Crisis has been a way of life here for as long as anyone can remember. "To survive with a measure of style and humor" could serve as the city's theme.

Essential Information

More than two years after the official unification of the two Germanys, the nuts-and-bolts work of joining up the two halves is by no means complete, and uncertainties still abound. We have given addresses, telephone numbers, and other logistical details based on the best available information, but please understand that changes are taking place at a furious pace in everything from street names to postal codes and telephone numbers. At press time (early summer 1991) callers from West Berlin to East Berlin dial "9" instead of the "02" city code. Callers from East Berlin to West Berlin dial "849" instead of the "030" city code. These procedures apply only to calls within Berlin. It is highly likely that by the spring of 1992 admission will be charged for public museums in West Berlin that are currently free, and that admission prices at East Berlin public museums will rise to equal those of their western counterparts.

Important Addresses and Numbers

Tourist Information The **Verkehrsamt Berlin** (main tourist office) is located in the heart of the city in the Europa Center (tel. 030/262–6031). If you want materials on the city before your trip, write **Verkehrsamt Berlin Europa Center** (D-1000 Berlin 30). For information on the spot, the office is open daily 7:30 AM–10:30 PM. There are also offices at **Tegel Airport** (tel. 030/410–13145; open daily 8 AM–11 PM); **Bahnhof Zoo** train station (tel. 030/313–9063; open daily 8 AM–11 PM); and at the former **Dreilinden** border crossing (tel. 030/803–9057; open daily 8 AM–11 PM). Berlin has an information center especially for women, offering help with accommodations and information on upcoming events. Contact **Fraueninfothek Berlin** (Leibizstr. 57, tel. 030/324–5078; open Tues.–Sat. 9–9, Sun. and public holidays 9–3).

The main office of the **Reisebüro** (the former East German tourist office) is at Alexanderplatz 5 (tel. 02/212–4675 or 02/210–4209; open Mon.–Fri. 8 AM–8 PM, Sat. 9–6). There's another branch at **Schönefeld Airport** (tel. 02/687–8248).

For information on all aspects of the city, pick up a copy of *Berlin Turns On,* free from any tourist office.

Embassies and Consulates **United States Consulate** (Clayallee 170, tel. 030/832–4087); **British Consulate** (Uhlandstr. 7–8, tel. 030/309–5292).

Following the unification of the city, the American and British embassies in former East Berlin have taken on the character of information centers. The **American** office is still at Neustädtische Kirchstrasse 4–5 (tel. 02/220–2741) and the **British** office remains at Unter den Linden 32–34 (tel. 02/220–2431). **Canada** has a Consulate-General at the Europa Center (tel. 030/2611161).

Emergencies **Police** (tel. 030/110). **Ambulance and emergency medical attention** (tel. 030/310–031). **Dentist** (tel. 030/1141 or after 9 PM, tel.

030/892–0379). **Pharmacies** in Berlin offer late-night service on a rotation basis. Every pharmacy displays a notice indicating the location of the nearest shop with evening hours. For emergency pharmaceutical assistance, call tel. 030/1141 or 030/247033.

English-language Bookstores **Marga Schoeller** (Knesebeckstr. 33, tel. 030/881–1112). **Buchhandlung Kiepert** (Hardenbergstr. 4–5, tel. 030/331-0090).

Travel Agencies **American Express Reisebüro** (Kurfürstendamm 11, tel. 030/882–7575). **American Lloyd** (Kurfürstendamm 36, tel. 030/883-7081).

Car Rental **Avis** (Tegel Airport, tel. 030/410–13148; Budapesterstr. 43, Am Europa Center, tel. 030/261–1881; Haus der Reise, Alexanderplatz 5, tel. 02/2125575).

Europcar (Kurfurstenstr. 101, tel. 030/213–7097).

Hertz (Tegel Airport, tel. 030/410–13315; Budapesterstr. 39, tel. 030/261–1053).

Where to Change Money The bank with the longest hours is the **Wechselstube** in the Bahnhof Zoo railway station. It's open Monday to Saturday 9–9, Sunday and public holidays 10–6. At other hours the leading hotels will change money, but at comparatively unfavorable rates.

Arriving and Departing by Plane

Airlines flying to West Berlin's **Tegel Airport** from major U.S. and European cities include Pan Am, TWA, Air France, British Airways, Lufthansa, Euro-Berlin, and some charter companies. Because of increased air traffic following unification, the former military airfield at Tempelhof is being used increasingly. Despite substantial government subsidies, domestic fares are high. Tegel is the most comfortable and best-equipped airport for international travelers, and it's only 6 kilometers (4 miles) from downtown Berlin. Tempelhof is even closer. Since most international flights start and end at Tegel, that's probably the airport you'll be using; for information on arrival and departure times there, call tel. 030/41011.

East Berlin's **Schönefeld Airport** is about 24 kilometers (15 miles) outside the downtown area. It is used principally by Soviet and Eastern European airlines, although with the increase in flights to Tegel, it's been taking more and more charter traffic. For information on arrival and departure times call tel. 02/672–4031. The former East German state airline, Interflug, has folded.

Between the Airport and Downtown A direct bus service links Tegel and Schönefeld, traversing the center of the city. There are six stops on the 31-kilometer (19-mile) route, four of them in the center of the city, handy to major hotels and shopping areas. The blue-white-and-yellow Airport-Transfer bus leaves each airport every half-hour and takes 80 minutes to cover the route. The travel time from each airport to the city center is 30–40 minutes. The fare for the Tegel–Schönefeld stretch is DM 15 adults (DM 7.50 children); for the stretch between Tegel and downtown, DM 7 (DM 3.50); and between Schönefeld and downtown, DM 10 (DM 5). Two other city bus services—Nos. 8 and 9—run regularly between Tegel and downtown.

Arriving and Departing by Train and Bus

By Train There are five major rail routes to Berlin from the western half of the country (from Hamburg, Hanover, Köln, Frankfurt, and Nürnberg) and the network is set to expand to make eastern German territory more accessible. At press time, trains are jointly run by the former East German Deutsche Reichsbahn (DR) and former West Germany's Deutsche Bundesbahn (DB), and reduced-price DB tickets are accepted. Check out the 10-day "Berlin Saver Ticket," sold at West German stations; it offers reductions of 33%. Trains from western Germany arrive at Berlin's main terminus, Bahnhof Zoologischer Garten (Bahnhof Zoo). The U-bahn (subway) and S-bahn (suburban railroad) stop here, too. Eastern Berlin's chief stations are at Friedrichstrasse or the Ostbahnhof. For details, call **Deutsche Bundesbahn Information** (tel. 030/19419) or **Deutsche Reichsbahn** (tel. 030/311–02116); **reservations** (tel. 030/311–0221–12).

By Bus Buses are slightly cheaper than trains; Berlin is linked by bus to 170 European cities. The main station is at the corner of Masurenallee and Messedam. Reserve through DER (state), commercial travel agencies, or the station itself. For information, call tel. 030/301–8028.

Getting Around

By Public Transportation Berlin is too large to be explored on foot. To compensate, the city has one of the most efficient public transportation systems in Europe, a smoothly integrated network of subway (U-bahn) and elevated (S-bahn) train lines, buses, trams (in East Berlin only), and even a ferry (across the Wannsee Lake), making every part of the city easily accessible. There's also an all-night bus service, indicated by the letter "N" next to route numbers. In summer, there are excursion buses linking the downtown area with the most popular recreation areas.

A DM 3 ticket (DM 2 for children) covers the entire system for two hours and allows you to make an unlimited number of changes between trains and buses. The best deal for visitors who plan to travel extensively around the city is the **Berlin Ticket,** valid for 24 hours and good for all trains and buses; it costs DM 12 (DM 6 for children). A six-day pass allowing unlimited travel on all city buses and trains between Monday and Saturday costs DM 28. If you plan to visit the Wannsee Lake, buy the **combined day ticket,** good for the entire network and the excursion boats of the Stern- und Kreisschiffahrt line; it costs DM 18.50 (DM 9.30 for children). If you are just making a short trip, buy a **Kurzstreckentarif.** It allows you to ride six bus stops or three U-bahn or S-bahn stops for DM 2 (DM 1.20 for children). Buy it in packs of five for the best value (DM 7 adults, DM 5 children). Finally, there's a ticket good only for rides along the Kurfürstendamm on buses 119 and 129; it costs DM 1.

All regular tickets are available from vending machines at U-bahn and S-bahn stations. Punch your ticket into the red machine on the platform. The Berlin Ticket and the combined day ticket can only be bought from the main BVG ticket offices at the Bahnhof Zoo station and at the Kleistpark U-bahn station. For information, either call the **BVG** (Berliner Verkehrsbetriebe, tel. 030/216–5088) or go to the information office on

Hardenbergplatz, directly in front of the Bahnhof Zoo train station.

The fare structure now covers transportation systems for both parts of Berlin, although cheap, subsidized tickets are still sold to East Berlin residents. Don't be tempted to buy one if you're traveling in East Berlin (it's difficult to do that anyway, because East Berliners normally have to show their identity documents in order to take advantage of the special fare); the fine is hefty if unauthorized travelers are found in possession of subsidized tickets. It doesn't help, either, to plead ignorance as a foreigner. For visitors and west Berlin residents, the fares are the same in both halves of the now-united city.

By Taxi Fares start at DM 3.40 and increase by DM 1.69 per kilometer (DM 2.69 after midnight). There's an additional charge of 50 pfennigs per piece of luggage. Figure on paying around DM 10 for a ride the length of the Kurfürstendamm. Hail cabs in the street or order one by calling tel. 030/6902, 030/21660, 030/261–026, 030/240–024, or 030/240–202, or 02/3646 in East Berlin.

By Bike Bicycling is popular in Berlin. While it's not recommended in the downtown area, it's ideal in outlying areas. Some bike paths have been set up and many stores that rent bikes carry the Berlin biker's atlas to help you find them. Outfits renting bicycles include: **Fahrradbüro** Berlin (Hauptstr. 146, tel. 030/784–5562), and **Räderwerk** (Körtestr. 14, by U-bahn station Südstern, tel. 030/691–8590), which offers a week's rental for only DM 40; for bike rental in the Grunewald forest go to the S-bahn station Grunewald, tel. 030/8115829.

Opening and Closing Times

Berlin shops usually stay open weekdays from 8:30 or 9 until 6 or 6:30, but only until 1 or 2 on Saturday. The larger shops and department stores stay open until 8 on Thursday. Banks are usually open weekdays 8–12:30 and 2–4; post offices, weekdays 8–6, Saturday 8–noon. The post office at the Bahnhof Zoo is open 24 hours daily.

Lodging

Berlin—particularly the eastern half of Berlin—suffers from a lack of reasonably priced accommodations. A crash program to boost East Berlin's hotel market is now under way, but it will be at least two years before any effect is felt. For now don't bother to look for a budget hotel in East Berlin. In the western half of the city, consider settling for a hotel in one of the outlying suburbs, such as Dahlem or Schöneberg. The city's excellent public transport system will guarantee you swift and regular access to the center from wherever you are staying. In the center, small, cheap pensions can be found in the side streets off the famous Kurfürstendamm (or Ku'damm), but the best of them are booked well in advance. On weekends, when the business travelers leave town, the bigger hotel chains offer reduced rates, which can sometimes make an expensive establishment enticingly affordable. The most spectacular weekend deal comes from InterContinental and Forum hotels, which charge as little as DM 120 a night for a double room. Call their toll-free number, 0130–3955 (no area code), for details and res-

Berlin Public Transit System

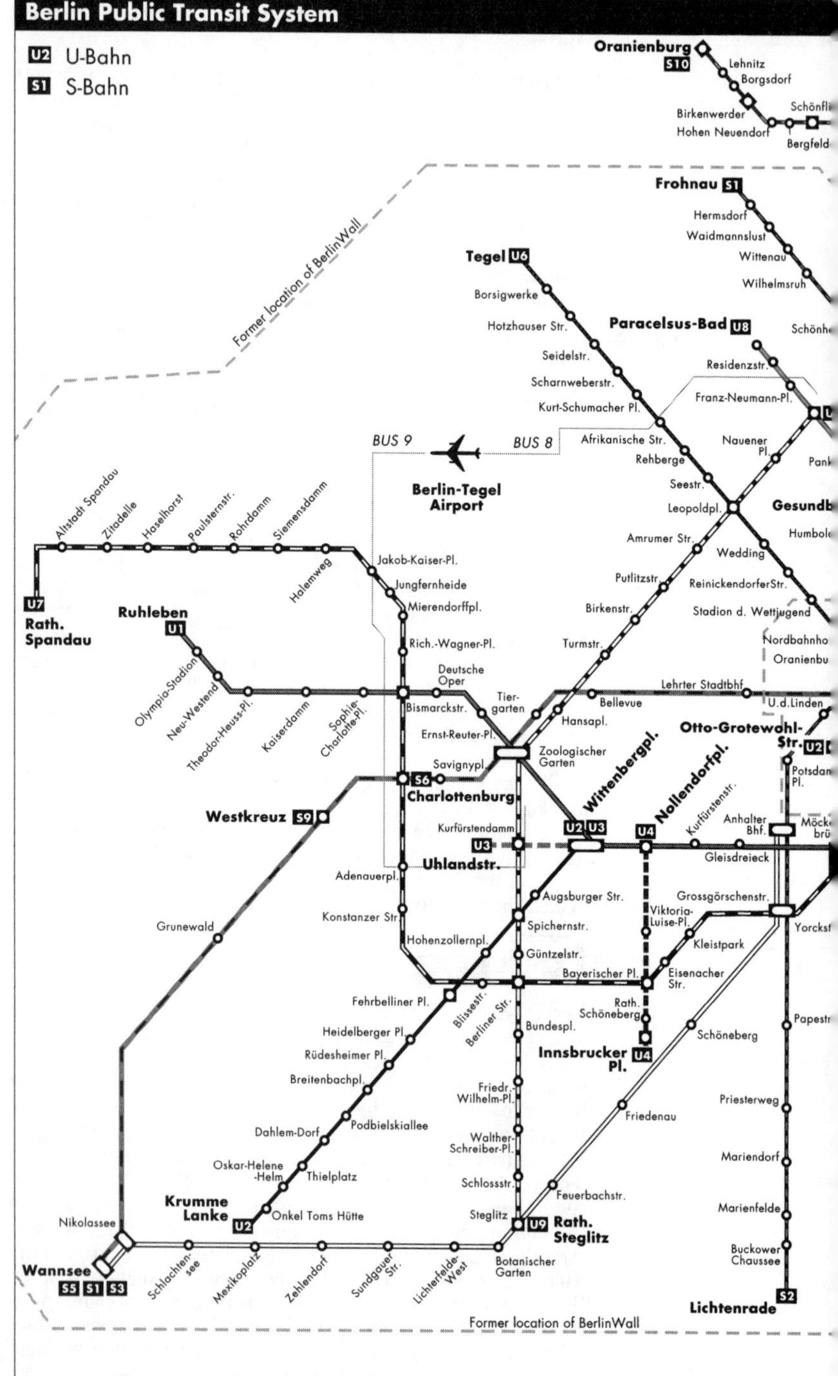

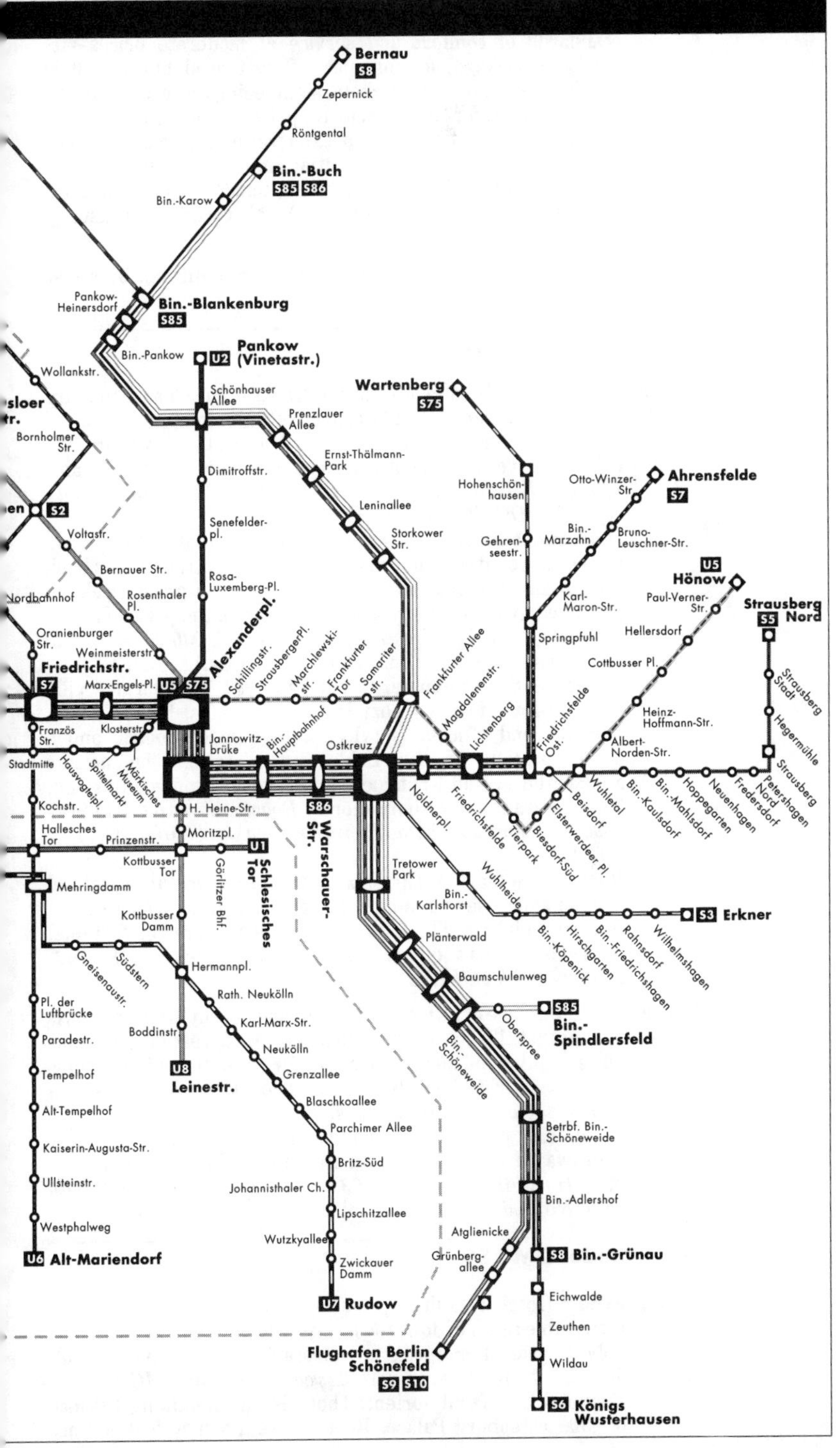

Bernau
S8
Zepernick
Röntgental
Bln.-Buch
S85 S86
Bln.-Karow
Pankow-Heinersdorf
Bln.-Blankenburg
S85
Bln.-Pankow
Pankow (Vinetastr.)
U2
Wollankstr.
Bornholmer Str.
S2
Voltastr.
Bernauer Str.
Nordbahnhof
Rosenthaler Pl.
Oranienburger Str.
Weinmeisterstr.
Friedrichstr.
S7
Marx-Engels-Pl.
U5 S75
Alexanderpl.
Schönhauser Allee
Dimitroffstr.
Senefelder-pl.
Rosa-Luxemberg-Pl.
Prenzlauer Allee
Ernst-Thälmann-Park
Leninallee
Storkower Str.
Wartenberg
S75
Hohenschön-hausen
Gehren-seestr.
Otto-Winzer-Str.
Ahrensfelde
S7
Bln.-Marzahn
Bruno-Leuschner-Str.
Karl-Maron-Str.
Springpfuhl
U5
Hönow
Paul-Verner-Str.
Hellersdorf
Strausberg Nord
S5
Strausberg Stadt
Hegermühle
Strausberg
Cottbusser Pl.
Heinz-Hoffmann-Str.
Albert-Norden-Str.
Schillingstr.
StrausbergerPl.
Marchlewski-str.
Frankfurter Tor
Samariter-str.
Frankfurter Allee
Magdalenenstr.
Lichtenberg
Friedrichsfelde Ost
Französ Str.
Klosterstr.
Jannowitz-brüke
Bln.-Hauptbahnhof
Ostkreuz
Stadtmitte
Hausvogteipl.
Spittelmarkt
Märkisches Museum
Kochstr.
H. Heine-Str.
Moritzpl.
Hallesches Tor
Prinzenstr.
Kottbusser Tor
U1
Görlitzer Bhf.
Schlesisches Tor
S86
Warschauer-Str.
Nöldnerpl.
Friedrichsfelde
Tierpark
Biesdorf-Süd
Elsterwerdeer Pl.
Beisdorf
Wuhletal
Bln.-Kaulsdorf
Bln.-Mahlsdorf
Hoppegarten
Neuenhagen
Fredersdorf
Petershagen Nord
Mehringdamm
Tretower Park
Bln.-Karlshorst
Wuhlheide
S3 Erkner
Bln.-Köpenick
Hirschgarten
Bln.-Friedrichshagen
Rahnsdorf
Wilhelmshagen
Kottbusser Damm
Gneisenaustr.
Südstern
Hermannpl.
Rath. Neukölln
Karl-Marx-Str.
Neukölln
Grenzallee
Blaschkoallee
Parchimer Allee
Britz-Süd
Johannisthaler Ch.
Lipschitzallee
Wutzkyallee
Zwickauer Damm
U7 Rudow
Plänterwald
Baumschulenweg
Oberspree
S85
Bln.-Spindlersfeld
Bln.-Schöneweide
Betrbf. Bln.-Schöneweide
Bln.-Adlershof
Atglienicke
Grünberg-allee
S8 Bln.-Grünau
Eichwalde
Zeuthen
Wildau
S6 Königs Wusterhausen
Flughafen Berlin Schönefeld
S9 S10
Pl. der Luftbrücke
Paradestr.
Tempelhof
Alt-Tempelhof
Kaiserin-Augusta-Str.
Ullsteinstr.
Westphalweg
U6 Alt-Mariendorf
Boddinstr.
U8
Leinestr.

ervations. The Ringhotel chain has built a reputation for high standards of comfort and service at moderate prices—its weekend package, for instance, offers two nights in central Berlin, theater or opera tickets, sightseeing tours, and a bottle of champagne, for the all-inclusive price of DM 299 per person. Hotel accommodation can be booked free of charge at all of Berlin's tourist offices (*see* Essential Information, *above*). The cheaper hotels and pensions usually include breakfast in their rates, but it's advisable to check. Double occupancy is usually about 30% higher than single rates.

Highly recommended establishments are indicated by a star ★.

Under DM 180

West Berlin

★ **Casino Hotel.** What was once a barracks in the Charlottenburg district has been skillfully converted into an appealing hotel with large, comfortable rooms. You'll detect the Bavarian owner's influence in the south German cuisine at the restaurant. *Königen-Elisabeth-Str. 47a, tel. 030/303–090. 24 rooms with bath. AE, DC, MC, V.*

Hotel Hamburg. The Ring group's Berlin establishment offers all the expected comforts in a quiet, handy location. If you book well in advance you can take advantage of a great weekend package (*see above*) for not much more than the price of a one-night stay. *Landgrafenstr. 4, Berlin 30, tel. 030/269–161. 240 rooms with bath. Facilities: restaurant, bar. AE, DC, MC, V.*

★ **Landhaus Schlachtensee.** Opened in 1987, this former villa (built in 1905) is now a cozy bed-and-breakfast hotel offering personal and efficient service, well-equipped rooms, and a quiet location in the Zehlendorf district. The nearby Schlachtensee and Krumme Lanke lakes beckon you to swim, boat, or walk along their shores. *Bogotastr. 9, tel. 030/816–0060. 19 rooms with bath. Facilities: breakfast buffet. AE, DC, MC, V.*

Riehmers Hofgarten. This small hotel in the colorful Kreuzberg district and close to Tempelhof airport is housed in a late-19th-century building. The high-ceilinged rooms are comfortable, with crisp linens and firm beds. *Yorckstr. 83, tel. 030/781–011. 21 rooms with bath. AE, DC, MC, V.*

East Berlin

★ **Adria.** Because of its moderate price and decent location, this is a hotel that fills up fairly far in advance. Its restaurant is also quite popular and inexpensive. Try for one of the quieter rooms at the back. *Friedrichstr. 134, tel. 02/2805105. 67 rooms with bath or shower. No credit cards.*

Newa. This popular older hotel is just a 10-minute streetcar ride away from the downtown area. Rooms in the back are quieter. *Invalidenstr. 115, tel. 02/282–5461. 57 rooms, most with bath. No credit cards.*

Under DM 130

West Berlin

Atrium Hotel. This little privately run hotel is located within reasonable reach of downtown. The modest rooms are comfortably furnished and clean, the staff efficient and helpful. *Motzstr. 87, tel. 030/244–057. 22 rooms with bath. MC.*

Econotel. This family-oriented hotel is within walking distance of Charlottenburg Palace. Rooms have a homey feel and are spotlessly clean. *Sommeringstr. 24, tel. 030/344–001. 205 rooms with bath. Facilities: snack bar. MC.*

Herbst. A plain and simple bed-and-breakfast pension in the Spandau district, where Hitler's mysterious deputy Rudolph Hess spent more than 40 years in jail, the Herbst has good connections to downtown by S-Bahn. *Moritzstr. 21, tel. 030/333–4032. 22 rooms with bath. AE, DC.*

Hotel-Pension Ambiente. Glistening dark-wood furniture contrasts with pale walls in this attractive lodging on a covenient corner of central Olivaerplatz. Most rooms have a fine view of the square and the Ku'damm. The Adenauerplatz underground station is two minutes away. *Konstanzer Str. 1, tel. 030/880–0070. 42 rooms with bath. AE, MC.*

Hotel Pension Arco. It's earned three stars, for comfort and friendly management, from a leading German consumer group. The rooms are small but individually furnished. The price includes a buffet breakfast, and if you settle for a room without bath you can bring it down below DM 90. The Ku'damm location is right in the thick of things. *Kurfürustendamm 30, tel. 030/881–9902. 21 rooms, 16 with bath. No credit cards.*

Hotel-Pension Arka. Try for one of the rooms under the mansard roof; the others can be cramped, but they're all comfortably furnished and spotlessly clean. A beamed lounge-restaurant with open hearth is one of the pleasant surprises behind the austere modern facade. The Ku'damm is right outside the front door; Halensee is the nearest S-bahn station. *Kurfürstendamm 103–104, tel. 030/892–9888. 40 rooms, most with bath (those without are up to DM 70 cheaper). AE, MC, V.*

★ **Hotel-Pension Dittberner.** Here you'll find a touch of grand-hotel luxury: thick carpeting, velvet drapes, comfortable armchairs in the large bedrooms, and Oriental rugs, screens, and antiques in the public rooms. The Ku'damm is two minutes away. *Wielandstr. 26, tel. 030/881–6485. 17 rooms, 10 with bath. MC.*

Ravenna. A small, friendly hotel in the Steglitz district, Ravenna is near the Botanical Garden and Dahlem museums. All the rooms are well equipped. *Grunewaldstr. 8–9, tel. 030/792–8031. 45 rooms with bath. AE, DC, MC, V.*

East Berlin

Charlottenhof. This popular hotel-pension on East Berlin's beautiful Platz der Akademie was acquired by a large West German group in 1991, and by 1992 it should have reopened in fine new style. If the moderate prices and friendly atmosphere remain, it will rank high among East Berlin's lodgings. *Charlottenstr. 52, tel. 02/356–754. 86 rooms with bath. AE, DC, MC, V.*

★ **Hospiz am Bahnhof Friedrichstrasse.** This Evangelical church-run hostel, both because of price and a convenient location, gets booked up months in advance. It is enormously popular with families, so the public areas are not always particularly restful. The restaurant is cheap and usually busy. *Albrechstr. 8, tel. 02/282–5396. 110 rooms, most with bath. No credit cards.*

Hospiz Auguststrasse. Comfortable rooms and friendly staff make this very low-priced hotel—also run by the Evangelical church—appealing. It is roughly a 10-minute streetcar ride into downtown Berlin. Breakfast is the only meal served here. *Augustr. 82, tel. 02/282–5321. 70 rooms, some with bath. No credit cards.*

Hotel Krone. The Krone, opened in 1991, shares the Dom Hotel's excellent location on East Berlin's Platz der Akademie.

Berlin Lodging

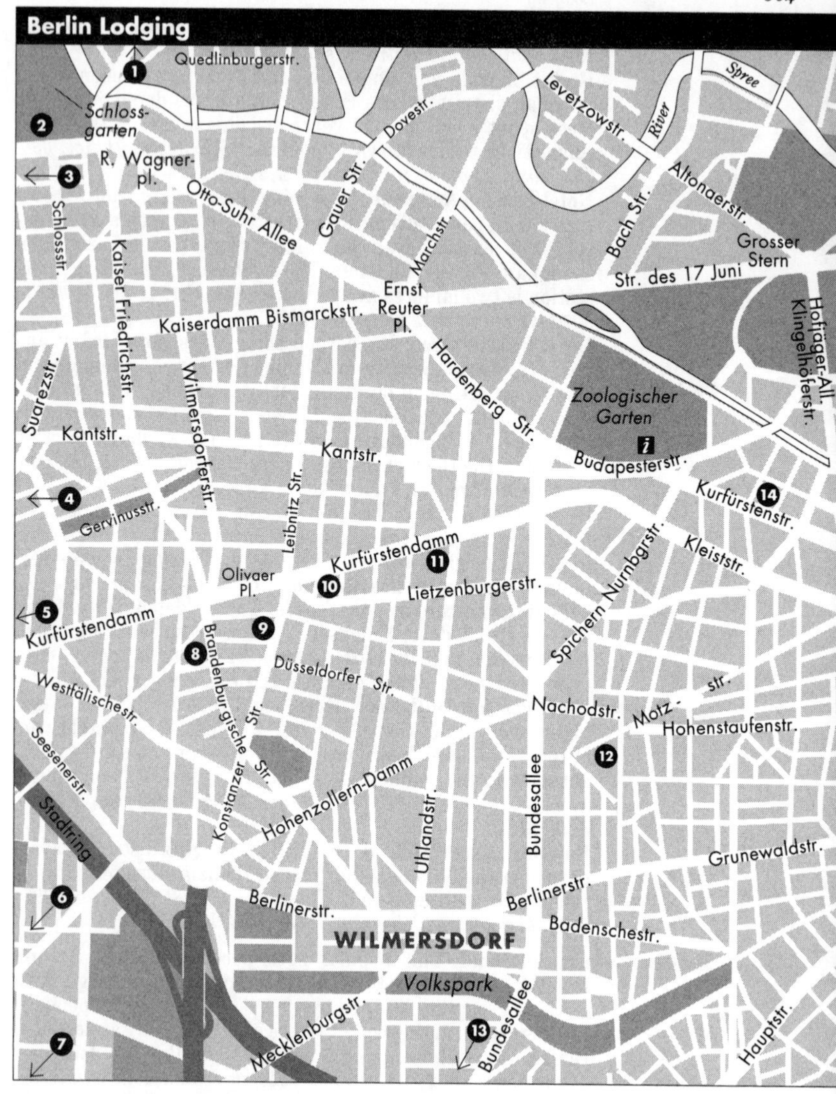

Adria, **19**
Atrium Hotel, **12**
Casino Hotel, **3**
Charlottenhof, **23**
Econotel, **2**
Ernst-Reuter Haus, **1**
Gästehaus am Wannsee, **7**
Gästehaus Berlin, **16**
Grand Hotel Esplanade, **15**
Herbst, **4**
Hospiz Auguststrasse, **20**
Hospiz am Bahnhof Friedrichstrasse, **18**
Hotel Hamburg, **14**
Hotel Krone, **22**
Hotel-Pension Ambiente, **9**
Hotel-Pension Arco, **11**
Hotel-Pension Arka, **5**
Hotel-Pension Dittberner, **10**
Landhaus Schlachtensee, **6**
Newa, **21**
Ravenna, **13**
Riehmers Hofgarten, **17**
Savigny, **8**

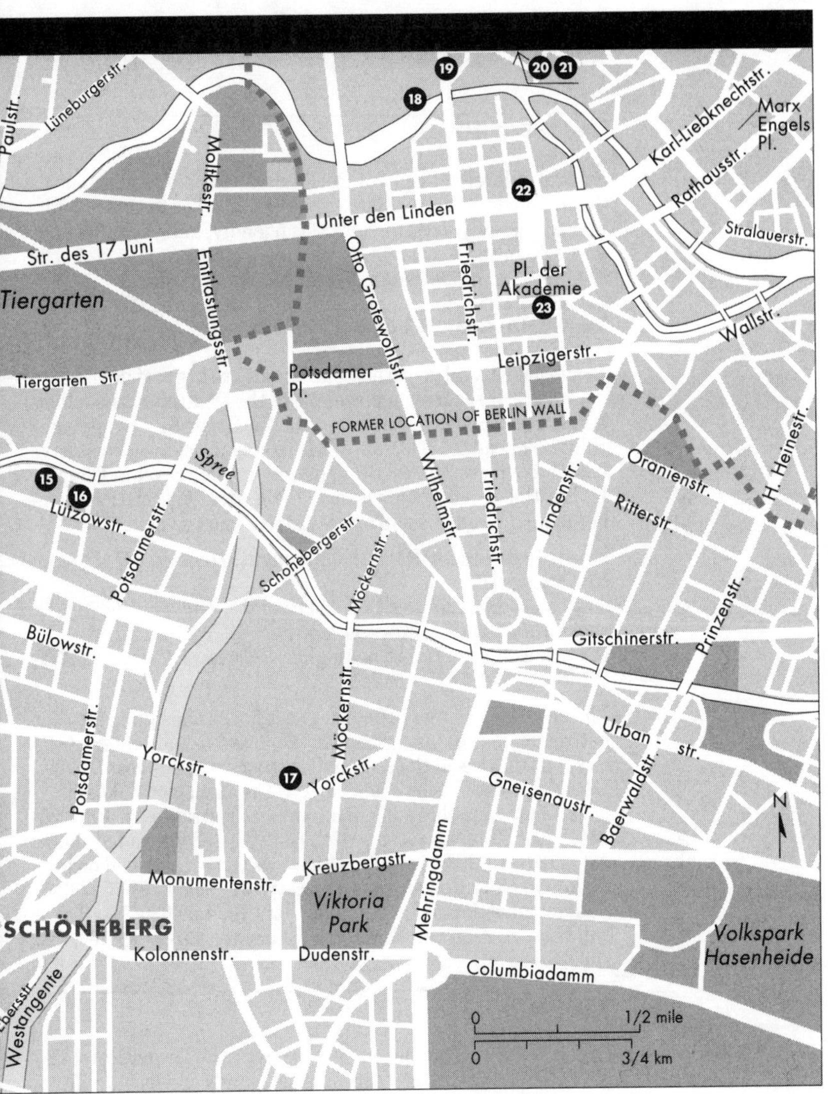

Paulstr.
Lüneburgerstr.
Moltkestr.
Unter den Linden
Str. des 17 Juni
Tiergarten
Entlastungsstr.
Otto Grotewohlstr.
Friedrichstr.
Pl. der Akademie
Karl-Liebknechtstr.
Marx Engels Pl.
Rathausstr.
Stralauerstr.
Wallstr.
Leipzigerstr.
Tiergarten Str.
Potsdamer Pl.
FORMER LOCATION OF BERLIN WALL
Spree
Lützowstr.
Potsdamerstr.
Schönebergerstr.
Möckernstr.
Wilhelmstr.
Friedrichstr.
Lindenstr.
Oranienstr.
Ritterstr.
H. Heinestr.
Bülowstr.
Gitschinerstr.
Prinzenstr.
Potsdamerstr.
Yorckstr.
Möckernstr.
Yorckstr.
Urban str.
Gneisenaustr.
Baerwaldstr.
N
Monumentenstr.
Kreuzbergstr.
Viktoria Park
Mehringdamm
SCHÖNEBERG
Kolonnenstr.
Dudenstr.
Columbiadamm
Volkspark Hasenheide
Eberstr.
Westangente
0
1/2 mile
0
3/4 km
15
16
17
18
19
20
21
22
23

The rooms are comfortable and adequately furnished. *Platz der Akademie, tel. 02/988–255. 148 rooms with bath. AE, DC, MC, V.*

Under DM 90

West Berlin **Savigny.** Hotels in central Berlin don't come any cheaper—a double, including breakfast, costs DM 70. The rooms are furnished basically, but the service is friendly, and you're just 500 yards from the Ku'damm. *Brandenburgische Str. 21, tel. 030/881–3001. 50 rooms without bath. No credit cards.*

Youth Hostels and Guest Houses

Berlin has several youth hostels. Rooms are in great demand; to make sure of securing a place, write the **Deutsches Jugendherbergswerk** (Landesverband Berlin e.V., Berlin 61, Templehofer Ufer 32) or call tel. 030/262–3024. To stay in one, you must have hostel membership (*see* Student and Youth Travel in Chapter 1), but this can be purchased at the hostel. Association membership is the only requirement; there is no age limit.

Ernst-Reuter Haus. DM 17.90 per night. *Hemersdorf (U-bahn station Tegel).*
Gästehaus am Wannsee. DM 22 per night. *Right on the lake, a short walk from the Wannsee station.*
Gästehaus Berlin. DM 22 per night. *Kluckstr. 3, Tiergarten (U-bahn station Kurfürstendamm).*

The city also has more than 20 guest houses designed for (but not restricted to) young people. None are in the center of the city, but they're all close to public transport. Beds cost DM 20–DM 40; private baths are a rarity. The **Haus der Zukunft** organization runs three of them, at Goethestrasse 37 (tel. 030/801–8704), Hagenstrasse 30 (tel. 030/826–38830), and Stuhmer Allee 12 (tel. 030/304–7495). Others we can recommend include **Paul-Schneider Jugendhaus** (Beisstr. 92, tel. 030/775–2424), **Studentenhotel Berlin** (Meiniger Str. 10, tel. 030/784–6720), and **Haus Anselm von Havelberg** (Sakrower Kirchweg 103, tel. 030/365–5674).

Splurge

West Berlin **Grand Hotel Esplanade.** Opened in 1988, the Grand Hotel Esplanade exudes luxury. Uncompromisingly modern architecture, chicly styled rooms, and works of art by acclaimed artists combine with superb facilities and impeccable service. A special weekend offer will secure you a double for not much more than DM 250. *Lützowufer 15, tel. 030/261–011. 369 rooms, 33 suites. Facilities: 2 restaurants, pub, poolside bar, pool, sauna, whirlpool, steam bath, solarium, masseur, hairdresser, boutique, medical station, library. AE, DC, MC, V.*

Exploring Berlin

Guided Tours

Orientation Tours Berlin is a vast city, so don't expect to be able to do your sightseeing on foot unless you stay for several days and pack each of them with several hours of solid walking. The most sensible way to see the city is to join any of the bus tours that leave at regular intervals from well-marked stops on the Ku'damm. Prices and services are basically the same (DM 30 for a 2½-hour tour of East and West Berlin), and four main companies share the business:

Berliner Bären Stadtrundfahrten (BBS, Rankestr. 35, tel. 030/ 213–4077). Groups depart from the corner of Rankestrasse and Kurfürstendamm.

Berolina Stadtrundfahrten (Meinekestr. 3, tel. 030/8822091). Groups depart from the corner of Kurfürstendamm and Meinekestrasse, and, in East Berlin, from the corner of Unter den Linden and Universitätstrasse.

Bus Verkehr Berlin (BVB, Kurfürstendamm 225, tel. 030/ 8826847). Tours leave from Kurfürstendamm 225.

Severin & Kühn (BVB, Kurfürstendamm 216, tel. 030/883–1015). Groups leave from clearly marked stops along the Kurfürstendamm and, in East Berlin, at the corner of Unter den Linden and Universitätstrasse.

Special-interest Tours

Sightseeing tours with a cultural/historical bias are offered by **Kultur Kontor** (Savignypl. 9–10, tel. 030/310–888). Tours include "Berlin Becoming Berlin," "Berlin 1933–45," and "The Roaring '20s." Departures are from the corner of Savignyplatz and Kantstrasse. **Berliner Geschichtswerkstatt** (Goltzstr. 49, tel. 030/215–4450) also offers historical tours and tours on foot, starting from the Naturkundemuseum, at Invalidenstrasse 43.

Boat Trips

A tour of the **Havel lakes** is the thing to do in summer. Trips begin at Wannsee (S-bahn: Wannsee) and at the Greenwich Promenade in Tegel (U-bahn: Tegel). You'll sail on either the whale-shaped vessel *Moby Dick* or the *Havel Queen*, a Mississippi-style boat, and cruise 27 kilometers (17 miles) through the lakes and past forests. Tours last 4½ hours and cost between DM 10 and DM 15. There are 20 operators. *See below* for the leading ones.

Tours of downtown Berlin's **canals** take in sights such as the Charlottenburg Palace and the Congress Hall. Tours depart from Kottbusser Bridge in Kreuzberg and cost around DM 10.

Tour Operators

Stern- und Kreisschiffahrt (Sachtlebenstr. 60, tel. 030/ 8100040).
Reederei Bruno Winkler (Levetzowstr. 16, tel. 030/391–7010).
Reederei Heinz Riedel (Planufer 78, tel. 030/6913782 or 030/ 6934646).

Berlin for Free—or Almost

There aren't many free rides in Berlin, but the one there is is quite spectacular: You literally float along, on the world's first officially sanctioned **magnetically operated railway system,** which travels between the M (for magnetic) stations Gleisdreieck and Bernburgerstrasse. It's a fine way to travel but it's not the fastest; the 1-mile stretch takes 10 minutes to cover. The service operates weekdays 2 PM–10:30 PM and weekends 8 AM–10:30 PM.

Street buskers may be a part of every German city scene, but the best seem to congregate in Berlin, livening up Breitscheidplatz, parts of the Ku'damm, and Tauenzianstrasse. It's free entertainment, but a mark or two thrown into an upturned hat or open violin case is always appreciated.

Classical-music fans can enjoy free **organ recitals** at most Berlin churches—check the calendar of events outside every church door, or call 030/319–00180 for program details. Organ recitals are given every Saturday at 4:30 at East Berlin's Marienkirche, on the edge of Alexanderplatz.

Berlin's radio and television stations RIAS (tel. 030/85030) and SFB (tel. 030/303–11123) sometimes issue **free tickets** to concert rehearsals.

Highlights for First-time Visitors

Ägyptisches Museum (*see* Tour 3)
Alexanderplatz (*see* Tour 2)
Brandenburger Tor (*see* Tour 1)
Gemäldegalerie, Dahlem (*see* Tour 3)
Haus am Checkpoint Charlie (Wall Museum) (*see* Tour 2)
KaDeWe department store (*see* Tour 1)
Kaiser Wilhelm Gedächtniskirche (*see* Tour 1)
Pergamon Museum (*see* Tour 2)
Reichstag (*see* Tour 1)
Schloss Charlottenburg (*see* Tour 3)
Zoologischer Garten (*see* Tour 1)

Tour 1: West Berlin

Numbers in the margin correspond to points of interest on the Berlin map.

Your tour of West Berlin begins on its best-known street, the
1 **Kurfürstendamm.** Berliners (and most visitors as well) refer to it affectionately as the Ku'damm. Its two-mile length is lined with shops, department stores, art galleries, theaters, movie houses, hotels, and some 100 restaurants, bars, clubs, and sidewalk cafés. It bustles with shoppers and strollers most of the day and fairly far into the night. Traffic can remain heavy into the wee hours of the morning.

This busy thoroughfare was first laid out in the 16th century as the path by which Elector Joachim II of Brandenburg traveled from his palace on the Spree River to his hunting lodge in the Grunewald. The Kurfürstendamm (Elector's Causeway) was developed into a major route in the late-19th century on the initiative of Chancellor Bismarck, the "Iron Chancellor," who was the force behind the original unification of Germany.

The Ku'damm is much more important today than it was to prewar Berlin. It was a busy shopping street, but by no means the city's most elegant one, being fairly far removed from the heart of the city, which was on the opposite side of the Brandenburg Gate in what became East Berlin. The Ku'damm's prewar fame was tied mainly to the rowdy bars and dance halls that studded much of its length and its side streets. Some of these were really low-down dives, scenes of erotic circuses, where kinky sex was the norm.

Similar clubs, along with cabarets and avant-garde theaters, were set on and along side streets of the Friedrichstrasse, in East Berlin. While there's no nighttime action at all on the now dreary Friedrichstrasse, Ku'damm certainly has its share of *Kneipen*, the German term for friendly neighborhood bars.

Along with the rest of Berlin, the Ku'damm suffered severe wartime bombing. Almost half of its 245 late-19th-century buildings were destroyed in the 1940s. The remaining buildings were damaged in varying degrees. What you see today (as in most of Berlin) is either restored, or was constructed over the past decades. While the street is frequently described as "glittering" and/or "sophisticated," there are those who are convinced it has lost whatever real charm and flair it may once have possessed. But it is certainly the liveliest stretch of roadway in Berlin, East or West, and definitely where the action is.

The Ku'damm starts at the western end of the Breitscheidplatz, a large square on which several notable landmarks stand.
2 The ruins of the **Kaiser Wilhelm Gedächtniskirche** (Memorial Church), built between 1891 and 1895, stand as a dramatic reminder of the war's destruction. The bell tower, now known as the "hollow tooth," is all that remains of this once-imposing church that was dedicated to the Emperor, Kaiser Wilhelm I. On the hour, you'll hear the chimes in the tower play a melody composed by the emperor's grandson, Prince Louis Ferdinand von Hohenzollern.

A historic exhibition inside the tower features a religious cross constructed of nails that were recovered from the ashes of the burned-out Coventry Cathedral in England, destroyed in a German bombing raid, November 1940. *Kaiser Wilhelm Memorial Church. Admission free. Open Tues.–Sat. 10–6, Sun. 11–6.*

In stark contrast to the old bell tower is the adjoining Memorial Church and tower built in 1959–61. This ultramodern octagonal church, with its myriad honeycomb windows, is perhaps best described by its nickname: the lipstick and powder box. The interior is dominated by the brilliant blue of its stained glass windows, imported from Chartres in France. Church music and organ concerts are presented in the church regularly.

3 Mere steps away from the new Memorial Church is the **Europa Center,** a vast shopping and business complex on the east side of the Brietscheidplatz often described as a "city within a city." This 1960s 22-story tower block—dubbed "Pepper's Manhattan" after its architect, K. H. Pepper—houses more than 100 shops, restaurants and cafés, an ice rink, two cinemas, a theater, a casino, and the Verkehrsamt (Tourist Information Center). You can even find thermal baths above the car park at the very top. For a spectacular view of the city, take the lift to the i-Punkt restaurant and observation platform on the top floor.

Across from the entrance to the Tourist Information Center is
4 Budapesterstrasse and the **Elefantor** (Elephant Gate), which is the main entrance to Berlin's aquarium, part of the adjoining zoo complex. Before visiting the zoo, take a stroll along Tauenzienstrasse, the boulevard that runs southeast away from the corner of the Europa Center. Tauenzienstrasse leads you
5 straight to Germany's largest department store, the **Kaufhaus des Westens** (Department Store of the West), known to Berliners as **KaDeWe.** An enormous selection of goods can be found on its six floors, but it is most renowned for its food and

Berlin

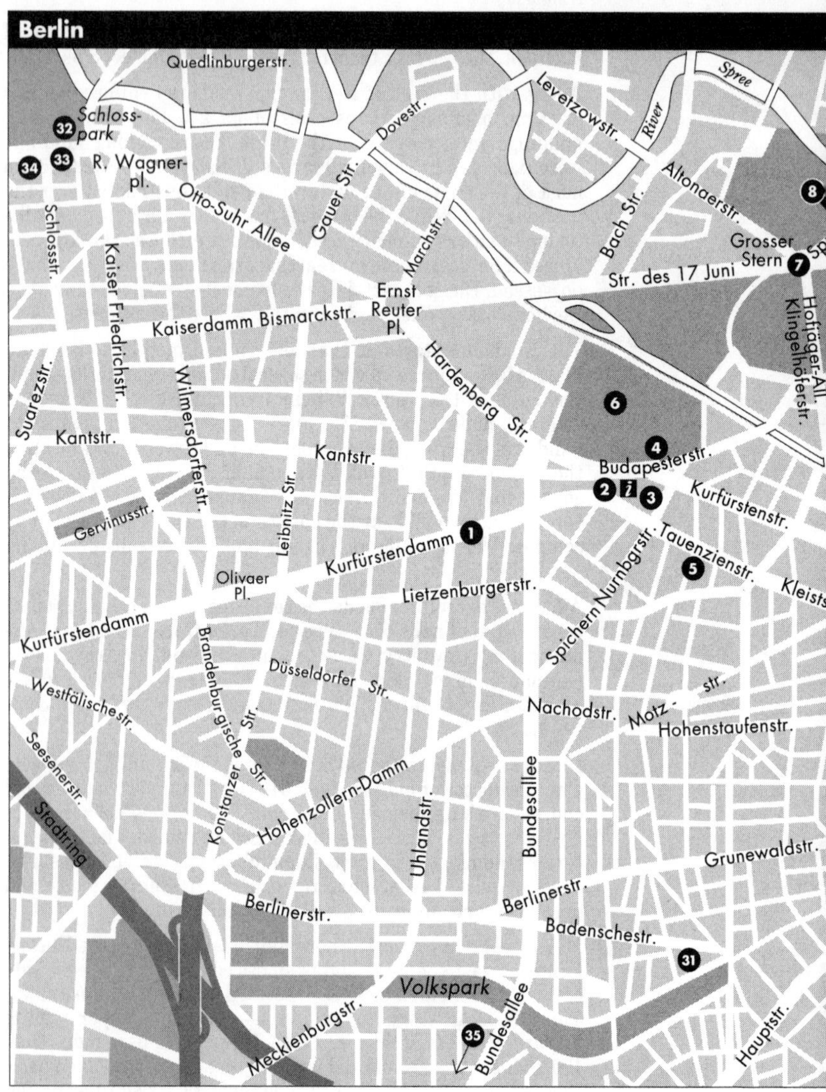

Ägyptisches Museum, **33**
Alexanderplatz, **25**
Alte Kammergericht, **14**
Antikenmuseum, **34**
Berlin Cathedral, **23**
Bertolt Brecht House and Museum, **28**
Brandenburger Tor, **11**
Checkpoint Charlie, **16**
Dahlem Museum Complex, **35**
Deutsche Staatsoper, **19**
Elefantor, **4**
Europa-Center, **3**
Fischerinsel, **26**
Kaiser Wilhelm Gedächtniskirche, **2**
Kaufhaus des Westens, **5**
Kongresshalle, **9**
Kreuzberg, **30**
Kulturforum, **15**
Kurfürstendamm, **1**
Marienkirche, **24**
Märkisches Museum, **27**
Museum für Deutsche Geschichte, **21**
Museumsinsel, **22**
Palais Unter den Linden, **20**
Platz der Akademie, **17**
Potsdamerplatz, **13**
Rathaus Schöneberg, **31**
Reichstag, **10**
Schloss Bellevue, **8**
Schloss Charlottenburg, **32**
Siegessäule, **7**

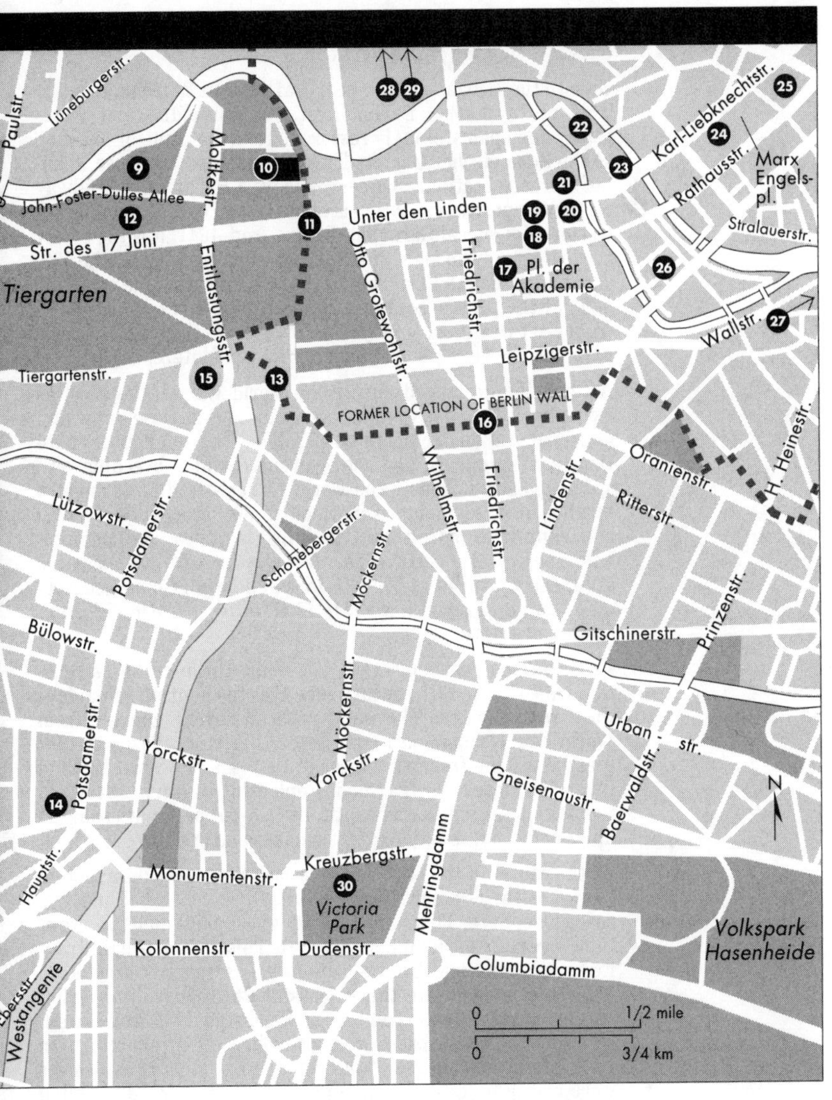

Lüneburgerstr.
Paulstr.
Moltkestr.
John-Foster-Dulles Allee
Str. des 17 Juni
Tiergarten
Entlastungsstr.
Tiergartenstr.
Unter den Linden
Otto Grotewohlstr.
Friedrichstr.
Pl. der Akademie
Karl-Liebknechtstr.
Rathausstr.
Marx Engels-pl.
Stralauerstr.
Wallstr.
Leipzigerstr.
FORMER LOCATION OF BERLIN WALL
Wilhelmstr.
Lindenstr.
Oranienstr.
Ritterstr.
H. Heinestr.
Lützowstr.
Potsdamerstr.
Schöneberger str.
Möckernstr.
Bülowstr.
Gitschinerstr.
Prinzenstr.
Urban str.
Yorckstr.
Gneisenaustr.
Baerwaldstr.
Hauptstr.
Monumentenstr.
Kreuzbergstr.
Victoria Park
Mehringdamm
Volkspark Hasenheide
Kolonnenstr.
Dudenstr.
Columbiadamm
Eberstr.
Westangente
1/2 mile
3/4 km
N

delicatessen counters, restaurants, champagne bars, and beer bars covering the entire top floor.

Go into the U-bahn station near KaDeWe on Wittenbergplatz. This subway station, Berlin's first, was built in 1913 and has recently been painstakingly restored. Take the train for one stop to the Zoologischer Garten. This station, also known as Bahnhof Zoo (Zoo Station), also serves as West Berlin's main railway
6 station. Opposite the station is the entrance to the **Zoologischer Garten** (Zoological Gardens). Dating from 1841, it is the oldest zoo in Germany and is set in the southwestern corner of the 630-acre park called the Tiergarten (Animal Garden). The northern edge of the park is bounded by the Spree River, which flows from East Berlin. Even if you're not a zoo enthusiast, both the park and the very modern zoo offer much of interest.

After being destroyed during the World War II, the zoo was carefully redesigned to create surroundings as close to the animals' natural environment as possible. The zoo houses more than 11,000 animals, and has been successful at breeding rare species. The zoo boasts the world's largest and most modern birdhouse, a terrarium renowned for its crocodiles, and an aquarium with more than 10,000 fish, reptiles, and amphibians. *Zoologischer Garten, Hardenbergpl. 8. Admission to zoo only: DM 7.50 adults, DM 4 children under 15. Combined tickets to zoo and aquarium: DM 12.50 adults, DM 6 children. Open daily 9–dusk.*

From the zoo, you can set off diagonally through the Tiergarten, which in the 17th century served as the hunting grounds of the Great Elector. The park suffered severe damage from World War II bombing raids. Later, Berliners, desperate for fuel during the freezing winter of 1945–46, cut down much of its ancient forest for firewood. Replanting began in 1949, and today's visitor will see a beautifully laid-out park with some 14 miles of footpaths and 6½ acres of lakes and ponds.

At the center of the park you approach the traffic intersection known as the Grosser Stern (Big Star), so-called because five roads meet here. This is the park's highest point, and the site of
7 the **Siegesäule** (Triumphal Column). This 227-foot-high granite, sandstone, and bronze column was originally erected in 1873 to commemorate the successful Prussian military campaigns; it was set up in front of the Reichstag, half a mile away. The column came close to being finished off by anarchists in 1921, after the collapse of the empire. Six kilos of explosives were placed in its stairwell, and the fuse was already sizzling when the bomb was discovered. In 1939, as Hitler was having Berlin redesigned according to his megalomaniacal plans, the column was moved to its present site. A climb of 285 steps up through the column to the observation platform affords splendid views across much of Berlin. *Siegessäule at Grosse Stern. Admission: DM 1.20 adults, 70 pf children under 14. Open Mon. 3–5:45, Tues.–Sun. 9–5:45.*

8 Follow the Spreeweg Road from the Grosser Stern to **Schloss Bellevue** (Bellevue Palace). Built on the Spree River in 1775 for Frederick the Great's youngest brother Prince Augustus-Ferdinand, it has served as the West German president's official residence in West Berlin since 1959. The 50-acre palace grounds have been transformed into a park with an English garden on its western edge. This park-within-a-park was origi-

nally dedicated by an English statesman, Anthony Eden, who later became one of Nazi Germany's staunchest political opponents. Berliners often refer to it jokingly as the Garden of Eden. *Schloss Bellevue Park. Open daily 8–dusk. Closed when the president is in residence.*

Leave the Schloss Bellevue and head east along the John-Foster-Dulles Allee, keeping the Spree River in sight on your left.
9 You'll soon arrive at the **Kongresshalle** (Congress Hall), a meeting and conference center that was a feat of engineering in its day. The hall was built in 1957 as the American contribution to the International Building Exhibition, Interbau. Its resemblance to an open oyster shell earned it the title "pregnant oyster." The roof collapsed in 1980 and has been rebuilt.

Rejoin John-Foster-Dulles Allee again and continue east to the
10 **Reichstag** (Parliament Building), which was erected in the late-19th century to house the Prussian parliament and later performed a similar function for the ill-fated Weimar Republic. The Reichstag was burned to a shell under mysterious circumstances on the night of February 28, 1933, an event that provided the Nazis with a convenient pretext for outlawing all opposition parties. After rebuilding, the Reichstag was again badly damaged in 1945 in the last Allied offensive of the war. Today the west wing houses a popular exhibition of German history since 1800, and a restaurant. The Bundestag will once again be meeting in the Reichstag, but at press time the timetable had not yet been determined. *Reichstag Exhibition: Questions of German History in the Reichstag. Pl. der Republik. Admission free. Open Tues.–Sun. 10–5.*

Behind the Reichstag is the old line of the Berlin Wall, few traces of which now remain. It was here, at the end of Strasse des 17 Juni (June 17 Street), that visiting western dignitaries as well as tourists stood on a wooden viewing platform to peek over the three-foot-thick Wall into the No Man's Land separating the two political halves of Berlin. Crosses still dot the neighborhood and the Spree river bank adjoining the Reichstag—grim reminders of lives lost as East Germans tried to escape to the West after the barrier was built.

Just south of the Reichstag, where Strasse des 17 Juni meets Unter den Linden, is another monumental symbol of German unity and of the long division of Berlin—the mighty
11 **Brandenburger Tor** (Brandenburg Gate). Ever since the Wall was built the Brandenburger Tor, once the pride of imperial Berlin, was stranded in the eerie No Man's Land. When the Wall came down, it was the focal point of much celebrating, for this evocative symbol of Berlin was finally restored to all the people of the newly united city. The Brandenburger Tor is the only remaining gate of an original group of 14 built by Carl Langhans in 1788–91, in virile classical style, as a triumphal arch for King Frederick Wilhelm II. The quadriga, a chariot drawn by four horses and driven by the Goddess of Peace, was added in 1793. The goddess was originally naked, but puritanical protesters persuaded the city fathers to clothe her in a sheath of sheet copper. Troops paraded through the gate after successful campaigns, the last time being in 1945 when victorious Red Army troops took Berlin. The upper part of the gate, together with its chariot and Goddess of Peace, were destroyed in the war, but in 1957 the original molds were discovered in West Berlin and a new quadriga was cast in copper and pre-

sented as a gift to the people of East Berlin—a remarkable, rare instance of Cold War–era East-West cooperation.

A short distance west, along Strasse des 17 Juni—a name that commemorates the unsuccessful 1953 uprising of East Berlin
12 workers against the Soviets—you will reach the **Soviet Victory Memorial,** until 1990 a Russian enclave in the West. Built directly after the end of World War II, before power plays between opposing sides had been set in motion, it was located in the western rather than the eastern sector. Through an East-West arrangement it has been allowed to remain there, although no longer guarded by Soviet troops, and now serves as a major attraction. The semicircular monument, which shows a bronze statue of a soldier, rests on a marble plinth taken from Hitler's former Berlin headquarters, flanked by what are said to be the first two tanks to have fought their way into Berlin in 1945.

Turn south from the memorial and cross the tip of the Tier-
13 garten to **Potsdamerplatz,** a somewhat dull-looking expanse that was once among the busiest squares in prewar Berlin. Potsdamerplatz is the point where the British, American, and Russian sectors met and is often referred to as the three-sector corner. The Wall cut through the center of the square. Not far from the square, on part of the wasteland on the other side of the dividing border, is a little knoll marking the remains of Hitler's reinforced concrete bunker where he spent his last days. At press time, discussions were under way on what to do with the site.

On nearby Potsdamerstrasse, on Heinrich-von-Kleist-Park, is
14 the former **Alte Kammergericht** (Prussian Court Building) in which many Nazi show trials were held before the infamous Judge Roland Freisler. The building was taken over by the Allies in 1945 and is still used by the Allied forces. It was here that the four-power agreement, which set the rules governing communication between the two halves of the city, was signed in 1971.

Several blocks north, in nearby Kemperplatz, lies the
15 **Kulturforum** (Cultural Forum), a large square where you'll find a series of fascinating museums and galleries. Their contents will shift as state collections that were stuck on opposite sides of the Wall are reunited. Two new buildings will join the complex. One, opening in 1993, will house the collection of drawings and prints currently at Dahlem (*see* Tour 3, *below*). The roof that resembles a great wave belongs to the **Philharmonie** (Philharmonic Hall). Built in 1963, it is home to the renowned Berlin Philharmonic Orchestra. The main hall is closed for renovation until spring 1992. Until that time the orchestra is performing at the smaller Kammermusiksaal next door and at other venues throughout the city (*see* The Arts and Nightlife, *below*). *Philharmonie ticket office: Matthäikirchstr. 1. Open weekdays 3:30–6 and weekends 11–2.*

The Philharmonie added the **Musikinstrumenten-Museum** (Musical Instruments Museum) to its attractions in 1984. It is well worth a visit for its fascinating collection of keyboard, string, wind, and percussion instruments. *Tiergartenstr. 1, tel. 030/254–810. Admission free. Open Tues.–Fri. 9–5, weekends 10–5. Guided tours on Saturday at 11 with a noon presentation of the Wurlitzer organ. Tour admission: DM 3.*

Opposite the Philharmonie is the **Kunstgewerbemuseum** (Museum of Decorative Arts). Inside this three-story building you'll find a display of the development of the arts and crafts in Europe from the Middle Ages to the present day. Among its treasures is the Welfenschatz (Guelph Treasure), a collection of 16th-century gold and silver plate from Nürnberg. The most impressive single piece is a reliquary in the form of a domed Byzantine church. Made in Köln in 1175, it is believed to have held the head of St. Gregory when it was brought back from Constantinople in 1773. Other displays of particular interest are the ceramics and porcelains. *Tiergartenstr. 6, tel. 030/266–2911. Admission free. Open Tues.–Fri. 9–5, weekends 10–5.*

Leave the museum and walk south past the mid-19th-century church of St. Matthaeus to the **Neue Nationalgalerie** (New National Gallery), a modern glass and steel building designed by Mies van der Rohe and built in the mid-1960s.

The gallery's collection comprises paintings, sculptures, and drawings from the 19th and 20th centuries, with an accent on works by Impressionists such as Manet, Monet, Renoir, and Pissarro. Other schools represented are German Romantics, Realists, Expressionists, Surrealists, and the Bauhaus. The gallery also has a growing collection of contemporary art from Europe and America. *Potsdamerstr. 50, tel. 030/266–2666. Admission free to downstairs gallery. Open Tues.–Fri. 9–5, weekends 10–5.*

The last stop on the tour of the Cultural Forum is the **Staatsbibliothek** (National Library), opposite the Neue Nationalgalerie. This modern building, housing one of the largest libraries in Europe, with four million volumes, was designed by Hans Scharoun, the architect of the Philharmonie. *Potsdamerstr. 33, tel. 030/2661. Admission free. Open Mon.–Fri. 9–9, Sat. 9–5.*

Tour 2: East Berlin

Much of eastern Berlin was cleaned and restored in recent years, the idea being that when you crossed from West Berlin you should see a modern, fresh, and above all orderly city. The lower end of the Friedrichstrasse has been rebuilt, and much of the 11-square-kilometer (4-square-mile) "Berlin Mitte" district, the center of the city, has been given a thorough face-lift. When you wander off the beaten path, however, you will frequently find the drabness and sameness for which the socialist eastern zone was better known. Massive showcase housing and other communal projects hastily built in the '50s and '60s now show their age and shoddy construction, but newer projects are being planned on a more human scale, with greater effort to incorporate them into their surroundings.

For a sense of déjà vu, enter the eastern part of Berlin at
16 **Checkpoint Charlie,** the most famous crossing point between the two Berlins during the Cold War, and the setting of numerous spy novels and films. On the West Berlin side, visit **Haus am Checkpoint Charlie** (the Wall Museum). The museum reviews the history of the events leading up to the construction of the Wall and displays records and photographs documenting methods used by East Germans to cross over into the West (one of the most ingenious instruments of escape was a miniature submarine). Also displayed are paintings, drawings, and exhibits

of Berlin history since the erection of the Wall. *Friedrichstr. 44. DM 5 adults, DM 3.50 children. Open daily 9 AM–10 PM.*

Follow busy, shop-lined Friedrichstrasse north for six blocks
to Johann-Dieckmann-Strasse (or ride the U-bahn to Stadtmitte station) and turn right to come to the large square called
17 **Platz der Akadamie,** still one of Europe's finest piazzas. It's the
site of the beautifully reconstructed **Schauspielhaus,** built in
1818 and East Berlin's main concert hall, and the rebuilt
German and **French cathedrals.** The French cathedral contains
the **Huguenot Museum,** with exhibits charting the history and
the art of the Protestant refugees from France—the Hugue-
nots—expelled at the end of the 17th century by Louis XIV.
Their energy and commercial expertise did much to help boost
Berlin in the 18th century. *Admission DM 1 adults, 50 pf children. Open Tues., Wed., Sat. 10–5; Thurs. 10–6; Sun. 11:30–5.*

18 Head down Französischestrasse to **St. Hedwig's Cathedral,** a substantial, circular building that's similar to the Pantheon in Rome. Note the tiny street called Hinter der Katholische Kirche; it means "Behind the Catholic Church." When the cathedral was built in 1747 it was the first Catholic church built in resolutely Protestant Berlin since the Reformation in the 16th century.

19 Head north one block and you reach the **Deutsche Staatsoper** (State Opera House), lavishly restored in the late '80s. A performance here can be memorable. *Unter den Linden 7. The box office is open weekdays, noon–5:45.*

You are now on **Unter den Linden,** the central thoroughfare of
old Berlin; its name means simply, "under the linden trees."
Something of its former cosmopolitan elegance is left, though
these days it can hardly claim to rival the Champs Élysées. On
the north side is **Humboldt University,** originally built in 1766 as
a palace for the brother of Friedrich II of Prussia. It became a
university in 1810, and Karl Marx and Friedrich Engels were
20 once among its students. The **Palais Unter den Linden** is also on
this boulevard; it's the former crown prince's palace, today
used as a government guest house. At the eastern end of Unter
den Linden, housed in the onetime arsenal (Zeughaus), is the
21 **Museum für Deutsche Geschichte** (Museum of German History), constructed from 1695 to 1705. This magnificent Baroque
building was later used as a hall of fame glorifying Prusso-
German militarism. Today, it provides a compendium of
German history from 1789 to the present. Displays focus on a
range of relics, from the hat Napoléon wore at the Battle of Waterloo to relief portrayals of faces of soldiers through the ages.
*Unter den Linden 2. Admission: DM 3 adults, DM 1.50 chil-
dren. Open Mon.–Thurs. 9–6, weekends 10–5.*

Turn left and follow the Spree Canal and you come to Museum
22 Island, or **Museumsinsel,** on the site of one of Berlin's two original settlements, Cölln, dating back to 1237. Today, you'll find a
complex of four remarkable museums here. *Admission: Varies
from free to DM 3 (extra if you want to take photographs). Open
Wed.–Sun. 10–6. Pergamon Museum open daily 10–6. Check
hours before visiting, as they can occasionally change.*

The **Altes Museum** (Old Museum; entrance Lustgarten) is an austere neoclassical building just north of Marx-Engels-Platz that features postwar East German art; its large etching and drawing collection, from the Old Masters to the present, is a treasure trove. The **Nationalgalerie** (National Gallery, entrance on Bodestrasse) houses an outstanding collection of 18th-, 19th-, and early-20th-century paintings and sculptures and often hosts special temporary exhibits. Works by Cézanne, Rodin, Degas, and one of Germany's most famous portrait artists, Max Liebermann, are part of the permanent exhibition.

Even if you aren't generally inclined toward the ancient world, make an exception for the **Pergamon Museum** (entrance on Am Kupfergraben). It is not only the standout in this complex; it is one of Europe's greatest museums. The museum's name is derived from its principal and best-loved display, the Pergamon altar, a monumental Greek temple found in what's now Turkey and dating from 180 BC. Adorning it are finely carved figures of gods locked in battle against giants. As much as anything, perhaps, this vast structure illustrates the zeal of Germany's 19th-century archaeologists, who had it shipped piece by piece from a mountaintop to Berlin. Equally impressive is the Babylonian Processional Way in the Asia Minor department. As you walk through the museum, you cannot help but wonder how they ever got away with dismantling and exporting these vast treasures.

Last in the complex is the **Bodemuseum** (entrance on Monbijoubrücke), with its superb Egyptian, Byzantine, and early Christian relics, sculpture collections, and coin gallery. The Sphinx of Hatshepsut, from around 1500 BC, is stunning, as are the Burial Cult Room and Papyrus Collection. There is also a representative collection of Italian Renaissance paintings.

From the museum complex, follow the Spree Canal back to Unter den Linden and the enormous, impressive 19th-century
23 **Berlin Cathedral** (Berliner Dom). A small museum in it (entrance on Unter den Linden) records the postwar reconstruction of the building, which was due to be completed by the end of 1991.

The stupendously hideous modern building across Unter den Linden is the **Palast der Republik** (Palace of the Republic), a ponderous, postwar monument to socialist progress. It houses a theater, a dance hall, and several restaurants.

Follow Karl-Liebknechtstrasse to take a look at the 13th-centu-
24 ry **Marienkirche** and its late-Gothic fresco *Den Totentanz (Dance of Death)*. Obscured for many years, it was restored in 1950, revealing the original in all its macabre allure. Like something out of an Ingmar Bergman movie, Death dances with everyone, from peasant to king. The fresco and the tower were both 15th-century additions. *Alexanderplatz. Open Mon.–Thurs. 10–12 and 1–4, Sat. 12–4. Organ recitals: Sat. 4:30.*

25 The Marienkirche borders **Alexanderplatz,** the square that formed the hub of Berlin city life. It's a bleak sort of place, open and windswept, surrounded by grimly ugly modern buildings, with not so much as a hint of its prewar elegance—a reminder not just of the Allied bombing of Berlin, but of the ruthlessness with which what remained of the old buildings was demolished by the East Germans. Finding Alexanderplatz from any other part of the city is no problem; just head toward the **Fernsehturm,** the unmissable TV tower (completed in 1969 and 1,198 feet high) that stands at its center.

In the base of the tower is the Berlin Information Office. Here, you'll be able to get an excellent brochure, listing (in English) every worthwhile sight in the city, along with the clearest of maps and a diagram of the public transportation system.

For DM 3 (DM 1.50 children) you can take the elevator to the viewing platform halfway up the tower, which is open 9 AM–midnight. On a clear day, you will see Berlin extend in all directions. The revolving café is ideal for a coffee break with a view, though the food is not worth the time you'll have waited in line to get up here. The area around the tower offers ample shopping opportunities, including the chance—at least for the time being—to buy goods from other formerly socialist countries. The focal point for shopping is the **Centrum Warenhaus** (department store), next to the Hotel Stadt Berlin at the very top of the plaza.

Walk across the lower end of the square past the **Rathaus** (Town Hall, also known as the Rotes Rathaus, or Red Town Hall), a marvel of red brick and friezes depicting the city's history. The complex of buildings next to the town hall has been handsomely rebuilt, centering around the remains of the twin-spired, 12th-century **Nikolaikirche** (St. Nicholas's Church), Berlin's oldest parish church. The quarter that has grown around it, the **Nikolai quarter,** is filled with stores, cafés, and restaurants.

Wander back down Rathausstrasse into the area around the Breite Strasse—there's an array of fine old buildings here, some rebuilt, some actually moved to this location from else-
26 where in Berlin—and on over to the **Fischerinsel** area. This was the heart of Berlin 750 years ago, and today retains some of its medieval character. It provides a refreshing change, too, from some of the heavy and uninspired postwar architecture, which you may by now feel the need to get away from.

Cross over the Gertraudenstrasse and wander up the south
27 bank of the canal to the red-brick **Märkisches Museum,** the museum of city history. It includes a special section on the city's theatrical past and a fascinating collection of mechanical musical instruments. These are demonstrated on Sunday 11–noon, Wednesday 3–4. Next door to the museum live the (live) bears, Berlin's symbol. *Am Köllnischen Park 5. Admission: DM 2 adults, DM 1 children. Open Wed.–Sun. 9–6.*

The upper Friedrichstrasse is undergoing reconstruction. Among its landmarks are the tall **International Trade Center,** next to the Friedrichstrasse rail station, and, farther up, the **Friedrichstadtpalast,** featuring a nightclub, dancing, and occasional musical shows. Despite the rebuilding, the street still houses a number of small shops, bookstores, and neighborhood establishments. Walk up beyond the bend where the street turns into the Chauseestrasse (or take the U-Bahn to Oranien-
28 burgerstr.) to find the **Bertolt Brecht House and Museum** and a library for Brecht scholars. *Chausseestr. 125. Admission: DM 2 adults, DM 1 children. Open Tues., Wed., Fri. 10–noon, Thurs. 5–7, Sat. 9:30–noon and 12:30–2.*

Brecht is actually buried next door, along with his wife Helene Weigel and more than 100 other celebrated Berliners, in the **Dorotheer Cemetery.** They include the neoclassical architects Schinkel and Schadow as well as the Berlin printer Litfass, the man who invented those stumpy cylindrical columns you'll find across Europe carrying advertisements and theater schedules.

Head back toward the center and turn left down Oranienbur-
29 gerstrasse to the ruins of the massive city **synagogue,** now being restored. It's an exotic amalgam of styles, the whole faintly Middle Eastern, built between 1894 and 1905. It was largely ruined on the night of November 11, 1938, the infamous "crystal night," when Nazi looters and soldiers rampaged across Germany and Austria, burning synagogues and smashing the few Jewish shops and homes left in the country. It was further ruined during the bombing of the city toward the end of the war. From here, take the U-bahn from Oranienburgertor back to the center of the city.

Tour 3: Outlying Sights and Attractions

30 West Berlin's highest natural hill, the **Kreuzberg** (Hill of the Cross) in Viktoriapark (Victoria Park) can be reached by taking the U-bahn at Kochstrasse, across from Checkpoint Charlie, and traveling two stops on the U-6 line to Mehringdamm station. Leave by the Kreuzbergstrasse exit.

The Kreuzberg is on your left, crowned by an iron cross. The monument was erected in 1821 to commemorate the 1813–15 Wars of Liberation. The view from the top embraces the center of East Berlin to the north and Tempelhof military airfield to the south. A vineyard on the sheltered southern slope of the Kreuzberg produces Germany's rarest wine, the Kreuznerberger. It is produced in such small quantities that it is only served at official Berlin functions.

Leave the park by the western exit on Monumentenstrasse and continue until you reach the intersection with Potsdamerstrasse on the right. Turn left into Hauptstrasse and continue south until you reach Dominicus-Strasse. Turn right here and take the first turning on your left, Elsas-Strasse. It will lead
31 you straight to the **Rathaus Schöneberg** (Schöneberg Town Hall).

Since the division of the two Berlins in 1948, the Rathaus Schöneberg has been home to the West Berlin Chamber of Deputies and their Senate. The Rathaus is of special interest to Americans, for it was here, on June 26, 1963, that John F. Kennedy made his memorable "Ich bin ein Berliner" speech just months before his assassination.

Completed in 1914, the Rathaus has a 237-foot-high tower from which a replica of the Liberty Bell is rung each day at noon. The bell was given by the American people as a symbol of their support for the West Berliners' struggle to preserve freedom. A document bears the signatures of 17 million Americans who pledged their solidarity with the people of West Berlin. *Rathaus Schöneberg Bell Tower. John-F.-Kennedy-Platz. Open Wed. and Sun. 10–4.*

From the Rathaus, head north up the Innsbrückestrasse to the U-bahn station at Bayerischer Platz. Take the U-7 line toward Rathaus Spandau eight stops and get off at Mierendorffplatz.
32 Head south along Mierendorffstrasse to the **Schloss Charlottenburg** (Charlottenburg Palace).

The Charlottenburg Palace complex can be considered the showplace of West Berlin, the most monumental memento of imperial days in the western sector. This sumptuous palace served as a city residence for the Prussian rulers. It has on occasion been referred to as Berlin's very own Versailles. Indeed, some claim that it was Napoléon, when he invaded Berlin in 1806, who first made the comparison to the Sun King's spectacular château near Paris. The comparison hardly seems appropriate. Charlottenburg is on a smaller, more intimate scale than Versailles. Its proportions and decoration are restrained; formal gardens are not nearly as vast. Nor are you likely to encounter the kind of crowds that flock to Versailles. But you are sure to be suitably impressed.

A full day is not too much time to devote to Charlottenburg. In addition to the apartments of the Prussian nobility, there are the landscaped gardens to be visited, and several excellent museums set within and just inside the grounds.

This gorgeous palace started as a modest royal summer residence in 1695, built on the orders of King Frederick I for his wife, Queen Sophie-Charlotte. Later, in the 18th century, Frederick the Great made a number of additions, such as the dome and several wings in the Rococo style. In time the complex evolved into the massive royal domain you see today. The palace was severely damaged during World War II but has been painstakingly restored. Many of the original furnishings and works of art survived the war and are on display today.

Behind heavy iron gates, the Court of Honor—the courtyard in front of the palace—is dominated by a fine Baroque statue, the Reiterstandbild des Grossen Kurfürsten (the equestrian statue of the Great Elector). A 156-foot-high domed tower capped by a gilded statue of Fortune rises above the main entrance to the palace.

Inside, in the main building, the suites of Friedrich I and his wife Sophie Charlotte are furnished in the prevailing style of the era. Paintings include royal portraits by Antoine Pesne, a noted court painter of the 18th century. On the first floor you can visit the Oak Gallery, the early 18th-century Palace Chapel, and the suites of Frederick Wilhelm II and Frederick Wilhelm III, furnished in the Biedermeier style. Visits to the royal apartments are by guided tour only; tours leave every hour on the hour from 9 to 4. Parks and gardens can be visited for free and offer a pleasant respite from sightseeing.

A gracious staircase leads up to the sumptuous State Dining Room and the 138-foot-long Golden Gallery. West of the staircase are the rooms of Frederick the Great, in which the king's extravagant collection of works by Watteau, Chardin, and Pesne are displayed. In one glass cupboard you'll see the coronation crown, stripped of its jewels by the king, who gave the most valuable gemstones to his wife. Also in the so-called New Wing is the National Gallery's collection of masterpieces from 19th-century German painters such as Caspar David Friedrich, the leading member of the German Romantic school. *Schloss Charlottenburg, Luisenpl., tel. 030/320–911. Admission (includes guided tour): DM 6. Open: Tues., Wed., Fri.–Sun. 10–5, Thurs. 10–8.*

There are several buildings in the park that deserve particular attention, among which are the Belvedere, a teahouse overlooking the lake and Spree River that now houses a collection of Berlin porcelain and the Schinkel Pavilion behind the palace near the river. The pavilion, modeled on a villa in Naples where the king stayed in 1822, was built in 1824–25 by Karl Friedrich

Schinkel, one of 19th-century Berlin's favorite architects. It houses paintings by Caspar David Friedrich and late-18th-century furniture. Also of interest in the park is the mausoleum, which contains the tombs of King Frederick Wilhelm II and Queen Louise.

Just to the south of the palace are a group of small, distinguished museums. The first, across from the palace, is the
33 **Ägyptisches Museum** (Egyptian Museum). The building, once the east guardhouse and residence of the king's bodyguard, is now home to the famous portrait bust of the exquisite Queen Nefertiti. The 3,300-year-old Egyptian queen is the centerpiece of a collection of works that spans Egypt's history since 4,000 BC and includes one of the best preserved mummies outside Cairo. *Schloss Str. 70, tel. 030/320–911. Admission free. Open Mon.–Thurs. 9–5, weekends 10–5.*

Opposite the Ägyptisches Museum in the former west guard-
34 house is the **Antikenmuseum** (Antique Museum). The collection comprises ceramics and bronzes as well as everyday utensils from ancient Greece and Rome and a number of Greek vases from the 6th to 4th centuries BC. Also on display is a collection of Scythian gold and silverware and jewelry found in the Mediterranean basin. *Schloss Str. 1, tel. 030/320–911. Admission free. Open Mon.–Thurs. 9–5, weekends 10–5.*

The final museum, the **Museum für Vor- und Frühgeschichte** (Museum of Pre- and Proto-history), is located in the western extension of the palace opposite Klausener Platz. The museum depicts the stages of the evolution of man from 1,000,000 BC to the Bronze Age. *Spandauer Damm. Admission free. Open Mon–Thurs. 9–5, weekends 10–5.*

Another stop on your tour of West Berlin is also a cluster of mu-
35 seums, the **Dahlem Museum complex.** The best way to get there is by the U-2 subway line, to Dahlem-Dorf station.

The Dahlem complex includes the **Gemäldegalerie** (Picture Gallery), the **Kupferstichkabinett** (Drawings and Prints Collection, currently closed), the **Museum fur Völkerkunde** (Ethnographic Museum), and the **Skulpturengalerie** (Sculpture Gallery).

Begin with the **Gemäldegalerie.** One of Germany's finest art galleries, it houses a broad selection of European paintings from the 13th to 18th centuries. Rembrandt devotees will be particularly pleased to find the world's second largest Rembrandt collection located on the second floor.

Several rooms on the first floor are reserved for paintings by German masters, among them Dürer, Cranach the Elder, and Holbein. An adjoining gallery houses the works of the Italian masters—Botticelli, Titian, Giotto, Filippo Lippi, and Raphael—and another gallery on the first floor is devoted to paintings by Dutch and Flemish masters of the 15th and 16th centuries: van Eyck, Bosch, Brueghel the Elder, and van der Weyden.

Flemish and Dutch paintings from the 17th century are displayed on the floor above. In the Rembrandt section, where there are 21 paintings by the master, you can see "The Man with the Golden Helmet," a painting formerly attributed to Rembrandt that has since proved by radioactive testing to have been the work of another artist of the same era. *Arnimallee 23–*

27, tel. 030/83011. Admission free. Open Tues.–Fri. 9–5, weekends 10–5.

The **Kupferstichkabinett** (Drawings and Prints Collection) includes European woodcuts and engravings from the 15th to 18th centuries, several pen-and-ink drawings by Dürer, and 150 drawings by Rembrandt. There is also a photographic archive, which is closed until 1993, when it will reopen in a new building at the Kulturforum. *Entrance: Arnimallee 23. Admission free. Open Tues.–Fri. 9–4, weekends 10–5.*

The **Museum für Völkerkunde** (Ethnographic Museum) is internationally famous for its arts and artifacts from Africa, Asia, the South Seas, and ancient America. American visitors homesick for a taste of their own history should look out for the North American Indian wigwams and the feather cape that once belonged to Hawaii's 18th-century King Kamehameha I. Also of interest is the display of native huts from New Guinea and New Zealand. *Entrance: Lansstr. 8, tel. 030/83011. Open Tues.–Fri. 9–5, weekends 10–5. Admission free.*

The **Skulpturengalerie** (Sculpture Gallery) houses Byzantine and European sculpture from the 3rd to 18th centuries. Included in its collection is Donatello's *Madonna and Child*, sculpted in 1422. *Entrance: Arnimallee 23–27. Admission free. Open Tues.–Fri. 9–5, weekends 10–5.*

Beyond the tour of monuments, museums, and other aspects relating to the Wall and the divided city, no visit to Berlin would be complete without seeing the vast world of lakes and greenery along its western extremities. In no other city has such an expanse of uninterrupted natural surroundings been preserved within city limits.

Along the city's fringe are some 60 lakes, connected by rivers, streams, and canals, in a verdant setting of meadows, woods, and forests. Excursion steamers ply the water wonderland of the Wannsee and Havel. (*See* Guided Tours in Essential Information, *above*, for details.) You can tramp for hours through the green belt of the Grunewald. On weekends in spring and fall and daily in summer the Berliners are out in force, swimming, sailing their boats, tramping through the woods, riding horseback. To the north, close to the line of the old barbed-wire political boundary, there are still a few working farms. Time and progress seem to have passed right by the rustic village of Lubars.

You can reach Grunewald and the Wannsee on the S-1 or S-3 suburban line from Zoo Station. To reach Lubars, take the U-6 subway to Tegel, then bus No. 222 to Lubars.

Shopping

Shopping Districts

The liveliest and most famous shopping area in West Berlin is the **Kurfürstendamm** and its side streets, especially between **Breitscheidplatz** and **Olivaer Platz.** Running east from Breitscheidplatz is **Tauenzienstrasse,** another shopping street. At the end of it is Berlin's most celebrated department store, **KaDeWe.**

East Berlin's chief shopping areas are along the Friedrichstrasse, Unter den Linden, and in the area around Alexanderplatz. The Palast and Grand hotels have small shopping malls. A number of smaller stores have sprung up in and around the Nikolai quarter; under the Communist regime, all were supplied from the same central sources, but they make fun places to shop for trinkets.

Department Stores

The classiest department store in Berlin is **KaDeWe,** the Kaufhaus des Westens (Department Store of the West, as it's modestly known in English), at Wittenbergplatz. The biggest department store in Europe, the KaDeWe is a grand-scale emporium in modern guise. Be sure to check out the food department, which occupies the whole sixth floor. The other main department store downtown is **Wertheim** on Ku'damm. Neither as big nor as attractive as the KaDeWe, Wertheim nonetheless offers a large selection of fine wares.

East Berlin's **Centrum** department store, at the north end of Alexanderplatz, offered ridiculously cheap subsidized prices under the old regime, though style was somewhat lacking. Prices have changed, but it's worth a visit for souvenirs and such eastern German specialties as wooden toys.

Street Markets

Berlin has more than 70 weekly markets, augmented in December by the annual Christmas fairs. The best of the weekly markets are in **Spandau, Schöneberg,** and **Kreuzberg,** but for inexpensive and imaginative Berlin handicrafts make for the **Strasse des 17 Juni** on any Saturday or Sunday: On the northern side between Ernst-Reuter-Platz and the Grosser Stern you'll find the city's largest street market. The stalls—offering everything from cheap kitsch to valuable antiques—go up at about 10 and disappear again around 5.

You can also find inexpensive bygones among the antiques shops that line **Keithstrasse,** not far from Wittenbergplatz.

Clothing

Berlin is Germany's fashion-trade center, and although many of the leading labels are expensive, you can find a wide range of good-quality locally made clothing. Try the clothing sections of department stores such as **KaDeWe** and **Wertheim,** or the **Horn Modenhaus** (Kurfurstendamm 213).

Gift Ideas

Berlin is a city of alluring stores and boutiques. Despite its cosmopolitan gloss, prices are generally lower than in cities like Munich and Hamburg. Berlin has one of Germany's finest **porcelain** works, the former Royal Porcelain Factory, known now by the initials **KPM.** This delicate, handmade china—identified by a blue scepter and by colorful flower motifs—isn't cheap, but you can find seconds at the factory salesroom (Wegelystrasse 1, tel. 030/390–090). There's another sales outlet at Kurfurstendamm 26A (tel. 030/881–1802). If you long to have the Egyptian Museum's Queen Nefertiti on your mantelpiece at home, try the **Gipsformerei der Staatlichen Museen Preussischer Kulturbesitz** (Sophie-Charlotte-Str. 17, tel. 030/321-7011, open weekdays 9–4). It sells plaster casts of this and other treasures from the city's museums.

Toy soldiers are another Berlin specialty, and one of the best-stocked shops is the **Berliner Zinnfigurenkabinett** (Knesebeckstr. 88).

Tax Refunds

Visitors from countries outside the European Community (that is, the United States and Canada) qualify for a refund of the sales tax on items purchased in Berlin. All stores should advise you on the procedure for getting the refund, but in practice try to shop at stores displaying a TAX FREE FOR TOURISTS sign. *See* Money-saving Tips at the beginning of this guide.

Dining

Dining in Berlin can mean sophisticated nouvelle specialties in upscale restaurants with linen tablecloths and hand-painted porcelain plates, or hearty local specialties in atmospheric and inexpensive inns: The range is as vast as the city. Specialties include *Eisbein mit Sauerkraut,* knuckle of pork with pickled cabbage; *Rouladen,* rolled stuffed beef; *Spanferkel,* suckling pig; *Berliner Schüsselsülze,* potted meat in aspic; *Schlachteplatte,* mixed grill; *Hackepeter,* ground beef; and *Kartoffelpuffer,* fried potato cakes. *Bockwurst* is a chubby frankfurter that's served in a variety of ways and sold in restaurants and at bockwurst stands all over the city. *Schlesisches Himmerlreich* is roast goose or pork served with potato dumplings in rich gravy. *Königsberger Klopse* consists of meatballs, herring, and capers—it tastes much better than it sounds.

Berlin is the city of the *Frühstückskneipe,* or breakfast tavern, with breakfast served round the clock; on Sunday morning it often comes complete with live jazz, a German institution known as *Frühschoppen.* The best of the breakfast taverns carry the name **Eierschale,** and the best of these is on the corner of Rankestrasse and Ku'damm (*see below*). You can choose between a Continental breakfast and a buffet brunch.

The Bavarian Bratwurst has made big inroads in Berlin, and you'll find this cheap and tasty lunchtime filler at street stalls throughout the city. For something more substantial, the **Churrasco** chain of steak restaurants is well represented, with three central addresses (Kurfürstendamm 177 and 214, and Rankestr. 35) and one in the Steglitz suburb (Schlosstr. 34–35).

Far as it lies from the sea, Berlin nevertheless has some excellent and moderately priced fish restaurants. The Hildebrandt group has four: the **Roter Sand** (Kurfurstenstr. 109), the **Bunte Kuh** (Wilmersdorfer Str. 95), **Seute Deern** (Berliner Str. 90–91), and the **Hamburger Fischstube** (Wexstr. 27). In fine weather, Berlin's parks, gardens, and riverbanks beckon picnickers. At the delicatessen counters of Berlin's biggest and best-stocked department store, the legendary **KaDeWe** (*see* Tour 1, *above*), you can take your pick of the delicacies and then stroll across to the Tiergarten park to enjoy them alfresco.

Highly recommended restaurants are indicated by a star ★.

Under DM 40

West Berlin

Alt-Nürnberg. The waitresses wear dirndls, the Bavarian colors of blue and white are everywhere, and that region's culinary delights dominate the menu. If you prefer to eat Prussian-style, order calves' liver *Berliner Art. Europa Center, tel. 030/261–4397. Reservations advised. AE, DC, MC, V.*

Hecker's Deele. Antique church pews complement the oak-beamed interior of this restaurant that specializes in Westphalian dishes. The Ku'damm is right outside. *Grolmannstr. 35, tel. 030/88901. Reservations advised. AE, DC, MC, V.*

★ **Ponte Vecchio.** Delicious Tuscan-style Italian food is served here in a handsome, light-wood dining room. Ask the friendly waiters for their recommendations—the food is excellent and simply presented. *Spielhagenstr. 3, tel. 030/342–1999. Reservations essential. Jacket and tie required. DC. Closed lunch (except Sun.), Tues., and 4 weeks in summer.*

East Berlin

★ **Berlin Esprit.** For authentic Berlin specialties you'll probably do no better; the atmosphere is also thoroughly relaxing. *Alexanderpl., in the Hotel Stadt Berlin, tel. 02/2190. Reservations advised. AE, DC, MC, V.*

★ **Cafe Flair.** This café is immensely popular despite its somewhat limited menu—more intended for snackers than diners—but what there is is good, and no complaints about the service, either. There are tables outside for warm-weather sidewalk dining. *Am Marstall (ground floor), Marx-Engels-Forum, tel. 02/212–6919. Reservations advised. No credit cards.*

Moskau. The strong Russian influence shows itself here in its food and drink offerings—superb chicken Kiev and real Russian vodka—but you'll also find a good range of Berlin-style fare to choose from. The restaurant is, however, less central and offers less atmosphere than many other restaurants listed here. *Karl-Marx-Allee 34, tel. 02/279–4052 and 02/279–2869. Reservations essential. Jacket and tie suggested. No credit cards.*

Ratskeller. This is actually two restaurants in one, a wine and a beer cellar, each highly popular, and each with great atmosphere (entrances at opposite corners of the building). Menus are somewhat limited, but include good solid Berlin fare. The brick-walled beer cellar is guaranteed to be packed during main dining hours, at which time reservations sometimes get ignored; Berliners simply line up to get in. The wine cellar is less crowded, in part because it is slightly more expensive. *Rathausstr. 15–18 (in the basement of the Rotes Rathaus, or Red Town Hall), tel. 02/212–4464 and 02/212–5301. Reservations advised. No credit cards.*

Under DM 30

West Berlin

Adriatic Grill. There's a huge menu, with emphasis on Yugoslavian cuisine, but schnitzel and other German meat dishes muscle in. On fine days you can dine outside and watch the Ku'damm crowds. *Kurfürstendamm 96, tel. 030/323–4027. AC, MC, V.*

Alt-Berliner Weissbierstube. A visit to the Berlin Museum must include a stop at the museum's pub-style restaurant. There's a buffet packed with Berlin specialties, and you can take in live jazz here on Saturday and Sunday morning. *Berlin Museum, Lindenstr. 14, tel. 030/251–0121. No credit cards. Closed Mon.*

Besenwirtschaft. The floor is bare boards, the tables rough wood, and the vegetarian-based food at this highly original pub is simple but imaginative, with a small menu that changes daily and an impressive wine list. The Ku'damm is a 10-minute walk away. *Uhlandstrasse 159, tel. 030/881-1623. No credit cards.*

Blockhaus Nikolskoe. Prussian King Wilhelm III built this Russian-style wooden lodge for his daughter Charlotte, wife of Russian Czar Nicholas I. Located south of the city on Glienecker Park, it offers open-air riverside dining in the summer. Game dishes are prominently featured. *Nikolskoer Weg, tel. 030/805–2914. Reservations advised. AE, DC, MC, V.*

★ **Hardtke.** This is about the most authentic old Berlin restaurant in the city. The decor is simple, with paneled walls and wood floor. The food is similarly traditional and hearty.*Meinekestr. 27, tel. 030/881–9827. Reservations advised. No credit cards.*

Historische Gaststätte auf der Zitadelle. Here you'll banquet like a medieval noble, served by Prussian maidens and serenaded by minstrels. In winter, a roaring fire helps warm the vaulted restaurant, which is part of Spandau's historic citadel. *Am Juliusturm, Spandau, tel. 030/334–2106. Reservations required. AE, DC, MC, V.*

★ **Ratskeller Schöneberg.** If you're visiting the Liberty Bell at the Rathaus Schöneberg, drop into the Ratskeller. Fixed-price menus keep costs low, but there's an à la carte menu, too. The food is resolutely traditional. *John-F.-Kennedy-Pl., tel. 030/783–2127. AE, DC, MC, V. Closed 3–6 PM and Thurs.*

Wirtshaus Moorlake. You need a car (or a taxi, about DM 25) to reach this enchanting lakeside restaurant deep in the Grunewald, which was built in 1840 as a royal hunting lodge. Reserve a table upstairs under the exposed beams. Weekdays are less crowded. Despite the Bavarian surroundings, the menu is mostly Berlin fare. *An der Moorlake, tel. 030/805–5809. Reservations advised. AE, DC, MC, V. Closed Tues. and winter evenings.*

East Berlin

Alex Grill. This cafeteria-style restaurant pulls in the crowds because of its range of offerings and the good value it gives for money—it is truly a feat to get in at lunchtime. *Alexanderpl., in the Hotel Berlin, tel. 02/2190. No credit cards.*

★ **Alt-Cöllner Schankstuben.** Four tiny restaurants are contained within this charming, historic Berlin house. The section to the side of the canal on the Kleine Gertraudenstrasse, where there are tables set outside, serves as a café. The menu is relatively limited, but quality, like the service, is good. *Friederichsgracht 50, tel. 02/212–5972. No credit cards.*

★ **Arkade.** The art deco-style interior is a refreshing change from other East Berlin restaurants, though in good weather you may choose to dine outside. Inside, the front section is more of a café, while the grill counter at the back offers a greater variety. This is a convenient place to grab a snack after a performance at the nearby Komische Oper (Comic Opera). *Französische Str. 25, tel. 02/208–0273. No credit cards.*

★ **Quick.** Low prices and tip-top quality have long made this self-service cafeteria popular. It's mobbed at noon; go slightly earlier or later if possible. Note that it closes at 8 PM. *Karl-Liebknecht-Str. 5, in the Palast Hotel, tel. 02/2410. No credit cards.*

★ **Zur letzten Instanz.** Unquestionably Berlin's oldest restaurant, established in 1525, this place is imbued with Old World charm.

The choice of food is, as usual, limited, but it is prepared in the genuine Berlin tradition and is truly hearty—you'll find beer in the cooking as well as in your mug. *Waisenstr. 14–16 (U-bahn Klosterstr.), tel. 02/212–5528. Reservations essential. No credit cards.*

Under DM 20

West Berlin **Eierschale.** This well-placed *Frühstückskneipe* (*see above*), on a central corner of the Ku'damm, serves breakfasts at all hours but really gets going in the evening, when jazz groups perform in a neighboring room. Lunch and supper tend toward filling Berlin fare, but the Mexican-style spare ribs are recommended. At the Sunday morning *Frühschoppen*, live jazz accompanies the buffet brunch. *Rankestr. 1, tel. 030/882–5305. MC.*

Karagiosi. A short walk from the Charlottenburg Palace, this simply furnished, friendly Greek restaurant offers food so authentic that you could be in Athens. If you're in luck, there'll be live music, too. *Klausenerpl. 5, tel. 030/798–2379. No credit cards.*

Splurge

West Berlin ★ **Bamberger Reiter.** The Tirolean chef at this leading restaurant relies on fresh market produce for his *neue deutsche Küche* (new German cuisine), so the menu changes daily. Fresh flowers set off this attractive oak-beamed restaurant. Expect to spend around DM 100 per person. *Regensburgerstr. 7, tel. 030/244–282. Reservations essential. Jacket and tie required. DC, V. Closed lunch, Sun., Mon., and Aug. 1–20.*

Rockendorf's. Only fixed-price menus, some up to nine courses, are offered in this elegant restaurant in the north of the city. Exquisitely presented on fine porcelain, the mainly nouvelle specialties are sometimes fused with classic German cuisine. Dinner for two should cost about DM 200. *Dusterhauptstr. 1, tel. 030/402–3099. Reservations essential. Jacket and tie required. AE, DC, MC, V. Closed Sun., Mon., 3 weeks in summer, Christmas, and New Year's.*

The Arts and Nightlife

The Arts

Today's Berlin has a tough task living up to the reputation it gained from the film *Cabaret*, but if nightlife is a little toned down since the '30s, the arts still flourish. In addition to the many hotels that book seats, there are several ticket agencies, including **Theaterkasse Sasse** (Ku'damm 24, tel. 030/882–7360), **Theater-kasse Centrum** (Mienekestr. 25, tel. 030/882–7611). Most of the big stores (Hertie, Wertheim, and Karstadt, for example) also have ticket agencies, while in East Berlin tickets can be obtained from the tourist office in Alexanderplatz, and at ticket offices in the Palast and Grand hotels. Detailed information about what's going on in Berlin can be found in *Berlin Programm*, a monthly guide to Berlin arts (DM 2.50), East Berlin's monthly *Wohin in Berlin?*, and the magazines *Tip* and *Zitty*, which appear every two weeks and provide full arts listings.

If you're a student with I.D. from any university or higher place of learning, you're in luck: the evening box offices of city-run theaters, opera houses, and concert halls will sell you any available tickets at half-price. Otherwise, the best way to keep theater costs to a minimum in expensive Berlin is to buy tickets at the box office—the ticket agencies demand a fee of DM 3 or more. For information on free organ recitals and concert rehearsals, *see* The City for Free—or Almost, *above*.

Theater Theater in Berlin is outstanding, but performances are usually in German. The exceptions are operettas and the (nonliterary) cabarets. Of the city's 18 theaters, the most renowned for both its modern and classical productions is the **Schaubühne am Lehniner Platz** (Kurfürstendamm 153, tel. 030/890–020. Also important are the **Schiller-Theater** (Bismarckstr. 110, tel. 030/319–5236), which has an excellent workshop—the **Werkstatt,** specializing in experimental and avant-garde theater; **the Schlosspark-Theater** (Schlossstr. 48, tel. 030/791123); **the Renaissance-Theater** (Hardenbergstr. 6, tel. 030/312–4202); the **Freie Volksbühne** (Schaperstr. 24, tel. 030/8812489). For *Boulevard* plays (fashionable social comedies), there is the **Komödie** (Kurfürstendamm 206, tel. 030/8827893), and at the same address the **Theater am Kurfürstendamm** (tel. 030/8842080), and the **Hansa Theater** (Alt Moabit 48, tel. 030/391–4460). Among the smaller, more experimental theaters is the **Tribune** (Otto-Suhr-Allee 18–20, tel. 030/341–2600), a youthful enterprise.

East Berlin's leading theaters include: the **Berliner Ensemble** (Bertolt-Brecht-Pl., tel. 02/2888155), dedicated to Brecht and works of other international playwrights; **Deutsches Theater** (Schumannstr. 13–14, tel. 02/287–1225), for outstanding classical and contemporary German drama; **Friedrichstadtpalais** (Friedrichstr. 107, tel. 02/28360), a glossy showcase for variety revues and historic old Berlin theater pieces; **Kammerspiele** (Schumannstr. 13–14, tel. 02/287–1226), a studio theater attached to the Deutsches Theater; **Maxim-Gorki-Theater** (Am Festungsgraben, tel. 02/2071790), featuring plays by local authors and some contemporary humor; and **Volksbühne** (Rosa-Luxemburg-Pl., tel. 02/2828978), featuring classical and contemporary drama.

Berlin's savage and debunking idiom is particularly suited to social and political satire, a long tradition in cabaret theaters here. The **Stachelschweine** (Europa Center, tel. 030/261–4795) and **die Wühlmäuse** (1/30 Nürnbergerstr. 33, tel. 030/213–7047) carry on that tradition with biting wit and style; East Berlin's equivalent is **Distel** (Friedrichstr. 100, tel. 02/287–1226). For children's theater, try **Klecks** (Schinkestr. 8/9, tel. 030/693–7731) or the **Literarisches Figurentheater** (Kleistr. 13–14, Schöneberg); **Puppentheater** (Greifswalderstr. 81–84, tel. 02/436–1343), East Berlin's puppet theater, is nominally for children but can be good entertainment for adults as well.

Concerts Berlin is the home of one of the world's leading orchestras, the **Berliner Philharmonisches Orchester** (Berlin Philharmonic), in addition to a number of other major symphony orchestras and orchestral ensembles. The **Berlin Festival Weeks,** held annually from August to October, combine a wide range of concerts, operas, ballet, theater, and art exhibitions. For information and reservations, write **Festspiele GmbH** (Kartenbüro, Budapesterstr. 50, 1000 Berlin 30).

Opera, Ballet, and Musicals The **Deutsche Oper Berlin** (Bismarckstr. 35, tel. 030/3410249) is one of Germany's leading opera houses and presents outstanding productions year-round. The ballet also performs here. Tickets for both are expensive and sell out quickly. At the **Neuköllner Oper** (Karl-Marx-Str. 131–133, tel. 030/687–6061) you'll find showy, fun performances of long-forgotten operas and humorous musical productions. The skillfully restored **Theater des Westens** (Kantstr. 12, tel. 030/31903193) is the ideal setting for comic operas and musicals like *West Side Story, A Chorus Line,* and *Cabaret.* Experimental ballet and modern dance are presented at the **Tanzfabrik** in Kreuzberg (Möckernstr. 66, tel. 030/786–5861).

East Berlin's main sites for opera, operettas, and dance are the **Deutsche Staatsoper** (Unter den Linden 7, tel. 02/2004762), the **Komische Oper** (Behrenstr. 55–57, tel. 02/2292555), and the **Metropol Theater** (Friedrichstr. 101, tel. 02/2082715).

Film Berlin has around 90 movie theaters, showing about 100 movies a day. International and German movies are shown in the big theaters around the Ku'damm; the "Off-Ku'damm" theaters show less commercial movies. For (un-dubbed) movies in English, go to the **Odeon** (Hauptstr. 116, tel. 030/781–5667) or the **Arsenal** (Welserstr. 25, tel. 030/246–848). Films from East Germany's state archives are shown Tuesday and Friday at 5:30 and 8 at **Filmtheater Babylon** (Rosa-Luxemburg-Str. 30, tel. 02/212–5076).

In February, Berlin hosts the **Internationale Filmfestspiele,** an internationally famous film festival, conferring "Golden Bear" awards on the best films, directors, and actors. The organizers, under pressure from an increasingly popular film festival that takes place in Munich every June, are considering moving the two-week event to summer. Call tel. 030/254890 for information.

Nightlife

Berlin's nightlife has always been notorious. There are scads of places in West Berlin to seek your nighttime entertainment, and the quality ranges widely from tacky to spectacular. East Berlin's nightlife has not been on a par with the western sector, although that is changing.

All Berlin tour operators offer **Night Club Tours** (around DM 100, including entrance fees to up to three shows, free drinks, and, in some cases, supper). Most places in West Berlin stay open late; some have all-night liquor licenses.

Clubs **Chez Nous** (Marburgerstr. 14, tel. 030/213–1810) lives up to Berlin's reputation as the drag-show center of Germany. Empire-style plush is the backdrop for two nightly shows (reservations recommended).

You'll find three more-conventional stage shows at **Dollywood** (Kurfürstenstr. 114, tel. 030/248–950) each night, plus a disco. **La Vie en Rose** (Europa Center, tel. 030/323–6006) is a revue theater with spectacular light shows that also showcases international stars (book ahead). If the strip show at the **New Eden** (Ku'damm 71, tel. 030/323–5849) doesn't grab you, maybe the dance music will (two bands nightly). All four clubs have a cover charge that won't break the bank. The cover includes one drink, which it pays to nurse before ordering another.

Jazz Clubs Berlin's lively music scene is dominated by jazz and rock. For jazz enthusiasts, *the* events of the year are the summer's **Jazz in the Garden** festival and the international autumn **Jazz Fest Berlin.** For information call the **Berlin Tourist Information Center** (Europa Center, tel. 030/262–6031).

Traditionally, the best **live jazz** can be found at:

Eierschale (Podbielskiallee 50, tel. 030/832–7097). A variety of jazz groups appear here at the "Egg Shell"; daily from 8:30 PM, admission free.
Flöz (Nassauischestr. 36A, tel. 030/861–1000). The sizzling jazz at this club is sometimes incorporated into theater presentations.
Kunstlerhaus Bethanien (Mariannenpl. 2, tel. 030/614–8010). Jazz and "Free Music" concerts are held at this big venue.
Quartier Latin (Potsdamerstr. 96, tel. 030/2629016). The Quartier Latin is one of the leaders in Berlin's jazz scene. Jazz and rock are both presented.

Discos **Blue Note** (Courbierestr. 13, tel. 030/247–248). For an escape from the usual disco sounds, try the Blue Note; you'll find a tasty mixture of jazz, bebop, and Latin American rhythms. Open until 6 AM.
Dschungel (Nürnbergerstr. 53, tel. 030/246–698). A funky disco, "Jungle," is a current "in" spot. Dance until you drop, or at least until 4 AM. Closed Tuesday.
Hafenbar (Chauseestr. 20). This is a popular East Berlin disco decorated in '50s style. Closed Wednesday.
Haifischbar (Unter den Linden 5). This East Berlin disco is part of the Opern Café complex.
Metropol (Nollendorfpl. 5, tel. 030/216–2787). Berlin's largest disco, which stages occasional concerts, is a hot spot for the younger tourist. The black dance floor upstairs is the scene for a magnificent light and laser show. The DM 10 cover includes your first drink.

Kneipen Berlin has roughly 5,000 bars and pubs; this includes the dives, too. All come under the heading of *Kneipen*—the place round the corner where you stop in for a beer, a snack, a conversation, and sometimes, to dance.

Bogen 597 (Savignypl., S-bahn passage). Sound effects are provided by the S-bahn—you'll hear and feel the trains passing on the tracks overhead. This is a cozy place that serves a fine selection of wines in addition to the inevitable beer.
Ku'dorf (Joachimstaler-Str. 15). The Ku'dorf makes it easy to go from one Kneipe to another—there are 18 located under one roof here, underground, just off the Ku'damm. Open Monday–Saturday from 8 PM.
Leydicke (Mansteinstr. 4). This historic spot is a must for out-of-towners. The proprietors operate their own distillery and have a superb selection of wines and liqueurs; definitely the right atmosphere in which to enjoy a few glasses.
Zur Nolle (Nollendorfpl.). You can sit in an old subway car in this converted (above-ground) subway station and enjoy live Dixieland music. Berlin specialties are served from the buffet. Check it out on a Sunday morning as you stroll around the local flea market.
Sperlingsgasse (Lietzenburgerstr. 82–84). Look for the replica of the Brandenburg Gate on the sidewalk. It'll point you in the direction of the 13 different Kneipen here. All open at 7 PM.

Wilhelm Hoeck (Wilmersdorferstr. 149). Berlin's oldest Kneipe is also its most beautiful. Its superb interior dates back to 1892—all original. Frequented by a colorful cross section of the public, this is a place that's definitely worth a visit.

Wirthaus Wuppke (Schlüterstr. 21). Come here if you're seeking a mellower, quieter atmosphere. It gets as crowded as the others, but it's not so hectic. The food is good and inexpensive.

Yorckschlösschen (Yorckstr. 15). In the summer you can sit in the garden and enjoy a beer and a snack or a hearty meal. If you're lucky, there may be live music.

Zwiebelfisch (Savignypl. 7). Literally translated as the "onion fish," this Kneipe has become the meeting place of literary Bohemians of all ages. It has a good atmosphere for getting to know people. The beer is good, the menu small.

14 Excursions from Berlin

Potsdam, Magdeburg, Dresden, Leipzig, and Meissen

Reunification has unleashed a surge of tourists on eastern Germany. Is the region ready for them? At press time the former German Democratic Republic was still in a state of flux. The transportation and communications systems of the two halves of a country so long divided have to be completely integrated, and that will take time. The former East German tourism ministry and tourist boards are being taken over by West German authorities, and the resultant bureaucratic problems are formidable.

Meanwhile, prices are shooting up to western levels. Travelers who remember East Germany as a low-budget paradise will be disappointed to find an area where the cost of comfortable lodgings has gone through the roof. As this process of price adjustment is still under way, it's difficult to predict costs (or much else) accurately. Museums and art galleries are still converting their old admission charges into the new Deutschemark currency. Telephone exchanges in eastern Germany are also being expanded to accommodate the sudden surge in calls from the West, and numbers are being altered at a frustrating rate.

As you travel here you'll see ample evidence of past grandeur. Alas, you'll also find the ongoing depredations of a modern industrial society: scarred landscapes, polluted air. It will take years before the dying forests in the south can rejuvenate, years before the ancient soot-stained factories are replaced. The deteriorating public housing projects of the '50s and '60s cannot be razed any faster than the acrid smell of brown coal smoke can be eliminated. Still, the towns of eastern Germany—in regions once known as Prussia, Saxony, Thuringia—tell more about an older Germany than do the frenetic lifestyles of the western cities. The Communist influence, hard-line as it was, never penetrated here as deeply as the American influence in the west did. East Germany clung to its German heritage, proudly preserving connections with such national heroes as Luther, Goethe, Schiller, Bach, and Wagner. And although bombing raids in World War II devastated most of its cities, the East Germans, over the years, carried out an extensive program of restoring and rebuilding the historic neighborhoods. Meissen porcelain, Frederick the Great's palace at Potsdam, the astounding collections of the Zwinger palace in Dresden will now be incorporated in the total national heritage.

The five side trips we offer here start with an easy day trip to Potsdam, but the remaining four—to cities lying two hours or more from Berlin—may make more sense as overnight excursions. The choice of hotels remains limited, and although private householders may now rent rooms, the demand is far greater than the supply. Contact the local tourist information offices for names of additional bed-and-breakfasts.

Potsdam

Tourist office: Friedrich-Ebert-Str. 5, tel. 033/23385 (in the center of town near Platz der Einheit).

From Berlin
By Train The trip takes a half-hour or so. Take the S-bahn (either the S-5 or the S-1 line) to Wannsee. Change there for the short rail trip to Potsdam Stadt (for Schloss Sanssouci), Potsdam West (for Schloss Charlottenhof), or Wildpark (for Neues Palais) station. You also can take the No. 113 bus from Wannsee to the Bassanplatz bus station, and walk from there down Brandenburgerstrasse to Platz der Nationen and on to the Green Gate, the main entrance to Sanssouci park; or you can take the No. 695 bus to the park.

By Bus There is regular bus service from the bus station at the Funkturm, Messedamm 8 (U-1 U-bahn station Kaiserdamm). It's a half-hour journey.

By Boat Boats leave hourly from Wannsee landing between 10 AM and 6 PM.

By Car From Berlin center (Strasse des 17 Juni) take the Potsdamerstrasse south until it becomes Route 1 and then follow the signs to Potsdam. City traffic is heavy, however, and the journey is easier by rail, even though there are no direct trains.

Guided Tours **Severin & Kühn** offers a whole-day tour for DM 89 (including lunch). **Berliner Bären Stadtrundfahrt** conducts an afternoon tour that includes tea in its DM 65 price. Berolina and Bus-Verkehr-Berlin also offer tours of Potsdam from Berlin (*see* Guided Tours in Chapter 13).

Exploring Potsdam is virtually a suburb of Berlin, some 20 kilometers (12 miles) southwest of the city center. Germany's most famous king, Friedrich II—Frederick the Great—spent more time at his summer residence there than at the official court in Berlin, and it's no wonder. Frederick was an aesthetic ruler, and he clearly fell for the sheer beauty of a sleepy township lost among the hills, meadows, and lakes of this rural corner of mighty Prussia. Frederick's father, Friedrich Wilhelm I, had established the Prussian court at Potsdam, but the royal castle didn't match the demanding tastes of his son and heir, who built a summer palace of his own amid green lawns above the Havel River. He called it "Sanssouci," meaning "without a care" in the French language he cultivated in his own private circle and within the court.

Some experts believe Frederick actually named the palace "Sans, Souci," which they translate as "with and without a care," a more apt name because its construction caused him a lot of trouble and expense and sparked furious rows with his master builder, Georg Wenzeslaus von Knobelsdorff (Frederick called him fat and lazy). Growing increasingly restive over the expense, Frederick told von Knobelsdorff he wanted the palace to last only his lifetime, but fortunately the Prussian architect ignored him, and his creation became one of Germany's greatest tourist attractions (5 million visitors a year file through the palace and grounds). In 1993 Potsdam celebrates its 1,000th birthday, so if you plan to visit that year book well in advance.

A double ceremony that took place in 1991 drew big crowds, when Frederick the Great was given the burial he requested in his will but that was denied him by his nephew and successor, Friedrich Wilhelm II. Frederick wanted to be buried beside his hunting dogs on the terrace of his beloved Sanssouci, with no pomp and ceremony; a "philosopher's funeral" was what he decreed. His shocked nephew ordered the body to be laid out in state and then consigned Frederick's remains to the garrison church of Potsdam. The coffin was removed to safety during World War II, after which time it went on a macabre peregrination that ended in the chapel of the Hohenzollern castle in southern Germany. The unification of Germany made it possible to grant Frederick his last wish. On the same day, the body of his father was reinterred, on the 250th anniversary of his death, at the so-called Peace Church, also on the Sanssouci grounds.

As you walk through Potsdam's own **Brandenburger Tor,** a victory arch built 25 years after Sanssouci, what you see today of the Hohenzollern palace complex, contained in a beautifully landscaped park and one of the most important European royal residences of its time, is largely re-created. Just weeks before the end of World War II, Potsdam was razed by British bombing, and the battle for Berlin finished it off. The East Germans did a magnificent restoration job. There is no charge to enter the grounds.

The vine-covered terraces on which **Sanssouci** stands are actually an artificial hill, rising in majestic steps from a side stream of the Havel, a few minutes' walk from the center of Potsdam.

Executed according to Frederick's impeccable, French-influenced taste, the palace is extravagantly Rococo, with scarcely a patch of wall left unadorned. Strangely, Frederick occupied only five rooms; his bedroom, study, and circular library (beautifully paneled with cedar wood) can be visited. Five rooms were kept for guests, one exclusively reserved for the French writer and philosopher Voltaire. Johann Sebastian Bach was also a welcome visitor; he and Frederick, a competent musician, performed together in the palace music chamber, considered one of Germany's finest Rococo interiors. To the west of the palace is the **New Chambers** (1747), which housed guests of the king's family; originally it functioned as a greenhouse until it was remodeled in 1771–74. Just east of Sanssouci palace is the **Picture Gallery** (1755–1763), which still displays Frederick's collection of 17th-century Italian and Dutch paintings.

At the end of the long, straight avenue that runs through Sanssouci Park you'll see a much larger and grander palace, the **Neues Palais** (New Palace). Frederick loosened the purse-strings in building this palace after the Seven Years War (1756–63), and it's said he wanted to demonstrate to his subjects that the state coffers hadn't been depleted too severely by the long conflict. Frederick rarely stayed here, however, preferring the relative coziness of Sanssouci. Still, the Neues Palais has much of interest, including an indoor grotto hall, a Jules Verne-like extravaganza of walls and columns set with shells, coral, and other aquatic decoration. There's a fascinating collection of musical instruments, which includes a 900-year-old portable organ; the Upper Gallery, which contains paintings by 17th-century Italian masters; and a bijou court theater in which performances are still given during an annual music festival held in June or July.

After Frederick died in 1786, the ambitious Sanssouci building program ground to a halt and the park fell into neglect. It was 50 years before another Prussian king, Frederick William III, restored Sanssouci's earlier glory. He engaged the great Berlin architect Karl Friedrich Schinkel to build a small palace for the crown prince. The result is the **Schloss Charlottenhof,** set in its own grounds in the southern part of the Sanssouci park. Schinkel gave it a classical, almost Roman appearance, and he let his imagination loose in the interior, too—decorating one of the rooms as a Roman tent, with its walls and ceiling draped in striped canvas.

Just north of the Schloss Charlottenhof, on the path back to Sanssouci, you'll find two other later additions to the park: Friedrich Wilhelm II's **Roman baths** (1836) and a **teahouse** built in 1757 in the Chinese style, which was all the rage at the time. (The teahouse was closed for restoration in 1991 and is expected to reopen in May 1992.) Between the Neues Palais and the Sanssouci is the **Orangerie** (completed in 1860), which, with two massive towers linked by a colonnade, evokes an Italian Renaissance palace. Today it houses 47 copies of paintings by Raphael. Halfway up the park's Drachenberg hill, above the Orangerie, stands the curious **Drachenhaus** (Dragon House), modeled in 1770 after the Pagoda at London's Kew Gardens and named for the gargoyles ornamenting the roof corners. When built, it served as the residence of the palace vintner; it now houses a popular café.

Elsewhere in the park, a delicious layer cake **"mosque"** disguises pump works that operated the fountains in the Sanssouci park; the minaret concealed the chimney. The Italianate **Peace Church** (1845–48) houses a 12th-century Byzantine mosaic taken from an island near Venice.

The final addition to the Sanssouci park is equally exotic. Resembling a rambling, half-timbered country manor house, the **Schloss Cecilienhof** was built for Crown Prince Wilhelm in 1913 in a newly laid out stretch of the park bordering the Heiliger See, called the New Garden. It was here that the Allied leaders

Truman, Atlee, and Stalin hammered out the fate of postwar Germany, at the 1945 Potsdam Conference. You can see the round table where they held their meetings; in fact, you can stay the night under the roof where they gathered to make history, for the Cecilienhof is today a very comfortable hotel (*see* Lodging, *below*). Also in the New Garden is the substantial two-story **Marble Palace,** completed in 1792, using gray-white Silesian marble to ornament the red brickwork. Formerly housing a military museum, it is closed for restoration until 2000. *Information Center, Sanssouci: tel. 033/22051. Open Apr.–Oct., daily 9–4:30. Schloss Sanssouci admission (guided tours only): DM 6 adults, DM 3 children. Open Apr.–mid-Oct., daily 9–5; mid-Oct.–Jan. 9–3, Feb., and Mar., daily 9–4; closed first and third Mon. of month. New Chambers admission: DM 4 adults, DM 2 children. Open Sat.–Thurs. 9–5. Picture Gallery admission: DM 3 adults, DM 1.50 children. Open mid-May–mid-Oct., daily 9–5, closed fourth Wed. of month. Neues Palais admission with tour: DM 6 adults, DM 3 children; without tour: DM 5 adults, DM 2.50 children. Open Apr.–mid-Oct., daily 9–5; mid-Oct.–Jan., daily 9–3; Feb. and Mar., daily 9–4; closed second and fourth Mon. of month. Schloss Charlottenhof admission (guided tour only): DM 3 adults, DM 2 children. Open mid-May–mid-Oct., daily 9–5; closed fourth Mon. of month. Roman baths admission (additional charge for special exhibitions): DM 2 adults, DM 1 children. Open mid-May–mid-Oct., daily 9–5; closed third Mon. of month. Chinese teahouse admission (closed for restoration; reopening May 1992): DM 1. Open mid-May–mid-Oct., daily 9–5; closed one Mon. a month. Orangerie admission (additional charge for special exhibitions): DM 3 adults, DM 1.50 children. Open mid-May–mid-Oct., daily 9–5; closed fourth Thurs. of month. Mosque admission: DM 3. Open mid-May–mid-Oct., daily 9–5; closed fourth Mon. in month. Schloss Cecilienhof admission (nonguests): DM 3, DM 1.50 children. Open daily 9–4:15, closed second and fourth Mon. of month.*

Don't leave Potsdam without looking over the town itself, which still retains the imperial character lent to it by the many years it served as royal residence and garrison quarters. The central market square, the **Alter Markt,** sums it all up: the stately, domed **Nikolaikirche** (1724), a square Baroque church with classical columns; an **Egyptian obelisk** erected by Sanssouci architect von Knobelsdorff; and the officious facade of the former **city hall** (1755), now the Haus Marchiwitza, with a gilded figure of Atlas atop the tower. Wander around some of the adjacent streets, particularly Wilhelm-Külz-Strasse, to admire the handsome restored burghers' houses.

Three blocks north of the Alter Markt is the **Holländisches Viertel,** built by Friedrich Wilhelm I in 1732 to induce Dutch artisans to settle in a city that needed migrant labor to support its rapid growth. (Few Dutch came, and the gabled, hip-roofed brick houses were used mostly to house staff.) The Dutch government has promised to finance some of the cost of repairing the damage done by more than four decades of Communist administration.

There's a chilling reminder of the Communist years a few steps away from the central shopping street, Brandenburgerstrasse. Turn down Otto-Nuschke-Strasse, and at number 54 you'll find an old guardhouse that served as a prison for victims of the

East German State Security Service, the dreaded Stasi. It's now empty of its political prisoners, and you can step through the outside door and into the tiny exercise yard, overlooked by small barred windows. The new political parties that replaced the Communists have taken over the administrative offices, together with an enterprising Potsdamer who has opened a café there!

Lodging
Under DM 130

Schloss Cecilienhof. This English country-style mansion is where Truman, Atlee, and Stalin drew up the 1945 Potsdam Agreement. The hotel rooms are somewhat mundane, although comfortable and adequately equipped. The Schloss is set in its own parkland bordering a lake and is a pleasant stroll from Sanssouci and the city center. *Neuer Garten, tel. 033/231141. 42 rooms with bath or shower. Facilities: sauna, masseur, restaurant. AE, DC, MC, V.*

Dining
Under DM 40

Am Stadttor. A five-minute walk from the Sanssouci palace on Potsdam's main shopping street, the Stadttor is the ideal spot for lunch. The soups are particularly wholesome, and the liver Berlin-style is as good as any you'll find in the city. *Brandenburgerstrasse 1–3, tel. 033/21729. Reservations advised. No credit cards.*

Magdeburg

Tourist office: Reisebüro, Wilhelm-Pieck-Allee 14 (near the main railway station), tel. 091/35352.

From Berlin
By Train

Trains leave approximately every two hours from Bahnhof Zoo in Berlin; the trip takes about two hours.

By Bus

Buses leave from the Funkturm bus station in Berlin for the 100-minute drive.

By Car

Magdeburg is located just off the E-8 motorway, the old transit road connecting Berlin and Hannover. It's 150 kilometers (90 miles) west of Berlin, a 90-minute drive as long as the motorway is clear. (In summer and at weekends, when the E-8 gets crowded, the two-hour train ride from Berlin might be preferable.) To get to the town center follow the signs for Magdeburg-Stadtmitte.

Exploring

Much of Magdeburg was rebuilt after the 1945 bombing in the dull utilitarian style favored by the Communists, but there are nevertheless corners where the town's 1,200-year history still lingers. If you arrive by train or bus, head east from the main railway station (the bus depot is beside it) for two blocks to the city center, the Alter Markt, which is dominated on the west side by the 17th-century **Rathaus** (City Hall), one of Magdeburg's few remaining Baroque buildings. In front of its arcaded facade is a 1966 bronze copy of Germany's oldest equestrian statue, the **Magdeburger Reiter,** completed by an unknown master around 1240. The sandstone original is now in the nearby **Kulturhistorisches Museum,** where you can also see the simple invention with which the 17th-century scientist Otto von Güricke proved the extraordinary power created by a vacuum. The device consisted of just two iron cups; von Güricke sealed them together by pumping out the air—and then attached the hollow sphere to two teams of eight cart-horses, which were urged to pull the cups apart. The vacuum proved stronger. *Otto-von-Güricke-Strasse 68–73. Admission: DM 3 adults, DM 1.50 children. Open Tues.–Sun. 10–6.*

Head down Breiter Weg (formerly Karl-Marx-Strasse, a name that was one of the first casualties of the fall of East German communism). To your left you'll see the mighty twin towers of Magdeburg's Gothic **cathedral** of saints Maurice and Catherine rearing up above the rooftops. Opposite the post office on Breiter Weg turn left into Domplatz, and there is the soaring west front of the cathedral before you. The awesome structure was begun in 1209, making it the oldest Gothic church in Germany; it was completed in 1520. The founder of the Holy Roman Empire, Otto I, lies buried beneath the choir, his tomb overshadowed by graceful columns of Ravenna marble. Study the representations of famous Christian martyrs on the walls of the nave; you'll find them all standing determinedly on the heads of their persecutors (that's Nero under the heel of St. Paul). A more recent memorial is Expressionist artist Ernst Barlach's sculptured group warning of the horrors of war. It was removed by the Nazis in 1933, but it's back with all its original force. *Open Mon.–Sat. 10–noon and 2–4; Sun. 2–4. Guided tours: Mon.–Sat. 10 and 2, Sun. 11:15 and 2.*

Just north of Domplatz and on the way back to the city center is Magdeburg's second great attraction, the Romanesque monastery church and cloisters of **Unser Lieben Frauen.** The church, built in the years 1064–1230, now serves as a concert hall and an art gallery. Gothic sculptures share space with modern east German works in sober surroundings which encourage meditation and reflection—there's also a café for more mundane requirements. *Regierungstr. 4–6, tel. 091/33741 (concert information). Open Tues.–Sun. 10–6.*

Both the cathedral and Unsere Lieben Frauen are a few strides from the Elbe River, where some fine walks open up through the wooded **Kulturpark.**

Magdeburg is an ideal center from which to explore the Elbe River countryside between the Harz Mountains and the Brandenburg plains. The tourist office (*see above*) offers bus tours of the region. Ships of the eastern German shipping line Weisse Flotte (tel. 091/31907) embark from Magdeburg on day trips and longer cruises on the Elbe.

Lodging
Under DM 130

Grüner Baum. This is one of the few hotels in eastern Germany to have remained in private hands throughout the years of Communist state control. At press time, there were plans to give it a long-overdue renovation (which will add private baths), so call beforehand to check on the availability of rooms (which are large). *Wilhelm-Pieck-Allee 40, tel. 091/30862. 40 rooms without bath. No credit cards.*

Dining
Under DM 40

Stadt Prag. The "City of Prague" restaurant has a menu that reads like a culinary tour of the former Hapsburg empire, from chicken Viennese style to Bohemian dumplings by way of Hungarian goulash. *Wilhelm-Pieck-Allee 10, tel. 091/51162. Reservations advised. No credit cards.*

Under DM 30

Böthelstube. Drop in after you tour the museum. Local specialties such as *Magdeburger Lose Wurst* and *Kochklops*—a variety of sausage and dumplings—are served with an excellent beer. *Alter Markt 3, tel. 091/35940. No credit cards. Closed Sat. dinner and Sun.*

Haus des Handwerks. The large, echoing restaurant has the atmosphere of an East European railway station buffet. It's not central, but is well worth the 10-minute journey (No. 10 tram).

Garaisstr. 10, tel. 091/51422. Reservations advised. No credit cards.

Dresden

Tourist office: Dresden Information, Prager Str. 10–11, tel. 051/495–5025.

From Berlin *By Train* Trains leave about once an hour from Berlin's Lichtenberg station for the two-hour run to Dresden.

By Bus There is no direct bus link between Berlin and Dresden, but all the major Berlin tour operators offer Dresden day trips, leaving Berlin at 8 or 9 and returning in the early evening. The cost is around DM 100 and sometimes includes lunch.

By Car Leave Berlin at Köpenick and head south on Autobahn E-15, following the Dresden signs. You can do the 170 kilometers (105 miles) comfortably in two hours.

Exploring *Numbers in the margin correspond to points of interest on the Dresden map.*

Splendidly situated on a bend in the Elbe River, Dresden is a compact city easy to explore. In its rococo yellows and greens, it is enormously appealing, and the effect is even more overwhelming when you compare what you see today—or what Canaletto paintings reflect of a Dresden centuries earlier—with the photographs of Dresden in 1945, after a British bombing raid almost destroyed it overnight. It was one of the architectural and cultural treasures of the civilized world, and the fact that, despite lack of funds and an often uncooperative Communist bureaucracy, the people of Dresden succeeded in rebuilding it is an enormous tribute to their skills and dedication.

Their efforts restored at least the riverside panorama to the appearance Canaletto would have recognized, but some of the other parts of the city center look halfway between construction and demolition. In the coming years the city will look more like a building site than ever as 20 new hotels are added to provide the accommodations the city so desperately needs. Don't think of staying in Dresden without reserving a hotel room well in advance.

Dresden was the capital of Saxony as early as the 15th century, although most of its architectural masterpieces date from the 18th century, when the enlightened Saxon ruler August the Strong and his son, Frederick Augustus II, brought leading Italian and Bavarian architects and designers up from the south. The predominantly Italianate influence is evident today in gloriously overblown Rococo architecture. *Streetcar tours leave from Postplatz Tues.–Sun. at 9, 11, and 1:30; bus tours, leaving from Dr.-Kulz-Ring, run on Tues., Wed., and Thurs., at 11 (call tel. 051/495–5025 for details).*

The starting point of our Dresden tour will be the main railway station (which has adequate parking for those traveling by car). To reach the old part of the city and its treasures you'll first have to cross a featureless expanse surrounded by postwar high rises, leading into the pedestrians-only Pragerstrasse (the tourist information office is at No. 10–11). Cross busy Dr.-Külz-Ring and you'll enter a far different scene, the broad
1 **Altmarkt,** whose colonnaded beauty has managed to survive the disfiguring efforts of city planners to turn it into a huge

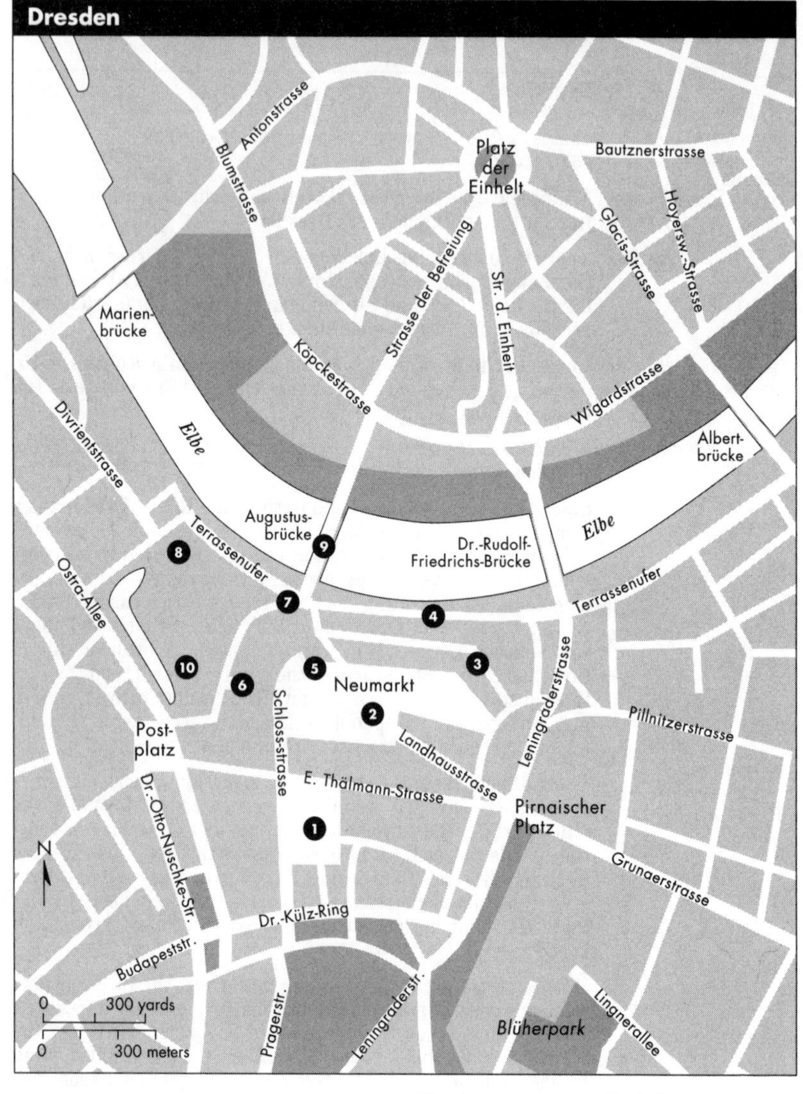

Albertinum, **3**
Altmarkt, **1**
Augustusbrücke, **9**
Brühlsche Terrasse, **4**
Frauenkirche, **2**
Herzogschloss, **6**
Johanneum, **5**
Katholische Hofkirche, **7**
Semperoper, **8**
Zwinger, **10**

outdoor parking lot. The church on your right, the Kreuzkirche, is an interesting combination of Baroque and Jugendstil architecture and decoration. A church stood here in the 13th century, but the present structure dates from the late-18th century. The rebuilt Rathaus is on your left, as is the yellow-stucco, 18th-century Landhaus, which contains the **Museum für Geschichte der Stadt Dresden** (City Historical Museum). *Ernst-Thälmann-Str. 2. Admission: DM 2 adults, DM 1 children. Open Mon.–Thurs. and Sat. 10–6, Sun. 10–4.*

At the northern end of the Altmarkt cross Ernst-Thälmann-Strasse (or pause for a window-shopping break on this broad boulevard) into the **Neumarkt** (New Market), which is, despite its name, the historic heart of old Dresden. The ruins on your right are all that remain of Germany's greatest Protestant church after the bombing raid of February 1945. These jagged, precariously tilting walls were once the mighty Baroque
2 **Frauenkirche,** so sturdily built that it withstood a three-day
bombardment during the Seven Years' War only to fall victim to the flames that followed the World War II raid. Like the Gedächtniskirche in Berlin, the Frauenkirche has been kept in its ruined state as a war memorial, although plans were announced in 1991 to rebuild it as a European cultural center.

The large, imperial-style building looming behind the Frauen-
3 kirche is the famous **Albertinum,** Dresden's leading art muse-
um. It is named after Saxony's King Albert, who between 1884 and 1887 converted a royal arsenal into a suitable setting for the treasures he and his forebears had collected. The upper story of the Albertinum, accessible from the Brühlsche Terrasse, houses the Gemäldegalerie Alte und Neue Meister (Gallery of Old and Modern Masters), temporarily displaying the highlights of the Sempergalerie while it is being restored (*see below*). Permanent exhibits include outstanding work by German masters of the 19th and 20th century (Caspar David Friedrich's haunting *Das Kreuz im Gebirge* is here) and French Impressionists and Post-Impressionists.

Impressive as the art gallery is, it's the Grünes Gewölbe (Green Vault) that draws the most attention. Named after a green room in the palace of August the Strong, this part of the Albertinum (entered from Georg-Treu-Platz) contains an exquisite collection of unique objects d'art fashioned from gold, silver, ivory, amber, and other precious and semiprecious materials. Among the crown jewels is the world's largest "green" diamond, 41 carats in weight, and a dazzling group of tiny gem-studded figures entitled *Hofstaat zu Delhi am Geburtstag des Grossmoguls Aureng-Zeb*. The name gives a false idea of the size of the work, dating from 1708, which represents a birthday gathering at the court of an Indian mogul; some parts of the tableau are so small that they can only be admired through a magnifying glass. Somewhat larger and less delicate is the drinking bowl of Ivan the Terrible, perhaps the most sensational of the treasures to be found in this extraordinary museum. Next door is the Skulpturensammlung (Sculpture Collection) that includes ancient Egyptian and classical works and examples by Giovanni da Bologna and Adriaen de Vries. Am Neumarkt. *Gemäldegalerie Alte und Neue Meister admission: DM 5 adults, DM 2.50 children. Open Tues. and Thurs.–Sun. 9–5, Wed. 9–6. Grünes Gewölbe and Skulpturen-*

sammlung admission: DM 5 adults, DM 2.50 children. Open Fri.–Tues. 9–5, Wed. 9–6.

4 If you leave the Albertinum by the **Brühlsche Terrasse** exit
you'll find yourself on what was once known as the "Balcony of
Europe," a terrace high above the Elbe, carved from a 16th-
century stretch of the city fortifications; from the terrace a
breathtaking vista of the Elbe and the Dresden skyline opens
up. The southern exit of the Albertinum brings you back to the
Neumarkt and to another former royal building that now serves
5 as a museum, the 16th-century **Johanneum,** once the regal stables. Instead of horses, the Johanneum now houses the
Verkehrsmuseum, a collection of historical vehicles, including
vintage automobiles and engines. *Neumarkt. Admission: DM
4 adults, DM 2 children. Open Wed.–Sun. 9–5, Tues. 9–6.*

Walk behind the Johanneum and into the former stable exercise yard, enclosed by elegant Renaissance arcades and used in the 16th century as an open-air festival ground. To spare the royalty on horseback the trouble of dismounting before ascending to the upper-story to watch the jousting and jollities in the yard below, a ramp was built to accommodate both two- and four-legged guests. You'll find the scene today much as it was centuries ago, complete with jousting markings in the ground. More popular even than jousting in those days was *Ringelstechen,* a risky pursuit in which riders at full gallop had to catch small rings on their lances. Horses and riders often came to grief in the narrow confines of the stable yard.

On the outside wall of the Johanneum is a remarkable example
of Meissen porcelain art: a painting on Meissen tiles of a royal
procession, 102 meters (336 feet) long. More than one hundred
members of the royal Saxon house of Wettin, half of them on
horseback, are represented on the giant jigsaw made up of
25,000 porcelain tiles, painted in 1904–07 after a design by Wilhelm Walther. Follow this unusual procession to the end and
6 you will come to the former royal palace, the **Herzogsschloss,**
where restoration work is under way behind the fine Renaissance facade. Although the work is expected to last well into
the 1990s, some of the finished rooms are hosting historical exhibitions. The main gate of the palace, the Georgentor, has acquired its original appearance, complete with an enormous
statue of the fully armed Saxon Count George, guarding the
portal that carries his name. The palace housed August the
Strong's Grünes Gewölbe before it was moved in its entirety to
the Albertinum. *Sophienstrasse. Admission: DM 5 adults, DM
2.50 children. Open Mon., Tues., and Thurs.–Sun. 9–5.*

Next to the Herzogschloss is the largest church in Saxony, the
7 **Katholische Hofkirche,** also known as the Cathedral of St.
Trinitas. The son of August the Strong, Frederick Augustus II
(ruled 1733–63), brought architects and builders from Italy to
construct a Catholic church in a city that had been the first
large center of Lutheran Protestantism. They worked away by
stealth, so the story goes, and Dresden's Protestant burgers
were presented with a fait accompli when the church was finally consecrated in 1754. Seventy-eight historical and biblical figures decorate the Italian High Baroque facade; inside, the
treasures include a beautiful stone pulpit by the royal sculptor
Balthasar Permoser and a 250-year-old church organ said to be
one of the finest ever to come from the mountain workshops of
the famous Silbermann family. In the cathedral's crypt are the

tombs of 49 Saxon rulers and a precious vessel containing the heart of August the Strong.

Opposite the cathedral on the Theaterplatz is the restored
8 **Semperoper** (Semper Opera house), justifiably one of Ger-
many's best-known and most popular theaters. Richard Wagner's *Rienzi, Der Fliegende Holländer*, and *Tannhäuser*, and Richard Strauss's *Salome, Elektra*, and *Der Rosenkavalier* all premiered here. The masterful Dresden architect Gottfried Semper built the opera house in 1838–41, in Italian Renaissance style, and then saw his work razed in a fire caused by a careless candle-lighter. Semper had to flee Dresden because of his participation in a democratic uprising, so his son Manfred rebuilt the theater, in the neo-Renaissance style you see today. Even Manfred Semper's version had to be rebuilt, after the devastating bombing raid of February 1945. On the 40th anniversary of that raid—February 13, 1985—the rebuilt Semperoper reopened with a performance of *Der Freischütz* by Carl Maria von Weber, another composer who did so much to make Dresden a leading center of German music and culture. The demand to experience the Semper Opera again in all its glory is enormous, and tickets are difficult to obtain in advance. If you're lucky enough to get in, however, an overwhelming experience awaits you. Even if you're no opera buff, the Semper's lavish interior, predominantly crimson, white, and gold, can't fail to impress. Marble, velvet, and brocade create an atmosphere of intimate luxury (it seats 1,323), and the uninterrupted views and flawless acoustics are renowned.

9 The impressive bridge behind the cathedral, the **Augustusbrücke,** is a rebuilt version of a historic 17th-century bridge blown up by the SS shortly before the end of World War II. Renamed for Georgi Dimitroff, the Bulgarian Communist accused by the Nazis of instigating the Reichstag fire, the restored bridge, after the fall of communism, has gotten back its original name honoring August the Strong. You'll find this process of curing the unpleasant hiccups of communist rule still underway throughout eastern Germany.

Back on the Theaterplatz, in the center of the square directly in front of the opera house, you'll see a proud equestrian statue of King Johann, who ruled Saxony when Gottfried Semper was at work. Don't be misled by Johann's confident pose in the saddle—he was terrified of horses and never learned to ride.

The southwestern side of the square is taken up by another
Gottfried Semper creation, the Sempergalerie, part of the
10 largely 18th-century **Zwinger** palace complex. Built by the
great architect to house parts of the art collections of the Saxon royal house, it contains the world-renowned Gemäldegalerie Alte Meister (Gallery of Old Masters). The Zwinger is being restored and is scheduled to reopen in October 1992. Until then, the Sempergalerie paintings are temporarily on display at the Albertinum (*see above*). The porcelain collection, zoological museum, and Mathematisch-Physikalischer Salon (displaying old scientific instruments) remain open at the palace (*see below*). Call the Zwinger (tel. 051/48420) for the latest information on when the collections will reopen at the palace complex.

Among the priceless paintings in the Sempergalerie collection are examples by Dürer, Holbein, Jan van Eyck, Rembrandt, Rubens, van Dyck, Hals, Vermeer, Raphael (The Sistine Madonna), Titian, Giorgione, Veronese, Velázquez, Murillo, Canaletto, and Watteau. On the wall of the entrance archway you'll see an inscription in Russian, one of the few amusing reminders of World War II in Dresden. It reads, in rhyme: "Museum checked. No mines. Chanutin did the checking." Chanutin, presumably, was the Russian soldier responsible for checking one of Germany's greatest art galleries for anything more explosive than a Rubens nude.

The Sempergalerie forms one side of the fabulous Zwinger, the pride of Dresden and perhaps one of the greatest examples of Baroque architecture. There are two entrances to the Zwinger; the Kronentor (Crown Gate), off of Ostra-Allee, is the one through which August the Strong and his royal retinue once paraded. August hired a small army of artists and artisans to create a "pleasure ground" worthy of the Saxon court, building it on a section of the original city fortifications (the "Zwinger"). They were placed under the general direction of the architect Matthaus Daniel Pöppelmann, who was called reluctantly out of retirement to design what came to be his greatest work, started in 1707 and completed in 1728. Completely enclosing a central courtyard, filled with lawns and pools, the complex comprises six linked pavilions, one of which boasts a carillon of Meissen, hence its name: Glockenspielpavillon. It's an extraordinary scene, a riot of garlands, nymphs, and other Baroque ornamentation and sculpture on the edge of an urban landscape etched in somber gray. The contrast would have been much greater if Semper had not closed in one side of the Zwinger, which was originally open to the riverbank. Stand in the center of this quiet oasis, where the city's roar is kept at bay by the palatial wings that form the outer framework of the Zwinger, and imagine the scene on summer evenings when August the Strong invited his favored guests to celebrate with him—the wedding, for instance, of his son, Prince Friedrich August, to Maria Joseph, Archduchess of Austria. The ornate carriage-style lamps shone, the fountains splashed in the shallow pools, and wide staircases beckoned to galleried walks and the romantic Nymphenbad, a coyly hidden courtyard where nude female statues are protected in alcoves from a fountain that spits unexpectedly at unwary visitors.

The Porcelain Museum, stretching from the curved gallery adjoining the Glockenspielpavillon to the long gallery on the east side, is considered one of the best of its kind in the world. The focus, naturally, is on Dresden and Meissen china, but there are also outstanding examples of Japanese, Chinese, and Korean porcelain. *Porcelain Museum admission: DM 5 adults, DM 2 children. Open Sat.–Thurs. 9–4:30. Zoological Museum, Mathematisch-Physikalischer Salon admission: DM 3 adults, DM 1.50 children. Open Fri.–Wed. 9–4.*

Other less central curiosities in Dresden include the **Armeemuseum** (Military Museum), which covers military history predating the German Democratic Republic (Dr.-Karl-Fischer-Pl., admission DM 3, open Tues.–Sun. 9–5); the **Buch Museum** (Book Museum), which traces the history of books from the Middle Ages to the present (Marienallee 12, admission free, open Mon.–Sat. 9–5); and the **Deutsches Hygene-Museum** (German Museum of Health), with historical displays of medical equipment and a unique glass anatomical figure (Lingnerpl.

1, admission DM 3 adults, DM 1.50 children, open Sat.–Thurs. 9–5).

Lodging Dresden, like the other cities of the former German Democratic Republic, is in the midst of a crash hotel-building program, but it's unlikely that it will be anywhere near completion by 1992. Moderately priced accommodation is desparately scarce, and what little the city has is booked months in advance. Your best bet is a room in a private home, which can be booked at a special counter at the tourist office. There is no fee.

Three moderately priced hotels were being refurbished in 1991:

Under DM 150 **Interhotel Prager Strasse.** This modern complex of two hotels in tandem, the **Königstein** and **Lilienstein,** which stand side-by-side on a pedestrian street between the train station and the city center. Rooms are modern if unexciting; the favored rooms (for the view) overlook the Prager Strasse, although the back rooms are slightly quieter. *Prager Str., tel. 051/48–460 and 051/48–560. 300 rooms each. Facilities: 3 restaurants, sauna, garage. AE, DC, MC, V.*

Parkhotel Weisser Hirsch. You'll be a considerable distance from city center here (if driving, take Bautzenerstrasse from Platz der Einheit) in pleasant country surroundings. *Bautzener Landstr. 7, tel. 051/36–851. 54 rooms without bath. Facilities: restaurant, café (dancing in evenings). No credit cards.*

Dining
Under DM 30 **Kügelgen-Haus.** The complex here includes a grill, coffee bar, restaurant, and historic beer cellar, all justifiably popular, so go early or book ahead. *Strasse der Befreiung, tel. 051/52791. Reservations advised. No credit cards.*

Sekundogenitur. This is one of the city's more famous wine restaurants, now connected to the Dresdner Hof hotel complex, situated on the riverbank with a view of the river. There is outside dining as well, weather permitting. *Brühlsche Terrasse, tel. 051/495–1435. Reservations advised. No credit cards. Closed Mon.*

Leipzig

Tourist office: Leipzig-Information, Sachsenplatz 1, tel. 041/79590.

From Berlin
By Train Trains leave Berlin's Lichtenberg station about once an hour for the 2½-hour run to Leipzig.

By Bus There is no direct bus service from Berlin to Leipzig.

By Car Leave Berlin on the Avus city autobahn (E-51) and join Autobahn E-6, exiting at the Leipzig junction. The 150-kilometer (90-mile) trip takes about 90 minutes.

Guided Tours Guided bus tours of Leipzig run daily at 10 and 1:30 (from March to mid-October, there's also a tour at 4); tours leave from the information center downtown at Sachsenplatz 1 (tel. 041/79590).

Exploring With a population of about 560,000, Leipzig is the second largest city in eastern Germany (Berlin is the largest) and has long been a center of printing and bookselling. Astride major trade routes, it was an important market town in the Middle Ages, and it continues to be a trading center to this day, thanks to the trade fairs that twice a year (March and September) bring together buyers from East and West.

Those familiar with music and German literature will associate Leipzig with the great composer Johann Sebastian Bach (1685–1750), who was organist and choir director at the Thomaskirche (St. Thomas's church); with the 19th-century composer Richard Wagner, who was born here in 1813; and with German Romantic poets Goethe and Schiller, both of whom lived and worked in the area.

In 1813 the Battle of the Nations, in which Prussian, Austrian, Russian, and Swedish forces stood ground against Napoléon's troops, was fought on the city's outskirts. This battle (*Völkerschlacht*) was instrumental in leading to the French general's defeat two years later at Waterloo, and thus helped to decide the national boundaries on the map of Europe for the remainder of the century.

Following the devastation of World War II, little is left of old Leipzig. Considerable restoration has been undertaken in the old city, however, and the impression is certainly that of a city with touches of Renaissance character, although some of the newer buildings (notably the university skyscraper tower) distort the perspective and proportions of the old city.

Numbers in the margin correspond to points of interest on the Leipzig map.

Railroad buffs may want to start their tour of Leipzig at the
1 **Hauptbahnhof,** the main train station. With its 26 platforms, it is the largest in Europe. In 1991 it was expanded to accommodate the anticipated increase in traffic after reunification. But its fin-de-siècle grandness remains, particularly the staircase that leads majestically up to the platforms. As you climb it, take a look at the great arched ceiling high above you; it's unique among German railway stations.

From the station, cross the broad expanse of the Platz der Republik, crowded with nascent capitalists selling everything from shaving soap to Czech Pilsner beer. Better shopping is to be found in the narrow streets opposite you. Behind them is a characterless square, Sachsenplatz, where you'll find Leipzig's main tourist office, Leipzig Information (open Mon.–Fri. 9–7, Sat. 9:30–2). Continue south one block, along Katharinenstrasse, passing the "Fregehaus," number 11, with its fine oriel and steep roof. In two minutes you'll enter Leipzig's showpiece plaza, the city's old market square, the **Markt,** only slightly smaller than St. Mark's Square in Venice. One side is occupied completely by the recently restored Renaissance city
2 hall, the **Altes Rathaus,** which now houses the municipal museum, where Leipzig's past is well documented. *Markt 1. Admission: DM 3 adults, DM 1.50 children. Open Tues.–Sun. 9–5.*

Starting from all sides of the Markt you'll find small streets that attest to Leipzig's rich trading past, and tucked in among them glass-roofed arcades of surprising beauty and elegance. Invent a headache and step into the Apotheke at Hainstrasse 9, into surroundings that haven't changed for 100 years or more, redolent of powders and perfumes, home cures, and foreign spices. It's spectacularly Jugendstil, with finely etched and stained glass and rich mahogany. Or make for the antiquarian bookshops of the nearby Neumarkt Passage. Around the cor-

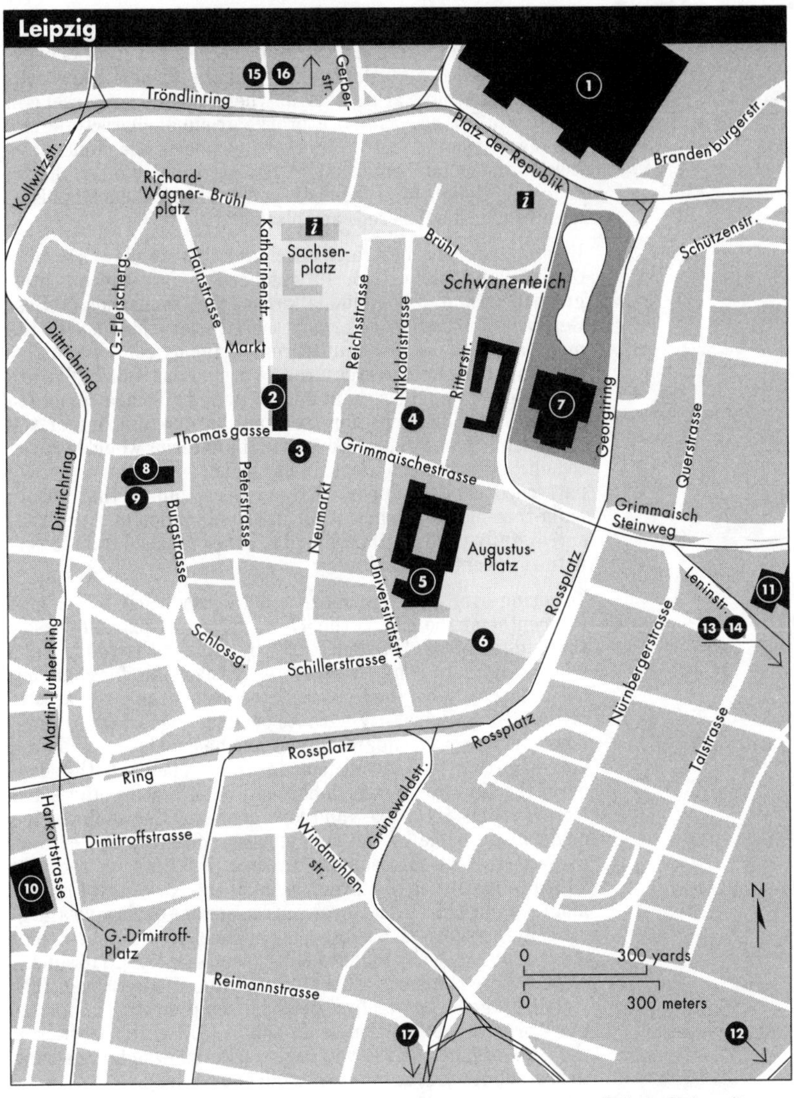

Altes Rathaus, **2**
Bosehaus, **9**
Botanischer Garten, **12**
Exhibition Pavilion, **13**
Gohliser Schlösschen, **15**
Grassimuseum, **11**
Hauptbahnhof, **1**
Leipzig University tower, **5**
Mädlerpassage, **3**
Museum der Bildenden Kunste, **10**
Neues Gewandhaus, **6**
Nikolaikirche, **4**
Opera House, **7**
Schiller's House, **16**
Schloss Dölitz, **17**
Thomaskirche, **8**
Völkerschlacht-denkmal, **14**

ner, on Grimmaischestrasse, is Leipzig's finest arcade, the
3 **Mädlerpassage,** where the ghost of Goethe's Faust lurks in ev-
ery marbled corner. Here you'll find the famous Auerbachs Keller restaurant, at number 2, where Goethe set a scene in *Faust* (*see* Dining, *below*). A bronze group of characters from the play, sculpted in 1913, beckons you down the stone staircase to the cellar restaurant. A few yards away down the arcade is a delightful Jugendstil coffee shop called Mephisto, decorated in devilish reds and blacks.

Behind Grimmaischestrasse is a church that stands as a symbol of German reunification. It was here, before the undistin-
4 guished facade of the **Nikolaikirche,** that thousands of East
Germans demanding reform gathered every Monday in the months before the Communist regime finally collapsed under the weight of popular pressure. "Wir sind das Volk" ("We are the people") was their chant as they defied official attempts to silence their demands for freedom. In the interior of the church, much more impressive than the exterior would lead you to believe, is a soaring Gothic choir and nave with an unusually patterned ceiling supported by classical pillars that end in palm-tree-like flourishes, a curious combination of styles that successfully meld. Luther is said to have preached from the ornate 16th-century pulpit.

Towering over the Nikolaikirche and every other building in
5 the center of the city is the 470-foot-high **Leipzig University**
tower, dubbed the "Jagged Tooth" by some of the young wags who study there. They were largely responsible for changing the official name of the university, replacing the postwar title of Karl Marx University with its original one. At press time, however, the vast square spread out below the tower like a space-age campus was still named after Karl Marx. In the shadow of the skyscraper, which houses administrative offices and
6 lecture rooms, is the glass and concrete **Neues Gewandhaus,** the
modernistic home of the eponymous orchestra, one of Germany's greatest. (Its popular director, Kurt Masur, recently added to his duties the directorship of the New York Philharmonic Orchestra.) In the foyer you can see one of Europe's largest ceiling paintings, a staggering allegorical work devoted to the muse of music by Sighard Gilles, who employed 716 square meters to monumental effect. The statue of Beethoven that stands in the foyer won first prize for sculptor Max Klinger at the World Art Exhibition in Vienna in 1912. The acoustics of the Gewandhaus, by the way, are world renowned, enhancing the resonance of every tone by a full two seconds.

Opposite the Gewandhaus, on the north side of the Augustus-
7 Platz, is the modern, boxy **Opera House,** the first postwar theater to be built in communist East Germany.

Continue west on Grimmaischestrasse to Thomasgasse and the
8 **Thomaskirche,** the Gothic church where Bach was choirmaster
for 27 years and where Martin Luther preached on Whit Sunday, 1539, signaling the arrival of Protestantism in Leipzig. Originally the center of a 13th-century monastery that was rebuilt in the 15th century, the tall church now stands by itself, but the names of adjacent streets recall the cloisters that once surrounded it. Bach wrote most of his cantatas for the church's famous boys' choir, the Thomasknabenchor, which was founded in the 13th century; the church continues as the choir's home as well as a center of Bach tradition. In the Middle Ages,

the choir was assembled to sing at every public function—from the installation of bishops to the execution of criminals. Its ranks thinned rapidly when the boys were engaged to sing while plague victims were carted to graves outside the city walls.

Bach's 12 children and the infant Richard Wagner were baptized in the church's early 17th-century font; Karl Marx and Friedrich Engels also stood before this same font, godfathers to Karl Liebknecht, who grew up to be a revolutionary too!

The great music Bach wrote in his Leipzig years commanded little attention in his lifetime, and when he died he was given a simple grave, without a headstone, in the city's Johannisfriedhof cemetery. It wasn't until 1894 that an effort was made to find where the great composer lay buried, and after a thorough, macabre search his coffin was removed to the cemetery church, the Johanniskirche. The church was destroyed by Allied bombs in December 1943, and Bach found his final resting place in the church he would have selected: the Thomaskirche. It's now a place of pilgrimage for music-lovers from all over the world, and his gravestone below the high altar is never without a floral tribute. Fresh flowers also constantly decorate the statue of Bach that stands before the church. *Thomaskirchhof. Admission free. Open daily 9–6.*

9 The Bach family home, the **Bosehaus,** still stands, opposite the church, and is now a museum devoted to the life and work of the composer. (The exhibits are in German only; a guide to the museum in English can be purchased in the shop.) Of particular interest is the display of musical instruments dating from Bach's time. *Thomaskirchhof 16. Admission: DM 2 adults, DM 1 children. Open Tues. and Thurs.–Sun. 9–5, Wed. 1–9.*

From the Thomaskirche, follow Burgstrasse southward, past
the 19th-century neo-Gothic monstrosity that now serves as
Leipzig's city hall, and you'll come to the city's most outstand-
10 ing museum, the **Museum der Bildenden Kunste,** an art gallery
of international standard. The art collection occupies the ground floor of the former Reichsgericht, the court where the Nazis held a show trial against the Bulgarian communist Georgi Dimitroff on a trumped-up charge of masterminding a plot to burn down the Reichstag in 1933. *Georgi-Dimitroff-Platz 1. Admission: DM 3 adults, DM 1.50 children. Open Tues. and Thurs.–Sun. 9–5, Wed. 1–9:30.*

Head across the Martin Luther-Ring up the short Grimmaisch
11 Steinweg to reach the **Grassimuseum** complex (Johannespl. 5–
11. Admission: DM 3.05 adults, DM 1.55 children). It includes the **Museum of Arts and Crafts** (open Tues.–Fri. 9:30–6, Sat. 10–4, Sun. 9–1), the **Geographical Museum** (open Tues.–Fri. 10–3, Sun. 9–1), and the **Musical Instruments Museum** (enter from Täubchenweg 2; open Tues.–Thurs. 3–6, Fri. and Sun. 10–1, Sat. 10–3).

12 The **Botanischer Garten** (Botanical Gardens) is a set of splendid open-air gardens and greenhouses. *Linnestr. 1. Admission: DM 2. Open weekdays 9–4, Sun. 10–4; greenhouses Sun. 10–12:30 and 2–4.*

Still farther out, via streetcars No. 15, 20, 21, or 25, is the
13 **Exhibition Pavilion** at Leninstrasse 210. Its main feature is a
vast diorama portraying the Battle of the Nations of 1813 (open

Tues.–Sun. 9–4). Slightly farther on Leninstrasse is the massive
14 **Völkerschlachtdenkmal,** a memorial in the formal park; it, too, commemorates the battle (open daily 9–4). Rising out of suburban Leipzig like some great Egyptian tomb, the somber, gray pile of granite and concrete is more than 300 feet high. Despite its ugliness, it's well worth a visit if only to wonder at the lengths—and heights—to which the Prussians went to celebrate their military victories, and to take in the view from a windy platform near the top (provided you can also climb the 500 steps to get there). The Prussians did make one concession to Napoléon in designing the monument: A stone marks the spot where he stood during the battle.

Outside of the center of Leipzig but reachable by public transportation (streetcars No. 20 and 24, then walk left up Poetenweg, or streetcar No. 6 to Menckestrasse) is the delightfully
15 Rococo **Gohliser Schlösschen** (Gohliser House), the site of frequent concerts. *Menckestr. 23. Open Mon. and Fri. 1–5, Tues., Thurs., and Sat. 9–1, Wed. 1–8.*

16 Beyond that is **Schiller's House,** for a time the home of the German poet and dramatist Friedrich Schiller. *Menckestr. 21. Admission: DM 2 adults, DM 1 children. Open Tues., Wed., Fri., and Sat. 11–5.*

17 **Schloss Dölitz** (streetcars No. 22 or 24, walk up Helenstrasse) contains an exhibition of *Zinnfiguren,* historical tin soldiers. *Torhaus, Schloss Dölitz, Helenstr. 24. Admission: DM 3. Open Sun. 9–1.*

Lodging Like Dresden, Leipzig suffers from an acute accommodations shortage. We advise booking a private room from the special counter at the tourist office. There are a few moderately priced hotels in the area of the main railway stations, the best of which are:

Under DM 150 **International.** You're within steps of the heart of the city. The spacious rooms offer old-fashioned comfort but with modern facilities. The sidewalk café is popular. *Tröndlinring 8, tel. 041/71–880. 108 rooms with bath. Facilities: restaurant, Bierstube, bar, café, garage. AE, DC, MC, V.*

Parkhotel. The location directly across from the train station could hardly be better, but the accommodations are simple if not downright spartan—virtually none of the rooms have baths. *Richard-Wagner-Str. 7, tel. 041/7821. 174 rooms. Facilities: restaurant, parking. No credit cards.*

Zum Löwen. This is a postwar modern hotel, personable and cheerful if not opulent. It's within an easy stroll of the city center. *Rudolf-Breitscheid-Str., tel. 041/7751. 108 rooms with bath. Facilities: restaurant. AE, DC, MC, V.*

Dining
Under DM 30 **Altes Kloster.** Game is featured in this fascinating Old World restaurant, once part of a cloister. *Klostergasse 5, tel. 041/282–252. Reservations advised. Jacket and tie required. No credit cards.*

Auerbachs Keller. This historic restaurant (built 1530) in the city center is immortalized in Goethe's *Faust.* Even if you don't eat here, stop by for a visit. *Grimmaische Str. 2–4, tel. 041/209–131. Jacket and tie required. AE, DC, MC, V.*

Paulaner. Intimate, attractive, and quiet, this small place offers a limited selection of good local food. *Klostergasse 3, tel. 041/281–985. Reservations advised. No credit cards.*

Meissen

Tourist office: Meissen-Information, Willy-Anker-Str. 32, tel. 053/4470.

From Berlin *By Train* Meissen is accessible via Dresden (*see above*). Trains leave Dresden every half-hour for the half-hour run to Meissen.

By Bus An hourly bus service leaves Dresden's main railway station. It's cheaper than the train but takes nearly double the time.

By Car Meissen is 18 kilometers (11 miles) west of Dresden on the B-6 highway.

Exploring This romantic city on the Elbe river is known the world over for its porcelain, bearing the trademark crossed blue swords. The first European porcelain was made in this area in 1708, and in 1710 the royal porcelain manufacturer was established in Meissen, close to the local raw materials.

The story of how porcelain came to be produced in Meissen reads like a German fairy-tale: Saxony's ruler, the free-spending August the Strong (ruled 1697–1704, 1710–33), urged alchemists at his court to search for the secret of making gold, which he badly needed to refill a Saxon state treasury depleted by his expensive building projects and extravagant lifestyle. The alchemists failed to produce gold, but one of them, Johann Friedrich Böttger, discovered a method for making something almost as precious: fine hard-paste porcelain. Prince August consigned Böttger and a team of craftsmen to a hilltop castle outside Dresden—Albrechtsburg in Meissen—and set them to work. August hoped to keep their recipe a state secret, but within a few years fine porcelain was being produced by Böttger's method in many parts of Europe.

The porcelain works outgrew their castle workshop in the mid-19th century, and you'll find them today in the town at the foot of the castle mount at Leninstrasse 9. There you can see demonstrations of pieces being prepared. In the same building, a museum displays Meissen porcelain, a collection that rivals that of the Porcelain Museum in Dresden. *Tel. 053/541. Open Apr.–Oct., Tues.–Sun. 8:30–4:30.*

Meissen porcelain is to be found in one form or another all over town. A set of porcelain bells at the late-Gothic **Frauenkirche,** on the central market square, the Marktplatz, was the first of its kind anywhere when installed in 1929. The largest set of porcelain figures ever crafted can be found in another Meissen church, the **Nikolaikirche,** which also houses remains of early Gothic frescoes. Also of interest in the town center is the 1569 Old Brewery, graced by a Renaissance gable; St. Francis, now housing a city museum; and St. Martins, with its late-Gothic altar.

It's a bit of a climb up Burgstrasse and Amtsstrasse to the **Albrechtsburg** castle, where the story of Meissen porcelain really began, but the effort is worthwhile. The 15th-century Albrechtsburg is Germany's first truly "residential" castle, a complete break with the earlier style of fortified bastion. It fell into disuse and neglect as nearby Dresden rose to local prominence, but it's still an imposing collection of late-Gothic and Renaissance buildings. In the central courtyard, a typical Gothic *Schutzhof* protected on three sides by high rough-stone walls, is an exterior spiral staircase, **the Wendelstein,** hewn from one massive stone block in 1525, a masterpiece of early masonry. Ceilings of the halls of the castle are richly decorated, although many date only to a restoration in 1870. Adjacent to the castle is a towered early Gothic cathedral.

Lodging and Dining
Under DM 150

Bahnhofshotel. This small hotel is right at the train station and convenient to the center of town. Rooms have a dated modern decor but are attractive, with satisfactory baths. The restaurant reminds one a bit of the train station, which is only appropriate. *Grossenhainer Str. 2, tel. 053/3320. 18 rooms with bath. Facilities: restaurant, parking. AE, DC, MC, V.*

15 The Baltic Coast

Including Rügen and Usedom Islands

The unspoiled Baltic Coast—a region of white-sand beaches, coves, chalk cliffs, ancient ports, and fishing villages—is about to become one of the new playgrounds of reunited Germany. Some of its beach resorts were already popular holiday destinations in the mid-19th century, when sunbathing and sea swimming first became fashionable. But the whole weaving coastline—1,130 kilometers (706 miles), including 338 kilometers (210 miles) of sandy beaches—plunged into isolation when the Iron Curtain came down just east of Lübeck. On the island of Rügen, for example, the clock stopped in the Nazi era: The architecture, the furnishings, the pace of life seem to exist in a time warp. Even the trains are steam-powered.

In addition to the scenic seaside locations and quiet islands, this chapter explores five of the most important Hanseatic League towns, whose rich merchants monopolized trade on the Baltic Sea between the 12th and 16th centuries. Much of their wealth went into fine buildings, many of which have survived the upheavals of this century: Some of the finest examples of north German redbrick architecture, with its dizzyingly steep gables, can be found here. Our base will be Rostock, the former East Germany's chief port.

Tourist information for the region can be obtained from Ostsee Tourist (Hermann-Duncker-Platz 3, Rostock, tel. 081/380–208).

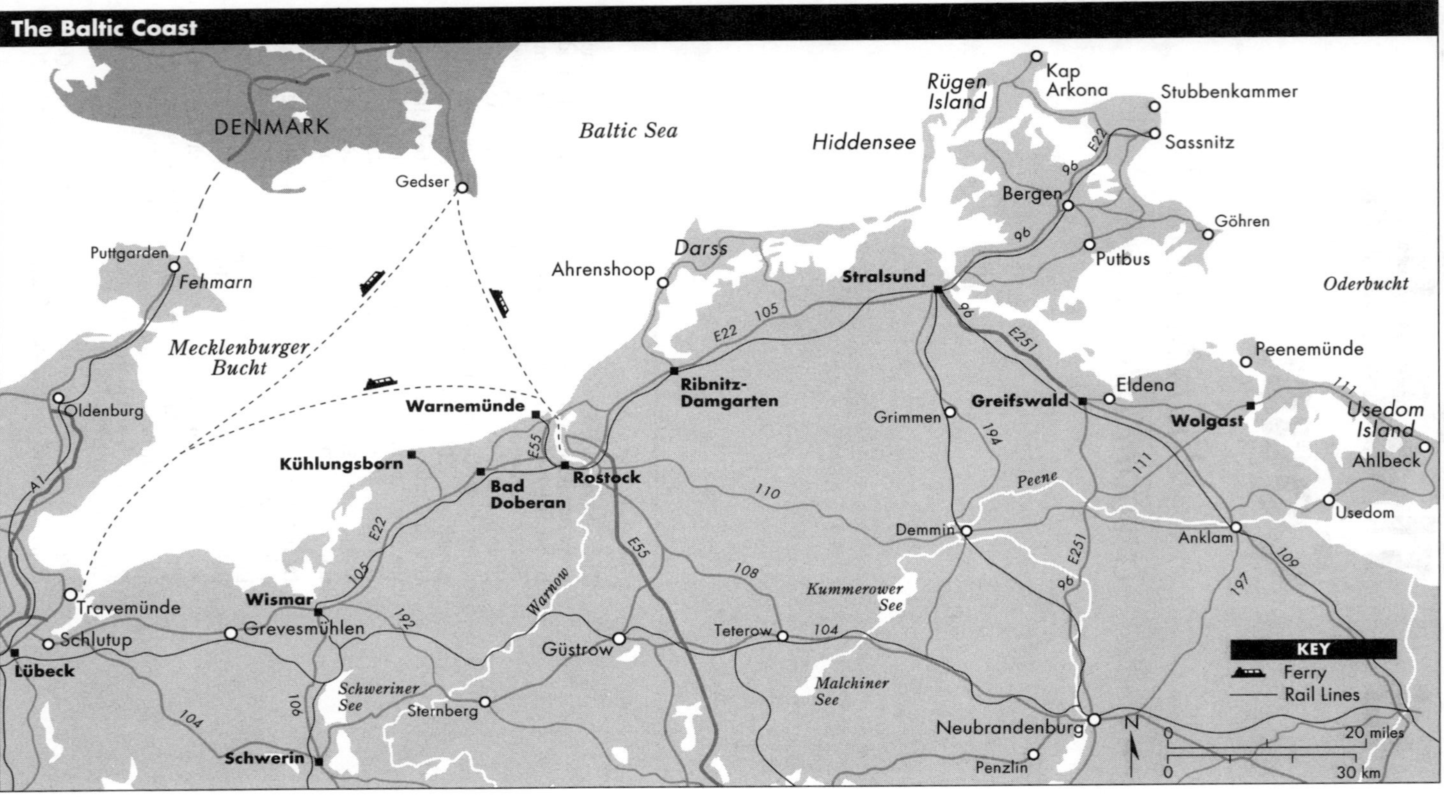
The Baltic Coast
DENMARK
Baltic Sea
Gedser
Puttgarden
Fehmarn
Mecklenburger Bucht
Oldenburg
A1
Travemünde
Schlutup
Lübeck
Warnemünde
Kühlungsborn
Bad Doberan
Rostock
E55
E22
105
Wismar
Grevesmühlen
192
106
104
Schwerin
Schweriner See
Sternberg
Warnow
Güstrow
Ahrenshoop
Darss
Ribnitz-Damgarten
110
108
Teterow
Kummerower See
Malchiner See
Hiddensee
Rügen Island
Kap Arkona
Stubbenkammer
Sassnitz
Bergen
96
Göhren
Putbus
Stralsund
E251
194
Grimmen
Greifswald
Eldena
Peene
Demmin
Neubrandenburg
Penzlin
Oderbucht
Peenemünde
111
Wolgast
Usedom Island
Ahlbeck
Usedom
Anklam
109
197
KEY
Ferry
Rail Lines
N
0
20 miles
30 km

Essential Information

Getting Around

By Train

At the time of this writing, the area's extensive railway network was still being operated by the old East German Reichsbahn. Trains are slower here than in western Germany because of the worn condition of the tracks. (The system is safe, though.)

By Bus

Buses link outlying villages with railway stations, but there is no firm network of long-distance services apart from the few between the big cities.

Guided Tours

For travelers with limited time, the Rostock tourist office (*see above*) operates several worthwhile and inexpensive half-day and full-day tours of the coastal region, taking in many of the attractions listed in this chapter.

Telephones

Phone connections between western and eastern Germany improved dramatically toward the end of 1991, after a period of near-chaos resulting from the overloaded and antiquated system of the Communist era. However, at present, if you direct-dial any destination in this chapter from anywhere in western Germany, you must still use the old international code for East Germany: 0037. All numbers cited in this chapter give the area code; if you use the prefix 0037, delete the "0" of the area code. For example, to call the Bad Doberan tourist office (tel. 08193/3001) from Hamburg, dial 0037/8193–3001. Within eastern Germany, just dial the full number given in the text. (This was the situation at press time, but conditions in eastern Germany are improving all the time, and area codes may change.)

Lodging

The choice of hotels in this area remains limited—smaller hotels and pensions range from the charming but basic to charmless and basic. In high season all accommodations, especially along the coast, are in great demand. During the past 40 years, the majority of East German summer visitors stayed at more than 150 campsites scattered along the coast. In the wake of reunification, plenty of bed-and-breakfast lodgings in private homes have sprung up. Try to book well in advance, but if this isn't possible, throw yourself on the mercy of the local tourist office, which will probably be able to find you simple, inexpensive bed-and-breakfast accommodation in a private home.

Highly recommended establishments are indicated by a star ★.

Dining

Restaurants, like lodgings, are sparser than in western Germany, and the quality of the food is generally lower. But given the entrepreneurial spirit of the Germans, the situation is improving all the time. A number of new restaurants are reviving or promoting the region's traditional dishes. Potatoes and fish remain the two main staples. Among the local specialties to look out for are *Mecklenburger Griebenroller,* a custardy casserole of grated potato, eggs, herbs, and chopped bacon; *Mecklenburger Fischsuppe,* a hearty fish soup with vegetables, tomatoes, and sour cream; and *Pannfisch,* the region's own fish patty. A delicacy that originated during the time of Sweden's influence is *Grützwurst,* an oatmeal-based liver sausage sweetened with raisins. A favorite local nightcap since the 17th century is *Eierbier* (egg beer), a concoction of egg white, beer, ginger, cinnamon, sugar, and water stirred vigorously and served warm. It's said to soothe the stomach, and it's guaranteed to give you a sound night's sleep.

Highly recommended restaurants are indicated by a star ★.

Shopping Amber (*Bernstein*) is the region's chief souvenir. You'll find it at the state-owned jewelry factory adjacent to the Bernsteinmuseum in **Ribnitz-Damgarten** (*see below*).

You might come across a bargain antique (including amber jewelry) in one of the bigger towns. During the Communist years, people hid heirlooms and anything else of value to protect them from heavy taxation or even confiscation. Now, as owners seek to raise capital, many of these treasures are finding their way into second-hand or antiques shops. The best places to look are **Schwerin** (on and around Schmiedestrasse and Schloss-strasse and **Rostock** (along Kröpellingerstrasse and side streets.)

Biking The coastal region is ideally flat for cycling, a fact that numerous entrepreneurs have been quick to note. So now, not only do the bigger hotels provide bicycles for guests, lots of shops are beginning to rent them on a daily or weekly basis at modest rates. However, train stations in this region are not yet renting bicycles. Escorted tours are being organized by the tourist offices; contact the regional tourist office in **Rostock** (*see above*) for more information.

Beaches Good beaches exist all along the Baltic coast. Virtually all the sandy beaches are clean and safe, sloping gently into the water. At the height of the season (July–August), the seaside resort beaches, with food services and toilets, are packed. The busiest are at **Bansin** (Usedom Island), **Binz** (Rügen Island), **Ostseebad Kühlungsborn,** and **Warnemünde.** More remote and quieter beaches can be found at: **Timmendorf** on **Poel Island,** where the water quality is particularly good (you can drive there from Wismar, or take a White Fleet boat); **Kap Arkona** (reachable on foot only); and **Hiddensee Island,** off Rügen. The prettiest coves and beaches are located at: **Ahrenshoop** on the Darss peninsula, **Nienhagen** (near Warnemünde), and the **Grosser Jasmunder Bodden** on Rügen Island to the west of Lietzow.

Some beaches allow nude bathing; in German it's known as *Freikörperkultur* (literally, free body culture), FKK for short. The most popular of these bare-all beaches are at Nienhagen and Prerow (on Darss).

After a sea storm, head for a beach and join the locals in the perennial quest for amber stone washed up among the seaweed. Your children may also stumble upon a little pebble with a hole worn in the middle. Prevalent on this coast, they are called *Hühnergötter* (chicken gods) by the locals, who believe they bring good luck.

The Arts A resurgence of traditional *Volksfeste*—popular festivals—is following in the wake of 1989, in particular *Fischerfeste* (fishermen's festivals) in the ports and coastal towns. For a schedule of events contact the local tourist offices.

The summer season brings with it a plethora of special concerts, the highlights being the "Music in May" concerts at **Rostock** and **Stralsund; Greifswald's** Bach Week in June, including open-air concerts at the ruins of the Eldena cloister; **Schwerin** Summerfest on the Lankowersee lake, also in June; an international brass band competition in **Rostock** in July; and a series of concerts in **Bad Doberan** in August.

Nightlife **Rostock, Schwerin,** and **Warnemünde** have the most to offer night owls. Nearly all the seaside resorts, even the smallest, have almost nightly dances during the summer months. The biggest hotels are the places to head for in search of fun.

Highlights for First-time Visitors

Marktplatz, Wismar
The medieval seaport of Stralsund
A ride on the steam train *Molli* to or from Bad Doberan
Rügen Island
Schloss Schwerin
Zisterzienser-Klosterkirche church, Bad Doberan

Exploring the Baltic Coast

Rostock, our tour base, may not be the prettiest place on the Baltic, but it's ideally located in the middle of our tour area, and it offers good train connections and reasonable facilities. The town adjoins the seaside resort of Warnemünde at the mouth of the River Warnow, which doubles the prospects for lodging and dining.

From Berlin
By Train The Berlin–Rostock trip takes two hours and 40 minutes; trains run every two hours.

By Car Autobahn 55 covers the entire 246 kilometers (154 miles) between Berlin and Rostock. Car-rental or tourist offices should be able to tell you whether the 100-kilometers-per-hour (62-miles-per-hour) speed restriction is still in force.

From Hamburg
By Train Trains run every two hours during the day; the trip takes just over three hours.

By Car It's 56 kilometers (35 miles) by Autobahn A-1 from Hamburg to Lübeck, where you switch to the B-104, then the B-105, for the remaining 80 kilometers (50 miles) to Rostock.

Rostock

Tourist office: Schnickmannstrasse 13, tel. 081/22619.

Rostock was one of the powerful merchant towns of the medieval Hanseatic League but became a backwater after the merchants' power was broken by the devastation of the Thirty Years War, in the 17th century. The town became important again in the late 1940s, when the newly created German Democratic Republic realized it needed a sea-trade outlet.

The city suffered severe damage in World War II bombings, but much of the old town's core has been rebuilt, including large segments of the medieval old town wall and the facades of the late-Gothic and Renaissance houses of the rich *Hanse* merchants. (One of the best views of old Rostock is from a boat in the harbor.) The finest examples are to be found along the main street, the pedestrian-only **Kröpelinerstrasse,** which begins at the old western gate, the Kröpeliner Tor, and leads into the town square (Markt/Ernst-Thälmann-Platz). You'll immediately notice the architectural potpourri that is the **Rathaus** (Town Hall). Basically 13th-century Gothic with a Baroque facade, the building spouts seven slender, decorative towers, looking like candles on a peculiar birthday cake. The square is surrounded by historic gabled houses. Head north on Langestrasse out of the square to reach the four-centuries-old **Marienkirche** (St. Mary's Church), the architectural gem of Rostock. The Gothic structure boasts a bronze baptismal font from 1290, and some interesting Baroque features, notably the oak altar (1720) and organ (1770). The unique attraction, however, is the huge astronomical clock dating from 1472; it has a calendar extending to the year 2017. At the rear of Marienkirche in Am Ziegenmarkt is Rostock's former mint, the **Münze.** The town started producing its own coins in 1361, and only relinquished this right in 1864. The Münze has a fine Renaissance arched entrance and a stone relief depicting coinmakers going about their work.

Just beyond the city walls, through the Steintor, you'll come to the **Schiffahrtmuseum,** at August-Babel-Strasse 1, which traces the history of shipping on the Baltic and displays models of ships throughout the ages. *Admission: DM 1.50 adults, 50 pf children. Open May–Sept., daily 9:30–4:30; Oct.–Apr., Tues.–Fri. 9:30–4:30.*

The **Zoologischer Garten** has one of the biggest collections of exotic animals and birds in northern Germany. This zoo is particularly noted for its polar bears, some of which have been bred in Rostock. *Tiergartenallee 10, tel. 081/37171. Admission: DM 3.50 adults, DM 2 children. Open May–Sept., daily 7:30 AM–8 PM; Oct.–April, daily 7:30–5:30.*

The nearby seaside resort-cum-fishing village of **Warnemünde,** at the mouth of the Warnow River, is now virtually a suburb of Rostock—a 10-minute ride on the suburban train from the main Rostock station, or a 9-mile ride north on Route 103. For years it has been a popular summer holiday destination for East German families, drawn by a 2-mile-long sandy beach. Children will also enjoy climbing to the top of the town landmark, a 115-foot-high **lighthouse,** which on clear days offers views of the coast and Rostock harbor. *Am Strom. Admission: 50 pf. Open daily.*

If the weather is too bad for outdoor swimming, children will be just as pleased to splash in the giant heated seawater pool (with artificial waves as high as 4 feet). *Seepromenadestr. Admission: DM 3.50 adults, DM 2 children. Open May–Sept. daily 9–7.*

Lodging

Under DM 150

Congress. Most facilities of the hotel, which resembles a 1960s-era university building, are geared to the business traveler. Rooms are bright but plain and cheaply furnished. *Leningraderstr. 45, tel. 081/7030. 250 rooms, most with bath or shower. Facilities: restaurant, bars. AE, DC.*

Warnow. This modern eight-story building is decorated in a clumsy mixture of styles. The rooms are cozy but dated. The Warnow does have its strong points: a central location and much-sought-after modern comforts. Warning: More than half of the rooms are singles. *Hermann-Duncker-Platz 4, tel. 081/37381. 312 rooms with bath. Facilities: 2 restaurants, café, 2 bars, beer garden. AE, DC, MC, V.*

Under DM 110

Hotel am Bahnhof. This threadbare but adequate hotel—close to the train station, as the name implies—was due to undergo renovations during 1992. *Gerhart Hauptmannstr. 13, tel. 081/ 36331. 73 rooms, most without bath. No credit cards.*

Promenadenhotel. The gray exterior of this small Warnemünde hotel belies the bright and friendly interior, which wears a 1960s look. Some of the rooms overlook the sea promenade. The in-house dance hall is a popular venue on weekends. *Seestr. 5, Warnemünde, tel. 081/52782. 23 rooms, most without bath, and 1 suite with bath. Facilities: restaurant, bar. No credit cards.*

Strandhotel. Despite its lack of facilities, this old-fashioned seaside-resort guest house on the beach promenade in Warnemünde, just a block from the Promenadenhotel (*see above*), is often booked months in advance. *Seestr. 12, tel. 081/ 5335. 47 rooms without bath. Facilities: restaurant. AE.*

Under DM 70

Haus Sonne. A plain guest house in the center of the old town close to the Rathaus, the Sonne used to specialize in accommodating seamen. A management change was expected to herald a major renovation program in late-1991. *Ernst-Thälmann-Platz 35, tel. 081/37101. 35 rooms without bath. No credit cards.*

Nordland. This simple hotel on a noisy street in the old town center hasn't changed much since the early 1950s. *Steinstr. 7, tel. 081/23706. 34 rooms without bath. Facilities: restaurant. No credit cards.*

Youth Hostel

Jugendtouristhotel. The museum-ship *Frieden* (Peace), moored on the River Warnow a few miles downriver toward Warnemünde in the suburb of Schmarl, is the site of this unusual youth hostel offering two-, three-, and four-berth cabins. It can be reached by bus or S-bahn train (get off at S-bahn station Schmarl) from the main train station. At press time, the DM 20–DM 24 price per person was expected to rise. *Tel. 081/ 716202.*

Dining

Under DM 30

Fünf Giebel Haus. This modern but rustic-style wine tavern serves regional fare. *Breitstr. 21, tel. 081/22660. Reservations advised. No credit cards.*

Under DM 20

Strandhotel. The restaurant of this Warnemünde hotel (*see* Lodging, *above*) provides solid but dull fare; nevertheless, it's popular, especially during the July–August holiday period. *Seestr. 12, tel. 081/5335. Reservations advised. AE.*

★ **Zur Kogge.** Looking like the cabin of some ancient marine, this old sailor's beer tavern serves mostly fish. Order the *Mecklenburger Fischsuppe* if it's on the menu; *Pannfisch* is also a popular choice. *Wokrenterstr. 27, tel. 081/34493. Reservations essential in evening. No credit cards.*

Under DM 15

Café Rostock. Spread over three floors, this no-frills eatery on the pedestrianized main street of the old town gives you the choice of a waitress-serviced café, a pizzeria, or a self-service snack bar featuring such solid fillers as sausages, sauerkraut, and *Spätzle* (egg noodles). *Kröpelinerstr. 7, tel. 081/22331. No credit cards.*

Ostseegaststätte. This is a traditional beer restaurant, handily placed in the town center. At DM 8 (1991 prices), the *Schweinesteak ungarisch* (spicy pork fillet) is just about the best deal in town. *Langestr. 9, tel. 081/34220. No credit cards.*

Teepott. A converted seaplane hangar next to Warnemünde's lighthouse provides an unusual setting where you can relax over a light meal or coffee and cake while gazing out onto the traffic at the mouth of the River Warnow. *Am Leuchtturm, tel. 081/5381. No credit cards.*

Zum alten Gewölbe. At this colorful old wine tavern, situated in a vaulted stone cellar on the main thoroughfare through the old town, you'll find an excellent selection of wines, expert service, and a small menu of well-prepared regional specialties. *Kröpelinerstr. 75, tel. 081/23584. No credit cards.*

Splurge ★ **Neptun Spezialitätenrestaurants.** Each of the six restaurants at the Neptun Hotel specializes in a national cuisine: north German, Swedish, Russian, Hungarian, Cuban, and Asian (a wide selection, from Malaysian to Vietnamese). Expect a three-course meal, excluding drinks, to cost DM 35–DM 65 at lunch, DM 50–DM 60 at dinner. *Schillerstr. 14, tel. 081/5381. Reservations advised, and necessary on summer weekends. AE, DC, MC, V.*

The Arts Rostock's **Volkstheater** (Doberanerstr. 134, tel. 081/244253) presents plays (in German) and concerts.

Nightlife The Warnow Hotel's **Newa Bar** has nightly dancing and cabaret; the **Sky Bar** on the 19th floor of the Neptun Hotel offers the chance to sit under the stars (the roof opens up) and watch the ship lights twinkling on the sea until 4 AM. The drinks are more expensive than in other local bars and restaurants, but there's no entrance charge. A disco worth trying is the **Kurhaus** in Warnemünde (Seestr.).

Bad Doberan

The trip from Rostock takes only 25 minutes, and between mid-morning and late afternoon trains depart almost hourly. Tourist office (also for the beach resorts of Heiligendamm and Kühlungsborn): Kurverwaltung, Am Markt 5, tel. 08193/3001.

This is the home of *Molli,* a 19th-century steam train that churns the 16 kilometers (10 miles) between Bad Doberan and the popular seaside resorts of **Heiligendamm** and **Kühlungsborn.** The scenic line was opened in 1886 to ferry the ever-increasing number of holidaymakers to the cure-all sea air at Heiligendamm, the oldest seaside bathing beach in Germany. (The practice was first popularized in 1793 by Duke Friedrich Franz I. But the social rules were strict—men and women were separated by screens on the beaches. Family bathing wasn't allowed until early in the 20th century.) The train acquired its name from a little dog that kicked up a big noise every time the steaming, smoking giant passed by. At the start of the journey the engine and its wood carriages chug through Bad Doberan along the town's cobbled streets. *Fare (one way): DM 4.50 adults, DM 2.50 children.* Molli *runs 13 times daily, from 5 AM until 10 PM, in both directions between Bad Doberan and Kühlungsborn. The trip takes about 40 minutes each way.*

Bad Doberan is also home to one of the best-preserved high-Gothic redbrick cloister churches in the region, the **Zisterzienser-Klosterkirche** in the town center. It was built by Cistercian monks between 1294 and 1368. The main altar, which is original, features a 45-foot cross. Many of the monastic buildings have been preserved; the former corn storehouse is today a school. *Kampplatz. Admission: DM 2 adults, 50 pf children. Guided tours Sept.–June, Tues.–Sat. (July–Aug., Mon.–Sat.) 9, 10, 2, and 3; Sun. 2 and 3.*

Horse racing aficionados may be interested to know that the first track on the Continent was established in Bad Doberan, in 1807. The site is remembered in the name *Rennbahn* (racecourse), one of *Molli*'s stops.

Lodging
Under DM 110

Hotel Kurhaus. This late-18th-century half-timbered building has been accommodating visitors for more than 125 years. It was completely renovated in 1986 to raise it to international standards. Rooms are plainly but comfortably furnished. *August-Bebelstr. 2, tel. 08193/3036. 37 rooms, most with bath or shower. Facilities: restaurant. AE.*

Dining
Under DM 20
★

Weisser Pavilion. A Chinese pagodalike structure built in the 19th century in an English-style park is an exotic setting for lunch or high tea (the café closes at 8 PM). Specialties are cheese and beef fondue and a fiery dessert-drink with the intimidating name of *Feuerzangenbowle*, a mélange of fruits flambéed with pear schnapps. *Am Kamp, tel. 08193/2326. Reservations advised. No credit cards. Closed Sat.*

Lodging and Dining
Under DM 150
★

Arendsee. This new low-rise hotel in Kühlungsborn offers exceptionally well-decorated rooms with patterned easy chairs as well as TVs and minibars. The Arendsee caters to families with young children, who need connecting rooms or extra beds. The restaurant, in the under DM 30 range, offers a mix of regional and international dishes. *Strandstr. 46, Kühlungsborn, tel. 08193/691. 66 rooms and 6 suites with bath. Facilities: indoor saltwater pool, sauna, solarium, sun terrace. AE, DC, MC, V.*

Wismar

There is a regular train service from Rostock via Bad Doberan; the trip takes 1 hour and 40 minutes. Tourist office: Touristbüro, Bohrstr. 5a, tel. 0824/2958.

The port of Wismar has probably the most colorful history of any town in the region. It was one of the original three sea-trading towns that banded together in 1259 to combat Baltic pirates (the other two were Lübeck and Rostock). From this mutual defense pact grew the great and powerful private trading block that dominated the Baltic for centuries: the Hanseatic League. The Thirty Years' War was particularly devastating for this region—the prewar population was halved—and the power of the Hanseatics was broken. Wismar became the victim of regular military tussles and finally fell to Sweden. The town was mortgaged to a German Mecklenburg duke in 1803 on a 100-year lease, and it was only when this expired in 1903 that Wismar legally rejoined Germany.

Despite its checkered history, the wealth originally generated by the Hanseatic merchants can still be seen in Wismar's rich and ornate architecture, particularly in the patrician gabled houses that frame the **Marktplatz,** the main square, one of the largest and most colorful in northern Germany. The style of buildings on the square ranges from red-brick late-Gothic through Dutch Renaissance to 19th-century neoclassical. Of particular interest is the **Wasserkunst,** the ornate pumping station in Dutch Renaissance style built in 1602 by the Dutch master Philipp Brandin. Not only was it a work of art, it supplied the town with water until the mid-19th century.

Walk west to reach the 250-foot-high tower of the ruined **Marienkirche** church, bombed in World War II, just behind the

Marktplatz. At noon, 3 PM, and 5 PM, listen for one of 14 hymns played on its clarion bells. Next to it stands the **Fürstenhof,** home of the former dukes of Mecklenburg, an early 16th-century Italian Renaissance structure with touches of late-Gothic. The facade is a series of fussy friezes depicting scenes from the Trojan War. Another victim of the war is adjacent to the Fürstenhof, the **Georgenkirche,** the cathedral of St. George. Today, it's the biggest Gothic religious ruin in Europe.

Backtrack through the Marktplatz and along Krämerstrasse to reach the **Nikolaikirche,** a late-Gothic church with a 37-meter-high (120-foot-high) nave. Important architectural relics rescued from the bombed ruins of other Wismar churches are displayed here, notably the Gothic high altar from the Georgenkirche. Across the street the Dutch Renaissance **Schabbelthaus** houses a fascinating museum of local history. *Schweinsbrücke 8. Admission: DM 2 adults, DM 1 children. Open May–Sept., Tues.–Sun. 10–4; Oct.–Apr., Tues.–Sat. 10–4.*

If you've got an hour to spare, wander among the jetties and quays of the port, a mix of the medieval and modern.

Lodging
Under DM 110
★ **Hotel Wismar.** Wismar's only hotel, it's handily located in the old town center a few strides from the market square and other attractions. It's small and well-worn but clean, with a reasonably priced restaurant serving regional dishes. *Breitstr. 10, tel. 0824/2498. 18 rooms without bath. No credit cards.*

Under DM 70
Mecklenburger Hof. This simple pension, clean and plainly furnished, stands in the old town center just a few minutes' walk from the old market square. *Gerberstr. 16, tel. 0824/2706. 10 rooms without bath. No credit cards.*

Dining
Under DM 20
★ **Alte Schwede.** One of the most attractive, authentic taverns on the Baltic—and correspondingly busy—the eatery has a cooking staff intent on reviving Mecklenburg's traditional cuisine, which features both game and fish dishes. *Am Markt 20, tel. 0824/3520. Reservations advised for dinner. No credit cards.*

Weinberg. An old wood-beamed wine tavern near the market square has the well-worn look you would expect of a place that has been in business since 1575. The menu is unspectacular, but there's an excellent wine list. *Lübschestr. 31, tel. 0824/3550. Reservations necessary on Fri. and Sat. evenings when dances are held. No credit cards. Closed Mon.*

Under DM 15
Gastmahl des Meeres. This small, no-frills fish restaurant, catering as much to locals as to visitors, is a good place to try Mecklenburger Fischsuppe or Pannfisch (*see* Dining, *above*). *Altböterstr. 6, tel. 0824/2134. No reservations. No credit cards.*

Schwerin

It's 70 minutes from Rostock by a fast hourly train service. Tourist office: Tourist-Information, Am Markt 11, tel. 084/864509.

Schwerin, with a population of 120,000, is the second-largest town in the region and the capital of the new state of Mecklenburg-Vorpommern. Until the end of the German monarchy, in 1918, it was the home of the Mecklenburg royal family. They have gone, but you can see their imposing **Schloss Schwerin** (Schwerin Palace), built in 1857 on an island adjoining

Schwerin's old town, in the southwest corner of the vast Schweriner See lake. A pastiche of historical styles, the palace, surmounted by 15 turrets large and small, is reminiscent of a French château, and, indeed, was modeled after Chambord in the Loire Valley. Surprisingly, the Communist government restored and maintained the fantastic opulence of this rambling 80-room reminder of an absolutist monarch system. Antique furniture, objets, silk tapestries, and paintings are sprinkled through the salons (the Throne Room is particularly extravagant), but of special interest are the ornately patterned and highly burnished inlaid wooden floors and wall panels. The palace stands on the site of an earlier Renaissance castle, of which only the chapel, 1560, survives, and is surrounded by parkland laid out in the 18th century and containing many beautiful species of trees. *Lennestr. Admission: DM 3 adults, DM 1.50 children. Palace and gardens open Tues.–Sun. 10–5.*

Schwerin's showpiece square, the **Alte Garten,** opposite the entrance to the palace island, was the scene of military parades during the years of Communist rule. It is dominated by two buildings, the ornate neo-Renaissance state theater (1883–86) and the Staatliche Galerie (admission free; open Tues.–Sun. 9–4), which houses an interesting collection of paintings by 19th-century German artists such as Max Liebermann and Lovis Corinth, plus an exhibition of Meissen porcelain. Another noteworthy sight in Schwerin's old town is the Gothic cathedral, or Dom. The bronze baptismal font dates from the 14th century, the altar was built in 1440. Religious scenes painted on the walls of the adjoining Marienkapelle (Chapel of Maria) date from the Middle Ages. Sweeping views of the old town and lake await those with the energy to climb the 219 steps to the top of the 320-foot-high cathedral tower. *Buschstr. Tower open Mon.–Sat. 11–12, 2:30–4:30, Sun. 2:30–4:30.*

Lodging
Under DM 110

Niederländischer Hof. The facilities at this small, comfortable, established hotel in the center of the old town are above average for the Baltic Coast. The restaurant specializes in Mecklenburg dishes. *Karl-Marx-Str. 12, tel. 084/83727. 32 rooms, most with bath. No credit cards.*

Dining
Under DM 30
★

Weinhaus Uhle. One of the best eating places in Schwerin, it's named after the wine merchant who opened the restaurant back in 1740. You can dine on regional specialties served in a colorful, unspoiled setting, accompanied by a small band that plays nightly. *Schusterstr. 13–15, tel. 084/864455. Reservations advised. No credit cards.*

Under DM 20

Waldburg. This cozy restaurant on the banks of the Schweriner See specializes in game. Be on the lookout for *geräucherten Gans* (smoked goose). *Schlossgartenallee 70, tel. 084/812552. Reservations advised. No credit cards.*

The Arts

Opera is staged regularly in Schwerin's **Mecklenburger Staatstheater** (Am Alten garten, tel. 084/83993); so are plays, but only in German. Tickets are reasonably priced, but of course you won't be seeing internationally known performers.

Nightlife

For nightlife, Schwerin has the **Achteck** (Neumühlerstr. 20), a big disco in a new octagonal building; the **Lesecafe am Pfaffenteich** (Wilhelm-Pieck-Str. 16), which attracts a very young coffee-and-Coca-Cola crowd; and the **Strandpavillon** (Am Strand 15), where discos are held Friday to Sunday until 4 AM.

Stralsund

An hourly train connects Rostock with Stralsund; the trip takes 70 minutes. Tourist office: Touristbüro, Rat der Stadt, Alter Markt, tel. 0821/2439.

In 1815 the Congress of Vienna awarded Stralsund, which had been under Swedish control, to the Prussians. Although it was rapidly industrialized, this jewel of the Baltic features a historic city center painstakingly rebuilt and restored.

Following an attack by the Lübeck fleet in 1249, a defensive wall was built around Stralsund; you'll see parts of it on your left as you come into the old town. The old market square, the **Alter Markt,** boasts the best local architecture, ranging from Gothic through Renaissance to Baroque. Most of the buildings were rich merchants' homes, notably the late-Gothic **Wulflamhaus,** with 17 ornate, steeply stepped gables. Stralsund's architectural masterpiece, however, is the 13th-century **Rathaus** (Town Hall), considered by many to be the finest secular example of redbrick Gothic in northern Germany. Note the coats of arms of the main towns that formed the exclusive membership of the Hanseatic League. The 13th-century Gothic **Nikolaikirche** (Church of St. Nicholas) also faces on to the square. Its treasures include a 15-foot-high crucifix from the 14th century and a Baroque altar. Walk down the pedestrian street Ossenreyerstrasse and along through the Apollonienmarkt to the Katherinenkloster, a former cloister, on Monchstrasse. Forty rooms of the cloister now house the **Meeresmuseum** (Sea Museum), which includes an **aquarium** of Baltic Sea life. It also displays the skeleton of a giant whale and a 25-foot-high chunk of coral. *Katharinenberg 14a. Admission: DM 2.50 adults, DM 1 children. Open daily May–Oct. 10–5; Nov.–Apr., Wed.–Sun. 10–5.*

Dining
Under DM 20
★

Scheelehaus. The 10-foot-high windows in this centuries-old restaurant with the air of a baronial hall still have their original thick, bull's-eye panes. House specialties include onion soup, and pork with peaches and *Kartoffelbällchen*—potato balls filled with an almond, apple, and cinnamon mixture. *Fährstr. 23, tel. 0821/2987. Reservations advised for dinner. No credit cards.*

Lodging and Dining
Under DM 110

Baltic. This simply furnished old hotel in the historic heart of town is often fully booked, especially in high summer. If you dine in the restaurant (in the under DM 30 range), try the spicy Hungarian goulash or the *Kasslerbraten,* smoked pork coated in honey. *Frankendamm 17, tel. 0821/5381. 21 rooms, 2 with bath, and 3 suites with bath. Facilities: restaurant, bar, disco. No credit cards.*

Shopping

The town's **spring markets** (April–May) precipitate a multitude of flea-market stalls for bargain hunters.

Nightlife

The **Baltic Hotel** (Frankendamm 22) hosts dances in its main bar. You'll also find dancing and cabaret in the **Störtebeker Keller** (Ossenreyerstr. 40).

Ribnitz-Damgarten

Frequent trains take 45 minutes from Rostock. Tourist information: Rostock Touristbüro, Schnickmannstr. 13, Rostock, tel. 081/22619.

The town of Ribnitz-Damgarten is the center of the amber (in German, *Bernstein*) business, unique to the Baltic Coast. You can see a fascinating exhibition of how the precious "Baltic gold" is collected from the sea and refined to make jewelry and objects of art in the **Bernsteinmuseum,** which adjoins the main factory. (You can buy amber at the factory, which is open the same hours as the museum.) The museum has examples of amber dating back 4,000 years. *Im Kloster 1–2, tel. 0825/2931. Admission free. Open June–Sept., Tues.–Sat. 9:30–5, Sun. 2–4; Oct.–May, Tues.–Sat. 9:30–4.*

Rügen Island

A number of trains run daily from Rostock, either to Bergen, the island's nominal capital, or to Sassnitz, on its seaward (western) side. The journey to Sassnitz via Ribnitz-Damgarten and Stralsund can take up to three hours, but express trains will do it in a little over two. The best train for a day trip is the 9 AM from Rostock; it reaches Bergen by 11 and Sassnitz at 11:25. In some cases you have to change trains at Stralsund.

The intermediate stations between Stralsund and Sassnitz are Bergen (change here to reach Putbus for the Racing Roland *steam train, or to catch a bus for Schaprode) and Lietzow (the stop for the Grosser Jasmunder Bodden). Take a bus from the Sassnitz train station to reach the Stubbenkammer or Kap Arkona. Train and bus schedules are in the process of being altered, so travelers should check first with the tourist office, at Hauptstrasse 9, 2337 Binz, tel. 08278/2241.*

What Rügen lacks in architectural interest it makes up for in natural beauty. From the chalk cliffs of the **Stubbenkammer** headland on the east coast of the island, through the blustery sand dunes of **Kap Arkona** in the north (its lighthouse marks the northernmost point in eastern Germany, and you can see the Danish island of Moen from a restored watchtower next door), to the quiet waters and coves of the **Grosser Jasmunder Bodden** in the center, this is a nature lover's paradise. Off the northwest corner of Rügen is a smaller island, the sticklike **Hiddensee.** Motorized transport is banned on Hiddensee, which adds to its tranquility. A ferry will take you there from the village of **Schaprode.**

Rügen has been joined to the mainland since 1936 by a causeway that carries road and train traffic. The main road over the causeway from Stralsund (Route 96) cuts straight across the island southwest to northeast, a distance of 51 kilometers (32 miles). The route runs between the Grosser Jasmunder Bodden, a giant sea inlet, and a smaller expanse of water—the Kleiner Jasmunder Bodden lake—to the port of **Sassnitz,** where ferries run to Sweden.

Rügen first became popular as a holiday destination with the development of the railways in the mid-19th century, and many of the grand mansions and villas on the island date from this period. Despite its continuing popularity during the Communist years, little new development has taken place since the mid-1930s, leaving the entire island in a kind of time warp. For example, dances—all the rage in the 1920s and 1930s—continue on Rügen with afternoon coffee dances at cafés and dinner dances at hotels, and the island still retains its own regular steam-train service, the *Rasender Roland* (Racing Roland), which runs daily at regular intervals from **Putbus,** in the south, for the hour-long chug (24½ kilometers/15 miles) to **Göhren,** at the southeast corner of the island. Call tel. 0859/27172 for timetable details.

Near Binz, on the coast north of Göhren, you can climb the 38-meter (125-foot) lookout tower by Jagdschloss Granitz for a splendid view in all directions.

Lodging
Under DM 110

Hotel Nordpferd. Comfortable and close to the sea promenade, this 1960s-style guest house is due to be renovated in 1992. *Nordpferdstr. 3, Göhren, tel. Göhren 381. 51 rooms without bath. No credit cards.*

Under DM 70

Mecklenburger Hof. This simple guest house, close to the train station, is set to undergo renovation in 1992. *Bahnhofstr. 67, Bergen, tel. Bergen 263 (still operator-connected in late 1991; there may be direct-dial by 1992). 19 rooms without bath.*

Youth Hostels

Youth Hostel Thomas Müntzer. There are 70 beds, mostly in dormitories, as well as several four-bed rooms at this plain but clean hostel. *Thomas-Müntzer-Weg 9, Bergen, tel. Bergen 320. No private baths.*

Youth Hostel Wilhelm Thews. This bargain dormitory lodging, with 75 beds and communal facilities, is close to the sea and offers lodging and breakfast for DM 15–DM 20. *Stubbenkammerstr. 2, 2355 Sassnitz, tel. 08277/22693 or 08277/32090.*

Dining
Under DM 20

Gastmahl des Meeres. The decor is faded but the fish is fresh at this lively and popular restaurant in Sassnitz. Regional dishes such as Pannfisch and Mecklenburger Fischsuppe are served, but go for the house specialty: *Zander* (pike-perch) in an herb cream sauce. *Strandpromenade 2, Sassnitz, tel. 08277/22320. Reservations advised for dinner. No credit cards. Closed Mon.*

Lodging and Dining
Splurge

Mitropa-Rügen-Hotel. Many of the rooms here provide views of the busy little port of Sassnitz, where ferries to Sweden (Trelleborg) operate. Among the hotel's attractions is a dance hall where locals and summer visitors congregate. Double rooms cost DM 140–DM 220; there are 59 doubles, 19 at the lower-price end. The best of the two restaurants is the rustically decorated Rügenklause, where three-course menus range from DM 45 to DM 60. *Seestr. 1, Sassnitz, tel. 08277/32090. 147 rooms and 2 suites with bath. Facilities: café, bars, indoor pool, sauna, solarium, sun terrace, hairdresser. No credit cards.*

Greifswald

*Take the train from Rostock to Stralsund (*see above*) for the local train to Greifswald, which takes 30 minutes. Tourist office: Informationsbüro, Strasse der Freundschaft 102, tel. 0822/3460.*

Greifswald was a busy sea trading center in the Middle Ages but became a backwater in the 19th century, when ships became too large to negotiate the shallow Ryck River leading to the sea. Today's visitors have German army commander Colonel Rudolf Petershagen to thank for being able to see many of its original buildings. In charge of Greifswald in early 1945, he surrendered the town to the approaching Soviet forces rather than see it destroyed. Ironically, lack of funds for restoration over the next 40 years left some historic buildings in desperate need of repair.

Stroll along the Strasse der Freundschaft to the **Platz der Freundschaft,** presided over by a medieval **Rathaus,** rebuilt in 1738–50 following a fire, modified in the 19th century and again in 1936. The square is surrounded by splendid old houses in red-brick Gothic styles. Three churches shape the silhouette of the city: the 13th-century **Dom St. Nikolai** (St. Nicholas's Cathedral) at the start of Martin-Luther-Strasse, a Gothic church from whose 300-foot-high tower one can get an impressive view; the 14th-century **Marienkirche** (St. Mary's Church), on the corner of Brüggstrasse and Friedrich-Loeffler-Strasse, the oldest surviving church in Greifswald, and noted for its remarkable 60-foot-high arches and a striking four-cornered tower; and the 13th-century **St. Jacob's,** later rebuilt to a three-nave design.

Just outside Greifswald, in the suburb of **Eldena,** stand the ruins of a 12th-century Cistercian monastery made famous in a painting by Caspar David Friedrich (now at the Gallery of Romantic Painting in Berlin), who was born in Greifswald, in 1774. The monastery, which led to the founding of Greifswald, was plundered by rampaging Swedish soldiers early in the Thirty Years' War and abandoned. The Gothic structure was further cannibalized by townsfolk over the next two centuries until it was made a protected national monument, a result of the publicity it gained from the celebrated Friedrich painting.

Lodging
Under DM 110

Boddenhus. A nondescript apartment-block-style building reflects the rooms within: drab furnishings and plain carpets and walls. The hotel's facilities, however, are generally excellent. *Karl-Liebknecht-Ring 1, tel. 0822/5241. 75 rooms, most with bath, and 9 suites with bath. Facilities: restaurant, café, 2 bars, sauna, solarium, beauty salon, tennis courts. AE, DC, MC, V. Closed Jan. 2–15.*

Dining
Under DM 20

Ratsweinkeller. Down in the dimly lit vaulted cellars of the medieval town hall, the kitchen offers an international menu. The game dishes, in season, are particularly mouth-watering. *Platz der Freundschaft 2, tel. 0822/3285. Reservations advised. No credit cards.*

Wolgast

Local trains via Greifswald run frequently out of Stralsund (see above). *The trip from Stralsund takes 65 minutes.*

This small town is the gateway to Usedom, the other principal German island off the Baltic coast. Wolgast's chief attraction is the old town square, **Karl-Liebknecht-Platz,** where the pretty mid-17th-century half-timbered house known locally as the **Kaffeemühle** and a Baroque **town hall** are situated. The Kaffeemühle, far from serving coffee, is the local history museum, the **Kreismuseum,** which tells the life story of another locally born artist of the Romantic era, Philipp Otto Runge. The museum also has an exhibition detailing the development of Germany's V2 rocket during World War II, spearheaded by scientist Werner von Braun (who later developed the United States space program). *Admission free. Open Tues.–Fri. 9–5, weekends 9–4.*

Usedom

You'll have to stay overnight if you plan to visit this island by public transportation. The trip from Rostock, including a train change in Stralsund, takes more than four hours all the way through to Ahlbeck. Tourist office: Kurverwaltung, Dünenstr. 45, Ahlbeck, tel. Ahlbeck 8228 (operator connections only).

On its seaboard side, 25-mile-long Usedom Island has almost 20 miles of sandy shoreline and a string of resorts. The best of them and the island's main town is **Ahlbeck,** which features an unusual 19th-century wooden pier with four towers. Ahlbeck's promenade is lined with turn-of-the-century villas, some of which are now small but as yet unsophisticated hotels. Much of the island is a nature reserve and provides refuge for a number of rare birds, including the giant sea eagle, which has a wing span of up to 8 feet. Most of Usedom is German territory, except for the most easterly corner, which belongs to Poland. If you stroll along the beach to the right of Ahlbeck's pier you'll come to the border. (At press time, there was still no border crossing point on the island, but this is expected to change.) Just west of Ahlbeck, you'll come to Heringsdorf, the oldest resort on the island, and the place chosen by Russian playwright Maxim Gorky for a quiet sojourn during 1922. He stayed in the villa called Irmgard, now a protected monument.

At the northern end of Usedom is **Peenemünde,** the launch site of the world's first jet rockets, the V1 and V2, developed by Germany toward the end of World War II and fired at London (*see* Wolgast, *above*). You can still see remnants of the project buildings scattered amid what is now a bird sanctuary. There is also a monument to the forced laborers who died working on the site and to the 2,000 people later killed in Allied air raids.

Lodging
Youth Hostel

Youth Hostel Herbert Tschäpe. Hikers in particular seem to like this simple but typical dormitory hostel, which charges DM 18 per night. *Puschkinstr. 7, Heringsdorf, tel. Seebad Heringsdorf 325.*

Dining
Under DM 20
★

Cafe Asgard. You'll dine amidst silk wallpaper, potted plants, crisp white napery, and fresh flowers. The specialty is *Feuertopf Göttergarten,* a spicy fondue. The restaurant, which dates from the 1920s, is open all day, so you can stop by between meal times and order the homemade pastry. If you're in a foot-tapping mood, visit the Golden Twenties dance hall above the restaurant. *Strandpromenade 13, Bansin, tel. Bansin 558 (operator only). Reservations advised for dinner in July and Aug. No credit cards.*

Lodging and Dining
Under DM 110
★

Ostseehotel. Generations of vacationing families have stayed at this snug, if slightly dated, hotel in a 19th-century villa on Ahlbeck's promenade. Most of the airy but spartan rooms have sea views; few have private bathrooms. The restaurant serves mainly hearty local pork and potato dishes, but the goulash soup is exceptional; also look for fresh pike-perch in season. Dances are held several times a week during the summer. *Dünenstr. 41, Ahlbeck, tel. Ahlbeck 8132 (operator only). 37 rooms, most without bath. No credit cards.*

Under DM 70

Hotel Stadt Berlin. This turn-of-the-century villa-turned-hotel in Heringsdorf has been accommodating summer visitors since the 1920s. Its facilities are rather well-worn, but there's a friendly holiday atmosphere. The bright little restaurant serves solid but predictable local fare. During the summer there are lively dances several times a week. *Ernt-Thälmann-str. 38, Heringsdorf, tel. Heringsdorf 413 (operator only). 26 rooms, none with bath. No credit cards. Closed Jan.*

German Vocabulary

Words and Phrases

	English	*German*	*Pronunciation*
Basics	Yes/no	Ja/nein	yah/nine
	Please	Bitte	**bit**-uh
	Thank you (very much)	Danke (vielen Dank)	**dahn**-kuh (**fee**-lun dahnk)
	Excuse me	Entschuldigen Sie	ent-**shool**-de-gen zee
	I'm sorry	Es tut mir leid.	es toot meer lite
	Good day	Guten Tag	**goo**-ten tahk
	Good bye	Auf Wiedersehen	auf **vee**-der-zane
	Mr./Mrs.	Herr/Frau	hair/frau
	Miss	Fräulein	**froy**-line
	Pleased to meet you.	Sehr erfreut.	zair air-**froit**
	How are you?	Wie geht es Ihnen?	vee **gate** es **ee**-nen?
	Very well, thanks.	Sehr gut, danke.	zair goot **dahn**-kuh
	And you?	Und Ihnen?	oont **ee**-nen

Numbers	1 eins	eints	6 sechs	zex
	2 zwei	tsvai	7 sieben	**zee**-ben
	3 drei	dry	8 acht	ahkt
	4 vier	fear	9 neun	noyn
	5 fünf	fumph	10 zehn	tsane

Days of the Week	Sunday	Sonntag	**zone**-tahk
	Monday	Montag	**moan**-tahk
	Tuesday	Dienstag	**deens**-tahk
	Wednesday	Mittwoch	**mit**-voah
	Thursday	Donnerstag	**doe**-ners-tahk
	Friday	Freitag	**fry**-tahk
	Saturday	Samstag	**zahm**-stahk

Useful Phrases	Do you speak English?	Sprechen Sie Englisch?	**shprek**-hun zee **eng**-glish?
	I don't speak German.	Ich spreche kein Deutsch.	ich **shprek**-uh kine doych
	Please speak slowly.	Bitte sprechen Sie langsam.	**bit**-uh **shprek**-en zee **lahng**-zahm
	I am American/British	Ich bin Amerikaner(in)/ Engländer(in)	ich bin a-mer-i-**kahn**-er(in) **eng**-glan-der(in)
	My name is . . .	Ich heiße . . .	ich **hi**-suh
	Yes please/No, thank you	Ja bitte/Nein danke	yah **bi**-tuh/**nine** dahng-kuh
	Where are the restrooms?	Wo ist die Toilette?	vo ist dee twah-**let**-uh
	Left/right	Links/rechts	links/rechts

Open/closed	Offen/geschlossen	O-fen/geh-**shloss**-en
Where is . . .	Wo ist . . .	**vo** ist
the train station?	der Bahnhof?	dare **bahn**-hof
the bus stop?	die Bushaltestelle?	dee **booss**-hahlt-uh-**shtel**-uh
the subway station?	die U-Bahn-Station?	dee OO-bahn-**staht**-sion
the airport?	der Flugplatz?	dare **floog**-plats
the post office?	die Post?	dee **post**
the bank?	die Bank?	dee **banhk**
the police station?	die Polizeistation?	dee po-lee-**tsai**-staht-sion
the American/ British consulate?	das amerikanische/ britische Konsulat?	dahs a-mare-i-**kahn**-ishuh/**brit**-ish-uh cone-tso-**laht**
the Hospital?	das Krankenhaus?	dahs **krahnk**-en-house
the telephone	das Telefon	dahs te-le-**fone**
I'd like to have . . .	Ich hätte gerne . . .	ich **het**-uh gairn
a room	ein Zimmer	I-nuh **tsim**-er
the key	den Schlüssel	den **shluh**-sul
a map	eine Karte	I-nuh **cart**-uh
How much is it?	Wieviel kostet das?	**vee**-feel **cost**-et dahs?
I am ill/sick	Ich bin krank	ich bin krahnk
I need . . .	Ich brauche . . .	ich **brow**-khuh
a doctor	einen Arzt	I-nen artst
the police	die Polizei	dee po-li-**tsai**
help	Hilfe	**hilf**-uh
Stop!	Halt!	hahlt
Fire!	Feuer!	**foy**-er
Caution/Look out!	Achtung!/Vorsicht!	**ahk**-tung/**for**-zicht

Dining Out

A bottle of . . .	eine Flasche . . .	I-nuh **flash**-uh
A cup of . . .	eine Tasse . . .	I-nuh **tahs**-uh
A glass of . . .	ein Glas . . .	ein glahss
Ashtray	der Aschenbecher	dare Ahsh-en-bekh-er
Bill/check	die Rechnung	dee **rekh**-nung
Do you have . . . ?	Haben Sie . . . ?	**hah**-ben zee

Food	Essen	**es**-en
I am a diabetic.	Ich bin Diabetiker.	ich bin dee-ah-**bet**-ik-er
I am on a diet.	Ich halte Diät.	ich **hahl**-tuh dee-**et**
I am a vegetarian.	Ich bin Vegetarier.	ich bin ve-guh-**tah**-re-er
I cannot eat . . .	Ich kann . . . nicht essen	ich kan . . . nicht **es**-en
I'd like to order	Ich möchte bestellen . . .	ich **mohr**-shtuh buh-shtel-en
Is the service included?	Ist die Bedienung inbegriffen?	ist dee beh-**dee**-nung **in**-beh-grig-en
Menu	die Speisekarte	dee **shpie**-zeh-car-tuh
Napkin	die Serviette	dee zair-vee-**eh**-tuh
Separate/all together	Getrennt/alles zusammen	ge-**trent/ah**-les tsu-**zah**-men

Menu Guide

English	*German*
Made to order	Auf Bestellung
Side dishes	Beilagen
Extra charge	Extraaufschlag
When available	Falls verfügbar
Entrees	Hauptspeisen
Homemade	Hausgemacht
. . . (not) included	. . . (nicht) inbegriffen
Depending on the season	je nach Saison
Local specialties	Lokalspezialitäten
Set menu	Menü
Lunch menu	Mittagskarte
Desserts	Nachspeisen
. . . style	. . . nach . . . Art
. . . at your choice	. . . nach Wahl
. . . at your request	. . . nach Wunsch
Prices are . . .	Preise sind . . .
Service included	*inklusive Bedienung*
Value added tax included	*inklusive Mehrwertsteuer (Mwst.)*
Specialty of the house	Spezialität des Hauses
Soup of the day	Tagessuppe
Appetizers	Vorspeisen
Is served from . . . to . . .	Wird von . . . bis . . . serviert

Breakfast

Bread	Brot
Roll(s)	Brötchen
Butter	Butter
Eggs	Eier
Hot	heiß
Cold	kalt
Decaffeinated	koffeinfrei
Jam	Konfitüre
Milk	Milch
Orange juice	Orangensaft
Scrambled eggs	Rühreier
Bacon	Speck
Fried eggs	Spiegeleier
White bread	Weißbrot
Lemon	Zitrone
Sugar	Zucker

Appetizers

Oysters	Austern
Frog legs	Froschschenkel
Goose liver paté	Gänseleberpastete
Lobster	Hummer
Shrimp	Krabben
Crawfish	Krebs
Salmon	Lachs
Mussels	Muscheln
Prosciutto with melon	Parmaschinken mit Melone

Mushrooms	Pilze
Smoked . . .	Räucher . . .
Ham	Schinken
Snails	Schnecken
Asparagus	Spargel

Soups

Stew	Eintopf
Semolina dumpling soup	Grießnockerlsuppe
Goulash soup	Gulaschsuppe
Chicken soup	Hühnersuppe
Potato soup	Kartoffelsuppe
Liver dumpling soup	Leberknödelsuppe
Oxtail soup	Ochsenschwanzsuppe
Tomato soup	Tomatensuppe
Onion soup	Zwiebelsuppe

Methods of Preparation

Blue (boiled in salt and vinegar)	Blau
Baked	Gebacken
Fried	Gebraten
Steamed	Gedämpft
Grilled (broiled)	Gegrillt
Boiled	Gekocht
Sauteed	In Butter geschwenkt
Breaded	Paniert
Raw	Roh

When ordering steak, the English words "rare, medium, (well) done" are used and understood in German.

Fish and Seafood

Eel	Aal
Oysters	Austern
Trout	Forelle
Flounder	Flunder
Prawns	Garnelen
Halibut	Heilbutt
Lobster	Hummer
Scallops	Jakobsmuscheln
Cod	Kabeljau
Crawfish	Krebs
Salmon	Lachs
Spiny lobster	Languste
Mackerel	Makrele
Herring	Matjes
Mussels	Muscheln
Red sea bass	Rotbarsch
Sole	Seezunge
Squid	Tintenfisch
Tuna	Thunfisch

Meats

Mutton	Hammel
Veal	Kalb(s)
Lamb	Lamm

Beef	Rind(er)
Pork	Schwein(e)

Cuts of Meat

Example: For "Lammkeule" see "Lamm" (above) + ". . . keule" (below)

breast	. . . brust
scallopini	. . . geschnetzeltes
knuckle	. . . haxe
leg	. . . keule
liver	. . . leber
tenderloin	. . . lende
kidney	. . . niere
rib	. . . rippe
Meat patty	Frikadelle
Meat loaf	Hackbraten
Cured pork ribs	Kasseler Rippchen
Liver meatloaf	Leberkäse
Ham	Schinken
Sausage and cold cut platter	Schlachtplatte
Brawn	Sülze
Cooked beef with horseradish and cream sauce	Tafelspitz

Game and Poultry

Duck	Ente
Pheasant	Fasan
Goose	Gans
Chicken	Hähnchen (Huhn)
Hare	Hase
Deer	Hirsch
Rabbit	Kaninchen
Capon	Kapaun
Venison	Reh
Pigeon	Taube
Turkey	Truthahn
Quail	Wachtel

Vegetables

Eggplant	Aubergine
Red cabbage	Blaukraut
Cauliflower	Blumenkohl
Beans	Bohnen
green	*grüne*
white	*weiße*
Button mushrooms	Champignons
Peas	Erbsen
Cucumber	Gurke
Cabbage	Kohl
Lettuce	Kopfsalat
Leek	Lauch
Asparagus, peas and carrots	Leipziger Allerlei
Corn	Mais
Carrots	Mohrrüben
Peppers	Paprika
Chanterelle mushrooms	Pfifferlinge
Mushrooms	Pilze
Brussels sprouts	Rosenkohl

Red beets	Rote Beete
Red cabbage	Rotkohl(kraut)
Celery	Sellerie
Asparagus (tips)	Spargel(spitzen)
Tomatoes	Tomaten
Cabbage	Weißkohl
Onions	Zwiebeln

Side dishes

Potato(s)	Kartoffel(n)
fried	*Brat . . .*
boiled in their jackets	*Pell . . .*
with parsley	*Petersilien . . .*
fried	*Röst . . .*
boiled in saltwater	*Salz . . .*
mashed	*. . . brei*
dumplings	*. . . klöße (knödel)*
pancakes	*. . . puffer*
salad	*. . . salat*
Pasta	Nudeln
French fries	Pommes Frittes
Rice	Reis
buttered	*Butter . . .*
steamed	*gedämpfter . . .*

Condiments

Basil	Basilikum
Vinegar	Essig
Spice	Gewürz
Garlic	Knoblauch
Herbs	Kräuter
Caraway	Kümmel
Bay leaf	Lorbeer
Horseradish	Meerettich
Nutmeg	Muskatnuß
Oil	Öl
Parsley	Petersilie
Saffron	Safran
Sage	Salbei
Chives	Schnittlauch
Mustard	Senf
Artificial sweetener	Süßstoff
Cinnamon	Zimt
Sugar	Zucker

Cheese

Mild:	Allgäuer Käse, Altenburger (goat cheese), Appenzeller, Greyerzer, Hüttenkäse (cottage cheese), Kümmelkäse (with carraway seeds), Quark, Räucherkäse (smoked cheese), Sahnekäse (creamy), Tilsiter.
Sharp:	Handkäse, Harzer Käse, Limburger.

curd	frisch
hard	hart
mild	mild

ripe	reif
sharp	scharf
soft	weich

Fruits

Apple	Apfel
Orange	Apfelsine
Apricot	Aprikose
Blueberry	Blaubeere
Blackberry	Brombeere
Strawberry	Erdbeere
Raspberry	Himbeere
Cherry	Kirsche
Grapefruit	Pampelmuse
Cranberry	Preiselbeere
Raisin	Rosine
Grape	Weintraube

Nuts

Peanuts	Erdnüsse
Hazelnuts	Haselnüsse
Coconut	Kokosnuß
Almonds	Mandeln
Chestnuts	Maronen

Desserts

. . . soufflé	. . . auflauf
. . . ice cream	. . . eis
. . . cake	. . . kuchen
Honey-almond cake	Bienenstich
Fruit cocktail	Obstsalat
Whipped cream	(Schlag)sahne
Black Forest cake	Schwarzwälder Kirschtorte

Drinks

chilled	eiskalt
with/without ice	mit/ohne Eis
with/without water	mit/ohne Wasser
straight	pur
room temperature	Zimmertemperatur
. . . brandy	. . . geist
. . . distilled liquor	. . . korn
. . . liqueur	. . . likör
. . . schnapps	. . . schnaps
Egg liquor	Eierlikör
Mulled claret	Glühwein
Caraway-flavored liquor	Kümmel
Fruit brandy	Obstler
Vermouth	Wermut

When ordering a Martini, you have to specify "gin (vodka) and vermouth", otherwise you will be given a vermouth (Martini & Rossi).

Beers

non-alcoholic	Alkoholfrei
A dark beer	Ein Dunkles

A light beer	Ein Helles
A mug (one quart)	Eine Maß
Draught	Vom Faß
Dark, bitter, high hops content	Altbier
Strong, high alcohol content	Bockbier (Doppelbock, Märzen)
Wheat beer with yeast	Hefeweizen
Light beer, strong hops aroma	Pils(ener)
Wheat beer	Weizen(bier)
Light beer and lemonade	Radlermaß
Wines	Wein
Red wine	Rotwein
White wine and mineral water	Schorle
Sparkling wine	Sekt
White wine	Weißwein
dry	herb
light	leicht
sweet	süß
dry	trocken
full-bodied	vollmundig

Non-alcoholic Drinks

Coffee	Kaffee
decaffeinated	*koffeinfrei*
with cream/sugar	*mit Milch/Zucker*
with artificial sweetener	*mit Süßstoff*
black	*schwarz*
Lemonade	Limonade
orange	*Orangen . . .*
lemon	*Zitronen . . .*
Milk	Milch
Mineral water	Mineralwasser
carbonated/non-carbonated	*mit/ohne Kohlensäure*
. . . juice	. . . saft
(hot) Chocolate	(heiße) Schokolade
Tea	Tee
iced tea	*Eistee*
herb tea	*Kräutertee*
with cream/lemon	*mit Milch/Zitrone*

Index

Personal Itinerary

Departure *Date*

Time

Transportation

Arrival *Date* *Time*

Departure *Date* *Time*

Transportation

Accommodations

Arrival *Date* *Time*

Departure *Date* *Time*

Transportation

Accommodations

Arrival *Date* *Time*

Departure *Date* *Time*

Transportation

Accommodations

Personal Itinerary

Arrival *Date* *Time*

Departure *Date* *Time*

Transportation

Accommodations

Arrival *Date* *Time*

Departure *Date* *Time*

Transportation

Accommodations

Arrival *Date* *Time*

Departure *Date* *Time*

Transportation

Accommodations

Arrival *Date* *Time*

Departure *Date* *Time*

Transportation

Accommodations

Personal Itinerary

Arrival *Date* *Time*

Departure *Date* *Time*

Transportation

Accommodations

Arrival *Date* *Time*

Departure *Date* *Time*

Transportation

Accommodations

Arrival *Date* *Time*

Departure *Date* *Time*

Transportation

Accommodations

Arrival *Date* *Time*

Departure *Date* *Time*

Transportation

Accommodations

Personal Itinerary

Arrival *Date* *Time*

Departure *Date* *Time*

Transportation

Accommodations

Arrival *Date* *Time*

Departure *Date* *Time*

Transportation

Accommodations

Arrival *Date* *Time*

Departure *Date* *Time*

Transportation

Accommodations

Arrival *Date* *Time*

Departure *Date* *Time*

Transportation

Accommodations

Personal Itinerary

Arrival *Date* *Time*

Departure *Date* *Time*

Transportation

Accommodations

Arrival *Date* *Time*

Departure *Date* *Time*

Transportation

Accommodations

Arrival *Date* *Time*

Departure *Date* *Time*

Transportation

Accommodations

Arrival *Date* *Time*

Departure *Date* *Time*

Transportation

Accommodations

Addresses

Name

Address

Telephone

Name

Address

Telephone

Name

Address

Telephone

Name

Address

Telephone

Name

Address

Telephone

Name

Address

Telephone

Name

Address

Telephone

Name

Address

Telephone

Name

Address

Telephone

Name

Address

Telephone

Name

Address

Telephone

Name

Address

Telephone

Name

Address

Telephone

Name

Address

Telephone

Name

Address

Telephone

Name

Address

Telephone

Addresses

Name

Address

Telephone

Name

Address

Telephone

Name

Address

Telephone

Name

Address

Telephone

Name

Address

Telephone

Name

Address

Telephone

Name

Address

Telephone

Name

Address

Telephone

Name

Address

Telephone

Name

Address

Telephone

Name

Address

Telephone

Name

Address

Telephone

Name

Address

Telephone

Name

Address

Telephone

Name

Address

Telephone

Name

Address

Telephone

Fodor's Travel Guides

U.S. Guides

Alaska
Arizona
Boston
California
Cape Cod, Martha's Vineyard, Nantucket
The Carolinas & the Georgia Coast
The Chesapeake Region
Chicago
Colorado
Disney World & the Orlando Area
Florida
Hawaii
Las Vegas, Reno, Tahoe
Los Angeles
Maine,Vermont, New Hampshire
Maui
Miami & the Keys
National Parks of the West
New England
New Mexico
New Orleans
New York City
New York City (Pocket Guide)
Pacific North Coast
Philadelphia & the Pennsylvania Dutch Country
Puerto Rico (Pocket Guide)
The Rockies
San Diego
San Francisco
San Francisco (Pocket Guide)
The South
Santa Fe, Taos, Albuquerque
Seattle & Vancouver
Texas
USA
The U. S. & British Virgin Islands
The Upper Great Lakes Region
Vacations in New York State
Vacations on the Jersey Shore
Virginia & Maryland
Waikiki
Washington, D.C.
Washington, D.C. (Pocket Guide)

Foreign Guides

Acapulco
Amsterdam
Australia
Austria
The Bahamas
The Bahamas (Pocket Guide)
Baja & Mexico's Pacific Coast Resorts
Barbados
Barcelona, Madrid, Seville
Belgium & Luxembourg
Berlin
Bermuda
Brazil
Budapest
Budget Europe
Canada
Canada's Atlantic Provinces
Cancun, Cozumel, Yucatan Peninsula
Caribbean
Central America
China
Czechoslovakia
Eastern Europe
Egypt
Europe
Europe's Great Cities
France
Germany
Great Britain
Greece
The Himalayan Countries
Holland
Hong Kong
India
Ireland
Israel
Italy
Italy 's Great Cities
Jamaica
Japan
Kenya, Tanzania, Seychelles
Korea
London
London (Pocket Guide)
London Companion
Mexico
Mexico City
Montreal & Quebec City
Morocco
New Zealand
Norway
Nova Scotia, New Brunswick, Prince Edward Island
Paris
Paris (Pocket Guide)
Portugal
Rome
Scandinavia
Scandinavian Cities
Scotland
Singapore
South America
South Pacific
Southeast Asia
Soviet Union
Spain
Sweden
Switzerland
Sydney
Thailand
Tokyo
Toronto
Turkey
Vienna & the Danube Valley
Yugoslavia

Wall Street Journal Guides to Business Travel

Europe
International Cities
Pacific Rim
USA & Canada

Special-Interest Guides

Bed & Breakfast and Country Inn Guides:
Mid-Atlantic Region
New England
The South
The West
Cruises and Ports of Call
Healthy Escapes
Fodor's Flashmaps New York
Fodor's Flashmaps Washington, D.C.
Shopping in Europe
Skiing in the USA & Canada
Smart Shopper's Guide to London
Sunday in New York
Touring Europe
Touring USA